The Evolution of Resource Property Rights

The Evolution of Resource Property Rights

Anthony Scott

OXFORD
UNIVERSITY PRESS

OXFORD
UNIVERSITY PRESS

Great Clarendon Street, Oxford, OX2 6DP,
United Kingdom

Oxford University Press is a department of the University of Oxford.
It furthers the University's objective of excellence in research, scholarship,
and education by publishing worldwide. Oxford is a registered trade mark of
Oxford University Press in the UK and in certain other countries

First Edition published in 2008

Published in the United States of America by Oxford University Press
198 Madison Avenue, New York, NY 10016, United States of America

British Library Cataloguing in Publication Data
Data available

Library of Congress Cataloging in Publication Data
Data available

ISBN 978–0–19–828603–5

For Barbara

Preface

I got involved in writing this in the aftermath of my work on the economics of the fishery. In the wake of Scott Gordon I had been trying to explain theoretically how the absence of individual property rights for fishermen could be the explanation of over-entry into the industry and over-fishing particular stocks. These inquiries led a group of us to look into how government fishery regulation actually worked, and thence into government's issuing only a limited number of permits. These permits, it seemed, had very nearly become property rights, at least as some economists write about them.

Our work on fisheries differed from the theoretical work on the presumed invention of property rights over land and other natural resources in that we had not a theoretical model but a healthy slice of the actual history of the permits' creation. Most of the theoretical work by economists had, it is true, showed evidence of some historical investigation. But at a certain point their work typically ceased showing interest in what actually happened to the composition and structure of rights and became confined to finding events or practices that backed up the theory.

My perception of that work—to which I contributed a little and of which I made much use—suggested that most of us didn't know much about the actual processes by which real property rights over resources had been shaped and re-shaped, nor about who it was that did the shaping, nor about how the attributes of the rights changed in response to technological change, new consumer demands or new business practices. Indeed we didn't even have an agreed list of 'attributes'. Some analysts emphasized the importance of rights' growing transferability almost to the exclusion of other attributes. Others emphasized the rights' durations; and many emphasized their exclusivity. Property lawyers meanwhile had their own emphases: the quality or security of the rights themselves in the face of changes in government policy or court decisions on inheritance practices or on trespassing.

This diversity in the experts' approaches probably explains why economists and a wide range of social scientists—from archaeologists and anthropologists to political scientists and sociologists—speak confidently of 'imperfect', 'incomplete', or 'attenuated' property rights over land and resources. They spoke as though there were some agreed perfect composition of a right. In contrast, in my approach I began to think of the right held by all land-users as having five or six attributes. The amounts or proportions differed. Perhaps, in some ideal world, the user's right would have 100 per cent of each of them. But my investigations show that while the amounts of each attribute in a 'standard' right over some resource did increase in some periods, those over other resources, or in other periods, declined. To describe these changes as moves toward perfection or imperfection is to miss the complexity: the blends of characteristics were and are frequently changing and it is these changes that economists will be called on to understand and work into their theories.

This book attempts to describe the 'standard' rights held by users of particular natural resources, and to describe their evolution in terms of changes in the amounts of the rights' characteristics. It builds on my own work on permits and rights for the ocean fishery. These studies were followed by work on English coal leases held in church estates, these by an international comparison of rights to water resources, and so on. Eventually I have asked a somewhat similar set of questions in describing the evolving of rights over seven or eight natural resources. This effort has necessitated giving a great deal of space to the institutions developed by government for holding, farming out, and disposing of the public lands (Crown lands, royal forests, royal fisheries, royal mines, state parks, forest reserves, navigable waters, etc.) because governments' rules and 'tenures' were and are lasting substitutes for rights emerging on private property, not always with the same attributes.

The writing and re-writing of these chapters has stretched over many years. It has been accomplished with the welcome help of the friends, and of the research assistants, whose names are mentioned at the start of the various chapters. I must mention the pleasure of my cooperation with Georgina Coustalin, who was my co-author when we learned about the law bearing on rights to rivers and streams, and together we wrote and published an early version of the chapter on this subject. Much of her work has deservedly survived my brutal shortening of our paper for this book.

My investigations have been greatly helped by generous support from various funds and organizations. Among these I would mention especially the Social Science and Humanities Research Council of Canada for research grants received, the Canada Council for a Killam Fellowship, the Reserve Bank of Australia for a Professorial Fellowship, the MacKenzie King Foundation for a MacKenzie King Fellowship at Harvard University, and assistance, support, and accommodation from generous departments of economics and research units at the University of York, Harvard University, University of Tasmania, University of Melbourne, Australian National University, Tokyo Fisheries University, University of Ottawa, and from my own economics department at the University of British Columbia.

I also mention the frequent encouragement for the whole magnum opus—as he called it—of Andrew Schuller, then of the Oxford University Press.

In writing earlier versions, I had welcome editorial and production help from Ann-Marie Metten. I must mention too the excellent editorial help of Laura Turner who has vigorously and with good taste joined me in the task of shortening some of the chapters and in the consequent bridging and re-arranging of some of the material for the present version.

My preoccupation with rights to resources has dominated too much of our family life, and I gratefully acknowledge the tolerance, cooperation and encouragement I have received over the long period of its writing from my wife Barbara.

Contents

Part I

Rights over Natural Resources

1

Concepts in Resource Property Rights

Introduction: identifying changes in resource property rights

Through exposure to economists' writings on European land enclosures and on agriculture in developing countries, most non-specialists understand that there can be various systems of property and that these systems can develop and change with the needs of society. Looking at the sheer volume of the historical and development literatures, one would think that scholars of property rights and institutions must also have looked in depth at the emergence of individuals' rights to natural resources, including minerals, water, forests, and fish. Yet, when I embarked on this project, it was largely because nobody seems yet to have assembled a unified body of knowledge that can familiarize the non-specialist with changes in the rights held by owners and users of natural resources.

My purpose in this book is to provide such a unified body. I compile accounts found in a variety of (mostly non-quantitative) sources, some of them primary research, some of them secondary writings, into a history of how individual property rights over natural resources emerged and developed in the West, with emphasis on England and the major British colonies, the United States, Canada, Australia and New Zealand. I have classified into two familiar categories the forces that produce change in and shape property law: demand-side forces and supply-side forces. The underlying idea is simple. In order for an existing property right (or for that matter for any legal, social or economic institution) to change, society requires not only a set of interested actors who can express a desire for the right to be amended in some way beneficial to them, but also some authority and set of procedures that can effectively respond to the demand. Only when both these forces are present can we expect to see property rights develop and change.[1]

[1] The demand-and-supply approach is implicit in much historical writing on the emergence of institutions. For a masterly use of a demand-and-supply framework to analyse an economic or social institution, see Stigler 1971. As soon as supply-and-demand are mentioned, we look for evidence of market-like relationships among the groups of demanders

This approach is in general harmony with a view of the emergence of institutions held by many historians of common law. In this view, institutions are not deliberately created; they evolve. F. A. Hayek compares this evolutionary approach, as it first emerged in the fifteenth century, with a 'design' approach in which thoughtful or tyrannical men are seen deliberately to invent and design social institutions, and put them in place:

> Complex and orderly and, in a very definite sense, purposive, institutions might grow up which owed little to design, which were not invented but arose from the separate actions of many men who did not know what they were doing. This demonstration that something better than man's individual mind may grow from men's fumbling efforts represented in some ways an even greater challenge to all design theories [Hayek elsewhere includes among these theories the Cartesian schemes of consistent law-making, such as is represented in Rousseau's social contract] than even the later theory of biological evolution. For the first time... [it] was shown... [that] the emergence of order [was] the result of adaptive evolution.[2]

Hayek falls back on describing a gradual process by which changes to the entire institutional structure arise only incrementally. In particular, he mentions the common-law process, within which property rights were formed and changed. The evolutionary process is a mechanism, working somewhat autonomously. He cites Hale: '[It] is not necessary that the reasons [for] the institution should be evident unto us'.[3] Just as in biological evolution the plants and animals do not plan natural selection, so in the evolution of institutions (including property rights) the users and the suppliers do not design the system or its progress.[4]

In economists' language, the phrase 'property right' is typically little more than a synonym for 'ownership' or perhaps 'possession'. Thus a contention like 'by the Victorian era the feudal system of tenure had given way to a system of private property rights' means simply that title to and control over the lands and resources had come under the control of individuals; that the *distribution* of landed wealth was changed. In this book, however, as in many works for

and among the supplying institutions. When Anthony Downs 1957, Howard Bowen 1943, and Macpherson 1962 followed Schumpeter 1942 in seeing voter and interest group rivalry as an extension of market competition, they launched the new field of public choice. Rivalry among governments (suppliers) is a newer idea: See Breton et al 1991.

[2] Hayek 1960, p. 59. Hayek mentions Carl Menger. His personal distaste for other explanations of the appearance of social institutions is that they tend to glorify single-minded rationality and, hence, totalitarianism.

[3] Hayek 1960, p. 58, citing Chief Justice Hale's criticism of Hobbes 1651.

[4] Although Hayek's approach is intuitively satisfying, he has almost nothing to say about an institution becoming widely accepted and so a sort of public good (see Scott 1983, Scott and Johnson 1985). See also Viktor Vanberg's (1986) critical examination of Hayek's theory of cultural evolution, which also has nothing to say about the difficulty created by public goods. For discussion of Darwinian selection of institutions, see Gordon 1989 and Sugden 1985.

lawyers and economic historians, the change with which I am concerned has less to do with the distribution of rights to land among persons than with *what* is included in a (standardized) right. In particular, we can consider the set of *powers* conveyed by a particularly named right over a piece of land. These powers, which have changed from century to century in different types of right, are given a convenient three-fold classification that we will encounter throughout this book. They are: powers to *use and manage* the land, powers to *transfer or alienate* it and powers to *take the income or rent* from its use. Legal economic analysts say a standard right is complete when it gives its holder healthy doses of all of these three powers.[5] Rights that people say have 'incomplete', 'deficient', or 'attenuated' powers may permit or even induce feeble or destructive economic performance from their holder.

Alternatively, a person's property right over a piece of land is often described by property-law scholars as a *'bundle'* of rights. The 'bundle' consists of the privileges and restrictions attached to a particular ownership, either in terms of the general powers just described or in terms of specific privileges, such as an easement or right of way granted across a neighbour's land, or duties or burdens benefiting someone else. In states or provinces where land titles must be entered in a land registry, most of the privileges and burdens that go with ownership of a particular piece of land are listed in the registry alongside the holder's title.

The focus of this book will be on the evolution of the *standard* bundle of rights associated with a property tenure—those enjoyed by every holder of the right, and recognized and enforced by the courts or government authority. The bundle of rights that goes with a standard modern freehold land ownership, for example, typically includes a right (or power) to cut timber on the land. In contrast, we will see in Chapter 12 on forest law that the holder of an entailed or leasehold right to forestland was and is often restricted from committing 'waste' by clearing the forest unless by a condition bundled into his rights there is an explicit agreement or stipulation in his contract (with his family or with the lessor) releasing him from 'impeachability for waste'. Titles to natural resources frequently contain such specialized rules, which may be individual or situation-specific and so depart from standardization. However, taken together, and through their adjudication and enforcement, these too can lead to the formation of *standard* bundles of rights, the emergence of which will be the theme of the following chapters.

In preference to classifying by groups of *powers*, or by standard *bundles* of specific liberties and privileges, I make reference throughout the following chapters to a third set of elements that compose individual property rights, especially those held by individuals who use and manage natural resources. These elements I call the *characteristics* of the right. Some of these characteristics

[5] See A. Honoré 1987.

will be familiar from standard economic literature on the efficient allocation of resources. My approach differs from this (mainly normative) literature in two ways. For one, I am not primarily interested in deriving solutions to an 'optimal' property holding problem, in the sense that more of the characteristics lead to better functioning regimes of property rights. We will see in the description of the characteristics and in the many discussions of their development that the story was often far more complicated. Second, I assume that the characteristics I describe are *quantitative*. I treat them as though they are continuous, measurable and changeable (rather than dichotomous, amorphous and fixed). The kind of analysis I want to avoid is one in which in which the resource holder has a property right with, say, full and complete liberty to transfer the right to another person, or to avoid interference and spillovers from neighbours. While such simplifications can be useful, for the purposes of this book, they assume away situations in which a holder may have existent but insufficient amounts of a characteristic, inducing him to understand the need for, and hence make a demand for, more.

The six characteristics of a property right

The six characteristics of property rights are ***exclusivity***, ***duration***, ***flexibility***, ***quality of title***, ***transferability*** and ***divisibility***.

I begin with the *exclusivity* characteristic. Property holders demand exclusivity in order to be independent—to free themselves from the losses and costs arising from such interferences as a forest fire that spreads from one treed property to another or sewage carried downstream from the emitting property through the lands of other riparians. Greater exclusivity implies greater freedom from these losses and costs. Making holders' rights more exclusive can be likened to heightening their fences.

Exclusivity has two fairly distinct situational meanings in this book. It can refer to the reduction or avoidance of physical interference with the right-holder's use of his resource, interference that amounts to having to *share* a resource with other owners, usually neighbours. Exclusivity can also refer to the right-holder's degree of independence or freedom from government regulations that restrict the ways in which he can use the resource in order to promote the public good or the government's own ends. Usually, the type of exclusivity being discussed will be obvious from the context.

Both the idea of exclusivity and the possibility of its measurement become more complicated where a land-holder's property has multiple uses. His right may in this case be an aggregation of various rights to grow trees, to hunt, to mine and so on. Each of these rights has its own specific measure of exclusivity, and the extents may differ, depending on the number of potential interfering neighbours and the number of interfering uses. At one extreme, the owner may be able to internalize all possible interferences with any use of his resource, for instance if his property is very large or isolated. At the other extreme, however, his right may include only one use of his natural resource, because any other interferes with the use of the first or with the uses of adjoining right-holders. This second extreme is not uncommon in the history of property rights: we will encounter situations close to it in Chapter 9 on petroleum rights, Chapter 8 on miners' surface rights, Chapter 3 on inland water rights, and Chapter 4 on fishing rights.

I turn next to a standard property-right's *duration* characteristic. Obviously quantitative, it might be measured by the length of time the property right gives the holder to exercise the three powers over the resource. Under most modern versions of common law, the duration of freehold or fee-simple tenure is 'indeterminate' or permanent, while that of leases, licences, and other tenures is determinate, limited to an agreed period of months or years for private transactions (and subject to renewal), or to a legislated period for holdings on public and Crown lands. Examples are given for public-land oil contracts in Chapter 9 and for private forestry in Chapter 12. The actual duration of a property right over a private resource has rarely been set by the courts or by the legislature. It may have been implied (for instance, entailed land is held for the current occupant's lifetime after which it passes automatically to the defined heir) or set explicitly by bargaining between the parties to a leasehold or licence.

The duration of a property right can be looked at in two ways. Seen one way, it measures the period of time within which the holder has liberty to carry on his resource-improving or resource-depleting operations—growing trees or exhausting a mine. Seen another way, it measures the period of time over which a second user must wait for the first user to finish his occupation. Medieval law was full of prescribed waits, such as a minor's wait to come of age in order to take over ownership of his family's mines; or the necessary interval—often twenty years—after which an illegal or legally vulnerable occupation or encroachment of land became legal possession or ownership (through prescription). Even today, statutes force an impatient landlord to wait before evicting a dilatory tenant.

The third characteristic is *flexibility*. This is the extent to which the powers and obligations a right bestows on the holder can be adjusted without weakening title. If his interest in land has zero flexibility, a holder can make no choices with respect to his or her three powers of ownership (management, disposal and receipt of income/enjoyment). Rather, the owner must confine his or her activities to one standard or agreed kind of use, sale and mode of payment. If it has flexibility, however, the holder's right may provide for renegotiation of the terms or conditions during the duration of the user's occupation. Probably the most flexible kind of holding is a permit or licence to use public lands or an open-access resource; only government-imposed regulations can make such a right less flexible.

Next I turn to *quality of title*, which refers to the extent to which a right is proof (*secure*) against others' claims to possession. Good quality of title is commonly assumed to be essential to the sustainable management and improvement of land, because it allows the property owner to be sure that he will in fact receive the payoff from his improvements. (The effects of good quality of title are often closely tied to the effects of long duration, mentioned above, since expropriation or nullification of a right in fact cuts the right's duration short.) As against the world, and as against the government, title is of a high quality if the holder can be confident of being able to maintain or recover possession of his land and his powers over it against potential usurpers. These ideas are simple enough, and they suggest how one may be able to distinguish between rights with different 'amounts' of quality of title.[6]

For the most part, the legal literature on quality of title sets out ways in which the characteristic may be missing. Quality of title historically has depended on three conditions: legitimacy, usually by inheritance, conveyance or custom; enforceability, which depends on the existence, quality and breadth of jurisdiction of relevant social institutions such as courts; and freedom and security from government seizure of the land. Early on in the history surveyed in these chapters, the third condition was increasingly satisfied as the late medieval Crown's power to take privately held property gradually fell into disuse. Faced by the same force that, after Magna Carta, had restricted its powers to tax, the Crown increasingly found it wise to stop taking private lands without paying for them. Centuries later the new United States banned this executive 'habit' with a constitutional amendment declaring a right to property.

As their powers of confiscation lapsed, governments themselves instituted procedures for restraining compulsory-purchase acquisition. Restraints are now found in most developed countries, where new measurements of 'contract enforceability and property rights security' are found to be associated with high incomes, education, and economic growth.[7] Where and when it does take place, expropriation tends to be highly controversial, perceived as a threat to the property rights of its citizens. For example, statutory interventions to make private land available for public recreation and for wildlife habitat have been opposed by the affected landowners, and some members

[6] One measure, for titles granted by private owners, is the inverse of the number of persons who might come forward with better titles. Another, for titles acquired from government, is the negative of the market's estimation of the likelihood that the grantor will interfere to dilute the rent or take the land. Proxies for measures such as these underlie recent comparative studies of countries' rates of economic growth. For this idea applied to forestry tenures, see Luckert 1991.

[7] Knack 1996, p. 209. Knack argues that differences in institutional quality, as measured by two private indexes of the risk of investing in a country, explain which relatively backward nations successfully catch up with relatively non-backward nations. The indexes have proxies for each nation's rule of law, the absence of the risk of expropriation and the absence of the risk of repudiation of contracts (p. 212). Thanks to John Helliwell for help on this subject.

of the public in sympathy with them, as threatening their ownership and exclusivity. (We will encounter examples in which imperfect quality of title leads to a reduction in the exclusivity characteristic, forcing property owners to in effect 'share' their resource with the public. In particular, see Chapter 12 on modern rights to private forest holding.)

The next characteristic is *transferability*, or alienability. An increase in a standard property right's transferability increases the extent to which the holder may bequeath, trade or sell his or her interest in a parcel of land or a natural resource.[8] Transferability, and its variants, is mentioned by some writers (particularly in the allocational economics literature mentioned above) as *the* indispensable aspect of ownership rights for good land and resource use—more so even than quality of title. It is the characteristic that allows for markets in property rights, with perfect transferability a prerequisite for the 'perfect' market. These authors, of course, advocate complete transferability—total freedom to transfer any part of ownership of a property right to any outside party in return for fair compensation. In the real world, and especially historically, a complete transferability of land rights is rare. At many points in the following chapters, we will see this ideal impeded by custom, laws and contracts.[9]

We will see also that extensive transferability in natural resource property in the West is a fairly modern invention. The main shift began as late as the seventeenth century when judges, asked to evaluate the legality of disputed land transfers, began to find against old laws and customs that called for inalienability. (As the judges were being increasingly recruited from an urban middle class, they may have tended to sympathize with would-be buyers who were excluded from land ownership because of inalienability in the titles of would-be sellers, a subject I discuss further below.)[10] The trend since then has generally been toward greater transferability. The general rule today, strengthened by the insistence of the English common-law courts, has become that the holder of a freehold right has an almost unconstrained right to transfer land. As for leaseholds, laws generally permit and enforce transfers but do allow lessors to prohibit further alienation by the lessee. A common example is the legality of 'no subletting' clauses in a modern rental lease.

[8] For a discussion of inalienability, not only of property but also of other rights and social duties, see Susan Rose-Ackerman 1985. She defines ownership as 'pure property' if it can be both given away and sold.

[9] To quantify transferability, the ideal index would capture the number of eligible persons to whom the right could legally be reassigned. This number could easily be close to zero, as in early feudal England, where the general rule was that holders of land were merely an overlord's tenants with almost no rights to sell or rent and had to pass land on according to the rules of primogeniture.

[10] See Barzel 1989 chapter 7 for conjectures about why land-holding governments and some resource users in the nineteenth century resisted the tide of increasing transferability.

This brings us to the *divisibility* characteristic—also encountered in the literature as 'partibility', 'fragmentability', and 'separability'—probably the least recognized of the characteristics. Economists may consider divisibility as a subset of transferability—the ability to transfer a part of a property right. Even authors who strongly support market approaches to natural resource allocation (such as farm economists who advocate breaking up very large private blocks of irrigation water) neglect to discuss the extent to which all property rights, or at least all water rights, are, or should be, divisible. To make clear what this characteristic permits or protects, I distinguish three kinds of divisibility: (1) horizontal; (2) vertical (including *temporal* division of one parcel among estates or successive possessors); and (3) multiple-use (dividing an interest in land into interests in each of its uses, products, attributes or purposes).

Horizontal divisibility of an interest in land allows its holder to subdivide his land or resource into rights over smaller, probably adjacent, parcels by lease, gift, will, or sale. (A variant of horizontal division was the widespread practice of dividing a landlord's arable 'common land' into strips or fields.) Division was and is sometimes forbidden or opposed because it destroys economies of scale and other advantages[11] of exploiting large blocks of a natural resource. In France and some parts of England, on the other hand, both law and custom once called for every decedent's lands to be divided equally among his sons.[12]

A less familiar kind of horizontal divisibility allows a landholder to divide his simple land ownership into a co-ownership—joint or common. The difference between these two types of co-ownership shows up when one party dies or drops out. The share of a joint owner simply vanishes, as with a member of a club who, in dropping out, sees his or her former interest in the club's assets melt into those of the remaining members. A share of an owner in common, however, passes intact to another person when he leaves, much like a corporate stock. The right to create co-ownerships this way has rarely been denied, and is commonly found today in the case of residential property held in the names of two spouses. More relevant to the subject of this book, common ownerships of placer sites were tried with varying success during the nineteenth-century gold rushes. We will see in Chapter 6 that such joint ownerships were tried in the first year of the California gold rush only to be replaced by individual claim holdings. On the other hand claim holders in Victoria during the slightly later Australian gold rush did successfully pool their

[11] The advantages of not dividing natural resources may be recreational or aesthetic, and may be captured by modern private or governmental zoning restrictions, on which see Ellickson 1973.

[12] Various laws and customs called for the land to go to the oldest descendant (primogeniture), the youngest descendant (borough English) or all male descendants equally (gavelkind). Typically when I look at English succession here and in future chapters, I am more concerned with families' concerns and legal provisions in their wills concerning the passing of estates intact to a single inheritor as provided by entail and strict settlement.

operations and so became owners in common, partly for companionship and partly to spread the labour and cost of deep alluvial diggings.

I turn now to *vertical* divisibility, a somewhat esoteric way of describing overlapping temporal claims to a unit of land or natural resource. A partial explanation was given, breathlessly, in *Walsingham's Case* (1579):

> The land itself is one thing, and the estate in land is another thing, for an estate in land is a time in the land, or land for a time, and there are diversities of estates, which are no more than diversities of time, for he who has a fee-simple in land has time in the land without end, or the land for time without end, and he who has land in tail has a time in the land or the land for a time as long as he has issues of his body, and he who has an estate in land for life has no time in it longer than his own life, and so of him who has an estate in land for the life of another, or for years.[13]

'Time in the land' is still a good way of getting started thinking about the right to divide ownership vertically, for dated future intervals of time.[14] The amount of this characteristic in a right may be measured by the number of estates (ownerships or interests conferring possession currently or in the future) in existence today in a piece of land. To illustrate, consider a territory now granted in leasehold for a known period of years, after which it returns to the possession of its freehold owner, after which possession will, sometime, pass to an heir under the family's succession arrangements. We may measure the vertical divisions by counting the 'estates' into which current 'ownership' was fragmented: three. When a right to land has vertical divisibility, each future estate is held as property today, and the estates' holders may be permitted to trade, mortgage or further divide them.

Third, we consider what I have called *multiple-use divisibility*, a characteristic that allows the right holder to divide his powers to create a separate right over each of the uses of the land. (Note the difference between this and the co-ownership of all the land described above as a kind of horizontal divisibility.) This kind of divisibility seems always to have been possible under the common law. As will be seen in subsequent chapters, particularly Chapter 8 on private-estate mining, medieval and early modern owners frequently severed their powers over the management, disposal and income/enjoyment of one or more of the natural resources growing or existing together on their land. They disposed of the severed 'estate' by freehold, leasehold, or contract, thereby partitioning or fragmenting their rights to allow private engagement in fishing, hunting, logging or mining on the land.[15] From the owners' point of view, this portioning for compensation may have provided an attractive alternative

[13] *Walsingham's Case* (1579), 2 Plowd. 547, 555, 75 E.R. 805, 817 (Exch.).

[14] In classical property law, estates in land could be classified according to their duration, the number and connection of their holders and the time of enjoyment I have dealt with the first under the heading of 'duration', the second under the heading of 'horizontal divisibility' and the third under the heading of 'vertical divisibility'.

[15] Alchian 1977, cited by Eggertsson 1990, p. 39.

to undertaking all of the fishing, logging, hunting and mining themselves, increasing operational specialization and bringing in cash.[16]

The six characteristics of a holder's property right in land can usefully be thought of graphically, as a six-pointed figure, where the length of each spoke represents the amount of the corresponding characteristic. If there is a legal development that has the effect of making a right more transferable, the diagram would show this by a lengthening of the transferability spoke. If there is a burst of government expropriation of private property, the diagram would show this by a shortening of the 'quality of title' (security) spoke. At its fullest length the spoke represents the (hypothetical) amount of the characteristic that would justify saying that it is 'complete' or 'perfect' in the sense that a holder of the right would have no reason to want or demand more of it.[17]

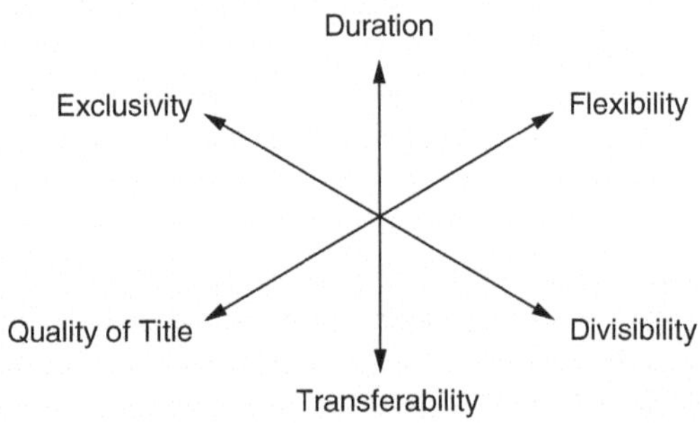

My strategy in this book is to identify changes and evolutions in the rights held by typical owners of property with changes in the characteristics of the kind of standard right they hold. For example, when a seventeenth-century court found that an upstream party could legally increase his diversion of a stream's flow, even at the expense of a miller downstream from him, this resulted a *reduction* of the exclusivity characteristic in the miller's right to water, and an increase in the upstream party's exclusivity characteristic. These changes are in principle measurable and can be represented by a respective shortening and lengthening of the 'exclusivity' spokes in the diagram above applied to each right.[18] Similarly, when governments first limited the number of commercial fishing-boat licences available to their citizens, as described in Chapter 4, they in effect added something to the exclusivity of each remaining fisherman's right (licence), though the interference might have been seen by all fishers as compromising their quality of title. These

[16] Whether to work a farm, share it, or lease it out completely is an old subject in political economy. It was revived and modernized by Cheung 1969 and by Eswaran and Kotwal 1985.

[17] For ingenious use of this diagram, see Devlin and Grafton 1998, chapters 3 and 4.

[18] It must be conceded, however, that some writers do agree that the amount of a characteristic can be quantitative, as when Barzel 1989, ch. 5, says that someone's right has become 'better delineated'.

effects could be captured through the lengthening of one and the shortening of another spoke for those fishers who retained their licenses.

To be sure, I do not share the Victorian notion that society's laws and institutions, like nature's mechanisms, are not only perfectible but are constantly in the process of perfecting themselves and, in so doing, are bringing to the service of humankind (and of God) more specialization, more economies of scale, and more diversity. At least, such a belief does not fit the historical evidence on the development of property rights. As historians and observers, we can generally know for certain what demanders are seeking, but not whether the judicial or governmental satisfaction of their demands, if it occurs, has actually improved the standard property right rather than simply improved the situation of one class of users relative to another. It is also unclear whether the improvement will last, be reversed, or prove to be inappropriate in the face of changing technology and use. This is not my concern. I seek to learn how and why the characteristics of property rights have changed, not—at least as a general principle—whether the changes were a good or a bad thing.

Taking action to add to a characteristic

The listing of characteristics leads on to examining more closely the private and social procedures followed by demanders and suppliers in amending them. I devote the remainder of this chapter to this task. I first present a listing of demanders and suppliers, in order of their appearance along a spectrum or range of what I consider to be the importance of their historical roles. On the demand side, the spectrum of demanders runs from holders of manors and large estates to individual owners of smaller holdings to small and residential tenants. Intermixed along this range are firms, collective holders of rights and groups of holders and users acting collectively.

On the supply side, government clearly appears as provider of rights to users of the public lands; as registrar of private property rights; and as maker of rules and regulations that restrict the powers of holders of property rights to natural resources. At various points in the following chapters, we will explicitly encounter government and government departments acting as demanders of characteristics of property rights, either to advance the private ends of politicians and bureaucrats or to protect a common or public aspect of property that private owners can not be trusted to supply in the absence of the characteristic. Indeed, before the modern era, the difference between the government landowning class and the strictly private landowning class was often very unclear, making supply and demand behaviour difficult to untangle. For brevity, I will leave this discussion to later chapters (see especially Chapter 8) and deal with government here only in its capacity as a supplier.

Beyond the government as supplier, along the spectrum, lie the courts. At places in this book it will appear that, at least until recently, the courts were in fact the primary supplier of changes in property rights. This was certainly true of the medieval courts. Later, as nineteenth and twentieth-century governments took the initiative in codifying property law and tort law, the courts' property-right role became the interpretation of the comprehensive statutes.

At the end of the spectrum we will find traces of ancient modes of providing and enforcing characteristics of property right, including 'custom' as a source of tenants' land rights, surviving from possibly fictional ancient feudal contracts; and scattered instances of collective, cooperative, and communal law-making and decision-making. These primitive suppliers, along with manorial courts and the law-making powers of private landlords over their demesne were once the main source of the characteristics of individual rights over open-access resources such as common lands, fisheries and waters. They declined in importance as government and judicial systems gained legitimacy and authority in the transition to modern society.

The notion of a spectrum of demanders and suppliers does not leave room for the private agreement or contract, the main device by which one private (or sometimes public) party transfers some of his rights and powers of property, along with some or all of its characteristics, to another. Nevertheless, we might well expect that there is a connection. The amounts of characteristics supplied by a standard (boilerplate) private contract are bounded above by the amounts of characteristics in the original right. We will see examples of this boundedness in Chapter 9 concerning individual leases between farmers and oil drilling companies on the American frontier. Sometimes as well the government would intervene as a supplier of sorts to specify what had to be conveyed by any private contract.

To illustrate the supply and demand process and its players consider the hypothetical case of a group of landowners who drain their properties by pouring their ditched floodwaters onto neighbouring lands. Suppose that the ability to do so has traditionally been regarded as within the powers bundled into their standard freehold property rights. At some point, however, the neighbours rebel by turning back the flow issuing from the ditches, harming the original landholders. The landholders sue, an 'upstream' party bringing suit against a 'downstream' party. The court hears the pair of landowners and finds (say) for the downstream party. Using the 'characteristic' vocabulary, the court finds that the flooded party's right has (or should have) sufficient exclusivity to protect him from the flood waters flowing unnaturally from upstream. As this is a new finding, the exclusivity characteristic in the downstream party's right is revealed to be greater than previously understood. The finding becomes, under the common law, a precedent for subsequent judgments on the same point.

If the complainant victim does not bring his flooding problem to the attention of a common-law court, he may nevertheless get his desired re-interpretation of the exclusivity characteristic in his right from a local court (whose terms include the discovery and interpretation of local customary rules about land and drainage). Or he and like-situated right-holders may turn to the government, seeking an administrative order or legislation. In selecting his court, governmental bureau or other potential right-supplier, the individual or firm weighs the likely actuarial benefit of un-flooding his land (weighted by the probability of success) against the costs of litigation and/or the costs of co-ordinating with other similar right-holders to lobby government.

Regardless of what supplier he turns to, the enhancement of exclusivity won by the demander(s) may become generalized and standardized through either statute or common-law precedent, available to all holders of the standard right held by the downstream party. In economists' language, this makes the increase in exclusivity a sort of public good, whose provision to one right-holder extends as a non-excludable and non-rival right to all other holders of the same right. (Of course, if the change in the law causes more harm to rival property holders than good to the winners, it could also be considered a 'public bad'.) Leaving aside the merits of the change, however, it is important to remember that the individuals and firms who appeal to the government or take private legal action in a dispute may be (though they certainly are not always) unaware of, or indifferent to, being 'demanders' of a change in the *standard* right. As in classical market theory, individual self-interested demands combine to produce public outcomes that indirectly affect all members of an industry or society.

I turn now to a formalization of the question of *why* demanders request a change in property rights. Demanders' (private) goals mainly fall into two categories. On the one hand, they may be almost entirely *distributional*. Individuals whose actions would increase some characteristic of a property right are doing so in order to protect and possibly to increase their own rights over some natural resource. How this resource or land is to be held, as personal property or real property, singly or jointly, is secondary to them. The cases and examples documented in the following chapters are often landowners trying to capture or re-capture rights on their own estates, from members of their own families, from their feudal tenants or from neighbours who are imposing externalities on them. A modern-day example, encountered in Chapter 4, involves international fishing conflicts. In addition to somewhat academic-level debates about the ideal method of setting-up and enforcing collective ownership and fishstock management, there are bitter underlying conflicts about distribution of rights. To whom and in what amounts should shares of the catch be allotted? More specifically, why should some fishers benefit from the increased exclusivity inherent in the individual catch quota when their gain requires that others be excluded from the industry?

The second category of demands is *allocational* in nature—demanders seek changes in property rights to affect the purpose for which the resource in question is used. For instance, in Chapter 12, competing demands for exclusivity in property rights applying to a private forest help determine which types of property rights, and which holders of such rights, may use the woods for timber and which for residential, recreational, hunting, fishing, food-collection or mining purposes.

To conclude this part, I return to the idea of weighing the benefits and the costs of strengthening property rights. Distributional and allocational changes in exclusivity and other characteristics of property rights introduce changes in demanders' costs, first of achieving and then of holding the improved right. Transactions costs can be divided into two main categories: *top level* costs include costs of searching for information, actual litigating, and organizing the group taking collective action. *Mid-level costs* include the costs of protecting, dividing or dealing in the land explicitly caused by the change from the right's old bundle of characteristics to the new one.[19] An important mid-level cost is enforcement of the new right against neighbours and free-riding outsiders.[20]

The levels of both top-level and mid-level transactions costs are sensitive to the characteristics of the firms' property rights. For instance, a firm with weak exclusivity provisions in its property rights may need to adopt costly personal contracting or fencing or guarding to protect its holdings. And a firm will expect to suffer (or enjoy) economies of scale in unit management costs if it experiences a change in the size or shape of its lands in the course of a change in the characteristics of its property rights. Field (1985, 1989)[21] imagines a community considering the division of a large common into smaller individual holdings and seeking to find one best number of identical small holdings.

[19] Given this terminology, we might also expect to encounter 'low-level' transactions costs. These would be changes in those costs first described by Ronald Coase: the right-holders' costs of co-coordinating, trading and organizing employment in using the natural resource under the modified right (not of adapting to the right). Unlike mid-level transaction costs, they are only indirectly caused by the achieved change in the property right. For instance, if a right-holder has acquired more exclusive rights over a forest, the low-level transaction cost of his doing so would be the resultant change if any in his costs of information, organizing and coordination within his forestry firm and of bargaining, trading with and delivering to his own suppliers or customers.

[20] This depiction of demanders incurring transactions and enforcement costs to obtain enhanced characteristics in a standard property right borrows from economists' 'naïve' public choice model, to which I return in Chapter 4. 'Naive' is the word used by Eggertsson 1990, chap. 8. To follow the literature see Coase 1960; Alchian 1965; and Demsetz 1967. Douglass North, in a related literature seeking to explain the historical transition from an earlier warrior society to a later property-owning society, emphasized the increasing availability of better or cheaper enforcement procedures, often not local but international. Later writers have adapted this model to discuss the enclosing of range lands, fields, fisheries and oil formations. See Eggertsson 1990, p. 254; Dennen 1976; Ault and Rutman 1979; Harper-Fender 1981; Johnson 1987; and Trebilcock 1984; also Stevenson 1991 and Netting 1976 on the so-called Swiss common, or Alp.

[21] See also Ellickson 1991.

He argues that this optimum size and number will change as the expected average internal management cost or expected average external transactions costs change. This, in turn, might change the holders' demands for other characteristics. If, for example, a change led to larger holdings, the increased size might induce landholders to demand enhanced divisibility, duration and transferability in their rights.[22] At the same time, if the unit costs of dealing with neighbours rise, it becomes worthwhile to deal less and spend more on internal management.[23] Calculations like these will come up below in Chapter 6, in which California placer miners are seen struggling to set an ideal size of their camp's individual claims, and the corresponding number of miners that the camp can accommodate.

The spectrum of official and unofficial suppliers

Because this is not a general history of economic development, and because a large literature already exists on the historical demanders of changes in property rights (mainly the wealthy, landholding classes), I focus for the remainder of this chapter on the forces of supply that, besieged by these demanders, determined the development of property rights and their characteristics in England and the New World from the Middle Ages to today. In the historical examples provided here and in the rest of the book, we will of course encounter the (mostly familiar) individuals, firms and organized lobbies who, by appealing to the suppliers, provided the other half of the transaction.

Government: the Crown and the legislature

Some economic theorists' writings on property-right development give the idea that it was politicians in government who disavowed the warrior

[22] Field's model is a descendant of Coase's pre-war 1937 model, which explains the optimum size of the corporation by a similar balancing of internal and external costs. It can also be used to illustrate the effects of changing in-migration, wage-rates and fencing prices. In this connection McManus 1975 argues for the idea that all institutions, from common property to firms and individual contractors, have enforcement or monitoring costs and that it should not be assumed that the private firm is better at handling these than are its alternatives. Buchanan and Tullock 1962 used a similar approach to explain the choice of optimum constitutional rules for voting. Breton and Scott 1978 adapted this idea in our explanation of the choice of allocation of powers between levels of government. For a related discussion see Godwin and Shepherd 1984.

[23] A practical problem for economists is that the naïve model may be followed to predict the direction of change, but not to discover the likely direction of causation. Does it predict that an expected relative decline in enforcement and transactions costs *causes* the upgrading of the exclusivity of property rights, or *is caused by* its expected upgrading? Did lower-cost barbed wire induce, or follow, more exclusive property rights? Although such chicken-and-egg problems abound, variants of the naïve model do illustrate theoretically how changes in transactions and management costs could be sufficient to create an active allocational demand for a resource-right characteristic. See also Godwin and Sheppard 1984 and Albert Breton 1996, pp. 181–227.

society and feudalism and turned to the creation by legislation of rights over land; and that thereafter they devoted themselves to repeated exercises in modernizing these rights. But politicians rarely did anything like this. Until the mid-nineteenth century, in England, legislation concerning property rights was infrequent and usually confined to supplying only relatively minor changes in the law of property. Exceptions included Parliament's modernizing of laws applying to the conditions governing bequests and successions to land; the tidying up of some legal anomalies dealing with property and urban leases; and—crucially—the establishment and protection of courts of law. But most of these activities could scarcely be said to reflect a desire of reforming politicians to improve the characteristics of the public's, or at least the landowning public's property rights. For centuries it was the judges, not the politicians, who had the job of enforcing and renewing the law of property.

As time passed, however, the participation of government in supplying characteristics became more necessary. Three examples we will encounter throughout this book are the legislation governing the occupation of and disposal of public land; legislation regulating the enclosure of common lands; and legislation regulating and dividing common pool or open-access natural resources. Parliament and the other legislatures did not merely take over the courts' property-rights work. We will see that the characteristic-changing decisions of politicians went in different directions from those implemented by the courts. When an ownership dispute before a court involved the exclusivity or transferability of a litigant's rights, the judges primarily saw their role as making the fairest possible application of the existing law. In situations where doing this led to unsatisfactory outcomes, they might seek to incorporate what usually amounted to a strengthening of the characteristics of property rights, often as a means of ensuring the better working of land and resource markets. This led them, for example, to admit and strengthen concepts such as reasonableness and seniority in resource use. By contrast, when similar issues appeared within demands put before Parliaments, the parliamentary committees wavered, sometimes weakening and sometimes strengthening the characteristics in standard rights. Their major (political) concern often seems to have been how changes in rights' characteristics would affect the *distribution* of property, finding fair or otherwise favourable outcomes for specific groups of demanders than with establishing rules that would make efficient outcomes more likely.

As government lost its monolithic structure, becoming a composite within which separate departments and offices dealt with particular topics, jurisdiction over law-making became widely diffused. Who, or what bureau, would have jurisdiction and responsibility for laws over private property rights was something of a mystery. The same is true for oversight of the Crown and public lands, including colonial holdings. In the early nineteenth century the Royal Navy was known to keep its eye on cutting rights in colonial forests (see Chapter 11) but it is very unlikely that a typical mid-century British official was well-informed about the rights and rules governing the colonies' gold rushes (Chapter 6), or their fisheries (Chapter 4).

It might therefore be possible to explain governments' property right-supplying activities as instances of interaction among bureaux or among politicians, competing on a personal basis or on behalf of the lobbies and jurisdictions they wished to oblige.[24] To the extent that government's internal structure was competitive, demanders and their interest groups would have been able to choose from which sector or level to seek a desired change in characteristics of property rights. However, the theory of competition in government is difficult to back up empirically. At most points in history, parliamentary or republican governments have endeavoured to present a unified appearance so that competitive elements within them may be difficult to identify. For example, nineteenth-century changes to the complex of British forest taxation discussed in Chapters 11 and 12 could have reflected certain MPs' personal, and possibly conflicting, concerns for the tax burden on their constituents and supporters, or it could have reflected the Treasury's impersonal campaign to reform the whole structure of land and income taxation, or it could have represented an agricultural department's sympathy with a pressure group seeking to strengthen the nation's forest cover.

This difficulty has forced me to avoid explanations that depend on the possible degrees of competition and cooperation within government in supplying rights, and refer only to 'government' (or Parliament or Congress or 'the legislature'). In a basic vision of the process, demanders appeal to politicians and their bureaucrats. Their demands are passed 'up' to a politician, 'down' to what is thought to be the administrative unit most appropriate, and back up again for formal ministerial adoption. Bureaucrats protect their minister, and he or she, as a member of the governing party, governs the extent to which any proposed change in policy encroaches on the domains of other ministers. Political alliance among governing politicians therefore dampens what might otherwise develop into visible inter-bureau competition.[25]

[24] In a 1991 conference paper I sketched a model for such an approach. See Scott 1991b, pp. 8 and 9. See also companion paper by Mattei and Pulitini that investigates competition within the judicial system. For the general competitive approach to understanding government see the comprehensive treatment in Albert Breton 1996.

[25] In a parliamentary system, each minister operates 'in the shadow of the prime minister'. See Breton 1991 and Breton 1996, pp. 70–95 for how this works in both parliamentary and congressional systems of government. Breton relies on the financial power of the governing party, a power that may or may not be relevant to decisions about the modification of private property rights. Another view of government emphasizes the competition between departments, with each minister supporting his or her own department's bureaucrats.

SUPPLY OF RIGHTS VIA PUBLIC LAND POLICIES

Public land disposal for settlement and raw-material production

In its traditional and most primitive role, government acted as a landowner, handing out ownership or tenure to private holders. In terms of European history this is hardly surprising; in Britain all land was originally Crown property. From the Norman Conquest onward, the holdings of every class of landholder were regarded as having at one time or another been taken out of the monarch's lands and disposed of to friends, allies, the church and buyers. The land rights—titles—of these recipients were first shaped by the feudal system. As will be seen below, the re-shaping of the rights of landholders gradually drifted from the monarchy to litigation and the courts.

I discuss the medieval royal forests further in Chapter 11; as an introduction, we can think of them as analogous to royal cattle ranches: very large areas set aside almost exclusively for game and the chase and reserved for use by the royal household.[26] However, farmers and peasants, and sometimes assembled villages, also lived in the forests, ruled by special officers enforcing a distinct code. Their rights over the land were different from those of outside land holders.[27] Even after the importance of the hunt to the Crown had dwindled, some of the enormous forests continued to be ruled by Crown forest law, including property provisions applying to forest inhabitants. And even when Crown lands were not technically designated as forests, there were royal prerogative rights governing transfer, division and exclusion. Writing about the Stuart period, Lord Macaulay comments: 'There can be no doubt that the Sovereign was, by the old policy of the realm, competent to give or let the domains of the Crown in such manner as seemed good to him. No statute defined the length of the term which he might grant, or the amount of the fee which he must reserve.'[28] Just as important, the Crown typically claimed similar absolute prerogative proprietorship over the lands in its newly discovered or conquered domains abroad. As all land in England had been originally the monarch's land, so in the new colonies rights over the lands were from the beginning claimed for the British Crown.

By the late eighteenth century, Parliament and the legislatures had replaced the monarch in making policy and establishing property rights. In the New World, in order to encourage settlement, Parliament distributed large acreages to its friends, and to the colonial governments, land companies, utopian communities, churches, schools and retired soldiers. In the new United States

[26] Remember that Robin Hood lived in Sherwood Forest, a large royal forest. When he is celebrated for 'robbing' the rich to feed the poor, a correct reference is not to his banditry but to his continuous slaughtering of the royal game, taking venison from the king's table. It took a generous royal pardon to relieve Robin of this outlawry. Both Crown and private lands where trees/timber were the specialty were referred to as 'wastes' (of the manors); as 'woods' (as in Chorley Wood); or as coppices, groves or spinneys.

[27] See Rackham 1980, pp. 175–88; Nisbet 1909.

[28] Macaulay 1885, chap. 23. Even today the constitutional division of powers between the executive and the legislature may leave some powers over the public lands undefined. Not every land transaction has been, or need be, authorized by the assembly.

the state legislatures adopted the English governments' disposal role in the remaining public lands, though they differed among themselves in the method of transfer adopted—through freehold, leasehold, sharecropping or another alternative. The political leaders of the new federal government debated even more vigorously how to dispose of the nation's 'empty' public lands, and how much of the transferability and divisibility characteristics the rights to these lands should be endowed. George Washington reflected the views of the old 'proprietary interest' in proposing gradual, compact settlement restrained by government. Against him, Thomas Jefferson argued for what was later to be called a free land policy, with rapid and unregulated granting of surveyed plots not less than one hundred acres each.[29]

This question reverberated in popular debates as well. Reacting against what they regarded as the remnants of the feudalism of rural England, most Americans adopted points of view mixing their allocational goals for the nation (economic development, mostly) and distributional goals for themselves and their children (free land, low taxes and the promise of eventual freehold tenure). But they were divided on the subjects of work and payment requirements, and on interim property rights. And there were some Americans who favoured extending the older tenures of the southern states, including plantations, various durations of tenancy and share-cropping. What in the colonies had been a matter of conferring land titles to encourage and reward supporters of the Crown became in the independent United States a matter of conferring land titles that were most fair and advantageous according to the various classes' views of the republic's nation-building.

There were more global discussions as well. A few years later the English Parliament followed the United States' governments in debating its settlement policies for colonial migration to the remaining British colonies, especially Australia. In 1823 R. J. Wilmot-Horton, a senior colonial-office official (and a political economist in his own right), showed his support for assisted emigration overseas. To create a colonial 'pull', he recommended not only cheap fares and free serviced land but also reformed colonial property rights, tending to freehold. Disposal ideas such as his were adopted as policy for a time, until the brilliant Edward Gibbon Wakefield, arguing against putting unskilled families on scattered plots, urged that migrants should first work for capitalistic farmers. To achieve this end, he recommended rationing land by price and withholding many government services. The workers could eventually acquire freehold land at the full price, which would also cover the cost of roads and other services.[30]

[29] The debate involved more than the leaders' views on individual property rights. Other associated issues were slavery, the acquisition of the western lands, the admittance of new states and property qualifications for the franchise. Thanks to Craig Yurish for help on this period.

[30] Wakefield modified his ideas about spending the proceeds of colonial land sales. Indeed, both Wakefield and Horton altered their proposals progressively; but their ideas did not converge, perhaps because of strong personal antipathy. See Shaw 1970 for an excellent collection of articles by D. N. Winch, E. R. Kittrell and R. N. Ghosh on the 1830s 'colonization controversy' in and out of Parliament.

Official British land disposal policy, already deterred by the costliness of Horton's scheme, shifted toward the self-financing aspects of Wakefield's proposal. But elements of Horton's outlook survived and echoed throughout nineteenth-century colonial policy-making. Like Jefferson's, this approach to land distribution involved dramatic shifts toward land giveaways and settler titles. The Wakefield approach simply entailed government offices offering compact units of the public domain under orthodox titles, with the property system remaining as given.[31]

The debates in England and the US were followed in the British colonies by frequent switching and experimentation among disposal methods: pre-emption, homesteading, appropriation, squatting as well as leasing, staking, recording and licensing for non-homesteading land uses. The rights held prior to final disposal seem not to have become models for new combinations of characteristics in private property rights. While a person held public/Crown land, he or she had one kind of tenure; when that person finally got a permanent title to this land he was granted a standard eighteenth or nineteenth-century common-law interest (typically freehold, sometimes termed a 'patent').[32] Presumably settlers were satisfied with, or even longed for, the quality of title carried by this standard right. There is little evidence that they tried to change its ration of transferability or exclusivity.

'Constitutional' limits on legislator's public-land disposal

By the late nineteenth century there seemed to be no effective limits to politicians' and legislators' ability to allot rights over the public lands, or on the conditions and characteristics they could attach to their allotments. However, the government suppliers had actually run into specific limitations, two of which I summarize here. The first was geographical. Legislatures, of course, could not grant extraterritorial rights, or change the characteristics of existing rights over lands located beyond the borders over which they had jurisdiction. Nor could they grant rights when the land or resource was fluid and not clearly subject to jurisdictional laws or ownership rights—we will encounter this type of situation in Chapter 3 on water rights and a somewhat similar one in Chapter 9 on fugacious mineral rights. In the UK and its former New World

[31] In British Columbia in 1858–9, for example, land policy was on the Wakefield basis, being auctioned or sold at a price high enough to produce a limited number of takers. This was unpopular, and in 1860 the governor allowed squatters to 'pre-empt' land until a survey had been made and other conditions met. This new policy matched that in the US and was in harmony with Horton but not with Colonial Secretary Lytton, who followed Wakefield. See Cail 1974, pp. 12–13.

[32] This may explain why, when Horwitz (1977) set out to write about the changing American concepts of property after 1780 he did not write about rights to land (where there was little development) but about rights to water. The main exception is in connection with aboriginal claims to natural resources and land in New Zealand, the United States, Australia and Canada. From these may flow new forms of right, disposal and tenure—some of which may be communal.

colonies, it has sometimes been uncertain which among the levels of domestic government, and which among the community of nations, had rights and powers sufficient to transfer title over offshore petroleum deposits.

The second limitation is now known in its American version as the 'Public Trust' doctrine. An earlier English version, without a specific label, applied to rights to navigate on tidal or fresh water navigable rivers. The doctrine holds that some resources should be regarded as the 'diffused' property of the public, available and reserved for public purposes. Modern legal literature (especially contributions by Joseph Sax) includes among these public purposes the activities necessary for sustaining the environment. Applied to issues in American states, it provides an exception to the general constitutional rule that the government must respect private property. It is as though the public at large holds an 'easement' (similar to a standard common-law right to build a road or to place an electrical transmission line across someone's land) over certain resources. The legislature can invoke the right when it seizes or withdraws land for environmental purposes that it deems are more in the public interest than would be some proposed private use. But while the legislature may depend on this doctrine, it must also respect it by avoiding seizing, for narrow government purposes, land and resources which would otherwise be for the general public benefit. That is, the government itself must respect the 'easement' over public land, waterways and even private land in its routine project and land-use decisions, just as it demands that citizens do.[33]

The American version of the doctrine has been enforced for the most part by state-level actions in the courts, imposing a duty on the legislature as would an article in the Constitution. Other common-law countries, in their water laws and in their emerging environmental regulation (such as refusing to issue private fish catch quotas beyond the number that would erode the publicly owned fishstock) may be said to have placed duties and limits on their governments that look like weaker versions of public-trust rules, restricting government's supplying powers to respond to private demands over rights to use natural resources.[34]

TAX AND EXPROPRIATION POLICIES AND THE SUPPLY OF CHARACTERISTICS

In the mind of its holder, the quality of title in a standard right to land is imperilled not only by the possibility that property law will be changed, but also by the possibility that his ownership will be compromised by an increase in tax rates or an invigorating of expropriation powers. For example, a person holding a right over a tree plantation might suffer from government's failure

[33] See Rose 2003.
[34] See Kidd 2006, pp. 187–207. See also Rose 2003, pp. 9–10.

to respect his title, or equally from government taxes that decrease the value of his title over the plantation.

Taxes

Changes in tax rates and tax bases have sometimes fuelled demands among landholders that are equivalent to changing their demands for characteristics in their rights (see the discussion in Chapter 12). An early example, to which I will refer back throughout this chapter, comes from the Tudor period in England. Many landowners adjusted to the king's feudal dues by placing their lands in trusts (known then as 'uses'). They retained only what was known as 'equitable ownership'. By thus relinquishing most of the legal responsibility these lords escaped the burden of the dues. (The lawyers who invented the Tudor trust did not intend that it be used for tax avoidance, but it served that purpose.) In order to protect his own revenues, Henry VIII in effect abolished equitable ownership, drastically changing taxpayers' rights over 'their' property.

This story contributes to the generalization that changes in taxation, reductions to encourage certain taxpayer activities or increases to raise public revenues stimulate taxpayers' attempts to hold property and wealth (including land) in ways that keep down their exposure to these taxes. These adjustments, the holders found, and find today, have weakened the characteristics of their property-rights, and may induce further private action to restore them. On the other hand, as I will argue in Chapter 12, land owners may also react passively to the tax by shifting their behaviour the ways presupposed by the designers of the tax policy.[35]

Expropriation

Expropriation from the private sector is even more likely than taxation to stir up public opposition, nominally (at least) based on the sanctity of property rights. Historically, this has certainly been the case. By 1539 the English monarchy's general prerogative over all lands had gone into disuse, except for its rights to gold and other royal metals. Expropriation powers had fallen into the hands of Parliament and colonial legislatures, where compensation for land taken was becoming the rule.[36] The new elected national

[35] The threat of capital gains tax, for example by changing the desirable timing of income from land also changes the effective *duration* of ownership of an interest. It can also be shown that estate tax, income tax and property tax affect duration and that taxation in general affects quality of title, transferability and divisibility. The invention of Zamindar system in India and Burma provides an outstanding instance of tax collection leading to a major change in the social system and the distribution of landed wealth property. See Ault and Rutman 1979. For a modern survey of property and taxation, see also Feeny 1988, pp. 288–90.

[36] In the US seizure had been authorized by the constitution but was limited by the Fifth Amendment's insistence on compensation. The legality and efficiency of 'taking' have been widely discussed for generations and are a staple of today's law-and-economics teaching literature. See Posner 1977; Cooter and Ulen 1988, pp. 191–211.

governments delegated much of their power of compulsory acquisition to junior governments (for public works) and to firms (for canals and railroads), while retaining some national-level expropriation powers for military installations among other things. At first, legislation was needed to acquire land for each project, but later governments routinely assigned decision-making to committees, tribunals and even to certain courts.

As with its reliance on taxation, the increasing governmental reliance on expropriative powers reduced the quality of title of private standard land rights. Private powers to manage, dispose and/or enjoy a piece of land were exposed to the risk of erosion, or of being passed to a public or private developer. A twentieth-century example will be seen in Chapter 3: in some American states, a right over a flow of water that the right holder is using for a low-value purpose may be confiscated and the water put to a more valued use. As a further example, in some Australian states government can expropriate unexploited private mining rights and, in effect, convert them into Crown resources for exploration and development by newcomers.

As with taxation, expropriative interferences with private property rights give the affected landholders an incentive to react by demanding protective legislation governing the use of expropriation by arms of government. If the expropriation policy weakens the quality of their title, its implicit duration and its transferability, they may seek public measures that can restore part of the lost characteristics of their rights. Or, again, they and the broader public may in turn react passively, accepting 'reasonable' compensation for their lost or weakened rights.

Government's role in directly changing private rights

Examples abound of governments' role as a direct legislative supplier of private property right characteristics, generally in situations where the needed interventions are simply beyond the powers of the courts. To supply quality of title and security, governments have passed laws forbidding trespass. They also provide property right registration not only for urban land but also for forests, farms and mineral sites. Land registration also strengthens the *transferability* and *divisibility* characteristics of a property-holder's rights. Law-making may also improve the *duration* characteristic by setting out statutory periods during which a land-holder is protected or has a right or privilege. For example, the English Prescription Act 1832 specified the number of years land must be used by another before the original owner loses his title.

However, it is arguable that government's main historical role, and its greatest potential role, has been as provider of *exclusivity* in private rights over land. The phenomenon is perhaps best illustrated by the long process of English enclosure, when land once used in common was in various ways parcelled out into individual ownerships available for fencing, cultivation, pasturage or sale.

Before the Normans, village lands, common arable fields, meadow and waste had been substantially the property of the villagers on the estate. After the Norman invasion, all soil became the property of the lord, but certain of its uses were dedicated to the use of the village (manorial) commoners. Many lords agreed to or succeeded to a division of rights under which they forfeited full powers over all their lands, specifically the right to consolidate (enclose) or divide the land in their own interest. Some of the Crown's medieval laws therefore can be thought of as responses to these lords' descendants' demands for relief from these 'ancient' divisions of the estates. The Statute of Merton (1235) was an early step, permitting the lord to occupy manorial waste, subject to showing that sufficient pasture and wood was left for the commoners. Consequently tenants' ensuing loss of common had to be 'voluntary' or 'contractual', in that an effort was made to obtain agreement to proposed exchanges of the land holdings and claims within the manor. Such voluntary enclosure was not universal. In some cases it could be and was refused by tenants; in others it was little better than imposition.

For three centuries voluntary and mandatory enclosures and their aftermaths proceeded, accompanied by continuing and widespread litigation. The Tudor parliaments re-enacted the thirteenth century enclosing statutes, but then reversed themselves. During the succeeding two hundred and fifty years government shifted in its role as representative of the great landowners to represent more closely the needs of local landowners and local politicians. In the matter of enclosure, landlords who had difficulty coming to agreement with their tenants turned to Parliament to pass private bills. These imposed new enclosures or legitimized old ones. So private were some of the private bills that, although enforceable, they did not even appear in parliamentary records. In the main, though, Parliament did take on a greater responsibility than merely passing private enclosure bills that it had not scrutinized. Committees were created that intervened and undertook to settle the non-specific land rights of certain English villagers, in effect drafting conditions that future applicants for private bills must meet.

The initial trickle of these parliamentary enclosures in the early seventeenth century swelled to over two hundred in the reign of George II and to over three thousand, sanctioned by at least fifteen hundred acts, in the reign of George III (coinciding with a new wave of private canal and railway charters and expropriations). The dividing line between public laws and private bills became unclear. Rydz suggests that originally a private bill was distinguished by whether it could extract fees from someone.[37] Unlike the enclosures of centuries earlier, those of the eighteenth century implemented by private bills in

[37] Rydz 1979, p. 3; Lambert 1971, chap. 6. Nearly all land-use acts authorized the partition and enclosure of the open arable fields into private 'farms'; less than one-half of them also provided for partial or complete enclosure of the common pastures, meadows and wastes (see Turner 1980). According to Christopher Hill 1967, p. 269, an Act of Parliament around 1750 cost about £2000.

Parliament did not necessarily call for balance between lord and commoners, or for compensation of any kind to those who saw their traditional commoner rights revoked. Supplying a right of enclosure—that is, increased exclusivity of landlords' rights—on such terms made Parliament and its committees into first-line suppliers in direct competition with the courts. The lords' savings, in thousands of cases, provided the base from which the clerks and representatives 'extracted' personal fees from the process.

Governmental procedure of using private bills to deal one by one with landlords' demands for exclusivity ended when a later, reformed, Victorian parliament insisted on uniform procedures. From then until the final demise of private enclosure in the 1850s, an enclosure was granted only after specified bureaucratic investigations and after the owner/promoter was shown to be granting his former feudal tenants access to woods and perhaps a share in rents or royalties from mines operated beneath the former common land. This result was something like a land-owner's standard ownership right, highly exclusive over pasture and arable, less so over woods and minerals—and a result of supply of property characteristics by legislation rather than by the courts.

Common pool resources: Supplying individual rights

Another major example of government supplying characteristics is the official provision of individual rights tailored to common pool (herein treated as synonymous with 'common property') resources. Following the introductory discussions here and in Chapter 2, examples of common pool resources are seen in following chapters in connection with evolution of rights to flowing water (Chapter 3), fisheries (Chapter 4) and petroleum (Chapter 9)—all 'fugacious' or flowing resources, though timber rights (Chapters 11 and 12) can also be an example. Legislation over common pool resources returns us to the earlier discussion of the origins of the Public Trust doctrine, under which government was found to have a duty to keep waterways (a common pool resource diffusely owned by and in the service of the public at large) open. Common pool resources are open to unique management problems—for users of the resource and for the surrounding community of land-users—as will be seen most clearly with respect to the history of American oil rights. These types of disabilities are well known, outlined by the static economic theory of common property and the 'tragedy of the commons'. Typically, common pool users in long-run equilibrium produce or obtain less economic rent than the resource is capable of producing—a problem that may be worsened by dynamic uncertainty and risk aversion, and by the scarcity and depletion of the resource, for instance in the international fishery. Because there is legally open access, and because such resources may well have many of the attributes of a public good, joint private action to manage and stabilize the rate of use is subject to private incentives to cheat, in line with the traditional theory. Instead, common users—or citizens affected by their inefficiency—may become demanders of political or litigative action to create some kind of reasonably exclusive private property right out of the common pool resource.

Litigative action has helped to clarify the situation in the past, but offers little hope for the future. In Chapters 3 and 9 respectively I will show how the courts assisted in refining both the riparian law governing stream diversion and the 'law of capture' applying to underground water and crude oil. Both actions (particularly the former) went a long way toward removing conflict among competing resource users. But they were unusual. Historically, the courts were more likely to be found enforcing and protecting widespread public liberties of open access. In general, they stood against the evolution of sole ownership powers or management for common pool resources.

When Victorian governments began to intervene their aim was to respond to demanders by halting the decline of output and the increase in resource waste, often with the assistance of technical experts (a relatively recent luxury). Two main types of solutions to the supply problem emerged, with a third alternative occasionally invoked. The first was to create a monopoly over the resource, converting the common pool into a single resource holding. In a water rights application, certain streams and bays were placed under local shellfish guilds. More common was the single-buyer's network for a natural product, like the Hudson's Bay Company's monopsony-based management of the fur trade in northern Canada.[38] In such all-inclusive legal arrangements, variously referred to as concessions, charters or franchises, the government authorized the holder to take control of production and so to avoid many of the results of common pool competition and exploitation. Since the 1900s probably the most through-going instance has been the Middle-East oil concession, handed over by local rulers to western oil companies.

The second supply solution was simply to invent new kinds of rights for individuals, adapted to the physical characteristics of the common pool resource. The simplest of these was the limited-access licence issued by governments. The holder obtained a right to do or take a named thing from a named place at a given time. The fishing licence (in English law technically not a property right) was the best example. In the late twentieth century, the fishing licence was strengthened in many countries by imposing a top limit on the number issued. This added a little to its exclusivity. As well, governments imposed additional regulation on the day to day use of the resource. Only licence holders who had undergone the costs of unpopular regulations were entitled to any benefits that the same regulations brought—presumably a higher catch in the long run. Finally, as licences and permits were given increasing amounts of the characteristics of standard private sector property rights, they began to take on the quantitative aspect of quotas. In some oil

[38] See Carlos and Lewis 1999.

fields (including Alberta's) and watersheds, a numerical right was issued, always accompanied by complementary regulations. In the fishery, this was the vessel or catch quota, requiring additional government intervention in arranging the entry and exit of licence holders so as to keep the sum of active quotas more or less constant and thereby maintain the resource.

The third, less common, supply alternative for government was to make licensees members of a self-governing firm. While there are many models and designs for such organizations, they are in practice relatively rare. Examples are provided by land control groups (property holders linked by covenants or a trust agreement); worker- or user-owned firms; condominiums and strata-titles;[39] or cooperative irrigation or oil-field organizations. In all these arrangements, the participants hold some individual property (vessels, oil wells, irrigation systems), some shared ownership of the rest of the common pool and a right to participate in group decisions. All of them lack the individual exclusivity that would enable them to survive without government charters or legislation. I discuss their possibilities in several chapters below, notably in my discussions of the fisheries and private multiple-use forests.

In the preceding discussion, I have implicitly argued that governments, exposed to pressure groups, have been fairly active in improvising tenures and management schemes for users of what, in the absence of government intervention to limit access, would be common property. In this, government stands in contrast to the courts whose judges were not and are not really in the business of 'inventing' new rights. The question remains, however, as to whether the government had any *general* advantages over the courts as a supplier.

The chief advantage that has been suggested is power, made available at low cost. In Robin Matthews' formulation, government can play a major role in changing institutions such as property because it has the power to force change with or without compensation. 'The state is likely to find it easier to alter institutions than private parties do: one of the main obstacles to privately initiated institutional changes is the need to secure the consent of other affected parties . . . whereas the use of compulsion is the specialty of the state,

[39] There is a long history, in early modern Roman-law countries and in England, of the courts allowing a simple land title to be subdivided into individual ownership of floors (or even of single rooms). Although courts accepted upper-storey freeholds in some form, it was found that residents had difficulty borrowing money on the security of their apartments, could not register them, and/or needed a web of bilateral covenants in order to share ownership. Government's condo legislation swept aside these difficulties. By legislation it created a new form of ownership, along with a new collective organization. Its details differed from place to place, but it always (1) allowed a developer to divide his or her standard property right, selling the fragments as individual apartments; (2) gave the occupants collective ownership of public parts of the building; and (3) provided for the creation of a council or government. By the end of the nineteenth century, condo legislation and use was making inroads in statutes throughout Western Europe and Latin America, and, soon after, in the United States (see Oosterhoff and Rayner 1985, p. 1781).

indeed its *raison d'être*.'[40] Simpson makes a similar point in connection with English changes in land law. The mechanism for change, he says, was not private property law, reformed or unreformed; it was the legislative power of Parliament to enact private bills for interested parties that made development (and eventual standardization of the development of rights) possible.[41] Demanders of characteristics were attracted to this power, which could untangle and modify old features of land law with a single statute (achieving impressive economies of scale relative to a series of court cases and appeals), and create collective institutions such as boards, councils or companies.

Beyond their greater 'power' to change the characteristics of property rights, however, governments also had a more fundamental institutional advantage over the courts. Without government to supply an initial real property right to be litigated, private demanders had no access to legal procedures, and the courts had no entrée. Government legislation was therefore indispensable as the original granter of property rights. But with governmental authority, and law enforcement, in place, it generally fell to the courts to shore up and interpret users' security and title characteristics, and thereby to guide the development of the characteristics of property rights.

Second official suppliers: the courts and judge-made law

EVOLUTION OF THE COURTS AS SUPPLIERS

In the common-law tradition, new property law has been and continues to be supplied with both a distributional and an allocational intent. Judges provide decisions about who owns which right to what land, and they also rule on the meaning or extent of the rights themselves. Their rulings become *precedents* for other courts, and, eventually, the combined rulings become the received law for all the courts.[42]

Although most common-law judges work in isolation, the systems of courts to which they belong have often been in competition. Indeed, in the system of medieval courts, individual judges (along with their dependent clerks, officers and the providers of specialized services) behaved as rivals. Some were slow to recognize precedent while others clung to it. Disputants, concerned with their rights to property, noted these differences and 'chose' whichever court or system of courts they thought might be most favourable to their cause (taking into account also the expected cost of litigation and the organization and coordination costs of implementing whatever the court ruled).

[40] Matthews 1986, p. 810.

[41] Simpson 1986, p. 291. At the same place he remarks on the remarkable continuity displayed by the judge-made law of property in England. It survived, but the big changes were supplied by statute.

[42] More general description of the developments of the English courts and branches of law here is found in Chapters 3 and 8 as preludes to more specific descriptions of the evolution of laws governing fresh water and mineral rights in England.

After the twelfth century, at the bottom of the heap the lowest order of courts contained the customary manorial courts where the common fields and grazing rights were administered—either as between the tenants and the lord or among the tenants. Just above them, though generally with relatively little property law jurisdiction, were the sheriff's and shire courts surviving from pre-Norman days. Above these were the Royal courts. There was a personal travelling court, consisting of the king's family and his councillors, available for legal petitions and appeals wherever it rested. When the king's train was not available, 'justices in Eyre'—circuit courts held by itinerant royal justices—performed many royal revenue, criminal and civil adjudication functions.

The king's common-law court developed around the 'writ', a sort of form letter a plaintiff acquired from an official representing the king. There was a stereotyped writ to be filled in for each kind of action (for recovery of possession of land, for example). The writ instructed the plaintiff's lord, or a sheriff or a judge to hear the case, declared what must be shown and who must be heard, and filled in other details of the particular action. As the system developed, the writs produced actions in one of three royal courts: the London-based Court of Common Pleas, the travelling Court of King's Bench and the Court of Exchequer. The lines between these courts fluctuated, although the king formally headed them all. King's Bench aggressively accumulated the litigation of freeholders not only from the manorial, ancient shire and county courts, but also from the Court of Common Pleas. New procedures accompanied new writs, enabling the judges, who were paid by fees, to attract land and property cases.

After about 1500, commoners with villein tenure had had their duty to provide labouring services commuted, leading to an obligation to pay a money rent to the lord for their holdings. The transactions whereby their ancestors had acquired their land were recorded in the manorial court roll so that tenants were said to 'hold by copy of the court roll'. Soon they were described as copyholders, akin to the freeholders who already lived in the manor with a minimum of duties. Both were now tenants and could have individual standing in the royal courts. As Maitland states, 'Owing rather to the ingenious devices of lawyers in search of business [than] to any legislation, the manorial courts had ceased to be of any great importance as tribunals for contentious business.'[43]

In property disputes the parties drafted the writs, got them endorsed in Chancery (for a fee), then pleaded them before the common-law judges. As the drafting of writs was perfected, they became part of a compulsory formulary, the 'forms of action', comprising many mandatory steps. As a result they were soon condemned as weak, mechanical and bound by precedent. As well, many cases were left undecided, for a medieval judge had no more authority to declare the law than did a senior lawyer: both aspired to explain what the

[43] Maitland 1911, p. 205. For further exposition with relevance to mining law, see Chapter 8 of this book.

profession in general thought about the law. Law was 'accepted [because of a belief in] its general rightness rather than because a court had declared it to be right'. Baker (1986) goes on to argue that medieval judges were seen rather as we see today's football referees: it was their duty to know the rules. If these were in any doubt, they readily consulted their colleagues and held debates. If there was no agreement, they did nothing. For at least two hundred years, while this approach was applied, the courts were not assisted—or threatened—by any alternative way of 'ascertaining' the characteristics of property rights.[44]

In the sixteenth century the king and council supplemented (but did not replace) the common-law courts by slowly developing more specialized 'prerogative' courts.[45] While the common-law courts used writs and forms of action and appeal to focus on statute law and on title to land, the court of equity sought to avoid fixed procedures. In addition to offering quicker judgments in actions on the case, the king engaged in the practice of systematically accepting petitions for his personal intervention, especially from poor persons. The Chancellor, a high cleric at court, was authorized to hear these petitions and to make binding decisions in the king's name. The Chancellor dealt with petitions on an ad hoc, personal basis—as questions of conscience. His only remedies were personal: for example, he could not restore land, but could punish a party severely for not restoring it himself. Through the Chancellor, someone learned in canon law, the morality of using one's neighbour's property crept back into the English law of property and tort. Later on, the Chancery became the Court of Equity, and equitable principles evolved in the fifteenth and sixteenth centuries.

The seventeenth-century system of justice is best characterized as a division of labour—somewhat competitive—between the common-law and equity courts. Both had an influence on real property rights. The common-law courts, stung by the intrusions of the court of equity, began vying with each other to offer quicker and less costly decisions. Litigants not only wanted their cases resolved, they also wanted understandable reasons for the resolutions. For the first time, lawyers and clients purchased a new style of law reports, in which the facts and the decisions, rather than the debates, were emphasized. When there was disagreement about the law, the common-law courts began to call a full bench to invoke majority rule and so come to a decision.[46] Although these changes enabled the common-law courts to hold on as a source of lasting

[44] This and the preceding paragraph have been derived from Baker 1986, pp. 472–3.

[45] In addition to the council itself, the prerogative bodies included the Chancery, its extensions the Council of Wales and the Council of the North, the Star Chamber, the Court of Requests (under the Lord Privy Seal), church courts (after the Reformation) and the Court of Exchequer (later under the Chancellor of the Exchequer).

[46] Baker 1986, p. 474. Juries were still required to follow a rule of unanimity, but the majority principle governed full courts from the sixteenth century on.

rulings on property,[47] they came too late to edge out the court of equity. It had become most important where the common-law courts held back—offering as remedies injunctions and specific performance instead merely of damages or seisin. I return to this important subject in Chapter 8. Finally, the court of equity, unlike the common-law courts, was not bound by precedent. Of course, creating a precedent would be no advantage to a litigant, but where common-law precedent was stacked against him, he might well prefer equity's disregard of previous decisions or even the possibility that more attention be paid to the persons involved than to their land claims.

The previously discussed law regarding trusts (called 'uses') is an outstanding example of competition for property law-making. If a land holder appointed a trustee to act for him, the trustee was to be passive;[48] decisions were left to the former landlord for a beneficiary (often an heir).[49] But the question of ownership remained. The common-law courts said clearly that the beneficiary had neither possession nor title and so was not protected against selfish behaviour by the trustee. This hard-hearted attitude gave a clear opening to the court of equity. Using other remedies than those available to the common-law courts, the court of equity first impelled trustees toward faithfulness to their promises, and then proceeded to build up a body of law concerning trustees' duties. Chagrined, the common-law courts and their lawyers challenged the jurisdiction of the court of equity. Bitter rivalry went on until Henry VIII, indifferent to the courts' battles, intervened with his Statute of Uses, 1536. This statute frustrated the court of equity's ambition. The 'equitable' estate was now to be the same as the common-law estate. Litigation business was restored to the common-law courts and their specialist lawyers.[50]

The rivalry between equity and common law gave way to reciprocal borrowing and convergence. Had they been private suppliers, they might even have merged. The equity principles that found their way into common land law were helped along later by statutes. And equity's later adoption of a rule of precedent (instead of full dependence on personal conscience) 'hardened' the spirit of equity judgments in land-right cases.

[47] Kerridge 1969, ch. 3.

[48] The expressions 'trust' and 'trustee' are anachronistic, but, for my purposes, they are simpler than 'feoffee to use'.

[49] See Joan Thirsk's essay in Goody, Thirsk, and Thompson 1976. Apart from making bequests of land, owners got other advantages from putting land in use. The new courts of equity backed this, protecting the beneficiary against exploitation by the trustee. See also Megarry and Wade 1984, p. 1,165, for various authorities holding the opinion that, by the time of the Wars of the Roses, the greater part of the lands in England were held in use.

[50] This episode was not the end of the struggle. In the next century uses and trusts were refurbished in both common-law courts and the courts of equity. Uses and trusts played a part in working the strict settlement (discussed below and especially in Chapter 12), especially in making sure that the widow and younger children of the late life tenant received incomes or bequests.

In 1875, after the merger of equity and law courts, it was enacted that where the rules of equity were inconsistent with those of common law, equity would prevail. By 1880 the seven English courts of common law and the courts of equity had been fused into a compact system that used only one body of judges. Common-law jurisdictions abroad followed suit. For example, in Pennsylvania equity has been tried in common-law courts since the mid-eighteenth century. But the sought-after equitable remedies (e.g., specific performance; injunction) could not be awarded in common-law courts until the 1850s.

In addition to choosing among the rival courts, litigants might choose between three types of law under which they could press their claims: the law of property, the law of tort (nuisance) and the law of contract. Again, the three branches of law differed both in terms of what remedies they could respectively provide and in the scope of their jurisdictions. Property law, narrowly defined, is the oldest type of law, its judgments usually made by comparing the plaintiff's claim or title to a piece of land or an estate with that of the defendant. In the eleventh century the procedure for doing this was reduced to a routine by the introduction of the Assize of Novel Disseisin (wrongful dispossession). From the start the courts gave disseisin a fairly wide and liberal interpretation—deprivation of almost any of the rights and privileges normally associated with and enjoyed by one who has seisin.

The second type of law to which demanders might turn began to appear in the thirteenth century with the introduction of the Assize of Nuisance, enabling the courts to deal with demanders in matters of trespass, negligence and nuisance to land. These were the forerunners of what was to become case law or, more fully, 'action on the case'. Originally, the range of disputes for which nuisance was available was narrow in two ways: the parties had to be freeholders and the accused's disputed actions had to have directly harmed the plaintiff or his or her property. Nevertheless, negligence or nuisance law could still attract a wide variety of disputes. Disputants sometimes turned to this branch of law when the intricacies of trespass and other forms of law-of-property action failed them.

We will see in later chapters that nuisance, negligence and tort law generally show up where the exclusivity characteristic was weak: in cases where plaintiffs were flooded or harmed by fire caused directly or indirectly by the defendant's activities spilling over across property boundaries. These sorts of disputes dragged on for centuries, a sort of complement to trespass actions in property law where the plaintiff could allege negligent behaviour by the other party. These were all handled as actions on the case: modern tort actions did not get under way until the late eighteenth and nineteenth centuries. They all had one drawback: the remedy was payment for damages. The common law court had not the powers of equity to order the defendant to prevent or undo the harm he was found to have caused.

Resource users who held their natural resources under contracts or covenants called upon a third type of law. Typically, a major landholder would get agreement, usually formally in writing, from users of various parts of his land as to the conditions for logging or mining or river diversion. These conditions were very like the items in the property-law concept of 'bundles' of property rights, and often provided 'easements' over land as known to property law. Typically, litigants appealed to the courts to interpret or enforce disputed contracts. However, the judges sometimes went beyond handing down their interpretations of the text of individual documents. In Chapters 8 and 9 on contracted rights to metallic and fluid minerals, we will see how the nineteenth-century courts began actually to insert or read implied stipulations into leases to protect one party from the other or to establish or resurrect a 'custom' in the industry (see p. 373 below). Remedies under contract law included damages or an order that the defendant carry out the terms of the contract ('specific performance').

THE COURTS' SHAPING OF INHERITANCE LAWS

A good—perhaps surprisingly good—deal of the discussion of the evolution of the courts, and of the legal definitions and enforcement of property rights, centres on the laws of inheritance and succession. *Distributional* questions arose frequently because, although a family's property holder/tenant would have a good land title as against outsiders, there was much doubt about his powers to bequeath the land and about the state in which the land must pass to the heir—that is over the powers over *transferability* held by a family head.

Henry VIII's Statute of Uses shows the king, as law-maker, trying to please two quite different parties: small landholders who welcomed the new freedom in bequest and large landholders who did not, as they wished to prevent their estates from being divided ('frittered away') among heirs, daughters, younger sons and other relatives. This discussion is something of an oversimplification; Norman property law was superimposed on that of the Saxons and the Danes. Under the Saxons some lands could be willed, and some inherited lands were divided equally among sons (failing sons, among daughters). Primogeniture was not automatic, as the Normans brought with them ideas concerning equal division between sons. Nevertheless, division of the land had become of great concern to large landholders in the sixteenth century who feared Henry's statute would diminish family status as well as land productivity.[51] Two instruments met the demands of these two parties: an old one known as the entail, and a later one known as the strict settlement.

In 1285 the king had introduced *De Donis Conditionalibus*, which helped create the estate in fee tail, the main alternative to the estate in fee simple. A landholder (whom we may call the 'ancestor') could convert his estate into

[51] Scale is among the subjects surveyed and analysed in R. Allen 1992.

the former type of holding, after which it would be passed down following the rules of primogeniture. Each heir in succession had ownership in fee tail, meaning that his right to the lands had a good title but reduced rights of alienation, i.e. less transferability than the estate in fee simple. For two centuries this arrangement was available to those bequeathing their lands. Like a chain, it linked entailed heir to entailed heir, unless one of the heirs cut the chain by a tricky legal procedure known as barring.

Fee tail was contentious. Some in the courts disliked the continuing respect given to the perpetual inheritance intentions of a long-dead ancestor. Others disapproved of the fictions involved in the barring procedures and felt the ancestor's intentions should be respected indefinitely. After a long period of inter-court competition, and of uncertainty, the matter was tackled under the leadership of the court of equity. The agreed solution was to retain the concept of entail but to shorten the number of generations that it would govern.

In 1600 the protected-inheritance controversy re-appeared. At issue was a device known as 'contingent remainders' to a will. Similar to an entail, this device enabled an estate owner to bequeath land to a successor for life and, after that, to one or two grandchildren not yet born. The device had been rejected by the common-law court based on the feudal principle that the land was held of an overlord and ultimately of the king, and that the current holder could not guarantee that his grandchildren could fulfill their feudal duties. However, it was accepted by the court of equity. The lawyers of the courts of common law were anxious not to lose their clients to the court of equity. Their approval of contingent remainders was soon forthcoming; in 1620 a common-law court enforced a will with contingent remainder.[52]

THE COURTS ON SUCCESSION, FAMILY SETTLEMENTS AND IMPEACHMENT FOR WASTE

Sixty years later the court of equity,[53] after vainly trying to get the informal support of common-law court judges, enunciated on its own a general Rule Against Perpetuities: a formula regarding the remoteness of the probable future births and deaths referred to in wills. By 1750 judge-made law had converged on the rule that the span of an entail should be one life-in-being plus twenty-one years (long enough for an heir's son to reach maturity). The common-law bench joined equity in this rule. Landowners who sought to keep their family lands under the undivided rule of a succession of chosen male family heads were displeased with these developments. On their behalf, lawyers worked out the single-generation 'strict settlement'.[54]

[52] *Pells v. Brown* (1620), Cro. Jac. 590, 2 Rolle 216. Reported by Plucknett 1956, p. 595.

[53] In the *Duke of Norfolk's Case* (1681), 3 Ch. Cas. 1, 2 Ch. Rep. 229, 2 Swans. 454, 460.

[54] See Spring 1977 and 1964; Lawson and Rudden 1982, pp. 164–75; Habbakuk 1950; and Bonfield 1983.

Strict settlement allowed some families to arrange and keep much of the concentration of land and wealth that their forbears would have obtained by a bequest of ownership in fee tail. On suitable occasions—births, marriages and majorities—the head of a family and his adult heir (usually his son) joined in the procedure of barring their ancestor's existing entail, as referred to earlier. Barring now made the father the new 'ancestor', a temporary owner in fee simple, free now to devise the family estate in any way by will. He would bequeath to his son a life tenancy in the land. The father's will provided that, on the son's death, the estate would go, again in entail, to the expected grandson.[55] Thus the idea behind the contingent remainder was achieved. A re-settlement between son and grandson would be needed when the grandson reached his majority. By a chain of such strict settlements families could keep their lands in the hands of successive life tenants, provide incomes for their heirs, and, through additional provisions, look after other children. The continual voluntary re-settlement (in every generation the son was free to refuse to re-settle and, thus, could break the chain) had accommodated the common-law court's unwillingness to allow a perpetual entail by a dead ancestor.

This excursion into the powers of the courts to sustain or change the inheritance aspects of general property law also leads us back to the quality of title, divisibility and transferability characteristics of his property right and to the effect of the new strict settlements on landowners' power over their woods, mines and other resources. On many estates, under the strict settlement the current owners were simply life tenants, responsible for keeping the estate's assets, including its resources, intact for future generations of the family, and liable to be sued by the heirs or the trustees if they diminished it. They might, that is, be 'impeached for waste' of the family's estate, making the strict settlement even more binding on the current generation than had been fee tail which had clearly allowed the estate to be mined or logged. Right up to the end of the nineteenth century some family settlements imposed this responsibility.

Though the literature makes much of this threat, I contend that careful reading suggests that most English holders of timber and minerals were not vulnerable to being impeached for waste. Impeachability for waste is frequently mentioned by legal-history writers as a serious limitation on

[55] For the meantime he granted his son an income, an immediate annuity against the estate until his (the father's) death. Other family members could also be provided for: the son's mother, brothers and sisters. They might be financed by a mortgage against the estate, which allowed mortgages and debts to pile up from generation to generation. Daughters could sometimes become heirs under an entail. The explanatory literature on entails and settlements is extensive. For a short non-historical treatment see Lawson and Rudden 1982, ch. 12. The full variety of historical and geographical arrangements is revealed in Goody, Thirsk, and Thompson 1976. Studies by Habakkuk 1950 examine families, class, savings, wealth and inheritance from the fifteenth century to the nineteenth century. Spring 1977 examines the Victorian 'abolition' of the strict settlement.

owners' powers of natural resource management and on the transferability and divisibility of rights to resources. However, settlements were not all the same. Strict settlements could be drafted so as to allow the heir to sell minerals or timber, though presumably there was a price to be paid for this concession. Life tenants who defied their settlement by selling minerals could redeem themselves by distributing the proceeds. Nor were the rights of customary tenants and copyholders all the same. In some manors they had strong, transferable rights; in others they had almost none. I revisit this important issue in Chapter 12 in the context of rights to harvest private timber.

DID JUDGES AND GOVERNMENTS SUPPLY WHAT DEMANDERS SOUGHT?

The courts had powers to act as suppliers and to respond to demanded changes in the characteristics of property rights. But the fact that changes emerged does not prove that they really answered the demanders' needs for different characteristics. Indeed it is not even clear that judges had a coherent conception of the emerging, or the desirable, structure of property law. The story of the evolution of the laws pertaining to strict settlement certainly suggests that the sequence of decisions and so the path of the law was far from orderly. There were contradictions and reversals. All authorities say the property law applicable to successions became steadily more complicated and bewildering.[56] Nevertheless the process of litigation and preference may have carried many demanders/litigants in the direction they wanted to go, depending in part on official attitudes and the selection of cases.

Judicial bias affecting the development of common-law rights to natural resources should be given some consideration.[57] Just as politicians in government must have had their own preferences about the property issues referred to them, so judges, as property-owners themselves, must have had opinions

[56] Indeed, there is an efficiency theory that judges' decisions emerge as though driven by a hidden hand. Precedent drives common-law courts and the laws developed are predictably *efficient*. By this specialists sometimes mean that judge-made changes in law reduce the costliness of future litigation, and sometimes that the changes improve the allocation of resources in the economy as a whole. Note that there is no claim that litigants are in search of efficiency. Just as the theory of markets does not claim that parties are consciously working to reach an equilibrium or efficient price, so efficient-litigation theories presume that litigants are concerned only with their own disputes and conflicts. The theory about the efficiency of precedent-produced law is still being debated.

The proposition has not really been advanced with regard to land and natural resource property rights. It has two weakening features. First, it is usually couched in terms that deal with a liability rule in tort law, not with a right under property law. Second, it assumes that one outcome is objectively or observably more efficient than another, which is a debatable proposition. See Posner 1977 and 1986

[57] See Posner 1977, p. 416, for the suggestion that judges seek to impose their preferences, tastes, values, etc. on society.

about the powers and characteristics of rights to land. For example, with regard to detailed provisions of a will, judges, in their own careers buying and creating their own landed estates, may well have sympathized with desires to keep new estates within the family[58] and so been content that the emerging tangle of case law was producing an entail-like result. Yet this conflicted with the courts' 'traditional' favour for transferability and free choice in land-ownership. As well, as Cohen (1982) has pointed out, successive generations of judges also sought the status that goes with land ownership.[59] Through purchasing estates and country houses, many of them sought to live with, and like, the aristocracy. With this attitude, judges may have acquired a personal enthusiasm for an active land market, and so a dislike of wills and trusts that reduced the transferability characteristics of the rights held by owners of old estates, preventing them from developing or selling out.

The leaders of the school of American academics known as legal realists offer many insights into how the social, economic and intellectual climate has influenced judges and their decisions—on how judges made rulings based on what 'he or she had for breakfast'.[60] What is not in dispute is that, during the shaping of property rights, a number of lawyers, and some of the judges (many of whom were elected from political ranks) must have shared their clients' attitudes. Their systematic recruitment from property-acquiring classes, in America as in England, must have affected the trend of their precedent-making judgments.[61] A concrete example in the following chapters is the nineteenth-century English rejection of eighteenth-century prior-use rights to flowing water, which I argue in Chapter 3 was produced largely by the changing attitude of English judges.

However, even were we to assume that judgments were impartial, it is still difficult to ascertain the ultimate effect of judges' collective decision-making on resource rights. Presumably, precedent-setting judgments typically benefited the litigants, but we cannot be sure that the decisions on one-at-a-time

[58] For a brief account of the changes in the classes from which judges were selected see Plucknett 1956, pp. 231–51. However, like many others, this account depends on knowledge of only the most able and famous judges.

[59] See Cohen 1982. Thanks to Dean Cohen for help on this subject.

[60] Fisher, Horwitz, and Reed 1993, xiv.

[61] If judges tend to produce judgments favourable to people with their own background, can they be said to take an interest in the income-distribution aspect of their cases? Various law-and-economics scholars say no, because most judges are appointed, not elected (Posner 1977, p. 405; Stigler 1971; Cooter and Ulen 1988, pp. 492–9). Where judges come from and an alleged preference for economic development may be connected. I will argue in the water-rights chapter that Judge Story's introduction of the reasonable-use criterion in river-use disputes in 1827 New England had an explicit economic-developmental rationale. His English colleagues adapted the criterion but not the rationale. I believe that in the US economic-value in river use was being taken seriously by the class from which lawyers and judges were drawn. But at that time English judges had other concerns. See Mclaren 1983; Lauer 1963; Griffith 1977, p. 214; and Spatt 1983.

lawsuits made or will make natural resource discovery and production more efficient. In touching off the common-law process, they may well lead to the emergence of more and other property-law changes that will force resource users and owners to arrangements, agreements and methods that are far from the best. Of course, optimistic economists will have faith that competition in the allocation of all resources will eventually work through courts and politics to reverse individual bad judicial decisions. Perhaps so. But the process of judicial retrieval and re-direction can be slow enough to induce real hardship and inefficiency, and when resource users and owners turn to the legislature for relief, they may encounter the non-competitive motives of government that I discussed earlier. Their cases and petitions may be seized on by politicians as instruments in the ongoing stresses of internal government competition.

The conditions of demand

Having reviewed two of the main sources of supply, I digress briefly into examining when, under what conditions and with what general results they were likely to be approached and put to use by demanders of new or modified property rights in land. Judges and politicians did not act in a vacuum. They were presented with cases and petitions that reflected the conditions, concerns and property-rights shortcomings of their time. Changing technology and land use patterns created waves of litigation and lobbying focusing on specific aspects of land, water and resource rights. In responding to these demands, the suppliers of property rights collectively produced changes in characteristics of standard property rights.

WHEN ARE DEMANDERS MOST ACTIVE?

Presumably there is always a stream of lawsuits and political actions designed to change or strengthen specific property rights. Presumably too, such a stream is not steady but rises and falls with economic events, inspiring periods of general intense examination of property law alternating with quieter periods. To illustrate this proposition, I mention certain kinds of economic events and the effect they may have.

An increase in total economic activity

An increase in economic activity often sharpens the business and industrial demand for, and thus the economic rent that can be taken from, raw materials derived from natural resources. Higher rents repay additional demand-for-characteristics activity by resource users and owners that previously may not have been considered worthwhile. For example, changes in laws governing claims to oil property have been in demand during periods of business prosperity (the 1950s) but not during business depressions (the 1930s).

A technical change

New natural resource uses almost always give rise to demand for changes in the powers and characteristics of the rights over of the resource, both among current holders and would-be users. For example, when in the Industrial Revolution British industry went over to steam power, coal-mining-firms demanded change in the bundles of rights and duties in their leases and contracts with landowners. Similarly, as the world shifted to gasoline and oil-powered transport, the increase in the demand for petroleum led to demand for more refined concession arrangements between developed-world firms and developing-world rulers and princes. Another example is in uranium mining. When after the Second World War nuclear power and the nuclear bomb increased the value of uranium deposits, buyers of the mining land demanded new regulations over (and ownership rights to) these deposits.

A change in the number of purposes

The same idea applies when new technology or demands make a resource profitable in multiple uses, with the additional concern that the resulting property right may have a difference degree of the exclusivity characteristic. For example, those who are concerned about the health, stock size and harvest of a particular fish stock may demand regulations that effectively prevent fishing of the stock by holders of non-specific fishing licences. When a forest becomes valuable for both timber and wildlife habitat, holders feel a need for rights that allow them to develop both these uses (or to enable holders of different uses to agree on the extent of their interference with each other). When farm land becomes valuable both for pasturing and for mining a demand arises for standardization of rights over both uses so that they have sufficient exclusivity to operate (more or less) independently of the other.

DEMANDERS' SELECTION OF A SUPPLIER

I have argued that pre-modern governments rarely directly intervened in the supply of property rights by statute. We have seen a few major exceptions: the Norman *De Donis Conditionalibus* creating the institution of fee tail; the Statute of Merton designed to promote enclosure and allow landlords to reclaim their lands from commoners; and Henry VIII's Statute of Uses governing the way the courts could rule regarding the duties of trustees. Until the late nineteenth century, in the long historical gaps between these government interventions, demanders relied on the courts. We cannot know whether this dependence satisfied them. Instead, I list and briefly discuss six factors that would have governed their choice in the periods when both kinds of official supplier—government and court—were available: cost, delay, jurisdiction, access, number and remedy.

The relative cost of litigation

Probably the most important influence on the differences in the costs of the competing suppliers was the necessary scales of their procedures. These would be associated with the differences among hoped-for benefits or awards (e.g. repossession; damages; political appeals; new legislation). We will see in the mining chapters that some American suits that became precedents in property-right law were relatively small affairs at the state or local level, and probably inexpensive. To have gone to a politician for help, mobilizing a pressure group, would have been disproportionately costly, as it was for much of English history.[62] My prediction is that differences in scale were definitive in determining the cost-benefits of different kinds of appeal. Large parliamentary confrontations could be very costly to the parties, but could have solid, widespread effects that were appealing to large resource users or groups of these users. By contrast, small law suits might be inexpensive, but, unless a litigant's suit was exactly representative of the disputes representing the same demand, typically had only an uncertain, and at least a delayed, effect on property or tort law when reinforced or refuted by similar judgments.

That said, it is worth noting that by the nineteenth century, with the expansion of the British Empire, a paradox had emerged. Demanders seeking legislation for the general good, or on behalf of a very large group, often preferred to go to Parliament, whose jurisdiction was of course limited to Britain. Local demanders whose aim was more strictly personal started with local courts. But the judgments they provoked contributed to the worldwide building of the common law of real property, adopted or adapted overseas.

Delay and the slowness of litigation

What may also be crucial in choosing between the court and the legislature is the difference in waiting time. In early centuries delays were often notoriously long. In theory, the court was faster than the legislature: an injured party could try for a settlement, go on to sue within a year and have a decision within two years. In practice, however, important suits were drawn out longer and might produce no decision at all. Government was not, however, often a speedier option. A demander approaching a political supplier might require an indeterminate period of coalition building and lobbying, followed by a period of debate and drafting and months of waiting for a possible legislative decision.

[62] See Offner 1981, chs. 1 and 2, esp. p. 26. His account of the activities of nineteenth-century solicitors rarely mentions going to court or even retaining a barrister. Most solicitors slogged away as conveyancers. Their defeats and victories would not have been precedents in the law. Legislative expenses/court expenses and bribe-type payments to politicians or to judges were not unknown in heated land-law disputes.

Jurisdiction and access

'Access' varied not only regionally but also with the degree of discrimination against particular groups over the centuries. Under the early Normans, aggrieved freemen had to be content with the decisions of the manorial or the sheriff's courts and had no access to government, while unfree persons had access only to the manorial courts serving the very lord with whom they may have been in dispute. The access of the classes changed as the royal courts took over, as villeins became free copyholders and as civil war and the growth of Parliament gave more people some access to politicians or to government. Of course, even in the early nineteenth century the English courts and the property law they shaped still discriminated against women, minors, Roman Catholics, Jews and persons with 'no standing' in a particular dispute. Equity, motivated by the chancellor's conscience, generally offered more flexibility in its property law rulings.

Differences in number, and class actions

Related to the discussion directly above, the wider the jurisdiction of a court or political body, the more demanders can exist for a change in characteristics of a standard property law. The importance of scale is especially important politically. Politicians would generally want to count heads in order to ascertain how supporting a given demand for new property characteristics is likely to affect their electoral position. The litigative route, in contrast, could work to effect change in property rights even when the jurisdiction is tiny. Some of the cases reviewed in later chapters show that certain decisions were influential in the development of property rights, even when the parties and the place were obscure. Nevertheless, a change in judge-made law does usually depend on the frequency with which an issue is taken before a lower court, which affects how likely similar issues are to eventually come before a higher court. Frequency, in turn, must depend on the number of people affected. In the case of the strict settlement, the potential beneficiaries were numerous, and the courts adapted the law to head off an 'avalanche' of cases.

Differences in remedy

As discussed above, in various periods English courts offered fairly widely different remedies, which of course affected the demanders' choice among the courts and between the courts and a politician. For example, a nineteenth-century plaintiff awarded an injunction in the new, unified, court would have been in a better position to choose, or bargain, a combination of future land uses than his eighteenth-century predecessor who would have been confined to an award of damages.[63] Demanders also had to choose whether to press

[63] A large, mostly normative, law-and-economics literature exists comparing remedies. See Calabresi and Melamed 1972 and Posner 1977, p. 51 for examples of the effects of differences in remedies. In most examples, bargaining or a market do not work because mid-level transactions costs are high. If transactions costs were low, an injunction would confirm one party's rights and set the stage for the other party to bargain with, or buy out, the first.

their cases under property law, tort law or contract law. The importance of all these differences between the courts shows up in Chapter 3 on water rights and Chapter 8 on mining rights. It is also worth noting the difference between this class of legal remedies and what could be achieved through political lobbying. Legislative actions usually merely provided new regulations and penalties, or at best authorized compulsory purchase of contested land or created a new subsidy or tax incentives. A resource user who had already been harmed might therefore prefer going to a common-law court, which could give him personal recompense in the form of damages.

STABILITY AND CYCLING

I introduced above the idea that, although suppliers responded to and generally attempted to satisfy many of the demands of their time for changes in property rights, it cannot be assumed that the regimes of property rights created by their responses were more efficient than what came before. I raise a similar point here with respect to stability. It is natural for economists to expect institutional stability in the property rights created by the interaction of supply and demand; to expect that, say, a standard property right changed to provide its holder more exclusivity will continue to do so. But this was not and may not always be the case.

Certainly in the following chapters we encounter cases in which the initial change is more than stable—it starts a trend that eventually alters the entire property right in the way original demanders would have wanted. For example, from the thirteenth to the nineteenth century the transferability characteristic of private ownership in woods steadily increased, not only permitting grants to family members not in the line of primogeniture but also to outsiders such as city merchants. However, there are also examples of property-right characteristic trend lines that could be said to bend back on themselves, producing cycles of increasing and decreasing levels of the given characteristic. In Chapter 3 we will see that the wavering of the historical private right to flowing water between periods of land-based (riparian) rights and use-based (appropriative) rights followed a pattern that is better described as cyclical than as a linear progression, changing the fortunes of different river users and riparian owners through the exclusivity and quality of title in their rights. In Chapter 4 we will see how early governments granted private proprietorship and good title over some shellfish fisheries, later reversing themselves by opening some of these as 'common property' with no individual title, then—in the modern era—re-assigning collective or even individual proprietorship and management rights. In Chapter 6 we see that gold miners' quality of the title was frequently compromised by nineteenth-century governments torn between the desire to reserve gold for the Crown and to promote development of the resource by private individuals. Certainly, from the prospector/miners' perspective, the governments' actions did not always go in the direction of increased individual security over gold discoveries.

Commentators have pointed to the arrival of new technologies and new user demands as responsible for some of these instabilities in a property-right's complement of characteristics. For instance, Elinor Ostrom points out that there is a delicate balance between the prevailing technology and the rules observed by 'members' of informal resource-using communities. 'The rapid introduction of a "more efficient" technology can trigger... the "tragedy of the commons"' a regime in which each participant thinks it has become imperative for him to ignore any exclusivity in the rights of other participants and to energetically exploit the resource as long as it lasts. Changes in fishing equipment and oil drilling methods are examples of technological changes that at one time or another plunged fugacious resource users back into the chaos of common property.[64]

Unofficial supply: custom, force and private producers

Finally I turn to a third source of supply of property rights characteristics. In older civilizations, land law and the accompanying individual property rights were matters of custom, or of private social or family arrangements. For the most part, their simple arrangements did not come from official sources whose business it would have been to respond to demands for changes in property-right characteristics. When eventually demands for changed rights did emerge, the response from early governments and courts took the form of weakening, abolishing or modifying customary rights. Still, some customary rights have survived and even seen support from resource users. Many have been adapted by official suppliers to form the basis of modern rights. We will encounter examples in Chapter 6 on gold rush camp law and its legal aftermath; in Chapter 4 on the historical development of fishing rights; and in Chapter 12 on the development of forest rights from the feudal manor to the modern freehold.

CUSTOMARY RIGHTS AND ORIGINAL CONTRACTING

For the natural resource rights examined here, the most important source of customary and unwritten law was the English feudal manor.[65] As systematized

[64] Ostrom 1990, p. 241 note 29. Thanks to Gordon Myers for correspondence on this subject. See also Marceau and Myers 2005.

[65] See Herskovits 1952, p. 318; Belshaw 1957, ch. 3; Thompson 1991, 1993, pp. 97–184, and Beaglehole 1968. In later chapters I refer to the literature concerning customs known to have affected modern common law. Particularly relevant is the literature on early forms of customary laws relating to water and fisheries (see Ruddle and others cited in Neher, Arnason, and Mollett, eds., 1989, pp. 73–85. See also Ostrom 1990 and Schlager 1990). In Ault and Rutman 1979 the authors apply a theoretical evolutionary process to African land law similar to, and perhaps derived from, Demsetz 1967. To make the Demsetz process fit, however, they are forced to regard all opposition, uncertainty and resistance as 'transactions costs'.

by manorial and local courts, manorial customs are said to have been the 'antecedents' of common law[66] and became recognized, from a distance, by the official agencies of royal government. One good illustration comes from the nineteenth-century increase in mining activity on private lands. The landlord who wished to open a coal or iron mine found himself in conflict with 'his' tenants' and copyholders' modern claims to ancient and customary rights over the same place. The nineteenth-century courts tested these alleged customs, focusing on the presumed *contracting* (between original lord and his tenants) from which each custom must have arisen.[67]

The courts presumed that the early customary rules and privileges had flourished when they made local everyday conduct more convenient. To be regarded as customary, these rules and rights could not be unduly one-sided, for they represented the result of a *bargain* between the lord and tenants, involving an exchange of various rights to hold and use land in return for feudal work and tax obligations. The nineteenth-century courts therefore posed the question: 'Would it have been reasonable? Would the forerunners of a modern party to a lawsuit have consented to provisions to a bargain that, depriving them of certain land uses, would have been well rewarded, or unbelievably onerous?'[68] If the courts deemed the (unwritten) contract unlikely or unreasonable, the custom was deemed invalid.

There was a related debate over how ancient these original contracts were, and specifically whether commoners' rights to use the land, river or forest antedated the Norman invasion or were products of feudal grants. That these customs could be considered to be the remnants of original contracts is supported by the authors of some modern land-law texts and histories (e.g., Plucknett, Milsom, and Simpson). Simpson, for example, describes a pre-Conquest communal, cooperative system of agriculture. Some of these communes had already fallen under the domination of powerful individuals. Some inhabitants became serfs, but '[many] of the humbler cultivators were men who were personally free, but who were bound by custom (which in individual cases may have originated in some form of contract) to perform [to supply work or produce]'.[69] The Normans had been willing to adopt this view. It made

[66] See Posner 1980 for a study of both primitive and ancient tort law. He also offers an economic analysis of customary law. A good source for customary law throughout Europe between 1200 and 1400 is Berman 1983, ch. 10, pp. 316–32. He relies in part on Hilton 1966.

[67] 'Contracting for property rights', a phrase of some importance in this book, is the title of a well-known study by Libecap of certain nineteenth and twentieth-century property rights.

[68] Allen 1958, p. 137 and Appendix I. Conflicting versions of local custom were invoked in proceedings to prevent a lord's developments of 'his' landed estate. Or custom might also be invoked to protect some of the people from encroachments on wastes and commons by outsiders. All the villagers were, from time to time, tempted to encroach on the fields, wastes and the surviving village greens or commons. Interesting material on encroachment since the Middle Ages is to be found in the United Kingdom's Royal Commission on Common Land, 1954, and in material interpreting the subsequent Common Registration Acts, 1964 and 1965. I am indebted to H. Baden-Fuller for a conversation on this subject.

[69] Simpson 1986, pp. 156–7.

little difference to them whether some cultivators were seen to 'own' their land and to have assumed contractual obligations to their lords or to 'hold' their lord's land subject to an imposed tenurial obligation.

Nevertheless, the courts' requirement of 'antiquity', or 'immemoriality' in assessing the validity of contracts should not be taken too literally. A neat explanation was given in the twentieth-century custom case of *Wolstanton and A.G. of Lanc. v. Newcastle Under Lyme Corp.* [1940] 3 All E.R. 101: 'it means that the custom must have been in existence from a time preceding the memory of man, which has been fixed as meaning 1189, the first year of the reign of King Richard. The courts, however, have decided that, in the case of an alleged custom, it is sufficient to prove facts from which it may be presumed that the custom existed at that remote date, and that this presumption should in general be raised by evidence showing continuous user as of right going back as far back as living testimony can go. The presumption is rebuttable and, for instance, can be rebutted by evidence that the custom alleged could not have existed in the time of Richard I. The presumption itself in most cases is little more than a fiction.'[70]

The courts' emphasis on the reasonableness of the original contract, however, was an important precedent for modern judicial ideas of utilitarianism and the balancing of interests, particularly as the eighteenth and nineteenth centuries witnessed a transition to modern types of contracting. In one-on-one bargaining to empower a miner to dig for coal, for instance, the eighteenth-century owner may have agreed to add provisions and covenants to their contract that created a coal lease quite unlike any that had gone before and that reflected changing industrial conditions. One upshot was that the content of the parties' agreed leases could sometimes touch off legislative or legal action that, in a party's own interest, restricted what he could agree to. One example is urban rent control; a second is rural land zoning; another, mentioned in Chapter 9, is the American government's effectively setting the minimum compensation a nineteenth-century farmer could accept in an oil lease.

INVASION, FORCE OR SELF-HELP

The Norman Conquest is the obvious example of a land reform by force. The Norman conception of land law involved a pyramid of military authority, with every human rung in the feudal ladder responsible for service to his overlord. William accordingly apportioned the land of England among his thousand senior officers as tenants-in-chief who redistributed their lands among knights. The rights they acquired did not reflect the rights of their Anglo-Saxon predecessors, nor did they much resemble the freeholder's rights that would later emerge in England. While the soldier-lords exercised broad powers over their manorial tenants, they were subject to intrusion and intervention

[70] At 110, per Viscount Maughm (House of Lords).

by their overlords, up to and including cancellation of the holding (if, for instance, the heir under primogeniture could not perform feudal duties). In other words, the conquering manorial lords, while powerful, had land rights in which the characteristics of duration, exclusivity and transferability were very limited. On the other hand, the new system brought stability, which guaranteed at least a minimum quality of title, particularly from a dynastic perspective. The force of the invasion meant that, for the most part, Norman rule not only introduced new property rights and their characteristics but also prevented their being revised again in further invasions.

Summarizing and looking forward

Summary of Chapter 1

In this chapter, I have introduced the idea that characteristics of property rights were *supplied*—they emerged and changed in response to *demands* for them made to official and unofficial sources. Sources of supply existed and exist separately and mostly independently from the sources of demand. My emphasis on the supply side of property rights evolution is intentional. Where historians and economic theorists have had anything to say about natural-resource property rights, they have looked at change from the demand point of view, as in their treatment of the enclosure movement; or as a matter of contract between several demanders, as in the treatment of property rights among hunters (Demsetz) or among miners (Libecap and many others) or among ranchers. Had a similar emphasis been put on supply, these writers would likely have focused more attention on the economics of the development of the courts' (or the Crown's) potential to deliver or withhold the main characteristics of rights, not just on changes in the details of, for example, the laws of property inheritance.

The supply and demand approach points to suppliers responding to the demanders, but not necessarily establishing rights endowed with the characteristics the latter sought. Demanders, mostly actual or potential land-users, are persons who would be better off with an increase in any of the six characteristics (exclusivity, duration, flexibility, quality of title, transferability and divisibility) that combine in their own, standardized, real property right. These characteristics are, in principle, observable and measurable. I conclude with the following nine generalizations:

(1) Because most demanders have been concerned with rights to their own property, and because most suppliers have not been equipped to produce afresh and in full the six characteristics of a new interest in natural resources, most innovations consist of increments in only one or two characteristics.

(2) Because demand for characteristics has been episodic and infrequent, there is no government department and no court that has had a steadily observable traditional role as the main supplier of strong characteristics in standard property rights.

(3) Because the demand for characteristics in a *standard* right is a demand for a public good, a governmental role as supplier is obvious. Such a role is reinforced when the demand is for a drastic redistribution of natural-resource ownership accompanying the modification of the right; only government can compel, and compensate for, such a hurtful change. The role is reinforced further when the new right introduced is part of a wider policy for, say, enforcing land tax collection, managing a common pool natural resource or disposing of public lands. Here in fact is one case where the supply and demand roles—usually independent—may overlap, with government itself acting as a *demander* for changes in property-rights characteristics on behalf of politicians or the polity.

(4) Judges have contributed to the introduction of new public-good-like property rights as a by-product of hearing disputed land-ownership and tort questions. Dealing with these questions one by one, they may not always have been influenced by thoughts about how their decisions will accumulate to create new standard rights over certain natural resources. At other times, however, broad philosophical or public-interest and/or narrow personal motives may have influenced the judges to make decisions that did not directly address or that went beyond the circumstances and demands of the litigants.

(5) If only because demanders and suppliers are not in continuous contact, property rights in land and resources have changed glacially. Bureaux and/or courts may foreshadow larger changes by later legislators and courts by producing innovations narrowly distinguished to serve the specific needs of the most persistent demanders.

(6) The general direction of changes in the characteristics of property rights is difficult to predict once it is recognized that a trend may turn back on itself; or that rights may cycle or alternate between types. Alternations have been observed both in the history of judge-made sets of property rights (such as that between riparian and use-based water rights) and in government-legislated rights (such as the discovery requirement governing the acquisition of mineral rights).

(7) The special holdings, permits and claims developed by government for the disposal of rights to use the public lands could theoretically harden into real standard rights to private lands. In general, this has not happened in practice, with the notable exception of some common pool, quasi-public resources such as fisheries. Rather, the public lands disposal laws set out procedures for

distributing licences and claims which the recipients may then convert into existing types of conventional private freeholds or leaseholds.

(8) Competition with government and with other courts spurred judges to be innovative in providing precedent for changes in property rights. However, the historical role of the courts was to prevent property injustice by using and defending existing law, including characteristics of property rights. Court-made changes were usually made in short steps.

(9) After a major innovation has disturbed the value or application of an existing set of characteristics, the courts were and are naturally more active than government in responding to demands for re-interpretation, reconciling and ironing-out of how the old characteristics now affect particular rights-holders. Knowing this, the demanders of new characteristics might tend to take their business to the courts rather than to government. Furthermore, government, when autonomously drafting the introduction of a new property characteristic, would take into account the courts' powers to reinforce or nullify its changes.

Outline of the rest of the book

The remainder of this book encompasses eleven chapters arranged in three overarching parts. Part II concerns property rights over 'fugacious' or flowing resources, and the related institutions, and problems, of common pool and common property reviewed above. After a brief introductory chapter on the challenge of fugacity and common pool resources in the legal, conceptual framework of land-based property rights, I turn to two specific resources that clearly fall under this heading. Chapter 3 covers the development of rights to flowing inland water and is adapted from an earlier article by myself and Georgina Coustalin. Chapter 4 discusses rights over fisheries, both ocean and inland. Crude-oil formations are a third type of fugacious resource (and interesting for the legal challenges they pose), but I postpone the discussion of the evolution of oil and gas rights until the second part of Chapter 9.

Part III covers the development of rights over (mostly) land-based mineral resources, from their origins in antiquity and medieval Europe (Chapter 5), through the New World gold rushes (Chapter 6) and into the era of modern, fully industrialized hard-rock mining for base metals (Chapter 7). Rights to energy resources—coal, oil and gas—are in Chapter 9. Chapters 5 through 7, and the first half of Chapter 9, deal with the interaction between rent-seeking public suppliers of rights and the mining interests—first individual prospectors, later capitalistic investors and corporations—who dealt with and obtained rights from them. Chapter 8, and the second half of Chapter 9 on the American freeheld oil lands, deal with the parallel development of mining rights on private lands, mostly through property and nuisance law disputes in the common-law courts and through the use and adjudication of contracts.

In the final Part IV I turn to the development of rights over the forest and timber lands. Again, after an introductory chapter on major concepts in forest property rights (Chapter 10) there are separate treatments of the development of rights and tenures on public lands (Chapter 11) and on private lands (Chapter 12).

In all the following chapters, I confine my focus to the common-law countries of Britain and her major colonies in the New World and Oceania. Consistency and general interest sometimes require me to make forays into the property-rights institutions in classical Greece and Rome and in certain European countries and in their empires in the developing world. Of course, limiting my geographical and historical foci in these ways leaves much unsaid about the development of property rights worldwide, including in the developing and currently industrializing world. As well, I must ignore or downplay some topics closely related to the creation of natural resource property rights, such as the re-distribution of resource rights in favour of aboriginals, the general conservation of resources for future generations and the protection of the ecosystem and the realization of sustainable development. Alas, delving further into these issues would fill another book.

Part II

Rights over Fugacious Resources

2

Fugacious Resources and Common Property

Concepts of fluid or fugacious resources

In this introductory chapter to Part II, I look at the nature and the general evolution of property rights over 'flowing' natural resources: flowing water (Chapter 3), fisheries (Chapter 4) and—also relevant, though postponed until Part III on mineral resources—oil and gas (Chapter 9). My consideration of these resources as a group is a consequence of their specific physical nature. Rights over fish and over the use of rivers for energy and water consumption are obviously both 'water-based' rights; but their important similarity for my purposes is their fluidity. It is this property that makes them naturally vulnerable, at least in the absence of direct intervention by government or another collective body, to a specific type of property-right arrangement: 'open-access' or 'common property' (called 'common pool' in Chapter 1). This is responsible for these resources coming under the property rights system at a later date than other resources and for developing property characteristics that generally have less weight or effectiveness than those over land-based, non-fugacious resources.

In a sense, rights over fluid resources are the most difficult type of natural resource property right to understand and improve, because, unlike resources such as minerals and timber, they cannot easily, or cheaply, be bounded spatially, into private estates. The difficulty that suppliers of property rights had in dealing with them will become seen in the following chapters. The common-law courts, struggling to make rules for ownership of flowing water and for other liquid resources, were driven to adapt rules originally applying to the ownership of wild animals—as with these, no one has either a personal or a real property right over individual gallons of flowing water, fish or barrels of oil unless and until they have impounded them in a cage, pool, box, net, tank or other bounded area.

'Fugacious', a word in the language of property rights, implies transience or non-permanence. From the user's perspective, this non-permanence of the resource—or of his ability to exploit it—has two connotations. One is that rivals may forestall his efforts, diverting or taking some of the resource and leaving less or nothing for him. The other is that the period of the resource's availability is naturally short, terminating when it flows or migrates away. Both of these meanings suggest that in the absence of suitable laws and property rights, resource users and their rivals will have to race against each other (and against nature) to claim a share of the resource, a phenomenon we will see in the fishery and in the private oil and gas sector in the pre-Second World War United States. Using the language of the characteristics of property rights, fugacious resources naturally lack *exclusivity*—both demanders and suppliers of rights to fugacious resources struggle to obtain it.

Categories of ownership: public, private and common property

Fluid or fugacious resources can be divided into three categories, depending on whether the rights to them are supplied publicly (by the government authority) or privately, and on whether current users of the resource have the powers to exclude others from the resource or from some delineated share of it.

In the case of private property, the holder is a private individual or firm who has acquired the resource from another private individual or firm by sale or contract and whose quality of title is protected in his holding by the common laws of property, nuisance and/or contract as discussed in Chapter 1. As well the physical nature of the resource can easily be such that the holder can at reasonable cost enforce his (legal) rights to exclude others. Although his resource may be fluid—like a pond with fish—it also may be containable and clearly of his possession.

In the second category of rights are those over public property. In this case, the government holds the land and either runs operations on it or else contracts it out to private firms who extract or exploit the resource for which they have contracted. The physical nature—that is, excludability—of the resource is the same as when it falls under private property. It may ultimately belong to the public, but the government like a private person can exclude all but a designated class.

The third category—and the one that is especially pertinent to fugacious resources—is the group of rights over common property (or open-access or common pool) resources. In Chapter 1, I looked at common property in the context of common pool resources open to exploitation by (possibly regulated) atomistic demanders. Looked at another way, in pure common property situations, there are *no* holders of the resource because exclusivity in its use is not feasible. In more qualified or limited common pool situations, would-be users of the resource may hold permits (also licences, leases or easements) authorizing them to join the other permit holders in their exploitation of the resource. In some cases, the government may participate by denying access to would-be users to whom permits or similar formal rights-of-access have not been issued—thus increasing the exclusivity of the remaining rights of access and bringing them closer to actual property rights. Just as the characteristics of a property right are quantitative or variable, so the extent to which a resource is common property or has open access is a matter of degree.

Not all fugacious or common pool resources are necessarily 'held' by their users as common property. And some non-fugacious resources can be 'held' as common property. Non-fugacious examples of common property (or just 'commons') are the fields or wastes governed by the 'commoners' of the medieval manor; the communal pastures (or Alps) of modern Switzerland; and the rural forests in India. In all these cases, the local people, in order to prevent a predictable degradation of their natural resources, have made their own institutional arrangements to exclude outsiders and manage their collective resource. The multiple-use forest to be described in Chapter 11 also has some elements of common property. As a general rule, however, there is such a large overlap between resources that have the physical attributes of a common pool and those that have the legal-law or property status of common property that it is sensible to consider them together. This is the practice of economists specializing in the field of industrial organization. For them unconfined fluid resources are typically assumed to be common property, subject mainly to administration by associations of users or by government agencies.

Understanding the absence or deficiency of rights over fluid and common property resources

A formal explanation of the absence or deficiency of standard (land-based) rights to fluid resources amounts to much the same thing as an explanation of the existence of common property in either the private or public sector. We can look at it in terms of supply and demand. On the demand side, the absence of resource users who are already owners or holders of conventional rights under common law has translated into an absence of the chief means by which users of other resources have exercised demand for modifications of their rights (i.e. the addition or strengthening of their characteristics). In the chapters of Parts III and IV we will see that changes in and formalizing of property rights were typically introduced to deal with legal disputes in which right-holders alleged that others had displaced them in the occupation and possession of such land resources as soil, forests and minerals. Decisions in the resulting litigation were essentially responses to demands for changes in the characteristics of pre-existing but (from the holder's private perspective) imperfect property rights—usually for increases in exclusivity.

This kind of action was difficult or impossible in the case of common-access resources. Under the customary rules of the common-law fishery, fishermen had no property in the swimming fish, and so had no grounds to bring suit to demand that one or other of the characteristics of their property rights be changed. As we will see, litigation was more possible in the case of rights over water and stream resources than of fishery rights. But the actual litigation has usually been to settle arguments over rights to divert or consume some of the flowing water, not to exclusively occupy and hold the water resource itself. And even then, irrigation, milling and mining establishments whose owners' rights did not extend to the stream water passing by had to wait until the nineteenth century for the law to change sufficiently for them to fruitfully challenge diverters. In the case of underground petroleum, lawsuits to protect or establish exclusivity were feasible in the rare cases where the formation was believed to lie entirely within the borders of a single property's surface area, but not—once the law of capture was established as the common-law precedent—for the majority that stretched and flowed beneath a number of surface properties. Drillers, aware that much of the formation they tapped lay in the property of others, had no grounds to sue when the oil and gas in the formation was depleted.

We may make a few more generalizations about the lack of demand. In all cases described above, potential litigants probably did not demand exclusive rights over these fluid resources because, even where victory in court was possible, the costs of excluding others—the costs of detection and enforcement under whatever right they might have gained through litigation—would have been too high. Again, this follows from the nature of fugacious resources, whose physical movement would make proof of origin difficult and intruders on the edge of property boundaries hard to exclude. As well, the lack of exclusivity provided resource users an incentive to invest in personal property and capital goods that made capturing a share of the resource easier in the absence of exclusivity: water diversion and storage systems; fishing vessels and catching equipment; and oil and gas transportation and storage systems. Paradoxically, it may well have been the protection of these individual protective and racing investments that sometimes led the water-users, fishermen and oil operators to eschew calls for a workable property system, and even government regulation, which would decrease their opportunities to use their technology to exploit their fugacious resources.

Problems arose on the supply side too. The courts were hampered by the necessity of sticking by ancient doctrines drawn from Roman law concerning water and navigation; from implications of more modern doctrines such as Magna Carta, the Freedom of the Seas and traditional rights of navigation; and their own precedents, such as the adoption of the Law of Capture to oil rights.

None of these doctrines enabled the courts to provide adjudication of disputes about ownership, or to nurse along the exclusivity characteristic so that property in fluid resources could gradually emerge.

Government provided something of an antidote, despite in some cases facing constitutional limitations. In Chapter 4, I provide examples of governments bestowing sole-owner-type rights over oysters (though these were sedentary) in particular bays or other marine locations. For water resources there are many examples of government conveying sole-owner-type rights over streams, lakes and aquifers for hydro-electric dams and lakes, urban water-supply operations and irrigation cooperatives. For oil and gas resources, Chapter 9 provides examples of 'unitized' oil fields where one firm or co-operative does all the drilling and pumping, or at least carries out certain group-level operations, for all the firms sharing the field. The rights bestowed on such fishery and oil-field firms may have had only minimal amounts of such ownership characteristics as transferability or divisibility but they do reflect the government's actions in supplying property rights with a measure of the exclusivity characteristic.

Government, however, has been slower to offer property-like rights over fluid resources to *individuals* who would share and independently draw from the common resource. It has backed up the courts by helping to enforce the few judge-made individual rights, especially to certain kinds of water diversions, but has gone no further. I offer the following reasons why not:

Lack of demand

A more concrete way of putting this is that more demanders typically opposed than favoured individual rights to common-access resources. Vessel owners and their crewmen, working hard to outwit and outrun other fishermen for the catch, have not lobbied politicians to undertake the creation of individual rights. Had politicians been able to come up with such rights (for instance to favour a single large firm or conglomerate), they could have been sure that, on balance, 'the fishing interest', composed of many smaller operators who feared being squeezed out, would oppose them. The same is true of ownership of rivers and lakes, and of the sea. Individual users, accustomed to open access to bodies of water, have not banded together to persuade politicians to hand these bodies over to favoured individuals. To the contrary. The same is true of oil and gas resources: individual explorers and drillers, racing each other to find and remove the oil from an underground formation, have not urged that the whole resource be assigned to one operator. In short, the government did not supply because the majority of resource users did not demand.

A regulatory duty

On the other hand, government has long felt a duty, enhanced by demands from the public and in some cases from the affected industries, to provide laws to protect and conserve liquid resources, to make rules under which these laws could be implemented and to enforce these rules. Regulations to conserve inland fisheries emerged during the medieval period. Regulation to conserve water resources began in Roman times, or earlier. To conserve the resources of oil and gas fields, state governments implemented rules governing the prevention of the waste of subterranean gas pressure and setting maximum efficient rates of extraction early in the twentieth century. In all events, the politicians and resource users accustomed themselves to the idea that the proper role of government was to regulate and protect fugacious resources, not to try to create individual rights to them.

Conflicts over distribution

If government had used its legislative powers to create individual property rights, the question would arise over whom to assign them. It is safe to assert that politicians have always, or at least from very early in the history I am examining here, found assigning wealth or rights to be a distasteful task, fraught with dangers of popular revolt. To avoid doing so (at least visibly) they have adopted an alternative strategy of making regulations, applicable to everyone, as mentioned just above. In some cases, though, the enforcement costs of implementing these regulations have driven government further, to give access under the regulations a quantitative dimension. In these cases, government has in fact landed itself with the distributive problem of deciding how access and product are to be divided. We will encounter this phenomenon—and the opposition and discord it naturally creates—explicitly in relation to marine fisheries, where the licence has gradually been modified and limited until it is a quota. Somewhat similar stories are also applicable to describe the gradual transformation of blanket water-using regulations to quantitative rights in some North American water disposal systems and the transformation of the output of oil wells into 'allowables'.

In short, the fugacious resources have traditionally lacked the sort of property rights that exist over minerals and trees, especially in regard to their exclusivity, because of a lack of effective demand for these rights, of a high cost of enforcement, and of an inability on the supply side to meet what demand did exist. Individual users of the fugacious resources, lacking property rights to the resource, have had no occasion and often no grounds to go to court and expose their 'common property' problems to the judges. Government has provided schemes of regulation and protection for the resources, but rarely property rights. Indeed, apart from putting the entire resource under a sole owner or trying to impose regulations that require joint management (as the US federal and state governments did for oil fields on public and private lands), they have had little idea what kind of private property right would work. The following chapters on the fugacious resources show that out of some crude regulatory systems have grown official systems of quantitative quotas or rights for some fugacious resources: for landing fish, for water diversion and for withdrawing oil and gas from petroleum formations. These are probably as close to individual property rights, with some kind of exclusivity, as these resources will ever get.

Tort law and contract law

Finally, given that exclusivity in fugacious resource holdings was an uncommon concept in the law of property, it is worth mentioning the importance of other types of law to the development of rights to these resources. The following chapters will show that the courts could and can help out in the efficient use of fugacious resources, quite apart from attempting to create conventional, exclusive rights. One of the ways they did so was by dealing with conflicts in which the parties were quarrelling about torts. Injury to a fish stock caused by water pollution is a good example. Settling nuisance and negligence matters helps to provide another kind of exclusivity than would be obtained if the law of property could be applied—specifically, protection against damage and externalities not involving the direct capture of the resource.

It is obvious too that contracts, enforced by the courts, can accompany government regulation in helping fugacious resource users avoid the high costs associated with common property. Neighbours can share water flows, for example, by contract, even if a basic property right is missing. Fishermen can co-operate with each other and enter into contracts with groups of other fishers and water-body users to avoid damage to their own fish stocks. Oil and gas operators can contract with each other over rates of withdrawal, spacing and so on. Whether or not they did so is a debatable historical question and likely depended on external conditions as well as the nature of the resource. We will see in Chapter 9 that, with respect to oil and gas, such contracting between adjoining oil field owners was in fact fairly rare.

3

Rights over Flowing Water

Anthony Scott and Georgina Coustalin

Introduction: changing regimes of water law

The water rights described in this chapter can be widely defined as the rights to use or enjoy the flowing water in a stream.[1] In the common-law world, before government allocation of streamflows, a person's water right was acquired in two ways. The first was through ownership of the land on the banks of the flowing stream, called a 'riparian right', or 'land-based right'. The second was by making early, exclusive use of the flow—called a 'prior use', 'prescriptive', 'appropriative' or 'use-based' right. There were indirect means of acquisition too: a user who was neither a riparian nor a first user might gain access to a flow by contracting with a person who held land-based or use-based rights. Today rights to enjoy flows in most river basins are issued, administered and controlled by government agencies. But there are still some jurisdictions in the common-law world in which the state leaves enforcement of land-based or use-based water right regimes to the courts.

A right based on *land ownership* has no specified limits. The holder is only bound to restrict his use so as to maintain a certain level and quality of

We gratefully acknowledge the suggestions and comments and the research help we have received, over nearly ten years, from many persons. Among them we would mention: Terry Anderson, Jamie Benidickson, Ljiljana Biukovic, Charles Bourne, Gardner Brown, Richard Campbell, Lindsay Cameron, Sandy Clark, Ronald Cummings, Anthony Dorcey, Mason Gaffney, David Getches, Mischa Gisser, Joel Hamilton, Linda Hannah, Charles Howe, Ian Keay, Stephen Kellett, Elizabeth Kirk, Alistair Lucas, Arthur Maass, Ben Marr, Cherie Metcalfe, Mary McGregor, Rachel Meyer, Christopher Nowlin, Peter H. Pearse, David Percy, Christine Riek, Ruth Picha, J. A. Raftis, A. Murray Rankin, Monique Ross, Bernadette Stale, Jennifer Stewart, Andrew Thompson, Stephen Wisenthal.

[1] Neither this nor the following chapter deals with the law governing rights over underground water. Some discussion of this topic can be found in Chapter 9, dealing with rights over petroleum, a similarly fugacious resource.

streamflow, and so make flow available to other landowners along the stream. His right is continuous and permanent. By contrast, a right based on (prior) *use* is limited and quantitative. It represents a fixed, measurable rate of flow to be put to the uses over which the right holders' right is defined.

The history of water rights in the western world can be seen as a series of alternations of water-right regimes in particular water-using regions. When the economic base of a region changed, its peoples' needs for amounts, locations and qualities of water often changed as well. This in turn gave rise to new types of demand for water, manifesting in disputes, litigation and awards and to exchanges, grants and contracts. The resultant regional systems of water rights can be very different from one another, even among countries that have the same general property system (for example the common-law countries) or—as we will see—even within a single country or along a single river. They can differ not only in their detailed rules and procedures but also in their general property-right characteristics, challenging legal and customary continuity. To relate and compare the 'twists and turns' of evolving water-right regimes is the main task of this chapter.

To simplify the analysis, we reduce the time during which water law and water rights have evolved into five successive periods or phases. We begin with rivers in the medieval period. We then assess the few changes to water law between the sixteenth and eighteenth centuries. Third comes the rapid period of change during the Industrial Revolution in England. Fourth, we examine the frontier period in the New World, before turning at last to modern water law. In keeping with the theme of this book, we keep an eye on changes in the six characteristics of property rights: duration or permanence, flexibility, exclusivity, quality of title or security, transferability and divisibility. We might expect to find that, however weak they were at the outset, the six characteristics of typical interests in water became stronger across successive periods, following the general march of economic history and the strengthening of legal and government authority. However, in keeping with the 'cycling' idea introduced in Chapter 1, our examination shows instead times of retrogression as well as times of progression in such key characteristics as exclusivity and transferability. The strength of the characteristics fluctuated like, or maybe with, the legal basis of the right, reflecting demand as well as the capacity of the appropriate institutions—the government, the courts, appeals to long-standing custom—to supply them.

Roman water law

As discussed in Chapter 1, although Roman law helped explain the English common law, it was *not* the law. Lord Denman made this point clear in the famous 1883 English water law case *Mason v. Hill*, stating: 'Roman Law... is no authority in ours... .' It was merely a filler of the spaces between precedents in the common law. Nevertheless, a philosophy or rationale can change the way a judge interprets a precedent-setting case, just as can the economic, social or political conditions of the time. These interpretations then become precedent. Viewed in this manner, Roman law may be seen as a dynamic factor in shaping the common law over time.

Independent of its transmission through British common law, Roman law has had more direct and independent influence in North American water law. Its influence was strong in mainland Europe, and from there it spread to Mexico with the Spanish discoverers in the sixteenth and seventeenth centuries, found its way directly into the southern or southwestern United States and finally achieved some expression in the appropriative rights doctrine.[2]

Roman law, as it spoke at the time of writing to life in the newly conquered territories, contained noticeable focus on personal property, possessions and agreements rather than on privately owned real property (land). All 'perennial' rivers (as opposed to freshets or torrential streams) were considered *res publici* (things owned by the public) and subject to the authority of a centralized administration. The state owned the riverbed as well as its banks, and recognized public rights of navigation, fishing and access. The right to divert water was also available to the public subject to state regulations. Nevertheless, a private right could be acquired from the public domain, resembling somewhat the later English 'prescriptive' right, similar to a squatter's right. Individuals diverting water with this right of *usucapio* could not be prevented by the state, after a certain period of time, from continuing to do so as long as they did not change the flow of the river from that of 'the previous summer'. An 'interdict' or prohibition from the praetor or governor laid down the rules regarding water diversion, with the penalty of restitution for disobeying them. Because the diversion of water in perennially flowing streams was open to the public, and because the banks of these streams were publicly owned but the land behind them was not, *praedial servitudes* were also recognized. These were private rights, comparable to 'easements' in land, by which a person had a 'way' through the land of another. The servitude of *aquaductus* was, as its name suggests, a right to lay a conduit—pipes—over another's land to bring water from the river to one's own land.

In this system's overall classification of 'things' the flowing water itself is viewed differently from publicly owned or privately owned streams. All flowing water in private or in public rivers is by its physical nature *res communes* because it is incapable of ownership. As soon as one user finishes his use, the water is released back into what is called the 'negative community'—a kind of communal pool—to be used by someone else.[3] In things classified as *res communes* there could only be usufructuary rights.

[2] See Johnson and DuMars 1989, pp. 348–9, and Hutchins 1928, p. 26.

[3] MacGrady 1975, pp. 511, 517–34 (citing Pothier circa 1762, translated in *Geer v. Connecticut*, 161 US 519 (1895)).

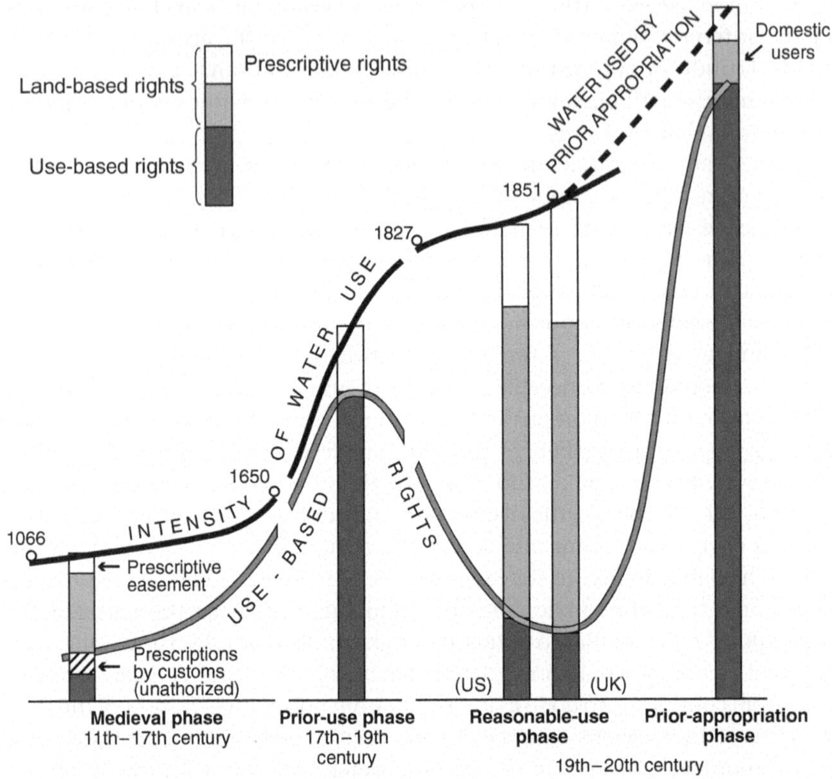

Figure 3.1 Twists and turns of water law.

Roman law required that all users of water respect a 'good neighbour' principle. They could not use water in such a way as to inflict damage on someone else's water use or on someone else's land. The general damage law, the *lex aquilian*, and its equivalent in the later Institutes of Justinian provided for compensation to those who had suffered damage at the hands of others.[4] One result of this legal structure was to give older or existing uses priority over newer or later uses, a priority noted by those who wrote 'seniority' and 'appropriation' into user-based water regimes.

As for temporary or 'torrential' rivers, private rights to divert them belong to the landowners on either side. These owners were riparians, considered to own the banks and the stream bed to its midway mark.

[4] Sanders 1876.

The twists and turns of water law

The medieval period of water law: 1066 to 1600

In the feudal, agrarian society of the Middle Ages, dated from after the Norman Conquest through to the waning of feudalism in the sixteenth century, water power was used for mills operated mainly to saw wood, to grind corn, to full yarn or in some locations to pound ore and metal.[5] Medieval records suggest only a few disputes between stream users, mainly over navigation and fishing. It is possible, however, that some competing water-power cases, now lost, did arise during this time.

There must have been rivalry over prime *sites* that placed the fewest demands on technology and transportation. Sites adjoining falls or in boroughs would attract new mills, reducing the power or the market of older ones. When the dispute was within one manor, it would receive rough justice from the lord's court, with no surviving records. When it was between neighbouring localities, it was heard by larger feudal assize courts or by King's courts, with records written often by students or other non-professionals. A report from the Year Books gives a typically uninformative example: 'The assize comes to recognize if Nicholas Sonka has unjustly and without judgment diverted a certain watercourse in Crowlas . . . to the damage of the free tenement of Gervase Blohicu in the same town within the assize. The jurors say that [Nicholas] has diverted it. Judgment: Let Gervase have seisin, and Nicholas is in mercy. Damages, two shillings.'[6]

The 'assize' or travelling court had heard the plaintiff, Gervase Blohicu. His case was that the defendant, Nicholas Sonka, had diverted the watercourse and deprived Blohicu of water. Gervase was a freeholder or landowner. The defendant presumably was not. The twelve 'jurors', after examining the situation, swore that the diversion had taken place, that the plaintiff had been 'disseised' or dispossessed of the watercourse, and that it was he who had the better right; therefore his possession and 'seisin' were to be restored. The defendant was required to cease his diversion activity and pay damages to the plaintiff.[7]

[5] The knowledge we have of the water right in the earlier part of the medieval period has been patched together from an appreciation of the system of land ownership or 'tenure' as well as a study of the various competing courts and the remedies they offered. During the period Glanvill and Bracton wrote on the common law. They incorporated some of the elements of Roman law into their reporting of somewhat scattered precedents from all levels of courts. They created a 'doctrine' of the common law, complete with flaws that later centuries would have to address and resolve. See Glanville 1130 (Hall ed. 1993); Bracton 1230 (Thorne ed. 1968).

[6] Baildon 1890, p. 82.

[7] Gervase Blohicu's case is especially relevant to our analysis to the extent that it illustrates the general importance of the possessory right of seisin throughout the evolution of water rights. Paraphrasing Maitland 1886, Berman 1983, p. 313, states: 'seisin was, in effect, a legal

The case shows how the medieval common law regarded a stream as though it were a piece of land. Rights were not attached to a thing flowing by land, but were a feature of land. In relation to the owner's vertical column of land, stretching from the centre of the earth to the heavens, water was 'situate' on the surface like a wood or field. The landowner 'owned' his portion of the watercourse, and technically had full rights to do with the water what he wished. If the river formed a boundary of his land, he owned the bed to the midway mark of the stream; the owner of land on the opposite bank owned the other half. Thus the miller who constructed an upstream diversion and deprived a downstream mill of its water or power took away the downstream landowner's property or, in feudal terms, 'disseised' him of his property.

The land-based water right, then, was contingent upon owning the bed of the river and was not defined in terms of flow. It was not attached to the banks of the stream except where the owner of the bed was also the owner of the banks. The word 'riparian' (owner of the riverbanks) was not in the legal lexicon.

As early as 1215, with the Magna Carta, a distinction was made between private and public rivers based on the presence of tidal influence. King John made an undertaking creating public rights of fishing (see Chapter 4) but applying only to *tidal* waters: mostly estuaries and seas. Even though the banks of these tidal public rivers may have been privately owned, the Crown owned their beds and promised not to grant them to others. Owners of the public riverbanks would have no rights over the river or the river water. As against upstream diverters, owners of the banks of tidal public rivers apparently had no rights. This would have posed little hardship, however, since there were no tidal-riparian millers, as millers needed a steady one-directional flow. Nor would downstream brewers or farmers suffer, since they needed fresh, not salt tidal water.

As well, the concept of personal damage overlapped with land ownership. As early as 1200 courts were awarding indemnification to injured plaintiffs for unjustly caused harm as well as for restoration of the right of which the plaintiffs had been deprived. With the progression of the medieval phase, some feudal land rights faded; but (as will be seen in Chapter 8 on private mining rights) the duty not to cause 'damages' to land took on increasing significance in the courts and drew attention in English theory books. Bracton, in his major 1230 work, was one of the first to explain the concept of damages as being a 'servitude' or obligation of each freeholder not to harm another's

right to continue in a factual situation, which right was derived from previously having been in that factual situation'. It was a right of possession independent both of ownership and contract—a concept unknown either to Germanic law or to the older Roman law. This idea of 'possessory right'—not possession but right of possession—has persisted in English and American law. Berman explains that '[the] concept of seisin was a product partly of the feudal concept of divided ownership and partly of the canonist concept of due process of law, with its antipathy to force and self-help. A person seised of land, goods, or rights could not be ousted by force even by the true owners' (p. 313).

land or impede his use of land. This philosophy was a carry-over from Roman law: *sic utere tuo ut alienum non laedas* was the phrase used most often.

The right corresponding to this duty—the right to the integrity of one's land—was a 'natural' right that accompanied land ownership. The 'assize' or travelling court enforced it. If one was not already a freeholder one could not bring action for harm caused to one's land or water use, and one had no means of enforcing an individual usufructuary right except by claiming a prescriptive right, to which we turn next.

'PRESCRIPTIVE EASEMENT' TO USE WATER

In the Middle Ages, prescription—or the 'prescriptive easement'—offered an important way for a land user to obtain rights over land from its legal owner. These rights were achieved through continuous and undisputed use of the land for a period of time—which the common-law courts settled on as twenty years. It is not surprising that a comparable prescriptive right to use flowing water also emerged with comparable power. It gave the holder greater quality of title over water use than any other formal interest he might achieve by grant, contract or licence because it could be asserted against 'the whole world'—not only against the acquiescing owner (equivalent to grantor) and his successors in title, but against all other users of the stream flow, upstream or downstream, past, present or future. It granted what amounted to a fixed quantity of water, although the exact location and specific use of this water has been held to be somewhat flexible.[8] Like a land easement, however, it was connected with the land from which it is exercised rather than with its user and transferable with that piece of land. Because the river itself was not owned, the creation or transfer of an easement did not take water from the bundle of rights of another property. It could be extinguished by intentional non-use over a period of time, usually the same period as needed to acquire it.

The early prescriptive easements to use the water were of a different nature than their later counterparts. They emerged from purely usufructuary rights granted by a lord to his tenant (for example, to use the stream to turn a mill). After a certain number of years of this use, the lord was no longer entitled to withdraw the right. From a relationship between two parties, the prescriptive easement expanded to be effective against other stream users. The plaintiff did not have to be a landowner himself to sue, so long as he could assert a use prior to that of the (landowning) defendant in the form of a prescriptive easement.

GROWTH OF THE ACTION 'ON THE CASE'

With the thirteenth-century introduction of personal action in trespass,[9] riparians and water users gained a convenient legal procedure for cases in

[8] *Hale v. Oldroyd* (1845), 153 E.R. 694 (Exch.).

[9] The writ of trespass was first seen around 1253. See Fifoot 1949, p. 54. We encounter it again in Chapter 8.

which, say, an upstream neighbour had interfered with the plaintiff's water use or a downstream neighbour had flooded his land. As seen in Chapter 1, in such cases a successful action would lead to an award of damages for lost income or repair rather than just abatement of the nuisance-causing action and possible arrest of the wrongdoer. Actions on the case, the forerunners of modern tort actions in nuisance, were grounded on the precept of just compensation for damage. Any relationship to 'land' was secondary.

The action on the case as it applied to water law was, then, a type of hybrid action combining elements of property law and personal law. It could be used instead of the old feudal assize for disseisin and for 'trying title'[10] such as in Blohiccu's case above.

SUPPLY: ACTIONS ON THE CASE CREATE USE-BASED RIGHTS

The transformation of the water rights of medieval land law into rights based on use was brought about by changes both on the supply side (almost entirely in the courts) and on the demand side (increased use of water power). As in Chapter 1, we begin here with the supply side.

By the beginning of the seventeenth century any water user could bring a personal legal action for enforcement of his rights, translated into rights of non-interference with *use*. A new legal concept of the *flow* of the river, with water either coming from another property or impeded in another property, represented a shift from the seisin concept of the *presence* of the water on land owned.

It is easy to see why the action on the case as a mechanism of enforcing land and water rights grew in popularity to the point where it virtually replaced the feudal 'real' actions. Not only was it simpler for the courts to dispense, it was cheaper and quicker for the litigants and allowed leaseholders as well as freeholders to sue. The large number of cases made for further efficiencies in operation, further decreasing the courts' costs and increasing their profits.

One apparent defect of the action on the case was that its compensation did not include 'rights restoration'—an order for the defendant to cease the activity for which he was being sued. Theoretically, a new mill, merely by paying 'actual damages', could continue to capture water from an old mill. That mill owners did not complain about this facet of the law probably means that the amount of the expected damage award was typically high enough to prevent newcomers from interfering with established mills. For one thing, the plaintiff mill could have continued with repeated suits, collecting multiple damages; certainly the burden of proving its case would be easier (and cheaper) with each repetition. As well, the cost to newcomers of new, non-interfering sites may have been relatively low.

[10] The 'real' or land-based assize for seisin of a stream continued to be also available to freeholders until 1833, when Parliament abolished it in the Real Property Limitation Act, 3 & 4 Will. 4, c. 27 (1833) (Eng.). See Maitland 1909. But we have come across no evidence of its use after 1600.

Finally, in this supply-side explanation of the switchover from the assize to the action on the case we should note that judges, court personnel and the king himself were involved competitively for litigation 'business'. The 'action on the case', because it offered cheaper forms of action, superior remedies and the privileges of 'royal justice' to his subjects, was a powerful tool for the king in terms of maintaining royal prestige and creating revenues. For this reason, and all those discussed above, disputes about water tended to be resolved by actions on the case, the new 'supplier' of changes in rights. The right to litigate was independent of land ownership; it was extended to all users. Thus the enforcement of court decisions created rights that were also independent of land ownership. They could no longer be described as land-based; they had become use-based. Later in the seventeenth century the land-based feudal actions would be abolished altogether.

DEMAND: THE IMPACT OF INCREASING USE

The shift of supply from the assize to the action on the case and the resultant transformation of water rights to those based on use were reinforced by changes on the demand side, in the direct demands of those who held, used and enjoyed water.

Medieval property law, with its emphasis on seisin and land, had not contemplated rights to running water. As long as the only conflict was about *sites* for mills, landowners and their millers were content with feudal law. But at the end of the medieval period, as lessees and contractees became more independent, they became active in their own right, contending with others for the use of streams. Static land law could scarcely help when the problem was that users with good title to their sites were nevertheless interfering with each others' enjoyment of the flow. Richard Holt estimated that there were already about 15,000 mills in England around 1300, most of them corn and fulling mills on or near manors.[11] This number increased as the medieval period waned.

The old remedy, restoration of property, could not compensate a lease-holding miller who had lost water power. It was too inflexible to accommodate the greater variety of uses, the notion of competition between uses and the complication of prescriptive easements. As diversions such as those for river navigation improvements, canals and town water supplies began to appear with greater frequency in the century leading up to the Industrial Revolution, land law's inadequacy became more acute. Water users sought to use the courts to straighten out their respective rights to stream flow directly against the perpetrators of disruption. The remedy of damages could give them a new defendable usufructuary 'title' to stream flow. As for riparian landowners who did *not* use the water, their legal recourse to protect the quality and quantity of

[11] See Holt 1988, and Langdon 1991, pp. 424–38.

the water that flowed by their land and the prospective commercial value of that land was fast diminishing. In brief, in late Medieval England it was demand that brought about a transition from an era in which water rights depended on land occupation to an era in which rights were conceded to those who *used* flowing water.

The prior-use period of water rights: 1600 to 1850

By 1600 the action on the case had clearly replaced the old feudal forms of property actions.[12] Thereafter there was an almost exclusive reliance on the law of torts and, particularly in cases about water, on the law of nuisance with its remedy of compensation or 'actual damages'. (The other side of tort law, negligence, had little specific relevance to water; it is discussed in later chapters.) The plaintiff could only bring an action on the case if an active use of the water had been hindered; otherwise he would be presumed to have accepted damage or the risk of damage.[13] Thus prior use, a form of seniority, became all-important.

The new prior-use phase established itself in England's age of expanded trade, high production and changing technology catering to an explosive textile export demand, mainly to Germany and the Netherlands.[14] Population, also growing rapidly, tended to concentrate in newly industrialized urban areas and mill town districts. Energy and heat were still provided by wood and even by coal, but to a large and growing extent running water provided mechanical energy not only for turning millwheels but also for blowing air into mines and for smelting lead and iron.[15] Mill after mill was set up on non-tidal streams at suitable sites, such as near a fall. The competition between some mills along the crowded streams became intense. Water disputes and litigation in the seventeenth and eighteenth centuries were almost all about diversion, arising between mills competing for the flow.[16]

PRESCRIPTIVE RIGHTS AGAIN, AND RECOGNIZING PRIOR RIGHTS

The courts were called on to clarify the prescriptive right's difference from traditional seisin. In the process they also came to recognize the lesser but significant personal right, the *prior-use right*, as establishing a basis for a plaintiff's action. This was a right based solely on use of the water for any period

[12] See Christopher Hill 1975. By an act of Charles II in 1660, feudal tenures had been abolished and land previously held in 'seisin' was now held in 'freehold' with no duties or obligations to the king and lord attached to it. In addition, freeholders could acquire written title to their land, good against any other party. Copyholders were not included in the freeing of the land; they were still completely dependent on their landlords.

[13] See *Bealey v. Shaw* (1805), 102 E.R. 1266 (K.B.).

[14] See Ramsay 1965, p. 22.

[15] See Harris 1988.

[16] Von Tunzelmann 1978 points out that after 1780 industries increasingly used water for steam power.

longer than the opposing party's. In this section we follow well-reported cases that step by step defined the prescriptive right and so, in distinguishing it from the emerging prior right, created a demand for the latter.

Shury v. Piggot[17] is perhaps the most frequently cited water rights case of the Cromwellian period.[18] It has been interpreted in very different ways, some scholars going so far as to claim it as authority for a land-based riparian right to river flow[19]—the opposite view to ours. Piggot, the defendant, had built a wall that cut off the flow of a stream into a pond where the plaintiff had been watering his cattle. By an action on the case the plaintiff sought damages for the interruption of the flow. The defendant argued that the plaintiff's 'right to the flow' had consisted merely of an easement. Thus, under the law of easement of passage on land as then understood, it had been automatically extinguished when the plaintiff had come into possession both of the pond and of the property now held by the defendant.[20] (The report is vague about this, but evidently Shury had once acquired then granted the property now held by Piggot.) None of the judges agreed with the defendant's submission. Instead, they said, *because the water once flowed, it should continue to flow.* The phenomenon of flowing water was, according to Justice Whitlock, *ex jure naturae* (it 'came from nature'); therefore it made no sense that the right to use it should be extinguished simply because of the technical rule applying to easements over land. Justice Jones remarked: 'This water-course is not extinct by the unity of possession, the same being a thing which ariseth out of the land, and no interest at all, by this claimed in the land, but *quod currere solebat*[21] this way, and so to have continuance of this.'

Neither land ownership nor prescriptive rights were mentioned as necessary ingredients by the judges. For this reason the case cannot be said to reaffirm a land-based or riparian right to water. Instead, it establishes a seniority right: in a dispute, earlier *enjoyment* or use of the river gives the better right, that is, the right to the maintained state of the river's levels and flows *as the owner found them* when he became owner of the banks or before the defendant's actions interfered. This finding was to assist the courts in establishing as precedent the doctrine that simple prior-use was a main basis for asserting or defending a right to the water.

[17] *Shury v. Piggot* (1625), 81 E.R. 280 (K.B.).

[18] In the earlier *Lutrel's Case* (1625), 76 E.R. 1065 (K.B.), an owner of two fulling mills with prescriptive rights to water replaced them with two corn mills. The court held his prescriptive rights were still valid as long as the alternation to the mills did not substantially affect the stream or further affect another user. The case defined the prescriptive right as quantitative.

[19] See Maass and Zobel 1960.

[20] Where two adjoining properties, one with an easement across the land of the other, come under the same possession or ownership ('unity'), the easement is no longer considered necessary and so is, by law, extinguished. As one of the judges in the case put it: 'the greater benefit [ownership of the whole land] shall drown the less [ownership of the easement]'. See *Shury v. Piggot* (1625), 81 E.R. 280 at 281 (K.B.).

[21] 'As it was accustomed to run', or 'as in the past'.

In two *Anonymous* cases a few years later[22] the plaintiffs did not plead a prescriptive right to divert water, but merely that they had already been diverting it and that another user had cut off the flow. In both cases the court decided in the plaintiffs' favour. The year after that, in *Sands v. Trefuses*,[23] the plaintiff was unable to show any entitlement at all to use the water (prescriptive or otherwise) but the court said it was enough that he be 'lawfully' using it.

The next main case was *Cox v. Matthews* (1673). It gave an opportunity for a pronouncement on the question by one of the great theorists of the time, Sir Matthew Hale. Although the case concerned the stopping of light, he gave the analogy of a watercourse, saying that an action for diversion might be brought by a mill owner without pleading prescriptive rights (*antiquum molendinum* or 'ancient mill'). The only defence against it could be that the defendant was using the water *before* the plaintiff. Even if the plaintiff had a new mill (that is, it arrived later than the defendant), unless the defendant was already *using* the water himself he would have no justification for cutting off the miller's flow.[24]

The cases in this early series demonstrate the emerging recognition in the courts that a person who is 'in possession' of, i.e. using or diverting water, may sue someone who interferes with its flow and does him damage merely by pleading that he was using the water first and that he had legal access to the river. The new right, purely possessory or usufructuary, was only relative. As between two users, the one who had made the *prior use* would win. Here and there one might find a user who still held a prescriptive usufructuary title once acquired under medieval law. Otherwise, the resulting prior-use regime of water rights had no ties to landowners or to land.

BLACKSTONE AND OWNERSHIP OF THE RIVER

Although the water regime of prior-use seems to have worked, as a system of property rights it lacked the quality of title characteristic: historical or theoretical foundation. Of course, Bracton's thirteenth-century Roman idea about the 'good neighbour principle' of land use (*sic utere tuo ut alienum non laedas*) still applied as between persons. But could this principle serve as the foundation of a property right? There was no clear answer for almost a century. Then, one of the greatest early modern legal theorists, Sir William Blackstone, in his treatise on the origins of property, reached back into Roman law for the same

[22] *Sands v. Trefuses* (1638), 79 E.R. 1094 (C.P.).

[23] *Shury v. Piggot* (1625), 81 E.R. 280 (K.B.).

[24] The fact that the law cited in *Cox v. Matthews* (1673), 86 E.R. 159 at 160 (K.B.), referred to in *Wheeldon v. Burrows v. Matthews* is both hypothetical and ambiguous has meant that it has been used to support both the old land-based law and the new 'prior-use' law. Our view is that Lord Hale's analogy with sunlight supports the view of *interference*; that is, the miller could succeed in a lawsuit because his prior use was interfered with and not because the defendant had merely diminished the flow.

idea. As flowing water had there been labelled *res communis* (a thing owned by all) subject to personal law respecting the first-comer, he observed:

> But after all there are some few things which notwithstanding the general introduction and continuance of property must still unavoidably remain in common, being such wherein nothing but a usufructuary property is capable of being had and they still belong to the first occupant during the time he holds possession of them and no longer. Such (among others) are the elements of light, air and water which a man may occupy by means of his . . . mills . . . . All these streams so long as they remain in possession every man has a right to enjoy without disturbance, but if once they escape from his custody and he voluntarily abandons the use of them, they return to the common stock and any man else has an equal right to seize and enjoy them afterwards.[25]

Blackstone's work, first published in the 1760s, was followed by a period of between forty and fifty years during which judges probably continued to apply the principles of this natural law (recognizing the prior right) to the growing number of cases on diversion. Few cases, however, applied the prior-use theory to the question of quality of title. Not until 1805 was there an important exception: *Bealey v. Shaw*.[26] The facts were that A, an upstream riparian, had diverted water for his mill for more than twenty years, thereby gaining a prescriptive right to continue doing so. B, the plaintiff, later built a mill downstream and used most of the surplus water from A's mill for a period of less than twenty years. A then enlarged his mill, depriving B of the surplus flow. The court held that B had a right to the surplus (although not a prescriptive right) and that A could not now deprive him of it and hinder his existing operations. This actionable right came only from the priority of use by B of the surplus water. Lord Ellenborough wrote:

> The general rule of law as applied to this subject is, that, independent of any particular enjoyment used to be had by another, every man has a right to have the advantage of a flow of water in his own land without diminution or alteration. But an adverse right may exist founded on the occupation of another. . . . [If] the occupation of the party so taking or using it have [*sic*] existed for so long time as may raise the presumption of a grant, the other party, whose land is below must take the stream, subject to such adverse right.[27]

It is important to note that while Lord Ellenborough is writing loftily about the prescriptive ('adverse') rights of A, the case was about the surplus water to which neither A nor B had prescriptive rights. If one followed a riparian-right approach, both had rights to the flow. But no *property* action was available to either A or B to sue on this basis other than an old feudal action of disseisin, by now out of the question. B prevailed over A because he had standing in *tort law* to sue A, being the prior user of the surplus water and having sustained damage.

[25] Blackstone 1789 Book 14, no. 2.
[26] *Bealey v. Shaw* (1805), 102 E.R. 1266.
[27] Id., p. 1269.

Further attempts at giving a legal or quality of title foundation to the priority-of-use right were made in two cases that took place some thirty years after Blackstone's 1789 *Commentaries*. In the first case, *Williams v. Morland*, Judge Bayley, still depending directly on Roman law, said: 'Flowing water is originally *publici juris*. So soon as it is appropriated by *an individual* his right is co-extensive with the beneficial use to which he appropriates it. Subject to that right all the rest of the water remains *publici juris*.'[28]

Seven years later this rationale was again recognized in a reported case, *Liggins v. Inge*. Lord Chief Justice Tindal wrote:

> Water flowing in a stream, it is well settled, by the law of England, is *publici juris*. By the Roman law, running water, light, and air were considered as some of those things which had the name of *res communes* and which were defined as 'things, the property of which belongs to no person, but the use to all.' And, by the law of England, the *person* who first appropriates any part of the water flowing through his land to his own use, has the right to the use of so much as he thus appropriates, against any other.[29]

This right lacked the characteristic that judges agreed was quality of title; nevertheless, it was seen to be secure.

TRANSFERABILITY: PRIVILEGES AND CONTRACTING FOR WATER

We know that parties have made arrangements to create water privileges of some sort since earliest times and that the tendency increased with time. In medieval times 'contracting', as it was known later, was rare, for water and mill sites were plentiful enough to meet the modest demand for them. One who wished to build and turn a mill would generally have other methods of procuring a water right than buying or leasing one from an owner of land by the river. In any event the common law had not yet evolved to enforce such a personal obligation.

In the fifteenth and sixteenth centuries, however, the *leasehold* became an increasingly popular method of holding a site and using the adjacent river water. This interest combined elements of both property and contract law.

In the seventeenth and eighteenth centuries, as the number of unused sites (especially those with both level and flow suitable for water power) diminished, the price of the water right increased. So did the use of contracts and other lease-type arrangements between owners of water rights and those who wished to acquire all or part of these rights. The *transferability* characteristic of water holdings, by now common to other property rights typically held by riparians and other water users, was on the increase.

[28] *Williams v. Morland* (1824), 107 E.R. 620 (K.B.).

[29] *Liggins v. Inge* (1831), 131 E.R. 263 (C.P.). A fallacy in these cases, conflation of the concepts *publici juris* and *res communes*, glosses over the distinction between private and public rights to flowing water. *Res communes* would have been the better term and it harkened back to the natural law discussion of Blackstone.

Thus, during the Industrial Revolution the contract for water rights was available for expanding use while protecting original titles. It was almost as good as a lease of land with water attached. Both could be time limited and subject to various conditions and covenants. They kept the land with its seniority of water right intact for reversion to the owner and they economized on both the landlords' and the industrialists' capital. A statement by one of the judges in an 1866 case shows just how important the system of water privileges (actual or supposed rights) had become:

> The application and use of flowing water to work machinery is as old as the law. Corn mills have existed from time immemorial, and it appears, from old legal authorities, that fulling and other mills worked by water for the purpose of manufacture are of a very ancient date. Until the last century, steam as a power was, if known, not much in use; and until it was introduced, water power was very generally used, and it is still the cheapest when available. The mill is sometimes situated upon the bank of the natural stream, but more usually at some little distance from it; the water is conveyed to it by a goit or artificial cut, leading from the stream, and then, after turning the wheel of the mill, flows away in what is commonly called the tail goit. So, also, water was and is very frequently conveyed from the natural stream in the same manner for purposes of irrigation. And it is not too much to say, that the value of actual or supposed water rights of this character throughout England may be estimated by hundreds of thousands, perhaps millions. The law has been supposed to be well settled.... [T]he law favours the exercise of such a right; it is at once beneficial to the owner and to the Commonwealth.[30]

We may say with some confidence that the regime of water law that enforced individual or use-based water rights and the intense level of personal contracting of stream water that took place during the Industrial Revolution facilitated and enhanced each other.

After 1800 the variety of ways of getting and holding water increased. In particular the government, restricting and even expropriating riparian owners' rights in favour of public uses, had recourse to water supply statutes and canal and railway incorporations. As we will see later in this chapter, the courts restricted the scope of contracting, perhaps to retain their own discretion to handle the swollen demand for water. They gradually formulated a concept of 'community of the river', tending to exclude (at least for enforcement of their rights against proprietor-riparians) those parties who had merely contracted for water. Perhaps under these discouragements, dependence on contracting decreased. Economic studies do speak of fewer, larger water works and enterprises, many of them government-owned, rather than a multitude of small private ones. This concentration may in turn be partly explained by the judicial attitudes.

[30] *Nuttall v. Bracewell* (1866), 2 Exch. 1 at 9–10 (Eng.).

QUESTIONING THE PRIOR-USE PRINCIPLE

In 1823 users of water who had established their use earlier than their neighbour's use could be confident of winning damages if a dispute between the two went to a common-law court. *Wright v. Howard* arose in the Court of Equity about a water lease, however, and had nothing to do with damage. Howard, the defendant, a prospective purchaser, had planned to build a cotton mill for which he would need to divert the stream flow and had found a suitable site along a little-used river in a rural district. The price of the site included a ninety-nine-year water lease from Wright, a downstream proprietor, giving him consent to make the necessary diversion. But upon investigation the would-be purchaser found that there were two other parties downstream on the river who had not given (or sold) their consent and who he feared might later sue him if he diverted their stream flow. We do not know whether the three parties were using the water. To justify his lack of desire to proceed with his purchasing of the site Howard argued that since there was no guarantee he could in the future make the planned diversion without facing legal action, the value of Wright's land was only worth one third of what it would be worth with a secure water right. Wright asked the court to oblige the defendant to go through with the deal.[31]

Blackstone's water-law teaching would probably have been that, once the defendant had constructed his mill and made the necessary diversion, downstream parties who were not using the water themselves would not have any legal redress. Howard's success might therefore have turned on whether the downstream parties had prior-use rights to sue. But the judge in the case, Vice-Chancellor Sir John Leach, agreed with the defendant more broadly, making a statement, two parts of which were eventually to shake up the common law of water. He attributed ownership of property rights to the waterflow to all of the riparian proprietors (those downstream as well as the defendant if he purchased the land) *whether or not they used the water.* Although he thereby identified a land-based water right, he agreed that only those riparian proprietors who had suffered damage could sue to enforce it. He was thereby recognizing a distinction between black-letter law and enforceable rights:

> The right to the use of water rests on clear and settled principles. *Prima facie*, the proprietor of each bank of a stream is the proprietor of half the land covered by the stream, but there is no property in the water. Every proprietor has an equal right to use the water which flows in the stream, and consequently no proprietor can have the right to use the water to the prejudice of any other proprietor. Without the consent of the other proprietors, who may be affected by his operations, no proprietor can either diminish the quantity of water, which would otherwise descend to the proprietors below, nor throw the water back upon the proprietors above... It appears to me that

[31] Wright had brought the case in Equity because he sought 'specific performance', a remedy that was not then available in the common-law courts.

no action will lie for diverting or throwing back water, except by a person who sustains an actual injury. . . .[32]

There were two new principles here. The first was later to be called the 'natural flow' principle. Applied strictly, it could mean that any use of the stream flow which changes its quality, quantity or manner of flow (except a prescriptive use) is wrongful without consent from riparians who *might* be affected by it, although the second of the new principles said that wrongful use was actionable only by those riparians who actually suffered damage to their existing use. It defined water rights uniquely in terms of land ownership. Although it did not specifically deny that persons other than property owners could acquire rights in the water, 'equality of right' among riparians certainly seems to exclude any idea of 'priority of right' among mere users.

Wright v. Howard is said to demonstrate how desperately the courts at the time were seeking a solution to the problem of excessive water use. According to Lauer,[33] the courts were unhappy about the extent to which both prescriptive and prior-use rights were being pressed into service to settle disputes arising when mills were enlarged. There seemed no criterion by which to limit the application of the priority idea. The judges worried that, without such a criterion, prior-use could 'bring to a standstill' the development of water resources by new entrants.[34] Lauer's treatment, otherwise excellent, seems to give too little weight to the opportunities for the two parties to contract, once prior-use had been established as an exclusive right.[35]

For a time, however, few judges seemed to notice the conundrum illustrated by the reasoning in *Wright v. Howard*. Heard in the Court of Equity, the decision was not binding in the common-law courts. And since it had nothing to do with actual damage, it was different from the vast majority of cases that came before them. The prior-use phase in the development of water rights continued for at least another ten years until the new river pollution problem changed the facts of the disputes coming before the courts. Facilitated by the existing law, industrial use had increased so much that all users were adversely affected by the pollution of the overburdened rivers. In response, judges at last reached back to 1823 and the natural flow approach of *Wright v. Howard* for a way to discontinue the prior-use principle—a change in the foundation of water rights they would later base on the American precedent set in *Tyler v Wilkinson* (1827) (see below).

[32] *Wright v. Howard* (1823), 57 E.R. 76 (V.C.).

[33] Lauer 1963, pp. 99–104.

[34] Id., *passim*.

[35] *Wright v Howard* can also be thought of as a foundation for the American public trust doctrine discussed in Chapter 1 and in fn 144 below. In his 1823 judgment Sir John Leach identified the riparian land owners as 'the public' who between them were the proprietors of the flow of the river. See Chapter 1 and Rose 2003.

LORD DENMAN AND A NEW INTERPRETATION OF 'PRECEDENT' CASES

To pick up the story in England we skip ten years beyond *Wright v Howard* to focus on the influential 1833 common-law case, *Mason v. Hill.*[36] It is notable among other things for the performance of Lord Denman, a well-respected judge of the Court of King's Bench, in supplying an alteration in the direction of water law in England while claiming continuity with the law arising from the precedent of earlier cases. He set aside a body of case law relying on the prior-use theory, denouncing the authority of Roman law on which he said it was based. In so doing he paved the way for later courts to supply an enforceable land-based water law in the place of the previous individual or use-based law. In four pages of the decision, Lord Denman went through a careful process to show that the prior rights law was 'misconceived' and that cases which had reflected the misconception should no longer be followed.[37]

The facts of the extremely complicated *Mason v. Hill* case relevant to this discussion are the following: the plaintiff was a downstream riparian owner (A) who had been using the stream water for more than twenty years, although for different purposes and in varying quantities. His upstream neighbour (B) moved onto the stream and began using the water, with A's permission, and A used the surplus from B's operations. This was at first sufficient for A's purposes. Part of B's use, however, had been to divert water from certain springs, which would have drained into the stream, into a reservoir. This B did without A's permission. When A later increased his operations, he did not have enough clear water and disputed, among other things, B's right to divert the spring water into the reservoir. A was able to prove 'damage' because subsequent additions to B's mill had thermally polluted the stream (water was returned to the stream in a heated condition), and this damaged A's *existing* operations. Had it not been for this proven damage, A would not have had standing to sue, since his operations had been increased *after* B had diverted the spring water.

However, the importance of the judgment actually concerned the question of whether the fact that B had used the stream water *first* gave him a right to divert part of the stream and deprive A of stream water which he would need *later.* Lord Denman emphatically found that B did *not* have this right. In so finding, he challenged the legal assumptions which had formed the law in the previous centuries, that priority of use created rights in all the circumstances. Thus he began the process of bringing the prior-use phase of water law to an end.

The lawyer for B cited a body of precedent to support his argument that priority of use gave rights of continued use. This included *Cox v. Mathews,*[38]

[36] *Mason v. Hill* (1833), 110 E.R. 692 (K.B.). [37] Id., at pp. 698–701.

[38] *Cox v. Matthews* (1673), 86 E.R. 159, 160 (K.B.), referred to in *Wheeldon v. Burrows v. Matthews* (1673), 86 E.R. 159 (K.B.).

Williams v. Morland,[39] *Liggins v. Inge,*[40] and *Bealey v. Shaw.*[41] Of these, the strongest was *Bealey v. Shaw.* Lord Denman set out in *Mason* to destroy its formulation. He first distinguished *Bealey* on its facts. In *Bealey* the prior-user was the party who had been damaged, while in *Mason* the prior-user was the party doing damage and preventing further use by his downstream neighbour. Lord Denman limited Bealey's principle of priority rights to a right not to suffer damage rather than the right to inflict it. More important, he emphasized a different basis for the rights: A's ownership of riparian land and B's lack of prescriptive title. Given such treatment, *Bealey v. Shaw* no longer had any precedent value for supporting prior-use rights in general. A quote from Lord Denman's judgment is illustrative of his technique: 'This decision [*Bealey v. Shaw*] is in exact accordance with the proposition contended for by the plaintiff; that the owner of the land through which the stream flows may, as soon as he has converted it to a purpose producing benefit to himself, maintain an action against the owner of the land above, for a subsequent act, by which that benefit is diminished; and *it does not in any degree support the position, that the first occupant of a stream of water has a right to it against the proprietor of land below.*'[42]

Cox v. Matthews was given similar treatment. *Williams v. Moreland,* was confined to its particular facts (plaintiff's ability to prove damage to the riverbanks from an upstream use which altered the flow of the river), and all broad reasonings supportive of prior rights were dismissed as non-binding '*dicta*'. *Liggins v. Inge* was interpreted narrowly, and Lord Tindal was said to have intended to express himself narrowly, even though he referred to broad principles. *Saunders v. Newman*[43] was discounted as being inapplicable. A logical reason was given by Lord Denman for not recognizing prior rights to divert or use water:

> But it is a very different question, whether he [the prior-user] can take away from the owner of the land below, one of its natural advantages, which is capable of being applied to profitable purposes, and generally increases the fertility of the soil, even when unapplied; and deprive him of it altogether by anticipating him in its application to a useful purpose. If this be so, a considerable part of the value of an estate, which, in manufacturing districts particularly, is much enhanced by the existence of an unappropriated stream of water with a fall, within its limits, might at any time be taken away. . . .[44]

Thus *Mason* made severe inroads into the theory of prior rights from a technical and logical point of view. Lord Denman went further than this, however, and attacked the philosophical underpinnings of 'prior-use' law:

[39] *Williams v. Morland* (1824), 107 E.R. 620 (K.B.).
[40] *Liggins v. Inge* (1831), 131 E.R. 263 (C.P.).
[41] *Bealey v. Shaw* (1805), 102 E.R. 1266 (K.B.).
[42] *Mason v. Hill* (1833), 110 E.R. 692 at 699 (K.B.) (emphasis added).
[43] *Saunders v. Newman* (1818), 106 E.R. 95 (K.B.). This was a case on prescription which also discussed prior rights, relying on *Bealey v. Shaw* (1805), 102 E.R. 1266 (K.B.).
[44] *Mason v. Hill* (1833), 110 E.R. 692 at 698–9 (K.B.).

namely, the public's use of river water. This analysis began with a reinterpretation of Roman law. Lord Denman first limited the Roman law principle (*res communes*) that the water in streams belonged to everyone and to no one (ideas reiterated by Blackstone), to find that only water which is used for domestic purposes was 'public'. Then, to be safe, he firmly announced that Roman law did not constitute binding precedent for English common law anyway. These findings were so crucial to the development of water law in later years that we quote them in full:

> It appears to us also, that the doctrine of Blackstone and the dicta of learned Judges, both in some of those cases [*Bealey v. Shaw, Saunders v. Newman, Williams v. Moreland*], and in that of *Cox v. Matthews*... have been misconceived....
>
> ...it appears to us there is no authority in our law, nor, as far as we know, in the Roman law (*which, however, is no authority in ours*), that the first occupant (though he may be the proprietor of the land above) has any right, by diverting the stream, to deprive the owner of the land below, of the special benefit and advantage of the natural flow of water therein.[45]

Finally, Lord Denman supported his reasoning by recalling from ten years earlier the 'luminous judgment' of Sir John Leach in the Court of Equity case *Wright v. Howard.*[46]

Lord Denman's activism in demolishing the 'public rights' theory of water law was certainly motivated by a concern for justice in the particular case. There may have also been a broader, societal factor in his consideration. A clue comes in a case fifty years later, *Ormerod v. Todmorden Mill Co.* (1883),[47] wherein Justice Cave, in a lower court, said that, 'Owing, however, to the greater demand for water for manufacturing purposes, it has been found necessary in our law to limit the right to running water, and as is pointed out in *Mason v. Hill*, running water can no longer be said to be *publici juris* in the original sense of those words.'[48]

THE TRANSITION TO REASONABLE USE: NATURAL FLOW DOCTRINE

Lord Denman's judgment in *Mason v. Hill* began a transition to what would be a new regime of legally recognized title to water: the 'reasonable use' regime, centred on land-based rights to water and a whole new philosophy of the river. A plaintiff who sustained damage by diversion and thermal pollution caused by the defendant still had standing to take his case to court. But Lord Denman, although advocating and supporting a land-based water right, recognized that a landowner who had not used the river could not have sustained any damage to his use, and therefore could not bring suit to enforce his rights to the river's 'natural flow'. He had commented that damage ought not to be necessary to

[45] *Mason v. Hill* (1833), 110 E.R. 692 at 699, 701 (K.B.) (emphasis added).
[46] *Wright v. Howard* (1823), 57 E.R. 76 (V.C.).
[47] *Ormerod v. Todmorden Mill Co.* (1883), 11 Q.B.D. 155 (Eng.).
[48] Id., at 160.

bring legal action for loss of natural flow, and that current tort-derived procedures in the law were not in accordance with the land-based right he was espousing.

Though this comment was not binding in the original opinion, it was reiterated in some later cases. For example, two years later in *Bower v. Hill*,[49] Chief Justice Tindal, after finding that the plaintiff had indeed suffered damage to an easement through permanent obstruction of it, proceeded to say that even if he hadn't, he should still have standing to sue. Failure to sue, he argued, would enable a prescriptive right to accrue to the defendant, giving the defendant an unfair advantage and decreasing the value of the plaintiff's land:

> But, independently of this narrower ground of decision, we think the erection of the tunnel is in the nature of, and, until removed, is to be considered as, a permanent obstruction to the Plaintiff's right, and therefore an injury to the Plaintiff, even though he receive no immediate damage thereby. The right of the Plaintiff to this way is injured, if there is an obstruction in its nature permanent. *If acquiesced in for twenty years, it would become evidence of a renunciation and abandonment of the right of way.* That is the ground upon which a reversioner is allowed to bring his action for an obstruction, apparently permanent. ... The Plaintiff's premises would sell for less whilst the tunnel is in existence, if now put up to sale.[50]

This idea, suing to prevent prescriptive rights from accruing, was generally adopted as an 'exception' to the otherwise strict requirement of actual damage in the action on the case. It smoothed the way for the theory that all riparians had an equal right to a natural flow.[51]

Fourteen years later the Court of the Exchequer (1849) picked up the idea articulated in *Bower v. Hill* of 'damage to right' (to receive the natural flow of the river), and applied it to a pollution case. In *Wood v. Waud*,[52] Chief Baron Pollock spoke of 'damage-in-law' (that is, damage to the right) as opposed to 'damage-in-fact' (actual damage). From it, he said, the court would *presume* that the plaintiff had suffered damage in fact, caused by the defendant. This reasoning also circumvented the causation problem encountered under tort law in a case of pollution: how to prove that the defendant, in particular, had caused the damage when many others were also contributing to it. These cases and the judgments that followed them[53] helped to open the way for a full rehabilitation of the law of land-based riparian rights. The key point was the new procedural ability for riparians to sue without having suffered (actual) damage-in-fact, and without having used the water at all, so that the other party's priority had become, for this purpose, irrelevant.

[49] *Bower v. Hill* (1835), 131 E.R. 1229 (C.P.).

[50] At 1231.

[51] It could also be compared with an early action against a trespasser in which it would not be necessary to prove actual damage, only that the person was on the land without permission.

[52] *Wood v. Waud* (1849), 154 E.R. 1047 (Exch. 1849).

[53] *Sampson v. Hoddinott* (1857), 140 E.R. 242 (C.P.); *Pennington v. Brinsop Hall Coal Co.* (1877), 5 Ch. D. 769 (Eng.).

The reasonable use period of water in England

The beginning of the reasonable use regime of water law in England may be set at the year 1851 when a judicial decision dealing with water rights—*Embrey v. Owen*—first made mention of the concept of 'reasonableness'.[54] As we will see below, the doctrine of natural flow, already ascendant in the English law courts, appeared attractive for the purposes of reducing pollution, but impractical when applied to water abstraction. At best, it would undermine those who had established their water rights back in the prior-use era. It would also put a new burden on old industries: the cost of buying out the right to sue from other riparians on the stream. These were problems to which 'reasonable use' theory, as a development from natural-flow theory, could be addressed while still providing the institutional groundwork to clean up the rivers.

POLLUTION: ADVANTAGES OF NATURAL-FLOW THEORY

By this time, in the second quarter of the nineteenth century, industry in England had crowded some rivers to their capacity. Cities, led by their manufacturing districts, doubled their population in as short a time as ten years. Demands on agriculture and even on irrigation increased with population. Where drinking and washing had once been small-scale direct uses of the water, they now depended on massive reservoirs and canals. Where there had been goits, there were now pipelines, diverting larger amounts of water out of the riverbeds. Mills were larger, wheels were larger. Location became less important as water could be carried longer distances from diversions. The use of steam for power modified dependence on water-power sites. What mattered was the ability to abstract water. On falling rivers or near towns, however, industrial sites continued to be packed together. Any mill's change in level, impoundment and releases could significantly affect several other establishments below and above.

If we turn from water quantity to water quality, we see that the waterways of England had become dumping grounds for wastes. Industry emitted new chemicals and its steam power created thermal pollution. At their outskirts, cities, towns and villages routinely dumped their sewage into rivers. So serious had river pollution become, and so extensive were the diversions, that the small farms and other properties alongside the rivers were now effectively deprived of the 'benefit and advantage of the natural flow of water' by their property.[55]

The aim of natural flow doctrine was to restore the pristine state of the rivers by giving each riparian landowner the right to receive water in an undiminished, unaltered state. His right of action was grounded on the right to a clean

[54] *Embrey v. Owen* (1851), 155 E.R. 579 (Exch.).

[55] The *Globe and Mail*, September 16, 1991, p. 18, mentioned Charles Dickens in 1849 sending an article entitled 'Dreadful Hardships' to *Punch* magazine. It was about the scandal-

river. The focus was on conservation. If applied generally the doctrine had potential for sweeping clean the fouled rivers of England in a way that tort (or nuisance) law simply had not.

Under the nineteenth-century law of nuisance (the successor to the late medieval action on the case) victims sued waste dischargers for damages. But the information and litigation costs of nuisance law litigation on rivers were alarmingly high. To establish that a certain polluter had caused specific damage was almost impossible when as many as fifty other polluters were also contributing to the river's pollution; and to establish the whole value of a cleanup was almost as difficult: how much were living organisms and fish worth to a riparian who did not operate a fishing business? While the wealthy might push a nuisance action through, ordinary users or landowners had virtually no redress.[56]

Natural-flow doctrine was stronger, cheaper and easier. Any riparian could sue any one of the many polluters. He would not have to show that a particular polluter was responsible for specified damage. Nor would he have to quantify any damage, because the damage was deemed to his riparian rights. The cost of a successful action was shifted away from the riparian plaintiff onto the defendant, who had to prove that he had not caused the stated damage.

Riparians were now further assisted by a powerful remedy, which had by the late nineteenth century made its way from the Court of Equity into the common law: the *injunction*. This discretionary remedy enabled the court to order an impugned activity to cease. It was an alternative remedy to damages, awarded if deemed 'sufficient' to redress the harm. Injunctions were most frequently awarded to avoid plaintiffs having to repeat their damage actions against defendants who resumed or continued their harmful operations. To determine which remedy to award, the court would weigh the 'balance of convenience' as between the benefit that an injunction would give the plaintiff and its detriment to the defendant. In pollution cases the injunction would invariably be awarded against the user-polluter defendant. Defendants who wished at all costs to continue their polluting operations could always try to buy out the plaintiff; some did so, probably paying the plaintiff considerably more than would have been received in one damage action.

The injunction gave individuals some power against rich and powerful corporations and cities. Consider the following two cases which, most likely, would not even have been brought forward if the only remedy had been damages. In *Attorney General v. Birmingham Borough Council*,[57] the plaintiff

ous state of London's water supply, arising from the air and water pollution of modern industry. See also John Ruskin 1871–84, pp. 21–9, and 1885–9, p. 35.

[56] On the inaccessibility of nuisance law in mid nineteenth century, see McLaren 1983; Brenner 1973; Horwitz 1977.

[57] *Attorney-General v. Birmingham (Borough) Council* (1858), 70 E.R. 220 (Ch.). This was a public nuisance action.

individuals (the Attorney-General was taking the case on their behalf) were applying for an injunction to stop the City from carrying out drainage operations which had the effect of killing the fish and preventing cattle from drinking the water seven miles downstream. The City argued that if the injunction were granted, an overflow of sewage would result, threatening the health of 250,000 people. The court was unmoved, referring the city to Parliament for relief.

In *Pennington v. Brinsop Hall Coal Co.*,[58] the plaintiff owners of a cotton mill were suing a large colliery because it had dumped sulphuric acid into the river, corroding the iron in their machinery. The defendants argued that they had neutralized the acid as far as technology allowed and that the only way of preventing any acid in the water would be to close the colliery, thereby losing £190,000 in capital and five hundred jobs. The plaintiffs had suffered 'a mere scintilla of damage', precisely £100 which it would cost to clean their machinery. But the court granted the injunction.

EARLY REASONABLE USE DOCTRINE: REASONABLE DAMAGE

To further pursue the development of the reasonable use doctrine we turn back to waterflow diversion cases. We begin, again, with *Embrey v. Owen* (1851). In his judgment, Baron Parkes of the Exchequer Court pronounced that 'the law as to flowing water [was] now put on its right footing'.

This case had belatedly followed the precedent of the American 1827 case *Tyler v. Wilkinson* regarding water use and water rights (see next section), emphasizing both exploitation and protection from damage.[59] The judgment proceeded along these lines: riparians were entitled to receive the natural flow of the rivers and to sue to protect those rights even if they had suffered no actual damage because of an upstream or downstream diversion or alteration of the flow. But if they had not suffered damage, or had suffered only minimal damage, they might not win their suit. This was because of a new emphasis on the rule that the law will not redress trivialities: *de minimis non curat lex*, first stated in *Embrey v. Owen*. Once the courts cited the requirement of minimal damage the riparian right to a natural flow in cases of diversion became a dead letter because, as in tort law so in property law, a damage claim could only work for a riparian who had some kind of seniority in use. But the new provision went further to allow diversion to proceed if it caused some provable but *minimal* damage. That is, the theory might protect industrial exploitation of the rivers to a certain 'reasonable' extent. The extent, said Baron Parke, was entirely a question of degree and depended on the facts of each case, including the size of the river.

[58] *Pennington v. Brinsop Hall Coal Co.* (1877), 5 Ch. D. 769 (Eng.). This was a riparian rights case.

[59] See *Tyler v. Wilkinson*, Fed. Cas. No. 14312, 4 Mason 397, 24 F. Cas. 472 (C.C.D.R.I. 1827). Embrey also referred to recent developments in English law which had relaxed the damage requirement for standing.

Thus, while the emphasis in natural-flow doctrine had been to protect a riparian's passive right to (continue to) receive the flow in its 'natural' state, it now shifted more to protect the riparian *user's* active right to divert a *reasonable* amount of water. Judgments from two contemporary cases would restate the importance of economic exploitation of property: 'The law favours the exercise of dominion by every one upon his own land, and his using it for the most beneficial purpose to himself.'[60] And: 'The great interests of society require that the cultivation of every man's land should be encouraged.'[61]

Embrey v. Owen (like *Tyler v. Wilkinson* in the United States) was a case about water diversion. While addressing the problem of determining which uses were 'reasonable', it offered nothing to protect the small landowners by the stream who were merely using the water in a 'domestic' way for drinking or washing or feeding cattle. The interests of these small parties were addressed specifically in *Miner v. Gilmour,*[62] a Canadian case brought to the English Privy Council. Lord Kingsdown, in words which were to be quoted many times afterwards as the 'riparian rights doctrine' said:

By the general law applicable to running streams, every riparian proprietor has a right to what may be called the ordinary use of the water flowing past his land; for instance, to the reasonable use of the water for his domestic purposes and for his cattle, and this without regard to the effect which such use may have, in case of a deficiency, upon proprietors lower down the stream. But, further, he has a right to the use of it for any purpose, or what may be deemed the extraordinary use of it, provided that he does not thereby interfere with the rights of other proprietors, either above or below him. Subject to this condition, he may dam up the stream for the purpose of a mill, or divert the water for the purpose of irrigation. But, he has no right to interrupt the regular flow of the stream, if he thereby interferes with the lawful use of the water by other proprietors, and inflicts upon them a sensible injury.[63]

What is interesting in this statement is that it gives 'ordinary' users an almost absolute right to their use, regardless of the effect it has on others. It suggests that 'ordinary' use is, *per se*, reasonable. The idea of protecting the ordinary user in his domestic use of the water[64] was now to solidify as one of the main tenets of the reasonable use doctrine in England.[65]

[60] *Bonomi v. Backhouse* (1859), 120 E.R. 643 (Exch.).

[61] *Chasemore v. Richards* (1859), 11 E.R. 140.

[62] *Miner v. Gilmour* (1858), 14 E.R. 861 (P.C.).

[63] Id., at 870 (emphasis added).

[64] The idea had already been referred to ten years earlier in *Wood v. Waud*. In this case, the Exchequer Court remarked that, 'if the stream were only used by the riparian proprietor and his family, by drinking it, or for the supply for domestic purposes, no action would lie for the ordinary use of it; and it may be conceived, that if a field be covered by houses, the ordinary use by the inhabitants might sensibly diminish the stream, yet no action would, we apprehend, lie, any more than if the air was rendered less pure and healthy by the increase of inhabitants in the neighbourhood, and by the smoke issuing from the chimneys of an increased number of houses.' *Wood v. Waud* (1849), 154 E.R. 1047 at 1060, 1061.

[65] The right is, nevertheless, subject to the level of the stream flow. This means that, in times of low flow, the ordinary users lower down on the stream may not be able to fulfil all their requirements because of upstream ordinary users against whom they will have no legal redress.

A complementary result of the reasonable use concept was that certain uses were also to be found to be *per se* unreasonable. These were the uses that by their very nature were clearly detrimental or wasteful. They destroyed river quality, killing the fish, or they failed to return the water after it had been diverted, or they were merely unnecessary. The common law moved swiftly to combine with the growing volume of statute law to discourage such obviously unreasonable water uses by making them sure losers under suit from another riparian. They included polluting uses,[66] wasteful or merely ornamental uses,[67] and uses which took the water out of the river basin or off the riparian tenement.[68] In the first two instances, for example, the user could not justify harm or damage for a socially useful purpose. Nor could he justify potential harm among other downstream users (not only the plaintiff) in the third instance. Damage was assumed.

By the courts' own doing, this new criterion further reduced the categories of uses left to the courts' discretion.[69] But here the process stopped. None of the other 'extraordinary' or non-domestic uses were actionable as unreasonable under the law of property unless they caused damage to other riparians. Indeed, the reasonable use innovation did not affect the majority of water users or the majority of river water used, which was governed by the accumulated law of prior-use. As well, tort law continued to develop its own approach to damages in water matters, although the degree of overlap with property law decreased. Nuisance law still prevented a riparian who had merely an intention to use the river from suing existing users to protect the potential commercial value of his property.

To what extent, then, had the law in fact escaped from the prior-use phase? In *Sampson v. Hoddinott* (1857), a case contemporary with *Miner v. Gilmour*, the court made it clear that, conceptually at least, it had escaped: 'all persons having lands on the margin of a flowing stream have, by nature, certain rights to use the water of that stream, whether they exercise those rights or not; and they may begin to exercise them whenever they will.'[70] The court in *Orr Ewing v. Colquoun* (1877) warned that these 'certain rights' must not be used vexatiously or spitefully against newcomers.[71] *Miner v. Gilmour* (1858) had explained that 'extraordinary' users of the flow would be subject to a requirement of reasonableness; they would not otherwise be permitted to cause

[66] *Attorney-General v. Birmingham (Borough) Council* (1858), 70 E.R. 220 (Ch.); *Pennington v. Brinsop Hall Coal Co.* (1877), 5 Ch. D. 769 (Eng.).

[67] *Lord Norbury v. Kitchin* (1862), 176 E.R. 132 (Cr. Cir.).

[68] *Wilts and Berks Canal Navigation Co. v. Swindon Waterworks Co.* (1872), 20 W.R. 353 (Ch.); *McCartney v. Londonderry & Lough Swilly Railway Co.* [1904] A.C. 301 (appeal taken from Ireland).

[69] This contrasts with the direction followed in American courts in the period, who were carving out for themselves a public interest role by *enlarging* the scope of their discretion.

[70] *Sampson v. Hoddinott* (1857), 140 E.R. 242 (C.P.).

[71] App. Cas 839 (1877), p. 856. The practical implications of this case and its 'dog in the manger' objection were far-reaching to the extent that legal actions regarding diversion, brought by non-user riparians against users to enforce the natural flow, were never actually attempted except perhaps in earlier cases such as *Wright v. Howard* (1823), 57 E.R. 76 (V.C.),

damage or hinder any other riparian's reasonable use of the flow. The reasonableness requirement was increasingly cited, and the reasonableness of the extraordinary uses was judged according to their impact elsewhere on the stream. If they caused damage, the court would, as in the past, order the diverter to modify or stop his activity or pay those who suffered from it. Thus, it should be understood that the concept of damage and so the protection of prior users from damage continued to play a major role in the law. English reasonable use judgments did little to disrupt the security inherent in the system for most existing users.

English stream users had one more recourse. The ordinary-use category might be expanded. A few non-domestic uses were found to be 'customary' or 'publicly necessary' in certain districts. There is authority to suggest that, as the law had discouraged certain detrimental extraordinary uses by calling them '*per se* unreasonable', so it encouraged and protected these necessary uses by calling them 'ordinary'. The case of *Ormerod v. Todmorden Joint Stock Mill Co.* offers the following comment: 'The question whether the use of a river is ordinary or extraordinary use depends upon the development of trade in its neighbourhood, and upon the use to which it is put by adjoining owners.'[72]

Indeed, as I discuss in Chapter 8 with regard to externalities from hard rock mining, existing 'reasonableness' standards were also being applied in nuisance cases in an attempt to modify the rights of traditional and casual landholders to be protected from the changing requirements and externalities of modernizing industry. The fact that nuisance actions persisted throughout this period is evidence of their popularity.[73] In every period of English law, protection of property from actionable damage at the hands of others has been recognized by law. As we will see, even Justice Story in *Tyler v. Wilkinson* agreed that *sic utere tuo ut alienum non laedas* ('use your land without harming your neighbour's') has always been part of the law.

CONTRACTING OR LICENSING THE RIPARIAN RIGHT

Contracting was also available in all phases of water law discussed here. It was particularly prevalent in the prior use phase owing to the prevailing system of rights enforcement. Persons who acquired rights by contract assumed the seniority of their contractual partner. If they suffered damage they could sue others less senior in use whether or not they were riparians.

where there were very few users on the stream. At a time when water was highly demanded, however, it was illogical to expect that all users would be able to contain their use so that it did not affect the amount passing by the property of any other riparians. For one non-using riparian owner to sue all existing users on the river would almost certainly be seen by the courts as vexatious and frivolous. We have not found a single case in which it was allowed. In this respect the prior user reaped the benefit of the court's scrutiny.

[72] *Ormerod v. Todmorden Mill Co.* (1883), 11 Q.B.D. 155 (Eng.).

[73] See Brenner 1973, pp. 422–3.

Contracting continued in the reasonable use phase but was cut back somewhat. Under land-based rights to the flow, the rights and obligations of the group of riparians toward each other eclipsed straight seniority in importance. Land-locked contractors were not part of this privileged 'community' and were not protected by riparian law. On the one hand, they did continue to use the water in their industries and maintained the right to take a nuisance action against outsiders who interfered with their water supply.[74] It was permissible for them to contract for stream water and even to direct and use it off a riparian's land, although not to carry it out of the watershed.[75] On the other hand, they were not entitled to benefit from the reasonable use rule. This applied only to riparians; and they had no recourse to a riparian-rights action.

This limitation affected contractors' quality of title in two ways. First, because they did not themselves have the right to use stream water 'reasonably', they could not change appreciably the flow they took without being vulnerable to suit by any riparian. Not changing the flow meant returning the water to the stream before it left the property from which they had abstracted it, in the same condition as they took it. This was often a tall order.[76] Second, the contractors could not sue riparians who caused them damage, even through unreasonable use of water. They could sue only their riparian contracting partner for not delivering under the contract, or, therefore, an 'unreasonable' riparian third party indirectly through, and in the name of, their partner. The case of *Stockport Waterworks Co. v. Potter*[77] set forth these newly defined and limited rights in the most complete way. It held:

> There seems to be no authority for contending that a riparian proprietor can keep the land abutting on the river the possession of which gives him his water rights, and at the same time transfer those rights or any of them, and thus create a right in gross [personal right independent of land] by assigning a portion of his rights appurtenant [land rights]. It seems to us clear that the rights which a riparian proprietor has with respect to the water are entirely derived from his possession of land abutting on the river. If he grants any portion of his land so abutting, then the grantee becomes a riparian proprietor and has similar rights. But if he grants away a portion of his estate not abutting on the river, then clearly the grantee of the land would have no water rights by virtue merely of his occupation. Can he have them by express grant? It seems to us that the true answer is

[74] *Laing v. Whaley* (1858), 157 E.R. 639 (Exch.), however, laid down the rule that they had to first establish their own entitlement to the flow. A mere parole licence would not suffice in this regard.

[75] *Kensit v. Great Eastern Railway Co.* (1884), 27 Ch. D. 122 (Eng.).

[76] In *Ormerod v. Todmorden Mill Co.* (1883), 11 Q.B.D. 155 (Eng.), where the contractors had returned the water slightly heated, Brett, M.R. said with regard to reasonable use: 'The law as to flowing water is part of the common law of England; but it only exists as between riparian owners; it does not extend to those whose lands do not abut on streams and rivers.' The obligation of contractors not to diminish or alter the flow at all is consistent with an obligation of riparians not to take river water out of the watershed.

[77] *Stockport Waterworks Co. v. Potter* (1864), 159 E.R. 545 (Exch.).

that *he can have them against the grantor* but not so as to sue other persons in his own name for an infringement of them.[78]

The *Stockport* case shows that a contractor of water rights, unless he was a lessee of the riparian land, was now in a very different position from a riparian water user. A riparian could not transfer his full riparian right unless he transferred his riparian land. He could not, in fact, even transfer part of the right (for example, the right to divert water) or 'deduct', as it were, any property rights from his riparian 'bundle' because this bundle was shared exclusively with the riparian community. He could, however, *authorize* an inland party to draw water from the stream by giving that party legal access. He would still retain full abstraction rights for himself to the level of 'reasonableness'. His contracting partner acquired none of his rights to the flow vis-à-vis other riparians but only rights under the contract. The riparian was confined, nonetheless, by his own onerous obligations toward the rest of the riparian community, in addition to the obligations he owed to his contractual partner.

Such shades of difference in water rights led to a good deal of litigation. The resulting clarification in the courts of the quality of title (and of the transferability) conveyed by the riparian right inevitably devalued the contracted water right, reducing its security and other characteristics. Yet the diminution of contractual rights did not create a political problem. By the third quarter of the nineteenth century the English version of the reasonable use theory was well established and widely accepted. Its application was now much narrower than that of the water law of the previous century. Water power, its chief beneficiary, was increasingly yielding to steam power. Other water uses such as city water supply and transportation and sewage removal were being authorized under special charters and statutes. In particular, Parliamentary regulation, such as the Alkali Act,[79] relieved the courts of most of the responsibility of 'supplying' new doctrines relating to river pollution. Consequently there were few new river users. Existing users could defend their rights to particular water uses as being prescriptive, or as based on survivals of prior-use or natural-flow theories, or as being clearly 'reasonable' according to modern categories of English judges. They, and those with whom they contracted, demanded nothing more and the English version of reasonable use remained essentially unchanged into the twentieth century.[80]

[78] Id., at 556 (emphasis added). In the case of *Holker v. Porritt* (1875), 10 Exch. 59 (Eng.), an exception to this rule was made for lessees of the entire estate, who assumed the riparian rights of the lessor for the duration of the lease.

[79] See McLaren 1983. When it was passed, The Alkali Act was impressive in principle but weak in effect. Seniority of rights took priority over public legislation.

[80] During the last century, the UK gradually introduced a system of regional water authorities, taking in not only the granting and monitoring of individual rights but also the provision of city water and sewage services. The role of government thus expanded enormously. See Craine 1969; Sewell and Barr 1977; and Foster and Sewell 1981. In the late 1980s, the British government denationalized many of the functions of these authorities.

Reasonable use rights in the United States

This section explores the American development of the reasonable use doctrine, contrasting it with the English version. Our division of the latter into various periods runs counter to the ideas of many American writers. To some of them, England never got beyond the natural-flow stage (America's second stage). These writers regard such a rule-of-thumb distinction as ordinary vs. extraordinary-use as necessary in England, just to make the natural-flow principle operational. But they do not regard reasonable use as a separate stage of English law. And they continue to reject non-damaging use as a basis for an action.

POLITICAL INTERVENTION

In water policy, as with taxation, road building and other natural resource interventions we will encounter in later chapters, the American legislatures' aims reflected their constituents' high priority for the promotion of settlement, investment and industrialization. The various localities feared that if their governments did not provide a helpful water policy to help economic development, it would never happen, or would happen elsewhere. Their legislatures' response differed from that in England where a laissez-faire Parliament had taken no responsibility for the industrial allocation of water except to assist with private bills on relatively large projects.

Americans also perceived different obstacles to their aims. This can be briefly explained by a rather sweeping generalization about the chronology of river development. At the start, there was on the North American rivers an agricultural period of 'unrivalrous and unpropertied plenty',[81] without disputes or conflict. This phase was succeeded by a period of disputes between water power and other uses of the river: between mills and farms. In the next phase, the main American issues arose between adjoining water-power users. In Britain, as we have seen, things happened the other way around. The developers of mills and water power seem first, and for centuries, to have been struggling with the owners of similar mills projects to make similar use of the rivers. Only later did the conflict with other water uses emerge, centring on the use of the river to carry away wastes versus the use of the river to provide urban water. The legal literature does not usually draw attention to the differences between these two successions of use mixtures.

Thus when the eighteenth-century English courts continued to preside over law suits between mills that were injuring each other, their judge-made law,

[81] Rose 1990, p. 274. In this article, she compares the stages of the appearance of individual property as outlined in Demsetz 1967 with three historical stages in English and US water law. Stage 1 is characterized by an absence of conflict among water users who are all in the same industry. All make much the same use of water. In stage 2 there is contract and cooperation as among waterpower producers up and down a stream, but conflict and disputes with users in agriculture and other industries. In Stage 3 there is individual ownership and a drop in disputes. Stage 3 never arrived in the eastern United States, but did so in the west.

imported into America, did little to help with the American agricultural obstacles to industrialization. For example, one important American problem was flowage, damage to land *upstream* of a water-power dam created for storage and head. A dam-builder, under threat of damages under English nuisance law, was forced to offer compensation to the upstream landowner. Indeed on a slowly falling river he might have to compensate a large number of landowners, some of them holding out for high amounts.

In America the adoption of such an English law was seen as especially antithetical to necessary industrial development. Around 1813 governments had grasped that paying flowage compensation would be too costly for new water-powered industries. As a remedy they offered the helpful Mill or Mill Dam Acts. These had encouraged the building of dams (many of them for grist mills for local farmers) by giving the mills a power to expropriate upstream flowage. This power was very similar to what the legislatures were then giving to road and canal projects.[82] Later, up to the mid nineteenth century, these mill flowage expropriation laws were applied to assist not just grist mills serving local farmers but industrial mills serving wide markets.[83]

The states armed these investors with the status of public utilities having, in Scheiber's words, the 'power to expropriate some of America's choicest water-power sites, such as those on the Connecticut River, the Delaware and the Merrimac'.[84] They defended their laws as preventing old riparians from blocking new industries. In this they were successful, redistributing the economic rent of river locations from landowners to new industrial developers.

DISPUTES BETWEEN MILLS: PRIOR-USE RIGHTS PRINCIPLE IN AMERICA[85]

There was no need for legislative action to resolve early conflicts among mill developers in the US. They could be satisfactorily resolved by English common law's offering of both prescriptive rights and prior-use rights. As well, in

[82] See Scheiber 1973 (reprinted 1988) p. 232. On laws governing the Delaware see Hart 1998.

[83] A mill law was also proposed to Ontario, or Canada West, in 1859, as a matter of public importance. See Benidickson 1983, pp. 365, 369.

[84] Scheiber 1988, p. 136.

[85] Horwitz 1977 is frequently cited here, for his innovative use of the nineteenth-century transformation of water law as an illustration of his larger theme that there was an important transformation of all American property and tort law from its original static agrarian conception protecting the landowner against disputes and conflict to an abstract, dynamic and implemental system operating to speed capitalistic and productive use and development. Since 1977 his chapters about the advent of capitalistic goals in the law have been widely attacked (and defended), both as to their general conclusions and as to the correctness of his illustrations in property, commercial law, tort law and so on. In what follows we make almost no use of the literature on Horwitz's general theme about a nation-wide transformation of all law; however, see especially Watson 1990, who does refer to water law, and also Schwartz 1981, on the change in tort law. As for changes in water law, we have gone beyond Massachusetts and New England water law. See again Lauer 1970; Maass and Zobel 1960; Rose 1990; Martin 1991. Each Atlantic state had its own rate of departure from the common-law water law received from England. Virginia, for example, changed the law in order to help older, agrarian

general eastern American rivers were sufficiently numerous and large to provide sites for all and even to give each mill a stretch in which to store water without affecting a neighbour's use.[86]

Indeed, when the new natural-flow theories arrived from England they were hardly needed. The disputes were such that natural-flow principles seemed merely to point to the same decision as prior-use principles. By then, as settlement and industrialization leapt across the American landscape, neighbouring river sites were being quickly chosen by new arrivals. When these were in conflict the downstream mill often had the stronger claim. Its owner could claim actual damage, violation of a prior-use right or, now, invasion of a property right to the natural flow. An 1837 Vermont judgment remarked that 'The common law of England seems to be that each landowner, through whose land a stream of water flows, has a right to the water in its natural course, and any diversion of the same to his injury, gives him a right of action... Should this principle be adopted here, its effect would be to let the man who should first erect mills upon a small river or brook, control the whole and defeat all the mill privileges from his mills [up to] the source.'[87] The judgment and others like it suggest that prior-use rights and natural-flow principles were seen to lead to the same outcome—protection of original users.

Also striking in similar judgments and later writings is the assumption that, if a party proposing to make a new use of the stream loses his case and is denied a water right, that use is thereby defeated. Judges wrote that the flowage rights of riparians to use the water entailed the power to exclude new uses. That the riparian could then sell or rent a 'privilege' is implicitly denied. Under the powerful stimulus of the growth of textile milling, Horwitz says, the judges believed that economic development ('capitalism') embodying water-powered plants could not proceed without displacing older uses and so must hurt the users. Perhaps they believed the transactions costs of a miller's settling with a number of riparians might be prohibitive. (The Mill Acts can be seen as offering a short-cut procedure for arriving at the price while dispensing with most transactions costs.) Under this way of thinking, only the courts and the legislature, not the markets, could bring about the reallocation of sites to more profitable uses. Horwitz states: 'The increasing frequency with which courts appealed to the idea of *damnum absque injuria* [damage without legal injury]

and industrial uses, not new industries; Martin 1991. Delaware relied much more on changes in legislation than on court decisions (Hart 1998). Other states had a proliferation of water-powered mills earlier than Massachusetts. Such interstate variety, however much damage it may do to Horwitz's generalizations, does not change much either our view that there were important changes in water rights, and that they may have spanned two of the turning points in the twists and turns we have discerned since medieval times.

[86] See Rose 1990, pp. 288–93, who observes this indivisibility on eastern streams used for power but employs it primarily to reinforce her contrasts of eastern and western law.

[87] *Martin v. Bigelow*, 2 Aik. 184, 187, cited in Horwitz 1977, p. 276, arguing that the natural flow rule would permit the first mill to control stream use not only up but also down, and so 'control the whole'.

seems to have occurred in direct proportion to their recognition that conflicting and injurious uses of property were essential to economic improvement.'[88]

So much for the changing law. In practice (as in England) prior rights, prescriptive rights, the right to press nuisance actions and the trade in water privileges all continued together. As late as 1821 the Massachusetts Supreme Court clearly adopted a rule of priority of occupation. Chancellor Kent, although he was very soon after to be the first to expound the reasonable use principle, wrote of this decision that the long-duration aspects of the prior-rights principle justified an owner's investing in a (durable) mill.[89] Presumably, the late eighteenth-century American courts' veneration of Blackstone would also have strengthened their belief in a prior-use water-right doctrine.[90]

TYLER V. WILKINSON: THE ADVENT OF REASONABLE USE

Still, some US cases from the first part of the nineteenth century foreshadowed the rejection of prior-use in favour of reasonable use in water. Maass and Zobel (1960) pinpoint three New York cases denying that a water-power site's prior occupant necessarily had a superior right. Both parties were entitled to the natural flow.[91] This entitlement was referred to in one case as a 'common right'; doubtless it was the first of many in which the American courts responded to conflict by increasing the extent of common use rather than the extent of exclusivity. The three cases set the course for the 1827 introduction of reasonable use criteria by Justice Story in *Tyler v. Wilkinson*.[92]

Interestingly, the actual decision in *Tyler v. Wilkinson* could quite as easily have been reached on prior-use or on natural-flow grounds. One party, the plaintiff, had a dam. The dam did not divert water, but allowed the plaintiff to store and release water so as to reinforce the current for his mills further downstream. The defendants had for some time diverted a certain amount of this released water into their canal (ditch) just below the dam. When the defendants increased their diversion sharply, injuring the plaintiff's milling business, he sued. Justice Story found for the plaintiff, his reasoning being more influential than his finding.

[88] Horwitz 1977, p. 40. Horwitz does not attribute his evidence for this increasing frequency, although his footnotes show that he has examined numerous cases. Possibly he deduced it from Joseph Angell, author of two editions of *Watercourses*, 1824 and 1833. For a later edition, see Angell 1877.

[89] See Horwitz 1977, pp. 36 and 274, n8, describing how in 1796 the commentator on *Perkins v. Dow*, 1 Root 535 (1793), a Connecticut case, illustrated the confusion that the 'first' user might merely be the user upstream, because there the flowing water came first. This use need not be temporally first—i.e., by a prior user.

[90] For example, prior occupancy by a reasonable user gives a prior title to such use against later comers. For an instance, see *Cary v. Daniels*, 8 Metc. 466, 41 Am. Dec. 532 (Mass. 1844).

[91] Maass and Zobel 1960, p. 142. The three cases cited are *Palmer v. Mulligan*, 3 Caines 307 (NY 1805); *Platt v. Johnson*, 15 Johns. R. 213 (N.Y. 1818); and *Merritt v. Brinkerhoff*, 17 Johns. R. 306 (NY 1820).

[92] *Tyler v. Wilkinson*, Fed. Cas. No. 14312, 4 Mason 397, 24 F. Cas. 472 (C.C.D.R.I. 1827).

First he rejected the plaintiff's mere priority of appropriation. He distinguished it from the homesteading of vacant public land. Water, especially this waterflow, was not unowned, although the running water itself could not be possessed but only the channel and the right to enjoy the flow. Since the right to enjoy the flow in the channel is an incident of the riparian land, every owner of the riparian land must own a right to use the flow. A riparian location is the source of ownership, not prior use. Such ownership of the flow is conceptually possible only if all riparian owners are considered to own it in common.

Next he rejected the idea that either the plaintiff or the defendant was entitled to the *natural flow* of the river. Since any use of the river entails some degree of retardation, acceleration or diminution of the flow, the test of the amount of the flow that can be diverted must be the extent of injury to others that can be tolerated. Story held that the tolerable amount is the amount indispensable to the general and valuable use of the water by the diverter. A person must not be prevented from making a valuable good or an enjoyment of the flow if its cost or inconvenience to another is trifling. Thus the 'golden rule', *sic utere tuo ut alienum non laedas*, can be seen to apply.

In an economist's eyes, Story's explanation is consistent with a utilitarian maxim: let water be used so that each person imposes less injury than can be counterbalanced by his own gains. While the 'golden rule' is an ethical idea, following it makes the sum of the gains to public convenience or general good more than the sum of the inconveniences or losses. Story's treatment is impressive, and controversial. Some writers cite isolated passages to suggest that Story was confusedly supporting all previous authorities and doctrines at once. Indeed, Story continued to cite approvingly such conflicting English cases as *Wright v. Howard* and *Williams v. Moreland*. Like *Bealey v. Shaw, Tyler v. Wilkinson* was later used to support divergent decisions.[93] And Story's judgment was disseminated the very next year in James Kent's *Commentaries* (1828).[94] But its precedent was strong, setting the stage for other American judges to conform to the reasonable use approach (at least for *new* uses. Some time was to elapse before those following the reasonable use approach began to cast doubts on *existing* users' water entitlements and privileges.) Eventually, as we saw above, English judges began to follow it in their own decisions. Notable among these was *Embrey v. Owen*, which picked up Story's quote of Kent's remark: 'Streams are for the use of man' [and so not to be left in an unused state].

PROCEDURE IN AMERICAN REASONABLE USE CONFLICTS

To conclude this description of the reasonable use phase in America, we briefly examine what now went on in an American state court where a plaintiff sued a

[93] For an analysis of Story's judgment, see Lauer 1958.
[94] Kent 1828.

defendant for diverting water. Since under the Story theory, 'reasonable' could mean 'more productive than the alternative', *both* parties' uses came under scrutiny for their legality with respect to their riparian status. *Were* they riparians? The many American reserves and transfers of water rights or of stream beds or banks to non-riparian parcels or uses had not been dealt with in English cases.

The plaintiff had to be aggrieved, but his argument did not need to be restricted to the defendant's disregard for his prior-use rights (as it would be in England). It could also be based on an apprehension that the plaintiff's water use would suffer actual damages if the defendant's less-reasonable use continued. The court determined whether or not the defendant's use was the cause of the injury and whether it was justified by a valid prescriptive right or by prior use. The court would also ascertain whether the defendant's use should be preferred to the plaintiff's by reason of being ordinary or natural. Although prior use was rarely explicitly given as a justification, American courts in practice rarely found for a defendant whose reasonable use was junior to the plaintiff's prior-use right.[95]

The courts next considered the problem of finding whether the defendant's use was unreasonable in the circumstances.[96] Dealing with this question committed the US courts to more searching and less predictable examinations of water uses by both parties than took place in England. Since the early nineteenth century trial judges in more than twenty states have instructed juries on what a defendant might reasonably do in the local circumstances. These, mentioned in the states' leading cases, indicate that reasonableness has been interpreted in many ways. One example is as follows:

> In determining what is a reasonable use, regard must be had to the subject-matter of the use; the occasion and manner of its application; the object, extent, necessity and duration of the use; the nature and size of the stream; the kind of business to which it is subservient; the importance and necessity of the use claimed by one party, and the extent of the injury to the other party; the state of improvement of the country in regard to mills and machinery, and the use of water as a propelling power; the general and established usages of the country in similar cases; and all the other and ever-varying circumstances in each particular case, bearing upon the question of the fitness and propriety of the use of the water under consideration.[97]

The affected US jurisdictions have accepted and used these classes or scales of reasonableness. According to Powell and Hanks, reasonableness is scored

[95] See Trelease 1979, p. 325, saying 'in some of the . . . cases, the court [used] natural flow language, some [spoke] of reasonable use and some of non-riparian use, but regardless of the form of statement, the downstream plaintiff with the priority receives protection'.

[96] Surveys have been made to attempt to find the meaning of reasonableness. See for example Lauer 1970, p. 10, where meanings of reasonableness are classified.

[97] *Red River Roller Mills v. Wright*, 30 Minn. 249, 15 N.W. 167 (1883). A similar, but modern, listing is published in the American *Restatement (Second) of Torts*, ch. 41.

along four dimensions: reasonableness of purpose, destination, quantity and pollution.[98]

BALANCING OF INTERESTS IN REASONABLE USE CASES

Balancing of the parties' interests meant something different in America than in England. Under English procedure the court would more or less have been conducting a search for evidence of one of several kinds of unreasonableness in the defendant's use of the natural flow: having caused damage to another riparian user; having prevented an 'ordinary user' from enjoying his domestic uses of the water; or having been engaged in a *per se* unreasonable use, such as a polluting one. Only after these 'facts' were established could the English court even begin to exercise discretion over whether to exercise the equitable remedy of an injunction or merely to award damages, and, if so, of what severity. At this late stage in the proceedings it would consider the interests of both parties, weighing the reasonableness of the plaintiff's own water uses and behaviour in the balance.

In the American procedure, consideration of the reasonableness of the plaintiff's actions came much earlier in the proceedings. Both plaintiff and defendant could be found to be acting reasonably. If the plaintiff was harmed by the defendant's actual or proposed water use, the American reasonable use procedure called for a decision that would balance the gains. The plaintiff's injury alone was not sufficient for such a finding. In particular, an inquiry essentially comparing the benefits and costs of acceding to the plaintiff's claims would be made to determine who should win the case. If paying for compliance would greatly exceed the plaintiff's injury, then the court would tend to find that the disputed rights to use the flow actually belonged to the defendant. The balance of harm would determine the ownership of the interest in water. But in determining the remedy to award, the court, including a jury, could moderate its finding, say by ordering that the disputed diversion be fixed at a given reasonable amount.[99]

In this respect, the victory of the prior user in the United States was less complete than it was in England. Some American courts considered prior use as only one of the factors in the determination of 'reasonableness' as between riparians, along with the utility of the use or additional factors such as the size of the river. Nevertheless, in the courts of almost all states the fact that one litigant had made a sizeable investment in the water-using activity was given some weight in the determination of what was reasonable.[100] That prior use

[98] Powell 1968, pp. 371–4; Hanks 1980 (reprinted in) Meyers and Tarlock 1980, p. 51.

[99] See for example *Prather v. Hoberg*, 24 Cal.2d 549, 150 P. 2d 405 (1944), as discussed in Trelease 1979, pp. 312–13.

[100] The influential case of *Cary v. Daniels*, 8 Metc. 466, 41 Am. Dec. 532 (Mass. 1844), favoured the prior-user or occupant of a river site; but later some state courts began to play down the role of prior-use in the balancing of factors contributing to reasonableness.

could be weighed against other factors in American courts must certainly be an important explanation of the parties' frequent resort to litigation.[101]

Note again that, seen from an economic point of view, the procedure need not have constituted the final step in resource allocation. The court's division of 'ownership' merely laid the way open for the litigants to adjust their respective flow entitlements by contracting with each other. Part of the courts' success was in creating an environment in which such contracting was likely. In the hands of the American courts, reasonableness proved to be familiar enough to be widely applicable; robust enough to threaten well-entrenched old users; yet flexible enough to be applied differently in different circumstances. Furthermore, where water power was scarce reasonableness provided for compromise and water-sharing and kept the peace.

STATUTORY PERMITS SUPERIMPOSED ON RIPARIANISM

All accounts agree that American and Canadian water law was quiescent in the late nineteenth and early twentieth centuries. New sources of power made falling water sites less valuable. Legislatures, some of which had earlier introduced the mill acts reviewed above, took some water-right problems away from the courts and the common law: water-supply, irrigation projects, fishing and pollution. But in their remaining applications the common law reasonable use rules, under the courts, were left undisturbed. To most people 'water policy' meant western streams and big-dam projects or the equivalent Tennessee Valley Authority (TVA) and Ontario Hydro, hotly debated by left and right and inland and coast.

It was apparently not until the 1950s that these eastern riparian-law jurisdictions became aware that their 'humid' environments did not always have enough water to go around for small-scale industry and other local uses. It was found that when droughts, pollution or dam-building were issues, reasonable use riparian law offered their users no security, no private priority system and no flows for public uses. Following water-shortage discussions in the 1950s, the states[102] resolved to take what they called a 'planning' role in river-basin management. Varying powers to deal with water supplies and with pollution were assumed and entrusted to new agencies whose directors adjudicated

[101] See American *Restatement (Second) of Torts*, ch. 41.

[102] This sketch of the history of permit systems is confirmed by research into the history of the Ontario system. Around 1960 that province was introducing new water institutions to deal with flooding, with city sewage disposal and with water pollution. There had been proposals to introduce a type of water-taking permit to reinforce these. But they were upstaged by the need to deal with a different problem: drought in the tobacco counties of western Ontario. We hypothesize that this drought led to a very hasty adoption of the permit system then being installed in neighbouring American states. We are grateful to Professor Dan Shrubsole of the University of Western Ontario for access to his studies of the history of these Ontario institutions, and to Professor Bruce Mitchell for comments on the period.

disputes, approved transfers and cancelled unused or misused permits. Among these powers was the issuance of water-taking 'permits'.

Under the permit statutes users acquired a primitive property right. Their permits allowed them to continue their use, while holding them to a certain volume at a given site. Permits had limited duration but were renewable. The managing agencies' decisions tended to be dominated by riparian law. Reasonable use criteria commanded some respect, and some agencies were given a scale of priorities for new applicants. Otherwise, prior use was the (riparian) principle most respected, as one might anyway expect of bureaucratic decision-makers. Rights to transfer water to other locations were usually not guaranteed, but they were not precluded either. Shortages and droughts were addressed by legislative provisions which, during a water emergency, the director might invoke to suspend water permits. He was then, generally, supposed to allocate water on a special legislated or commissioned scale of priorities (with most states sensibly exempting domestic and certain other basic water uses from permit requirements).[103] Directors and agencies in the humid east have rarely been called on to make tough decisions on such matters.

The common-law rights of most permit-state (and Ontario) users have not been extinguished. Having a permit improves its holder's quality of title, but not to a fixed amount of water. Hence, when a state's water-power or water-supply demands exceed river flow, some users will still get less than their customary amount. The conflicts of many users who now are governed by a lumpy mixture of reasonable use and natural-flow with administrative rules then find their way to the courts for resolution, generating decisions, precedents and new characteristics of common-law rights.[104]

However, recent permit-state developments are of little consequence to most North American users of river levels and flows. Since the mid nineteenth century these users have held their rights under the radically different appropriative-rights system, to which we turn next.

The appropriative-rights phase in the western United States

INTRODUCTION AND GEOGRAPHY

By 1850, a quarter century after *Tyler v. Wilkinson*, in the eastern United States the concept of reasonable use was well entrenched. With the rest of the common law it was filtering westward with settlement. But in California, as in many of the states adopting reasonable use, there were as yet no water rights

[103] Unfortunately the exemption made water agencies' lists of users incomplete, so that their permit systems failed to clarify the status of persons and rights for water-shortage planning. See Meyers and Tarlock 1980, pp. 196–7.

[104] For a study of Ontario's provincial permit system, and estimates of the effects of placing a royalty-like price on permits, see Renzetti and Dupont 1999. For a brief discussion of tradable provincial permits, see id., p. 367.

in place, either because the jurisdictions had not yet formally received the common law of England or because the land alongside its rivers had not yet been claimed and brought into operation by ranchers and farmers. In this property void began the establishment and enforcement of an entirely different use-based system of appropriative rights.

This regime emerged on the American frontier. It held that a water user who had arrived and begun to draw an amount of water for irrigation and domestic purposes was considered entitled to continue drawing that amount in perpetuity. This entitlement protected him against later arrivals whose water use might reduce his appropriated flow. In some places farmers and ranchers who had been granted riverside lands held both their acquired appropriative rights and their common-law, constitutionally protected, riparian rights.

The results of these arrangements are visible on a North American map. The eastern states (and Ontario) have systems of reasonable use riparian water rights, supplemented since the Second World War by government systems of statutory water permits. The hundredth meridian roughly divides these jurisdictions from the appropriative-right areas to the west. Eight mountain states and four western Canadian provinces have pure appropriative right systems, now government-administered. Nine other western states on the Pacific Coast or in the Great Plains have 'mixed' systems of appropriative and riparian rights.[105] Irrigation is the chief variable; states having agriculture in dry areas and states located in high mountain regions can be predicted to have appropriative or at least mixed water-right regimes. We will see below that the appropriative-right system also influenced the development of the mixed water laws in Australia and New Zealand.

The evolution of water rights in the prior-appropriation region was quite different from any earlier process in England or New England. The lands and the rivers being largely untouched, early developments did not lead to major disputes or conflicts and litigation was comparatively rare. Instead, the water rights were first demanded from quickly devised 'customary' local procedures. Though slightly reminiscent of those by which the customary rules governing medieval English common land had emerged, the American processes were more rushed, called on to produce water law for impatient settlers and for transient gold miners. Those who participated in the procedures demanded political support; where necessary, they invented jurisdictions, legislatures, administrative bureaux, law courts and water statutes all at once. The rights produced by these customary local procedures were not left in their original profusion but, with the supply-side intervention of legislative committees and higher courts, were rather quickly made uniform by the demands of users' migratory competition.

[105] Only appropriative rights: Idaho, Wyoming, Montana, Nevada, Utah, Colorado, Arizona, New Mexico and British Columbia, Alberta, Saskatchewan and Manitoba. Mixed systems: Washington, Oregon, California, North Dakota, Nebraska, Kansas, Texas and Oklahoma.

A PARADE OF ORIGINATORS OF THE APPROPRIATIVE-RIGHTS DOCTRINE

Historians have looked to three groups of persons in their search for the true forerunners of the present water system. The best known are the California gold miners; second, the mountain-state open-country settlers and ranchers. A third is land developers and promoters who should be regarded as regional boosters—perhaps speculators—rather than as farmers and settlers. Some historians identify a fourth source of water law: the Spanish, Mexican and Indian irrigators in the southwestern states. Historians have sometimes written about these four groups as rivals, for a distinct spirit or purpose in water law can be attributed to each originating group. Their commonality was in requiring a new, home-made water law to address their problems.

Mining camps in California

As we will see in greater detail in Chapter 6, in some regions the first water users were placer miners. From 1849, they worked up the creeks in search of gold. As California gold became scarcer, many miners rushed off to new discoveries in Colorado and Australia in 1851, and to the north-west and the Fraser River in 1858–9. Even if the miners had wished to settle, they could not easily have acquired good titles to riparian land. In the crucial 1847–9 period in the United States, the western American resources lay where land-granting offices, courts, assemblies and police had yet to appear. Thus a very generally accepted theory about the choice of an appropriative-rights system makes much of the gold rush 'self-help'.[106] The miners, assembling in their camps, devised, agreed on and enforced new mining laws, including provisions about water rights. Because water rights were incident to mining claims, they were implemented and enforced in the same way: by recognizing seniority of 'active' claims and by applying force to defend them.[107] It is widely agreed that the use of force, or threat, was influential in the rule-making by the camps.

These simplifications mask a diversity in water use and water law.[108] In the first months of the California boom, only a few placer miners spread up and down along the creeks and used the running water for pans, rockers and long toms or sluice boxes. Their water diversions were therefore trivial in relation to the stream's flow and did not call for the appropriation of water. Indeed it seems likely that riparian law suited their needs.[109]

[106] See Hutchins 1971.

[107] The leading contemporary source is Shinn 1884. An influential legal study was Wiel 1911. Many histories and legal treatises enlarge on these. Economists are indebted to work by Umbeck collected in Umbeck 1977 and 1981.

[108] The next three paragraphs are much influenced by the rationalization of California water-rights history by Pisani 1986, p. 117, especially his emphasis on the ditch companies.

[109] See Scott 1991a, discussing the first (1859) British Columbia gold-mining proclamation which referred to water rights as though they were riparian leases.

Perhaps as a result no official steps were taken in California to disavow riparian law. In 1848 the military authority had pronounced that Mexican mining law did not apply.[110] In 1850 the first legislature embraced common law, not excepting common-law water rights. In 1854 it enacted a water code somewhat along the appropriative-rights lines accepted in irrigation states and territories, but it excepted the mining counties.

The rules of the appropriative water system probably came in 1850. By then waves of miners were being excluded by the first-comers from creek-side claims. These newcomers took up claims higher up the banks, called dry diggings. Needing to wash the gold out of their dry gravel, they chose between taking the gravel to the water and taking the water to the gravel by ditching hillside or mountain sources to their claims. For ditching, their choice was between digging their own or taking water from a 'ditch company' who would divert water to the workings. The mining camps may have made rulings on the behaviour of these ditch companies, including their rights of access and competition for the few sources. It is these ditch-company rulings that may be identified as the ancestors of miners' appropriative law. Apparently there were problems of definitions of amounts of water because the sources alternated between flood and drought, and the ditches could sometimes take more water than was currently available. The rules of seniority may have first applied here if one ditch company, in starting its operations, reduced the amount of water being taken by another.[111]

Pisani explains how the ditch companies competed with another group of water users: the driers or drainers. Holding claims on the stream, driers temporarily diverted stream flow into a flume. (One massive 1850 diversion turned the Feather River out of its channel for forty miles.) Drying needed cooperative organization for money-raising, doing the work and dealing with holdouts. Though it faded away as a source of mining law, it created a great commotion at the time. Pisani says:

> Most of the violence in 1850 arose because miners who turned streams either deprived other miners of water or gave them too much [for example, miners were submerged by bursting flumes]. All too frequently, unsuccessful negotiations, during which the injured parties were usually asked to join the company, culminated in attempts to tear down dams and flumes. Miners disagreed over which water rights were stronger: those senior in time, those used on land closest to the water, or those whose holders had invested the greatest amounts of money developing their claims.[112]

[110] Pisani 1992, p. 13.

[111] Hutchins 1971 says that early rights to appropriate water in California were derived in part from 'local customs formulated and applied in the mining camps of the Sierra Nevada foothills'. If it is to be taken seriously this observation suggests that water works were staked like mining claims or like pre-empted farm land.

[112] Pisani 1992, pp. 19–20.

These three classes of water-using miners fought, argued and litigated until the legislature intervened. The best evidence seems to be that the influence of alluvial mining on appropriative rights was temporary.[113]

Homesteaders and farmers

Other modern writers, while acknowledging a gold-mining influence, trace current western water law to the reaction of early farmers to the mountainous topography and the dry climate. To win land under the land laws and Homestead Act of 1862, they were required to cultivate it. In many regions that meant bringing water onto the land. Water law was not sought to provide rules for users seeking water privileges for milling or manufacturing as in the east, but for irrigation. The common law—even had its courts been available, which they were not—would have allowed only riparians to withdraw water, in small amounts, and would have denied them diversion rights to carry water beyond their boundaries or to return it at a distant point. Few settlers planned to farm as riparians of the high mountain creeks from which piped water was withdrawn.

Like the miners, the settlers developed their own rule. Just as homesteaded land was acquired by the first to claim it, so the necessary amounts of water were assigned to the first to divert them.[114]

In the other western states, farmer irrigation developments followed soon after the miners in the 1850s. Dunbar says that the farmers' first ditches were short and small, constructed to irrigate the bottom lands bordering the streams. Sometimes they were dug by individual farmers, sometimes by groups of farmers, and tended to be 'crooked, steep and subject to erosion'.[115] The ditch diggers' individual or group efforts later gave way to ditch and canal companies, mutual irrigation companies and irrigation districts, and they became the dominant class of right holders on the basis of prior appropriation.

Land developers and beneficial use

Coming from another direction, a third explanation of the appropriative water right lays stress on its beneficial-use requirement. The theory, rather complicated, holds that it was developers who originated and exploited appropriative rights. Amplifying the public outcry against riparian rights, they complained they were going without water and so could not dispose of their land at higher elevations, forcing them instead to acquire land from the

[113] Anderson and Hill 1975, p. 163, start from this premise and argue that early farmers and ranchers, already investing in water storage and control, borrowed the miner's water property system.

[114] See Mass and Anderson 1978, p. 325 This seniority rule may have been the basis of the Mormon 'tradition' of enforcing the exclusive rights of those who found water and put it to use—possibly later carried from Utah to Alberta, influencing the formulation of Canadian territorial law. See Percy 1988, p. 281, Thomas 1920, pp. 29–57 and Dunbar 1983, pp. 9–17.

[115] Dunbar 1983, p. 19.

earliest-arriving ranchers, pre-emptors and squatters who had occupied the best locations lower down along the streams. Instead of simply contracting with these first-comers, the developers urged the appropriative doctrine coupled with a stringent beneficial-use condition. Many joined in arguing that a water right with a beneficial-use requirement and easy marketability was a helpful instrument for dynamic development. It helped prevent a speculative overhang of unsold land from depressing land prices and brought underused land into the market.

Spaniards and Mexicans

A fourth theory is that western water users adapted locally existing Mexican and Spanish customs and traditions until they became modern appropriative law. William Blomquist gives the water supply of Los Angeles as an example.[116] Blomquist gives Hutchins as authority for a claim that, under the law as it had existed in Spain, waters were held by pueblos as a common property for domestic use and irrigation as administered by the town officials.[117] He paraphrases Mann and Blevins as saying '[as] long as the community was diverting and using less than the total amount of waters provided by the River, others could use the surplus, provided that their diversions did not interfere with the needs of the Pueblo'.[118]

Other historians have described instances which appear to lend credibility to a Spanish-law origin. But Pisani (1992) has rejected it outright.[119]

FROM CALIFORNIA TO THE COLONIES

Whichever of the above theories we accept, the California explanation holds that the new appropriative system of water rights emerged in the absence of governments and courts to implement a common-law system that would deal quickly and acceptably with the water disputes of the time. Such an

[116] Blomquist 1992, p. 198, says, 'the City of Los Angeles was, by California law, the successor in interest to the Pueblo of Los Angeles which dated back to 1781. One of the Pueblo's interests to which the City succeeded was the Pueblo's interest in the waters of the Los Angeles River. It was understood by the Pueblo's (later the City's) inhabitants and leaders that the settlement had a prior and paramount right to all of the waters of the River.'

[117] Ibid. See also Hutchins 1957.

[118] Ibid. See also Mann and Blevins 1986.

[119] Johnson and DuMars 1989, p. 349, say that Native Americans dug community ditches for agricultural purposes, and that some of these ditches were later used by northern Spanish military outposts and missions. In this sense the Spanish and the Mexicans in the southwest appeared to be well ahead of American miners, ranchers or settlers in using a prior-appropriation system for water. See also Trelease 1979, pp. 22–3, and Hutchins 1928, p. 261; Glick 1971 and Meyer 1984 all discussing whether specific legal grants of water diverted onto lands in Mexican or Spanish territories were later ceded to the United States. These granted rights had some of the characteristics of appropriative rights. Pisani 1992, p. 39, is firm: 'A few western historians have mistakenly argued that prior appropriation was a legacy from Mexico. Nothing could be further than the truth.'

explanation is subjected to a different kind of test in the Australian colonies of Victoria and New South Wales[120] and in British Columbia, Canada. All these regions were on the frontier of settlement by Europeans. Their lands were mostly 'public', owned by the Crown, and all experienced gold-mining booms in the 1850s and 60s as well as a rapid change of agriculture from extensive grazing and ranching to dry farming and on to intensive irrigation. They also abandoned the common-law rules regarding water, but differently, for, unlike California and Utah, they were not without (colonial) governments, councils and courts.

British Columbia during the Fraser gold rush borrowed from California.[121] Its official 1859 gold mining ordinance declared that ditch or water privileges could be obtained by non-riparians and those without an appurtenancy to any property. It can be seen that, at least until 1875, these official water law rules were strictly an extension of Crown mineral disposal law. They were confusing. At different places, the rules were completely *ad hoc* and unsuitable for expansion into water law. Later, they were broadened periodically to recognize domestic and agricultural uses, and continued to have the flavour of the public-lands disposal system. In 1892 a government declaration placed all water under Crown ownership, a strategy that had not been available to American states. Licences that were the lineal descendant of miners' water rights were to be issued for any use and some attempt was made to give administrators a priority ordering.[122] The resulting system had and has many California-like features: appropriative rights, seniority, beneficial-use and effective transferability. Nevertheless, it is also a paternalistic administrative system, in some ways more akin to the system of tree-cutting rights on Crown lands and in US national forests than to California's water property system.[123]

The Canadian prairie region, while most of its territorial lands and resources were still under federal control,[124] was settled in the 1880s and early 1890s. A water law, largely riparian, was hastily dropped in 1892, replaced by an administrative licence system that reflected the irrigation-influenced water laws

[120] See Clark and Renard 1970 and 1974.

[121] There being already a riparian law in effect in the sister colony of Vancouver Island, British Columbia's first official proclamation in 1859 was ambiguous, linking water rights to land leases and mining claims, as we have seen happened in California. See Scott 1991a, p. 355, and Percy 1988, p. 289.

[122] A report by Grunsky 1913 noted that legislation directed to irrigation arrangements had to wait until the Water Act of 1909. See also Wilson 1989b, suggesting that irrigation legislation lagged because, compared to mining and water works, government received little or no revenue from early irrigation projects.

[123] Lucas 1990. See also Farrow 1949 and Scott 1985 and 1991.

[124] Rupert's Land and the North-western Territory were admitted into Canada in 1870 as federal territories. The same year, the province of Manitoba was created out of Rupert's Land, and everything else was renamed the North-western Territory. In 1898, in response to the influx of population caused by the gold rush, the Yukon Territory was made a separate territory. In 1905, the provinces of Alberta and Saskatchewan were created from the North-western Territory. The dates for all provinces' reception of English law was kept at 1870.

of Utah and the northern tier of American states.[125] The features of British Columbia's water law were largely ignored. Indeed, competition for settlers probably induced British Columbia to follow Alberta and Saskatchewan in copying features of US water law suitable for creating irrigated acreage. Fifteen years later, when Alberta and Saskatchewan divided as separate provinces, they inserted the principles of seniority, beneficial use and licence transferability. These and other features were deliberately shaped by bureaucrats.

Water law in Australia, described as irrigation law, was considered by legal draftsmen in North America. A system of riparian rights had been applied in Victoria and New South Wales before the gold rush and was not abandoned. Government did innovate by introducing long-term water licences allowing reservoirs and ditches and finding water to put into them.[126] Soon after the gold rush the governments dusted off riparian rights and also introduced the first of a series of statutes governing city waterworks and mining and agriculture water systems, particularly for irrigation.[127] By 1865 riparian rights still existed, without a trace of a US-style appropriative-rights system. In 1880 a commission from Victoria, having inspected the California system, showed enthusiasm about its escape from the riparian system but disliked its litigation costs. In 1886 Victoria instead opted for tight state government control of all water uses and the issuing of non-transferable rights. These were appurtenant to land, without precedence by seniority.

Not until the age of widespread irrigation were all these jurisdictions to see individual water rights as a component in a whole system of procuring, using, storing and recycling water. The Australian states made government storage and irrigation projects with equal user rights central to their irrigation laws. Their strong governments had decided to use the practice of US irrigation institutions, rather than US state water laws, as models.

DEBATES IN THE AGE OF IRRIGATION

In the 1880s and 1890s American water-law debates moved on from disputes about government licensing versus private rights. Politicians were now subjected to a renewal of disputes regarding the virtues of common-law water rights versus appropriative rights. Holders of water rights, fearful of losing them, were subjected to explanations of what the two systems amounted to. Politicians typically held a brief for one of their two 'schools'.[128] To make their points, writers jobbed backward forty years or more, imputing their current arguments to the pioneers of the appropriative system.

[125] See Percy 1988.

[126] See the statute cited in Clark and Renard 1974, p. 153.

[127] Id., pp. 154, 157.

[128] Wiel 1911 is among the earliest investigations of the legal origins of western water law. Wiel fiercely propounded his belief in the appropriative system. See also Wiel 1918, 1919 and 1936. In this last title he takes a more neutral position.

In their debates, these American writers greatly exaggerated the power and rigidity of any system of water law. They affected to believe that, had the system of appropriative rights not been introduced, a riparian system would have prevented western resources from being developed. Even today some text-book authors write as though retention of the common law would have been disastrous for the spread of mining and irrigation, the growth of the American and the Canadian west, and most of the states of Australia.

ECONOMIC CHARACTERISTICS UNDERLYING THE APPROPRIATIVE SYSTEM

Debates over the merits of the two systems dwelt on the distributional aspects of water law—for instance, the seniority, beneficial use and greater transferability (but reduced flexibility) of the appropriative right. In this section, we frame the debate by associating each of the features of the appropriative system with one of three characteristics of any property right: beneficial use with quality of title; seniority with exclusivity; and, of course, transferability with itself. The mapping is not perfect, for the seniority feature provides security as well as exclusivity; the transferability feature provides both transferability and divisibility; and the details of the beneficial-use feature determine both duration and quality of title. Nevertheless, they are fair associations considering that a water right, merely an interest in using a flowing liquid in a common pool, is quite unlike the right to hold land, to which the six characteristics most directly apply.

Beneficial use: quality of title

Once the new holder of a water right complied with the rules of acquisition and registry and established the seniority of his right, the continuing security of his legal entitlement depended on the continuance of his beneficial use of the water. The requirement had an intended and an unintended effect. The intended effect was to encourage holders to release underemployed water, passing it toward more productive uses. The unintended effect was to encourage new right-holders to put water to work too early on too lavish a scale. The law compelled a water right holder to use the water beneficially but not as efficiently as possible.[129]

How intensively the water was used depended on how the courts of the day defined 'beneficial'. Originally, their interpretations differed widely, much as the common-law courts had differed on the meaning of 'reasonable use'. Later, consistent definitions were introduced by higher courts, legislation and the licence-issuing administrative agencies. These typically relied on the premise that the right holder should have made an expenditure on diversion and delivery works, and should subsequently maintain them so that all corners

[129] This remark of Mason Gaffney was said to be in Gaffney 1968 but we cannot find the precise citation.

of the appurtenant area could be irrigated. Given the area over which water use was to be beneficial, a standard ratio known as 'the duty of water' per unit of land per period (the amount required to irrigate a given acre of a given crop) was applied to arrive at the flow per period to which the right should give title.

To many, this formula was not limiting enough. That a farmer was visibly using his water did not prove that he was meeting the conditions for quality of title. He might merely be marking time, holding the water right speculatively for a value increase.[130] He might be substituting free water for other inputs.

Nevertheless, beneficial use continued as a condition for the quality of the holder's title, though it was weakened through the outcomes of actual disputes between applicants for water rights. One party would argue that his adversary's proposed water use did not come within the current definition of 'beneficial'. These definitions were arbitrary; Nevada and Utah treated conserved or stored water as 'unappropriated' while California classified storage as a beneficial use. Tregarthen[131] cites an illustration in which a Colorado water judge ruled that using water for dust control or land reclamation would not be beneficial, using it for cooling might be beneficial and using it for slurry in pipelines would be beneficial.

Some legislatures augmented the benefit requirement with an official water-use 'preference ordering'; a typical one would run from most-preferred home and farm uses, through manufacturing, to power and mining uses. This schedule upset the original requirement by its implication that all users were not making equally beneficial use of water and that, in cases of conflict, some users should yield their title to others.

Legislative preference ordering has had a few effects on the water rights system. These include strengthening the claim of domestic users and helping resolve rare disputes between new applicants for permits with the same seniority.[132] These effects are mostly distributional. In addition, preference ordering has served as the basis for some governments' actual expropriation policies: re-capturing old low-value use rights to make way for new higher-value or in-stream uses.[133] This feature of ordering would seem on balance to have weakened the right's quality of title or security, making users vulnerable to intrusive legal and political reductions in their entitlements that would have been unthinkable in the past.

Seniority: exclusivity

Appropriative water rights are quantitative. When it is working well, the appropriative system entitles users to measured amounts regardless of the quantities taken by other users, and is thus strongly exclusive. The greatest challenge to its exclusivity is the natural variability of stream flows. In dry

[130] Gaffney 1969 and 1992.
[131] 1989, p. 1529.
[132] See Lucas 1990, describing this phenomenon in four Canadian provinces.
[133] See Trelease 1979, pp. 221–2 and Johnson and Dumars 1989, pp. 351–61.

seasons, or in dry years, even normally compatible water rights come into conflict. The prevailing rule is that the available stream flow is allotted among right holders according to the date of issue of their rights: the most senior user gets *all* his water before the next gets any. Consequently his right may well be completely exclusive, unaffected by and independent of the water-using operations of other users. The most junior right-holder on a given stream gets his water only after all right-holders senior to him have obtained the full amounts to which they are entitled. Even if his right seems to entitle him to the same quantity as the most senior user, he will experience long periods without any water and uncertainty about when these periods will occur. His right has approximately zero exclusivity.

This drastic range of the exclusivity characteristic is changing. As water rights have become more transferable and divisible, seniority has lost some of its all-or-nothing aspect. A right-holder can combine fractions of his rights to riskier, low-flow streams with those to safer, high-flow stream rights to create a 'portfolio' like an investor's portfolio, balancing risk and return. Or users who seek a larger share in dry periods can demand protection against the seniority principle from government legislation. For example, where a senior raises an injunctive action, the court may be subject to legislation instructing that the injunction be qualified so as to permit the junior to continue taking water while providing practical protection for the plaintiff senior. The junior is to bear the burden of accommodation. The process amounts to a compulsory water transfer to the junior, part sale and part gift. In New Mexico, under the preference system mentioned earlier, if a junior's proposed use is preferred to that now made by the senior, administrative law gives the junior a 'right of replacement' to expropriate part or all of a senior right.[134] Even low-preference users are entitled to some water under the practices in some American states with appropriative-rights and mixed systems.[135] In most of the Australian states' administered water systems, equal sharing is the rule, with sometimes an extra apportionment being made to water users with the most water-sensitive crops. In Alberta shortages are shared equally according to a negotiated procedure, even though it 'is not in accordance with the Alberta Water Resources Act and thus leaves the government open to legal challenge'.[136]

Nevertheless there is no doubt that senior rights are still in a strong position everywhere where appropriative rights systems dominate. The reason is that in

[134] The word 'replacement' refers to a computer simulation of water availability and net expected withdrawals. The junior's proposed withdrawals replace the senior's. This compulsory-purchase procedure can lead to the same compromising result as reasonable use procedure. See Schaab 1983, p. 42.

[135] On Utah, see Maass and Anderson 1978, p. 337. On Colorado, Idaho and Nebraska, where in dry seasons domestic and farm uses are preferred but low preference users must also be accommodated, see Hirshleifer 1960, p. 236.

[136] Birch and MacLock 1992, p. 221. A new Water Act R.S.A. 2000, c. W-3, brought into force in Alberta in 1999 allows for a legislative order in times of emergency.

riparian-law states, mandatory transfers and sharing are facilitated by the use of permits with weak status as property rights (though, as discussed above, they share some of the characteristics of a property right), whereas similar intervention in appropriative rights states is limited by the well-established tenets of the prior-appropriation law. Even in the worst water shortages, in terms of acre-feet of water diverted, many governments do almost nothing to force holders of senior rights to share with junior holders.

The seniority principle thus provides an ingenious way by which at least some users have rights with high exclusivity and quality of title even where water availability fluctuates widely. The holders' resolute demand for retention of these characteristics in rights systems means that rights may well have become more exclusive and secure than originally, a process aided by improvements in such administrative tools as stream-adjudication procedures, flow records and seniority registrations. In spite of ever more serious variability in climate and natural flows, senior holders are increasingly independent of the use decisions of other users, though more junior users may find their right less exclusive than in a riparian-right permit system.

Transferability

We expect to find water being traded between rights-holders. Incentives lie in the differences between locations, between the water requirements of various uses and between the pressures to conform to a beneficial-use requirement. And there are indeed many recorded transfers. According to a 1986 survey by the Western States Water Council, few transfers of appropriative rights occur in North Dakota, Alaska, Nebraska or South Dakota. At the other extreme, 'Colorado, Idaho, Nevada, New Mexico, Utah, Washington and Wyoming reported that fifty or more transfers occur annually. Colorado, Nevada and Utah reported that more than 300 transfers occur each year.'[137]

In the latter three states and in California transferability allows water-right holders to participate in organized water markets. These markets are by no means perfect; the lots of water on offer are restricted in various ways by duration, security, seniority, region and quality. Nevertheless, arbitrage and speculation tend to cause divergent local prices to converge, and local markets to coalesce into one wider water market.[138]

In the other seven states, water transfers, sales and exchanges are more fragmented. A single market-wide price does not emerge. One reason is specificity: owners who sell water lose the value of their specific water-oriented real-estate improvements. A second reason is that physical transfer is in some regions costly or impractical. A third reason is that holders may be speculating, holding onto their rights for an expected future capital gain. The fourth,

[137] Johnson and DuMars 1989, p. 373. How much was transferred is another question.
[138] On the water-broker's point of view, see Shupe et al. 1989, p. 414 and Huffaker 2000.

perhaps the chief, reason for the fewness of complete or partial transfers is that they are actually discouraged by state laws and administrative procedures.

Almost everywhere transfers require the approval of a court or a government agency. The procedure is usually relatively simple if the transfer is to keep the water appurtenant to the same land; if it is temporary as with a lease or rental;[139] or if it can be handled by transferring a share in an irrigation district.[140] But it is not simple if the law calls for the legal protection of parties not included in the transaction. If the transferred water is to be diverted at a new point and/or appurtenant to a new location, the law usually calls for the administrative agency or the court to consider the extent to which the transfer injures third-party water users, and hear their protests.

There are three types of third-party injuries. The first, most talked-about, type is caused by reduced water spillovers. These occur when a holder's water transfer (sale or lease) reduces the amounts available as 'return flows' from his former operations to the stream or seepages to water-table levels.[141] The second type consists of injuries borne by the local society, families and businesses within the affected community. Injuries of the third type arise when a private water transfer damages public in-stream uses such as fish migration and habitat, commercial navigation, recreation and enjoyment of water quality. Modern remedies call for political intervention not only to reduce private transfers to new private users but also to increase private transfers to new public in-stream uses.[142]

The new procedures aim to verify and reduce these sources of injury. In some jurisdictions, the courts or water-right agency may simply enjoin the holder from transferring all or part of his water right. They may also order compensation payments. These, like nuisance damages, can win over groups of third-group objectors, such as commercial fishermen. But the groups' consent may be contractual and temporary, requiring costly renewal each time the water is transferred again. Traditionally, the transferor can also make a compulsory outright purchase of third parties' rights—as once occurred under legislation to facilitate English canal building, and under the New England Mill Dam Acts. Analogous procedures are used today in the transfer of key appropriative water rights. Sellers

[139] The disadvantages or short rentals can be overcome. According to Shupe et al. 1989, pp. 417–22, some large users, such as cities, may assemble a revolving portfolio of permanent and temporary water rights, from different sources.

[140] See Rosen 1990, pp. 10–14, reporting on the incentive by members of irrigation districts to approve capital expenditures to store more water rather than experience an internal redistribution of water.

[141] See Gould 1989.

[142] See Sax 1990 describing how groups have argued that the government must be governed by a public trust role under the constitution to protect navigable waters. See also Sax and Abrams 1986. Public uses are protected in Canada and Australia by statutory arrangements that over-ride individual licences. See also Sax and Abrams 1986 and Huffaker, Whittlesey, and Hamilton 2000.

may be compelled to transfer water not only to irrigation and ditch projects but also to favoured manufacturing plants in injured communities.[143]

The payment for third parties' consent is only part of the expense of making a water transfer. Perhaps exceeding it is the legal transaction cost. In general, transaction costs encompass spending for post-transfer monitoring, verification and enforcement activities, and also for the information on which transactions can be based—including information regarding the third parties who might protest to the transfer. In some American states, litigating parties must go through a judge's adjudication of the rights at all sites along a stretch of the river.[144] The official routine may be easier in places with administrative water systems, such as New Mexico, the Canadian provinces and the Australian states. But even here there are inevitable costs, which the agencies do not handle for nothing.[145] It is safe to say that many transfers that would once have been simple and informal—especially temporary diversions and rentals—have become more complicated, calling on more professionals to handle the skilful protests of interests potentially harmed by changes in diversions and appurtenances. The costs of these must be preventing many potential water-right transfers from occurring.

Flexibility

Related to its transferability is the water-right's flexibility—the extent to which the holder continues to have a secure and transferable interest even as changing technology or market demand diverts the water to a new use. For example, common-law land-based water rights were found to be fairly flexible when run-of-the-river flour milling gave way to water storage and release for large-scale textile mills.

Appropriative rights have been less flexible. Most systems of appropriative water rights do have the flexibility to support transfers between users many miles apart or even between users with technologies having widely different seasonal storage patterns.[146] But if the right is transferred to a holder who wishes to make other *uses* of the water, the appropriative right may be too specialized. It cannot prevent conflicts between new-use users and right holders using water for more traditional purposes.

THE LEGAL BASIS OF THE APPROPRIATIVE RIGHT: ENGLISH PRIOR-USE AND THE NEW WORLD'S PRIOR-APPROPRIATION

Appropriative rights can be referred to as the latest in the succession of use-based legal regimes, likening them to their seventeenth and eighteenth-century forerunners. But this view has been contested. As stated at the outset,

143 See Mitchell 1991 and Mitchell 1993 for studies of steps for improving water transfers to urban uses, by a flexible market, with compensation to rural communities.

144 On litigation costs, see Brajer et al. 1989, pp. 489–502.

145 For an analysis of costs under administrative agencies, see Howe et al. 1990, p. 20.

146 Some governments allow the creation of 'water trusts'. These may act as non-profit middlemen, acquiring rights to water in one place and making it available elsewhere.

Maass and Zobel were particularly influential in rejecting the notion that there ever was a phase when English water law was based solely on seniority of use.[147] Such denial echoes similar contentions in early nineteenth-century judgments ushering out the prior-use regime and introducing the natural-flow theory. The English courts in question asserted that to be a property right in water, the roots of an entitlement must be traced back to some grant of ownership, preferably by a document that describes the original sale or devise of the land. A tort-law-begotten prior-use right was not enough.[148]

In this section, we explore the debate by examining directly the legitimacy of American appropriative rights. Following this we examine three challenges to its legitimacy: in American states where the two systems survive together; in irrigation organizations; and in situations calling for in-stream and non-diversionary (public) water uses.

The legitimacy of American appropriative rights

American systems of appropriative rights emerged where there was a pronounced 'absence of land ownership', raising questions as to whether a legal basis for an appropriative right could be provided by the new legislatures in the absence of a root or connection to earlier land and water ownership. Yet in both the prior-use regime and in the western system of appropriative rights, rights were implicitly recognized by their enforceability and transferability, regardless of whether one could identify their original owner. They were usufructuary, 'belonging' or attributed to individuals. Today's lawyers would call them 'personal' rights in the same way that economists oriented toward legal foundations of markets would call them 'property' rights, the designation they would also give to contractual rights. No matter how named, they are rights to water.

An often quoted concept in law, and in this book, is that there is no right without a remedy.[149] Whenever there is no legal means of enforcing a 'property right', there is no right in law. Consequently, ability to defend and enforce them is the *measure* of rights. Applying this criterion, the absence of enforceability for riparian rights after the medieval period means they ceased to be rights. After the decline of riparian rights, even before the courts took it on themselves to affirm the enforceability of prior-use doctrine, use-based rights were enforceable. It could be said that they were rights before they were legally recognized as such.

Courts in nineteenth-century England were not prepared, however, to make an enforceability argument. As seen earlier in this chapter, Lord Denman recognized in *Mason v. Hill* that damage law had always been the law of

147 Maass and Zobel 1960.
148 See *Mason v. Hill* (1833), 110 E.R. 692 (K.B.).
149 *Ashby v. White* (1904), 92 E.R. 126 (K.B.).

England. But he vehemently denied that senior users had a *right* to damage junior users' entitlements simply because the juniors could not enforce their entitlements against seniors.[150] Those following in his footsteps said that the seniority system alone did not constitute a legal basis for a water right, and turned first to natural-flow theory and later to reasonable use theory as the English law of water.

American courts, faced with the similar problem of tracing a legal foundation for their new appropriative right, settled the problem a different way: by protecting the new system. They turned to the legislature for statutory recognition of appropriative rights. (The English courts could have taken a similar path in 1851. Instead, they reached back to salvage the old feudal system of riparian law;[151] then they provided, in the doctrines of reasonable use, new mechanisms for its enforcement.)

Co-existence of the two systems

When flows were low, there was a serious possibility that a claim made by a holder under riparian law would clash with claims to the same flow by holders under the appropriation system. Could riparianism tolerate such a clash or did it always yield?

In western Canada and in the Australian states, the lesson was that riparianism could be contained but might well survive. For instance, a clash occurred in British Columbia where those drafting their new water statutes failed to foresee all the situations that could provide an opportunity for a riparian argument. Crown-granted riparian common-law rights had been transferred back to the Crown and the way cleared for a statutory system of administrative water licences.[152] But these licences did not apply in a 'railway belt', where the loggers to whom the Dominion had issued timber berths successfully claimed riparian rights.[153] A Board, appointed by the two governments, spent a decade reconciling the riparian rights of some users with the recorded water licences of others.[154] As in many North American jurisdictions, no limit had been placed on the number of licences issued, the seniority system being relied on to sort out conflicts. But it could not do so for riparian rights. Somehow, possibly because some loggers eventually ran out of trees and opted to move on, a government Board muddled through to issuing new licences to the riparian rights holders, giving them precedence and appurtenance.

[150] *Mason v. Hill* (1833), 110 E.R. 692 (K.B.).

[151] For similar remarks about the opportunity missed see Lucas 1990 and Clark and Renard 1970.

[152] *Cook v. Vancouver (City)*, [1914] A.C. 1077 (P.C.) (appeal taken from B.C.); *Pasco v. Canadian National Railway Co.* (1985), 69 B.C.L.R. 76 (S.C.).

[153] These riparian rights were confirmed by the Privy Council in 1911 in *Burrard Power Co. Ltd. v. R.* (1910), [1911] A.C. 87 (P.C.) (appeal taken from Can.). See also Cail 1974 and Scott 1991, pp. 357–8.

[154] Cail 1974, p. 357.

This crisis, combined with western Canadian irrigators' fears that riparian rights would mandate that water be prorated during low flows, induced legislatures to pass laws wiping out riparian rights, and made appropriative rights universal in western Canada.[155] Even so, some riparian doctrine survived, even after the introduction of a modern permit system in 1961. The legislation did not impose a licence requirement on prospectors or on domestic and small farm users, allowing the latter to take water even in time of drought, and (roughly speaking), leaving them subject to riparian, reasonable use doctrine, not to the legislation that created the permit system.[156] Yet the survival of these riparian tenets has not created serious disputes. One explanation is that the division of nearly all western Canadian streams is so slack that the volume taken by small farmers is insignificant. It does worry legal scholars, however, because it concedes that riparianism is still acceptable modern water law.[157]

For Australian experience with the two systems, consider Victoria's statutory rights co-existing with common-law rights.[158] Water had come under an administrative licensing system in the gold rush. Nevertheless riparian rights continued to be respected, unaffected by the legislation setting up waterworks, sewage and irrigation districts. The situation lasted thirty years until in 1886 Alfred Deakin's Irrigation Act[159] forestalled new claims to riparian rights by vesting the right to use all water in the Crown. A significant group of riparian owners did already exist, although Clark and Renard claim that after 1905 the 'vast majority' of users held the gold rush era licences.[160] One is impressed that Deakin and his contemporaries, having been religiously converted to state provision of irrigation works, almost feverishly set about stamping out riparian rights. As Clark and Renard remark:

> It seemed to be the opinion of Deakin that, in order both to confer adequate powers on government, and, at the same time, to discourage the wasteful private litigation which plagued the Western United States, it was necessary to abolish all private rights to water. To his mind, the concept of administrative apportionment of resources was mutually inconsistent with the continued existence of private rights of action between individual water users. This attitude persists....[161]

[155] See Lucas 1990, p. 92 on the irrigators' fear of prorating.

[156] For a full account see Marcia Valiante 2003 'The Future of Common Law Water Rights in Ontario', *Journal of Environmental Law and Practice* 14, pp. 293–313.

[157] See Lucas 1990, pp. 49–51; Percy 1988, pp. 17–22.

[158] Clark and Renard 1974, pp. 140–271, mostly on water law in the state of Victoria.

[159] Irrigation Act (1886) (Vict.).

[160] Clark and Renard 1974, p. 186. This was partly because the Lands Offices had reserved stream-side strips of land for the Crown to forestall settlers' grants from being, technically, riparian properties. However, many lands evidently held under grants made before this policy began had often been sub-divided, remaining as an irritating exception to the universality of the licence system in Victoria.

[161] Id., pp. 196–7, 198. The phrase 'apportionment of resources' here means something like the state's universal distribution of water. Deakin was not yet thirty when the legislation was introduced. He was immensely influential in Victoria, bringing in such social legislation as the factory and arbitration acts. In the 1890s he devoted himself to the federation of the colonies,

American experience of two systems of flowing water rights can be illuminated by considering the cases of Oregon and California. In Oregon, and similarly in neighbouring Washington, the two systems coexisted for a time, thanks to the Constitutional guarantee to property and also to the historical precedence of riparian law, but the appropriative system finally won the day. California, by contrast, worked its way toward a mixed system.

In Oregon the transition to an appropriative regime was accomplished in four steps. First in 1909 there was an Oregon Supreme Court reinterpretation of the federal Desert Lands Act of 1877.[162] This, abrogating riparian rights on lands to be settled in later years, considerably reduced the number of riparian rights holders.[163] Second, in 1909 the Oregon water code grandfathered old riparian rights into its new appropriative system, confining recognition of old riparian rights to sites where beneficial use had been made of the water, and to the quantities of water beneficially used. Third, Oregon mobilized the state's powers of regulation. As in British Columbia, it provided for stream adjudications to determine the relative rights of water claimants. The US 9th Circuit Court of Appeals decided that the code did not destroy the usufructuary privileges of riparians, but only changed the conditions under which they could be exercised.[164] This advanced the idea that the holders' titles to their rights were still strong but the rights, being now subject to reasonable state regulation, had less of the exclusivity characteristic.[165] Fourth, from 1914 a series of cases began to reduce the rights of some users who were claiming riparian rights while holding appropriative entitlements, forcing them to choose.

and became second prime minister in 1903. See Clark 1979, p. 179. All Deakin's delegation and other Australian visitors to the United States seem to have been over-impressed by the volume of litigation, especially in Colorado. Later Victoria governments brought Elwood Mead, designer of the Wyoming version of the irrigation district to design legislation. The resulting legislation reinforced the water-sharing idea instead of seniority, an idea Mead had pushed within US irrigation districts. Powell 1976, pp. 127–41.

[162] *Hough v. Porter*, 51 Or. 318, 95 P. 732 (1908) and 98 P. 1083 (1909).

[163] See Desert Lands Act, 43 USCA 321 (1877). The federal court case which adopted 'beneficial-use' as the test of the riparian right was *Eastern Oregon Land Co. v. Willow River Land and Irrigation Co.*, 187 F 466 (D. Ore. 1910), reversed, *Land Co. v. Willow River Land and Irrigation Co.*, 187 F 466 (D. Ore. 1910).

[164] See *California-Oregon Power Co. v. Beaver Portland Cement Co.*, 73 F.2d 555 (C.C.A. Or. 1934). See Hutchins 1957, p. 210. The effect of the US Court of Appeals decision in *California-Oregon Power Co.* was also to uphold the interpretation given to the water code by the majority of the Oregon Supreme Court in *In re Hood River*, 114 Or.112, 227 P. 1065 (1924). See also the statement of Hutchins 1957, p. 207: 'the Oregon Supreme Court ... construed the water code as having validly abrogated the common law riparian rule as to the "continuous flow" of a stream except where the water had been actually applied to beneficial use'.

[165] This had been the view in 1914 of the Oregon Supreme Court in *In re Willow Creek*, 74 Or. 592, 144 P. 505 (1914), modified on rehearing, 74 Or. 592, 146 P. 475 (1914). See also Hutchins 1957, p. 206. Exception was made in the 1909 water code for those with works in progress, the amount of the right being limited to the quantity of water used a reasonable time after the passage of the act.

Even these four steps failed to erase some remaining advantages of holding on to riparian rights. In particular, in a conflict with another user holding a riparian right, a user might be best off if he too held a riparian right. Another advantage would be that, under some versions of riparian law, an owner's 'ordinary' uses of water for stock and home would be completely protected. Finally, a right holder might find his postponed future use best protected by a riparian right (though in many states, including Washington, the riparian must prove he will use the water within a reasonable time). Oregon's riparianism was battered, but it did not vanish.

California, in contrast to Oregon, upheld riparian rights. It upheld even those rights in conflict with appropriative rights[166] and those not claimed until after the federal Desert Lands Act 1887. It limited appropriative rights to public lands not federally reserved. This decision actually reintroduced a system of water rights believed by some to have been abolished. Their chief fear was that, by exercising a natural-flow right, riparians would prevent water from reaching irrigated fields away from streams and would reduce the courts' ability to deal with cases involving non-riparians.

Resigned to a survival of riparian rights in some areas, the legislature invented two steps to modify the riparian-right impact throughout the state. First, the legislature encouraged holders of appropriative rights to try for *prescriptive rights* by shortening the waiting period to a mere five years. As Maass and Anderson (1978) put it, 'The courts held that the actual appropriation of water, followed by open, continuous and exclusive possession for the prescriptive term, gave the right.' Often, 'large diversions in rivers were made near the point of emergence of the streams from the mountains. The riparian lands that would be seriously affected were so far downstream that the diversions frequently provoked no immediate opposition, and sometimes they ripened into prescriptive rights before they were opposed.'[167] Once obtained, California's legislated prescriptive right was very similar to its common-law cousins in other jurisdictions. A hybrid, partly land-based, partly use-based, it became a third type of water right.

The second step also radically changed the traditional rules restraining the riparian land-holder. A new law allowed him to transfer flows of water out of the 'riparian tenement' (although not out of the watershed). This political modification detached the water right from the riparian's land and could potentially have undermined the 'riparian community' and the basis for riparian law. Instead, the law had the unexpected effect of allowing upstream irrigators to use water diverted from downstream locations without reducing the water available to riparians along the way.[168]

[166] *Lux v. Haggin*, 69 Cal.255, 10 P. 674 (1886).

[167] Maass and Anderson 1978, p. 229.

[168] Of course there was a high cost of pumping over long diversions. For an account of the flexible features of riparianism see Freyfogle 1989, p. 1529.

Conflict of laws on boundary-crossing streams

Another type of mixed system is found on boundary-crossing streams, where upstream and downstream users hold rights under different governments or courts.[169]

In principle, it would seem that a boundary would provide few problems for the recognition of riparian rights. Each riparian's water rights stem from his land proprietorship. All riparians have the same property or ownership rights and responsibilities as members of the 'community of the river' as judged on either the natural-flow or the reasonable use theory. These rights and responsibilities are not created by governments and so need not terminate at frontiers.

What the frontier does terminate is the jurisdiction of a complainant's court. As among federal states or provinces enforcement requires either cross-boundary agreements about court jurisdiction or an appeal procedure to a higher federal court. For example, in 1931 upstream Massachusetts threatened to divert water that would otherwise flow by riparian lands in downstream Connecticut.[170] The latter sought an injunction from the US Supreme Court. That court did mention the downstream state's claim to an uninterrupted flow but, in the absence of evidence of a diversion's causing actual damage or detriment to navigation, it refused to act. It preferred a reasonable use (termed 'equitable apportionment') criterion to a primitive natural-flow right.[171] Increasingly, the Court has balanced the benefits or damages in alternative schemes of division, leading to decisions to allow old uses to be replaced by new uses of higher value.

The question of whether a user's right would be recognized across the state frontier, especially if the states have different water laws, takes us again to the legal basis of the appropriative right. One theory holds that a user's right is merely a regulatory permit.[172] It is not robust enough to be enforceable in another state unless there are agreements (compacts) between the two. A second, related, theory based on public ownership holds that a user's water right is based on his state's claims that all rights to use flows of water are vested in the people, the Crown or the government. These rights would otherwise belong to others; to riparians, in fact. The implications of this theory in the United States differ from those in Canada and Australia.

[169] The brevity of our treatment prevents us from displaying the variety of boundary water disputes. We should distinguish between disputes among governments and those among individuals; and also between conflicts arising when the stream forms the boundary and when it crosses the boundary, which involve different types of law. See Scott 1993, pp. 141–81; Gallob 1991, p. 85; the papers in Saunders 1986; and Pisani 1986.

[170] *Connecticut v. Massachusetts (Commonwealth of)*, 282 US 660, 51 S.Ct. 286, 75 L.Ed. 602 (1931).

[171] See also *New Jersey v. New York (State of)*, 283 US 336, 51 S.Ct. 478, 75 L.Ed. 1104 (1931).

[172] A complication is that appropriative rights systems do not remove some riparian rights, such as to divert water for 'ordinary' uses, or to sue when injured by pollution.

Most American courts treated water rights, even those issued as 'permits' by administrators (in the event a permit dispute reached the courts), as transferable, usually real, property rights. Declarations of state vesting or ownership were discounted, and in 1982 they were described by the US Supreme Court as a fiction: hence, in interstate commerce, water rights were likened to a commodity.[173] This judgment did not pronounce on the basis of individual rights except to recognize that they existed. The states were not the ultimate owners under the second theory so the rights were not merely administrative devices. From this approach emerges one American doctrine that individual appropriative water rights should be respected outside the state. Individuals may trade them up and down the river.[174] Other approaches are available: the states may join in a water-sharing compact, usually with federal government participation, but without litigation.

In Canada the governments' claims to provincial ownership or possessory rights to water (as to other resources) have been more successful. The conclusion for Canadian water users is a complicated one. A user holds an appropriable water right issued by his province that is not necessarily compatible in volume, benefit or seniority with rights issued by other provinces. But cross-border interference with a flow to which a water right is held cannot be corrected by individual litigation.

Neither can it be corrected by inter-province litigation. In provincial eyes, the vesting of water rights in the provincial Crown is a form of riparian ownership because it is confined to watercourses and also because it emerges from the taking of individual riparian rights. Therefore, the provinces are each adjoining riparians. Yet, in the Canadian constitutional framework, their riparian disputes may not be dealt with by the senior national courts, nor may these or any courts become involved in making reasonable use, equitable allotments. In despair various authorities have urged that, in order to achieve something like nationally efficient water allocations, the provinces must proceed by negotiated 'cooperative' management.[175] They predict too that the final basis for litigation—mediation, most likely—across provincial boundaries will be the common solution.[176]

Among Australia's Crown-property states, the outstanding instance of boundary conflict and compact is in the Murray-Darling system. The River Murray Agreement between three states and the new Commonwealth, which reconciled navigation with river irrigation, was settled by contract in 1915. It provided

[173] *Colorado v. New Mexico*, 459 US 176 at 181 (1982). See Tarlock 1985.

[174] Ausness 1983.

[175] See Barton 1986, p. 235, for the argument that Canadian courts would not substitute their own opinions for the negotiated agreements between the provinces.

[176] Percy 1988 suggested that the Supreme Court will eventually be faced with suits on a sort of interprovincial riparian right to clean water. Zimmerman 1969 predicted that common-law riparian rules will govern in interprovincial affairs. On the other hand, Gibson 1969 favoured outright federal jurisdiction over interprovincial waters.

joint development of storage, locks and weirs and provided for dividing irrigation waters. No other interstate stream has comparable importance.[177] Its 'basin-wide' contracting and engineering approaches were influential in planning the TVA, the St Lawrence waterway and a few other projects.[178]

Water storage organizations

That non-government irrigation organizations and individual water users exist side by side leads to another kind of mixed system. Most western settlers became the customers of commercial ditch and canal companies, many of which were linked to land-development companies that promised water to potential buyers. As a result, many users found themselves tied to monopolistic water sellers. Disputes over quantities and price were a commonplace.

There resulted three changes in irrigation institutions. First, farmers' demands in the courts and the legislature resulted in their water rights becoming appurtenant to their own addresses rather than to the ditch company's point of diversion.[179] In any case, the farmers were tending to take over the ditch companies' assets. Their favoured institutional form was a cooperative or mutual irrigation company, each share giving its holder a unit water entitlement. They were demanding that the legislature create public irrigation districts. This tendency, around 1900, led to a demand for a tax on water entitlement and one for expenses, both based on members' acreages. There was also a water charge. Users were allocated a fixed percentage share of the total amount of water available to the organization in a given period, an amount based on one or more appropriative water rights held by the organization for its members.[180] Throughout the American states, as in the western Canadian provinces and the

[177] See Powell 1976, pp. 139–40.

[178] Possibly the difference between the US equitable apportionment approach and the Canadian/Australian Crown-property approach could be explained by geography: As American states are relatively small there are relatively more interstate streams along which disputes can arise. The literature yields few explorations of this approach.

[179] Dunbar 1983, pp. 103–5.

[180] Schlager 1994, in research on the institutional implications of storage for certain kinds of common-pool resources, concludes that users 'of cell 1 types of resources [fisheries with no storage, some irrigation systems with no storage], in many instances, do not attempt to directly manage the mobile flows, since such flows are often unpredictable, and what benefits users would produce may be captured by others who also have access to those flows. Users of cell 2 [grazing areas with no storage], 3 [some irrigation systems with storage], and 4 [groundwater basins with storage] types of resources, because of storage, stationary flows or both, however, can exert direct control over the flow units, and do, as is exhibited by the types of allocation rules that such users adopt. Instead of allocating access to flow units through time slots, access may be achieved by granting fixed or proportionate shares of the flow units to each resource user. For instance, in each of the California groundwater basins examined, except for one, pumpers owned transferable shares of water.' See also Maass and Anderson 1978, pp. 379–81, on the value of storage in all sharing systems. The rights-based system mentioned will be seen to be similar to the idea of the foresters' or fishermen's 'condominium' organizations discussed in later chapters.

Australian states, such districts have more recently pointed the way for distributing water from high-dam projects.[181]

The member's entitlement, seen as a water right, had all the quality of title that could be set into irrigation legislation. Its transferability, however, depended on the decisions of those who set up the district. At one extreme are organizations where memberships, acres or both can be sold to anyone. At the other extreme are organizations whose original formation wiped out any idea of wider transferability; they devote themselves to irrigating the lands in one area. Between these extremes are organizations whose members may not sell their water right or share but may sell their water for a season or less.[182]

While the connection between irrigation organizations and larger institutions is too complex to be taken up here, it is worth noting that an increasing proportion of water users hold contracts, leases or shares issued by their organization rather than by an official agency. This is mainly because water scarcity necessitates an increasing investment in storage and delivery systems. Legal scholars neglect this trend because the shares are not legal water rights. But the development may foreshadow a reshaping of water right systems. Today, many non-government irrigation districts and storage organizations dispense with the ideas both of seniority and of beneficial use in favour of equal sharing of surpluses or shortages.[183]

Multiple rights systems and multiple stream purposes

The total utility of a stream is much more than the sum of the utilities of the individual diversions along its banks. Just as in the earliest times, streams are in public-good demand for navigation and for a multitude of such public, collective or individual services as drainage, waste disposal, transportation, wildlife habitat, fish habitat and migration, fishing and recreation. To these should be added the new 'public good' demand for protection of the ecological chain, biological diversity and local sustainable development. All these rely on water being left in the stream, sources of 'in-stream' or 'natural-state'[184] demands.

Consider now four ways by which the *appropriative* system can be used to answer to these demands on the stream. First, and formally, regulators can make provision for issuing regular permits to leave water in the stream.[185] Second, if

[181] Clark and Renard 1970, pp. 164–9 describe how the first Australian district equivalents were trusts, given ownership of whole streams with the purpose of providing for their proper administration. These were replaced by a water commission, which oversaw all the trusts.

[182] Trelease 1974, p. 207.

[183] Interesting examples are found in Australia. More generally, Maass and Anderson 1978, pp. 375–9, show that there are actually seven systems available, of which equal sharing is only one.

[184] 'Natural state', along with 'naturally occurring' are the expressions appearing in Alberta's Water Act, R.S.A. 2000, c. W-3.

[185] For a summary on American procedures, see Johnson and DuMars 1989, pp. 361–7. See also Alberta Water Resources Act, R.S.A. 1980, c. W-5, s. 11(1)(c), authorizing the issuing of a water licence for conservation, recreation or the propagation of fish or wildlife or any like purpose.

they are legally permitted, private charities and trusts can use donations to buy or lease flows for in-stream purposes. Third, regulators can place an in-stream flow requirement on the conditions of private diversion. Fourth, as at present, regulators at all three levels of government can whip up a tangle of customary, constitutional or statutory in-stream regulations. That these are all improvised adaptations of the basic appropriative diversion regime reflects a political reluctance to see water taken from 'productive' uses. In all three common-law countries, many users and their politicians (as evidenced by their adherence to seniority and beneficial use principles) believe *all* the water in a stream ought to be diverted to such uses as irrigation and mining, without 'waste'. They view allocations to in-stream uses as an almost shocking reversal.

Instead, consider provision of in-stream water under the riparian system. The reader will recall that the nineteenth-century system of land-based rights took as one of its points of departure the legal obligation of each riparian user to maintain the level and flow of the stream, thereby providing 'natural' flow or a related concept to the other riparians. These legal concepts could be revived to provide for 'a natural state' as one of a stream's multiple uses. The natural level and flow concept might thereby prevent total exploitation of a river by making every user responsible for natural-state maintenance.[186]

TRANSFERABILITY IN MODERN APPROPRIATIVE-RIGHT SYSTEMS

The extent to which appropriative water rights should be transferable and marketed has long been a controversial matter. Therefore, a few final remarks on this important subject are in order. In the original home-made court-enforced version of the appropriative-rights system, persons acquired a right to use or divert a volume of the flow of the stream by doing so at a specific location. Once obtained, the right was subject to the rights of prior users according to their dated seniority and to a requirement to make beneficial use. Storage of water was not originally considered a 'beneficial use'. Today members of irrigation organizations pool their rights and by formula share the organizations' total available water. (Their share is not a divided appropriative right, but may be regarded as one.)

In all three countries the levels of the property-right-characteristics of the appropriative right—duration, flexibility, security and exclusivity—have

[186] American streams fall into two legal categories. Navigable streams are subject to federal powers to regulate commerce, but nevertheless the state has title to the bed of federal streams rather than the riparian owner or the water appropriator. Streams that are not navigable are mainly subject to state water law. A state could not and cannot easily grant the bed for a private use, for since 1892 the courts have held that it is owned subject to a public trust to use the river for public purposes. At one time the main public purpose was navigation, a federal responsibility. But today, decisions such as *National Audubon Society v. Superior Court of Alpine County*, 189 Cal. Reptr. 346 (1983), call on states, in their administering of prior-appropriative rights, to exercise the trust to assure in-stream flows for what are essentially environmental purposes. In Canada, as suggested in an earlier section, provincial jurisdiction over most water resources is chiefly a result of constitutional provisions for provincial ownership of, and jurisdiction over, 'natural resources' as defined by a series of cases.

survived well from the origin of the systems. *Transferability*, however, is in greater demand for in-stream and commercial uses and is the subject of controversy. In the American west, many of the demanders of wider transferability of water rights have been urban elites who wish to melt the iron control of farmer groups over captured irrigation water for non-farm uses. These elites and pressure groups have played leading roles in policy battles concerning water rights that cross jurisdictional boundaries, water projects which involve more than one government and the holding of water rights in both riparian and appropriative systems. Winning these battles has promised more additional water than simply revising water rights.

Conclusion: change and stability in water rights

We have shown that individual rights to take flowing water have alternated between periods of land-based rights and periods of use-based rights. Prescriptive rights, which are both land-based and use-based, have acted as a braking force on the magnitude of the shift between the two regimes. As well, old rights are not extinguished when the legal basis shifts so that countries with mature legal systems tend to experience periods in which the two bases of rights co-exist.

To conclude the chapter we return to the theme of historical 'twists and turns' in water rights. We attempt to go beyond the generalization above, about alternation between the bases of water rights, to develop a general rule about why alternation between the bases takes place. With such a theory, we might be able to better predict the future course of legal water rights.

The alternation of the periods between land- and use-based rights: theories

Several obvious theories emerge in the histories laid out above to explain the alternation phenomenon. First, we might argue that changes were driven mainly by courts and the prevailing judges of the time. For instance, in the nineteenth century the concept of the 'reasonable man' spread from the tort law of negligence to water law, giving wide scope to enforcement of water level and quality maintenance by riparians, both users and non-users of the system. Although the courts did not so much drive this important change as convey it from tort cases to property cases, there can be no doubt that it was a change on the supply side, resulting in improved exclusivity and quality of title in water rights. Second, we might surmise that changes were a response to increases on the demand side, due perhaps to demographic or technological developments that increased the industrial need for flowing water. But we argue that it is difficult to see how increased cumulative demand for water power and other attributes must, *in itself*, be a cause of changes in the basis of water rights. Instead, we focus more narrowly on changes over time in the *composition* of users' needs for water—some indeed driven by changing technology—and the resulting change in users' demands for rights suitable to the new mix of water applications.

We start with periods in which the search for water, and conflicts about rights to water, seem to have been related to a single purpose. Water power for mills was such a single purpose. In a single-purpose period a use-based system of rights entails fewer sources of transaction cost than a land-based system. Transactions in water's few important attributes can rely on inexpensive and quick measurement of quantifiable amounts or flows of water, in comparable units. If little value is placed on other uses (such as preserving the stream's ecosystem), water may be transported or diverted from the natural watercourse. The sought-after attributes of water sources create a demand for certain characteristics of the right—divisibility and transferability—inherent to use-based rights. In short, those now participating in the resulting rights market, having a single purpose for stream flows, create a continuing demand for characteristics of water rights that collectively become a use-based rights system.

In contrast, in periods when there are strong demands for more than one attribute or purpose of the water, transactions cannot so easily rely on inexpensive and quick measurement of quantifiable amounts or flows of water in comparable units. Attributes can not be transformed into one another. The riparian right may be limited to a 'reasonable' use of the water, but what is reasonable is not definite and what is defined can change according to local circumstances of demand and supply. For example, the mix of using industries, and the mix of water uses they create, may differ widely from area to area, even on the same stream.

Because of these complexities, any water-rights market that has survived the use-based right period is handicapped by high transactions costs. The users may have little in common and their needs and potential losses may be legally difficult to compare, complicating the meaning of 'exclusivity' in use. Those who might create a market but do not share a single purpose for stream flows may therefore be expected to reject use-based rights and support the revival of a land-based system, with its approaches to reasonable use and natural flow better able to accommodate demands for multiple uses.

While important, the period-to-period changes in the basis of water were not necessarily reflected in instant or drastic changes in system or in users. A reading of the economic history of industries depending on particular attributes of water use suggests that the water users whom, it seemed, would have lost out under a new system in fact somehow kept going. Unlike the enclosures of common land and the Scottish clearances, the advent of a new water law was not actually a disaster for holders under the old system.

There are several explanations of this survival of old rights from earlier systems and bases. First, those who had acquired a prescriptive right over water were allowed to keep it, regardless of the changing phases in general water law. Second, the various principles of seniority or priority, usually introduced in periods with use-based systems of law, seem also to have been persuasive in periods with land-based systems. 'Ordinary' farm and domestic users were increasingly invulnerable to encroachments on the water they had customarily used. The holders of 'senior' or 'prior' rights, even without prescriptive rights, also seemed to lead a charmed existence, beyond the reach of revivals of natural-flow theory or of the actual workings of reasonable use and appropriative laws. The record shows that the judges rarely, if ever, found against a person who could be said to be 'in possession' of a flow of water, held by a title that he previously was believed to have enjoyed by actual use. As with a man's home, so with his mill: his home was his castle and his water was his moat! Third, security and permanence of water-right ownership led to an increase in stable contracting between right-holders and actual users. Non-holders of rights joined holders of older rights from whom their water was transferred as demanders that these rights remain secure and enforceable.

Collective water right holdings

Making use of the services of a river has many similarities to making use of the attributes of a fish stock or of a petroleum formation. Because, in their natural state, such resources are fluid, it is difficult or costly to assign and enforce rights to parts of them. The record of change in rights in a stream, however, is different from that of fish or petroleum in that there seems to have been no phase or experimental period in which the whole fluid resource was held and managed collectively. There are, of course, irrigation associations and districts, but these are rarely incorporated to make collective use of a stream. Rather they are intended to achieve economies of scale in storage and distributive networks, and typically draw their water from several sources: wells, springs and streams.

When one observes the ambitious organizations that may take over whole fisheries or whole oil fields, one is struck by the absence of schemes for whole streams to be managed by their users or by their riparian owners. The question of why this lack of initiative emerges will be raised in a later chapter about multiple-use forests. The answer appears to be, in all such cases, even in fisheries, that many users, who have a 'right' to make some use of the natural resource do not hold an individual property right to it or to its use. What 'right' they do have lacks exclusivity, transferability and divisibility. We will see that without rights that have these characteristics, individual users cannot be identified. They have no rights to pool and no power to use their own action to change the rate at or purposes for which a stream is used.

Of course, a government could, by statute, create exclusive and transferable quantitative rights and hand them to selected individuals. Failing the creation of such rights, however, we are unlikely to see river management evolving into the control of a collective of individuals whose chief claim is use of, or propinquity to, a stream.

4

Rights over Fisheries and Fish

Introduction: from the fishery commons toward property in fish

Economic analysts have long regarded ocean fisheries as a common-property resource. This label has been justified by the usual facts: the typical fishery is not a private-property resource, and those who fish it do so in common with others, all of whom have had, at least traditionally, unrestricted access.[1] I want to attempt, in what follows, to explain why *qualified* open-access fisheries have long been the usual arrangement. While many kinds of persons have been chased away in one century or another, their exclusion has rarely enabled whatever group has remained to enjoy any kind of private property over, or sole ownership of, the sea fishery. This has been true under most kinds of European law for almost a millennium. In England and its colonies open access took the form of an explicitly declared universal public right of fishing, protected by the courts and discussed below under the heading of *Magna Carta*.

These chapters have evolved from my earlier papers on fisheries regulations and on ITQs. I have revised them in the light of very helpful comments from journal editors and readers and from members of classes and seminars (not least of which was my class at the University of Ottawa). In particular, I would like to thank my generous friends and past co-authors Peter H. Pearse, Philip A. Neher and Mukesh Eswaran, as well as Lee Anderson, Ragnar Arnason, Trond Bjorndal, Harry Campbell, Jon Conrad, Jim Crutchfield, Scott Gordon, Gary Libecap, Gordon Munro, Jason Tolland, Rognvaldur Hannesson, Richard Unger, Irene Spry, John Sutinen and Jim Wilen. On particular matters I would also thank Dori Bixler, Parzival Copes, Colin Clark, Diane Dupont, Alex Fraser, Pat Marchak, Nina Mollett, and John Wilson. In matters of help with direct research, there are traces, great and small, of contributions by Laura Armstrong, Bette Bono, Chris Nowlin and, especially, Jason Tolland and Michael Cooper—all learned in the law.

[1] Some economists have disputed the term 'common property' applied to the fisheries, either because a fishery is not 'property' at all, or—conversely—because the management of fisheries has always involved some exclusion: of foreign fishermen, of those without licences, of those using forbidden gear, etc., and is therefore not really a 'common'. See Ronald J. Oakerson, Common Property Resource Management, US National Research Council 1986. Outline enlarged upon by Elinor Ostrom, David Feeny, Fikret Berkes and others.

I begin this chapter with a very brief account of the 'fishery' under English law. Since the Norman Conquest, rights have existed over inland fishing places (e.g., on a lake or stream). Turning to sea fisheries, I then show how, since the thirteenth century, the law of England has rejected the concept of a territorial right of fishery in tidal waters. I also touch upon the harmony between English institutions and Roman law as well as the budding international law of the sea. I examine why the public right of sea fishing lasted for so long: who in those days would have demanded a more exclusive or private sea-fishing right, and who would have been in a position to supply it?

I later show that when, in the eighteenth and nineteenth centuries, it was at last becoming clear that sea fish stocks were not limitless, there arose an opportunity to produce a less open public right to sea fishing. Indeed, the Demsetz or 'naive' approach to the demand for property rights would have predicted the emergence of an exclusive communal or individual fishing right. Nowhere did this occur. Rather, there emerged a role for government—that of fisheries regulator. Instead of touching off the crafting of a private fishing right, the recognition of the scarcity of sea fish seems always to have pushed the government to *deny* a pure public right of fishing, mostly by closing fishing at certain times or in certain areas. I survey the forms this political intervention took, with particular reference to the administrative licence and its 'limitation' as a means of decreasing total fishing effort.

In conclusion, I bring the story to the end of the twentieth century by showing how limited licensing gave way to landing quotas. (There are several official names for quotas in different countries, including 'vessel', 'catch' and 'fisherman' quotas. *Individual transferable quotas*, abbreviated to ITQs, are the name that will be used here.) Transforming the licence regime into an ITQ regime reduced the tendency of vessels to race in order to find and land the catch during the short period when the regulated fishery was open. Title to a given number of fish provided a kind of exclusivity, and the new quotas also had traces of the other private property characteristics that had been missing from earlier regulatory instruments. The move away from regulated licences and toward what we might understand to be a modern property right in fish did not, however, eliminate the perceived need or enduring role of government regulation of the fisheries, both for purposes of quota enforcement and for purposes of redistribution.

Medieval fishing rights

Early individual rights to inland fishing

In the common law, the 'ownership' of a fish depended on many things: whether it was swimming or captured and whether, when at large, it was found in the sea, a river or a pond. The common-law metaphor of wild animal ownership—seen again in Chapter 9 on American oil rights—developed from early Roman law. The *Institutes of Gaius* described fish as belonging to the category of wild beasts, which, until capture, were *res nullius* (no one's property). This Roman idea carried through to the game laws of England. While the fish was swimming, the common-law concept of the capture of wild things (*ferae naturae*) applied.

In Europe, it was widely held that the monarch had sole property in game, which could be allocated to anyone. All persons had a right to pursue and capture wild animals, unless restrained by property rights such as those pertaining to royal hunting grounds. Once captured, fish became the qualified, not the absolute, property of the captor for, though legally like a domesticated animal, they would be lost upon returning to the wild.[2] Upon the death of the animal, the owner's right over it became absolute.

The qualified right over a captured live animal was protected by law as a possessory right and in this sense remained absolute as against others.[3] One way of reducing swimming wild fish to possessions was to keep them in a pond. Many English manors had ponds, although the extent to which they were held, stocked and harvested in common rather than as part of the lord's private demesne is less clear.[4] Since the right to these ponds was possessory, a poacher could not be charged with wrongful conversion (for having caught fish on another's land).[5] The owner of the fishery could, however, find a remedy in damages in order to recover the value of the fish via a trespass claim or an action on the case—early real actions that, as we saw in Chapter 1, preceded tort or nuisance actions.

FISHERIES IN STREAMS

Leaving aside the ownership of the individual fish, I turn to the right of fishery itself. The characteristics of this right varied widely from place to place, probably because nothing automatic about allocating the privilege of catching local fish was included in the original Norman land grant. It was not until the nineteenth century that courts began to assert a 'natural right' of land to carry with it not only riparian rights to the enjoyment of the level, flow and quality of the stream (see Chapter 3) but also the right to fish the stream. Hundreds of years earlier, during the process of subinfeudation, lands were passed down in smaller and subordinated holdings (some of them carved out as non-feudal

[2] Case of Swans (1592), 7 Coke 15.

[3] Year Book (1473), 18 Ed. 3, and (1528) 19 Hen. 8.

[4] Gras 1930 writes of a fishpond at Crawley, near Winchester; Harvey 1965 writes of a thirteenth century Oxfordshire village having a pond for bream; Hey 1986, pp. 81 and 99, writes of a seventeenth-century Shropshire pond shared by the lord with an adjoining manor.

[5] Property rights in or over fish contained in a pond cannot be lost, the fish cannot escape and are equivalent to chattels: *R. v. Steer* (1704), 6 Mod. Rep. 183, 87 E.R. 939; *Greyes Case* (1594), Owen 20.

holdings such as abbeys or towns). Fisheries were severed from the grants of the adjoining lands and became 'several' fisheries.[6] The grantors sometimes made these fresh-water several fisheries appurtenant to lands other than those adjoining the stream, but others were highly transferable and divisible, conveyable from holder to holder.[7] Independent medieval towns or boroughs located along rivers gained ownership of adjoining fisheries, and owned or leased fisheries in nearby manors.[8]

The rights included in the bundle referred to as a 'fishery'[9] varied according to the extent of the entitlement. A grant could be of a fishery in common, a common of fishery, a fishery in gross, a several fishery or a free fishery. A fishery in common belonged to partners; on a partner's death, his share passed to his own heirs. A common of fishery, like a common of pasture, was available to all a lord's tenants, especially freeholders. A fishery in gross, almost indistinguishable from a profit-à-prendre in gross (the right to enter and take from another's land), could be held by a person and need not be attached to land. A several fishery was the most comprehensive private right of fishery, imposing the exclusion of all others from the land around.[10] Despite the variance in provision, all these types carried rights to catch fish in a specified stretch of a flowing stream or lake. Along with these went implied rights to perform actions on the adjoining land deemed necessary to enjoying the fishing right: to enter, to tend fixed gear, even to cut timber and switches to maintain the necessary weirs and traps.[11] Like a profit-à-prendre a fishery could be held without term or by lease for a specified term.[12] The owner usually specified in the deed the

[6] Finberg 1969, p. 163 describes how the royal Duchy of Cornwall, held by the Black Prince, leased a salmon fishery to Tavistock Abbey (fourteenth century).

[7] For example, Cottenham, a manor near Cambridge, was subsidiary to Crowland Abbey. The manor included, in addition to roughly 1,300 acres of land, two windmills, a common and one fishery. A separate rent was paid to the abbey for the fishery (Page 1934, pp. 86 and 92).

[8] For example, the town of Lincoln owned an adjoining fishery in 1455 (Hill 1967, p. 341). One of many arrangements occurred in Ludlow, Shropshire, where fishing was, in some sense, 'free' until 1367 but was leased out as a whole thereafter. In 1468 the town court heard prosecutions for water pollution and for using a small-mesh net; but it is not clear how the fishery was then held. See Faraday 1991, p. 107.

[9] See Paterson 1863 for further discussion. For judicial analysis, see the Case of the Fishery in the Banne (1611), Davis 55.

[10] A free fishery, often confused in the jurisprudence with a several fishery, was a right coexisting with the rights of others (*Seymour v. Courtney* (1771), 5 Burr. 2814) or granted via deed (Year Book (1477), 17 Edw. 4), without an attached grant of land, usually in the sea or tidal waters.

[11] See a medieval dispute about the right to cut wood for fishing in Finberg 1969 ch. 6. In 1 Jac. 1, the fishers of Somerset, Devon and Cornwall got a right to enter on coastal land to fish for herring and pilchards (Encyclopedia Britannica, 1910 edn, vol. 10). The same sort of thing occurred in Scotland (100 yards from high water) II Geo. 3, c. 31.

[12] Indeed, a right of fishery can be described as a profit of 'piscary'. It must be exclusive, but this word must be defined very narrowly, for it has long been possible for the fishing at one place to be granted or hired out to different persons at different times (Megarry and Wade 1984, pp. 911–12). Such a grant of any fishery would be accomplished by a written deed (*Duke of Somerset v. Fogwell* [1826] 5 B. & C. 875).

amount and means of payment, the species to be caught and type of gear to be used. He could grant fisheries at the same place for different species or in different seasons.

THE COMMON OF FISHERY AND STINTING

A freshwater fishery was normally granted to and held by a single user.[13] In cases where fisheries were held by custom or grant 'in common', it is unclear whether or not they were managed by the local people (as were the fields) and, if so, whether or not they were over-used (as were common-property open-access marine fisheries). A commoner's right might have been similar to, and sometimes identical to, her right to use the common meadow or the waste land for pasture and fuel, but this parallelism has not been established. J. A. Raftis' 1957 study, *The Estates of Ramsey Abbey*, suggests that the fishery could be regarded as part of the demesne; that is, in the abbey's lands fishing was at the disposal of the local lord of the manor. He may have 'farmed' (leased) it or he may have made it available to his tenants on terms of his choosing.

It is likely that the fishery provided a service to the village like that provided by the lord's ferry or his flourmill, yielding revenue to the lord. We have evidence of manorial revenues (to the lord) from the fishery. Still another possibility is that the fishery was leased to the village to be collectively managed by the village court. Paterson (1863) notes that established tenants would have cause for an action against their lord in the event of overuse of the commons arising because he had failed to restrict rights in the face of increasing population. Discussing eleventh-century medieval Yorkshire McDonnell contrasts the *Domesday* survey's mention of river fisheries (based on constructed weirs, traps and other installations) with its failure to mention commons of fishery. He turns to 'later documents', including Halsbury's *Laws of England*, to reason that many of the local resources of fish must have been contained in customary rights of manorial copy holders, freeholders and town burgesses, as is mentioned in documents of 1086, 1235, 1285 and the fourteenth century.[14] McDonnell's glimpses are few, but they are more numerous than are what is available elsewhere. The paucity of his examples is compatible with two contending views: (1) that fisheries held in common were widespread but taken for granted and thus almost never mentioned and (2) that they were very rare.

Turning from England to the Continent,[15] scattered evidence suggests that in the early Middle Ages villages and other corporate communities did hold

[13] Halsbury's Laws of England, 4th edn, vol. 6, para. 582, citing *Ward v. Creswell* (1741), Willes 265. Domesday mentions fisheries 'belonging to' villeins, but with no clarification. It lists scores of fisheries, probably ones with a fixed weir, probably private, and probably rendering a rent. See Darby 1977, pp. 66 and 279–86.

[14] McDonnell 1981, p. 13.

[15] Summarized from European sources by Professor Richard Hoffman, York University, Toronto (personal correspondence, 31 October 1988).

collective fishing rights. These often (perhaps usually) stemmed from a royal right comparable to that claimed over certain minerals. According to Richard Hoffman, these regalian rights were the basis not only of grants to persons and communities, but also of royal and princely orders and regulations issued in the fifteenth and sixteenth centuries.

Comparing late medieval English sources with those from the Continent, I am of the opinion that, on English rivers, the common of fishery had once been widespread but died out—a process that probably accounts for the imprecision of modern legal references to commons of fishery in England. Commons of fishery may have been frequent, as customary arrangements (or tolerances), in the *early* middle ages; however, as in Europe so in England, trade and the increasing market value of fish led to steady lordly repossession. As fish eventually took on a higher cash value than what would have allowed mass public consumption, landlords recaptured rights to their local wild fisheries and often granted them to outsiders such as fish merchants to manage new pond fisheries and hatcheries. Common fisheries were squeezed out or made subject (by lease or by ordnance) to regulation of species and gear, often with tenants providing forced labour (or paying a comparable rent called 'fishsilver') to maintain the lords' weirs.[16]

By the eighteenth century the commons of fishery had essentially disappeared and the several fishery had taken its place. The original commons arrangement became rare enough to have had no impact on the modern law of fisheries, either in fresh water or at sea.

TIDAL AND OCEAN FISHING RIGHTS

There had evidently been a system of private rights to fish in tidal waters, or perhaps a public right with exceptions, before the Norman Conquest.[17] Whatever the details and origin of this earlier system, it was assimilated into the Norman system of feudal land grants, in which the general presumption held that the soil beneath tidal waters adjoining land was capable of ownership, as was the fishery over this soil, and that the owner might exclude the public. That is, it was decided early on that, like all the lands and water of England, fishing rights belonged, or had belonged, to the Crown.[18]

This decision, taken as it was after the process of subinfeudation had begun, led to the related question of current ownership: which classes of submerged

[16] Hoffman has summarized information on 165 Polish ponds built before 1475. Eighty per cent of the rights had been sold to townspeople for rents that exceeded those of the local village.

[17] See the discussion in *Attorney-General (B.C.) v. Attorney-General (Canada)* (1914), A.C. 153 at 170.

[18] Moore and Moore, 1908, x/iii and x/iv, following an extensive essay on the subject, show that as early as the Domesday Book 1086, the ownership of some several fisheries in tidal waters could have carried over from pre-Norman times, but most were probably granted by the conqueror and his followers. See also Domesday, p. 1.

lands and fisheries the Crown had and would continue to grant automatically in a parcel with adjoining riparian or coastal lands, and which it must grant separately. The general legal tendency was to discard depth and navigability as criteria. Tidal action was all that mattered. As a result, the Roman-law practice discussed in Chapter 3 was not followed: no distinction was made between the soils, fisheries, and waters within the tidal portions of rivers, their estuaries, and the areas in and outside bays and inlets. Where any body of water was tidal, its fisheries did not go with the adjoining lands but remained with the Crown until explicitly granted to private owners.

MAGNA CARTA, CHAPTER 33

Evidently the Crown in the eleventh and twelfth centuries actively granted these tidal 'lands' as severed fisheries, most likely to large-scale consumers such as abbeys, as well as to merchants in the fish trade. These royal grants usurped the right of riparian landowners who might otherwise have been able to sell or lease the 'lands' or the fishing rights on them as they could forest or mining rights. This may be why, in the charters of London of 1196 and 1199, the Crown agreed not to grant fisheries[19]—a concession that would have protected (or restored) the market position of the local landowners.

To extend this protection to the rest of England, such landlords and their commercial tenants would have supported the barons, who were planning to confront the king over his vigorous use of his royal powers in levying taxes and in squeezing the users of the Royal forests. As a result, in Chapter 33 of Magna Carta 1215 the king undertook to prohibit the granting of rights to install *kydelli* in certain tidal waters: 'Henceforth all fish-weirs shall be completely removed from the Thames and Medway and throughout all England, except upon the sea coast.'[20] King John's agreement to this was repeated by Henry III in the revised charter of 1225. It was gradually generalized by the courts, first to become a royal undertaking not to grant a right to fish with *any* gear (not just fixed gear) and, second, to see that this prohibition applied in *all* rivers and, hence, all tidal waters, including coastal waters. In a third, fundamental, step, the Crown's obligation to refrain from granting fishing rights became the doctrine that denied all modern claims to private ownership of fishing rights in tidal waters. At least in English common law this denial became a positive obligation to protect and enforce today's public right of fishing.

Thus from the Norman Crown's claim to the original ownership of lands, waters and fisheries was subtracted a public right of fishing. This may have been regarded as a return to an older public right believed to have existed in

[19] Holt 1992, p. 57.

[20] MacGrady 1975, p. 554, citing the translation of J. Holt. Also see ch. 23 for a further possible provision on angling or sport fishing and the threat to navigation, and McKechnie 1913, pp. 299–304. For photographs and descriptions of modern kydelli in Wales, see Jenkins 1974, chs. 2 & 3.

Roman and Continental law, or perhaps to the practice in some Saxon kingdoms. If Chapter 33 of the Magna Carta did benefit the barons economically, it was not for long; ironically it soon also barred *them* from installing or granting weirs. Much of their control over shore fisheries disappeared. Furthermore, it seems that Magna Carta triggered an economic transformation: English fishers turned from supplying seafood by means of fixed gear to supplying it from small boats, most of which owed allegiance (and rents) to no one.

The available literature suggests that the arrival in England of a public right of fishing predated its arrival elsewhere in Europe, in law and in practice. Modern commentators on Magna Carta are more interested in Chapter 23's opening up the rivers to inland navigation than in Chapter 33's opening up tidal fisheries to everyone. In these commentators' view, the tidal rivers were like the King's highway and Magna Carta was a statute that guaranteed that it must be kept open.[21] In any case, common-law private rights of fishing are found only on fresh-water streams.

The impact of international law on individual fishing rights

In this subpart, we briefly take note of early 'international law' as a source of limitations on the wide-open public right of fishing in tidal water.[22] Later, we will see how the modern international law of the sea developed from these medieval and early-modern notions of sovereignty and international common access.

ROMAN AND MEDIEVAL

The western nations' concept of a common fishery in the seas of the world goes back to the Romans. Looking outward over the Mediterranean, the Romans held the sea was *res communis*, common to all persons both in ownership and use.[23] This included a state's coastline—defined as the extent to which winter tides could reach, as measured from the sea—free access to which for fishing purposes was placed in the *ius gentium* (the body of rules everywhere observed).

For centuries after the decline of Rome's Western Empire, the nations of Continental Europe clung to these concepts. Indeed, the notion of a common right to fish in the sea went unchallenged in Europe from the sixth century to

[21] Indeed, modern decisions in England suggest that, in the common law stemming from Magna Carta, a tidal river is open to all public uses, including navigation and fishing. A non-tidal river is open only to public navigation, if it is in fact navigable. Thus there is only a private right of fishing (in common law) on fresh-water streams. See *Dougleston Manor v. Bahrakis*, 89 N.Y. 2d 472 (1997).

[22] My earlier views on this subject may be found in Scott 1964; and Christy and Scott 1965.

[23] Book 8, 1st Title of the Institutes of Justinian. See also Fenn 1926, p. 23. The concept of individual ownership of the sea was introduced by Paulus in the first century AD, but it was not reconsidered for some centuries.

the twelfth century AD. However, along the way there developed the suggestion that a personal right to fish in public waters could arise through prescription, basically as a non-transferable extension or refinement of a fisher's public right. The suggestion—understood as the right of a monarch to impose a servitude on the sea—was developed further in feudal courts by the glossators, scholars who provided commentary and interpretation of Roman law in order to adapt it to Dark Age conditions. With the arrival of the twelfth century continental Europe (whose monarchs, recall, were not constrained yet by their own *Magna Cartas*) saw an upsurge in the number of royal grants of public fisheries to private bodies. On fresh-water streams, these grants reflected the royal right to dispose of the use at will, which was probably tied to ownership of the soil. At sea, the European monarch did not hold the soil but, at best, title to the fisheries, meaning the places where the fish were caught.[24] Such developments, which had geographical limits, tended to merge the right of fishery with real property concepts, a tendency to work personal status into land tenures that is found elsewhere in feudal law.

In England, throughout the period leading up to and following *Magna Carta*, fishers felt no domestic restraint on the extent to which they could explore and exploit the world's fish stocks. Emerging rights developed in an environment without scarcity. Foreign claimants did frequently 'intrude' on fishing grounds. Attempts to exclude them would have been motivated by attempts to monopolize particular local fish markets and perhaps by attempts to safeguard (or prevent) navigation, rather than by claims to sovereignty over territory or fisheries at sea. Claims to territory first appeared in the fourteenth century, with the development of Italian jurisconsult Bartolus' legal theory of the adjacent sea (*mare adjacens*) which assigned police power to a state over its adjacent sea. Under this theory state authority might be exercised over the inshore fishery mainly as a means of assisting coastal trade. It was the logical predecessor of the disputed doctrines presented two centuries later by the jurists Hugo Grotius for Holland and John Selden for England. Their debate was to shape the future of international law regarding the sea and its resources.

The right of fishing in the sea had limited significance to the larger scheme of geographical control desired by Europe's powers in the sixteenth and seventeenth centuries. Denmark claimed a sweeping monopoly over northern waters; in 1493 Spain and Portugal were each 'granted', by special papal edict, one-half of the world via a division of the Atlantic Ocean (the eastern Atlantic went to Portugal and the western Atlantic went to Spain). Britain, Holland and France wrestled for rights over the North Sea and the north-eastern Atlantic Ocean. Sometimes their claims also included a right to license

[24] For examples, see Fenn 1926, p. 53 where he describes the earliest known grant of a fishery in perpetuity (from Charlemagne to an unnamed monastery in the Rhine).

or to exclude foreign fleets from fishing grounds that served profitable markets.[25] In such ways did international law limit the public right of fishing.

These national pretensions were diminished when Britain, Holland and France, singly and together, rejected the Spanish and Portuguese overseas claims and set about defining rights for themselves. Grotius, on behalf of Holland, published his *Mare Liberum* (1609), a scholarly attack on the entire idea of a nation owning or having sovereignty over the sea, based largely on the concept of freedom to trade under contract. (Grotius' work served Dutch desires to gain access to England's coastal fisheries and markets and to secure its eastern trade routes.)

In rebuttal, the English Privy Council proclaimed that no unlicensed foreigner could fish in English seas without paying. The erudite Selden responded to Grotius on the scholarly level, insisting in his *Mare Clausum* (1614) that the sea could be appropriated through law and custom. English sovereignty in territorial waters was based on long and continuous possession.

Under the pressure of naval war, the Netherlands eventually yielded to much of the English case and conceded that every country could take possession of its coastal waters. Grotius formalized the territorial concession in his *De Jure Belli et Pacis* (1625), but he continued to maintain that the high seas were free to all. Indeed, Grotius's assumptions and arguments concerning the high seas amounted to an economic theory of exclusive property (and so sovereignty), suggesting two conditions for its existence: appropriability (enforceability) and exhaustibility (scarcity). First, a nation could not and should not try to appropriate territory in the high seas to the exclusion of others, for the ocean is infinite and, thus, appropriation or enclosure would be unacceptably costly. Second, a nation (and the global society) could not benefit from enclosing the high seas, for high seas resources were inexhaustible. Without scarcity a nation's fishers and consumers could not gain from excluding foreigners. Many political economists and legal scholars have since built upon Grotius' approach. John Umbeck's 1981 study of the property rights of California gold-rush miners (encountered in Chapter 6) makes use of a trade-off between enforcement and value of rights to the gold in a claim. Given Grotius' acceptance that these two arguments did not apply to coastal resources (and the similar distinction made in the Continental theory of *Dominium Maris*),[26] a central question became how to define the width of the territorial sea and

[25] Revenue from licensing was not trivial. 'The Emperor of Russia, the Kings of Denmark and Sweden, the Duke of Medina, and the Princes of Italy all derived great revenues from the taxation of fishermen fishing on the high seas off their coasts.' Elder 1912, p. 5, quoting Cal. S. P. Dom. Car. II vol. 339, pp. 1–5.

[26] Dominium Maris considered the interest of a state in territorial waters to be similar to that of a property owner (Fenn 1926, p. 213). This concept has remained central to international law, and it represents the last link in the chain of development from Roman law's freedom of the seas. Interestingly, Grotius accepted that fish, while abundant, might be exhaustible.

whether its boundaries should be uniform. Selden was silent on the subject. Grotius's first argument suggested the so-called 'gunshot rule', later very popular as an explanation of the three-mile limit.

Much of the development of the international law on fishing rights was merely incidental to the naval and commercial principles of freedom of the high seas and to the emergence of territorial and navigation rights, supplemented by the Stuart kings' concern, under pressure from English and Scottish fishers, to protect their home industry from the huge Dutch herring fleet. Further development occurred between the late seventeenth and early nineteenth centuries, with the birth of concepts such as inland waters, straight closing lines across bays, and related refinements of the idea of a territorial sea. Offshore fishing became free in waters beyond any state's jurisdiction, each vessel remaining subject to its own nation's laws. Under this 'freedom of the seas' doctrine, European vessels crossed the ocean in search of the cod fisheries and later circled the globe in pursuit of whale and seal fisheries. The high seas were *res nullius*: beyond the domain where a person could be granted any monopoly or right or licence that would be valid against anyone except his own countrymen.

FISHERIES AS THE SUBJECT OF TREATY MAKING

The rights of fishers from particular countries were also much affected by, and sometimes influential in the drafting of, the series of peace and boundary treaties that settled disputes such as those in the northwest Atlantic Ocean (i.e., Newfoundland and the Gulf of St Lawrence) between France, Britain and the new United States. Portions of the North Sea, the Baltic and the Mediterranean were also assigned and re-assigned.[27] Each nation sought access to certain foreign shores and/or fisheries for its own fleet and to close access to its own shores. But, with the possible exception of James I's war with Holland over Dutch access to Scotland's fish, wars were rarely declared over fishing issues, and one suspects that some of the periodic reallotments of fishing grounds, ports and shores were pushed through by diplomats whose knowledge of the differing goals of interest groups was far from complete.[28]

Most fisheries seemed endlessly prolific.[29] The number of fishers that sailed to distant waters was limited only by the extent or access to foreign markets. Consequently, vessel owners were concerned not only about their transport

[27] See Cushing 1988, ch. 4 for an account of the shifting medieval herring fishery in the North Sea, and Hey 1986, p. 81 for an account of Scarborough herring fishers ranging north to Iceland in the fifteenth century (citing Heath 1968).

[28] On the endless seventeenth and eighteenth-century politicking within the English camp concerning rights to bait, to lobsters, and to shore access to Newfoundland, see Thompson 1961, pp. 1–47.

[29] This statement may appear to be contradicted by the failure of the herring fishery off south Sweden in the early sixteenth century. However, the theory was that the herring merely moved elsewhere (Heaton 1936, pp. 149 and 256).

and preservation costs but also about getting themselves into grounds close to good markets. They sought access to certain shores where boats could be repaired and fish salted and smoked.[30] In response, some coastal states were forced to concede extra-territorial rights to fish their inland and territorial waters and shores as well as rights to land to purchase supplies, repair nets, and process and trade the catch.[31] For example, from 1713 to 1904, though hounded out of territorial claims around Newfoundland, France doggedly retained rights on the west coast's 'French shore'. And, during various periods after 1776, fishers from New England had shore rights along the so-called 'American shore'.

At least until late in the nineteenth century, the drafters of the fisheries clauses of bilateral treaties were apparently oblivious to the possibility that the fish stocks in disputed fisheries were exhaustible. When their governments began making laws to protect fish at home, the diplomats did not insert provisions that recognized a multinational need to protect certain fisheries by regulating the harvesting. Some governments reasoned that, because it was difficult to enforce fish conservation regulation at home when the same fishery was exploited by foreigners without regulation, the first conservation priority should be to evict foreigners–an approach that Thompson (1961) sees as defining the English–French rivalry over the nineteenth-century lobster fishery. It was not until the twentieth century that the makers of international law became seriously concerned with conservation, and the general law of the sea applying to all nations more clearly differentiated from bilateral treaties intended to protect shared fish stocks. I return to this subject later.

How to relate the developments in the international law of the seas to those in pre-twentieth-century private or individual rights? Because the issue under debate in international law was the position of the ocean boundary of the nation state, one might have expected private property law to have been affected as during the medieval, or 'primitive', period of international law. But the two were rarely connected. When Grotius and his contemporaries ushered in the 'classical' period they tended to ignore the various doctrines and concepts of domestic law.[32] Grotius' treatment made no distinction between the sovereign's right to the fishing in bays and his subjects' rights, if any, to the fishing adjoining their private lands. On the contrary, as would other scholars of international law for the next four hundred years, he pronounced on the open sea and, implicitly, on its boundaries with no reference to individual rights. This lack of attention to fishing rules is surprising, for Grotius and his followers had taken pains to understand the high-seas rules of private mercantile trading and of whaling.

[30] Thompson 1961, p. 10.
[31] Innis 1954 for specific references.
[32] Brierley 1963, p. 30.

Medieval demand and supply fail to produce exclusivity

While the inland fishery right continued to develop, the idea of an individual ocean fishery right remained in limbo in England and in common law for the 500 years following *Magna Carta*. We will see that, although the potential sources of supply for a new property right were not promising, the real obstacle was on the demand side: fishermen, not needing greater exclusivity, did not raise a demand for it.

The demand side

In theory, fishermen demanded an individual property right in order to benefit from property's five characteristics:[33] *quality of title*, best conceived of as the negative of the market's estimation of the likelihood that the holder would be deprived of the power to manage, alienate or take income from his property; *transferability*, which provided incentive to enhance a fishery beyond the period in which the holder intends to fish; *divisibility*, under which the quantity of fish landed, the hours of fishing or the area of the right may be divided and disposed of; *duration*, which gave the right holder time to profitably invest in fish stock, fishing capital or management arrangements; and *exclusivity*, measured by the inverse of the number of other fishers with whom a right-holder must contract in order to internalize the management of the fishery.

Exclusivity is the subject of what follows. As a number, it varied continuously from a right of high-seas open access (zero) to fish-pond sole ownership (infinite). The typical fisher's right lacked not only exclusivity in the right to harvest but also to occupy the space within the fishing ground and thereby to avoid externalities or 'diseconomies' from other users. Thus, to the extent there was a demand for any property-right characteristic it was almost always for exclusivity. Until this characteristic was provided, the others were irrelevant.

THE DEMSETZ OR 'NAIVE' APPROACH

In thinking of an effective demand for exclusivity in a property right over a fishery we may follow Harold Demsetz's (1967) approach.[34] Demsetz imagined the demander as acquiring an exclusive property right by forcibly excluding or ejecting other users. He did not make much distinction between the cost of gaining the right to expel other users and of enforcing their exclusion, i.e. between what I have defined as top-level and mid-level transactions costs.

[33] The sixth characteristic, flexibility, I ignore until the section on ITQs.

[34] Demsetz 1967. See also the survey in Eggertsson 1990, pp. 248–80; and development of the cost-of-exclusion idea in Lueck 1989 and Allen 1991. Becker 1977, ch. 5 treats Demsetz's exposition of the demand for property as a justification for the existence of private property.

Medieval fishers would not be creating property by physically excluding others; rather, they would be starting with a primitive public-use right to which they would seek to add exclusivity and other characteristics. Making these additions would likely entail top-level transactions costs. Political lobbying costs would be the modern equivalent.

While the reader of Demsetz will look for that single event that 'raises' the right to use the resource to the status of a property right, I look for incremental accretions spread over time and, eventually, across all property-right characteristics. Progress toward a better property right would be strong whenever the expected benefits increased and slow when the required transactions costs made the net gain from exclusivity less attractive.

EXPECTED BENEFITS FROM EXCLUSIVITY

I believe that, in the four-hundred-year period between 1400 and 1800, the net benefits to be expected from the appearance of an exclusive property right to an ocean fishery were few. From the early, pre-1215, right to place fixed gear and obstructions in (mainly inshore) tidal waters, the technology of sea-fishing changed over the later medieval and early modern period to offshore and distant-water operations that relied upon ships and boats to carry the gear to fish located in the Baltic, the North Atlantic, the North Sea and Newfoundland. This new technology reduced the rents of the river lands and greatly increased the opportunities of the ocean vessel owners in the seaports, the sea-fishers and those upon whom they relied to ship fish to markets inland and abroad.

These parties therefore should have emerged as relatively wealthy demanders of an exclusive, individual standard property right analogous to that held by landlords and farmers: either a profit-à-prendre (somewhat like the old fixed-gear area right or a modern oil field right) or a territorial right. Combinations of these alternatives could also be devised; however, none of them would have justified the costs they entailed. For medieval governments and society were not capable of protecting the exclusivity elements in these rights at sea. The lack of viable enforcement was common knowledge. It had informed medieval legal decisions and statutes that had explicitly avoided assigning rights over wild animals, birds, underground waters or fish in streams due to the impossibly high transactions costs involved in enforcing them. What rights existed were generally made incidental to an interest in land (and, it may be added, placed under the surveillance of the holder of such an interest).[35] On the profit- or rent-earning side, the assumed inexhaustibility

[35] In law, and in the places I use the term in this book, 'incidental' means 'attached to'. Historically, incidents were not personal privileges; each was attached to a kind of land tenure. In Chapter 8, for instance, we will see the courts attempting to attach incidental rights to the mineral estate.

of the stock meant that an exclusive individual right was clearly not advantageous unless it included excluding others from the spot where one liked to fish, or the place where one docked, or one's *market*.

One exception to this general rule was the creation of monopolies. During the age of mercantilism the fact that the king had conceded a general public right did not prevent rent-seekers and supplicants of various kinds from attempting to exclude others from a fishery so as to control its catch and to monopolize its market. For example, in 1572 Humphrey Gilbert received a monopoly of the Newfoundland fishery.[36] In 1630 a group in London sought and may have acquired a monopoly over the pilchard fishery southwest of Ireland.[37] Between 1632 and 1670 three charters for large fishing and trading monopolies were granted, on the understanding that the monopolists would raise capital, to match the challenges of the Dutch fleets off British coasts in various markets. None of these ambitious monopolies succeeded.[38] But at the local level fishing laws, monopolies statutes and simple royal charters often had the effect of reducing local competition and closing local fisheries *and* markets to outsiders.

Promoters of these 'rights' usually wanted to protect an existing group of fishers, buyers or merchants against outsiders. They sought to work upstream and downstream: to limit access to the fishery and fish market for all but their own vessels and catches. The existence of their restrictions shows that absolute open access did give rise to some restlessness in the fishing industry. But as the demand for monopolies can occur within almost any market, its appearance in the fishery does not really reveal a wide interest in creating an exclusive fishing right for any fish stock, with the exceptions of salmon and shellfish, which are discussed below.

EVIDENCE FROM MEDIEVAL EUROPE

I have already pointed out that Europe did not follow England in creating a public tidal-water fishing right. More detailed information pertaining to fishing rights along the coasts of medieval Europe is scanty. Compared to European inland and beach fishing, which I have already discussed, European fishing from boats had been, until the sixteenth and seventeenth centuries,

[36] Gilbert sought primarily to exploit Newfoundland but he also became the fishery proprietor. See Lounsbury 1934, pp. 19–54; Thompson 1961, p. 8; Cushing 1993, pp. 53–76, for subsequent events. Braudel 1979 surveys the sixteenth and seventeenth-century markets for Newfoundland cod in France.

[37] Elder 1912, p. 6, citing MSS in the Edinburgh Advocates' Library.

[38] Under Charles I, the famous Association for Fishing received a monopoly of the fish around the Scottish Isle of Lewis from 1632 to 1640. This company was reborn in 1661, when Charles II granted it rights in English waters. Another offspring was set up in Scotland in 1670. In addition to their charters, all monopolies received some protection from navigation acts and from royal claims to a territorial sea. Though all failed to become active fishing companies, the one established in 1750 did collect royalties from independent fishers. See Elder 1912, passim; Langford 1989, p. 178; and Scott 1951, vol. 2, p. 378.

still a minor activity. It was usually prosecuted for part of each year by smallholders or farmer-fishers and by foreigners who had crossed the open sea.[39] The main gear was the hand-line. There was no trawling or long-lining, although the ancestor of the modern drift net may have been used. Limited by this range of gear, both locals and foreigners are described as having remained within sight of land. There were other factors too: the usefulness of mountains for identifying fishing grounds, the threat of pirates and the seasonal concentration of cod in shallow water—all these contributed to persuading most fishers not to stray far from bays and visible landmarks, a tradition that prevailed in most nations into the eighteenth century.[40]

Thus it should not be presumed that the powers of private owners to grant exclusive fishing rights were unimportant in Europe. They held, and could monitor and enforce fishing rights along, the territories and littorals stretching seaward off their coastal properties. In some places these fishing rights may have been absolute and permanent, and may have included the floor of the sea, the water itself and the swimming fish. Indeed, some such medieval arrangements have survived. Rough private litright still existed in Norway's Lofoten Islands in 1816, when they were surveyed and rationalized.[41] In Finland today some shore owners' private ownerships still stretch across the strait to adjoining islands, from which government-licensed fishers are excluded—a vestige of an arrangement once typical of northern Europe and preserved by Finland's century under Russian legal control.

However strong, though, the European lords' rights over their littoral strips could not continue out beyond the high-seas claims of their kings and princes. We know more about the claims and rights of the kings than about those of their subjects. British kings and queens from Edward III to Charles I licensed Dutch and other fishers to fish in British waters, while Mary actually leased a whole fishing ground off the north Irish coast to foreigners. Thus, they followed the kings, princes and dukes of Russia, Denmark and Sweden as well as the dukes and princes of Medina in Italy, who in 1633 were said to have 'taxed' the fishers using the high seas off their coasts.[42] It is unclear who, if anyone,

[39] The information on medieval salt-water fishing is limited, but on technology it is better (for a review, see Cushing 1993, ch. 1). On the local fishery, especially for herring, see Coull 1993, pp. 33–4.

[40] See Michel Mollat du Jourdin 1993, p. 143. Citing Henri Touchard, Mollat says that fishers in Brittany did not adopt offshore fishing techniques until the fourteenth century. Even the Vikings are known to have sailed in sight of land to the extent possible. When, in the fifteenth century, the English sailed to Iceland, they did not fish en route but only after they had arrived. In the sixteenth century, in the English and French dry-fish fishery in Newfoundland, some crews dwelt onshore and fished nearby in small boats. See Lounsbury 1834, pp. 55–9 and 249–50. Thanks to Ragnar Arnason and Rognvaldur Hannesson for discussions of inshore fishing by foreign fleets.

[41] In 1857 they were assembled and turned into open-access fishing places for specific gear types. This had happened earlier, between 1800 and 1815, in other parts of northern Europe. See Mead 1958, p. 188 on Norway.

[42] Elder 1912, p. 5.

had the power to permit larger vessels to go on fishing expeditions across the sea. In the sixteenth-century Portuguese and Basque vessels ventured to Ireland, Iceland and Newfoundland, while Dutch, French and Hanseatic vessels had long roamed the North Sea and the North Atlantic, seeking cod and herring.[43] If the local capitalist owners of these vessels needed to hold rights granted by some authority or owner, they did not need exclusivity in those rights, for there was no scarcity of fish at sea. They chiefly valued permits or charters for providing access to otherwise closed or monopolized markets.

Eventually, French seamen did get a formal public right of fishing. It appears that French landowners kept their feudal powers over both people and resources well into the seventeenth century (at least formally, for enforcement must have been difficult). This legal regime is said to have been brought to an end by Louis XIV's minister Colbert, who was bent on expanding the French navy. In order to create a national corps of trained naval seamen he reasoned that France needed an expanded sea fishery. For this, open access would be essential.

France's new public right could be seen as restoring the Roman *res nullius* category to the open sea, with the *res gentium* category applying only to internal waters. Gradually, a public right spread to other European countries, though the extent and timing of its progress is still unclear. What *is* clear is that, while English fishers may conceivably have begun to articulate a demand for a more exclusive right (if only for commercial and marketing reasons), fishers and boat owners in France and the rest of northern Europe were still tied up in feudal concepts of landowner control. Far from seeking an exclusive individual right, they sought more freedom.

The supply side

If and when the medieval fishermen exercised a demand to replace the public right of fishing with a more exclusive standard right they would have had recourse to four different medieval sources, the first two of which may be regarded as local, the second two as national.

LOCAL SOURCES: CUSTOM

Access arrangements recognized or created by local custom generally came to be enforced in the royal courts. Thus we should not be surprised to find that fishers recognized the powers and rights not only of kings and princes but also of lesser proprietors. Indeed it is startling to learn that, as late as 1633, in the western parts of England, 'it was the custom for pilchard fishers to pay a tithe of their catch as tribute to the lords of the manors next the coast'.[44] Centuries

[43] Unger 1980, p. 257.

[44] Elder 1911, p. 5. His authority is 'A collection of divers particulars touching the King's Dominions and Sovereignty [sic] in ye Fishing as well in Scotland as in the British Ocean, presented April, 1644. Chronicon Malmsbury, John Haywood', Cal. S. P. Dom. Car. II, vol. 339, 1–5.

after *Magna Carta*, the rights of the landowner to grant fishing rights over the littoral had, owing solely to the strength of custom, survived—though whether to the benefit of the lords or the independent vessel owners is unclear. Modern research has shown that many years later, European fishers and whalers, reaching far out from their home ports, made some explicit (albeit customary) rules that, by precisely defining the law of capture, ended disorder on the distant fishing grounds. But this research does not show any trace of the procedures by which the earlier open entry, or public right of fishing, had been challenged.[45]

FORCE

No doubt force and coercion played some role in the early medieval allotment of fishing and market access. Generally, though, violence and invasion of rights took place only on an international scale. As between countrymen or with regard to trespass by foreigners on inland waters, rights obtained by force existed for the duration of their period of enforcement. Precisely because they arose from forceful occupation, it was unlikely that the courts would allow them to ripen into common-law prescriptive rights.

NATIONAL SOURCES: LITIGATION

Lawcourt activity, confined to inland fisheries, included some rough-and-ready methods to preserve vulnerable and migratory species like eel, sturgeon and salmon, as well as a body of law to resolve more typical disputes between inland fishers. Interfering with vessels in coastal fisheries attracted none of this legal activity. As there was a public right of fishing in tidal waters, there could be no basis for conflicting private claims. A vessel that sought an exclusive freedom from crowded fishing grounds had nothing to take before the courts. Thus, after *Magna Carta* the common-law litigation process did almost nothing to shape a private fishing right in salt water.

GOVERNMENT AND LEGISLATION

Those who wanted a new and more exclusive right could appeal to the Crown to create one. King and government responded occasionally by creating some local monopolies and a very few territorial rights in shallow coastal waters. These few mercantilist actions may, however, have been unenforced window-dressing. In general, government was silent on domestic fishing rights in tidal waters.

[45] The authority (as is often the case) is Ellickson 1991, pp. 184–206. To show that neighbours settle disputes following customary norms, rather than formal legal rules, he examined early modern whaling. Nowhere, I believe, does he suggest that individual fishers were ever able to rely on custom to 'build fences' between themselves.

Comment on supply

In all, I believe the inactivity of these four potentially active, even competitive, potential suppliers of changes in medieval sea fishery property rights is to be explained by the weak demand among medieval fishermen. While common-law courts could not act under Magna Carta's elimination of a legally recognized individual right of fishing, paths were available through tort law or the Court of Equity. Similar obstacles had been overcome in the courts, as seen in Chapter 3 on water rights. The medieval courts did not start on those paths because demanders gave them no occasion to do so. As for government inaction, some vocal fishery interests sought protection from international or commercial interference. Over the centuries governments showed they could respond to such demands with military, naval and diplomatic activity. But they did not apparently hear of a corresponding need for a medieval ocean fishing right with the exclusivity characteristic.

The nineteenth century and political intervention

Recognition of a fisheries 'problem'

Largely unmodified and free of government interference, the public right of fishing survived through the eighteenth century.[46] Even by the early nineteenth century the British parliament had not yet been made aware by fishing interests that open-access fishing presented a 'problem'. Indeed, one source of fisher complaint was the non-totality of open access. Wars and their peace treaties had determined who might have rights to the best fishing grounds. The resulting allocations were helpful to some fishers, damaging to others. Those who were excluded clamoured to be let back in.

Biological over-fishing was not yet recognized as a serious problem. Fishers everywhere shared real problems ranging from risk of injury to hard work, poor food, bad accommodation and low pay. In comparison to these everyday difficulties, the idea of depletion of some fish stocks produced little concern. It was known that certain inshore stocks had fallen; that the grounds periodically shifted; that some whales and seals were less plentiful; and that in some places stocks of oysters and of Atlantic salmon had actually failed. But these were the days of the frontier. Like North Americans, Europeans expected fields, trees, wildlife and minerals to disappear so that people could be 'getting on to something else'.

Of the world's really important pelagic and demersal fish stocks, there had been no recognized failure. The great fishing grounds of the North Sea and the

[46] Since my first essays on this subject, earlier scattered sources of information on catches, science and regulation have been impressively collected and rationalized for the general scholar by Cushing 1988.

Grand Banks did not seem depleted. Indeed, L. Z. Joncas, who attended the 1883 International Fisheries Exhibition in London on behalf of Canada, believed that they *could* not be depleted—at least on their feeding grounds (although perhaps they were vulnerable when they approached shore to spawn).[47] The influential economist Alfred Marshall agreed. Drawn into the question, he likened the supply of fish to a perennial stream where not even the new steam trawlers could run into diminishing returns. The sea is 'vast, and fish are very prolific; and some think that a practically unlimited supply can be drawn from the sea by man without appreciably affecting the numbers that remain there.'[48] Additionally, regulating access to the fishery would not solve the fishers' main problems—locating the stock and speeding the catch back to market.

A few forces did push in the direction of greater regulation. Fishers fretted about low or unpredictable prices. In some places the catches by new trawlers and seine nets were overwhelming traditional markets. Owners welcomed the idea of regulation that might prevent this over-supply. Paradoxically, however, some owners supported open access. Foreshadowing later conventional wisdom, they argued that over-fishing could result in smaller stocks and, thus, higher fishing costs. These higher costs would drive out new arrivals and cause price to rise again—an incomplete argument indeed!

Related to these strange arguments were those concerned with quality of the product and the price it could command. The Dutch herring combine of the seventeenth century had forced Dutch fishers to use large-mesh nets to land larger and more uniform herring. Thereby, Dutch pickled herring sold at a premium.

Fishers also disliked racing and congestion. Many of them suffered from overcrowded fishing grounds, ports, beaches and shore facilities, and some believed that this congestion caused declining catches: the vessels impeded each other. Regulation, such as the nineteenth-century banning of large seines to prevent one vessel's net from sweeping up a whole school to the detriment of competitors, could be an answer.

These two side-benefits of regulation, however, were over-balanced by fishermen's general and profound disbelief in the need to regulate in order to preserve stocks. Other observers, reflecting the classical economist's campaign against mercantilism, condemned any government regulation as illiberal. Laws passed between 1200 and 1842 (especially those restricting the use of

[47] See generally Joncas 1883 and Cushing 1988, p. 117. The leading scientific voice at the exhibition and elsewhere was that of T. H. Huxley. A few years earlier the US Congress had created the US Fisheries Commission (1871), sometimes seen as official recognition that the seas and the frontier were not inexhaustible. See McEvoy 1986, p. 101.

[48] Marshall 1920, pp. 166–7 went on to mention that others argued that some fisheries had been overworked and were falling off. He seems to have agreed with the optimistic position mentioned in the text. That there may have been steam-trawler over-fishing of some North Sea stocks was tentatively but officially recognized in Britain in 1893. See H. S. Gordon 1951.

salmon streams) were scrutinized for evidence that they had helped maintain the catch, and sometimes repealed.[49]

The emergence of demanders and suppliers of change in fishing rights

The nineteenth-century fishery was not a powerful political constituency. Lack of private ownership meant that there were no great landlords to wield power. The fishers themselves were rarely organized. Even within one country they were divided in many ways: they fished with different gear, from different ports, in different grounds, on different coasts, at different times and in different weather. Captains (vessel owners), crew and shore workers all had different information, methods and goals. To cap it all, captains and crews were not regarded in the common law as employees but as individual entrepreneurs and share-men, nominally separated by ownership and control from the companies and their workers' unions.

Thus, although fishers were skilled, reflective workers, often very articulate about their own problems, they did not easily organize for fisheries-oriented collective action.[50] When they did, it was, as Mancur Olson (1965) would predict, based on such problems as price or pay, perhaps augmented by common values such as race, location or family. In his 1984 worldwide survey, R. Hannesson found that fishers' organizations rarely participated in fisheries management.

A consolidated demand for individual rights appeared late in the nineteenth century when inshore and offshore catches began to change noticeably. Some herring, menhaden and mackerel stocks migrated for the first time in centuries. Worse, ground fish stocks of cod, haddock and plaice seemed to have declined. Looking for explanations, fishermen now became convinced that the cause of these upsetting events was the fish stocks' exposure to the new concerted fishing power of steam power, new nets and catching techniques and longer trip ranges from port. Fishermen were also disturbed by the 'industrialization' of many fisheries as wealthy and corporate investors such as Lever Brothers financed motor fleet expansion and took over processing and shore establishments. Deaf to intellectual voices for liberalism, they turned to government for relief. In our terms, confronted with a new scarcity of fish each sought exclusivity in his rights as protection against increasing spillover effects from other fishermen's operations.

Governments did not rush into a role as fisheries regulators. They were slowed down by their lack of knowledge about the impact of man on fish

[49] See Derham 1987, pp. 71–2 for the unusual view that regulation of fisheries was common.

[50] Opinions have differed about whether, across the globe, modern fishers as a group should be described as 'outspoken' or 'inarticulate'. Experts have used both terms in trying to explain why governments have difficulty understanding the fishers' point of view. See Thomson 1983, p. 33; and Shackleton 1986.

stocks; their adherence to the principles of laissez-faire;[51] the public right of fishing in tidal waters and the freedom of the high seas; and respect (especially in the United States) for an inviolable right to hunt or fish for subsistence. In America too regulations sometimes emerged merely as irritated responses to congestion or to conflict between gear types. To paraphrase McEvoy (1986), a government presented with a fishery problem would come under political pressure to fix the blame so that the legislature could eliminate the source: 'Just as Americans placed their faith in individual enterprise as an engine of social progress, they tended also to seek fault for social problems in individuals or identifiable groups. The fisher's suggestion for solving the fisher's problem, typically, is "burn every other... boat but mine."'[52]

Apparently such American state laws as did emerge to protect either fish or game in their fresh and boundary salt waters were never, or only briefly, enforced.[53] For instance, Lund (1980) notes that the right to sell fish was often granted to specific parties along certain rivers, giving them virtual monopolies within their area (though for commercial rather than conservation reasons). These grants were revoked when municipalities concluded that the enterprises' price-setting activities gave too much incentive to intensive fishing by individuals. As well, in many areas of the United States after the Revolutionary War, problems of damage or of ownership arose only with respect to inland fisheries, for which the law was an extension of the law governing wildlife. Inherited British law was not regarded as automatically applicable to a country where game was wild and plentiful, and where hunting and fishing for food was widespread. The colonies hated the class structure of the British hunting 'Black Laws', and this affected later attitudes to fishing laws. In this environment state and local governments evidently responded to local pressures with many highly specific, locally limited and often sporadically enforced fishery rules,[54] rather than with the systems that would later be adopted to comprehensively protect fish stocks.

[51] Gough 1993, pp. 13–14 mentions a nineteenth century reluctance to introduce licensing or leasing for sea fishing due to reasons of 'incentive'.

[52] McEvoy 1986, p. 102.

[53] This point is made explicitly by Tober 1973, pp. 7–54 but mostly with respect to deer and other game. It is implicit in other writers' historical chapters (e.g., see Christy 1964 on the Chesapeake Bay fishery and McEvoy 1986). The sources of information on early local fishing rules and general doctrine are very limited. Some, like Bean 1983 and Tober, are spread over both hunting and fishing laws. The sources for the United Kingdom and Canada are even rarer. See, for a start, Johnson 1981; Frankel 1969.

[54] I have found no author who describes these nineteenth-century state and local regulations as a group. Studies by Tober 1973 and Lund 1980, however, are suggestive. McEvoy 1986 mentions other states' laws in addition to California's. While many authors deal with or mention the fishery policies and actions of the federal government in the nineteenth century, this is not relevant to the states' regulation of nearly all stocks.

Two regulatory models: salmon and oyster rights

To be fair, nineteenth-century governments were presented with few models of rights or regulation in tidal waters. Among these, as suggested earlier, politicians could hardly distinguish between rules intended to protect a fishing group's monopoly and those intended to protect the fish stocks themselves.

SALMON PROTECTION

The first clear model in British jurisdictions was the salmon legislation of the 1860s. We can trace its antecedents almost back to Anglo-Saxon laws, when it appears there may have been a right of free fishing in some rivers and tidal estuaries, and to pre-Magna Carta rules that certain streams had to be kept clear of obstructions and the fishery closed on certain days. Provisions in the Magna Carta forbade not only the granting of fishing rights in tidal waters but also the obstructing of fresh-water navigable rivers (i.e. the obstructing of routes to salmon spawning grounds).[55] Soon a new series of statutes began regulating the obstruction of certain rivers and setting closed seasons. A 1393 statute of Richard II on this subject was still in force in 1861.

Salmon streams and closed seasons were a preoccupation in Scotland. According to Russell (1864):

> The commencement of Scottish law-making on this subject, indeed, was contemporary with anything like a settled order of affairs under Robert Bruce [1320], and continued to occupy an incredible share of the attention of Parliaments of his successors for several hundreds of years; so that, in reading the collections of ancient Scottish Statutes, one is apt to think that the chief thing which Scotland achieved on the field of Bannockburn was 'Acts anent the preservation of Salmonde'.[56]

Combined with the property rights of riparians and with the public right of fishing, Scottish and English laws created regimes of salmon rights and regulations lasting nearly 400 years. Seen through the eyes of the returning salmon, the regulations of the era divided streams into three stretches. As the fish entered the tidal portion of the stream, they were the prey of the 'public', using small nets and hand lines from the shore or small vessels. Fixed gear, though banned by Magna Carta, might also be encountered. The salmon that escaped beyond tidal waters encountered weirs and fixed gear of many kinds (as well as rod-and-line fishing) based on the lands of riparian owners and their merchant and recreational tenants.[57] In streams deemed not to be 'navigable'

[55] See Chitty 1812, p. 247; Russell 1864, p. 134; McKechie 1913, pp. 299–304; Howarth 1987, ch. 2. The clause dealing with tidal waters was quickly interpreted to create a public right of sea fishing. It could hardly have contributed to the conservation of salmon at sea.

[56] Russell 1864, p. 136. This flow of legislation died out after Union, to be replaced at Westminster by a flow of bills, many of them based on studies by Parliamentary committees. Almost none of them passed.

[57] By 'tenants', I mean the holders of rights of free fishery, common of fishery, and others. Some were customary, some had been granted by deed, and some were merely contractual.

the migrating fish were likely to find this second stretch very seriously obstructed. (Indeed, Parliament and common law both had permitted dams to be built even if they blocked all fish migration.) Salmon that penetrated higher to the third stretch of the river entered their spawning areas, where typically there were larger and fewer estates.

The residents, fishers and landowners associated with these three stretches of the river did not work together. Neither regulations nor rights proved enough to arrest the decline of English salmon stocks after the fifteenth or sixteenth centuries. Little was done until the nineteenth century when in 1861 a royal commission's report led to the Salmon Fishery Act. The commissioners suggested managing the river as a whole, each 'basin' (as we might now say) having its governing board responsible for removing obstacles to salmon migration, harmonizing the existing strategically chosen closed times, tackling pollution and enforcing the rules. Parliament's adoption of this act signalled that a common-law property-rights approach to assisting migratory salmon was being replaced by enforced systems of regulation.[58]

These English and Scottish regulatory instruments were adopted in other common-law countries—notably Canada, New Zealand and Australia. Reacting to the decline in salmon runs that began in Canada East in the 1840s,[59] the Canadian Confederation of 1867 shifted responsibility for salmon fisheries from local jurisdictions to the national government, prompting creation of a national fisheries act inspired by the British legislation. It called for some licensing and for the assembly of a national staff of officers to enforce regulations, some special to each stream or basin. Unlike the British approach, however, there were no local councils to make regulations and no specific licensing to help contain angling and netting in particular fishing places and streams.[60]

As for state regulation in the United States, information is extremely scattered. It seems doubtful that laws were much influenced by British salmon legislation. Laws in New England and California forbade fixed gear and set closed seasons for particular streams.[61] Along the East Coast there was a

Most of these were 'property rights' in land. Their existence is a reminder to modern advocates of the 'property-right solution' to the fishing problem that property institutions alone were not enough to save the English salmon; and that it was property, not government, that presided over the loss of the salmon stocks. Much modern writing on public access neglects the fact that there were, and are, some participants who do hold a property right of a kind. That is why it is useful, in policy making, to look past the mere existence of 'property' to discover what characteristics are not present in the rights held by property owners.

[58] For salmon law and its implementation in Wales, see Jenkins 1974, pp. 13–30.

[59] On French Canada, see Harris 1968, especially pp. 120–1. On law in Canada outside Quebec, see Lambert and Pross 1967; Dunfield 1985; Lyons 1969; Gregory and Barnes 1939; and Scott and Neher 1981 (relying on research by Alex Fraser).

[60] See Dunfield 1985, pp. 151–2. As well, the separate Sea Fisheries Regulation Act, 1888 (and 1903), set up some committees to regulate local non-salmon fisheries.

[61] See Gordon 1951.

general understanding of the salmon's reproductive and migratory cycles so that assisting escapement was a matter of distributing and enforcing rights. But on the West Coast it was not at first understood that Pacific salmon species reproduced in multi-year cycles and did *not* return to the sea after spawning. This rendered state regulation doubly ineffective.

There were a few areas of progress. In Britain, Canada and the US more headway was made in propagating salmon artificially than in protecting or managing the runs to which they were released. Also, exclusive property law was not altogether forsaken. Some new Canadian and American regimes, surprisingly, included the establishment of a few sole ownerships of smallish salmon streams. An 1859 California law assigned salmon-landing powers on the Eel River exclusively to riparian owners; and an 1880 Oregon law confirmed one capitalist's monopoly of the Rogue River.[62] Legislators must have been confused about whether they were being lobbied to set up monopolies or to establish and maintain regulatory regimes that would protect the fish.

OYSTER PROTECTION

A second tidal-waters model for regulation was oyster protection: based not primarily on government decrees and their enforcement but rather on individual participants in the fishery who developed their own version of a suitable property right, then turned to courts and legislatures to enhance and support it.

Sedentary and shellfish species such as oysters, clams, mussels and seaweed are dug, dredged or trapped in shallow water. In their wild state female oysters are fertilized by floating milt or sperm. Their fertilized eggs, or spat, drop to the bottom, attaching themselves in 'beds' to rocks or other hard objects from which they are dredged or raked by boats. There are strong interdependencies between adjoining beds, as the eggs and milt may float widely.

The natural oyster beds of Europe and North America were once immense. In southern England, the people in Roman towns may have depended on oysters.[63] Almost two thousand years later Atlantic oysters were still thriving. Oysters were an important product in Europe, and they became the main fishery product of New England in the nineteenth century. Earlier, in various places, including Scotland, oysters were designated as 'royal fish', a status that denied a public right of fishing for oysters and removed them from the application of some common law and statutory doctrines governing other shellfish and swimming fish. The value of oysters rose between the fourteenth and nineteenth centuries. Where beds of wild oysters were damaged or depleted, a specialized industry emerged to culture spat and to plant it in prepared beds or parks.

[62] See McEvoy 1986, p. 110; Higgs 1982; Cushing 1988, pp. 49–50.
[63] Appelbaum 1972, pp. 64 and 247.

Improving individual property rights to oysters

For an oyster enterprise to thrive required a property right with some exclusivity.[64] The chief impediment, of course, was the public right of fishing in tidal waters. The English courts generally allowed grants (and supposed grants) of fishery dating from before Magna Carta to be continued. The legal difficulties facing a would-be oyster proprietor stemmed not just from the public right of fishing but also from the law of capture.[65] As the seed, spat and oysters had not been 'reduced to possession', they could be likened to wild animals roaming over the land. There was an exception where oysters that had been gathered elsewhere were not 'growing' on the bed but were essentially being stored there. Attached to the land like timber, they were protected against 'stealing' by property law. In other places, the owners had seeded the oysters. But only in cases where the owner could show that she both owned rights to the space *and* had appropriated the shellfish—reduced them to possession as if they were in a pond—was her situation analogous to that of the owner of both the field and the cattle; simply having planted them herself was not enough.[66]

Such facts as whether the oysters were actually roaming or were attached to the soil were minutely examined in the various cases in England and Scotland. Even if a court found that the owner did have an exclusive right, the analogy to farming ownership was not complete, for she might then be faced with interference by persons entitled to make other uses of the space for navigation, waste-disposal or other fisheries. In short, despite centuries of demand in the form of litigation, the courts were unable to supply a general exclusive standard property right to an oyster bed beyond a few special cases.[67]

Consequently, demanders of a more robust, territorial farm right turned from the courts to the government. A first step had been taken in a 1602 enactment whereby oysters could be claimed as a fishery. They were defined as chattels or wild animals tamed, akin to farm livestock. Anyone taking oysters without authority would be poaching, a felony.[68] Tried out in various fishery jurisdictions, the rules under this criminal-law approach to ownership rights proved difficult to enforce. An 1808 statute of George III enabled the

[64] The next few pages deal with the chronology of oyster and salmon regulation and rights in Europe. Interestingly, a similar sequence of oyster (and scallop) regimes was observable in New Zealand, but began as late as 1977. See Arbuckle and Drummond 1999, p. 733.

[65] My survey here is very brief. A well-known survey is contained in the decision in *Attorney-General for British Columbia v. Attorney-General for Canada* [1914] A.C. 153.

[66] For more, see Coull 1993, p. 33, following Cutting 1955, pp. 18–24; and Howarth 1990, pp. 193–6.

[67] *Bagot v. Orr* (1801), 2 B. & S. 472. Note that some of the cases refer to modern multiple use, classified as 'coastal zone' management. See Miles et al. 1986; Miles and Geselbracht 1987; and Huppert 1982.

[68] 3 Jas. 1 c. 12. Later legislation and litigation laid down that the person charged or sued must have known that there was a private oyster fishery there. In general, a legal occupier of an oyster bed is entitled to maintain an action for trespass, irrespective of whether he owns or leases the soil. See *Foster v. Warblington* [1906] 1 K.B. 648 (C.A.).

owner to sue any party who knowingly took oysters or seed from his bed.[69] In the 1860s Parliament began writing a series of modern statutes for England and Scotland that created, extended and clarified property rights over shellfish by endowing them with the personal-property characteristics of rights over domestic animals.

These statutory rights over oyster beds rarely conveyed complete special exclusivity. Nevertheless, the policy of using them prevailed over general government oyster-bed regulation. In England, as in most countries, the synthesizing of statutory types of 'ownership' has allowed an oyster industry to survive in a few places. The best natural oyster beds, now public beaches or industrial sites, are lost as habitat. But in more secluded locations, where conflicting uses of the water space are at a minimum and where protection against theft is feasible, oyster culture in tidal waters can flourish.

Governments developed the various statutory systems of rights over a fishery in line with their contract-based disposal and management of Crown or public lands, in the form of oyster or shellfish leases or licences. In some cases politicians may have simply preferred creating such rights to inventing regulations. For instance, Scottish law created a special regalian status for oysters that differed from that for other shellfish.[70] German and French laws dating from the 1800s produced an array of private reserves, parks and leases for northern German and French oyster beds. While from the point of view of the holders these European tenures were not seen as being perfectly secure, they did improve on the judge-made arrangements of early England in providing some ownership-like exclusivity against the coastal landowner, adjoining municipalities and even fishers of other species.[71]

Oyster regulations supplant individual property rights

Leaving the property characteristics of oyster tenures, I turn to the demand for and supply of regulatory rules to deal directly with the depletion of oyster stocks. The first British supply response we know of came in a national law of 1577. There were also some local enactments. First a closed season was imposed: oyster beds were to be open only in the months without an 'R' in their names. Then, around 1600 a minimum size limit was imposed, as with salmon.

The demand for this kind of regulatory law may well have been derived more from concern about the quality and price of the marketed oyster than from concern to protect the species. And it may have come mostly from fishmongers, for in practice the closed season was usually most easily enforced by banning the selling of oysters at that time. The laws were only a modest start

[69] 48 Geo. 3 c. 144. The general tendency of the nineteenth-century common law, as it has travelled abroad, is well summarized in Seale and Thompson 1979.

[70] See discussions in Howarth 1990, pp. 196–8 and 222–6.

[71] Seale and Thompson 1979.

for they gave oyster beds no protection from predators, poaching, over-fishing, water pollution or damage by dredges and anchors. When salmon regulation was formalized in the 1860s, oyster regulation (by closures) was also modified as recommended in the 1861 commission report. Under the Sea Fisheries Act 1867 the government could make orders governing a particular oyster bed. In an effort to mix ownership with local regulatory control, these orders on size and season could be administered by a 'body' to which the site had been granted.[72] This body could also levy tolls and royalties, and it could seed and propagate the fishery. An 1888 act went further, allowing a local 'committee' to make by-laws regarding size and protective measures. Much of the legislation was concerned with protecting the group and its bed from other water users.

Since that time Britain has experimented with a number of regulations of the oyster fishery as well as with regulations to protect it from outsiders and, especially, from pollution. It also has grounds where the seeding is organized or even carried out by government—a type of policy followed intensively in Japan, and elsewhere for other species. New Zealand for example seeds scallops and collects a 'voluntary' levy from harvesters.[73]

WHY SALMON AND OYSTER REGIMES WERE MODELS FOR LATER FISHERY REGULATION

I have presented these details of regulations because many modern jurisdictional statutory regulations of ocean and inland fisheries have their origins in variants of British salmon regulation and oyster-bed ownership.

There are several reasons why salmon and oysters received earlier attention than other fish. First, both species were valuable enough to justify their protection and regulation costs. Second, they were well known to social classes who had litigation and lobbying power both in Britain and in the colonies. Third, many voters were people who enjoyed fishing for salmon and collecting oysters. Fourth, laymen could see oyster beds and observe their vulnerability (as is demonstrated in the *Walrus and the Carpenter*) and could literally observe the obstructions in salmon rivers.[74]

There was also the matter of necessity fathering invention. The visible migration of salmon made it clear that protecting them on the basis of small territorial property rights would not work. Regulation was therefore essential and, fortunately, feasible since salmon harvesting was more concentrated in time and place than most other types of wildlife and ocean fishes.[75] Salmon regulation therefore served as an early model for sea-fishery regulation.

[72] The 'body' could have a duration of sixty years. See Moore and Moore 1903, pp. 199–201.

[73] See Arbuckle and Drummond 1999, p. 374.

[74] Though white arrivals on the west coast of North America were slow to learn about the different migration paths and periods of species of Pacific salmon.

[75] This reason is extended by Johnsen 1986, p. 66 to explain why the southern Kwakiutl established property institutions while their inland neighbours did not.

Oysters, on the other hand, were known to be more sedentary than most other sea fish, making them more likely candidates for protection via an exclusive property right, fortified as necessary by regulation, as displayed in modern English legislation. And when the government did regulate oyster harvesting, a large part of both rule-making and enforcement was farmed out to local committees in small coastal districts, which may have taken responsibility for seeding the beds within their jurisdictions. While the law governing aquaculture in tidal waters has evolved from the law governing wild and cultivated shellfisheries, laws over oyster beds would not serve as a model until the advent of leases and ownership analogous to those in the public forests.

Learning about over-fishing

Early twentieth-century governments learned something about fisheries biology from observing salmon and oyster and the effectiveness of their regulation. But for truly effective regulation they needed similar information about demersal and pelagic ocean species. Ironically, this became available as a result of naval operations in the Great War. To the fishery scientist the importance of the First World War at sea was that it brought about a considerable and measurable reduction of fishing pressure and harvests for several years. Then, in peacetime, when full fishing pressure was resumed it created a more than proportionate increase in total catch and catch per unit of effort. These North Sea swings seemed to parallel hypotheses about declining catches per trip in the Pacific halibut fishery.

From this evidence, biologists surmised that a drastic decline in fishing would allow the fish stock to grow, age and increase its own annual yield. When a stock was heavily harvested, the fish in the population were reduced both in number and in average age and size, decreasing the population's capacity to produce an annual increment that could be steadily harvested. From a previous almost total lack of measurable data, the wartime natural experiment led to investigations showing to everyone that some ocean stocks could become, and were then becoming, dangerously small.

The results of this general biological process, slowly recognized,[76] were increasingly described as the 'over-fishing problem'. Biologists sought evidence of its magnitude and strove to distinguish between natural fluctuations and fishing-induced shortages. Mathematical theories of greater sophistication were developed. From this growing consensus emerged the first serious systematic efforts to regulate the fisheries in order to preserve stocks. I turn to them next.

[76] For the recognition of the stock problem, see Graham 1943; Walford 1958; and Cushing 1988, pp. 186–202.

Regulation gains approval

Pre-First World War fishing laws and controls, at first limited to salmon then extended to sport fishing and to a few other exposed commercial species, tended to be imposed *ad hoc* with a lavish but erratic hand in attempts to satisfy unrelated complaints. As consensus about over-fishing and the need to control it strengthened, however, stock-oriented fishery regulation took on a life of its own. Laypeople, sports fishers and others with some political strength all gave political approval to fisheries regulation as a form of conservation. Even before the biological overfishing problem was largely or officially understood, public interest showed up in support of nineteenth-century marine-mammal treaties (seals, then whales and otters) as well as of fish hatcheries, fish ladders and fishing gear regulation. There was resistance to any move to relax 'conservation' laws, especially those that would expose the game of the sporting angler to commercial fishing.

These attitudes received bureaucratic support in the twentieth century. With time, the new administrators and experts sought to perfect the new regulatory regimes that employed them. As early regulations had at first been imprecise, sometimes misdirected and almost always under-enforced, they left plenty of scope for evidence of improvement to show voters and bosses. Increasingly, commercial fishing interests also agreed with regulation, though their acceptance was not smooth. More accurately, perhaps, each kind of licensee became cautiously suspicious of regulators, the government and other kinds of fishers. The new administrative arrangements tended to divide those with access into quarrelling interest groups.[77] Any political initiative to reduce the domain of regulation encountered fearful resistance from one protected group or another, but the pockets of opposition were not the political deterrent that a united industry would have been.

Given all the above considerations, it is not surprising that the variety of resulting regulations was staggering. Those fishing for the most coveted and valued stocks were subjected to a wide variety of rules. The stocks' habitats were placed under protective controls. Some regulations were alarmingly inflexible while others were so frequently amended as to bring them into contempt—discounted alike by fishermen and enforcers. Types of regulation were combined within boundaries around bays or geometrical areas.

Certain types of vessel or gear were banned, seasonally or permanently. Well-known extreme examples included the prohibition of shellfish dredges

[77] In Alaska, for example, proposed territorial rights to protect certain fish were undermined by the White Act, 1924, which, in effect, prohibited any exclusivity in fishing rights (Rogers 1979, p. 784). Even though there was general agreement to closures and gear limits, no fisherman would agree to be excluded from a territory open to another group of fishers, as part of the strategy to reduce the concentrations of effort. Fishermen wanted identical access everywhere. A similar fate had been met by attempts in the 1870s to bring lobster fisheries under territorial rights (De Wolf 1974, pp. 15–29).

in Maryland waters, of powered vessels in Bristol Bay, and of salmon traps in many waters.[78]

Despite the haphazard nature of the pre-Second World War experimental phase of fisheries regulation, some successful regulations and types of regulations did emerge. Probably the most significant of these was net mesh-size regulation, especially in North Sea and North Atlantic waters. While some gear regulation was merely intended to deal with the costly excesses of inter-vessel competition, mesh regulation was intended to have an effect on stock reproduction and growth. From the 1860s onward, governments had experimented with rules about the size or kind of fish that could be landed. At first they had prohibited the capturing or landing of, for example, egg-bearing female lobsters, those with soft shells, or those whose length was less than nine inches.[79] Later, the lessons of such regulation were applied to rules limiting the characteristics of the physical apparatus with which fish were caught.

Net-mesh regulations were a success. They were supported by a good percentage of the fishermen who came to see that large net meshes would increase the survival of large fish, restore the stock to its pre-fishing age structure and increase the value of their vessels' landings. They were readily supported in the legislatures. Many lawmakers were anglers, already familiar with size limits in fresh-water sports fisheries.[80] Sophisticated stock-dynamic theories, such as those of Beverton and Holt 1957, were developed to reduce the roughness of the early analyses of mesh-sizes and to guide mesh selection.[81]

Naturally, net size regulation worked best where, of a number of stocks mixed on the fishing grounds, fishers wished to take the physically largest. In this case, regulators could propose to enforce mesh sizes large enough to allow many of the vulnerable 'by-catch' species to escape. But, if the species with the largest individuals were neither the most valuable nor the target of the area fishery, extra rules had to be made. Governments sought additional information about vessels' by-catches to provide data for biologists attempting to estimate the size and structure of the mixed stocks.[82] Such requirements were difficult and costly to enforce and might merely encourage a crew in throwing overboard its unwanted by-catch.

[78] See Christy 1964 on oysters; Cooley 1963 on traps and Bristol Bay; Christy and Scott 1965, pp. 84–6 and Russell 1864 on salmon.

[79] See De Wolf 1974, p. 7; Scott and Tugwell 1981; and Rutherford et al. 1967 for rules of the Canadian lobster fishery after 1872. In the private leases of fishing rights on inland rivers it had long been customary to specify the species and size of the fish that could be caught and the dates during which the catching could take place.

[80] Politicians may also be especially prone to accept those gear regulations that happen to favour small scale local fishers in their constituencies. Arnason 1995, p. 139.

[81] Some net-mesh regulation was unpopular with fishers who believed unregulated offshore fishers, or foreigners, would not conform to the rules. White 1954, pp. 103–5 and 177 and Dewar 1983, pp. 119–20 recount the decades-long refusal of New England haddock vessel owners and their union to adopt a larger mesh. For an economist's defence of net-mesh regulations, see Turvey 1964.

[82] See Gulland 1977, p. 123.

From public right of fishing to individual licences

William Royce's researches on the history of fishery science and management in the United States (where trawling and net-mesh regulation were relatively less important than in European waters) led him to generalize about the years before 1950:

> [This was] a period of slowly increasing research, but the findings had very little effect on fishery management. Conservation was fundamentally a political issue... The freshwater regulations were based on common sense, avoiding waste, protecting young animals so they could grow, protecting breeding animals so they could reproduce, and spreading the catches through the prevention of any excessive ingenuity in the use of nets. When fish became scarce, waters were stocked from hatcheries... The marine fisheries regulations on the other hand were very few, and there was little regulation of marine fisheries in [the United States], aside from inshore shellfisheries and perhaps the inshore herring fishery of New England, until recent years. What regulations there were, were largely designed to promote orderly marketing and orderly fishing, not really for the purpose of conservation.[83]

After the 1950s, however, things were different. A long period of increasingly 'knee-jerk' marine fishery regulation had run its course in the United States. As well, an influential economic theory of the fishery that could inform regulation and management and explain the problems of unregulated fishery was taking shape.

Economists and regulatory alternatives

Scott Gordon's pioneering economic analysis of the fishery changed the way economists thought about regulation and licensing. Between the wars, few economists had seen anything special about the fishery. Harold Innis' great 1931 book on the cod fishery had not dwelt on its open-access nature, though he was acquainted with property-conscious institutional economists. It was just another staple industry. Twenty years before that, Alfred Marshall, in his famous chapter distinguishing between short run and long run market responses,[84] had casually used the output of a local fishery as his example. As we saw above, he basically dismissed the possibility that the fish might be depleted. The words of modern fishery analysis, such as 'open access', 'common property' and 'over-fishing' were unknown.

Gordon (1954)[85] approached the matter as the cause of a distortion of the allocation of the economy's labour and capital. If allocation was undistorted,

[83] Royce 1988, p. 32. See also Royce 1989. European and other industrial nations with fisheries set up biological research stations during the inter-war period; all had an association with ICES: the International Council for the Exploration of the Sea.

[84] Marshall 1920, p. 371.

[85] Jens Warming, G. Gerhardsen and D. McGregor had anticipated various aspects of Gordon's initial paper.

competition among industries bidding for factors of production would tend to bring about a maximization of the whole economy's value of production. However, if an open-access fishery was one of the industries, the maximization would not be achieved. The reason was the paradox that would later become known, in Garrett Hardin's famous phrase (1968), as 'the tragedy of the commons'.

Briefly, in a two-industry Walrasian model, workers in a competitive industry are paid their marginal product (the marginal product of labour). In the fishery, however, workers' earnings are equal to their shares of the industry's surplus or rent. Assuming that all the workers in a fishery have the same skill and gear, their individual shares will be roughly proportional to the fleet's average catch, and they will enter the fishery until deterred by the decline of the *average* product of the fishery to the outside general wage level. Because, in the simple neoclassical model, marginal product falls faster than average product, the resulting labour-market equilibrium will be one in which the last labourer to enter the fishery adds less value there than he would if he had been directed to an alternative industry. The fish stock will be smaller and the cost of fishing will be higher than if a rent-maximizing fishery sole-owner were doing the hiring.

Gordon's innovative analysis—and those of several other analysts who tackled the allocation of labour in an open-access situation[86]—reinforced the conviction of government administrators and their biologist colleagues that even if all the fishing crews were breaking even financially, there was, somehow, too much 'effort' (people and boats) being allocated to fishing. Government regulation was evidently needed. But Gordon's paradigm suggested that it should be geared less toward modifying the behaviour of existing fishers than toward discouraging the entry of new ones.

As in many kinds of government regulation, the fishing licence came into focus as an essential administrative tool.[87] But later empirical analyses in the 1970s and 1980s showed that merely restricting licences would cause surviving licence holders to equip their vessels with more capital, leaving the biologists' effective 'effort' relatively unchanged.[88] Below we will see that this was one of the perceptions that led to an interest in ITQs.

[86] Gordon was inspired by Frank Knight's work on a no-property economy. Crutchfield's first published fisheries papers (1955 and 1956) directed attention to open access, the fishers unions, and labour misallocation. This fisheries' labour-market subject was also discussed by Jamieson and Gladstone 1950 and, later, by Johnson and Libecap 1982. All recognized that unions might become an organizing and restricting force in open-access resources. My own 1955 paper (Scott 1955) dealt with the possibilities of sole ownership, comparing that regime with common property in various aspects, including incentives to invest in the stock and to optimize over time.

[87] Another kind of 'regulation', mentioned below, was economic: taxing the catch. Crutchfield and Zellner (1962), pp. 380–2 advised against this on the grounds of political feasibility. In any case, taxing the catch was never implemented.

[88] See Munro and Scott 1985 for the distinction between fishery problems of over-entry and fishery problems of regulation.

1960s: instruments of economic regulation classified

Soon economists became united in opposing the intensification of fishery regulation by lengthening closed periods or by forbidding effective gear. Some argued for restricting fishery inputs, some for outputs; some focused on quantity, some on value-added. Their five proposed major 'economic' regulatory instruments and their targets were: (1) *'Sole ownership'* (including aquaculture) to internalize input and output decisions; (2) *licence fees*, a form of tax on inputs into fishing; (3) *royalty or negative subsidies*, a taxation of output (the catch); (4) *licence limitation* to ration access/inputs to the fishery; and (5) *individual catch quotas (ITQs)*, to ration the size of the catch or the output of the industry.

The most important of these regulatory instruments, the ITQ, is dealt with later in the chapter. First I survey the other four suggested instruments, with emphasis on the practice of licensing and its limitation that became widespread in and after the 1960s.

SOLE OWNERSHIP

Sole ownership is the most drastic solution to the 'common property' problem, in that it takes the remaining right holder from approximately zero to a (potentially) infinite degree of exclusivity. As in the Gordon paradigm (without transactions costs and assuming competitive markets for fish and fishing inputs), the theoretical sole owner would not distort the allocation of factors among productive enterprises. Economists have used the monopoly or sole-owner idea to make predictions about open-access situations that might come under some form of unified management.[89] The results of these investigations show some differences; however, in general, under standard (competitive) assumptions pertaining to price, wage and transactions costs, two types of institution, a monopsony fish buyer/processor (who sets a price for fish that cannot be bid up by competing buyers) and a sole owner (who continues catching only until marginal cost of effort equals the marginal value of more fish)—can be predicted to approach an 'efficient' rate of output and stock size.

The sole ownership ideal had evidently been considered by the designers of the Pacific Fur Seal Treaty organization.[90] As noted above single-management had emerged briefly in salmon rivers in California, Oregon, Alaska and British Columbia. Between 1871 and 1920 there was a policy of granting exclusive salmon licences on certain Ontario and Quebec waters; fishers'

[89] I have used sole ownership to examine the size of the catch over time and the output choices of an internationally owned 'Swiss Corporation': Scott 1955 and 1957; and Jones, Pearse, and Scott 1980. Crutchfield and Pontecorvo 1969 considered a variant: a monopsonistic fish-buying and processing company dealing with a competitive catching fleet. Their results were considered dynamically by Clark and Munro (1980) and were generalized by Schworm (1983) to include a comparison with an integrated sole owner.

[90] Christy and Scott 1965, p. 196; Paterson and Wilen 1977; Paterson 1977. See also Waite 1985, pp. 276–7 and passim for an account of the Bering Sea crisis that led to the treaty.

licences were attached to these. Neglected examples include the South African pelagic fishery of the 1960s and the West Australian exclusive shrimp fishery of the 1970s.[91] Such arrangements could be extremely unpopular with captains and crews since, in law or in fact, the individual vessels had only whatever rights were bestowed on them by the company for whom they caught fish. Politicians found them a handy subject for patronage; and it is for this very reason that they were later swept away. Nevertheless, hardly a year passes without a suggestion that this property approach be adopted for some international shared or straddling stock.

FINANCIAL REGULATION

Few, if any, financial (or Pigovian) instruments have been adopted for ocean fisheries, though discussion of them has helped to clarify the choice among regulatory instruments. One of the most serious administrative disadvantages of taxes on inputs or outputs arises because these instruments may have to be re-set frequently, even during the season, according to changes in the expected size of the stock, catch or fleet. Defenders of tax changes say that this may not be a serious disadvantage, pointing to the acceptability of frequent changes of certain government fees, excises and customs duties. They argue that, apart from political or constitutional issues, charges and taxes might be automatically re-set by a computerized iterative procedure.[92] Nevertheless, the chief reason for neglecting them here is that their role in the development of individual property rights in the fishery has been minor compared to the theoretical and practical role played by licensing and licence limitation.

LICENSING AND LICENCE LIMITATION

Modern sea-fishery licences are quite unlike the public and private land licences discussed in previous chapters. They are better thought of as resembling permits authorizing the holder to sell or to buy spirits, get married or carry firearms. Fishery licences may be issued in different contexts as a source of public revenue or as part of an overall scheme for stock management. In either case, an issuance in no way makes the licensee a holder of rights over lands adjoining or below the fishing ground or over the waters that are the fish-stock's habitat.

The introduction of the commercial fishing licence symbolized the end of the centuries-long practice of complete open-access (common property) fishing. In the first place, the new power to issue or refuse a licence gave governments a routine, bureaucratic means of enforcing other regulations: fishermen caught

[91] For discussions of the Pacific coast exclusive salmon rights, see Libecap 1989, pp. 79–80; Gregory and Barnes 1939; and Warriner 1987, p. 331. South African fisheries are discussed by Gertenbach 1962 and 1973. Today, the South African hake fishery TAC is assigned to only two or three firms. The exclusive Australian shrimp fishery is discussed by Meany 1979.

[92] See Clark 1976, pp. 77–87 and 116–25 and articles by Martin Weitzman reviving the argument that, in an uncertain world, adjusting taxes may be preferable to adjusting quantities.

violating various regulations risked losing their licences. Another advantage was to give governments an instrument for keeping out fishermen in foreign vessels and for discriminating among various classes of local fishermen, or users of various types of gear. Probably the most important advantage of licensing, however, appeared later: by withholding or conditioning licences governments could control in a quite new way the total amount of effort the fishing fleet applied to a stock.

In the 1960s biologists formalized a means of controlling fishing mortality that depended directly and entirely on fixing the amount harvested as the Total Allowable Catch (TAC). Some countries' licensing systems provided data on the amounts being caught and landed relative to the TAC. But in other jurisdictions where keeping track of the catch was too difficult, the regulators/biologists fell back on using the licensing system to keep track of the number of vessels, and perhaps of the length of their presence on the fishing grounds. These data were combined into measures of 'effort'. In either case, the TAC regulatory goal could be met by setting and adjusting the level of fishing effort. This could be done if, instead of issuing licences to all applicants, government controlled and *limited* the number of licenses issued to meet the effort target.

Licence limitation spread quickly across Western fishing nations. In the 1970s the UK and the Netherlands began to issue limited-entry permits and licences to fishermen catching herring, mackerel and roundfish. In the 1980s the US regional fishery councils began placing 'moratoria' on issue of licences to catch certain species. By the later 1990s there were almost thirty of these binding under US law. In 1982 New South Wales restricted entry into its abalone-dive fishery and in 1993 into its rock lobster (trap) fishery. In the 1990s Victoria limited the issue of scallop dredging licences in Port Philip Bay. In the 1980s Canada adopted the farm economist Sol Sinclair's recommended version of licence limitation to cope with its west-coast salmon fishery. Other countries followed suit.

Licensing as the creation of property, and the characteristics of a licence

In most instances, the introduction of licence limitation fit into an on-going history of attempts to use regulation to rescue over-exploited stocks. The logical next step from gear and fishing-season, licence limitation conveyed to licence holders some of the characteristics of a property right, and their associated benefits.[93] Indeed, in what follows, I discuss licences as if they are rudimentary *property rights* somewhat analogous to the profit-à-prendre and easement in real property law.[94]

[93] See Wilen 1989.

[94] See Beddington and Rettig 1984 for a discussion of technical biological modelling, including work by Colin Clark, Beddington and May, and Gulland. In several papers Rognvaldur Hannesson contrasts fixed effort (licences) with fixed catch (quotas). See Munro and Scott 1985; Hannesson and Steinshamn 1991.

Governments hoped that adding licence limitation to their armoury of instruments would reverse the trend in many sea fisheries toward ever-shorter open periods, which induced racing and inefficient competition among the vessels.[95] Unfortunately, there was a catch: early fleet reductions by limitation induced remaining licence holders to improve their vessels' and equipment's catching powers—a process called 'capital stuffing'. Governments were forced to reinforce their limited-licensing policy by stepping up their old regulatory measures, including shortened fishing seasons. In the halibut fishery this meant that the annual harvests, now caught in a few weeks, had to be frozen and stored for release to market over the whole year. Although licence limitation plus short seasons did keep annual effort at a lower level than that it would otherwise have been, the reduction imposed higher unit fishing costs, storage costs and administration and enforcement expenditures.[96] One mitigation was for governments to offer licences only to 'vessels' as defined by a maximum length, tonnage, engine power and/or other characteristics related to their 'effort' potential. The revival of older rules and limits such as quantitative net, net-mesh, trap or hook limits, trip limits and combinations of these was also maintained.

The actual cutting-back of the number of 'vessels' was handled gently. It was generally accomplished in fisheries already under government regulation by discontinuing the issuing of licences to new entrants along with reduction of licences still outstanding by non-renewal. The policy could be toughened by simple cancellation of unlucky individuals' licences, or softened by 'buyback' of their licences (and perhaps of their vessels), and even more by allowing politicians to issue unofficial licences at the back door to their friends.[97] In general, those commercial fishermen who expected to be excluded by the policy disapproved of it. Others, after a period of suspicion, came to approve of limited licensing. The introduction of scarcity meant that they held a marketable near-ownership interest in the fishery that was worth passing on to their children.[98]

At least five impersonal alternatives were suggested for licence disposal: by sale; by auction; by rotation (a kind of divisibility); by buyback; or by lottery. These systems of disposal could also be used to redistribute licences when they expired or when their holders retired or died, and would allow government to expropriate much of the rent from the fishery.[99]

[95] The important subject of the timing of fishing effort within the year is briefly mentioned on p. 182. See also Bradley 1970 and Agnello and Donnelly 1977.

[96] See Pearse and Wilen 1979 for the leading discussion. See also the balanced account of Wilen 1989 (in Neher et al. 1989, ch. 6). Cross-country comparisons may be found in Rettig 1984; recent developments in Australia may be found in FAO 1999.

[97] Among the very first proposals was that of Sinclair 1960, which was adopted in 1968. See Campbell 1974 and Pearse 1982, chs. 7, 8, and 9.

[98] Despite these drawbacks, Rognvaldur Hannesson, among others, has continued to examine limited licensing as a type of input regulation that is superior to quota regulation. See, for example, Hannesson and Steinshamn 1991.

[99] Pearse 1982.

In the 1960s, however, most politicians who were in touch with fishers decided on a less impersonal and mechanical hand-out. I use management of Canada's Pacific salmon fisheries as an example. Licences were first 'grandfathered'—issued to the fishers currently active when the policy went into effect. No active fishermen would be deprived of a licence, but no new licences would be issued. To reduce the number of fishers, the government would cancel the licences of those who retired (a policy with potentially disastrous consequences, such as forcing older fishers with dependants to stay on as licence holders into their old age). Fishermen opposed that plan, and any other with a time dimension or limit on intergenerational transferability.

Instead, Canadian fishermen campaigned to have their licences given a permanent *duration*, and to be allowed to transfer them whenever they chose. This was the idea that politicians in most jurisdictions accepted: an idea of the licence as a once-for-all, transferable permanent endowment administered to active fishers through a kind of squatters' right or pre-emption. Their acceptance in turn paved the way for a solution to the fleet-reduction problem: periodically the government should purchase a certain number back from their holders at full market price. The finances could be provided by the remaining licence-holders or by the government; a government-financed buy-back policy was usually preferred. Regulation by licence limitation therefore required that the licence have two characteristics: very long or permanent duration and wide or complete transferability (including by bequest).

Fishers confronted with a limited licence regime also came to demand greater *exclusivity*, which gave them a measure of freedom from inter-boat congestion. For example, fishermen pushed for further regulations to protect their fishing from other vessels' spillovers and externalities and perhaps even to protect improvements of the stock and its habitat from others' interference and free riding.

By contrast, licence limitation did not induce a demand for more of the *divisibility* characteristic in licences. If limited rights were divisible then their holders could split them or add to them until they had the requisite size fishing allowance. But because the limited licensing regime did not limit the amount that each vessel or licence holder could land, dividing the licence into two or more (for instance, by dividing the fishing year into seasons and assigning licence holders one of the seasons) had little appeal.[100] Absent very severe time constraints (extremely short openings could make a licence into a sort of catch quota), licences to fish, even when limited in number, had no quantitative dimension.

As for *quality of title*, governments' moves to limit licences ushered in a period of uneasiness and insecurity. It was clear to most fishermen that their government's proposed target number of licences, usually a round number,

[100] Rotation ideas did not catch on. Having two licences would probably mean that the holder could run two vessels. But half a licence has no meaning. See Bromley 1989, p. 203; Becker 1977, ch. 2 and Stevenson 1991, pp. 48–52.

had been picked out of the air—an arbitrariness reflected in the willingness of some politicians to use their influence to get licences issued to constituents who had been refused by administrators. As well, the units of licensing, such as 'vessels', called for the administrators later to produce artificial equivalences between units of different sizes, capacities, speeds or gear types. True, fishers had long been accustomed to there being different closed seasons or areas for different gear types. But, while arbitrary, these rules had been periodic, temporary and debatable. In contrast, the new decisions to limit licensing permanently threatened the opportunity of some to fish at all.

As fishers had no appeal procedure, they had nothing to lose by investing heavily in argument, protest and political action.[101] They came to describe their grandfathers' and fathers' annual permission to fish, as conveyed by their simple administrative licences, as something like a 'right'. What was now being discussed, they felt, was the security or quality of that right. As the debate continued, the conceived injustice of depriving an active fisher of a customary right, of destroying what was traditional, was forced on administrators and easily accepted by politicians. In response, governments—including those in Canada and Australia—introduced painfully negotiated phasing-in, retrial or buyback schemes to 'compensate' those whose 'rights' had been withdrawn.[102] The proposals provoked unexpected discussions of rights and titles, with the end result that some lucky fishers eventually received a better quality of title than had ever been intended by the invention of licence limitation.

Other evolutionary paths[103]

Not all modern ocean fishing rights emerged from the earlier regulatory licences. In this subsection I briefly examine two other sources of new systems of individual rights: the international fisheries treaty and the set of territorial and traditional fishing arrangements in developing economies.

RIGHTS UNDER CHANGING INTERNATIONAL LAW

Nations have periodically acted together to reduce stock-threatening fishing competition on the high seas.[104] Under the Laws of the Sea (LOS), developed

[101] Australia has been exceptional in that its federal administrative review system can hear some fisher complaints. See Australia 1988.

[102] For discussions of the northern fisheries buyback scheme in Australia, see Lilburn 1986; Campbell 1989; and Wesney 1989. For the same scheme in Canada, see Pearse 1979; Rettig 1984; and Scott and Neher 1981.

[103] Thanks to Gordon Munro for help and material on the subject of this section.

[104] The discussion here is brief. To learn how the Laws of the Sea developed historically, see McDougal and Burke 1962. On the management and sharing of boundary-straddling and highly migratory fish stocks and their effect on fishing communities involved, see the series of excellent papers by my colleague Gordon Munro and several co-authors, starting perhaps with his 'Approaches. . . .' in the *Canadian Journal of Economics* 1996, 29, p. S 157

after the UNCLOS's 1958 Convention on the High Seas, the fishing nations put aside their rights under the old doctrine of freedom of the seas and submitted to be told which parts of the ocean should be subject to the domestic fishery regulations of the various coastal states. By this decision most states fronting on the oceans were handed jurisdictions not only over their bays, inlets and nearby coastal waters but also over a two hundred mile wide Extended Economic Zone (EEZ). In complementary moves, various groupings of fishing nations came to ad hoc agreements for the management of particular ocean territories or stocks and of specific shared 'straddling' and 'migrating' stocks.

Before the First World War, national governments drafting domestic laws to protect their own neighbouring fisheries rarely spared a thought for a regulatory regime governing the more distant high-seas fisheries. At the turn of the century the advent of the steam trawler had caused treaty drafters to include provisions about restricting the intensity of fishing. But real progress had to wait until after the First World War when, for example, government representatives convened to lay the groundwork for the US–Canada halibut and salmon treaties and for various international control commissions. The powers around the North Sea, attempting to agree on the minimum mesh of trawls so as to relieve fishing pressure on small and young fish, took the first steps in coordinated research, mesh control and closed seasons.

After the distraction of the Second World War, pairs and groups of governments started again. Their efforts produced three types of international regulation. The first included treaties between nations to coordinate their research on particular regions: that for the Mediterranean, assisted by Food and Agriculture Organization of the United Nations (FAO), is the best known. The second type was concerned with particular species: whales, salmon, halibut, tuna and other wide-ranging, straddling and migratory species. The third, most ambitious, type was geography-based. The parties undertook to study and then to regulate all the stocks in an ocean region. In 1960 the North West Atlantic Treaty (ICNAF) actually created and allotted quantitative national landing quotas.[105] Since then the recourse to such national quotas has spread, inducing member states to contemplate the introduction of individual or vessel quotas as a means of carrying out their treaty obligations.

The European Community provides an example. Its founding fathers acted around 1970 to set up a Common Fisheries Policy analogous to their common policy for agriculture. They were slow to understand that such a 'policy' might involve their members jointly managing and sharing fish stocks in common parts of the high seas. Years of discussion resulted in the setting of national quotas. The Netherlands further subdivided its national quota into individual

[105] See Christy and Scott 1965 for a review of treaties and commissions; also Eckert 1979, p. 142; Crutchfield 1979; Needler 1979, pp. 718–20. Thanks again to Frank Iacobucci for treaties research.

or vessel quotas. The UK achieved somewhat the same result by dividing its national quota among nineteen regional fishing cooperative Producer Organizations (POs). Some of these UK POs have assigned shares in their sub-quotas to their members' vessels, so that an ITQ-like ownership structure of the type I examine in the next section seems to be emerging. Norway and Iceland, not directly party to the E.U. Common Fisheries Policy, have also established their own ITQ systems.

The European regional treaty and the Pacific halibut species treaty both illustrate how international agreements can serve as the basis for national, local and individual quota rights. Though their basis is international, they are beginning to take on characteristics of individual property: quantitative and therefore with some exclusivity and transferability. Support for these individual property-like rights may reflect the aspirations and understanding of the individual rights-holders. But the ideas for quotas and self-government would not have emerged without the actions of the diplomats and scientists who assembled the conservation treaties. Their emphasis on national quotas provided scope for the member nations' subdivision of these quotas into individual or vessel quotas. In a sense, therefore, the individual quota ideas and arrangements have spread from the top (the international treaty-makers) down, as well as from the bottom (local politicians and fishery lobbies) up.[106]

RIGHTS UNDER LOCAL COMMUNITIES AND TURFS

Here I turn briefly to fisheries in developing economies, especially those that, after years of self-sufficiency, have come into contact with foreign fleets or foreign economic developers. In some of these countries, in spite of their coastal position, there were no well-established traditional salt-water fishing institutions. In others, local 'artisanal' fisheries worked in small boats or canoes, sometimes on behalf of a capitalist owner of several such vessels. The former had no role, and the latter a minor role, in the shaping of modern LDC fishing institutions.

As recently as the 1950s, in much of the coastal developing world offshore stocks were freely exploited by the distant-water (DW) fleets and factory ships of a few developed nations. Until the 1960s, when the LOS assigned these waters to the coastal state, the host countries typically had no share, in money or in fish, in the catches of the foreign fleets operating off their coasts.

After the LOS changed the international legal regime in fishing, some of the DW fleets bargained with the host state and obtained an annual licence for an annual payment. The licence typically provided that the foreign nation's DW fleet could fish the host country's waters at least with a specified number of vessels and for a given period each year. This arrangement was fairly stable in countries with stocks of large and distinct offshore species. However, in countries

[106] See Symes 1999; Goodlad 1999; Davidse 1999.

where the 'offshore species' were mainly the inshore stocks during their annual migration, there was over-fishing and conflict.[107]

Generally, the host government lacked establishments or experience to acquire information about these local stocks; impose biologically helpful regulations on their fishing; or benefit from complementary investments. There was little governments could do for their coastal communities. Some governments, in agreement with the foreign fleet, intervened to clear away the congestion caused by the fishing of the traditional low-capital inshore fishers. In the worst scenario, both offshore and inshore fishers were left with lowered stocks, high costs and reduced yields.[108]

One way out of this trap was to integrate the DW fishery with a more developed local fish processing and shipping industry. Berkes (1986) recommended placing the offshore vessels under the control of local communities of inshore fishers based on the biological reality that offshore fisheries are 'unproductive'. Cordell and McKean (1986) describe a vast informal Brazilian system of 'sea tenures' under which individual territorial rights, both of DWs and of locals, are recognized and enforced.[109] A more general approach was, with the help of the fishing nation and agencies such as the FAO, to import capital and key personnel to start joint ventures in which the local government and the DW companies initiated new industries including ports, plants, crews and vessels.

It appears that, gradually, both parties to this new type of contract realized that their interests would be better served if their concession arrangement were quantitative or quota-based (in contrast, say, to the Brazilian territorial 'sea tenure' strategy mentioned above). It was not necessary for quota allotments to be fixed for all time; the negotiated concession could provide for a gradually changing percentage of the shared stock to be caught by the inshore or local fishers. (It should not be assumed that simple local gears take fish of lower quality or at a higher cost.) If quotas were issued to the inshore or local fishermen, then the central government's policy toward them could be implemented through an official decision regarding the transferability of their quota allotments. Developing the local fishery could be promoted by making the local quotas non-transferable and by pushing locals in the direction of equipping themselves to make use of them. Phasing out the local fishery could be promoted by making quotas partly or fully transferable to government or joint-venture buyers.[110]

[107] For an excellent survey of the tuna fishery at this period in the Pacific islands, see Campbell, Menz, and Waugh 1989.

[108] Berkes 1986. See also Cruz 1986.

[109] Cordell and McKean 1986. See also Cruz 1986.

[110] That ITQs would facilitate local development was suggested in Scott 1989, following the scheme for one-way transferability of quotas proposed by the Economic Council of Canada in 1980. The idea has found no favour in recent discussions, such as those in Campbell and Owen 1994, p. 33, where little concern is shown for guaranteeing a catch for 'locally based tuna operators'. The same is true for Payne 1994, who also deals with tuna (for canning). He apparently sees a growth of shoreside canning and port facilities only as a consequence of effort limitation and price increases, and he does not concede that ITQs could do this without a price increase.

At the same time, other nations provided grist for an expanding specialist literature on 'native', 'customary', 'co-managed', 'communal' and 'traditional' organizations.[111] The fisheries examined in this literature were common-property institutions; they had never come under local 'management', with or without a governmental presence or foreign participation. Nevertheless, they are not necessarily anarchic; in addition to enforcing its rules and ensuring a viable distribution of fishing opportunities, such an arrangement may implicitly or explicitly function to protect the stocks from over-fishing or to raise the total catch in weight or value. The extent to which common-property fisheries did and do so apparently varies over a very wide range.

It does appear that, as a group, traditional fisheries are mainly worked by poor people, are territorial, and are, in some places, losing out to intruders from more capitalistic neighbouring territorial fisheries.[112] The 1995 global report of the FAO summarized the matter:

> With the advent of rapid social change, population increases, urbanization, the rise of commercial opportunities for sales of fish and fisheries products, and the introduction of more effective mobile gears, these traditional management systems have come under extreme pressure and have, in some cases, started to disintegrate. However, the merits of fostering community control over vulnerable coastal fisheries are apparent and, given the mixed results that have been achieved with other conservation and management approaches, traditional management practices provide a viable alternative, in some cases, for regulating the use of coastal fisheries resources.[113]

This is a reference to the TURF (Territorial Use Rights of Fisheries) idea, which the FAO has fostered to help create and develop local inshore fisheries organizations, to supplant uniform national administrative and management centralization and to prevent friction between adjoining villages and communities. TURFs were typically to be applied to an inshore area, a bay, a lagoon or a reef (where many species mixed and were exploited) rather than to the open seas (where international fleets sought single species). They could involve local villages or communities in fishery regulation and could be held collectively or else broken down to be held by groups concentrating on narrower autonomous law-making areas. This sometimes meant confirming or supporting an old communal arrangement. More often, however, it meant devolving

[111] See Acheson 1975; Johannes 1978; Ruddle and Johannes 1985; and Berkes 1986. Schlager 1990 has brought together and compared studies of local fisheries. See also a collected volume edited by Ostrom et al. 1988. For an excellent forerunner of what has become an avalanche of common-property studies of resource use in many countries, by scholars from several disciplines, see US National Research Council 1986. There is a related literature on the quality of husbandry of Northwest Coast First Nations over the salmon fisheries and the role of the potlatch in the annual cycle of 'management'. See Herskovits 1952; Rettig, Berkes, and Pinkerton 1989.

[112] For closely reasoned analyses of traditional and under-developed territorial fisheries, see Ruddle 1989 together with an adjoining commentary by Panayotou.

[113] FAO 1995, p. 23.

responsibility to local authorities for coping with new problems of pollution, overfilling, crowding and excessive investment.[114]

All the experts agree that an important characteristic of successful customary systems has been their basis in territoriality. In customary territorial regimes of fishing rights, much emphasis is given to individuals' exclusivity (by the assignment of individual fishing spots) and to the exclusion of fishermen from neighbouring communities. Territorial dependence on land-based authority will undoubtedly feature in any future fisher-centred system of regulation. It has, for example, featured strongly in the development of the Japanese inshore fisheries, closely controlled, mile by mile along the coast by the adjacent farming-and-fishery village communities.[115]

Looking forward again to the discussion of ITQs, the research and evidence to date provides little evidence that foreign investment and LDC policy adjustments to international competition must or will lead to ITQ regimes. Local ITQ regimes might be introduced as fish stocks become scarce and as local fishers become readier to participate in and to take over what were once foreign-exploited DW fisheries. But as suggested in the discussion above, the process of modernization is largely independent of whether or not the ITQ for the individual or vessel is adopted as a method of stock management, as an alternative to closures and other types of area-based control. Indeed, the possibility of a TURF arrangement with continuing village or community customary shares suggests a permanent alternative to an individual property-right regime.

The 1980s and individual catch quotas

The late 1980s idea of basing fishery regulation on individual quantitative non-territorial rights involved further evolution of the licensing system. Indeed, most officials originally regarded quotas as one further experiment with instruments of fishery management. But it soon turned out that, in fine-tuning a proposed quota system, regulators were in fact modifying an individual right with property characteristics far more complete than those that had composed the limited licence.

[114] Though space constraints limit the discussion of traditional fisheries here, some outstanding studies are now available, including Acheson 1975; Johannes 1978; Ruddle and Johannes 1985; and Berkes 1986. There are many others. Schlager 1990 has brought together and compared studies of local fisheries. See also a collected volume edited by Ostrom et al. 1988. For an excellent forerunner of what has become an avalanche of common-property studies of resource use in many countries, by scholars from several disciplines, see US National Research Council 1986.

[115] For an excellent study of community-based management systems and fishery co-operative associations (Zengyoren) developed in Japan see Yamamoto and Short, eds. 1992, pp. 3–159.

The transition

The basic ideas of the ITQ are simple, and the variations among different countries' versions are not fundamental.[116] In a typical scheme, each licence-holder (or vessel) acquires the right to fish and to land a specified amount or 'quota' of a particular species per period, the holder's portion of that period's total target quota (the TAC). The variants of this basic arrangement involve *units* (the denomination of the quota in weight, pieces, value or percentage of the TAC); *geography* (the area from which the quota can be taken); *biology* (the species to which it applies); *duration* (the length of time in which the stated quota can be taken); *flexibility* (the carryover of unused quota to the next season); *permanence* (the length of the holder's ownership of the quota right); *renewal* (automatic, or by price, auction or another means); and *transferability*. There are also international differences in means of enforcement and in procedures for setting the TAC.

As ITQ regimes gained prominence, fishermen and administrators quickly grasped the basic idea of the quota and began to worry instead about their initial distribution. Should every fisherman receive a quota, or only those who had held a licence in the specific fishery? Should every initial quota carry the same (standard) catch entitlement? Should those who were most committed, having invested most in large vessels and larger crews, receive more quota? Unsurprisingly, such questions received different answers in different countries and fisheries.

Most countries, at least at the outset, parcelled out equal quota to the fishermen in each species fishery: Iceland for its pelagic fisheries; Canada for geoduck clams; the United States for bluefin tuna; New South Wales for abalone. The justification was roughly that what was being 'grandfathered' to the fishermen was not a right to catch a certain amount but a right such as that they had already enjoyed under licensing: to enter the fishery and take a catch.[117] Those who had previously landed larger-than-average catches had already received a market reward for them; there was no serious ethical or efficiency rationale to reward them again with larger-than-average quotas.

However, as the authorities turned from large high-value fisheries and began introducing quotas for older mixed stocks—typically exploited by vessels of various types, using several gear-types, from several different ports or in different seasons—the fishermen became less willing to accept equal or standardized vessel quotas. As a result, ingenious compromises differentiated between amounts of quota to the various classes of vessel depending on crew

[116] The ideas were not invented by academics, but introduced more or less autonomously by fisheries agencies in Iceland and New Zealand. As for scientific or academic recognition, it is interesting to note the crescendo of publication. The first published article on ITQs was by Francis Christy Jr., and it appeared in 1973. Moloney and Pearse published an original paper on the subject in 1979. Both had wide influence. Earlier, Crutchfield 1965, and Christy and Scott 1965, p. 238, had suggested aspects of the idea.

[117] On equal-shares before, and after, limited entry, see Lueck 1994.

size, racial composition, distance of the catch from port, season of catch, market served and other features of the fishery and fishers.

In most jurisdictions the transferability of the quota provided a lubricant in the distributional discussions because it allowed fishermen to sell—transfer—out or buy in based on characteristics that might be unobservable to the administrators. In many countries critics of the whole scheme's seeming discrimination were amazed by some of the win-win results. Initially excluded fishermen who had to buy quota did so and made money. Fishermen who were seduced by capitalists to sell out their quota did so and made money.

However, many criticisms remain, several of which I discuss below.[118] A major complaint is that the introduction and selling of the quotas led to wealth concentration; the value of the people's fishery was winding up in the fortunes of the wealthy few who have done nothing to deserve their enrichment.[119] Apparently regarding a permanent quota and a property right as much the same thing, these critics often attack the duration aspect of ITQs, preferring licences or quotas that must be frequently renewed, perhaps by auction or tender. In their eyes, increasing permanence is merely a way of transferring the ownership of the fishery from the public domain to a selected group of rentiers.[120]

Most countries figured out their transitional arrangements under emergency conditions such as the failure of a fish population or the takeover of the LOS' Extended Economic Zones from foreign distant-water fleets during the 1970s. This could lead to makeshift policy in the short run. In Iceland after 1976, for example, there was an almost continuous sequence of licence types to complement the first-time setting of TACs: limited entry, limited effort quotas, catch quotas, mixed systems and, finally, catch quotas alone.[121] However, by 1979–80 Iceland's herring quota rights had become permanent (or renewable) and transferable; and by 1984 this was also true of quotas for demersal fish and capelin. Since 1990 there has been a uniform system of transferable vessel catch quotas in all of Iceland's fisheries.

Similar crises spurred action in New Zealand.[122] In its new EEZ, domestic fishers taking over fisheries from foreign DW fleets required a management policy to be developed quickly. At the same time, the government had political

[118] For an overview of these disputes, and some evidence from the US and Canada scallop fisheries, see Repetto 2001.

[119] In the late 1990s ITQ holders' enrichment became an important political issue in Iceland. See Thorolfur Matthiasson 1999 and other chapters in Arnason and Gissurarson 1999.

[120] A good defence of this policy is to be found in Pearse 1982.

[121] In 1966 declining stocks in Iceland's herring fishery led to introduction of an overall quota, reinforced by closed seasons, licensing and even a complete moratorium on herring landings. Then, between 1976 and 1981 these policy instruments were discarded and replaced by vessel/catch quotas in both the faltering herring and capelin fisheries. These quotas were treated as optional and were subject to modification. See Arnason 1995, ch. 5.

[122] See Clark and Duncan 1986 and Major 1999. Conference papers looking at the evolution of NZ ITQs from the point of view of politicians, public servants, and industry can be found in the proceedings of FAO 2000.

reasons for presiding over a fairly radical 'privatization' of resources and a reduction in regulation and subsidies. Accordingly, in 1982 individual quotas were introduced in seven deep-water fisheries and later, under very general Quota Management System legislation, in about forty fisheries (including 85 per cent of the older inshore fisheries). In the next decade it was possible to settle Maori fishing claims by redistributing 20 per cent of all quotas to the tribes.[123]

In nearby Australia, certain states also introduced ITQ systems about this time, notably Western Australia for rock lobsters and southern bluefin tuna.

In the 1960s, partially in response to the EEZ opportunities but mostly due to ominous reductions in Atlantic groundfish catches, Canada introduced and allotted 'enterprise' quotas[124] not to persons or vessels but to four large vessel-owning companies.[125] In the 1990s the Canadian government created ITQs for the important Pacific halibut fishery and for several smaller fisheries.[126] More recently, the United States, having already placed Atlantic tuna under a form of quota, followed Canada in creating ITQs for the Pacific halibut and sablefish fisheries. In 1998–9, Congress placed a moratorium on the creation of further ITQ systems, pending an investigation. This moratorium has expired and by 2004 regional fishery management councils were working on several new ITQ systems, including one for Pacific Coast deep-trawl vessels.[127]

Across the Atlantic, apart from Iceland, only the United Kingdom and the Netherlands have allowed their limited-entry management systems for certain species to evolve into ITQ systems. Iceland and Australia[128] experimented with another form of quota: effort or input quotas. Norway introduced a variant of this approach: a system of inshore input quotas, lacking exclusivity and transferability. In the Norwegian system, the total of all quotas is reckoned to be greater than the TAC so that the fishery must be closed before all vessels have taken their quotas. Thus, in Norway the boats face the old incentive to engage in capital-stuffing in order to out-fish their colleagues.

Regarding input quotas in general, if we assume that the scientist designing a limited-licence regime had some idea of the amount of effort (denominated in vessels, vessel-hours, net-hours, etc.) needed to produce a desired fishing mortality, then we can see that the next step would be to distribute this ideal amount of effort among the licence holders. As suggested earlier, however, units of effort have sometimes proved difficult to quantify or enforce. One

[123] See McClurg 1997 and Major 1999.

[124] As has been mentioned, this is an old idea. In Alaska and elsewhere on the Canadian and American west coast, canneries, catching vessels and trap sites had once been assigned to a single company. See Lyons 1969, pp. 174–5; Hill 1967; and Gregory and Barnes 1939. Gertenbach 1973 refers to a pilchard enterprise quota off the coast of southwest Africa.

[125] Grafton 1996, pp. 154–8; Burke and Brander 1999, pp. 151–9. Actually, Canada's first IQ system began on Lake Winnipeg in the 1970s. See Gislason 2000.

[126] Macgillivray 1997.

[127] Thanks to Daniel Huppert for update information.

[128] See Cooper and Joll 1999.

obvious unit of measurement is the pot or trap. If the number of vessels is limited, as well as the number of pots each may drop per trip, the number of trips per year and the mesh of the net, the combined input of the boats' entitlements is very constrained. Under these demanding circumstances the effect would be similar to that of an output quota.

The exclusivity characteristic of quotas

In the section on comment on supply, I reviewed the property characteristics of the licence under limited licensing. In the next four subparts, I repeat the exercise, now looking for the major property characteristics of the individual quota licence, with attention to the specific criticisms of, and responses to, their creation.

Exclusivity is perhaps the defining characteristic, and major benefit, of the ITQ. In a simple single-stock offshore fishery under a constant-percentage ITQ regime,[129] the amount a vessel may land is held down to the owner's quota—her part of the TAC. This alone tends to keep the holder's fishing costs at the lowest level—just enough to land the catch at the date it is wanted. In an ITQ regime, holders have no motive to subject their vessels to capital stuffing by upgrade, elaborate gear or larger crews. Instead 'their' fish can be thought of as swimming around, securely waiting to be taken by whatever simplicity or sophistication of gear is chosen to land them.

In a year-round fishery, racing is pointless for fishers. They and their regulators have an incentive to stretch out the season from its short duration under the previous system of regulation. During this elongated season smaller vessels make regular trips. In the Pacific halibut fishery, for example, owners under a property right regime are now permitted to fish over more *months* than they did *days* under the previous regulated regime. Thus they can sell a fresher fish at a higher price, and, if they wish, downgrade the complexity and cost of their vessel and equipment.

However, the exclusivity of the ITQ is not complete. An ITQ gains exclusivity when, for example, it confines each vessel to a specific sub-area, sub-season, or age or size of fish.[130] Even then, in most cases the holders still have weather and market reasons for bunching into short fishing periods during which they may interfere with each other. The ITQ licence is generally not yet exclusive enough to allow complete optimization by its holder: to fish intensively, cut costs, build up his capital in his vessel, cash in on swings in market price, sustain his crew's morale, use his vessel in a second fishery, take a chance on the stock and/or rent out his quota.

[129] As opposed to quotas denominated as an absolute number of pieces.

[130] There are many New Zealand examples. See Pearse 1991, pp. 16–24 for discussion of a New Zealand experience involving integrating an old regulatory regime into an ITQ system.

Given these benefits and constraints, the attitudes of fishers under an ITQ system toward government regulatory decisions differ from those under a licensing regime. The biggest difference is that under the ITQ a fisher 'owns' the same (presumably unchanging) fraction of the swimming stock into the future. This gives him a proprietorial reason to support investment in measuring, predicting and enforcing the TAC; to listen to biologists; and even to take calmly the proposal that fishers pay for their own scientific research.[131] If the measures taken cause the stock and catch to increase, he will get his share of the larger stock with more certainty than will the traditional licence holder. For the same reason, the ITQ holder should be expected to acquire more knowledge, join with other fishers and regulators in constructive talks about policy and payoffs and take greater interest in preventing poaching than a similar participant in a licensing regime.[132]

However, the fishers' increased exclusivity from adoption of ITQs does not reduce the costs of enforcement, and may even increase them. First, as much or more enforcement may be required. Theoretically, each owner-and-crew has an increased incentive to exceed their vessel's quota: if they cheat now, they receive 100 percent of their present illegal gain, yet suffer only their quota percentage of the resultant future pain from a reduction in the stock. Second, even if the community of owners and fishers does create an ownership ethic strong enough to prevent large amounts of cheating, it may find that the actual mechanics of enforcement are more costly. Under the older restrictions on the length of the fishing season, the 'police' had only to make sure that no vessel was out fishing when the grounds were supposed to be closed. Under an ITQ regime, by contrast, vessels are allowed—encouraged—to be on the grounds when other vessels are not. Effective monitoring therefore requires more costly techniques, such as auditing account books; making sure balances are up to date and checking actual landings against them; or even placing observers on boats to ensure that no vessel exceeds its quota.[133] Third, the complexity of the necessary bookkeeping and auditing is also increased if holders are allowed to exceed their own quotas by buying or renting quota from other holders. If the net result is to increase the cost of the fishery, then ITQs and exclusivity-enhancing modifications may be opposed by fishermen, administrators and government.

As a simple rule, the more exclusivity a fisher's property right has, the lower the costs of fishing and the greater fisher support for its introduction. However,

[131] See Walters and Pearse 1996.

[132] One caveat is that the fisher will probably discount future net benefits more than do government employees. See Marglin 1963 and Sen 1967; for the social opportunity cost of funds, see Burgess et al. 1989; and for the public opportunity to spread risks, see Arrow and Lind 1970.

[133] See Clark et al. 1989, pp. 131–3. I am indebted to G. Peacock, Bruce Turris and Peter D. Wilson for information about observers.

as discussed just above, some fishers will expect to lose by the transition from a limited-licence to a more exclusive ITQ-based fishery and will therefore be hostile to it. Smaller fishers may expect to be squeezed out if they are confined to their small initial quota by the new ITQ regime. (As suggested above, however, such fishers have historically been well compensated for selling out as the market values of fish quotas have climbed worldwide.)

Another group hostile to quotas is made up of 'high liners'—those vessels whose captains consistently got the largest catches in the competitive racing regime under whatever system preceded ITQs. Such captains, through a self-reinforcing process, continuously attracted the most capital and the best crews. Government statistics consistently showed a wide gap between the catch of the highest-yield vessels and the median. The high liners did not benefit much from the introduction of quotas even when their past success caused them to be assigned larger-than-average initial quotas. Under an ITQ regime such captains and crews, along with the smaller vessels discussed above, would gradually leave the industry and be replaced by quota-holders more friendly to the calmer ITQ lifestyle. In this way the regime could be expected to 'select' its membership: the kind of fishers who would willingly work under it and eventually sustain demand for it.[134]

The transferability characteristic and quota markets

The transferability characteristic measures the freedom of any right-holder to grant (assign, give, lend, sell or rent) her right to any willing grantee, or to put it in the hands of a broker for offering on an impersonal market. People who thereby acquire more quota may land more fish; and if they land too much they may seek more quota. In the long run, each vessel may assemble just enough quota to suit its capacity and the crew's available time.

Quotas in actual systems usually have a good deal of transferability; indeed, on a worldwide basis the basic unit of most rights systems is labelled the individual *transferable* quota (ITQ), and it is sometimes fully as tradable as a city lot, a mining lease or a water right.[135] The presence of transferability can be signified by the existence of a market and current price for quotas. To maintain the market and keep the price up, quota-holders have an incentive to cooperate with regulators to police the industry and prevent free riding and quota-busting.

ITQ TRANSFERABILITY AND FISHER MOBILITY

An increase in the transferability of quotas makes possible a re-allocation of labour (along with other inputs). Licence holders who have been trapped in

[134] For an analysis of what kind of fishery is suitable for fixed quotas, see R. Hannesson in Neher et al. 1989, pp. 459–65.

[135] For a scheme for limiting quota transferability, see Economic Council of Canada 1980, ch. 6.

one fishery can move on to another, or to other industries and occupations, or into retirement without the loss to themselves and their heirs that would be felt in the absence of transferability. In theory, the fishers who buy quota probably expect a larger stream of income or rent from it than do those who sell out. There could be many rational reasons for optimism: greater strength, skill, patience, better labour management, easier access to capital, better complementarity with other fisheries or any combination of these. Over time, then, the fishery's crews, vessels and gear are altered so that the total fleet is more productive or 'efficient' than if the original quotas had been non-transferable. This improvement in inter-industry allocation is a fairly robust, though 'partial', theoretical prediction.

TRANSFERABILITY COSTS AND MARKET CONCENTRATION

Whether the transferability characteristic in quotas is demanded depends on whether markets work sufficiently well that transfers are smooth and easy. In turn, this depends upon whether fishermen and middlemen keep the market busy. The trading mechanism can get a boost not only from full-time quota brokers but also from allied boat brokers, fish middlemen and lenders such as the banks and (possibly) government. On the other hand, some intrinsic factors work against participation and efficiency of quota markets. In the short run, second-hand quotas may be partly used up and so not really sufficiently standardized to produce a smooth sale. A related concern is the *transactions costs* of using the market, notably the users' information costs. The two influences cannot easily be distinguished, because one reason for the existence of organized markets is precisely to make information available inexpensively. One effect when many fishers have frequent recourse to the quota market is the creation of economies of scale in producing and distributing information, or in the trading of products complementary to holding a quota.[136] But if the market is underused, transactions costs may remain discouragingly high. Finally, there are transitional fears, for instance that the government will tax transactions or introduce new costs to holding quota. In general, however, experience shows that fishers quickly understand quota markets and opt to participate. This is perhaps unsurprising since many modern fishers already own many kinds of property—boats, nets, land, cars, trucks—which they regularly sell and rent on markets.

A more basic fear is that capitalistic fish buyers and large-scale vessel operators will use the ITQ market to capture and hoard quotas, driving up their price. This is an aspect of the industry concentration that some fear may follow the transition to quotas. Transferability may accommodate a dominant player

[136] See Munro and Neher 1995, pp. 91–2. Finding and buying both a new vessel and a quota of the right size to go with it involves dealing in a surprisingly wide range of costly services. See Milgrom and Roberts 1992, pp. 147–8.

who sets the price or controls the amount of quota traded.[137] This player could be a speculator, a large firm, or a group of smaller vessel owners. Small fishers (except those who may be in on the price-fixing) hate this kind of manipulation because it can deprive them of expected gains, prevent entry or force small operators out.

However, people who grumble about a lack of competition in the quota market are usually less worried about quota price and fishing-cost effects than about the holding-down of the price of raw fish. Fears of price fixing are so widespread that governments (Iceland's, for example) have been persuaded to prevent a single buyer or group from acquiring a significant percentage of ITQs. That is, they have reduced the transferability of quota in order to prevent fish buyers from becoming price setters—despite the fact that potential ITQ concentration is only one of the factors that could reduce competitiveness in fish pricing.

Does concentration of the fishing industry actually increase when a licence regime is transformed into an ITQ regime as critics fear? Regarding horizontal integration at least the concern seems ill-founded; there is little evidence that introducing ITQs causes large firms to try to consolidate or expand their ownership 'backward' into land or resource ownership, or to acquire more vessels or expand into complementary industries. (By reducing racing behaviour and the need to squeeze competitors, introducing ITQs may even reduce firms' desire for horizontal or backward integration.) Turning to vertical integration, if concentration is measured by, say, the percentage of the catch taken by the ten holders with the largest catches, then concentration is almost arithmetically bound to increase, since the ten holders will be an increasing fraction of all holders. The data show that this is what happened in New Zealand and Iceland as well as in later regimes when ITQs were introduced. If instead the numbers are put into a ratio of percentages—the percentage of the total catch taken by the ten per cent of holders who have the largest quota holdings—then the evidence so far does not suggest an increase in concentration.[138]

TRANSFERABILITY, COMMUNITY AND FISHING AS A WAY OF LIFE

Some critics worry that the kind of restructuring brought about by the introduction of transferability in quotas will upset the life of fishing communities.[139] And they are right, as the subsection above on mobility suggests. In a world where

[137] See Robinson 1985 and Lilburn 1986.

[138] I am grateful for conversation with Birgir Runolfsson (Rekjavik), Tom McLurg (Wellington), Leslie Burke (Halifax), and Bruce Moffat (Vancouver) on this matter. For recent calculations, see Connor 1999 and Liew 1999.

[139] In 1996 this fear was often expressed when quota licences were introduced into Canadian fisheries. The effect of transferability is also indicated by the analysis of new treaties assigning salmon quotas to B.C. First Nations bands. The effect is similar to what it would be should a percentage catch quota held by existing commercial fishers in salt water be transferred to First Nations peoples upstream. Both sides believe that, because of this transfer, some First Nations communities will grow while some coastal fishing centres will shrink.

property has become transferable, a child may less frequently follow in his or her parents' footsteps. And decades of experience in agriculture have shown that the transferability of crop marketing quotas causes some regions to become important specialized centres for growing particular crops while other regions decline as producers. Similarly in the fishing world quota transferability facilitates and encourages relocation of fishing and people and of their communities. It may produce a shift in activity and eventually a general exodus to where fish can be better processed or rushed fresh to market; or to where people would prefer to have their homes and schools; or to where there are more or different off-season jobs. These moves are particularly likely when the coming of an ITQ regime lengthens the fishing season and so reduces the value of living near the grounds. Almost any kind of population migration within the fishing industry hurts those continuing to dwell in remote or declining communities. These individuals might be counted among opponents of greater transferability.

Views of duration of an ITQ

The duration characteristic of ITQs is of less interest than the duration of rights over such other natural resources as standing timber or mineral deposits.[140] As a concept it flounders in the confusion between two suggested meanings: the length of time during which an ITQ's rules and specification will not be changed; and the length of the period until a particular holder's entitlement lapses. These concepts are slippery. Most governments' long-term quota rights convey an entitlement to an amount of a total variable catch. The holder's *percentage* of the TAC will remain unchanged, but the TAC to be landed by all quota-holders may be reduced or increased frequently (or infrequently), within or between fishing seasons. By changing the TAC the government biologists and administrators whose business it is to manipulate the pressure on the stock can adjust the catch to which each holder is entitled without the hassle of introducing and disposing of new instruments of entitlement (i.e. new formal quotas).

Under the second meaning of duration, discussion arises about the distribution of jobs, income and wealth among potential quota holders. Some governments can and do issue quotas with limited duration, subject to a renewal fee. On the expiry of an ITQ its holder can pay to renew it or can allow it to be sold (or given) to the next person in line under whatever distribution policy is in place. But with transferability the owner of an expiring ITQ can also buy a replacement quota from another holder. Thus, a reasonable conclusion is that ITQs are always 'permanent' in the sense that no fisher need go without quota because it has expired, so long as he is willing to pay the going market price to acquire a replacement. The concept of duration is replaced by the concepts of TAC, renewal and replacement.

[140] For a discussion of quota valuation during the transition to an ITQ system (and the related property-tax problem), see Lindner, Campbell, and Bevin 1990.

Demands for quality of title or security

Governments' enhancement of their fishing rights in adding to exclusivity, transferability and duration has been met by fishermen's demand for better quality of title.[141] This in turn meets resistance from lawyers, who respond that the fisherman's claim to anything like title to a property right has *not* been strengthened by the transition to ITQs. Like government spokesmen, lawyers have insisted that the ITQ remains a mere administratively justified licence or permit, issued by the relevant government agency.[142] ITQs do not fall under the law of property. The ITQ system does not provide a 'root' for a holder's title or even anything like registries of mining claims or land titles.[143] Consequently, if there were a dispute about who owned an ITQ, the procedure for its settlement would be unlike the legal proceedings that have long protected title to real private property.

The fisherman's interpretation of the degree of security in his ITQ would be less obvious. The government agency from whom he acquired his licence and quota has continuously tinkered with fishing rights, offering successive refinements to licence and regulatory regimes that have reduced the holder's right to choose place, time, species and/or gear. It also intervened by creating ITQs and granting them to some fishers but not to others. Fishermen may have little faith in governments' will to fight off public complaints about the ITQ holders' unearned gains from increases in the value of the quotas (and about the failure of government to capture these fishing rents). In short, while he may know that his 'title' is fairly secure as against other fishermen (largely through government enforcement) he may be less sanguine about his security against future government policies.[144]

In my opinion, governments' slowness to reassure the world that ITQs are secure in the hands of their holders reflects official surprise at having stumbled into creating or supplying an interest that has plentiful measures of the characteristics of property. Its purpose was to continue to improve stock protection by using measures introduced by biologically trained administrators and officers, not to grant its holder a right of property, including

[141] A number of papers at the FAO property rights conference in Fremantle in 1999 presented lawyers' views. See Fitzpatrick, pp. 53–6; and Arbuckle and Drummond 1999, pp. 370–82.

[142] In countries with competitive forms of government (such as federations), the level of government with power over fishery regulation may not be the level that has powers to enforce or even to recognize individual real property rights. In such countries, constitutions and/or courts may prevent the regulating and licensing sectors of government from taking the final step toward private ownership. See Wildsmith et al. 1985; and Scott 1982.

[143] For the importance of a good registry, see Pearse 1991, pp. 12–13; and Wildsmith et al. 1985.

[144] These paragraphs omit discussion of the constitutional protection of the right to property which may, in the United States and perhaps under the European convention, be invoked in the future to prevent a fishery agency, in the name of fish stock management, from reducing the TAC and hence 'property' in individual landings, at least without compensation.

immunity from interference. If governments chose they now could take steps to *declare* the ITQ to be a property right. Their silence confirms some fishers' scepticism about the quality of their title. But it does not prevent others from continuing to assume functioning markets and good title.

What roles for governments?

THE TRANSITIONAL, DISTRIBUTIVE ROLE

When Western governments introduced ITQs they greatly reduced the burden of regulation they had unknowingly assumed a century earlier. Nevertheless, in the transition to ITQs governments' roles have broadened rather than declined. More than when they were content to regulate openings and gear, fishery ministries have been called on to make distributive choices and to explain, adjudicate and compensate while changing the fishery from a competitive racecourse to a place where ITQ-holders can work side by side.

I have already discussed some of the difficulties governments encountered in this role. Because the transition to an ITQ regime has often been precipitated or catalysed by a crisis in the fishery concerned, the fishers involved often had unrealistic expectations and widespread distrust of policy changes, disagreeing with government and with each other. Concepts of justice and fairness often conflicted with concepts of efficiency. In assigning quota, fishers who happen to have taken small catches during the historical period will be genuinely outraged that this should be used to deny them as much quota as the average fisher when, had they known that the past record was to dictate their future quota endowment, they would have invested in more equipment, larger crews, longer hours and larger catches. They may demand to know why fishing preferences or abilities should even serve as criteria for the division of wealth under transferable quotas.

In wading through this distributional quagmire, government fishery agencies are not detached arbiters of distributional matters. As mentioned, they will be under industry and political pressure to favour certain classes of fishermen. More important, they must cope with governments' own revenue targets, ranging from the imposition of general income and capital-gains systems to special royalty-like charges and fees. Under ITQs the rents of some fisheries may be high, and some finance ministers be as determined to capture part of them as they are to obtain public-land revenues from oil and gas operators, loggers and miners. One may predict that agency managers will sometimes be torn three ways about ITQs: on some occasions anxious to see justice in distribution as among commercial fishermen holding quotas; on some occasions considering private benefits as against society's claim to the rent of the resource; and on yet other occasions fearful that the sum of public revenue and private profit-taking will reduce their freedom to conduct sound fish stock management.

A CONTINUING REGULATORY ROLE

Once the ITQs have been distributed some fisheries will not need much regulation, especially enforcement of closures. In others, however, the incompleteness of exclusivity in the ITQ and/or the incentive to cheat will necessitate a continuing regulatory role for government to manage the fish stock and to prevent waste of labour and capital. Even where increased monitoring of the fishers' vessels or accounts is not required, regulators will still have to set and modify the TAC and related individual quotas for each year, area and/or species; set overall closures and/or size and gear restrictions to achieve the desired distribution of size and age within the stock; and balance the interests of the commercial fishing and sport fishing industries.[145]

Generally, official intervention in and regulation of the fishery is necessary because fisheries lack certainty and stability. Where the stocks and catches are not stable or predictable it is impossible to dispense with irregular closures. Fluctuating natural conditions (such as water temperatures, currents and quality, and unexpected changes in reproduction and mortality) require that TACs be quickly set and adjusted *during the season*. Pre-season forecasts are generally not credible. However, if governments do promptly adjust quotas in the face of new contingencies during the fishing season, vessel owners may make a long-run adjustment to instability by acting as though early closures are probable and engaging in the same high-cost capital-stuffing and racing behaviour that blighted pre-quota regulatory eras.

The world's salmon and other anadromous fisheries are the leading examples of this type of instability. Under the early regulatory regimes they received a disproportionate amount of attention and were the subject of experimental law making, a process that continues today. Each species has sub-species that are specific to rivers and adjoining coastal feeding grounds. At each stage in their life histories, they are best caught by, or are particularly vulnerable to, special fishing gears. As a result government is required to regulate in different ways, depending on place and time. The introduction of an ITQ regime hardly relaxes this obligation. Indeed, though some concrete proposals for bringing some salmon races under ITQ regimes exist, many ITQ enthusiasts believe that simple ITQs are not appropriate for stocks as unstable as salmon and other anadromous species, or even for migratory species such as tuna and halibut.

This brings us to the major challenge posed for government by multi-species fisheries. The introduction of ITQs into a fishery that catches more than one species will add great complexity to the management problems referred to earlier. A multi-species fishery—either one that catches multiple species or

[145] For more on sport fishing quotas, see Clawson and Knetsch 1966 and Scott 1965, Brubaker 1995, ch. 13 and passim; and Leal 1996, pp. 199–220. Allocation in ocean waters between sports and commercial fishermen is best presented in discussions of the problem in New Zealand. See Pearse 1991, pp. 8–9; New Zealand 1992, ch. 6; and McMurran 1999.

members of the same species at different points in the lifecycle—is said to be difficult (costly) to run under ITQs because of a heightened by-catch problem; but managing it without ITQs has been extremely difficult and costly (chiefly because it requires different closures for different species).[146] If costs of managing by using an ITQ regime are unacceptably high, then government can stay with managing by closure or, if incentives allow, push the costs onto the fishers.

Who will bear the high costs of managing a multi-species fishery with an ITQ regime? One may predict that government could be pressed into accepting this job, unless some of the by-catch species were unusually valuable. In that case, fishers might be willing to share in the costs. Studies of New Zealand and Australian fisheries show that most really low-value harvests and by-catches have not been placed under ITQs but instead remain under government regulation by closure or gear control.

GOVERNMENTS HARVEST FISHING RENTS

In this chapter I have left implicit how the advent of property allowed the economic rent of fisheries to appear. While pointing out how the champions of regulation and of fishing rights acted in their own interest, I have omitted reporting on the subsequent redistribution of the benefits and costs of an ITQ regime (beyond the initial distribution of quotas). Indeed, the information available on this topic is very limited. It appears, however, that the modern fishing institutions discussed here have finally produced a positive rent of fishing—one that, it must be noted, is in sharp contrast to the economic position of many of the West's largest fisheries that have yet to adopt quotas, and whose stocks are in some cases at or near collapse. In Newfoundland, for instance, after the cod fishery collapsed in 1992, most of the approximately 40,000 fishers were forced into unemployment, and the stocks have not recovered.

But where fisheries under ITQ and related regimes have flourished, the financial rents must somehow be allocated among owners, crews,[147] processors/buyers and, through taxation and the quota-selling, governments. Disputes and bitterness have naturally ensued. As a general proposition, however, it is fair to say that fishermen have long been at the lowest end of the economy's income scale. Now more of them, not only quota holders but crewmen as well, are entering the income-tax paying classes. If for no other reason than this, tax-collecting governments should be added to the list of beneficiaries from fisheries regulation, limited licensing and quotas.

[146] See McIlgorm and Tsamenyi 1999, p. 151.

[147] In western economies the crews of very large vessels will be on hourly or weekly pay. On middle-sized vessels, crew incomes are based on customary shares, the lay. When catches increase and prices rise, crew members get larger incomes. However, increases in the capital value of the fishing licence when it becomes an ITQ belongs to the licence-holder not to crew members. See Anderson 1999 and Johnson 1999.

GOVERNMENTS AND SELF-GOVERNING FISHERIES

The discussion above has shown that among the chief benefits of introducing ITQs is help in getting rid of over-crowding and racing, short seasons, low-quality products and certain kinds of gear regulation. But even when ITQs work perfectly they still leave each fishery in the hunting and gathering stage of economic development. The problem is that this highly individualistic mode of production does not encourage its participants to better pool information, to protect its stocks, to achieve economies of scale or to try other modes of co-operative production.

It could be replied that, because regulations, TAC and stock information are in effect local undivided public goods, one cannot expect a non-government cooperative, without powers of compulsion, to provide them efficiently—indeed to provide them at all. But since the late 1970s commissions and consultants have been looking into the possibilities of deregulating bits and pieces of the entire economy. In the process, they have been led to question government's role in many industries, including the fishery. In New Zealand in the late 1980s, politicians, knowing little about the subject, automatically included the fisheries service among the government branches to be downsized. One principle to which they swore fealty was that everything should pay for itself; another was that government should not provide what an industry needed privately. Governments were leaving farmers to look after themselves; why should fishermen not also look after their own needs?

A possibility I introduce elsewhere in this book (in Chapter 12 for an open-access, multiple-use forest) is that the users of a particular resource could form an organization similar to a condo or strata-title institution. The various users (here, fishers of the same or different species in the same or different seasons) form the membership and become the officers of the unit with names like 'share management regime', 'conservation cooperative', 'harvesters' association', 'management company', 'advisory board' or 'co-management organization'. Such fishing arrangements among ITQ holders have been coming into existence since the 1990s. Some provide services to the fleet that were not provided before; some have taken their roles over from government; some raise money and spend it on enforcement, information, research, storage or marketing. New South Wales for abalone (1996), Western Australia for rock lobsters (1994), New Zealand for orange roughy (1991) and scallops (1992), British Columbia for geoduck (1988), sablefish (1989), and halibut (1992), Nova Scotia communities for groundfish (1996) and the United States for West Coast whiting and pollock (1997–8) are all examples of such emerging organizations listed in a recent conference report.[148]

[148] R. Shotton, ed. Use of Property Rights in Fisheries Management FAO Fisheries Technical Papers 404/1 and 404/2 Rome 2000.

Is there a reason why a fishery, organizing itself as a cooperative, must depend on government regulation? Preventing unfair income or catch distribution is not the reason, for ITQs look after that once and for all. Neither is discriminating fishery regulation (laid on to help particular groups) the reason, for ITQs ensure that all regulations affect all fishermen for a given species and on a given fishing ground equally. Neither are overall enforcement and monitoring the reasons, since they cannot be avoided by choice of institution.

Does the answer lie in a special capacity of government to look after fish stocks? For example, is there a reason why the fishermen, working as a cooperative, cannot provide their own TAC? For an industry cooperative to do as well as the government's biological scientists in setting each year's TAC, it needs a long-run management goal, a plan, and good information about the size, growth and composition of the fishstocks. But fishermen are already the source of much, if not most, information used by government scientists. Their vessels can seek and provide most kinds of data, of better quality than in the past. They have time and incentive to collect such data, for under an ITQ regime they need not be frantically busy during the traditional short open seasons designed to preserve stocks before ITQs. Theoretically, scientific analysis of the collected data can be provided as well by private consultants as by government. Similar arguments can be made for organizing and arranging joint-fishing operations built around the participants' quotas: running docks, storage facilities or markets for fish or quotas.

Even in light of these speculations, however, just as with the transition and sharing of ITQs, so with the setting-up of cooperatives: the government has initial duties that will not and cannot be provided otherwise.

- *Fishing*: to prevent free riding on the cooperative management while ignoring its rules, government may need to provide enforcement of compulsory membership. Government ITQs have already made this possible.
- *Organization*: to prevent corruption and dishonesty within the cooperative, government may need to provide voting and reporting rules. Attaching votes to quotas makes this easier.[149]
- *Contracting*: to facilitate the carrying-out of agreements and bargains between cooperatives concerning harvesting of mixed species and using of the fishing grounds for other purposes, government may need to endorse

[149] Recent papers by Ragnar Arneson argue that neither government initiative nor fisherman's cooperative organizations are needed to make fishery policies for a particular stock. A working market in quotas is sufficient. For a particular fishery for which there are transferable ITQs, badly conceived fishery policies will lead to a decline in the market value of ITQs. Good policies will lead to an increase in fisherman profits and a rise in the market value of their quotas. Arnason argues that fishermen's political pressure or that of external ITQ-holding investors will induce the government to introduce and enforce ITQ-value-maximizing policies of the fishery's choosing. No formal cooperative organization is even needed.

contracts. Sharing any contractual burdens in proportion to members' quotas makes this more manageable and predictable.

There are other reasons that explain why ITQ-holding fishermen would sometimes rather depend on government than on their own fisheries' co-operative. Coping with multiple fleets harvesting overlapping multiple stocks may be one, preventing ocean pollution another, and defence against DW fleets from other nations may be a third. Yet some argue the most convincing reason is money. From a fisherman's hard-headed point of view, the best reason for retaining a paternalistic government to make regulations and set the TAC is that the government may continue to do so either for 'free' (from the fisher's perspective) or far below cost.

Nevertheless, the success of ITQs may allow participants to draw breath and consider which route to follow to further reduce costs, increase landing values and conserve the stock at the optimal level. Merely having a government-controlled ITQ regime may not always be enough. It is important to consider that with ITQs the fishermen have already achieved the two indispensable features for joint management. First, their membership is closed. Second, they already have a sharing of the catch through an individual (if still informal) property right with high levels of quality of title, transferability, divisibility, duration and, especially, exclusivity. This sharing is secure and as reliable as that of the equity of shareholders in a business corporation, members in a housing condominium or farmers in an irrigation district. ITQ fisheries would therefore seem a logical place to test the efficacy of private natural resource cooperatives.

Part III

Rights over Mineral Resources

5

Mineral Disposal and Mining Rights to 1850

Introduction: concepts and regimes in mining rights

This and the following four chapters concern the development of mining and mineral rights both as legal matters and as motivating events in the history of mineral development and use. With the exception of oil and gas, the subject of the second (major) section of Chapter 9, mineral resources differ from the 'flowing' resources discussed in Part II in that they obviously, and legally, go with the land from which they are taken. Property rights over minerals, both in the public and private domains, are therefore much closer to and are bound up with the 'standard' property interests in farm and urban land stemming from Roman and early common law and statutes. Though mineral owners imposed externalities on each other (for instance by breaking a water table and flooding a neighbouring mine) they could expect that their minerals would remain physically secure inside the borders of their property and that no outside party could legally take the minerals from within the land without express provision.

As a subject in the literature, the development of rights over mineral resources takes a back seat to the subjects of 'mineral disposal' law and 'mineral acquisition' law—that is, to the policies and laws governing the disposal by governments and private landholders of lands thought to be valuable for their subterranean mineral deposits. In the following four chapters (as in the subsequent chapters on rights to forest resources) I examine development in two distinct though overlapping spheres: that of rights in 'public' or Crown lands and that of rights in private lands. Rights in public land are those devised by authorities to protect and promote the government or Crown's own ownership and financial interest, or else to forward the 'public interest' as the politicians and legislators define it. Rights in private lands emerged as responses to demand for resolution of two types of conflict: conflicts arising between subsurface users (mainly miners) and users of the associated surface estate (such as farmers); and conflicts arising between neighbouring mining estates whose operations imposed externalities and spillovers on each other.[1]

As we will see, however, a public–private distinction was not always clear. The concept of a 'private mineral owner' was less clear-cut during the medieval and Enlightenment periods and even in the nineteenth century than it is today. Public and private owners of mineral rights, such as the recipients of British colonial charters, or the hereditary minor nobility of feudal Europe, were not easily classified as either law-making public entities or as private self-interested individuals making the best use of their own property. Often, they combined elements of both. For instance, the European Crowns and nobility had many of the trappings of 'public' landowners, such as law-making and presiding over medieval courts. But very often they acted like private profit- or utility-maximizing entities in choosing how best to dispose of the minerals on the land under their jurisdictions. The minor nobility had their own lawmaking and judicial powers over their tenant communities and were responsible for providing forest maintenance. Yet like private landlords, they disposed of their mineral rights within a largely exogenous, publicly defined set of laws and customs that pertained to all at their level. With respect to this latter group, I am most interested in their purely private behaviour as mineral landlords, the discussion of which is a subject of Chapter 8 on the development of private mining law.

In general, I have found the readiest explanations of the development of mining right characteristics come from examining the needs and policies of those disposing of the rights, rather than from the specific financial

[1] Regarding the development of private rights, I must say a few words about two expository approaches that fell by the wayside. One consisted of tracing the evolution of leasing. I became interested in leasing almost fifteen years ago and actually collected a sample of more than 100 ancient and early-modern English coal- and lead-mining leases. In spite of generous helpers' work to collect, translate and compare these documents, the results were disappointing. Little was revealed about the evolution of property rights. This work did lead me on to study the history of mining conveyancing, where I learned that scholars such as J. U. Nef, relying on leases and other deeds from other sources, had already brought to light much of what could be learned. I did use this material for a number of workshops and seminars, and it served me well by arousing interest in the study of property rights in natural resources.

A second possible approach to the development of private mining rights focused on three of the characteristics of leaseholding rights: one on the development of exclusivity, one on the development of flexibility, and one on the development of duration. The part on exclusivity eventually developed into the present chapter and is no longer confined to leases. The part on flexibility grew into an essay on the bargaining between landowner and miner before the completion of discovery. Interesting in itself, it was difficult to relate to the actual leases in my sample or to the parallel changes in property laws. The part on duration soon became dominated by speculation about the economics of planned renewal of mining leases. This could be an important subject, but its development seemed not to be much reflected in the development of standard mining rights.

and technical requirements of mining. For example, the size of the typical nineteenth-century holding was usually determined by general land policies or by settlement policies negotiated or demanded by those who held or desired to hold title to the land. The size of holding that would have allowed the miner to optimize his operation with respect to shafts, tunnels and mills seems often to have scarcely been considered. The property-right characteristic that the miners eventually obtained, crucial on feudal estates, in the California camps and in modern corporate mining, was not size, depth or area, but *exclusivity*.

Another thing to consider in approaching the history of mining rights is that systems of mining law are not easily classified into distinct national or theoretical types. Most systems are very old and have survived only because demanders and suppliers have from time to time greatly modified them to suit changing opportunities. Such alterations mean that I can offer only a general guide rather than a detailed, large-scale map of mining law development. I am not the first to be forced to experiment with various methods of classification. According to John Leshy, a modern authority on twentieth-century American federal mining law, Curtis Lindley warned early in the century that mining law is 'one of the most difficult branches of the law to . . . logically arrange for the purpose of treatment, and the embarrassments surrounding its exposition are almost insurmountable'.[2]

With these caveats out of the way, I proceed in the rest of this chapter to provide a short sketch of the history of mining and its conception as a system of property in the nation-state, up to the middle of the nineteenth century. In Chapter 6 I look at the development of one particular form of mining on public lands: the institution of free mining and its application to the New World gold rushes of the nineteenth century. In Chapter 7 I turn to the subject of how modern (post-colonial) governments established and developed systems of disposal for mineral lands and in particular how they reacted to the emergence of the modern corporate mining enterprise. Chapter 8 looks at mining rights in the situations where government was not a direct player: that is, rights as defined and developed between private mineral holders, particularly through their recourse to the courts. Most of the examples from Chapters 5 through 8 concern rights over metallic mining. Chapter 9 provides a specific overview of two equally important areas of mineral extraction: coal and oil and gas, both of which also developed in both the 'public' and 'private' spheres. Rights over these minerals were introduced in Chapter 2 and stand somewhat apart from those over the other minerals discussed in this part.

[2] Leshy 1987, p. 8, citing Curtis Lindley 1914, vol. 1, p. 125.

Original ownership and the state control of mineral rights in Europe and the early Spanish colonies

One of the major questions facing legal historians is the extent of the state's 'public' ownership over minerals inside its territorial boundaries, and in particular whether the early 'state'—as represented by the assembly, emperor or Crown—once assumed all the minerals within its territorial boundaries or just the gold and silver. The answer emphasizes an important practical difference between English (common) law and Roman (civil) law. Under English law there exists the presumption that anyone exploring or mining minerals does so under licence of the present landowner, who himself received the right to grant such licences by a previous owner, who in turn received the right or title from the previous owner in a dynastic line reaching back to the original, often ancient, landowner. That original holder might well have been the Crown (or, more generally, the state), by virtue of its original prerogatives,[3] but common law does not require this presumption in order to give an individual quality of title.

This stands in direct contrast to Roman law and to the modern legal systems that derive from it. In these systems—which persist in France and Spain and countries once under their dominion—the norm is state ownership of mines, ranging from those yielding precious metals and gems to open pits and quarries.

Roman mining law

GREECE AND ROME

Most modern writers casually assert that modern state ownership of resource-rich land can be traced back to the classical Greek city-state. Actually, this assumption is somewhat indefinite owing to the 'extreme paucity of evidence for the archaic and classical periods' which requires any honest assessment of property rights in ancient Greece to proceed cautiously.[4] Healy concludes that privately owned mines existed in ancient Greece but were rare, though some public reservation of minerals on private land certainly took place. In particular, surviving references to the silver mines at Laurion indicate that public functionaries auctioned contracts to freemen, who worked their own sites, and

[3] In addition, there is under common law a presumption that the Crown is the ultimate owner of the land: proprietors occupy or hold from, or of, the Crown. After the Conquest the Norman feudal land grants were revocable, but were made without term. Thus private ownership is not absolute, not alloidial. See Megarry and Wade 1984, chs. 2 and 3, pp. 12–13, 64. Today, in practice, when the Crown owns minerals it is not an instance of the fundamental doctrine of Crown ownership of all land but, rather, of the Crown having acquired particular land by right of discovery, conquest, occupation, or purchase.

[4] Healy 1978, p. 103. The matter is considered at length in Healy's ch. 5, pp. 103–38. See also Rickard 1932a, vol. 2, pp. 571–93, who cites different sources and tends to emphasize the large mines owned by the state or Emperor.

to larger operators who depended on slave labour. In Athens, original mineral ownership appears to have been casual and not a matter of high principle.

In the Roman republic's earliest days isolated mines and deposits went with the soil as the property of the landowner. In those days Rome was not regarded by its citizens as a mining economy, and some historians today believe that mining was actually regarded with disfavour. As Roman rule expanded, the state began to take over some of the rich mineral sites. Some mines did remain private though. In Spain there were mines once run by the Carthaginian regime that fell into the hands of Roman 'capitalists', who took over the management and also opened new base-metal and gold mines. Increasingly, everywhere in the Roman world, very large-scale private ownership and state ownership under the administration of provincial praetors supplanted small enterprises.

Historians hold that when imperial Rome succeeded the republic, the emperors, starting with Tiberius, began a personal seizing of the ownership of the mines—implying, at least, that a grant of land from the state no longer included the granting of its minerals. Citizens were evidently free to explore and to open mines, but if successful in their efforts they paid a hefty royalty on their takings (about 50 per cent) and a number of additional taxes remitted to the Emperor. The scanty evidence suggests that few mines were actually ever established on private lands in the Roman Empire, or at least not enough to require a formal set of laws defining the state's (later, the Emperor's) prerogative as against the rights of the landowner. Isay concludes that there was simply 'no occasion to separate the rights of mining from those of [private] land tenure or to assign the former to the state; nor is there any evidence that this was done'. A scanning of the literature suggests too that the regimes in various parts of the Empire were not uniform. Under the republic and under the Emperors, local and regional systems of administration and taxation in Britain, Gaul and Spain were apparently adaptations of whatever had been in effect before Rome arrived.

MEDIEVAL EUROPE

Though it is unlikely that either Greece or Rome ever took a profound, definite, view of the state's role in mineral ownership (and in particular never codified a mineral ownership or mining law), medieval scholars found it convenient to presume that they had done so. A leading question for hundreds of years was whether European mineral ownership was to follow the alleged dogmas of republican or of imperial Rome, in the former case conveying ownership of potential mines to the surface owner or, in the latter, to the state. The issue was not just a matter of scholarship. At stake was the distribution of the revenues from the great mines of eastern Europe, the Alps and Spain during the centuries when land and power were as often in the hands of regional magnates as in the hands of their royal rulers. On the one hand, the

Roman republican principle, maintained in French civil law up to the sixteenth century, pronounced that the local surface owner held both surface and subsurface rights. In the European (especially French) and British feudal system, this rule was supported mainly by the minor nobility (the 'lords of the soil') and was opposed by the monarchy.[5] On the other hand, the imperial principle, which held that all private property was merely a right of usufruct granted by the monarchy, prevailed in eastern regions, whose rulers and scholars subscribed to a Germanic theory of royal prerogative. In these countries, the interest and exploitation rights of the regional landholders and seigneurs went only plough-deep.[6]

From the very early medieval period, in certain remote and mountainous regions of England and Europe, a third, separate system of mining rights existed. Forms of 'free mining'—the subject of Chapter 6—had existed in the stanneries of tin mines of Cornwall,[7] south Germany, and Bohemia from before the fall of the Roman Empire and survived into the modern era, influencing the development of mining in the New World. The European granters of free mining rights allowed wide rights of exploration to groups of miners. When the monarchy granted free mining rights, it allowed its free miners to cross the surface boundaries of local lords and owners. In countries governed mostly by republican law, the local lords had more effective control over the territory and the underground minerals on their lands and were more likely to be the authority granting free mining rights to their estates.

In addition to geographic distinctions between prevalent systems of mineral law, the republican, imperial and free mining principles also waxed and waned over time. In the early medieval period the relatively powerful local lords generally prevailed in combining their surface rights with mineral rights within their fiefdoms. In the later feudal era, however, and in particular during the 'first industrial revolution'[8] of the late-fifteenth and sixteenth centuries, the increasingly powerful kings and princes struggled and generally succeeded in 'reclaiming' their regal powers and revenues from their subject seigneurs. The seigneurs naturally remained defiant in the face of the monarchies' growing control and

[5] J. U. Nef pointed out that our modern knowledge of the law of republican Rome creates a difficulty for any historian who argues that the late-medieval revival of Roman law helped the European princes to extend their regalian rights from gold and silver to base metals. 'It is true nevertheless. The use to which Roman law was put rested, to some extent, on the misinterpretation.' Late-medieval scholars believed that under the Empire property in land did not include property in minerals, this having been retained by the Emperor. This misconception was not cleared up until the work of Achenbach was published in 1869 (see Nef 1952 and 1987, p. 750, n93). As we will see below, French statutes accorded with an especially generous view of the Emperor's rights. See the full review of the old mining laws of France in (22 December 1883), *Legal News* 6, no. 51: 402–8, referring to the Custom of Paris; and Crabbé 1983, referring to Lamé-Fleury, *Legislation des Mines*. Thanks to Rachel Meyer for help on this.

[6] See Weber 1923 and 1961, p. 140; Nef 1952 and 1987; and Isay 1933, p. 514.

[7] Hatcher 1973; Lewis 1907; Pennington 1973.

[8] Nef 1932 and 1966.

their own consequent loss of tax revenue. In the course of this conflict the European Crowns, for instance Spain (1387) and France (1413), brought selected miners under their direct patronage and passed laws requiring the seigneurs and local lords to assist these miners with their explorations and investments.[9] These kings, great magnates and overlords were generally well-served by their royal scholars, who supported the legitimacy of their respective claims.

The French political example was especially influential. In 1413 Charles VI passed a law confirming the royal right to French minerals and cutting the seigneur out of the revenue stream, to the advantage of the miner. Then in 1471 Louis XI, not wholly disregarding his own seigneurs, created a royal mining administration. His intervention did not put the search for and extraction of all minerals under direct state control but set up some special local enterprises and assumed a managerial or regulatory role over the seigneurs (see below).[10] Such centralization could not make the French Crown, which ruled a mineral-poor country, into a great mining power, but the new laws' revenue implications were noted and emulated by other imperial Roman-law nations. Central European kingdoms cited the imperial Roman model and followed France in claiming a regalian right not only over the traditional prerogative precious metals (gold and silver), but also over such base metals as iron, lead and tin.[11]

SPAIN AND ITS COLONIES

In 1525 in a newly united Spain, King Carlos followed the French precedent in asserting royal rights to precious metals and to other minerals. This prerogative applied not only to old Spain's mining districts but also to Carlos's new gold and silver mines overseas. His successor, Philip, followed the French precedent even more closely. His 1559 mining law drastically centralized mineral ownership and control, expropriated certain private mines and authorized royal-sanctioned miners (concessionaires) to explore widely. Philip's intention was to reduce the nobles to, at best, minor rentiers in the revenue-collection and management of mines. In practice, however, his law provoked resistance not only from the nobility but also from the miners, who complained that royalties were too high and that their mobility was too restricted as they were confined, for monitoring purposes, to pre-selected locations. Such miner resistance, combined with the recalcitrance of the nobles, was eventually effective. By the late 1770s the Crown and its representatives in the colonies

[9] Reforms of 1387 in Spain (Don Juan) and of Charles VI of France 1413. See judgment in *Regina v. DeLéry et. al.* (22 December 1883), *Legal News* 6, no. 51: 402–8; Lacasse 1985; and Crabbé 1983.

[10] Edict of 1471. See Nef 1952 and 1987, pp. 748–9.

[11] Nef 1952 and 1987, pp. 749–50, refers to the regalian claims of the French Crown spreading to cover most of modern France. Adjoining rulers in Lorraine and Franche-Comté followed similar policies. Even the emperor and the lesser princes in central Europe followed France in claiming wider regalian rights.

were thinking of loosening the imperial-Roman leash. In 1783, under royal pressure to get revenue from a mutinous mining sector, the viceroy of Mexico tried to appease conflicting interests by forming a council of mining deputies and commanding it to help reframe the laws and principles to harmonize them with the demands of industry.[12] The viceroys in Peru also found it necessary to supplement the Spanish centralized approach with more localized mining incentives and assistance. Thus there was widespread local tinkering with the implementation of the Crown's authority in both the motherland and the colonies. Despite this backsliding, however, the essential element in the official mining law of imperial Spain into the nineteenth century was an absolute royal prerogative over minerals. This dogma pervaded the systems of government, in particular, of the Spanish Americas and of the Philippines.

THE NAPOLEONIC COMPROMISE OF THE IMPERIAL ROMAN LAW

The European royalty who sought to apply imperial Roman law to mining rights had as a goal maximizing revenue from precious metals, in part by cutting out the minor noble middleman. These rulers' mining policies and claims to minerals harmonized with their mercantilist trade policies and, as in the customs regime, induced their subjects to evade their laws. That the rulers might impose royalties, levy taxes and claim shares of mining discoveries did not guarantee that they would actually receive the demanded revenues. Some mining interests did not report their new mines, or undercounted their production, and some promoters simply postponed going into production until they got a more sympathetic or pliable government. In economic jargon, the Crown may have anointed itself as the principal, but the miners often refused to act as its agents.

The optimal extent of state rights was debated in France in the 1700s. In mid-century the physiocrat Turgot argued in favour of more free ownership for miners and explorers.[13] The younger Mirabeau disputed Turgot's position, urging a continued state prerogative. During the Revolution the Assembly adopted Mirabeau's position, so that surface owners were again largely dispossessed of their minerals and revenues as they had been since the days of Louis XI.

Twenty years later, although Napoleon codified this statist position, it was only weakly adhered to in Spain and France; more vigorously in the Saar, Belgium and Prussia. We have seen that, in Mexico, the Spanish viceroy was in no position to fully enforce the regalian rights he proclaimed against rebellious miners and other local interests. And in France too the state became

[12] The viceroy's proclamation creating the council seemed to restate 1774 legislation asserting royal ownership of anything to do with mining, but it was interpreted as a partial relinquishment. See also the comments in Shinn 1884, p. 55; and Ely 1964, pp. 86–7.

[13] *Memoir on Mines and Quarries*, 1768, as cited by Crabbé 1985. Turgot was then Intendant of Limoges. As a physiocrat, he believed all state revenue should come from rent, and the return from mines was not a rent. He favoured a non-governmental right of miners to enter property and open mines. See Crabbé 1985.

less the owner and more the supreme administrator of mines. Technically it had full responsibility for exploration and full powers to alienate minerals.[14] In practice, what emerged was a more cooperative working relationship between the emperor's court and the surface landholders than had been envisioned during the royal-nobility conflicts of the late feudal era. The Napoleonic state shared the rent of a mine with the surface owner and sometimes facilitated privately initiated mining development.

Original mineral ownership in English law

Roman law is less familiar to us than common law, as it is the latter that prevails today in England and its former colonies. Under common law the holder of land in fee simple is entitled to all the mineral wealth beneath his or her land and has full property powers to manage mines, to dispose of them and especially to receive their rents or royalties. The state's rights over minerals extend only to gold and silver. These limited rights were vaguely derived from the Roman and French royal prerogative over minerals, supported by appeal to coinage of precious metal.[15] In fact, the Crown's prerogative over gold and silver was rarely tested in feudal England, both metals being a rarity there. It was not until the first appearance of silver in lead and tin ores during the sixteenth century, and the Queen Elizabeth's subsequent demand to find more of these ores, that the matter came to a legal head. It was settled by the famous Case of Mines (1568) which found the Crown, rather than the minor landowner, entitled to gold and silver when and wherever it was found in concentrations high enough to be mined economically, including the right to annex the non-precious metals in the surrounding areas.[16] The implications of this decision lasted through the nineteenth-century gold rushes, giving Australian and British Columbian colonial governments the prerogative to reserve gold lands and grant them to free miners (see Chapter 6).

In the earliest British overseas colonies the Crown appropriated all land, including the land containing mines and other resources. It then granted lands and resources to various monopolies and proprietors—sometimes reserving for

[14] The possibility that the state may take the initiative in exploration and development may be explained by France's relatively poor mineralization. Prussia's super-efficient implementation of the French approach led to actual state enterprise in coal mining. See Nef 1932 and 1966, vol. 2, pp. 274–5 and Brose 1993, 45, p. 142. Quebec's quest for *domanialité* in mining is perhaps one version of the Napoleonic version of regalian mining rights; this is described below.

[15] As has been seen, throughout Europe rights to gold and silver were a royal prerogative, quite apart from royal claims to all minerals. Blackstone, writing in 1765, agreed with Gamboa, his contemporary, that this right originated in the coinage prerogative and was therefore a sort of seigneurage. Blackstone 1809, I.I.12.; Gamboa [1761] 1830, 16 (Heathfield translation); Rickard 1932a, vol. 2, ch. 11; Gregory 1980, p. 193.

[16] *Case of Mines*, 1568, 1 Plowd. 310. With this title went the power to enter, dig and remove, and to do such other things as were necessary in mining. This remained the English law until the Mines Royal Act in the reign of William III.

itself all minerals, sometimes only precious metals, sometimes nothing. The royal charters of these private land interests usually stipulated the reservation of precious metals and required that a royalty be paid to the Crown upon their extraction.[17] In the thirteen Colonies the chartered 'proprietors' then granted land to settlers, where land rights included management, disposal and revenue right to any minerals not reserved by the royal charter. In this way deposits of iron, coal, lead and zinc passed to the first landholders. In 1785, in an early ordinance, the revolutionary American government followed the then most recent British policy of the time, declaring a one-third federal interest in gold and silver. But this idea came too late. The states were by then following the common-law, settler-friendly norm of granting the surface and subsurface together, without exception for any specific precious metal. The state interests within the new federal government therefore rejected the 1785 ordinance, also nullifying the Elizabethan Case of Mines as a precedent in the former colonies.

Surprisingly, even as American settlers gained ownership rights over base and, in some cases, precious minerals, other British colonies witnessed a gradual increase in reservation of minerals to the Crown over the course of the late eighteenth and early nineteenth centuries. While general colonial histories have not had much to say about the issue, evidence from histories of particular minerals or of particular colonies suggests that mineral reservation emerged in the age of Adam Smith, soon after the constitutional monarchy had renounced many of its long-proclaimed personal and prerogative rights. The mineral reservation stood as one of the main centralist policies that defined British colonial resource-disposal policy during the later decades of the wars with France and the United States, including the reservation of coal in Nova Scotia, and the implementation of the Broad Arrow policies by which the Crown reserved certain types of trees for royal use as masts for the navy (see Chapter 11).

Summary: public lands and crown mineral reserves

The working-out of these various systems of European mineral ownership law during the age of colonialism placed much of the world's geology, or at least its commercially valuable minerals, under state control. As well, after the medieval period resources that were originally regarded as *res nullius*—the property of no one—were increasingly proclaimed to be, under the systems of laws adopted and enforced by the various European Crowns, state property.

[17] Virginia (Walter Raleigh 1606) reserved 20 per cent of its gold and silver and about 6 per cent of its copper; New England (Plymouth colony, 1620) did much the same; Carolina and New York reserved a fixed lump sum every year. As an example, Article IV of the Maryland charter (Lord Balitmore 1632) grants to the proprietor, without qualification, domain over every conceivable form of property, including 'gold, silver, gems and precious stones and any other whatsoever, whether they be of stones or metals of any other thing metal'. However, according to Article V, the king was to receive a fifth part of gold and silver. See Andrews 1933, p. 41. In general, see Cushing 1978, pp. 118 and 191; Harris 1953, pp. 83 and 99; Lewin 1931, p. 245; and Thorpe 1909.

Between 1066 and 1850:

(1) In all European countries, the Crown/state owned rights to precious metals (gold and silver). In both the Roman imperial and Roman republican systems of property rights law, rights to these precious metals were usually separated from the ownership of the surface lands.

(2) The Crown and the surface landlords disputed the ownership of non-precious minerals. In England after 1600 the decision went completely in favour of the landlord. On the Continent it swung back and forth. By 1800, due to the rise of the great European monarchies, it had tended to the king/state and away from the surface landlord.

(3) In England and its colonies the Crown continued to hold a respectable portion of all minerals until 1850, owing in part to the Crown's victory in the Case of Mines (1568), and in part to the wide extent of Crown lands.

(4) The concept of the separation of mineral rights from both private and public surface rights, which had defined imperial as distinct from republican Roman law, was accepted on the Continent.

(5) Rights to mined-out and abandoned holdings reverted to the landowner or to the state. Also, the state could reclaim private land by charging that the private landholder or land user had not complied with official payment, tax, occupation or work conditions. In most jurisdictions, such abandoned resources rejoined the general reserve, once again becoming ripe for the picking; some also went into a 'special reserve'.[18]

(6) The Crown rarely directly involved itself in mining, even during the early-modern period of relatively centralized control. It was usually content to impose a royalty on all precious minerals and a share on mines in its fields. These royalties and shares were collected by the king's tenants.

Mineral ownership and disposal in the later colonial era

New World gold, silver and base metals in the century before 1850

The mid-1700s saw genuine gold rushes in Siberia and in Brazil. In Siberia the leading discovery came around 1750 in the quartz mines of the Ural Mountains, monopolized by the Russian Crown until 1814 when landowners

[18] The implementation of special-reserve policies has usually required that the mineral be put under the control of a specialized government agency, modern equivalents including the British National Coal Board, the US Atomic Energy Commission, or Canada's Eldorado Mining and Refining Ltd. Otherwise the reserve is and has long been ignored or abused by other agencies. We will see in a later chapter that certain trees on Crown lands in Britain and in its colonies were marked to reserve them for the navy's use. While in reserve they were not generally under navy control.

obtained the right to work the gold beneath their own soil. The Crown then introduced a system of handing over Crown exploration and mining to private concessionaires, modelled on the French or German systems. The Crown and these large-scale concessionaires moved prospectors eastward toward the Yenisei and on to the Lena. When placer mining succeeded excavation, thousands of independent miners moved in. In the end, the Siberian placer gold rush was said to have involved twenty thousand miners, mostly Siberians, in about one hundred mines[19] before production levelled off in 1847.

Brazil's gold rush was better known and longer lasting. Before 1700, prospectors had made discoveries in what would later become the state of Minas Gerais ('Various Mines'). Until the 1820s the widely separated discoveries were worked mostly by placer operations.[20] Theoretically, the early Brazilian placer miners were subject to European-derived concession-type arrangements with local administrators collecting a royal revenue. As the rush intensified around 1750, the state moved to impose a free miner-type system of awarding claims to discoverers. But individualized placer mining gave way to the open-pit operations of principal-family 'owners' holding many claims and relying on slave labour to work them. In response, the government abandoned its royalty, substituting an import duty and a head tax. By 1800 these taxes too were fading and the claim-and-royalty system was re-appearing. There was also a vigorous, informal (and illegal) gold-mining sector, the 'garinpagem', that provided an early example of a phenomenon we encounter in the next chapter: regulations imposed by the colonial governments, if perceived as unfriendly to miners, simply encouraging the miners to operate outside the regulatory system.[21]

The Siberian and Brazilian gold rushes respectively attracted sufficient mobile young labourers that there was never a time when the authorities had to offer the temptation of withdrawing mining regulations in order to attract workers. However, as these rushes did not attract much foreign capital there were recurring problems of production and transportation. Because lack of capital and poor transportation of the mined minerals precluded racing to get ores to market as fast as possible, the miners tended to be patient on their claims and to adapt to their conditions rather than to innovate. This stands in direct contrast to the later experience of the California gold boom. There, gold

[19] Gregory 1980, p. 114. The author gives no source for this estimate. Other writers put the numbers lower.

[20] Morrell 1941, p. 53 and ch. 3.

[21] Eventually, the government gave up trying to regulate the industry and keep garinpagem off the land. As Morrell puts it, 'the multitudes that flocked to new discoveries in Minas Gerais at any rate made application of the mining regulations difficult. In 1728, on a rush . . . it was proclaimed that no grants would be made, but that the ground should be open to all, though a certain distance was to be left between pits.' This hands-off solution apparently became more common as, throughout Brazil, major new discoveries became fewer and the incentive to keep miners within the government revenue-generating system weakened. Only when congestion, increased by the drifting of freed slaves into the garimpeiro sector, became a risk to social order did local magnates intervene to divvy up and assign property rights to individual miners.

values would be much higher, physical capital both easier to come by and less vital to profitable operation and miner control and organization left untouched by government authorities. Indeed, California would have no government structures and revenue demands such as those found in the established colonies of Siberia and Brazil and later in Australia and Canada.

In contrast to gold, there are no recorded historical 'silver rushes'. After initial finds in England during the Elizabethan era, silver had been produced almost everywhere in the eastern hemisphere, often as a by-product of the smelting of the ores of base metals. After the opening of the western hemisphere, large amounts of silver, sometimes jointly found with deposits of gold, were obtained using rather simple techniques in many of the cordilleran districts of Peru and Mexico. Owing to its more commonplace production everywhere silver was less exciting than gold to historians, but far more influential in establishing systems of mining rights.

The world's supply of silver was increasingly provided by two American silver districts: Potosi in southern Peru and Zacotacas in western Mexico. By 1700 the mines in Potosi were nearly depleted, and some were relying on scavenging units to maintain a flow of silver. The mines of Zacotacas, however, remained active from 1520 until the 1920s, producing probably more than 60 per cent of world silver output over that period.[22]

Silver rights were dispensed similarly to gold rights, using the European concession system. Examined in the property-rights characteristics framework used here, the concessions were usually of very long *duration* (conditional on a work requirement that the mine be active for eight months of the year, with activity defined as having four workers present) but had little effective *exclusivity*. The concessionaires' limited exclusive control over their mining enterprises arose not from their contracts but from the fact that the Spanish Crown continued to maintain direct control over downstream and horizontal industries associated with silver mining. For instance, the mercury required for processing the silver ores flowed from Crown-monopolized mines. The Crown also dominated purchases of silver ore and supervised the supply of slave and indentured labour that wealthier free miners depended on for search and extraction. Shipping and transport were also subject to royal control.

In addition to the Crown's indirect control through its monopoly of downstream industries, the direct Spanish mining law—formalized and amended in 1783—was draconian, as if designed to repel venturesome prospectors and investors. It set up a Miner's Tribunal, a group of locals responsible for establishing mining rights (and also supposedly for giving the miners some voice and protection from inexperienced bureaucrats and senior governors). The Tribunal was supposed to operate like the free miners' bergmeister,[23] but it

[22] Gregory 1980, p. 113.
[23] See Chapter 6, for the definition and discussion of bergmeisters.

was clumsier and slower.[24] Its unpopular requirements did contain one important concession to miners worth mentioning here: it introduced the right to a finder's reward, an idea that would go on to play an important role in the California camp systems and the government-legislated free mining systems of the following decades. The 1783 law defined and instituted a *pertinencia*, a standard claim measured along the mineral vein, similar in concept to the English 'meer' (see Chapter 6). Discoverers were to receive three *pertinencia*. Finders in old districts received two and non-finders one *pertinencia*. In addition, the laws mandated that title was to depend strictly on staking.

Taken together, the features of the 1783 laws constituted a discouragement of exploring and mining. This may indicate that the Spanish-Mexican administrators thought themselves pretty much in control near the end of the eighteenth century, willing to assert their authority and engage in the costs of monitoring. It is unclear, but probable, that they had to relax their rules and regulations in the next seventy years, though some were still visible in the former Spanish colonies by the time of the very different California gold rush. There was still the unpopular requirement for elaborate mine documentation, much of which survives. On the other hand, it seems 'title' to small placer locations was awarded very casually.[25]

During this period of industrial revolution, the search for other minerals was catching up on that for gold and silver, producing their own booms and mining laws. By 1800 coal—especially from Britain—had rendered charcoal obsolete and had come into demand for use in both metallurgy and steam power. In 1850 British output was about five times that of the rest of the world, with Belgium and Germany's Silesia province also producing significant amounts. Coal districts were also emerging as global players in Virginia, Ohio, Pennsylvania and Nova Scotia.[26] I return to the emergence of New World coal briefly in Chapter 9.

Iron was the leading metal of the industrial revolution. In 1750 Britain was the world's chief source of iron ore, much of it coming from shallow bell mines and shaft mines, many of them the subject of the type of mining lease between lord and miner that I discuss in detail in Chapter 8. By the beginning of the nineteenth century, though, iron mines had to be dug much deeper, using the

[24] Within ten days of making a discovery, the miner had to submit a written statement to this Tribunal. This statement was to provide a complete description of the geographical characteristics of the finder's claim, and copies displayed throughout the claimed area. During the ensuing 90-day waiting period, anyone asserting a prior claim might file for a hearing, while the finder was to dig an opening one and a half yards wide and ten yards deep to enable an expert and two witnesses to ascertain the direction and dip of the vein along with the important minerals to be found within.

[25] Rickard 1932b, pp. 20–4.

[26] Limited production for fuelling steam-powered vessels commenced at or near coastal points all around the world. For a quick survey of American iron and coal discovery and production before 1850, see Rickard 1932b, pp. 8–17.

new technology of the period. The quality of the iron extracted began to drop as the industry reached capacity.[27] To compensate, sources in Scandinavia, Spain, Lorraine, Germany and overseas came into prominence. In the New World, Quebec and the American colonies began to produce small but significant quantities of bog iron. By 1850 production overseas—especially in the Lake Superior mining district—was beginning to catch European production.

Lead and copper, found in silver-lead-zinc or copper-lead ores, came in modest amounts from many European sources, including lead from England's Pennine district, where mining was revived in the late 1700s, and copper and lead from the Harz Mountains in Germany. As early as 1720 the Missouri region began to produce lead. Copper was obtained throughout Spanish America and later in North America beginning in the 1840s in upper Michigan.

Note that neither in Britain nor in the British colonies had the idea of a right or permit to search and produce minerals on Crown lands been developed. The usual procedure in British colonies was to buy land from the Crown. The purchase would include the coal or other subjacent minerals. Otherwise, there was no generally available 'coal right'. As well, the 'proprietors', the holders of the extensive overseas lands granted by the Crown, could sell or lease their minerals. In some colonies most of the land had been transferred in this way, and consequently various private tenure arrangements between the proprietor and the miner were emerging.

Early post-colonial evolution of public mineral disposals in the New World

In contrast to the Crown's disposal of colonial mineral land to proprietors by concession and charter, in the late eighteenth and early nineteenth century the nascent North American national governments increasingly found themselves in active charge of new mining resources and in a position to dictate how most miners would acquire and hold rights to them. They had few colonial innovations to work with. For previous colonial governments, the crafting of any law that affected mining had been concerned with answering two basic questions: (1) which minerals could the Crown claim; and (2) how was exploration to be conducted? To a lesser extent, the lawmakers concerned themselves with a third question: to whom should mineral rights be granted?

AMERICAN MINERAL GRANTS FROM PUBLIC LANDS

The establishment and diffusion of the American system of mining rights on public land stemmed from the gold rush of 1850 and remains one of the most

[27] More accurately, the remaining reserves were of steadily lower quality. See Schubert 1957. The demand for iron ore had been localized, depending on the availability of local wood or charcoal, until in 1709 Abraham Darby started the long series of coal-using inventions that were to make Britain a major exporter of iron.

fascinating and relevant periods in the history of mineral rights. For most of the century after the Revolution, the mineral disposal methods were deliberate extensions of agricultural soil-disposal methods (such as those that became defined in the Preemption Act of 1841 and the Homestead Act of 1862).

In 1785 Congress reserved one-third of mines for the treasury by classifying some lands as 'mineral lands'.[28] Naturally, settlers and homesteaders made efforts, ranging from politics to bribery, to shield their lands from being so classified. There was widespread law-breaking: trespass, plunder and illegal entry onto federal lands. In the event, the Congress's reserve effort was somewhat half-hearted, for visible showings were an unreliable guide to labelling lands as 'mineral' or 'non-mineral'. Historians have often deplored the fact that a more serious attempt was not made to classify and protect minerals from malapropriation, but it would surely have been impossible to carry out the intended reserve in the nineteenth century.[29]

Generally the federal resource-distribution arrangements did not grant 'mining rights' but simply vacant land. Miners competed with settlers under the rules of the Pre-emption Act (1841–9), which established a single set of fees independent of the relative demands of miners or homesteaders for any given piece of land. Squatters were allowed to take over ('locate') 160 acres of public land and, after six months, to buy it for less than the standard price would be after it was officially surveyed and sold. This pre-emption approach to land disposal and settlement was supplanted in 1862 by the free land policy of the Homestead Act.

The Homestead Act was welcomed by land-settlement spokesmen. They saw it as allowing lucky farmers whose homesteaded areas turned out to be mineral-rich to re-sell their land or to detach and lease their mineral rights while maintaining surface rights. Mining interests, on the other hand, pressed for policy changes that would prevent farmers from buying up mineral lands that they could resell at inflated prices. In spite of the earlier unfortunate experience with 'mineral reserves', and in spite of the absence of an official Geological Survey, they supported efforts to complement the farm-oriented pre-emption and homestead systems with blocks available for sale only to miners. Where such blocks were created, some miners did pay for mineral-land mining sites.[30] But most would-be miners paid alleged farmers (royalties ranged from 6 to 33 per cent

[28] In 1804 Congress began a series of reserves of lead-bearing lands. They were linked by a policy best-known for its reliance on leasing (for royalties) rather than outright sale of mining rights. See Leshy 1987, p. 10.

[29] See Gates 1968b, pp. 699–765.

[30] Before 1841 the Cash Purchase Act, 1820, was the chief policy instrument regulating land disposal. One of its effects was to encourage speculation by those who had the cash to invest. Before it was repealed later in the century, it was the means by which large resource acreages, especially iron and timber, were brought under the control of a small number of people. No royalty was payable. For a classic study of its workings in the iron-ore region in the 1890s, see Wirth 1927.

by 1840)[31] for land or for severed mineral rights, by which they acquired either by a patent or a freehold deed to subsurface resources.

The government's sale of mineral-land blocks was known as the survey-and-sale system. Dissatisfaction with it led to another approach: the government dusted off its earlier lead-mine leasing system and began in the 1820s directly to lease mines in the Missouri region for a rent or a royalty.[32] Compared to the continuing royalty-free survey-and-sale system used elsewhere, the leasing and royalty system was wildly unpopular with both farmers and miners. Their opposition was hardened by the fact that the simple legislation made little provision for administrative machinery. Except perhaps for Galena, where administration was handed to a military officer who licensed miners and smelters, and collected a royalty at the smelter gate—leasing systems did not produce enough revenue in the lead districts to make the political disaster of leasing worthwhile. A similar failure attended leasing in the 1840s rush to a vast copper discovery in an Upper Michigan district. Conditional on successful exploration, production required a royalty-bearing lease available on posting a $20,000 bond. The exploration permits allowed feverish searching but the bond deterred deep development. In all cases, the hapless administrators got little support from the government, and the entire policy collapsed less than a decade later,[33] to be revived fitfully in other areas throughout the 1830s and 1840s, before being abandoned by Congresses after 1850 in favour of a system preferred by the spokesmen for the emerging hard-rock mining companies.[34]

The failure of this attempt at a public-land leasing policy can be ascribed to a mix of politics, economics and lack of information. Some of the political opposition to leasing stemmed simply from a preference for the traditional institution of ownership over 'newfangled' leasing, especially as the power of the young federal government to classify, lease and manage property of any kind was untested. As well, small active miners—those who were least able to pay—found themselves most vulnerable to royalties under the leasing system and hated being saddled with the continuous payments.

As for information, there was a basic problem in setting the price for unexplored sites in a non-arbitrary fashion. It was made more difficult by the fact that there were simply no competent professionals to attend to the making of

[31] See Swenson 1968, p. 705.

[32] The leasing system may have been inspired by the French theory of state ownership, which was already vaguely in effect in the Louisiana Purchase. Opposition came in part from Missouri miners who cited their existing French or Spanish mineral title. In Galena, leasing lasted until the 1840s; elsewhere in the Midwest it lasted until the 1860s. See Shinn 1965, pp. 40–1 and, especially, Lake 1962, pp. 53–4.

[33] See Swenson 1968, p. 706. However, on the question of the rights of miners whose occupation of the Missouri mines began under Spain or France, Swenson's brief treatment must be complemented by Gates 1968b (cited in Gates 1968b, pp. 96–115).

[34] Good, short descriptions bringing in modern scholarship are found in Swenson 1968; and Mayer and Riley 1985, ch. 2. The standard historical source on Galena is Wright 1966.

mine and/or mineral-land valuations. (A similar problem for public forest land and its non-classification will be seen in Chapter 11.) Even competent officials would have found it extremely difficult to correctly identify lead, silver or zinc ore-bearing lands in a way the miners would trust. For officials to then locate paying veins in these metals, their direction and dip, would be technically even harder, more error-prone than locating deposits of iron and coal. I return to some of these issues in my discussion of the public land hard-rock profile in Chapter 7.

DISPOSING OF CROWN MINERAL RIGHTS IN AUSTRALIA AND CANADA

Australia's mineral reserves, like those in British North America, were hardly recognized before 1850. Iron deposits were known to exist, and small amounts of coal were discovered and exported after 1812. Prospectors found gold in the 1820s and 1830s. That little happened to follow up produces a suspicion that the colonial authorities, in accordance with their perceived responsibility for the security of exiled convicts, had actually suppressed the news. No special mineral ownership or mineral disposal law was yet in place in Australia in the early nineteenth century. The Crown reserved gold and silver. Otherwise, Colonial Secretary Lord John Russell, in an 1840 communication to the governor of New South Wales, advised that the colony should not reserve mineralized lands because 'the small amount of profit derived from mines throughout the great extent of the British Colonial empire would appear to us sufficient reason why such reservations would, as a general rule, be as unnecessary as they would be inconvenient to the progress of the settlement'.[35] His implication was that miners should acquire acreage from the Crown by purchase, just like settlers. This was the law in place when, in late 1850, Hargraves and his friends rushed back to Australia to press the California model (see the next chapter) for an alluvial gold rush.[36]

In eastern Canada, after France left Quebec, and after the American Revolution, there was little mining and scarcely any special mineral disposal procedure for the public lands. Ontario locations were being sold on a fee-simple basis, surface and all,[37] without royalty. Some miners found it less trouble, and just as efficient, to put in for a farm land grant and hope to mine the resulting allotment. In Quebec, although larger acreages were already private or seigneurial by the 1800s, the government made some freehold grants of mineral land. The

[35] Rickard 1932a, vol. 2, p. 629 (quoting Veatch 1911, p. 91).

[36] Blainey 1978, p. 14.

[37] When, in 1820, iron works were opened in southeastern Ontario (Marmora), the promoter was granted ten thousand acres of likely iron reserves. See Smith 1986, p. 19. And when, around 1845, copper was promoted in the Upper Great Lakes region, the tracts were freehold, large (ten square miles) and sold on installments. Newell 1986, p. 63; Gibson 1933; George 1987, pp. 54–6; Nelles 1974, p. 20; and Zaslow 1971, p. 12.

famous Forges of St Maurice had presumably been originally based on a French royal concession of the bog iron resource, continued by the English.[38]

Finally, in Nova Scotia, coal, copper and iron were already in production by 1750 so that the Crown did not need to consider exploration incentives in developing its disposal system. For instance, the famous lease to the assignees of the Duke of York had been simply the Crown's way of transferring monopoly wealth. The Duke's company used more capital-intensive methods than the locals would have chosen.[39]

Free mining and its legacy in the United States

In contrast to the British and Spanish colonial governments, whose mercantilist worldviews led them to view the minerals within their conquered territories as chattels to be exploited for the state, the nineteenth-century American federal government apparently was as indifferent to mineral revenues as it was to the accumulation of mineral information and the comparison of alternative approaches to mineral production. Its mineral disposal policy was a small part of the larger policy aimed at ensuring fairness and efficiency in the distribution of land and resources: first, during the western settlement rush to homesteaders, and later to eager miners (once it could be ensured that mineral land reached those who would use it to its maximum advantage). Until the Mineral Leasing Act of 1920 (see Chapter 7), one fair and peaceful system of disposal was as good as any other from the government's point of view.

The government did have a model to go on, however, for the efficient and peaceable disposal of mineral land: free mining. We have already seen how this system had made its way from remote areas of feudal Europe across the Atlantic to the Spanish colonies, where elements of it emerged in the 1783 mining law. In the next half-century it made its way to the camps of the California argonauts, where the miners more or less independently chose it as their preferred method of disposing of land and granting rights over the minerals beneath it. It is to this system, its development and modern ramifications, that I turn next in Chapter 6.

[38] The distribution of Quebec mineral rights among seigneurs, private land-owners and the province was analysed in the outstanding judgment in *Regina v. Delery* (22 December 1883), *Legal News* 6, no. 51: 402–8. See Crabbé 1979, 1983a; Armstrong 1978, p. 10; Armstrong 1984, pp. 177–86; and Ouellet 1980, pp. 249, 388 and 514.

[39] See Gerriets 1991.

6

Free Mining from Medieval Europe to the Gold Rushes

Free mining persisted as an institution from at least the time of the Roman Empire, through the Dark Ages and later feudal period, into the gold rush era of the New World. One of the most remarkable aspects of free mining is directly suggested by its name. In an era defined by strict hierarchy and land bondage, a free miner enjoyed the right to explore unrestrictedly for minerals within the wide boundaries of the sponsoring Crown or noble estate, and also to participate in making and enforcing the rules to which he was subject. These were wide departures from standard feudal land practice. The miners were never rulers themselves and, in fact, usually came from the labouring class, closer in status to the serfs and free labourers than to yeomen, tradesmen or members of the land-owning class. Generally, the land-owner appointed the chief miner of the district (called the bergmeister or, in English, barmaster). He was responsible to the lord for his revenues and the relaying of information. He took a share of each mineral discovery made by the miners in the district. Miners' law was evidently tailored over time and space to reflect the realities of deposits of widely varying grade occurring in what were often difficult-to-discover veins.

To begin this chapter I offer in the first section below an account of free mining as an institution and source of mining rights, first in Europe, then in the New World colonies. Then I discuss the reasons for its endurance (through a very long decline), its costs and benefits to landowners and its political and legal support. I later turn to the experience and property characteristics of free mining in the post-colonial New World, from the California gold rush until the decline of placer mining in the last decades of the nineteenth century.

Free mining from the Roman Empire to the Enlightenment

Free mining in the Dark Ages and feudal Europe

Though information on ancient sources is very scant, there was apparently something like free mining in classical Greece and in the Roman mines. It was re-invented or revived in early medieval Europe and became widely distributed in Germany and Austria, mainly but not exclusively in difficult mountain and coastal terrains where individual initiative was particularly useful. Rulers who embraced free mining typically granted individuals the right to roam freely, to cross the land boundaries of subordinate landholding lords and to claim and work the deposits they found. The extent of dependence on this institution varied but in some instances it was very prevalent. In fourteenth-century Bohemia, for instance, Wenceslas II gave all citizens the liberties of free miners.[1] A similar regime was found in France and along the Mediterranean coast.[2]

Agricola describes the process as it typically existed in medieval and early modern Europe. After making a discovery, a miner in a free mining district would be rewarded by the lord's regional appointee (the bergmeister) with a double-sized 'meer' along the vein, while later miners along this vein were awarded a regular-sized meer. The claim entitled the holder to acquire something like a production lease. Usually his lord did not require that he pay for either the status of free miner or the registration or rental of his meer. Payment of a royalty was sufficient. In the free mining regions of Europe, the group of free miners sanctioned by the lord usually constituted a community, and some even elected their bergmeister.

The long decline of central European free mining has been traced to the rise of the kings and the emperors who displaced the free mining-supporting landowners and nobles just as they wrested royal prerogative over minerals back from their lesser nobility. Free mining regimes dwindled under the Crown. Although some royal rulers continued to offer the freedom to explore, they reduced local free miner self-government and took a larger royalty from the finds.

Free mining rules, and the laws of free mining communities, appear to have been brought to England by invited German miners before the Norman invasion in 1066. The rights and even the terminology found in surviving free mining law documents are very similar to those found in the Austrian, Bohemian and Moravian systems. The exceptional liberties that English free mining offered to individual miners contrasted starkly with the bondage of other rural people under Norman feudalism. Later, as previously in Europe, free miners came into conflict with the growing concessionary strength of the British Crown. In the absence of any statutory 'mining law' or code to

[1] Nef 1952 and 1987, describing silver mining in Bohemia.

[2] The story of Massa Marittima is smoothly told in Fabretti 1995. In this Tuscan port rich ancient silver-copper mines were rediscovered around 1066. Mining was revived by the Lord Bishop with a corporation of local partners. After about two hundred years, the corporation had been transformed into a type of free mining regime that was built into the constitution of Massa itself, whereby all citizens had the freedom to explore. Discoverers faced a rather stiff work requirement. Thanks to Peter Pearse for this reference.

distinguish them, free mining rules developed concurrently and in close association with the common-law leases for iron, bedded materials and coal. As on the Continent, the class implications of these competing systems of disposal were themselves interesting: though free miners were free of serfdom, they would otherwise have been landless workers, whereas most mineral leaseholders who contracted with the lord were employers, even gentry.

There were distinct free mining areas in medieval England, notably those of tin-mining in Cornwall and Devon, lead-mining in Somerset, iron and coal mining in the Forest of Dean (Gloucestershire), lead-mining the Peak district of Derbyshire, lead and zinc mining in Flintshire (Wales) and several lead and zinc districts in the northern Pennines, particularly north Yorkshire, north Durham and Cumberland. Those in the north and in Derbyshire were in mountainous country. They were protected by the Crown and not closely bound by tenure to any village or manor, their status comparable to the exceptional position of people living in the royal forest. Indeed, the Forest of Dean mining community *was* forested in the legal sense.

In the northern districts the discoverer's claim was converted into two standard meers, each about one hundred feet along the vein. Once this was done, the holder could explore anywhere within his area,[3] mine and extract whatever ore he found there. The free miner's claim was permanent, transferable and heritable so long as the holder fulfilled prescribed minimal activity requirements and paid a conventional royalty to the lord. The holder and all the miners were ruled by the barmaster. He was sometimes elected (as in Europe) but usually appointed, his status comparable to that of a reeve in a manor or a warden in a royal forest. Disputes involving the facts of a discovery's priority in relation to extensive local customary mining property law were heard by local tribunals.[4] Most groups of free miners had immunity from the jurisdiction of the surface owners' own manorial courts and many had immunity from the courts of common law. Their free miners' courts survived for centuries.[5] Even older were the stannary courts of Cornwall, which oversaw somewhat similar customary arrangements for tin mining.

Free mining and disposal of mineral lands by private landowners

In Chapter 8 I will touch on the two main ways a landlord living in early modern Europe or England during the decline of feudalism and the transition to the modern concept of the private land-owner went about disposing of rights to

[3] Or, in certain free mining communities, *outside* his meer, in pursuit of a vein or seam. See Nef 1932 and 1966, pp. 271 and 276.

[4] These have been well described by Nef 1932 and 1966, vol. 1, pp. 265–80; Lewis 1907; Raistrick and Jennings 1965; Shinn 1884; Agricola 1556, Book 4.

[5] Pennington 1973, p. 16.

the minerals beneath his lands—either through direct investment and operation of his mines, or through leasing his mineral land to professional miners. A third option, of course, was for the lord to place the mining activities in his lands in the hands of free miners. In some districts the option to invite free miners onto the land could scarcely be called a 'choice' for the system may actually have been in place locally for years, perhaps for centuries. In other districts, for the family to turn to free miners would have been novel, to be reviewed from time to time. Old or new, the free miner would be licensed by the lord to prospect for a vein or deposit on his land. If successful, he received a mining right (a meer) in return for a manageable lump-sum payment or a royalty on his takings. The lord's family got not only the payment/royalty but also mineralization information about their lands: the location and grade of the deposit. This latter effect is extremely important in understanding the persistence of free mining through otherwise fairly unique historical periods and socio-economic orders as England and Europe moved toward the modern era. I return to it below.

Free mining communities

Free mining existed as an institution in many variants scattered across Europe. As for their influence on later mining rights, it is useful to classify two main forms. The first is best identified by its reliance on self-government and elements of collective 'ownership'—or effective use—of land. Miners worked away at the same collective beds for many decades in a row. Neither their technology nor their meers' geology led to dramatic mineral discoveries. In some of these communities, for instance in Cornwall and the Forest of Dean, some miners eventually became small proprietors, holding inheritable meers.

Free mining communities of the second form were less collective and more individualistic. The essence of the miner's 'freedom' had less to do with belonging to a self-governing community outside of the feudal hierarchy, and more to do with the right to explore and prospect widely and individually, as encouraged by the landowner's promise to grant him a production right upon discovery of a vein. Communities of this type were found in the broken geology of Germany and Austria and in the lead districts of Derbyshire and northern England.

The two institutions overlapped. The first naturally needed a free system of access to minerals for opening new mines, while the second required some kind of collective participation in enforcing claim-acquisition rules. Both forms—the community and the individual search—were later to influence the development of mining rights during the gold rush period, explored later in this chapter, though the second was perhaps the most important and enduring. Today there are essentially no miner-run communities, but a modern miner licensed to prospect on Crown or public lands relies on his right to roam freely in search of previously untapped deposits.

The claiming and enforcement systems were built around the concept of the meer, which, in most base metal mining districts, had a standard length, just under a hundred feet along the vein.[6] In some places it also had a standard width—in medieval Bohemia, for instance, equal to roughly half the meer's length. However, as a general rule, the width of a miner's holding depended on the dip, or slope, of his stretch of the vein from its *apex* (its outcrop or surface showing) downwards. The dependence illustrates the difference between the mining claim and the (fixed) agricultural furlong strip, or acre. The latter could be regarded as a unit of *input*. The meer, by contrast, approximated a unit of *output*. If the vein, deposit or seam was flat, then a 90-foot-wide meer would contain a predictable amount of ore. If the vein sloped sideways and downward, a smaller allotted surface width would provide the same amount of ore. Hence, where veins dipped steeply local standard meers were predictably narrow. The bergmeister granted the miners in his area the right to follow 'their' veins underground from the apex straight down. If the vein sloped flatly to left or right, the bergmeister awarded a more-than-standard width, enough to follow the dip as the mining might require. Thus the boundaries of each meer were dictated by the dip, rather than by an urban-type pre-discovery map.

This aspect of free mining—the output-based approach to the unit of property—was again revived centuries later, and adapted to government land disposal policies in the New World. We have already seen its application to the Spanish law of 1783 that defined the *pertenacia*. Later, during the homesteading period in the US, settlers received standard, pre-surveyed surface homestead areas, but miners were given more flexible rights. Like their European predecessors, they were entitled to follow the vein of their allotted claim from its apex. In some jurisdictions, they might do so even when it took them outside the left and right boundaries that had been assigned to them. This variant on a standard mineral right became known as the 'extra-lateral right'. As we will see in Chapter 7, it became important in the development of mining law in the late nineteenth century, particularly in disputes concerning overlapping claims.

Free mining and the demand for information

Costs and benefits of free mining to the landlord

It has been suggested that the second form of free mining described above, with its emphasis on the miner's right to wander without concern for legal

[6] For the size of the meer in 1550 in Bohemia see Agricola, Book 4, pp. 77–100. Although there was a standard meer of perhaps eighty to ninety feet, the number of such standard units to be awarded differed from time to time. The length was ninety six feet in Derbyshire in 1285, according to Raistrick and Jennings 1965, p. 57, and slightly over a hundred feet in the Forest of Dean in 1900, according to Bainbridge 1900, p. 156.

boundaries within a very wide district, was a system by which the landowners who appointed the bergmeister and patronized the community paid for information—in kind rather than in cash. Paying in kind for mineral information is loosely related to another feature of mining: learning by doing. Continuous investment in prospecting, discovery, proving and stepping out is everywhere part of actual operations for any mineral exploitation. In such activities, the mining industry's exploration is much like other industries' R&D expenditures, routinely performed but subject to variable returns.

During the medieval and early-modern periods not all landowners had the same need for the 'R&D' or for the fluctuating stream of revelations provided by one or more free miners searching for deposits on their lands. Landowners who believed they already had sufficient geological information about their lands—for instance those whose lands were marked with indications of coal or limestone—would have little use for the further information that free miners could provide. At the other end of the scale, very large landowners or benevolent land interests such as modern governments seeking to maximize mining's contribution to national income or welfare might have a demand for information revelation that was simply too large in scope to be addressed by a free mining approach within a lifetime. Such a government would require instead mineral information on a scale that could only be provided by, say, a geological survey.[7]

Historically, the most intense demand for free-miner-revealed information emanated from those feudal and later post-feudal private landowners whose estates were large but had a non-uniform geology. The larger the estate, the greater absolute potential value of a single discovery, and the more likely the owner would make area available to a small-scale free miner. If the estate was large enough to include dozens of separate deposits, then the owner had a mineral reserve from which to reward one or several prospectors in return for

[7] Consequently, I am excluding from the book consideration of large national mineral surveys as determinants of the decision to give mineral rights to miners in return for exploration. The boundary between such surveys and local reconnaissance is not clear. Small owners can make some initial investment in general information, hoping to stumble on indicators similar to those in better-known districts. As well, a general reconnaissance based on a very large grid can lead to more specialized inquiries into smaller areas. Maurice Allais 1957 is well known for his pioneering papers on this subject. If strategically useful, the information provided at these early stages could be kept secret and, hence, exclusive. It has long been recognized as a public good, but it is clear that there is also some rivalry between different users of geological maps. Also, it is quite feasible to keep map information private or exclusive.

There are official geological surveys whose mapping information is released to anyone. It is difficult to interpret their political existence, for they sometimes merely provide privately useful information. Leaving such doubts aside, I interpret most public surveys as either classic cases of providing a public good or as instances of the state as owner of mineral rights providing itself with the information it needs for their disposal. This latter is the theory often advanced to explain the key role in land disposal played by the US Geological Survey (as founded by J. W. Powell) and the US National Academy of Sciences. See Gates 1968b, pp. 419–20.

the information they revealed about the precise locations, or location characteristics, of the deposits, the remainder of which he could either work himself or lease out, perhaps to larger-scale mining interests.[8] Conversely, if the landholding was so small as to include only a single possible mine location, then its owner would have much less to gain from a miner's prospecting (that is, he would have little additional scope to apply the information gained from the miner). This reasoning helps to explain why it was great landowners like the Dukes of Devonshire, and not the one-farm landowners, who commissioned and rewarded free miners for working over their lands.

Non-uniformity was important. The owner who believed his acres to be homogenous might decide that the exploration of one acre would provide sufficient information about all of them, thus leaving him with no need for a whole community of free miners. The more the total area of owner's land was believed to be divided into distinct acres and plays, perhaps home to different types or grades of mineral, the more numerous the free miners the owner would recruit.[9] This helps to explain why in certain European Alpine areas such as Bohemia the rulers and nobles turned over whole mountain regions to communities of free miners, a practice less common in Europe's homogenous and well-mapped lowlands.

Free mining also had drawbacks, even for those landlords who had the most to gain from the information revelation it provided. Owners became heavily dependent on those who interpreted what the free miners said they were finding, the bergmeister or head miners of the districts. Some owners must have found it difficult to recruit responsible and successful miners from villages and towns. In each new region the special status of free miners (part employees, part entrepreneurs) would have to be invented and could interfere with the status of the lord's more traditional tenants who might have resented the free miners' freedom to roam and to make their own laws. Additionally, miners' uses of the surface might have interfered with that of traditional tenants. Their conflicts reverberated back to the lord. Finally, hiring free miners was less lucrative to the lord than leasing out land, since a lease ensured a fixed return and defined regular payments for the right to mine.[10] In contrast, the lord could only extract a royalty (which was also easier to evade) when his free miners made a discovery.

[8] See Ballem 1973, Parts 1 and 2 and ch. 5.

[9] At least to a point: If his holdings are totally heterogeneous, the owner will act as though he held numerous separated small holdings. He will expect no spillover of exploratory information. Giving away tracts to expand his information would make little sense.

[10] As in Germany, the discoverer took two meers and the king or his tenant took one; the king or his tenant also took a one-thirteenth share of the product, and there might also be a tithe. The shares were different in other places. The king's tenant paid a once-for-all or annual rent for the privilege.

The relative attractiveness of free mining to a lord would have depended additionally on the expected level of these royalties, which likely moved with prices of the metals. How exactly this dependence worked would have depended on the relative metal-price elasticities of royalties and rentals. If rentals were less flexible than royalties—for instance, because they were fixed in a multi-year lease—a fall in the price of metals would lead a landlord to choose to be paid by royalty—that is, to choose free mining rather than lease out his land at a low rental rate. But if institutions allowed both rentals and royalties to rise and fall parallel to mineral prices, landlords would have no particular price incentive to turn to free miners.

Alternative views of free mining

In the analysis here I have emphasized the role that free mining played in providing the land-owner with information. I should acknowledge, however, that in the mining history literature we find three other emphases, which can be seen as complementary views of the role for which free mining was tolerated and valued.

The first is the 'social institution' view of free mining. This view holds that the lord should be seen less as a land-owner than as an employer who sought a skilled and committed workforce through the free mining contract. He offered miners immunity from the burdens and interruptions of feudal status and duties as well as a right to keep some discovery share. In this view, free mining was an instance of the piece-rate system frequently found throughout medieval Europe, and particularly in the growing mercantile classes, by which employers gave workers a private incentive to work with and improve the owner's resources.[11]

A second view holds that the outstanding feature of free mining was its tenacity. This view gives weight to institutional inertia or path-dependence.[12] John Nef, for example, treats medieval free mining as the survival of an unexplained ancient customary regime even in the face of incentives on the part of the principles (the lords) to discontinue it in order to reclaim their feudal rights over minerals. Whatever its remote origins, the privileges of free mining were difficult to get rid of, especially if the miners had become relatively wealthy and obtained additional protection through royal charters and the like.[13] Because of its tenacity it did not disappear but merely waxed and

[11] This explanation is offered by Rickard 1932a, vol. 2, pp. 596–9. It is implicit in many older mining histories, such as Nef 1932 and 1966.

[12] Lewis 1907, pp. 82–4, specializing in the history of the Cornish tin mines, argues that not just Cornish but all English free mining districts may be survivals of pre-Roman mining regimes.

[13] Nef 1952 and 1987, p. 714, noted the likeness to guilds.

waned over the centuries leading up to the modern era. Ancient families who had once introduced free mining later found themselves resisting it. But free mining hung on while landowners blew hot and cold about needing it, thereby following the more general alternating patterns of the development of property rights and institutions discovered in this book.

A third view of free mining stresses its isolation, both in the European Alpine free mining regions and in the English free mining districts. The explanation holds that, while all great lords welcomed free mining benefits, few relished having non-feudal 'free' institutions among their manors and villages. Hence, English free mining became rare in closely settled areas, only surviving deep in the forest, on the moors and on the peaks. However, since remote areas were usually also the least explored, evidence supporting this isolation view of free mining fits well with the basic exploration and information explanations of the institution.

Taking all these aspects into consideration, my view is that the essential difference between the position of owners who remained as common-law lessors and those who retained and opted for free mining had to do with land-owner demands discussed in the subpart above: the need for help with exploration in increasing the lord's information about his own lands. The miners themselves tended always to support free mining. With exceptions in which the royalty charged by some lords might have been unattractively high relative to a leasing fee, the miners favoured free mining not only for its economic benefits, but also for the status and freedom that it bestowed in an era not known for its freedoms. The onus for the survival and health of the institution therefore was on the lords, the feudal and post-feudal suppliers of free mining patronage.

Historical evidence: the waxing and waning of English free mining

The preceding discussion might suggest that the intensity of free mining activity rose and fell several times through the centuries. Evidence of regular cycling is thin, but it does appear that owners who customarily depended on free miners typically wanted to free themselves of them when the market for their minerals or metals was either at a sustained low or at an extreme buoyant high. In periods of low demand and low prices, landowners preferred to speculate and naturally reduced the activity of free miners on their lands. In the second circumstance, when sustained high demand was forcing recourse to deeper pits, landowners wanted to turn from the relatively high costs of free mining to some lower-cost organization—typically to leasing their properties to commercial miners ('adventurers') and receiving rents.

History provides some more solid micro-evidence for the persistence of free mining in spite of the cycles of landlord preference for the institution. In the English lead-mining districts, which had been active since Roman times, the survival of free mining was attributed to ancient custom.[14] At various times, from soon after the Conquest until well into the thirteenth century, the king leased lead-mining rights in two Derbyshire fields to various nobles and gentle tenants. Perhaps the king just wanted some finance, or perhaps he was weary of the high costs of free mining when demand was buoyant. In any case, when these lessees attempted to prevent the Ashbourne (Derbyshire) free miners from 'trespassing' in search of mines, a royal inquiry (1228) found for the miners. It declared the king's right to have been merely that of a feudal lord, conditioned by the customary rights of the miners to search and mine at liberty. This interpretation persisted. As late as 1720 when, in a period of recovering demand for lead, the London Lead Company[15] entered a derelict field in Derbyshire to drain and reconstruct old workings, it was bound to acquire rights one by one from survivors and successors of the former free mining community. Free mining, under the name of the Custom of Derby, as fully described and confirmed by the inquiry, had become the legal basis for rights in all the king's mining fields, not only in Derbyshire, but also in Devonshire, Somerset, Wales, Yorkshire and the northern counties, at least partially beyond the whims of the king and the landowners' changing tastes in disposal.[16]

Another illustration can be found in the fortunes of the free miners in the Forest of Dean in Gloucestershire. Producing and exporting timber and general minerals for themselves and for the Crown they had a more or less unbroken social history of free mining and free forestry, along with other extra-feudal privileges. In 1612, near the end of a late-medieval mining boom in England, the Crown changed its ways and granted a mining concession in the Forest to the Earl of Pembroke. As our cycle model above suggests, the Earl attempted to hold back and limit the exploration rights of the local free miners and, presumably, to undertake exploitation with his own men. When his lease eventually expired, the Earl and his miners entered another phase of the cycle, expanding the demand for exploration and development, and thus calling on the skills of the free miners.

[14] As in Germany, the discoverer took two meers and the king or his tenant took one; the king or his tenant also took a one-thirteenth share of the product, and there might also have been a tithe. The shares were different in other places. The king's tenant paid a once-for-all or annual rent for the privilege.

[15] See Moss 1924, p. 329 and Nef 1932 and 1966, vol. 1, pp. 276–80. For evidence about the entry and drainage investments of the London Lead Company, see Stokes 1964, p. 96; Raistrick and Jennings 1965, p. 123; and the geographic historians Millward and Robinson 1975, p. 201. But these writers are not interested in the alternating or cyclical activity in the field.

[16] Also see Raistrick and Jennings 1965, pp. 97–8 for examples of thirteenth-century campaigns inviting miners to help to re-open royal mine fields.

Mining rights in California: 1850 and after

Medieval and early-modern free mining were much referred to by lawmakers, legal experts and authors in the nineteenth century. Thus when the miners in the New World, particularly in California, ran their own mining camps and allotted claims by priority of discovery, it seemed to many observers that history was repeating itself. Similarly, at least some of the California rule-makers must surely have known that they were following in the footsteps of the earlier rule-makers in the English and German free mining communities. Nevertheless, the Californians did not simply copy their forebears. On the contrary, they showed great originality in hammering out what amounted to nothing less than a social contract. Shinn (1884) conveys some of the atmosphere in which the demanders and suppliers of a new social institution interacted to produce it:

> The mining-camps, whose white tents and rude cabins rose so rapidly beside these rivers in this new Colchis in early '49, have found an enduring place in literature. The Argonaut himself has become one of the heroic figures of the past, and is likely enough to survive, as real and strong a type in the story of America as Viking or Crusader in that of Europe. But it is the place held by the Argonaut as an organizer of society, that is most important. He often appears in literature as a dialect-speaking rowdy, savagely picturesque, rudely turbulent: in reality he was a plain American citizen cut loose from authority, freed from the restraints and protections of the law, and forced to make the defence and organization of society a part of his daily business. In its best estate, the mining-camp of California was a manifestation of the inherent capacities of the race for self-government. That political instinct, deep-rooted in Lex Saxonum, to blossom in Magna Charta and in English unwritten constitution, has seldom in modern times afforded a finer illustration of its seemingly inexhaustible force. Here, in a new land, under new conditions, subjected to tremendous pressure and strain, but successfully resisting them, were associated bodies of freemen bound together for a time by common interests, ruled by equal laws, and owning allegiance to no higher authority than their own sense of right and wrong. They held meetings, chose officers, decided disputes, meted out a stern and swift punishment to offenders, and managed their local affairs with entire success; and the growth of their communities was proceeding at such a rapid rate, that days and weeks were often sufficient for vital changes, which in more staid communities, would have required months or even years.[17]

In addition to the romance of the California camps (a feeling mostly missing from the awkward history of free mining as it contended with the rigidities of feudalism in medieval Europe), Shinn touches on the major difference that existed between the frontier version of free mining and its European predecessor. While the California gold rush miners were operating in unchartered

[17] Shinn 1965, pp. 135–6. Colchis was where Jason sought the Golden Fleece. Rhetoric to the contrary, a large minority of these miners were not Americans. There were numerous Mexicans, although most were later excluded from holding claims.

and largely ungoverned lands, responsible only to themselves, nearly all active free miners in Europe had been subject to a land-owner who alternatively tolerated and encouraged free mining in order to deal with his exploration problems. The tussle between supply and demand and the economic forces behind the existence and temporal fortunes of free mining in Europe were almost entirely absent from the camps in California, where the miners were at once the suppliers and demanders of mineral rights and custom.

Camp life at the beginning of the California gold rush

In 1848 miners discovered gold in California, which Mexico had only recently transferred into American possession. The successful prospectors found themselves in a legal vacuum regarding the rights to their finds since, having as yet created no civil authority in California, Congress could neither endorse Mexican mineral law nor enforce any federal mining regulation of its own. Consequently the miners who quickly began to flood into California overland from the eastern states and from Mexico and overseas from Europe were literally left to their own devices in constructing a workable and reasonably secure mining and mineral policy around a mining right. Congregated in tent camps near the river sand bars and diggings, they soon began to create institutions to serve that purpose.

Early ad-hoc attempts to self-regulate the mining life hinged on the development of two-person or three-person cooperative and partnership mining ventures, really based on private contracts rather than property rights. The problem, however, was that, just as there were no enforceable rights to hold minerals, so there were no enforceable contractual rights (to share the work and the gold) between partners. These defects only worsened as more miners arrived. In 1849 the cooperative approach to mining was scrapped. Instead, the miners in their camp meetings began to devise a collective approach[18] in which individual miners collectively subjected themselves to rules for behaviour and for land use that their camps *could* enforce.

The agreements the miners hammered out in their camps amounted to regimes of mining law based on custom. As in any customary regime, the drafting of the rules mixed formal property law with elements borrowed from criminal law, nuisance law and familiar related policy regimes, notably from Washington's rules for the disposal of public lands. The details of the laws and rules that emerged differed from camp to camp, but their main provisions were remarkably similar, reflecting the similarity of the demands and the constraints faced by the atomistic miner across the gold rush lands, disseminated by individual miner mobility from camp to camp.

[18] Umbeck 1977, p. 212; Zerbe 1987.

As individuals, miners asserted above all a right to free prospecting and mining on previously unclaimed public lands. Within their camps they agreed to respect and protect each other's free prospecting and staking rights by establishing rules to fix camp or district boundaries, to set the size and number of claims per person, and to control the working, marking, recording and abandonment of claims. They also agreed to provide and ensure enforcement of these rules. Typically, these regimes contained the following basic provisions:[19]

Claims: The general eligibility rule was one claim per person, and (particularly in the early days when sufficient space was available) two to the first discoverer of a gold deposit. Somewhat similar provisions had been common under European free mining, and also under the Spanish concession system after 1783. Each camp standardized its own claim, and at first the claims varied across camps in accordance with local conditions, not only geological but also demographic, such as the size of the inflow of new miners into the area (see below). Each camp agreed internally on standardized steps to be taken to acquire a claim, such as marking, boundary ditching, staking, noticing and recording. Claims could be bought and sold in most but not all mining camps, and the transferability rules varied as to who the buyers could be. There was usually a work requirement: miners lost a claim in default of a fixed amount or value of work per week. Generally, there was no more than one week's grace before a camp would move to repudiate an inactive miner's claim right.[20]

Payments: There was no fee, rent or royalty paid to any government, but there was a small internal tax charged proportional to a camp's own collective expenses.

Enforcement: The meetings that agreed on the rules also enforced them by adjudicating disputes and alleged infractions between members. The camps also punished or expelled proven claim jumpers and required that all their members participate in enforcement and protection.

With these provisions, the camps created enforceable mining titles that were perceived by holders and observers alike as good against all comers. The power of the camp's customs was such that its rules for adjudication and enforcement were eventually adopted by the courts—both state courts and later federal civil courts—when the time came for the national government to assert its control over the region and before the transition to hard-rock mining rendered some aspects of the free mining-style laws obsolete.

[19] In this list I rely on Umbeck 1981 and Shinn 1965. There is a similar list in Leshy 1987, pp. 379–80, following a 1969 study done for the US Public Land Law Review Commission.

[20] This is similar to the requirement that a water-right holder make 'beneficial use' of the resource. As discussed in Chapter 3, water rights and mining rights developed simultaneously in California camps. Both Shinn 1965 and Umbeck 1981 emphasize the costs of enforcement and protection to explain the size of claims and the refusal of the camps to protect apparently abandoned claims or water sources.

Later camp law and the introduction of government and courts

There was an event-filled two-year period from the start of the gold rush in 1848–9 until the California territory came under American civil rule and its lands under Congressionally legislated mining laws, with local courts authorized to enforce them. The change in the 'suppliers' of mining law coincided with changes on the demand side brought about by newer gold mining organization and technology. As placer mining contracted in the later years of the gold rush in favour of larger-scale, more capital-intensive methods such as hydraulicking, the camps' role in 'supplying' placer laws and enforcement also waned relative to that of the government. State and federal government, and the new state court system, did their best to oblige the new demands for adjustments in miner's rights and security of title.

Generally, Congress became and remained supreme in its jurisdiction over the formerly Mexican public lands, while lands that had earlier been privatized fell under the jurisdiction of state courts and the new state legislature. Just as the other western states had passed a new appropriative law that jibed with earlier ad-hoc ranchers' and farmers' customary water law, so the California legislature adopted as a pattern the existing, geographically varying customary laws created in the camps. It did not hasten to impose state-wide (or industry-wide) uniformity or to impose on the earlier system the principles of common law.

In fact it was not for another twenty years—until 1866—that Congress finally began the process of legislating a set of uniform national mining laws for its public lands. The process culminated in the Mining Law of 1872, which constituted a disposal statute. Even this formal law retained from the original camp law the free mining provision that public lands were wide open to mineral exploration. It also kept many of the requirements for claiming, including the standardized claim, the finder's reward and the claiming work requirement mentioned above.

Camp law and later gold rushes

While discoveries were slowing down in California, goldfields were opening up elsewhere. Miners left California to search in Colorado, Nevada and other mountain states. They also joined gold rushes abroad following discoveries in New South Wales and Victoria (1851), Chile (1852), the Fraser River (1858), New Zealand (1861), and later in South Africa (1884) and Alaska and the Klondike mainly in the 1890s. Although many of the principles of the California camps survived the jump to the new placer-mining districts, miners found nothing there like the freedom they had enjoyed in California. Only California had had a two-year hiatus from established public law. By the 1850s almost the entire population of the New World had become citizens and their land subject to the laws of either young national or older colonial governments. Everywhere, the miners' customary camp law had to be modified into conformity with already-established and legitimate laws and institutions.

THE AUSTRALIAN GOLD FIELDS

New South Wales' (NSW) mining laws were representative of the variety of mining laws in force in the Australian states when the first miners arrived to take advantage of placer gold deposits found in 1851. Thousands of workers made their way to these diggings in the following years. There they were joined by thousands of experienced placer miners from California, delayed by the overseas journey to the fresh finds, all of whom had two years of mining experience when they arrived.[21]

In establishing local mining law, these miners had to contend with several important differences from their situation in California. The first was geology, and the technological requirements it imposed. Although the miners at first found nuggets and gold dust at the surface and in gravel, sand and clay, they soon discovered more gold underground in the sands of buried watercourses at Ballarat. The deep-shaft technology meant the miners had now to work together as partners or even in employer–employee relationships, with one miner functioning as the risk-taking 'capitalist' and hiring workers for wages. California's one-man one-claim rule was abandoned.

The second difference, already mentioned above, was that miners familiar with the free entry and localized camp-rule of California found that New South Wales already had a government, property law, courts, military and police. The colonial government had even gained some slight experience dealing with minor mineral finds and their subsequent exploitation dating back to the 1820s, though none that corresponded in scope or in details to the current gold rush. Conforming to colonial settlement policy and common-law practices, the government had been prepared to grant mineral rights in a package with surface rights to miners or to settlers for a substantial upfront price. Indeed, in keeping with Wakefieldian theory, the pricing of land was supposed to lead to an efficient disposal of empty land to the relevant interests. Miners who had not paid the price for entry found themselves 'trespassing' on Crown lands.

Now that they had to contend with both mineral and settlement demands, however, the New South Wales, Victorian and other colonial governments reacted with a coolness born of nervousness to the first gold miners arriving from the West. The colonial administrators had heard of the 'anarchic' and 'lynch-law' California rules and resolved that nothing similar should prevail in their colonies. In fact, their aversion to the absence of central control over

[21] On the effect of the gold rush on labour supply and mobility, see Jackson 1977, pp. 59–62. On the role of convicts in the labour force in the gold-rush years, see Hughes 1987, ch. 16.

the Californian goldfields made the NSW government intensely suspicious of the dangers of 'a mob that craved gold'.[22] But it was less clear about what kind of law would both prevent anarchy and satisfy the miners' demands for freedom and title. Complicating the situation was the fact that no English or colonial precedent for dealing with placer gold rushes existed. Gold had never played a significant role in either Great Britain or its colonies, though in 1851 the governor at Sydney did invoke the *Case of Mines* to reserve gold and silver to the Crown.[23] As well, the government faced determined domestic opposition to the gold miners from existing land users. In particular, the politically powerful pastoral landowners in the Australian states feared losing their workers to the new capitalistic miners, and perhaps also their mineral rights during a flurry of activity and pro-miner legislation.[24] They lobbied hard against expansion of the gold rush and accommodation of the miners' demands for California-model mineral rights.

The Australian governments can be seen as having attempted to satisfy four major aims: (1) to stem the migration from farm and town jobs and to reduce congestion in the field in keeping with their own basic distaste for anarchy and with landowners' fears of the disruption of their industries; (2) to raise a revenue for the Crown or colonial intermediaries through newly valuable disposal rights; (3) to assist the gold industry by matching claim size to technology; and (4) to extend somehow the Wakefieldian compact-settlement goal to mining in order to achieve an efficient and orderly parcelling out of land. To achieve these aims, the colonial administrators had only two real instruments: variation in the size of the claim and variation in the price of mining rights.[25]

The experience of the state of Victoria after 1851 illustrates typical policies adopted for both claim size and price.[26] Its initial settings had made the claim very small (eight feet by eight feet for one miner, and about three times this for a four-person operation), thereby accommodating a potentially vast number of miners. The government soon found that this small size led to costly, over-rapid depletion. It increased the claim area by 75 per cent accordingly.[27]

[22] Blainey 1962, p. 134. Much of the text here draws on Blainey 1962 and Blainey 1978. I have omitted Blainey's footnoted reference to the proceedings of the NSW select committees of 1852.

[23] The governor's proclamation was a precursor to the various Gold Field Acts (see fn. 30 below). The proclaimed policy echoed instructions issued by the Colonial Office in 1831 London to British North American and Australian colonial governors that gold and silver should be withheld from future grants of land. In NSW, land grants had excluded gold and silver since 1828. Lang & Crommelin 1979, p. 13.

[24] See Jackson 1977, p. 61.

[25] In revising this chapter I have been greatly stimulated by S. J. La Croix (1992) whose paper deals with these main points.

[26] I am, of course, guided by my sources, most of which focus on Victoria from 1851 on.

[27] Blainey 1978, pp. 22 and 50; La Croix 1992, pp. 206–7.

At the same time, in order to deter further in-migration to the diggings, the government increased the price of a mining licence more than proportionally to the increase in claim size. This price increase was sufficiently severe to provoke serious evasion, causing licence revenue actually to fall, which in turn led the Victoria government to cut it in 1853–4.[28] By this time, however, the damage to the government's authority as an enforcement agency had been done. The steep licensing fees of 1852 and the first part of 1853 had little effect on in-migration of small miners from California.[29] One estimate holds that approximately one hundred fifty thousand persons were working in the Victorian goldfields in early 1855, of which only one thousand paid fees to the government. Revenues vanished.

In 1854 a dramatic miner confrontation (the 'Eureka Stockade') challenged the government of Victoria to create policies more conducive to miner claim acquisition and working. The colony responded with a Gold Fields Act,[30] which took mining tenure much closer to the California model (and remains more or less in force today). Under this law, 'free miners' were issued a new, and very generous, 'miner's right'. This gave them entry to explore Crown lands, a right to stake a claim, a discoverer's priority in staking a claim, a right to occupy the claim (including a necessary surface area), a personal right to the minerals in place, a right to participate in the making of local mining rules and the right to participate in judging disputes and charges coming under these rules.[31] Indeed, the Act transcended its California forerunners in incorporating most of the features of European free mining. It was drafted as though the Crown were a feudal lord, seeking information, issuing rights, rewarding successful discoverers and conceding self-rule not available to other citizens.[32]

The government set the fee for this free miner's right at one pound per year. In view of the failure of the earlier licensing attempts, this fee was no

[28] Lang and Crommelin 1979, p. 2, indicate that after 1853 one month cost £1, three months £2, six months £4, and one year £8.

[29] Though Blainey suggests it may have had a major adverse effect on more capital-intensive syndicates who had hoped to install gear to exploit deep underground leads and who therefore had a harder time evading payment. Blainey 1978, p. 48.

[30] The precursor to Victoria's 1855 Gold Fields Act was the governor's 1851 proclamation that gold mining on the queen's lands could not be carried out without a permit. This initial ordinance was expanded in 1852 legislation to include a summary procedure for dealing with conflicts between miners; in 1853 to offer miners the option of a lease; and then to the comprehensive 1855 and 1857 Gold Fields Acts. In 1860, the Act was further amended to formally extend the provisions of the 'miner's right' to prospectors seeking other metals than gold, the subject of Chapter 7.

[31] The rules covered the procedure, size and characteristics of claiming. For a contemporary account, see Boldrewood's 1880 novel, *The Miner's Right* (1973), p. 120. See Lang and Crommelin 1979, p. 3; Jackson 1977, pp. 84–5; and Blainey 1978, pp. 42 and 57.

[32] It also set up individual 'mining courts' with nine elected members. These were later re-modelled, with rule-making going to mining 'boards' and dispute-judging to quasi courts. See Lang and Crommelin 1979, p. 4, and Blainey 1978, pp. 57 and 69–71. True to their miner membership, these boards later resisted the advent of large corporate mines.

longer intended to ration the supply of rights or stem the inflow of miners demanding them. Adding further flexibility, the government starting in 1853 also offered mining leases, presumably attached to specific claims, though few miners took them up.[33] For revenue, the government now introduced and collected an export tax on each ounce of gold.

BRITISH COLUMBIA AND THE FRASER RIVER RUSH

The Fraser River gold rush in British Columbia began in earnest in 1858, three years after the establishment of the Gold Fields Act in Victoria. When the first miners arrived, there was far less government in the region than there had been in Australia in 1851. This situation prevailed at least until elements of the government of the older colony of Vancouver Island took over the mainland region, including the Fraser River from the Hudson's Bay Company in 1858. At that time only some aboriginal bands lived along the river.

The government of the new colony intended to provide a mining law, preferably having most of the features of California camp rules. But hearing from the colonial office about the prevalence of vigilante justice in California, Governor Douglas reacted with the same distaste as the Sydney authorities had displayed earlier, and decided to model his 1859 law on the new Australian code. Meanwhile, miners just off the boats from California and Australia streamed up the river, built their own camps, made claiming rules and laws and began mining.[34]

Douglas's law created a now-familiar class of free miners with a right of entry to explore, stake a claim and mine. After holding a claim for a certain period of time, a miner could obtain a lease. After 1869 he could obtain a patent or Crown grant of a freehold interest, but in practice few bothered to do so, for a claim conveyed all the rights any surface placer miner needed for the few months that his sand and gravel would yield gold. The law adopted the rule of giving a claim site to the first miner to register a given bit of land. Since the miner had to take several preparatory steps before registering, the law insured that there were to be few disputes about priority.

As in the Californian and the later Australian models, Douglas's provisions left scope for miner laws and courts[35] and other miner-specific institutions. An earlier mining 'ordinance' legitimizing the mining-camp system of staking

[33] See Lang and Crommelin 1979.

[34] Cail 1974, pp. 72–4; Easterbrook and Aitken 1956, p. 337; Barton 1993, ch. 5; see also Clark 1942 for a full study of the miners' social system in relation both to local law and order and to a feared American takeover.

[35] The handling of the courts was slightly different in the new British Columbia law than it had been in the Gold Fields Act. Where the Victorian authorities had decreed a joint elected official- and judge-headed court to settle disputes, most of the tasks of enforcement and dispute settlement in B.C. fell on newly appointed local courts (magistracies) that dealt with claim-jumping and registration errors.

claims had been proclaimed without much legal authority in 1857; his new law also recognized local 'miners' boards'.[36] Rules pertaining to mining rights were evidently sketched out at the meetings of these boards. The board system did not become completely authoritative, however, because the individual miners flitted from camp to camp (and board jurisdiction to jurisdiction) and even left the country altogether when the river level was too high or the winter weather too unpleasant. As each 'bar' became exhausted, rumours of new finds emptied the camps. Successive discoveries took the miners from the lower Fraser into the upper canyon and then into the creek and Cariboo plateau country of the Interior.

For two decades, there were few adjustments to provincial claiming law. Indeed, most of the new government's mining efforts were not devoted to gold mining but to providing a disposal and legal framework for the coal industry. In each new northern district that came into play as gold discoveries were made, officials simply legalized the self-government latent in mining camps. As Zaslow put it, 'a measure of local organization and a good deal of cooperative action [between government and miners]—to determine local rules respecting land and water rights . . . provide public facilities, settle disputes, and petition government for various kinds of assistance—were essential to the proper functioning of a mining camp'.[37]

The system of mining rights chosen for British Columbia had the additional function of providing government revenue. The two obvious sources of revenue—rental and royalty fees—were not feasible: at flat rates they would have been collectible but unremunerative; at more discriminating rates they would have been easily evaded (or collection costs would have become prohibitive). The next best candidate was a head tax, a source that was disallowed by the colonial office. The authorities also examined, experimented with unsuccessfully and/or rejected out of hand other types of taxes, including the Australian front-end entry licence fee, an export tax, a mint and indirect charges such as customs tariffs. In the end the colony's government actually extracted little revenue from the claim system, leaving miners with most of the rents. As in Australia, the inability of the young government to administer and enforce compliance among the placer miners eventually led to a hands-off approach. This persisted until the more capitalistic deep-working methods of the 1870s decreased miners' ability to avoid payment while simultaneously increasing their reliance on publicly provided protection and transportation to their property.

[36] 'Boards' were mentioned in the 1959 Act. Apparently no eye-witness accounts and no records of miners' meetings have survived. See Howay and Scholefield 1914, vol. 2, pp. 32–3; Williams 1977, pp. 66–7 and 73, following W. N. Sage.

[37] Zaslow 1971, p. 51 (evidently following Vowell and Spence 1878, MS in Bancroft Library, Berkeley).

THE KLONDIKE GOLD RUSH

Following the Fraser River rush, small gold discoveries in Alaska, the Yukon Territory and northern British Columbia kept gold prospecting and placer mining going through the 1880s and 1890s. In Alaska, the prospectors on public lands were subject to the public lands General Mining Law (albeit slightly modified; see Chapter 7) that had emerged in the 1880s. Its existence may explain why a mining camp law similar to the one that had kept peace in California did not appear in Alaska. After discoveries in Juneau in 1880, individual prospectors roamed the whole state, seeking to stake claims under the general law. They sometimes crossed the border to Dawson in Canada.

When in 1898 a gold-rush camp did emerge on Alaska's Seward Peninsula, the three original finders saw their claims jumped by other prospectors two or three times over. According to Rickard, 'Anarchy ensued, culminating in a disgraceful litigation, rendered long and costly by a conspiracy among the local authorities at Nome.'[38] Eventually, in 1899 the US Senate came to the aid of the victims, and a US federal court in San Francisco restored their claims. Such lofty intervention had been unnecessary in California during the 1850s and even in the Yukon River rush of the 1880s where camp law was strong and legitimate enough to look after its members' needs.

Inland, smaller discoveries and fewer amateur prospectors meant that more orderly camps took shape along the Yukon River, on both sides of the Canadian–American boundary. The US camps essentially administered the now general law on claim size for the entire area.[39]

On the Canadian side, the federal mining law was a throwback to the free mining provisions developed in British Columbia forty years earlier. When applied to the Yukon region, it provided opportunities for determined prospectors and for thousands of young men crowding through narrow gateways to settle down in isolated camps to mine along streams. The new North-West Territories (which then included not only the northern territories but also what are now the three Prairie Provinces) were effectively governed by a council sitting in Regina.[40] This council was chiefly concerned with prairie land settlement. Much of its far-northern enforcement of the federal mining law and its provisions on claiming and federal remuneration was left in the hands of various local agents and of the specially created North-West Mounted Police.

Several types of placer mining subject to seasonal variation emerged in the Yukon that made direct application of the earlier B.C. law difficult. The techniques were not all applicable to every creek, so it was up to the local miners' meetings to decide which customary rules to adopt.[41] Harold A. Innis tells us about the rules in such camps:

[38] Rickard 1932b, p. 49. Rickard's chapter on Alaska is outstanding.

[39] Morrell 1968, p. 379.

[40] For N.W.T. government see Waite 1971, chs. 4 and 9; Zaslow 1971, ch. 1.

[41] Brown 1907, p. 7.

> Ogilvie noted the difficulties involved in the application of British Columbia mining laws which by then limited placer claims to 100 feet square. Work on the bars restricted diggings to the shallow limits because of the danger of water and to the banks of steams because of frost. It was generally agreed that the claims were too small, and recommendations were made suggesting that claims be measured three hundred or five hundred along the length of the stream and to extend from rim to rim. Unfortunately, carelessness in marking 500 foot claims led to immediate difficulties following the finding of Bonanza [Creek].[42]

In a footnote, Innis cites an unnamed miner whose experiences were later printed in sessional papers in Ottawa:

> All of this gave rise to such conflict and confusion, there being no one to take charge of matters, the agent being unable to go up and attend to the thing, and myself not yet knowing what to do, that the miners held a meeting and appointed one of themselves to measure off and stake the claims, and record the owners' names in connection therewith, for which they got a fee of $2, it being of course understood that each claimholder would have to record his claim with the Dominion agent and pay his fee of $15.[43]

This particular meeting ended with the decision to divide up the large claims to enable a larger number to share in this section of the creek. 'Improper marking of posts on the claims contributed to the difficulties until a survey was carried out and readjustments were made... With enforcement of regulations and an understanding of their general character, large numbers of claims were staked and recorded.'[44] These anecdotes give a flavour of the many complaints and disputes prevalent in the Yukon gold rush of the 1890s. With numerous claims and claimants, there were many trespasses and encroachments, as there had also been in Alaska before the camps took charge.

There was also during this period a shift in the supplying of property rights and enforcement. The increasingly well-established federal government took over from 'custom' and from the camps. By most accounts the mining camps lost their effectiveness in maintaining the authority to enforce order as the Yukon rush wore on: mining was seasonal; the camps were temporary; and their effectiveness at rule-making apparently faded out before the peak of the boom in 1898. Yet by October of that year, in spite of drinking, crime, poor health and the general social disorganization within mining communities, the Dominion government was finding it possible to keep order with regard to the disposal of claims. In fact, it was almost lavish in its provision of judicial, administrative and police personnel. Its local staffs, including

[42] Innis, 1936, p. 197; see also Brown 1907, p. 7.

[43] Ibid., p. 197, n48.

[44] Ibid., p. 197. When properties were resurveyed, it was often found that, when staking, the miners had overestimated the size of their claims. The subsequent corrections created various odd-shaped fractions and gores, which were available for restaking by another miner and possible resale to the miner from whose claim they had been cut.

surveyors, commissioners, recorders, magistrates and other functionaries, were able to select the rules to be enforced where the federal law did not precisely conform to regional needs—thus demonstrating some of the flexibility of the camps. The system was not, however, perfectly efficient, especially on the adjudication end where court justice took more time than the vigilante justice and decisions by majority vote that had prevailed in the camps. The gold commissioner's court heard more and more protests until in 1901—one year following the peak year for gold production—a record 425 protests were entered. More often than not, the parties to the dispute were represented by lawyers or other specialists because, while the hearings dragged on, the alleged trespassers were busy mining. Some infringers simply emptied the claim and disappeared before the case was finally decided.[45]

In summary, the British Columbia and Klondike gold rushes started off with few rules and rights. The set-up was broadly similar to that which had prevailed in the California miners' camps in, say, 1850. There were, however, three differences. In the first place, the camps were less important than those in California because the northern miners' routines included much more movement for exploration and staking, a result both of the huge geographical space available on the northern frontier and of distances between the deposits. In the second place, the geological variations among the northern workings necessitated that claim size, rules and laws be less standardized than those that could apply to California's relatively homogenous placer and alluvial locations. In the third place, because arms of the national governments were already in charge, law and order were more easily maintained than in California's government-less environment.

Theory of placer mining rights and free mining in the New World

The mining claim as a property right

In this final section I present a less historical and more analytical account of the evolution of mining rights during the New World gold booms. The mining right can be seen as a property right endowed with more or less of the six characteristics outlined in Chapter 1. The treatment below is organized around four of these: exclusivity, duration, quality of title and transferability. The miners' demands were five-fold: the freedom to explore, a reward for the first finder, protection from claim jumpers, the setting of a fair claim size and quick dispute settlement in the event one of these rights was violated. To the

[45] Foster and McLaren 1993, p. 471 and Foster and McLaren 1995, p. 465. In the peak year, 1900, gold worth more than $22 million was produced, according to the *Report of the Department of Mines to Parliament*, 1906, pp. 16 and 24.

extent that these goals could be satisfied by supplying property right characteristics, the emphasis was on exclusivity. For most New World miners, freedom from interference during exploration was the essence of free mining.

I limit the discussion here to California, contrasting its experience to the earlier European free mining experience and ignoring the Australian/New Zealand and Canadian rushes discussed above. This is drastic, but there are two justifications: first, in the California camps, more so than in the later gold rushes which were supervised by nascent national and state/provincial governments, the demanders of property rights characteristics were also the suppliers. Whatever changes in characteristics came to be widely accepted between 1848 and 1850 must have corresponded fairly closely to what miners actually wanted. Second, the sources of data with which to compare the theory are especially good for California. In particular, archival sources and historical literature provide evidence for multiple camps in the California gold rush.

The characteristics needed for discovery and acquisition

EXCLUSIVITY

The exclusivity characteristic in a miner's right can be thought of as appearing chronologically in three forms: exclusivity when the right-holder is engaged in prospecting; exclusivity when he has discovered a mineral showing; and exclusivity when he is fully engaged in recovering the mineral.

I begin with exclusivity—or rather its opposite—in prospecting for a mineral discovery. On the public lands reclaimed from Mexico, California's placer miners revived the freedom to explore that had been a staple of European free mining. This was not much of a triumph when one considers that the booms mostly took place where there were no surface owners to give opposition; and what few surface owners did live in mining districts in 1849 had a fair title to subsurface minerals, so exploration on their land was not free. But most European free miners, and later most of their California camp counterparts, had been convinced a prospector's right on the relevant lands should not exclude other *prospectors*. Nineteenth-century industry and governments gradually came to agree with them, in spite of their apprehensions about miners' vigilante and lynch law. Nonetheless, governments confronted with the difficulty of preventing trespassing and collecting revenues from the thousands of placer miners who formed the gold rushes (as we saw in the case of New South Wales) also perceived how wide access promoted racing, which promoted discoveries, which promoted production, which promoted public revenues and general economic prosperity. Thus, gold rush governments, including the post-1850 American Congress, tried to limit, but also to price, the number of issued permits.

Therefore, the characteristic that everyone knew about and promised was, paradoxically, *non*-exclusivity in searching. In placer mining, the prospector and the miner were the same person, and the prospectors' overwhelming demand to be free to roam everywhere searching for gold dominated the demands for every other miner's right. The possibly disadvantageous ramifications of this characteristic were never fully tested in California, where open access to unclaimed territory was more or less a geographical fact, as it also would be later in the far northern gold rushes. As well, the technology of placer gold discovery did not call for protected exploration sites; indeed, it was then (as it is now) fanatically argued that much gold would never be found unless many prospectors were free to work over the same countryside.

There is scarcely any break between the first and the second stage of placer mining, but it is between these two stages that the historical demand for exclusivity changes fundamentally. In the second stage, the discoverer of a likely location is in somewhat the same position as an inventor; he will be in a strong position if he can keep his find quiet. But he is vulnerable to the curiosity of other explorers who, by searching intensively close to his discovery, could deprive him of most of the area that would have been his if his right had been *exclusive*.

The early European base metal free miners had recognized this as a problem and had devised various rules that would protect a miner's find. As we saw earlier, the exclusive assignment of a discoverer's 'meer' to him had been automatic, and the bergmeister and local miners' tribunals were on hand to enforce its assignment. But this kind of exclusivity, suitable for an established free mining community seeking underground base metal on fief or royal lands, differed from the sort of exclusivity that could be effectively achieved in the sometimes lawless nineteenth-century gold fields.

The problem of achieving and enforcing exclusivity in finds can be seen in anecdotal evidence from the period. Consider the example of a discovery made two years into the California gold rush at Yankee Hill, a camp in the Columbia district, which Shinn says is typical of the area in that period. In March 1850 five New England prospectors camped beside a gulch and tested the gravel:

> [They] found they could make eight or ten ounces a day to the man, though water was very scarce. They named the place Kennebec Hill, and proceeded to wash gravel with their utmost energy, knowing others would soon find the gulch. Within a week, another prospector joined them, and succeeded in taking out two pounds and a half of gold during his first day's work. Within thirteen days from the time the five original prospectors camped on Kennebec Hill, there were eight thousand miners in the new town.[46]

[46] Shinn 1884, pp. 244–5. Later miners had to dig deep, often waiting months for water to wash their spoil. Camp rules awarded large claims to these late arrivals in marginal locations. For a parallel Australian example of discoverers overwhelmed by other prospectors, illustrating that Australian discoverers sought to keep their finds quiet, see Blainey 1978, pp. 32–8 and 42–3. For a British Columbia example, see Howay and Scholefield 1914, pp. 74–5 and Taylor 1978, p. 30. For a Klondike example, see Berton 1958, p. 52.

The five miners' problem was that there was no exclusion rule. This was largely because there was as yet no camp at Yankee Hill to make such a rule. There was no camp because, until the discoverer's find, there had been no placer mining in the area. It would take about four weeks for a mass-meeting to be convened and for the miners (mostly newly arrived, many new to mining, and generally suspicious of the idea of special treatment for anyone) to draw up a law similar to those in other camps about discovery claim staking, claim registering and claim size.

Thus, under California 'law' original finders at the second stage came to focus simply on how much gold they could take from a find before other miners arrived. Had they been able to remain alone as 'sole owners' of the discovery site, they would certainly have spread their exploration over a wide area and proceeded at a more careful, leisurely pace.[47] But everyone throughout the history of free mining—Crown interests, landowners, governments and especially the gold-rush miners themselves—opposed 'sole ownership'[48] because they feared any interference with their customary modes of competing. Consequently, until the miner had registered his claim, he was extremely vulnerable. Fully visible to all, he had to reconnoitre, choose the best location to work for himself, decide how much gold to take immediately before risking leaving the claim and, finally, hike to the camp to get the claim recorded. In some cases, unless a pre-existing camp had reached an agreement about the 'finders' claim', finders were technically limited to the same claim size and number as everyone else who followed them back to the deposit site, even assuming it wasn't gutted in their absence at camp.

This brings us to the third stage of exclusivity in holding claims for immediate or later production. The chief goal at this stage was to protect the active miners as their finds were brought into recovery and production. This had not traditionally been a problem. Medieval and early nineteenth-century free mining operations for base metals had been most prevalent in remote or mountainous areas, hence substantially inaccessible to outsiders. In the European free mining communities, decade-to-decade changes in numbers of miners had been relatively small. In contrast, in the California gold rush of 1848–50 and in subsequent New World rushes, the annual increases in the numbers of miners and would-be miners was, as we have seen, enormous and brought with it new difficulties in protecting those already on the land.

[47] The customs of modern Brazilian mining camps illustrate this part of the story. The first finder often becomes the boss of the nascent mining camp. He divides the space into claims, takes one or two for himself, licenses the rest for a royalty, and establishes himself as well as the monopoly operator of a local store, airport and so on. See Cleary 1990.

[48] As seen in Chapter 4, 'sole ownership' is the term given to a hypothetical ideal for a common-property, open-access fishery. See Scott 1956. Before exploration and appropriation, a mining district can be likened to a common-property resource, in which over-spending on discovery and racing to stake and register are analogous to racing to catch fish.

There was often no break in the California miner's activities between the second and third stages of his operation: he quickly followed his discovery and staking of a claim by beginning to take gold from it. Of course he valued rules and laws as provided first by the camps and later by nascent government and courts. A system of rules, however rudimentary, might protect his workings from the effects of spillovers of water or fire from neighbouring miners' workings (like civil nuisance law) or might protect him from intrusion and trespassing (like property law). Indeed, it was providing such instruments of exclusivity in the production of gold that was probably the chief motivator in the creation and endurance of the California mining camps. In their proceedings, miners and their neighbours made the rules of claiming; heard disputes about claim overlaps; made decisions about boundaries; and enforced their rules and rulings.

The enforcement problem was closely related to questions of admission of new miners to the camp and the size of the camp's standard claim. It too relied on the camp's powers of exclusion. In their decisions the miners had to recognize that the continuing influx of new arrivals into the camp area created a high-pressure demand for claims. For a given total area over which the camp could claim authority, the smaller the members' chosen claim size, the more new arrivals could be accommodated.

John Umbeck discusses a probable relationship between camp size and claim size.[49] Larger camps contain more individuals who can share the time and cost of patrolling the camp area. By producing economies of scale with regard to protection and enforcement, increasing the camp size thus reduces per-miner cost. One way of keeping a camp at a size effective in providing protection was to keep down absenteeism and insist that claims be worked steadily (and when abandoned by their holder, sold only to outsiders who do not yet hold a claim in the area). Another way was to admit new miners to replace those departing or to achieve a stronger defensive network through numbers. But if the returns to scale in patrolling actually increased camp production of gold, or if other miners got word that a camp in a lucrative area was expanding, then the larger camp size might attract too many new arrivals, increasing rather than decreasing the pressure on the area. In any case, as most arrivals would be disappointed in their hopes of attaining a claim of their own, they might instead turn to crime: claim-jumping, trespass, theft or burglary. In this case, they would reduce the camp's ability to defend itself or at least increase its per-capita security costs, measured in time spent patrolling the camp's perimeter instead of mining.

The international gold rush experience varied in how efficiently and satisfactorily the changing of claim size worked out. In some camps, farsighted

[49] Umbeck 1981.

miners managed to set a claim size as if they were incrementally balancing a predicted change in the cost of defence against the loss in the values of the claim shares being forfeit.[50] More generally, the dynamics of size adjustment probably speeded the process in some fields and delayed it in others. For example, when new arrivals kept coming at a relentless pace, the 'old' miners would tend to make room for them by hastily reducing claim size. However, where miners had little foreknowledge of the rush that was to come, they might organize themselves in an attempt to hold the line against cuts in claim size. And, of course, even if adopted, the process of reducing claim size could not continue indefinitely. As individual claims were depleted, the idea of dividing them would become less and less attractive, and miners would begin to *combine* low-grade sites instead, seeking economies of scale in places where a lot of gravel would yield only a little gold. Other miners would return to sites previously passed over—away from rivers, on hillsides or underground. In the Spanish Bar district in California, claims on the river were originally one hundred feet in length. Sometimes, though, when a camp was crowded and all the best claims taken up, a new company of miners would come along and, calling a public meeting of the miners, *persuade* them to diminish the prescribed size of claims so as to give all an equal chance.[51]

In general, in California, as on the Fraser River and in the Klondike, the adjustment mechanisms worked well: the chosen claim sizes even in the heat of the rushes were comfortably workable.[52] But elsewhere, in Brazil, Kimberley, South Africa (for diamonds) and in Victoria, Australia, especially when operations moved underground, there was much complaining. All too often the standard claim was found to be too small. Miners likened it to a grave twenty, fifty or a hundred feet deep.

DURATION AND RENEWAL

As one might expect, the duration characteristic of the placer miner's right was not of great importance to him compared to its exclusivity, especially given the strong incentives he faced to search and produce very rapidly. To the extent that duration did matter, however, it was in relation to the same three stages of mining as exclusivity: the prospecting phase; the period

[50] These sentences are derived from my earlier work and an essay on rule-making and camp and claim size. Its inspiration was work done by John Umbeck; see Umbeck 1981. As it developed I was in correspondence with Umbeck and with R. O. Zerbe, Ross McKitrick and James Johnston to all of whom I am grateful.

[51] 1884, pp. 174–5. Emphasis added.

[52] Regarding larger claims in California: away from water or on a hillside, see Umbeck 1981, p. 103; underground, see Shinn 1884, p. 239. Elsewhere, many miners went underground to old creek beds: for British Columbia, see Howay and Scholefield 1914, p. 78; for Victoria, Australia, see Blainey 1978, pp. 46–58.

between the discovery and gaining the legal (or recognized) title to the claim; and the subsequent panning and mining operations.

As discussed at length above, in Old World free mining, the issuance of rights to search for minerals had been typically under the control of either the Crown or the feudal or post-feudal landowner. In districts where claims or meers were not strictly heritable within the miner's family, the lord had some authority to set the rights' duration and thus the necessary frequency of their renewal. By adjusting the length of duration and ease of renewal, he could control the size of his free mining community to some extent, and thereby increase or downgrade the rate of discovery and, eventually, the rate of production on his lands. Since there were no landowners in California, however, and more generally no powerful private actors interested in substituting away from the free miner system toward a land ownership and leasing system, these 'supply' effects had little bearing on the development of the duration characteristic during the New World gold booms.

This conclusion reveals a more interesting question on the demand side of the equation: whether the California and other gold rush miners can be seen as demanding a longer-lived claim than what the staking and camp system naturally provided. To start, we may ask how the (variable) claim size influenced the life of the claim. In the early days of the gold rushes, when the gold miners used pans or rockers, mining exhibited constant costs or constant returns to scale in claim size (that is, ignoring the defence costs which, ceteris paribus, exhibited decreasing returns to claim size). As long as labour (either the miner alone or in tandem with slaves or claimless miners willing to work for wages) and water were available, a creek could be mined out in a year or a season regardless of the size of the individual claims.[53] However, if additional labour were not freely available, then the larger the claim, the longer the time required for the holder to mine it out, working alone. Operations could even extend over multiple years and might be inefficient as the restless claim holder would move on before mining the lowest-grade sand and gravel.

As against scale-based benefits from stretching out the period of production, the miner would also run up against various reasons for shortening his period of production. The first reason was discounting, stemming either from the market rate of interest (particularly if the miner was in debt to lenders and suppliers) or the miner's own impatience. The second reason for speeding up production came from the continuing burden of total expenses, or overheads,

[53] Marshall 1920, p. 167, wrote that mining out of a mineral property was like pumping out of a reservoir: The more nearly a reservoir is exhausted, the greater is the labour of pumping from it; but if one man could pump it out in ten days, then ten men could pump it out in one day. If the plans had been properly laid in advance, and the requisite specialized capital and skill got ready for the work, ten years' supply of coal might have been raised in one year without any difficulty. This contention has been disputed in detail but is widely accepted as the orthodox rule for coal-mining.

both those pertaining to security as discussed above and those pertaining to more mundane requirements such as dam and ditch repair, which remained necessary only so long as the mine remained active but could thereafter be forgotten. A third reason to speed up would come from the eventually declining output and activity on *other* claims. An aggregate drying up of claims would signal that the whole camp was preparing to close down, leaving any miner with an unusually prolonged production plan in danger of being abandoned by his camp fellows and overrun by newcomers and outsiders.

In general, it seems clear that, so long as placer mining dominated and the rushes kept the claims small, miners in their camps did not want or need claims of long duration; in fact, they raced to keep their duration on their claims as short as possible. Later, when the grade of surface mineral declined and a more capitalistic mining required underground tunnels and shafts or hydraulicking, miners began requiring bigger claims in order to take advantage of returns to scale. These larger claims had longer lives and the average cost of leaving some mineral unexploited grew too large for miners not to be thorough, which took time. The duration characteristic of their claim and implicit in their claim rights became more important.

QUALITY OF TITLE

The titles of the European free miners, like those of medieval private mining lease holders, had stemmed from the recognized land titles held by their feudal landlords, whose titles usually came from a system of dynastic inheritance stretching into the ancient past and whose 'quality' depended on the verifiability and acceptance of this lineage. Thus the rights to search and to hold mineral lands and minerals had deep roots. The legitimacy of the medieval and early modern free miner was intrinsically related to the legitimacy and stature of the supplier of his rights.

Nineteenth-century New World placer-mining titles were a different matter entirely. These rights, especially those held by placer miners in the California gold rushes, looked insecure to lawyers of the period precisely because, unlike in Europe, they had no root in an original grant. Indeed, they had no root even in some government action or law, but only in government forbearance or absence. In the earliest stages of the gold rush, miners' quality of title rested on even less than that: on the acceptance of their claim rights by their peers in the camps.

I discuss the quality of title characteristic and its impact on placer mining in the context of the same three stages as above: prospecting, claiming and working. I begin, again, with the miner's right to go prospecting. In the first California placer-mining gold rush the miners did not, of course, require permits as there was no government authority to issue them. Access to later gold rushes in the American states, in Canada and in Australia, did require a permit. However, once one was acquired, the free right of prospecting was always regarded by both demanders and suppliers as secure. The literature does not mention any occasion in which individual miners threatened, or camps or governments revoked, a prospector's right. In later years governments opted to limit the issuance of new licences in order to control the flow of miners or ensure a decent average return in revenue, but they never cancelled existing or previously issued prospecting and mining rights.

Quality of title became a dicier proposition at the second and third stages at which a miner required title: while proving up his discovery and deciding how to dispose of it, and then, if he opted to work the claim himself, while actually taking the gold from it. To overcome their lack of a title with a root in an original grant, the original gold rush miners in their camps took the initiative in creating and enforcing 'titles' for holders who met three conditions: (1) the right race/colour and/or citizenship; (2) evidence of an acceptably discovered, staked and recorded claim; and (3) evidence that the mine was being continuously worked through the duration of the claim (a 'use it or lose it' rule). Title was wholly dependent on the continued acceptance by, and existence of, the camp. Essentially, miners acted on the hope that for the short period of months for which they needed a title to a particular placer location, the camp-granted title would remain secure against other miners and against the camp.[54]

In later placer-gold rushes, of course, governments took the place of the camps and of an earlier royal or noble land grantor in providing title through their permits or more generally through legislation and a legal code. If anything, this official title had better roots than those conferred by the mining camps and was therefore one dimension in which, as mentioned above, the otherwise fiercely libertarian free miners welcomed the authority of the new state and national governments.

As discussed in the subsection on exclusivity, the miners did not necessarily find it easy to satisfy the second camp-made condition for title: evidence of an acceptably discovered, staked and recorded claim. The heart of the problem was that if a find was in a truly isolated location there would be no organized camp to provide a grant of title, however informal, and to help the prospector protect his claim. Thus, the title available in the camp system was not likely what the first finder would have desired from an impartial authority like a government or great landowner. One ramification was that the proliferation of new claims eventually prevented there being much extra space to award to the first finder. We do not know from the literature what most miners expected

[54] The possessory titles had many features of acquisition by prescription, or squatting. However, the latter were valid because the courts accepted that pretence that the person in possession held from someone who, in the remote past, had granted them the property. The deed had been mislaid. No such pretence lay behind a miner's right. See also Shinn 1884, pp. 274–6, for a summary of how the state courts interpreted the California titles.

from a real first discovery in terms of extra space, such as an additional 'finder's claim'. What most first finders did unchallengeably get, however, in addition to their initial takings before going in to register the claim, was the first choice of *location*. The first finder might choose the site of his original find or, if the initial site was sufficiently depleted by the time he registered the claim, he might also claim a newer, less worked-over site on the same deposit. In this regard, the gold rush miners were no different from contemporary land settlers, water users, fishers and loggers: all worked within public resource disposal 'systems' that gave priority to the first arrival's or first user's choice of location.

TRANSFERABILITY

Today transferability is a crucial feature of any mining right. The opportunity to sell a good find provides much of the incentive to prospect. Due to the capital demands of modern mining, transferability makes it possible to assemble neighbouring claims into a workable, fundable, promotable unit. So it comes as a surprise to find that miners in early gold rush mining camps apparently did not seek this characteristic in their property right.

Clearly, the nature of early gold rushes points to a great demand for transferability. Gold properties were always changing ownership. The miners were young, impetuous and optimistic. Many of them enjoyed making a good find more than they enjoyed doing a good day's work on the claim with pick, shovel and rocker, as evidenced by the obvious ease with which they would leave one bar or camp and join a rush to a new one. In addition, every miner knew that news of a find might come at any time and that he might want to go to it without delay. Transferability and marketability, therefore, should have been welcome, for they would have enabled a claim holder to get some value for anything he had put into the claim, any gold that was left, and any knowledge he could pass on. Put another way, miners should have demanded transferability because, along with exclusivity, it increased the payoff from a discovery.

One explanation for their not doing so is that, given problems of asymmetric information between seller and buyer, second-hand claims did not command prices high enough to make advertising and selling them worthwhile. However, this explanation does not explain why miners opposed transferability for those of their companions who did want to divest themselves of their claims. Many individual miners must have shared the same attitudes toward transferability as did lawyers and classical political economists. To make an interest in land or natural resources inalienable was inefficient and unfair. It was inefficient because it prevented people from allocating themselves to jobs or places where they had a comparative economic advantage. It was unfair because it favoured those who were happy staying in one place and penalized those who wanted to leave. Collectively, however, the miners had other reasons for denying the individual right to transfer a claim.

The camp meetings revealed attitudes that were hostile to the buying and selling of mining claims, couched in an appeal to what the Australian miners called 'mateship'. That is, they were reluctant to extend their friendly co-operative efforts to just anyone who might want to buy in. They couldn't know how good a community member the replacement miner would be. Beyond this 'membership quality' criterion, the camps had a population maintenance rationale for preventing their members from selling out: every individual miner had an incentive to make sure the camp did not start to disperse while his own claim was still workable. Thus in general miners opposed the sale of claims to other miners in the camp. But these 'insiders' might be the only buyers from which a prospective seller could command a worthwhile price because they would have better information about the claims than somebody arriving from another camp or another state.

The historical outcome of all these countervailing concerns was a compromise. According to Shinn and Umbeck,[55] many camps started with a total ban on claim sales but increasingly adjusted to permit such sales on a sort of individual basis. Additionally, some transfers were apparently made tacitly, outside the camp's common-policy requirements. For instance, while sales of claims to other camp members were frowned on, partnerships were permitted. These deals often served to conceal that a miner had sold out, as one 'partner' continued to mine in the departed 'partner's' name. As simple placer operations gave way to more elaborate alluvial mining, partnerships and syndicates became more common in the camps, presumably entailing within a camp frequent sales and divisions of claims and shares.[56]

Concluding notes on characteristics of early rights

The camps were looked at in different ways: as co-operative, pooling, mining enterprises; as tent sites for individual miners, each protecting his claim; and as a form of government and *supplier of rights* operated through majority rule. It was the third interpretation that stuck and is of most interest to historians of natural resource use and property rights. Under majority rule, the camp meeting acquired many aspects of the landlord. It could be seen as negotiating with each miner over his rights and responsibilities, much as if a lease were being drawn up. The landlord represented and supplied individual rights in the (collective) interest of all the miners, while the individual miner demanded

[55] Umbeck 1981, p. 95.

[56] See Libecap 1989, pp. 29–50, for a good account of the transition of California placer mining to underground operation.

the conditions that the camp had to concede in order for membership to be worthwhile to him individually.

But the claim was not a lease. The negotiations did not lead to a set of bilateral bargains, each adapted to the particular lessee; rather, they led over time to a set of rules, uniformly applicable to all claims. The camp voting reflected what each voter wanted *for himself* as a claim-holder; but in aggregate, the camp's terms represented the collective goals of the community. The miner was the demander, out to keep characteristics in his mining rights that were at least the equal of those granted in other camps and those he could get working on his own.

In summary, the functions of the characteristics were as follows: *Exclusivity* was given to the mining claim for law and order reasons, to replace violence. *Security and quality of title* were to some extent byproducts of increasing exclusivity achieved through camp decisions and cooperation. As the gold rush continued, security became even more highly valued because it protected durable investments in capital-intensive mining. *Duration* was rarely defined in the camps, except for the application of a use-it-or-lose-it rule that persisted through the transition to hard-rock mining and became enshrined in the official government regulations of the 1870s. *Transferability* was rarely encouraged because camp consensus both distrusted outsiders and wanted to keep population levels up, but it emerged implicitly, even where forbidden. It was needed first to accommodate the miners' intrinsic restlessness and, later, to facilitate land assembly when new, larger-scale methods were introduced on older claims.

Characteristics of camp law during the later part of the California gold rush

Collectivism and cooperation within the camp system

Some kinds of individual property rights serve as the basis for proportionate division of collective benefits and costs. For example, in medieval Europe the benefits of grazing on common land were often stinted (shared) in proportion to villagers' own plots. The California mining claim also served such a purpose. The claim was essentially a personal share in a larger collective property, one that, except for the possibility of a first finder's advantage, imposed fairly strict equality between neighbouring claim holders. It also made it possible for miners to meet together, to make decisions and to work together on joint projects.

Again, understanding the role of the claim in collectivism requires turning to examine miner self-governance. The journalistic and academic accounts of the mining camps contain many fascinating accounts of miner control and justice. The miners were well able to make collective decisions about matters of collective interest, especially in the granting and adjudicating of mining claims. What is not often realized is that the individual claim system was itself calculated to reinforce self-government. In the absence of government-mandated and enforced property rights, the chief enemy of introducing individual rights and shares is not a fondness for open access but a fear of being squeezed out or otherwise overridden by outsiders. Put another way, the miners needed assurance that submitting to a given code of conduct would not expose them to defectors, free riders, cheaters and shirkers who chose to ignore it. The mining camps plus the claiming system offered this assurance. Because each miner held his claim at the pleasure of the other miners, defection and claim jumping were difficult. Certain kinds of free riding and shirking (but not all) were also difficult because, again, the group could penalize a nonperformer by withdrawing his title to his claim (the use-it-or-lose it rules). Another natural fear was of the group ganging up on an individual member who became unpopular, but the camps reduced this risk somewhat by adhering to one-man one-claim one-vote procedures and by refusing to accommodate absentees. Certainly, there was not perfect democracy. There is no doubt that some domineering miners were more equal than others; that the justice dispensed was very rough; and that Spanish-Americans, French and Chinese, if they were even allowed to work claims, were otherwise excluded from the camp organization. Yet the typical miner who acquired a claim by meeting the camp's conditions would feel at home in the camp system of governance and would support and defend it.

But collective action and cooperation took on new prominence as the simplest forms of placer mining gave way to more complicated, large-scale operations in the later days of the gold rush. The best examples of placer miner collectivism (apart, of course, from the essential issue of claim enforcement) are found by examining the historical records on underground water drainage and stream damming and diversion, first encountered in Chapter 3. Typically, the miners would work together to drain an area, then each would mine his own property/claim within that area. The records suggest that the ditching ventures may well have divided the costs equally among the claims served, while the damming and drainage syndicates actually divided them in accordance with the gold discovered on each drained claim.

Doubtless, the mining camps sheltered and encouraged these ventures, at least implicitly. Even if they did not actively encourage such cooperation, they implicitly made it possible by enforcing the mining claim. Hence, Umbeck's belief that individual ownership helped to 'get things done' is very plausible. Less is known about the disadvantages or costs of joint ventures in draining. The problem would have been to make sure that free-riding miners did not resist labouring on precursor projects that might take many weeks to complete when they would prefer to be working their own claims (a major issue in England during the period as well—see Chapter 8). The camps might have helped to enforce a joint work requirement to complement their claim work requirement, but there is no record of this.

In the later years of the placer stage of the California gold rush, drainage of the sort that required joint effort was beyond the organizing ability of the camps and was sometimes supplied by external sources such as water or ditch companies. Some of these companies were hybrids: they relied on voluntary miner labour but provided the necessary capital. But most companies were simple private enterprises out to make a profit by providing a service to a related industry (mining).[57] Ditches in especially waterlogged areas must have taken months to complete and often required external financing that a ditching company could provide. Often the companies that provided them lived on after the camp was closed, serving other customers. Ditching and drainage were therefore one area in which the camp was not sovereign. While the exclusivity of individual mining claims and the strength of the mining camp were of some help in the organization of the damming, diversion and drainage ventures, they were not necessarily self-sufficient.

Miners' rights versus surface rights

One of the main themes in the study of natural resource property rights is how subsets of these rights—say, mining and ranching rights—interact with each other. This will be a major focus of Chapters 8 and 9 on modern, private mining rights and oil rights. The question here, in the context of nineteenth-century placer mining, is whether the mining claim administered by the districts and camps had enough of the characteristics of exclusivity and quality of title to help its holders establish users' rights as against other users of the same space. If we think of gold-bearing lands as a multi-purpose natural resource, then placer and hydraulic miners were just one group of possible users. If their uses conflicted with those of, say, ranchers or freshwater fishers, whose rights prevailed?

In fact, prospector/miner conflict with holders of surface rights was *not* an important question in the 1850s and early 1860s. Placer miners said little about the subject in their personal records, reflecting the fact that they rarely ran into a non-miner wishing to make some other use of the same land or

[57] In 1854, three hundred miners in the Columbia camp (out of about five thousand inhabitants) each gave several weeks' work to the local water company, which was building forty-four miles of canal and flume to serve twenty-four square miles. See Shinn 1884, p. 246. There is little record of companies being set up for drainage or other works; apparently groups of miners had to work together informally for this purpose. The reason may be that the ditches had longer service lives than the dams or drainage canals that served particular claims (which were soon mined out). But water-supply ditch companies could go on serving new camps and other users.

water.[58] Historically this is because there were actually very few people around: there were no urban developers, ranchers or settlers in the unoccupied frontier public lands in California, British Columbia or the Yukon, and not many in Australia. Additionally, to the extent that alternative users did make demands on a fixed amount of land, the original technology of placer mining was not provocative of land-use conflicts as it dumped little waste and caused no lasting surface upset. As a result, the first mining camp law said nothing at all about the rights of non-miners or the sharing of land. It did not fight for legitimacy with other potential land users.

All this changed in the 1860s when, first in California and then in the other gold-rush regions, pans and rockers gave way to more bulky, permanent, capital-intensive technologies. Among the first were damming and draining, for which groups of miners and private companies diverted water into sluice boxes and built dams to lay bare lower bars and beds. Soon after came hydraulicking and its need for water under pressure, sometimes carried many miles; to be followed by dredging and subsurface or alluvial gold mining. All these techniques, requiring water, roads and space for waste dumps, could in one way or another interfere with surface uses of the land above or adjoining the deposits. Conflict over rights and access to running water, among mining operations and between mining and urban populations and agricultural users, required the development of new systems of water rights, discussed at greater length in Chapter 3. In brief, the miners, apparently inspired by mining claims, relied on the ethic that the first user to divert a stated amount of the stream-flow at a certain place along the stream was deemed to have *appropriated* an exclusive right to make this diversion and to divert a stated amount of water. The state government then adopted the system which then became the model for many governments' appropriative water law.

When the various countries' gold-rush areas were set up as political units, the governments did set to work to place mining-camp law within a context of more general homesteading, settlement and land-use laws, not to mention property, contract and even criminal laws. But neither the camps nor the governments did much to resolve conflicts with other land users. Essentially this was because such rules could not be adapted to cover persons who had never contracted into them. The camps' authority had never extended beyond the camps' self-selected mining populations. Only the governments in their role as owners had the authority required to create and enforce novel surface-rights with sufficient quality of title applicable to both miners and, say,

[58] Surface water, also valued by ranchers, is an exceptional illustration. Normally, its use would have been dedicated to the needs of surface riparian owners. But this class was missing in the gold rush. When riparian owners did arrive, most of them adhered to miners' water law. Thus, as I noted in Chapter 3, historians are justified in concluding that the California miners shaped the modern appropriative surface water right for both rural and urban users.

farmers. But to do so meant either to continue to show constitutional respect for the placer rights that had been created and tolerated outside a legislative framework, or to disavow them—a drastic course of action for which there was no popular demand or political payoff.

How the placer gold claiming system was shaped by the functions it performed

With the first gold discoveries in 1848 the miners who flocked to the California gold rush found themselves faced with open-access common property and virtually no civil or legal authority to administer it. They are famed for their reaction to this situation: forming their own institutions for managing and distributing this resource, creating what some have referred to as a working model of the social contract spoken of by the Enlightenment philosophers. This process was helped by their having found a resource of both extraordinarily high value and extremely high accessibility—permitting them the luxury to experiment with high-cost organizations and institutions (such as placer partnerships), and to do without most capital goods and special training. Miners gained the ability to form socially cohesive institutions through their professional homogeneity, avoiding the class frictions prevalent in Europe. They had models in European self-governing free mining, including the tin, lead and copper miners' communities, free mining societies whose rules they imitated.[59] All of these advantages meant that, when the open-access common property was overwhelmed by thousands of new arrivals to the gold rush, the established miners in their self-made camps were flexible enough to make the adjustments of claim size and transferability needed to absorb many of them and preserve social order and profitability of the resource.

At the heart of the placer mining system was the 'claim', loosely inherited from the Old World base metal free miners and their lords. Under common law (by which mineral leases, for instance, were administered and enforced), one body of law—property law—governed the acquisition and holding of private mining rights, while other laws, both tort laws and regulations, governed the operation of the mine. By contrast, under the mining camp and the 'claim' system it endorsed, the rights and duties governing the explorer/prospector were closely integrated with the rules governing mine operation.

And it must be repeated that the California miners were unique in the external institutional framework in which they found themselves, one that was and is very rare in property rights history. The lack of existing government and the essential emptiness of the frontier districts where gold was found

[59] Though, of course, it is difficult to judge the extent of this precedent since few of the first miners, who designed the mining-camp institutions, knew much about Europe. They were more aware of Spanish-Mexican mining law, US federal land sale and leasing practices, and the Anglo-American common law of private mining, the latter of which' tenets they tended to reject.

meant that there were essentially no conflicting motives among demanders and suppliers of rights (like that of a government seeking to use the mining system to increase its own revenue) and no damaging or restricting spillovers from the land uses of other parties. Beyond the military or civil service and the merchants, no vested interests were affected by the conduct of mining. Unlike common law, and earlier disposal and leasing laws in Europe, mining law could therefore disregard both surface land uses and surface land-ownership. This was just as well, for, as nominal trespassers, miners certainly had no jurisdiction to make rules or laws for users in other economic sectors.

The placer miners reflected their own problems and needs when they designed their camps and supplied themselves with property rights. They needed a government of some sort, however rudimentary, for collective security and for the allocation of land. Beyond that, the search for gold ensured that their ideas about claims would be fiercely individualistic. After a few initial and inefficient attempts at partnerships, Californian miners showed little tendency to develop a claim to make it suitable for joint ventures. Of four main characteristics of property rights—exclusivity, quality of title, transferability and duration—the first two were most sought by early placer miners while the latter two, for reasons discussed at length in the last section, were of secondary importance. Both exclusivity and quality of title impacted on a miner's security in his claim. Concern about exclusivity was most visible in discussions of freedom of access in prospecting and of claim size which had to be varied to maintain a level of security conducive to profitability and personal safety. Quality of title depended on the functioning of the camp and the miner's place within it and was determined by majority voting decisions in the camp meetings.

Besides a fascinating story of cultural history and the archetypical example of the American frontier dynamic, the California gold rush of the 1850s was a milestone in the evolution of mining disposal systems and holders' property rights. Until that time, governments and quasi-private landowners (like the feudal landlords) had granted mineral rights and used methods that were basically indistinguishable from those used in the private sector. They were also similar to those used for disposing of farm soil and other resources. Only the ancient system of Roman-European free mining, enduring in remote pockets of Germany, Austria, the Mediterranean countries and England, provided an exception to this generalization.

In Chapter 7 I broaden the discussion from the mining of gold to include mineral mining more generally as it confronted governments and private mining interests. I show that the goldfield claim-staking procedure created by the camps was taken over and formalized by governments as mining shifted toward capital-intensive, time-consuming underground technologies. By the 1870s placer mining was rapidly becoming a thing of the past. Formerly, governments in Victoria and the Yukon and British Columbia had barely tolerated the thousands of new arrivals who flocked to the gold-rush camps. But with the new quest for underground gold and silver (not to mention veins and deposits of base metals, coal and industrial materials), they began to trim their mineral-disposal laws. Their idea was not to avert the miner inflow but to attract more miners, ranging from individual prospectors to large, advanced mining firms. Led by the passage of the American Mining Law in 1872, jurisdiction after jurisdiction re-examined the advisability of a prior discovery requirement, as well as other conditions for acquiring a mineral claim or lease, the major ones of which are the subject of the next chapter. Miner control gave way to government control, anxiously steered by prospecting, mining-company and financial lobbying groups. In the early part of the twentieth century, this procedure had to be revised again in order to accommodate the disposal of oil and gas land, the subject, at last, of Chapter 9.

7

After the Gold Rush: Alluvial and Hard Rock Mining on Public Land in the New World

Introduction: adapting placer mining rights to hard-rock mining

As we have seen, during the placer mining rushes of the mid-nineteenth century, the prospector's right to enter public lands was much the same thing as the miner's right to stake a claim and remove the mineral from it. A single right, essentially the free miner's right, entitled the miner-prospector to go where he pleased, stake where he wanted, pan for gold and divert water as suited his purposes. Once the early period of violence was past, miners rarely ran into the sort of conflicts with each other that could not be addressed by the camp-made or government-adapted claiming system, and rarely imposed any burden on other public land occupants, the few who were present being largely unbothered by small-scale, low-surface-damage placer operations.

As time passed, several changes to the technology and methodology of mining rendered the simple free mining claiming system inadequate for allocating mining rights on public land. As new deposits of gold in the alluvial stream beds dried up, miners began to look elsewhere—underground and into the hills—to find sources of gold, and later of other less valuable metals. They encountered remote deposits in new geographical features, the working of which required new technologies and new forms of equipment. The wider scale of operations in turn meant that miners were no longer so autonomous: their individual operations imposed new inconveniences and disruptions on each other and on other users of the land. At the same time, the need for cooperation in certain large-scale activities peripheral to mining increased with the scale of the operation on each claim.

In economists' language, the claiming system as perfected by the placer miners in their camps had little need to make provision for dealing with *externalities* and almost none for a division of labour. But as governments grew stronger and mining techniques grew more complex, the miners lost or surrendered their role as suppliers or adjudicators of their own rights. Instead, 'mining interests' turned to the government to provide the missing features. Governments, in turn, included in these formal rights increasingly specific details about what the holders might and must do as occupiers of the public land and as neighbours of other miners and other land users. This chapter surveys the development of these modern alluvial and hard-rock mining rights in the countries where the mineralized public lands were most extensive: the United States, Canada and Australia. (South Africa was also an important new source of gold but most operations there were on private agricultural land.)

Transition to deep diggings: deep alluvial mining and industrialization

Tradition and change

Harold Innis made the point that gold mining commanded the greatest possible mobility of labour and capital and that its institutions were designed to enhance this mobility.[1] Many placer miners had valued this restless aspect of their lives and opposed measures and institutions that would tie them down. Throughout the range of gold-rush districts—in California, Australia, the Fraser Canyon-Cariboo region and South Africa—miners had behaved as though making their fortune was only one of their ambitions. They were also travellers and gamblers who enjoyed their gold-camp experiences. Naturally, their enthusiasm lasted as long as the easy surface workings for gold held out and as long as the value of the deposits was sufficient to cover the lavish allocation of their often wasteful, competitive and interference-ridden activity.

After about 1860 the rules of the typical California placer-mining camp tended to converge in a standard set of miners' rights.[2] These were awarded with decreasing insistence on the continuous working of a claim (partly because of the shortage of water) and with increasing permissiveness about sales, transfers and subdivisions compared to the 1850s-era rules surveyed in Chapter 6. To some extent the consolidating of the camps' claim right systems coincided with the move to hard-rock mining. As surface and stream-bed gold became scarcer, miners began to trace the deposits to their sources: underground, in the alluvial beds of gold located in ancient river beds, and in the hills from which the streams had torn the gold flakes and dust. Not surprisingly, moving out of the streams and going underground imposed new technological requirements: shafts and tunnels to lead the miners to the underground deposits; hydraulicking for breaking up the banks of gravel in

[1] Innis 1936, p. 78. [2] Van Wagenen 1918, p. 99

which gold dust might be found; and dredging in the rich sand and gravel beds beneath streams. In all these techniques the gold particles then had to be extracted mechanically or by sluicing from large amounts of spoil.

The advent of deep digging in Victoria, Australia provides a good case study. With the precursor to the Gold Fields Act, 1851, Victoria's mining rules had set the stage for the gold rush yet to come.[3] Again, with its law-making for the transition from surface to underground placer mining, the colony anticipated and influenced the legislative response to similar transitions in California and elsewhere.

Around Ballarat in 1852–3, the miners found the creeks they were exploiting to be merely the surface trackings of much older creek beds far underground. Once an opening or cavern had been dug, it became necessary to sink a deep shaft, sometimes one hundred feet or more, in order to remove the sand and gravel and to pump flood water. While such mining did not require great technical expertise, each mine required an unprecedented amount of working capital for months of digging and construction.

To an outsider, the surprising aspect of the property demands then expressed by Australian miners was an insistence on maintaining placer-mining tradition: keeping ventures small, active and autonomous. For example, when a deep miner began to install a steam pump, it was attacked in Luddite fashion by miners who argued 'that the machine would enable the owners to win too much gold and would dispense with the need for so many working partners in each claim'.[4] 'Winning too much gold' meant both that the current owners would mine their claim so thoroughly that there would be nothing left for later miners and that, with the aid of a pump, they might even take material from adjoining claims where the miners' technology did not allow them to reach everywhere beneath their markings. At the same time, miners were expected to consider their responsibilities to comrades on adjoining mines. Those who had arrived first were expected to pump their mines regularly to prevent newer mines from being flooded. In their letters home, and in their petitions to the authorities, the miners often mentioned their responsibilities to each other. Perhaps in response to the populist sentiment, their official miners' courts supplied only small, grudging changes to the rights laid out according to mining law.

Other difficulties presented themselves. As the depth of their leads increased, miners became less confident that their surface staking had actually been placed over their claimed deposit in the ancient creek bed. This problem led to a large volume of disputes to be resolved. Perhaps more important, it encouraged miners to hang back from sinking their own shafts. The right

[3] For the chronology of the Gold Fields Acts, see the discussion in the previous chapter, especially fn. 30.

[4] Blainey 1978, p. 51.

moment to sink was *after* one's neighbours had discovered the direction of the lead but *before* they had time to invade one's own. Dozens of shafts might then be sunk adjoining a discovery shaft. To deal with hanging back, miners increasingly turned to authorities and to the courts to demand enforcement of continuous-mining, use-it-or-lose-it-type rules. These rules might be considered as constituting a weakening in the exclusivity characteristic in the holder's licence as they limited his powers to set his own rate of mining, forcing him to mine at a rate also acceptable to adjoining miners.

Of course, not all the miners' interdependencies were unwelcome. While the miners were tempted to free-ride on others' risk-taking in sinking shafts, they also were drawn into joint projects, including locating claims for all the miners in the area, drainage, support, illumination and ventilation. These projects improved the efficiency of every individual miner working on his own claim and had much the flavour of a public (producer's) good. The original concept of ad-hoc, camp-centric 'mateship' needed rewriting to comprehend good-faith partnerships needed to achieve joint-venture economies of scale while protecting individual claims from harm.

The Australian miners promoted an increase in holding size in proportion to depth and to the number of partners: under Victoria's law a single miner was entitled to one hundred forty four square feet while teams of four men or more were entitled to five hundred seventy six square feet.[5] One of the biggest concessions to the new alluvial realities was the granting of the right for miners to unite their claims,[6] a weak form of transferability. The mining courts, consistent with their leanings toward traditional claiming law and reflecting the individualistic egalitarian style of the original surface placer rush, were none too keen to assist these partnerships, let alone larger-scale enterprises.[7] However, since they also reflected the miners' opposition to speculation (at least when it took the form of holding claims inactive while other claim holders laboriously developed and probed), the same mining courts were driven gradually to approve larger, united claims. Thereby they acted to foil the free riders—the 'shepherds' of the unworked claims.[8]

As time marched on, underground alluvial gold mining gave way to lode or hard-rock mining: for gold, but also for copper, silver, various base metals and coal. Its new operations were even more inappropriate for the application of surviving placer mining rules than had been the procedure for deep

[5] Blainey 1978, pp. 47–9.

[6] Ibid., pp. 57–8. See also Morrell 1941, pp. 250–1.

[7] They encouraged the states to legislate to allow prospectors to enter private lands and remove gold in Crown reserves and, later, even to explore for and remove privately owned gold. See Lang and Crommelin 1979, pp. 4–5 and ch. 10.

[8] For an entirely different perspective, in which claim size is seen as set by official attempts to get revenue and to keep order, see La Croix 1992.

alluvial mining.[9] The hard rock mining process consisted of standardized, highly capitalistic operations, well beyond the scope of the individual miner-prospector whose needs had inspired the legislation leading up to Victoria's 1855 Gold Fields Act and similar statutes in New South Wales (1866) and other placer mining districts. In particular, less attention now had to be paid to the demands for characteristics in the rights of individual miners. More attention had to be paid to the demands of large mining firms, who primarily sought quality of title and security in their rights over their lands and constructions. They had less reason to be worried about exclusivity to prevent interference or about the mere priority of their discovery. For the first time, the 'mining interest' superseded the prospecting interest in demand for characteristics.

From this Australian example I turn to North American mining's transition from placer mining law. We can pick up the story with the discovery of enormous silver deposits in what was to become Nevada.[10] In 1859 the Comstock deposits were gradually revealed to be a mountain of ore. Individual miners flocked to the area and surface workings multiplied, but it soon became clear that the biggest reserves were far below the surface, and far beyond the reach of individuals and their surface working technology. Large mines like Ophir and Bonanza were incorporated not only to undertake drilling deep underground but also to invest in crushing, concentrating, transporting and refining facilities. These all required unprecedented investment in what was then cutting-edge technology.

Large service firms set up shop. One of them, Joseph Sutro's tunnel enterprise (to be discussed further in Chapter 8), drilled a four-mile drainage adit in order to remove water from two thousand vertical feet of waterlogged, ore-rich mountain in return for a share of the mines' ores.

Many of the new hard-rock or lode developments of silver, base metals and coal were set up beyond the established gold districts: in Michigan, Wisconsin, Minnesota, Ontario, Quebec, certain Australian states and the British parts of South Africa. In these areas the authorities had no experience with placer mining, its conventions and its camps. This was just as well since by the mid

[9] I am omitting the extended periods during which low-grade alluvial gravels were exploited for gold by dredging. This technique, sometimes scavenging where panning and digging no longer paid, survived in some fields for over a hundred years. Tin dredging is still an important industry. Dredging became a kind of land use, like quarrying or open-pit mining, and as such came less under mineral disposal laws and more under special land-use regulations. Innis's chapter on Klondike mining, 'Settlement and the Mining Frontier', contains some discussion of the transition from small-scale digging to dredging. See Innis 1936, pp. 178–212.

[10] The lodes contained silver, gold and antimony. There are many accounts of the first lode mines of the period between 1850 and 1860 in Nevada, California and other western and mountain states. My earlier sources serve here too: Libecap 1989, pp. 37–50; Libecap 1978; Morrell 1941, chs. 5 and 6; Rickard 1932, vol. 2; Van Wagenen 1932, ch. 13. See also collections of accounts by near-contemporaries such as Shinn 1884 and 1965, pp. 253–8, and Willison 1952 on Pike's Peak and other Colorado rushes 1858–65.

1860s many hard-rock deposits had in fact been known for years but had languished due to the unavailability of technology and capital, especially the means of concentrating and refining the very complex, sometimes low-grade ores.[11] As technology and means of networking improved, some of these regions came rapidly into play as mineral centres. But their 'rushes' had less to do with making new exciting discoveries than with finding financial backing, merging properties and planning production for what had already been found.

In these new plays, the outdated placer-gold claiming system might have been disregarded completely had it not been for the mobile miners. Many had migrated from placer workings to hard-rock mining jobs, bringing their traditions and traditional demands with them. Their presence brought the remnants of the system of placer-mining rights into contact with very big business, requiring new federal mining laws to deal with the newly relevant institutions and to satisfy the sometimes complementary and sometimes divergent demands of each. Unsurprisingly, the leading effective demanders and lobbies for these laws were not the active prospectors/miners and their local communities but rather the corporate mining interests, often headquartered in cities far away, whose fortunes in mining depended less on the luck of discovery than on their ability to shape favourable mining law and influence its interpretation. I now turn to their demands.

Sources of demand for changes in mining rights

New demands for mining law and more specifically for the characteristics of mining rights are well illustrated by the rapid growth of copper mining on public lands. For one thing, because of copper's capital requirements the international copper industry acquired relatively homogenous characteristics across copper-producing districts and nations—and so sought relatively homogenous legislative frameworks and institutions in which to operate. Until the 1850s mine owners in many countries had sent copper ores to smelters and refineries in the United Kingdom, which was then described as having a 'monopoly' on the world copper trade.[12] The international gold rushes made no direct difference to the copper trade. But around the same time that gold was first discovered in California other prospectors were uncovering copper deposits in Michigan (the Lake Superior district), Montana and Chile. In the 1880s, copper mining and processing spread to British Columbia and Ontario. Later still, the introduction of the Jackling method for mining porphyries and of the flotation

[11] See Newell 1986 for an investigation of the diffusion of technologies into and within Ontario.

[12] There are good economic histories of aspects of the copper industry. See Mikesell 1979; Harris 1964; Herfindahl 1959; and Gates 1969. For the migration of Michigan copper-mining methods into eastern Canada, see Newell 1986, pp. 65–72.

concentration process around 1900 enabled the industry to open new mines around the world, notably in Latin America and Africa. International companies such as Anaconda, Kennecott, Newmont, Rio Tinto and Noranda began to explore, produce, refine and ship from their mines in many countries. Similar widespread openings of regions with relatively low-grade base metals, such as lead-zinc ores, also showed that the types of mining law derived from California's placer-mining conditions had no particular superiority to mining laws worked out locally and perhaps derived from common-law procedures. Indeed, firms in the base-metal industries had for many years been subject to common-law property laws adapted for mining, as discussed in the next chapter. Discoveries of their metals and minerals on public lands brought them, along with gold, under the federal public-land mining laws.

Previously, host-country governments and politicians had dealt with the needs and demands of hoards of individual prospector-miners, accompanied by engineers who worked on designing the mines and traders who bought and sold the recovered ores. Now, however, these governments might encounter the demands of a single invading enterprise incorporating the functions of all these actors and a highly centralized lobby acting as an agent for a predictable international framework for public-land disposal procedures. Unsurprisingly, negotiations between government and industry quickly led to the forming and conveying of property interests (leases, freehold rights or wider concession-like tenures) in the public lands that tended to look the same across countries, with only slight variations designed to accommodate local labour practices, taxation or road-building.

The individual-prospecting interest, encompassing veterans of the gold rushes, did not however totally abandon its political role as an influential demander of claiming and owning rights to minerals. Sometimes prospectors allied themselves with the industry in lawsuits or in legislative campaigns for claim disposal laws that retained important roles for prospecting. On other matters, including rules governing the discovery requirement (that a right or claim would not be granted unless the applicant had made an actual discovery); changes in standard and finders' claim sizes; and adoption or rejection of the apex principle, prospectors differed from the companies in principle or in emphasis. In these circumstances the companies often used their heft to threaten that, without the legal changes they advocated, economic considerations would lead to their withdrawal from a local mining project. The prospectors on the other hand retained what political power they had from their status as 'lonely wanderers in the outdoors' who could call on sentimental political support for the retention or modification of policies affecting them directly.

The prospectors should not be visualized as a collection of superannuated Davids struggling against a few corporate Goliaths. For one thing, the prospectors differed among themselves. Optimistic prospectors—those who believed they would become holders of commercial claims that they could sell to mining companies—advocated large claims. Those who were more pessimistic about the likelihood of their making a real discovery sought laws that would allow them to share in the good fortune of those who had been lucky. To this end, they advocated that claims be granted even to those who had not made a discovery; that the authorized claim size be small enough that several holders would find themselves the neighbours of adjoining discovery claims; and that claims be subject to the 'apex principle' whereby a neighbour might be able to prove that the discovery vein peaked in his land, and that it therefore belonged to him. (The apex principle is discussed below.) The evidence suggests that, with the advent of hard-rock mining, prospectors became more willing to settle for relatively numerous but small pay-off claims. In fact, the prospectors' lobbies settled down to a century of guarding demands for a near-parasitical method of claim granting.

Though the big mine-development companies sometimes hired paid prospectors, they did not rely on making their own discoveries of lode sites. Instead they relied on a sort of information market in which they could acquire promising claims from prospectors who had made discoveries, or small firms that had already bought out and consolidated these prospectors' claims. The big companies were not therefore seriously interested in the choice among variants of discovery rules, so long as the laws provided for secure, transferable claims that could eventually be transferred to them.

Suppliers: providers of changes in rights and laws

Three main suppliers, now distinct from the self-government of the miners' camps, emerged in the post-gold-rush era as authorities to whom the miners could explicitly or implicitly turn with their property rights demands. I discuss each of the three, familiar from Chapter 1, in turn: (1) custom or tradition; (2) the courts; and (3) the governments.

CUSTOM

Custom had been a powerful force in free mining communities, both the traditional European free mining societies and the nineteenth-century New World ones. But tradition could not keep up with the modernization of mining. Even within the placer mining camps, rules had been open to some change as miners encountered different laws and procedures elsewhere or brought old traditions with them to new rushes. The eclipse of custom continued in the lode-mining era as miners welcomed mobile suppliers, experts, managers and capitalists from outside who were much less committed to local communities than were the placer miners themselves. The age of miner-created mining law was quickly coming to an end. Courts and government, already the overseers of land conveyancing or of public-land disposal, stepped in.

THE COURTS

In-camp majority voting or tribunals could not resolve boundary disputes between capitalist mine owners claiming and commanding separate jurisdictions. New institutions were needed: some to administer the new statutory disposal laws and others to hear conflicts arising from the weaknesses of these laws. A district's disposal arrangements would be administered by a government bureau and would be bolstered by rulings from special officers, magistrates and/or mining boards or courts.

The stakes became so high that the miners and their backers were often not satisfied by administrative methods of conflict resolution. To deal with their dissatisfaction frontier governments arranged that the tasks of the general court system should include the interpretation and adjudication of mining law. The US federal government obliged by explicitly handing over to the states the powers to make laws applying to the disposal and holding of mineral claims within each state's boundaries. As well, each state court involved itself in interpreting and applying federal law (see next subpart). A judge-made common law of interpretation was grafted onto extant statutes by the state courts, the federal courts and the US Supreme Court. The result was substantial: as the many hundreds of 'early court decisions suggest, the history and therefore the law of the early West was dominated by mining'.[13] Indeed, having delegated these regulatory roles to the states, the federal government found itself obliged to hasten the process of carving state governments and judiciaries out of unorganized territories.[14]

There were equivalent expansions of administrative and judicial systems in other countries. In the Australian states, in the aftermath of the 1854 Eureka Stockade, a fairly elaborate system of local mining courts had been created in the placer-mining districts. Such bodies were reconstituted several times, first taking over as mine-claim assignors, then continuing as courts or tribunals.[15] In British Columbia and in eastern Canada the miners' own courts had played a smaller role than in the US or Australia. In the Fraser River rush (1858–9), the government soon set up its own courts to supplant those of the miners, and the two co-existed for a short time. But when in the 1880s hard-rock mining emerged in the Ontario, Quebec and in the Kootenay region, big firms buying in insisted and won the right to take their disputes before the same formal

[13] This argument closely follows Leshy 1987, p. 20.

[14] Libecap 1979 fully discusses the role of judicial activity and mining legislation in the new state of Nevada from 1858 to 1895. For his own summary, see Libecap 1989, pp. 41–50.

[15] Blainey 1978, p. 57.

court systems that had jurisdiction throughout the colony or province and heard cases involving other landowners.

GOVERNMENTS

In the later nineteenth century governments were slowly becoming aware of themselves not only as land owners and dealers but also as providers, perhaps inventors, of the characteristics of the rights to be held by their mining clients. That is, in contrast to the governments discussed in Chapter 5, the new national governments were becoming increasingly aware of their *public* role, providing sets of property rights and revenue policies that maximized the welfare of the polity and defined the role of the private agent in relation to it.

As previously seen, as late as the 1800s the imperial Spanish, Portuguese and British governments were still attempting to act as mineral landlords, rather like the medieval estate owner with his free mining community: promoting discovery; selling or giving away mineral rights as patronage concessions; and profiting from revenues such as those brought in by licences, royalties and export levies. Great Britain's home government acted on behalf of its manufacturing and other concessionary interests, creating and changing laws as needed to accommodate and protect their trade. But its colonial governments did little to set up an enduring 'public' set of mining rights, leaving this task to the new national governments of the mid-nineteenth century.

In the United States, it took the transition from individualistic placer gold mining to the corporate mining of base metals to seemingly shake the Congress out of its tendency to regard its mineral-disposal procedures as merely a branch of its farm-land settlement policy. It was one thing to have sentimentally protected remote armies of young gold miners and indulged them in their determined avoidance of royalties, taxes and fees. But to allow rents from iron, copper, lead and zinc—not to mention coal—to be given away to promoters and to the great corporate 'exploiters' of the public lands was quite another. Lawmakers and voters apparently felt that these new millionaires ought to pay for what they were taking from the polity's resource endowment.

This determination was signalled by new statutes. Following the Homestead Act of 1862 (discussed in Chapter 5), a general US mining-land and mining law was finally introduced in 1866. It looked backward: in continuing to allow gold miners to take gold from the public lands, it explicitly legitimized the prior claim-disposal rules of the surviving districts or mining camps. Then it looked forward: it offered a title to those who 'located' (staked) a deposit or lode. A supplementary placer law in 1870 introduced the idea of 'patenting' (gaining freehold ownership) over a mineral claim in the public lands, for the first time establishing a parallelism between land settlement and claim-staking regimes. It also stated which kinds of minerals could be patented (most), the claim sizes for each, and clarified that the word 'deposit' could be used of both placer and quartz findings. A third General Mining Law, 1872, consolidated the first two acts and formally established separate, but overlapping, procedures for placer and for lode mining. Particularly significant was Congress's decision to carry over to lode or quartz mining the open-access no-royalty feature of placer mining.

Lawmakers elsewhere, perhaps under the guidance of the Colonial Office in London, scurried to follow this lead. In Australia, Victoria passed its new mining statute in 1865, while Queensland and New South Wales did so in 1870 (as did South Africa).[16] The Canadian provinces of Ontario, Quebec and British Columbia also adjusted their public land mineral laws to conform to US legislation. For a while, disappointed by a dearth of hard-rock mining activity, they introduced a number of gimmicky subsidies and concessions to lure foreign investors and miners. But when hard-rock mining did finally get under way, the provinces instituted American-model laws that permitted international competition for mining development. Even South Africa, where the lands in the diamond and gold-mining districts were already privately owned, strove to introduce access and disposal laws whose effects would replicate those of American hard-rock mining law.

The American set of mining laws was in part a modern political response to electorates who now looked to government for more than mere police activity. By the first decade of the twentieth century, the US government was committed to trust-busting and regulating to protect workers and consumers from such big-business entities as the Rockefeller and Carnegie interests. Politicians were becoming aware that many voters, taking seriously the pronouncements of the new conservation movement, were disturbed by the full-speed-ahead attitude of those exhausting known resource reserves. Activists in the conservation movement helped to organize a public awareness of the strengths and weaknesses of the mineral disposal laws, and of the ability of many in big business to manipulate these laws for their own benefit—perhaps fraudulently.[17] Politicians learned that their electorates no longer regarded mineral public-land exploration policy as merely a way of satisfying prospectors, their rural friends and their big corporate brothers. Public sympathy with lonely prospectors roaming the hills did persist. But voters, even those with no direct stake in mining, increasingly demanded that the interests of big business be seriously scrutinized and mining law given a hard look.

In the United States and elsewhere politicians were also hearing more from their treasury departments, as mining was revealed both as an economic base

[16] Lang and Crommelin 1979, p. 3. Victoria: Mining Act, 1865, 29 Vict. 291; Queensland: Mining Act, 1874, 36 Vict. 11; New South Wales: Mining Act, 1874, 36 Vict. 13.

[17] Even before the Leasing Act, 1920, American presidents under pressure from the conservationists, had removed non-metallic minerals from the general mining law (e.g., President Roosevelt in 1906). That these were strategic materials may have added to the pressure. The eventual policy was to lease these materials for five-year terms (with royalties). See Ise 1926.

for some not-yet developed regions and as a potential source of government revenue. In response to these pressures and self-evaluations governments created new bureaux charged with exploring, surveying, sometimes classifying and registering mining rights, and set up tribunals, all manned by new cadres of mining officials, to consider conflicts.

A profile of requirements in the United States, Canada and Australia

The respective national laws that emerged in the US, Canada and Australia of the late nineteenth century all had *requirements* that a miner had to fulfill before being issued a right to mine on public land. These conditions can be classified under the eight headings in the 'profile' below. They are distinct from the 'characteristics' of mining-camp claims surveyed in the previous chapter in that they constituted *conditions for acquiring* a mineral right rather than a *description* of the right. The conditions were constantly debated, and were sometimes changed for all mining, and often for particular regions, minerals or types of mining. The industry negotiated them frequently, reflecting not only its changed circumstances in the switch-over from alluvial to hard-rock mining, but also its members' reactions to the changing aims and needs of governments.

Profile of a mine disposal law

Free access/free removal	Patentability
Priority of possession	Surface rights and split estates
Uniformity	Discovery requirement
Claim size and extra-lateral rights	Work requirement

Some of these conditions, such as the work and discovery requirements, were carried over from camp law. Others, like patentability and the rights and responsibilities of the split estate, were new, and were thought to be ways of adapting mining rights to such new circumstances as the growth of non-mining populations and the expansion of land-use on public lands. Below I touch on three aspects of each of these conditions. The first aspect is the extent of similarity among the three counties where gold rushes had taken place and where placer mining culture had been supplanted by hard-rock mining and by other large-scale mineral resource operations such as oil and gas extraction. As we will see, governments differed in their impositions of new conditions on mining interests.

The second aspect is the *distributional* effect of granting policies: how governments affected the distribution of income between prospectors and firms; between those who explored and those who acquired the rights; and between the holders of the rights and those who actually did the mining. In placer mining regimes the prospector who made a discovery had usually been the same individual who had sought the right to claim and mine it. But with specialization in highly capitalized mining enterprises, these functions were split. The suppliers of mining law faced new demand challenges in allocating the resource wealth among the claimants, not to mention the challenge of dealing with the political demands of nearby communities seeking a source of jobs.

The third aspect is the relationship between changes in the profile of acquisition requirements and changes in the combination of the 'characteristics' in the rights themselves. We will see that the changes in the mining law profile generally improved upon the bundle of characteristics held by a miner that fulfilled its conditions—in particular endowing the claim-holder with more *transferability* than he would have had, under camp law, a generation earlier. On the other hand, the new requirements did not, or could not, prevent some weakening of the typical hard rock miner's *exclusivity* brought about by increasing externalities or spillovers from adjoining industrial properties. A miner's operations were simply not as independent as they had once been.

In the rest of this section, I focus on the first two aspects of the eight conditions in the disposal law profile. An overview of the third aspect, the relation to 'characteristics' implied and imparted in the changing mining-law requirements, is postponed until the next section.

Free access/free removal

This first item differs from the others in the profile in that it was as much a privilege as a requirement. Following European free- and placer-mining precedents, US public-land disposal law began as an extension of homestead law, with open access to those public lands that contained desired minerals. In Canada too open access was the rule. The provinces had originally required prospectors and miners to buy permits allowing entry into designated areas of the Crown lands. After the gold rush, they sold prospectors a cheap permit allowing them to explore and to locate a claim almost anywhere in the public lands. Nothing prevented permit-holders from exploring the same place.

Australia presented a contrast. Much of the colonies' mineral wealth lay beneath the private lands of farmers and pastoralists. As we saw in Chapter 6, this had presented land-use (and labour-use) conflicts even in the 1850s placer-mining stage. Additionally, to an extent undreamed of in the US or Canada, holders of agricultural land also owned the rights to minerals beneath. The 'opening up' of the mineral lands was not, therefore, a process by which government extricated itself from ownership by distributing rights and title over land to mining applicants. To the contrary, it was a process by which governments, one by one, reserved, acquired or re-acquired all minerals for the state. Following a kind of expropriation procedure, laws of the 1880s and 1890s in most states gave miners the rights to enter old strictly private lands to prospect for and recover the minerals beneath. (Depending on the state, the surface owner received compensation for damage to his property, or a royalty.) By this quite different route, miners in Australia were given the freedom to enter, explore and claim almost all lands—as in the US and Canada.

In all three countries free access to the public lands implied two policies: tolerance of racing behaviour and procedural openness. From the beginning, however, racing was considered a problem, either because it caused over-rapid depletion of resources or simply because it was considered disorderly. The subsequent claim staking removed the overlapping and interference and was retained by most of the governments. Once a miner had staked a claim, he was allotted the time and privacy to develop and produce it at his own pace.

By procedural openness, I mean a way of disposing of mining rights by imposing conditions that almost any applicant could satisfy (such as discovery and work conditions) without personal, bidding or other financial requirements. (An 'open' procedure will probably also have uniformity conditions, as discussed below.) In the late nineteenth century, American claimants' titles were not subject to any official's discretion. More so than the homesteaded farm, the mineral claim was possessory, acquired by a process with some similarity to that by which a squatter obtained a prescriptive title under common law.[18] Below, discussing patenting, I show that under US disposal law a patent (freehold) was also supposed to be possessory, automatically acquired by all who met the simple, verifiable conditions of the mining law. The rules of patenting in the other two countries, however, were not as open as those in the US.

Priority of possession

In the opening of the lands of all three countries, the slogan 'first-come, first served' was universally observed. In the settling of public land, the first comer was judged to be the first occupier or user, be it for farming or for prospecting/mining. When miners turned to hard-rock and to base metals under government rules, the implicit bargain continued to observe the placer-mining rule: the site belonged to the current occupier, be it the prospector who had staked the claim or the firm to whom he had transferred title.

Following the common law in the US, the discovery site was deemed to include both the mineral in the ground and all the soil and surface above it. However, if a settler first occupied then acquired a site on the surface of public

[18] Of course, a claim was statutory and carved out of public lands, while a prescriptive right was originally customary and under common law was carved out of a private holding or right.

lands the mining law no longer applied, for both the surface and the land below it had passed out of public ownership. The corollary was that if a miner first 'occupied' the site by staking a claim, the claim had a statutory area on the surface. By either disposal route, rights over the mineral underground were not severed from rights over the surface.

Priority of possession was a familiar basis for title on the US frontier. Only rarely did either state or federal government opt to ration pieces of land by price, bidding, status (except for Indian lands) or lottery procedures. Exceptionally, some American states, endowed with relatively small areas of public lands at the time they achieved statehood, did adopt a leasing system. Their methods of implementation differed, but all such states charged rents and/or royalties.

In the three Canadian provinces hard-rock properties were also acquired on a first-come, first-served basis. But there were differences from the US federal system. For most of the nineteenth century the Canadian provinces offered a variant of common-law real-estate law to dispose of minerals.[19] We have already encountered this as the survey-and-sale, or purchase, system (also confusingly known as the 'location' system).[20] Anyone, miner or speculator, could specify a map location and buy it from the government for a standard price per acre (plus surveying costs, if necessary) in large parcels of ten square miles.[21]

The first big test of 'location' mining law in Canada occurred after 1881 in the acquisition of rights from the Ontario government to Sudbury's massive deposits of copper and nickel. Railway building had already resulted in parts of the discovery area being surveyed and mapped, making it easy for miners and speculators to apply for a sale (patent) without having to invest in making sure the selected site was actually worth patenting.[22] When the first news of copper and nickel discoveries circulated, the entire area was blanketed with applications for patents (mostly sight unseen) by or on behalf of about six companies. These companies then patented their applications at a one-dollar price, locating them on a map in the registry. This final step was a little like the US patenting procedure, which also charged one dollar per acre; but it totally lacked the prior American requirements of discovery, work and three-year delay (all discussed in separate sections below).[23]

[19] See Cail 1974, pp. 75–7. Although location or survey-and-sale were available, nearly all B.C. miners staked their claims. This may have been an indication of the absence of surveys rather than a preference.

[20] Under American 1872 mining law 'to locate' meant, roughly, to stake a claim under the California system. But in eastern Canada 'to locate' usually meant to acquire by the survey-and-sale system.

[21] Barton 1993, pp. 131 and 136.

[22] Main 1955, p. 11.

[23] Because it was an outright sale, the royalties the companies would have paid under provincial leasing laws did not apply. Taxes and financial arrangements were not always a part of the mining law for the public lands, but could exist independently, from impositions of local (property) laws and from uncoordinated state and national tax laws. See fn. 28.

The Canadian approach to public disposal did not suit the prospectors as well as it did the industry. Most prospectors were reduced under survey-and-sale to merely exploring for wages on the wide acreages acquired by the few patentees.[24] In Ontario, staking was not mandatory on surveyed land[25] so that a prospector had difficulty learning which lands were still worth independently prospecting. Worse, when a prospector did make a discovery, he ran the risk of some distant speculator, having heard a rumour about a discovery on surveyed land, simply going to an office and patenting it.[26] Since it was these autonomous prospectors who formed the prospecting lobby, they mounted resistance—in particular, a campaign for 'reform' of a system in which fortunes were made but in which they played a minor role. As it happened, governments, dissatisfied with their revenues from big plays such as Sudbury, found themselves on the prospectors' side.[27] By 1906 in all three mining provinces the local variants of the survey-and-sale method and its little-work requirement were dropped. Claim-staking laws were re-introduced.

Over the next ten years, faced with a depression in mining, the Canadian governments tinkered with their disposal systems, introducing various combinations of leasing, patenting and claiming with various royalty and tax features. After a while, they dropped the leasing alternative for Crown lands (see below). They closely copied the claim-size, staking rules and patenting rules in the US and, less closely,[28] copied the American practice of giving priority to the first staker. Again, the Australian states adopted similar rules.

[24] The literature does not say they worked for wages only. Perhaps they also got a share of what they found for the patent-holder. The miners in Ontario and Quebec were said to favour patenting, following a work period. They did not favour the survey-and-sale. See Smith 1986, pp. 82–3; Armstrong 1984, p. 179. Sometimes location required discovery, sometimes it did not.

[25] The 1890 Mineral Resources Commission of Ontario, referred to by Main 1955, p. 11.

[26] See Cail 1974, pp. 75–7. Until 1869 the miners had been personally licensed to stake only gold. Although they were entitled to stake hard-rock gold mines, the records suggest to Cail that few discoveries were worth staking.

[27] In this discussion I have omitted the very frequent changes in revenue arrangements. In some years these tied in with leasing arrangements. When fees for located patents were high, all three provinces introduced leases, which spread the acquisition costs over as many years as the lease was held (e.g., British Columbia—from 1859; Ontario—1891 to 1906; Quebec—no leasing). Leases were sometimes accompanied, or paid for, by royalties. However, the provincial governments did not hesitate to impose royalties on patented mineral freeholds (even retrospectively) as well as on leases. Royalty rates varied from year to year and, in Ontario and Quebec, from place to place. They were usually stated in round numbers and, for the short periods they were in effect, brought in little revenue. One suspects that they were sometimes aimed at particular properties or, sometimes, were imposed only so that they could be forgiven or reduced (i.e. as an incentive).

[28] For example, in all provinces royalty was dropped and replaced by a tax on mining profits. This tax had plenty of defects but, as was seldom realized, it was much closer to economists' efficient or ideal mining taxes than were most royalties. See Ontario 1967, Bradley 1986, Perry 1989, pp. 409–12.

Uniformity

If the expression 'complete uniformity' is used of a public lands mining law, it means that miners get the same benefits and must pay the same price and meet the same conditions in every district and for every mineral. Location or geography make no difference to claiming rules or permitted claim size. (In farm-land disposition, uniformity, combined with the government's incentive to settle, was also referred to as the 'dollar per acre' rule.)

Such 'complete uniformity' was rare in practice. There was a constitutional rule against personal discrimination of any kind, but Congress could escape it by setting a different procedure or price for each mineral. This was a fortunate out, for it was soon realized that a state-wide or nation-wide uniformity of discovery requirement across the whole spectrum of minerals created real difficulties in the exploration and production phases, given that different types of mining and mineral required different prospecting intensities; different capital requirements; and different time periods before complete exhaustion. Accordingly the US, Canadian and Australian governments all set special terms and procedures in separate laws for coal mining and petroleum. Various hard-rock minerals were also specially catered to, though less consistently.

Special arrangements were nominally introduced into US mining law in 1872, although conflicts over staking and recording remained the jurisdiction of the state courts, introducing regional variation in the means and rights of disposal. (The lawyers made their arguments by citing precedents based on both national disposal law and state-made statutes that had applied before the federal mining law of 1872.) In general, however, the (less than complete) uniformity provision was popular. As had been the case with free mining arrangements throughout history, once free and non-discriminating prospecting was introduced, attempts to limit or condition it were hotly resented and effectively opposed by the prospectors affected. Prospectors within any specific mineral industry sought and cherished a uniform discovery procedure that specified the procedures, requirements and costs to making a claim, and limited their risks to those involved with reconnaissance and discovery itself, rather than post-discovery negotiations over title. Since the uniformity of procedures and terms of staking was of little interest to the capitalistic firms who were accustomed to buying out and investing in one mine at a time, there was no effective opposition to it. In the post-discovery phase, claim uniformity across all hard-rock minerals was the general rule. The firms satisfied their needs for large producing areas by holding multiple claims of the uniform size provided for in the law. If they held leases, they satisfied their needs for long production life by periodic renewals.

Each Canadian province and each Australian state developed its own staking and discovery laws for specific minerals, at about the same dates as in the US. The Australian state governments had it both ways: their mining laws indicated uniformity but ministerial discretion allowed (and allows) special arrangements for some lessees, restrained only a little by the quasi-judicial powers of mining wardens and magistrates.[29] Violations to uniformity procedures existed by mineral type and by the number of prospectors making the claim. With hard-rock mining, there was a tendency for the states to grant a range of permit and claim sizes, each for a different purpose or mineral. These were generally smaller than those under the American law, but in most states a miner would stake as many as he wished,[30] which reduced the prospector demand for greater uniformity in scale.[31]

Claim size and extra-lateral rights (the apex rule)

The US law's provision of extra-lateral rights was another consequence of the shift of the mining industry from alluvial gold to hard-rock (lode or quartz) deposits. Despite pressure from the industry, the Congressional framers of mining law had not responded to the new costs and difficulties of discovery and mining hard-rock deposits by materially changing standard claim size, finder's claim size or number of claims a miner might stake. Instead, the 1872 law introduced extra-lateral rights.[32] This was surprising in that it ran counter to the old common-law principle, much treasured among US policy makers, that the lateral boundaries of any interest in land extended vertically to the centre of the earth.

The apex rule works as follows: claims on or near the surface had, under the original mining law, been described in terms of their prescribed surface dimensions—that is, in terms of their surface areas. Now, however, claims to minerals situated in deep veins were to be described in terms of their relation to the revealed or discovered vein. The law dealt with the vein as if it were a thick blanket, mostly buried beneath certain surface claims. Perhaps it lay as a raking plain; perhaps it rose to or through the surface and dipped down again. Whatever its underground shape, the part of it nearest the surface was accessible for surface discovery and was (usually) discovered first. This exposed or nearly exposed part was referred to as an apex. The lawmakers, and lawyers who argued in subsequent cases brought under the law, pictured it as a line of ore snaking on the surface across the hill or countryside. The law said that

[29] Lang and Crommelin 1979, pp. 128–34.

[30] In some states, he was required to buy a miner's right for each claim staked. Van Wagenen 1918.

[31] Furthermore, beyond the mining laws governing claims and leases lay the Australian governments' powers to negotiate discretionary concessions, or 'agreements' (see Bradley 1986 or Crommelin 1982). Similar mining arrangements exist in many countries (see Gillis & Beal 1980 or Smith & Wells 1975) not to mention public forest disposal agreements (see Chapter 11) and oil and gas exploitation concessions (see Chapter 9).

[32] Leshy 1987, pp. 169–89. The length along the vein was about fifteen hundred feet and the width about three hundred feet.

miners' individual claims should be located or staked along this line, each, say, with two hundred feet between its sides (or lateral boundaries).

A holder mining such an apex claim would follow his length of the blanket-like vein underground, away from the apex. The law said that he might also follow it beneath one of his claim's two hundred-foot side or lateral boundaries, even beneath an adjoining claim belonging to another, as far down as it was feasible to mine. Sometimes, the law worked smoothly. But often the holder of the neighbouring claim refused to recognize that his lode was an extension of the apex vein. The ensuing dispute could go to court and could lead to long and expensive procedures.

Two explanations exist for the re-introduction (from late medieval European mining) of the extra-lateral right. The first is that it was borrowed from the rules of those European free miners who had mined lode or quartz deposits. The borrowing took place during the western states' 1860s-era transition from placer to deep-lode mining.[33] One example is the development of properties along Nevada's Comstock gold and silver lode, as early as 1859–60.[34] The typical description of a claim in Eldorado County specified the number of feet (usually two hundred) along the ledge or lode and an equal number on each side of the lode. No US mining rule had previously included wording about 'along the ledge' or 'along the vein', nor had it mentioned dips and spurs. Some medieval terminology, such as 'dip right' and 'rake right', reappeared when California gold mining turned to hard-rock mining.[35] In fact, it is difficult to find any line of transmission from English or German free mining districts to California (except through Cornwall) that did *not* provide for veins that extended beyond claim boundaries.

The second, related, explanation is that the extra-lateral-right was reinvented to deal with the same questions that had been dealt with by medieval landowners: how to distribute an ore discovery of dimensions unknown until preliminary mining showed if and where it dipped or stretched the first claim's boundaries. Everybody agreed that the answer to the question should be acceptably fair and just and should help maintain an incentive to explore and to add to knowledge. Setting a very broad standard claim size might have dealt with an indistinct discovery's strain on hard-rock boundaries, but such broadness would also have discouraged many prospectors from even bothering to participate in the search for hard-rock showings.

The trouble with these two suggested explanations (based on the medieval European discovery and mining problem) is that the US Congress of 1865–70, in drafting its mineral-disposal rules, did not recognize an incentive problem.

[33] Shinn 1884 and 1965, p. 35. [34] Umbeck 1981, p. 40.

[35] See Agricola 1556; Van Wagenen 1918, ch. 14, especially pp. 292–4 ('Spanish Mines in the 17th and Eighteenth Centuries'); Nef 1932 and 1966, vol. 1, pp. 276 and 300–1 ('Apex Principle Not Confined to Europe or to Metals'); Raistrick and Jennings 1965, p. 57 ('Apex Principle in Yorkshire Lead Mines').

Its public-lands mining goals had been designed neither to encourage the discoveries of latent minerals nor to provide the Congress with information about future bonanzas. It had simply sought to dispose of existing resources in a fair and orderly fashion, to help prospectors and to encourage land settlement. It was the large mining firms and the single prospectors who had preferences in the matter. The former did not care who got the finders' reward—they sought only that at least one of the lode-mining parties had a defensible title on which they could rely in building a mining and milling enterprise. A strongly enforced apex principle might be good enough. The prospectors and small miners had their own reasons for urging Congress to introduce the apex rule. They liked the apparent continuity of the principle with the first-comer principle in placer mining. They apparently had no trouble explaining the procedure to themselves, law-makers and judges. Where they *did* have trouble was agreeing on the application of the extra-lateral right to sites characterized by multiple outcrops, multiple veins and discontinuous features of all kinds. Each holder in a pair of claims could easily believe or assert that his contained *the* apex, effectively entitling him to both claims. To win a dispute would require much more information than would normally be sought when developing a mine. Uncertainty prevailed and, ultimately, resulted in difficult and costly litigation.

So easy was it for any holder to assert that he held an apex that, in some mineral plays, the large companies who hired the prospectors or bought out their staked claims agreed not to invoke the extra-lateral rights law against each other.[36] They had seen the sickening delays and high litigation that such nuisance suits—based on asserted rights that were sometimes completely fraudulent—could cause. Among the most famous of these costly suits were the eighty brought by F. Augustus Heinze between 1895 and 1906 against the Montana forerunners of the Anaconda Copper Company. Heinze stalled Anaconda's Butte developments until he was paid off to the tune of around $10 million.

In general, the Australian state governments legislating for lode mining preferred the larger-claim-size route over the apex-rule route. They moved away from the apex rule during the period in question. Under an 1858 law, in Maldon, Victoria miners could follow the vein in any direction, if the dip was at least twenty degrees.[37] This 'Maldon rule' did not survive the 1860s[38] largely because it was not needed.[39] Most Australian miners were then still working

[36] Spence 1970, p. 225 (citing J. Spurr's 1921 article in *Engineering and Mining Journal*, p. 254).

[37] Veatch 1911, p. 135.

[38] Blainey 1978, pp. 66–8; Rickard 1932, p. 628; Veatch 1911, pp. 116 and 136. According to Veatch, New South Wales introduced extra-lateral rights and maintained them until 1865, just when the US adopted them.

[39] Although a year earlier the famous Clunes underground war had been, in part, about the rights of miners to push their workings into adjoining mines, the trespassing in question was into private land.

deep alluvial layers and had not moved on to hard-rock veins. In any case, because the extra-lateral right was associated with large companies and elitist British ownership, most prospectors and small miners were instinctively against it. But they must have been tempted. At Ballarat in 1854, syndicates holding claims with tiny surface areas had sunk shafts to depths of eighteen stories in search of ancient alluvial stream beds. Disputes about small holdings and encroachment into other claims were inevitable and helped provoke the Eureka revolt of 1854. Apparently, however, even in these extreme circumstances the groups did not cooperate with each other underground, nor join in drafting an alluvial-stream anticipation of an extra-lateral rights law.[40]

Today, the idea of referring to the apex rule as a means of conveying the fullness of a discovery to its finder does not fit the spirit of modern Australian public-land hard-rock mining laws. Unlike the American mining law, the modern Australian laws do not require that the claim or lease be aligned on the vein. They do not even require that a vein or lode be known or asserted, merely that the claim be aligned on compass bearings. Therefore, the state's invitation to explore and to apply for a right to mine is not an undertaking to grant a discovered deposit to its finder, which undermines the essential purpose of the apex rule.

In the Canadian provinces, as in Australia, hard-rock claim sizes were comparable in size to those in the US, but miners might stake more than one. In the early 1870s provincial laws conceded extra-lateral rights as a way of competing with the US for prospectors.[41] The Canadians cited in their laws some special advantages of the apex principle. One was that it allowed the government to offer more land to a finder, minus the cost of also offering more to also-ran miners as under the traditional claim system. Another was that it allowed the opening of small inactive claims sandwiched between other claims in old mining districts, as apex-holders followed their vein beneath them.[42] According to Van Wagenen, the apex principle 'did produce discoveries' in the Canadian provinces.[43]

Commentators have said that in Canada, as elsewhere, the apex principle led to 'much litigation' and to 'inconclusive inspections and to long parades of experts'.[44] Because of the settlements and side agreements, it is probably impossible to discover how often it was invoked, let alone litigated. Perhaps because of all the lawsuits, the provinces had by 1905, after a thirty-year run,

[40] See Blainey 1978, ch. 4, pp. 46–58; and Gibson 1933, p. 5. Possibly the work requirements precluded working together underground.

[41] In 1869 Ontario introduced the apex principle for claims, but mining rights located by the survey-and-sale procedure did not have extra-lateral rights. See 27–8 Vict. 9, s. 20; Ontario Mining Commission 1890; Barton 1993, p. 132. Quebec never had extra-lateral rights. Thanks to Dr. J-P LaCasse for correspondence on this (1 January 1996). See also Lacasse 1976, p. 108. British Columbia, practically copying the wording of the US law, introduced the principle in 1872.

[42] Crowe 1932, p. 52. Cail 1974 is, surprisingly, silent on the apex principle.

[43] Van Wagenen 1918. [44] Barton 1993, p. 15n.

all withdrawn the apex principle. The B.C. government in particular may have been concerned: the above-mentioned F. A. Heinze, who had cleaned up on apex-based nuisance suits in Montana, was by this time becoming a major operator in the province.[45]

Two-stage routes to patenting

To maintain their implicit contract with rights-holders when hard-rock mining supplanted placer mining, governments offered two new procedures for obtaining the right to apply for a 'higher' category of tenure than the one invoked by discovery alone (i.e., for a right with greater quality of title, transferability and duration). One of these was patenting, by which the holder and operator of a traditional mining claim could, by performing extra work, become eligible to purchase a patent or freehold right to the same claim. The other became known as the two-stage mineral acquisition, in which the claim was greatly enlarged in size but reduced in status to that of an exploration permit. It gave increased 'pre-discovery rights' to a prospector in a given area. After this first stage the permit holder who had explored, made a discovery and done work on the site graduated to the second stage, where he applied for, and generally received, a lease or patent. Our three countries experimented with several variants of patenting and of two-stage claiming.

Governments may have intended the simple mining patent as a way of placing the miner on the same property footing as the homesteader or settler. Indeed, in the period after homesteading and other free-land policies, mineral claiming with patenting became the only way to acquire ownership of a piece of the surface of government lands. This holding could be used for purposes other than mining.[46] Introducing the patent possibility was one of the few examples of the US government responding to mining's demands for a secure hard-rock possessory claim. That was the theory. In fact, however, most US claim holders (mainly firms) did not take up the government's offer: they never bothered to go to patent when they made a discovery or opened a mine. This may be because getting a patent was a bother compared to the simple 1872-law requirements for just staking a claim. In some states there might be no requirement to pay a fee, advertise or register. But getting a patent required all these things as well as extra work and the subsequent payment of

[45] Indeed, after Heinze arrived in Canada, he devoted himself not to staking claims, but to establishing a 'nuisance' smelter that others had to buy out.

[46] Locators of mining gained exclusive rights of possession and enjoyment of the surface of their claims (20 acres). The law did not compel them to use this exclusive possession for mineral purposes. See Leshy 1987, p. 398 n18. Those who moved on to get a freehold of their claim gained freehold ownership of the land. This included an even less questionable right to use the surface for any purpose, and the right to ignore the mineral discovery that had justified the original land disposal.

local taxes. At any rate, only about a thousand patents were granted annually until the 1920s, when the number declined to hundreds.

In Canada the eastern provinces of Ontario and Quebec, having retreated from survey-and-sale toward claim staking, kept a close competitive eye on American and B.C. law with regard to patenting. Because their earliest disposal system had led to freehold mineral ownership, eastern miners and government apparently agreed that the staked claim system should also offer complete ownership, and followed the US in enabling a claim holder who had put in enough hours to acquire a patent for a small charge. British Columbia at this time was practically forcing patents on its miners. After 1871 any claim-staker who did the minimum amount of work for just three years virtually owned his site, surface and all.[47]

In contrast to their American counterparts, most holders of staked discoveries in Canada opted to take up the governments' patent offers. As operators in both countries were generally distrustful of government, explaining the difference comes from examining the differing historical bases of the two countries' respective mining laws. Unlike American mining law with its secure possessory claim, the Canadian mining industry had seen its treasured staked claim system abandoned by the governments in Ontario and Quebec, first in favour of survey-and-sale, and later in favour of various combinations of disposal systems. In all three provinces, the system had been subjected to decades of immoderate government experiment with locations, leases, concessions, durations, work requirements, rents, royalties and numbers. Most of these innovations had applied to new claims, but a few had been retroactive and invoked to cancel existing holdings.

Not until 1913 did all provinces finally return to offering claim-staking as the principal route to mineral right acquisition. Even after this date, industry probably believed that further government changes were likely and were most likely to apply to short-term licensing. Whereas the infrequent changes in US mineral lands policy had reflected differing opinions concerning one subject (i.e., the fairness of land disposal as between miners and other groups), the changes in Canadian policies reflected changing opinions concerning several subjects, including the regional development of competing land-use industries. Thus, predicting that a good way to protect themselves would be to become all-round owners, firms determined to accept the offer of a patent. In fact, the prediction did not pan out. By the middle of the twentieth century

[47] Cail 1974, p. 75, and Barton 1993, p. 123, say that British Columbia's freehold-grant policy was the logical corollary of its free-land grant policy (to settlers). Indeed it was, but the need for logical consistency in the land-disposal systems was not often a political imperative.

the provincial governments preferred that new firms acquire leases rather than patents or freehold rights. (See below.)

In Australia patents were not even offered. There was no progression from claim-staking to freehold ownership. Leasing continued to be the predominant form of mineral disposal, as it had been from well before the gold rushes. Indeed, during and after the gold rush, claim staking overwhelmed the demand for leases, and became the main form of property holding legislated in the Gold Fields Acts. Later as hard-rock mining's capital requirements became clear, the claim's limited transferability as a financial asset became something of a liability. Leasing staged a comeback, though it too had its short-duration limitations. These transitions are illustrated by the story of the syndicate that was promoting the great base-metal Broken Hill mine around 1883. The syndicate acquired some old properties severed from the holdings of various agricultural land owners. It then acquired seven of New South Wales's new twenty-year leases, totalling about three hundred acres and two miles along the vein at five pounds per acre annually. A combination of liquidity constraints and caution prevented the syndicate from buying outright the freehold and the mineral rights of all the ground in the area. Blainey explains further: '[In the earlier Silverton play nearby, many companies] had been optimistic and had bought the freehold, but the [Broken Hill people] missed their chance. In 1884 [the colony] virtually ceased to sell the freehold of mineral lands. Thus when the twenty years of the lease expired, the owners of the Broken Hill were at the mercy of the government and, for the privilege of renewing their lease, paid millions of pounds in royalties.'[48]

This story brings out the difference between two ways of disposing of hard-rock mineral property at the end of the nineteenth century. On one side of the ocean was an automatic recognition of possessory staked claims to Crown/public minerals, enticing firms with the promise of large capital gains. On the Australian side was the miner's lease of Crown mineral lands, granted only at government discretion, with constant concern over duration and renewal and with work and royalty fees always due.[49] The difference to mining firms between these types of arrangements was obviously large, and was made more so by the difficulty in changing any property-rights regime once it was in place. For one thing, seen as a possible security for a loan or mortgage, a government mining lease was inferior to a patent because it had a restricted duration and might not be renewed. One would expect mining firms in leasing regimes to have been more capital-constrained than their counterparts in patent regimes.

[48] Blainey 1978, p. 145.

[49] Australia's apparent inhospitality to hard-rock miners and prospectors was balanced by its legislative efforts to open private as well as public lands to exploration. See below.

The second new procedure was the two-stage route to patenting: a pre-discovery right (usually a permit) followed by a lease or patent. Here the Australian states, in formalizing their leasing procedures for hard-rock minerals, were the pioneers of the sequence that in the twentieth century was to become the main approach to the leasing of coal and of petroleum rights (the subject of Chapter 9). Though the pre-discovery permit was generally implemented in expectation of a leasehold (in Australia and Canada), in what follows I consider the pre-discovery permit in isolation.

Like the governments in other nations, the governments of Victoria and the other Australian states recognized the importance of 'pre-discovery protection' to hard-rock mining. A wide area had to be subjected to extensive exploration in searching for hard-rock formations. Then the policy called for a narrower area to be subjected to a more capital-intensive development and to mining. This sequence was unknown to the placer camps. Instead of adopting it, the US government had 'solved' this problem by weakening the discovery requirement. In a typical sequence, an American prospector with an idea could stake a claim and sell it to a firm with the capital to mine it; the buyer could then rely on the claim's exclusivity (a product of priority of discovery) while he explored it in depth. The advantage of this American sequence was its simplicity; the disadvantage was that it encouraged holders to speculate, thus closing potential discoveries to later exploration.[50]

The Australian states took a different tack: around 1900 they began to redefine the claim as an easily acquired first-stage exploration permit followed by a less easily acquired second-stage lease.[51] During the First World War, an unexplored area was replaced by a 'prospecting area' of less than five hundred acres.[52] Holding a right to one of these areas, a registered miner might securely search for specified minerals for up to two years. Upon making a find, he could confidently expect to be able to proceed to the second-stage lease.

Five hundred acres seems small today, but it was twenty-five times larger than the twenty-acre claim and was evidently enough to quiet some Australian explorers' complaints about the danger of being forestalled by the claim-staking of other miners. Since the Second World War, in response to the exploratory needs of the petroleum industry which was deploying airborne or geophysical instruments, the states have offered even larger areas, running to thousands of acres. These first-stage rights can be given on land or at sea, for metallic or oil exploration; here, the Australian states may have been inspired

[50] This is one of the main points of Leshy 1987. See his concluding chapter, pp. 347–70.

[51] Van Wagenen, in his worldwide survey of mining laws (1918, p. 311), wrote that by that time prospecting area licences were available 'in a large number of countries'. In fact, however, he mentions only Australia's prospecting area licences. See Lang and Crommelin 1979, pp. 5, 6 and 87–106.

[52] The 1918 spectrum of licences, prospecting areas, claims and leases in each Australian state is described in Van Wagenen 1918, pp. 115–54.

by the example of American coal laws and the public-land oil leasing law to be discussed in Chapter 9. Usually, the Australian governments have coupled the first-stage right with the right to procure a second-stage or production lease should the exploration lead to a real discovery.[53]

In the twentieth century the Canadian provinces followed Australia's lead, reducing the role of the staked claim to that of an exploration permit and converting patents to leases, sometimes even retroactively. The claim now forms part of a two-stage procedure wherein a discovery, plus work on a staked claim, gives the holder a preferred right to a lease. Some provinces have increased the area of the claim so that it may serve this first-stage purpose. Most provinces have also introduced the exclusive short-term exploration permit. Holders of these permits may, after exploration and work, stake a production claim (or apply for a lease) on a small part of their extensive exploration area, while relinquishing the rest to the government.[54]

The movement in the two Commonwealth countries toward this type of system was an obvious response to new circumstances. Easy-to-find mineral deposits were disappearing, while the new search technologies appearing were best adapted over wide areas. Both circumstances induced much of the mining industry to favour the granting of wide-area permits. However, these advantages were not good news for everyone in mining. Prospectors saw the pre-discovery permit as offering larger companies an 'exclusive monopoly' on an area, closing it to individual prospectors, and dedicated their lobby into talking the US state and federal governments out of implementing it. The prospectors' opposition was supported by some large companies who disliked the opportunity for the government to make discretionary decisions in granting permits. These interests also disliked the delay that could arise between a theory about a find by a discovery permit holder and the eventual granting of a secure title to it. To the large mining companies, the delay was not just a costly waiting period but also an interval during which the government could be preyed on by prospectors, miners, rent-seekers, lobbyists, litigants, environmentalists and others who wanted to prevent, or share in, the development. The companies and their allies were effective enough to ensure that two-stage procedures, common in Australia and in Canada, and in the petroleum industry everywhere, were very slow to arrive on the US public lands.

Rights of surface users and split estates

As mining went underground and operations became more capital- and land-intensive, conflicts between mining and surface land interests inevitably became

[53] Lang and Crommelin 1979, chs. 8 and 15.

[54] See Barton 1993, pp. 263–6. For a discussion of both Canada and Australia see Crommelin 1974.

more pronounced. Indeed, these conflicts and their resolution are at the heart of the modern *private* mineral-land law, to be discussed in Chapter 8. Here, I provide a brief overview of how, in their implicit bargaining with governments over the terms of the disposal and holding of mineral rights on public and Crown land, miners' fears about losing out to surface interests led to their demand for rights to the public-land surface above the hard-rock discoveries.

After initial attempts, detailed in Chapter 5, to parcel land among its best uses (mineral extraction, forestry and settlement being the major ones), the US mining law of 1872 essentially declared all public lands (with the exception of relatively small parks and military-use areas) open to staking and mining. Upon staking, the miner was entitled to the 'exclusive right of possession and enjoyment' of the mineral estate and of the surface estate, at least for purposes connected with mining. Other units of land were homesteaded by settlers. Once land was staked or homesteaded, respectively, mining and settlement were mutually exclusive: one government department might not dispose of staked land to farming interests; nor might the other government department dispose of the minerals beneath homesteaded land. Miners who wished to search for minerals on homesteaded land were forced to acquire rights directly from the farmer through the land market under common property law.

There were exceptional regions. After the Civil War some land recipients—notably railways and a new generation of homesteaders—were granted the surface only by way of subsidy. The legal presumption behind the new policy was that the government, acting like a private landlord, would be able at any point in the future to make separate grants of the severed mineral rights. A miner would then have access to the staked minerals, along with (common-law) rights of entry; rights to disturb or build on the surface; and rights to remove the minerals. Around 1900 the Congress began to adapt this policy by confining all applicant miners to sub-surface claims and leases and all farmers and ranchers to surface rights. Public land with such divided rights became colloquially known to lawyers as the 'split estate', where the word estate was borrowed from the law of property and referred to the totality of a holder's rights or interests or privileges in a piece of land. The two-estate concept was common enough in private property law, but had not been much contemplated at the time of the American drafting of the 1872 public-land mining law, nor of the earliest version of the homestead law.

Naturally, the splitting of surface and mining rights led to disputes between the occupants. Clarifying the respective surface and mining rights inherent in the split estate fell mainly to local and state courts,[55] amendments to federal law,[56] and to state legislation. These local sources of public-land mining law

[55] Leshy 1987, ch. 12 on the split estate, and Rocky Mountain Mineral Law Foundation 1984, s. 3.23, pp. 532–3.

[56] The Stock-Raising Homestead Act of 1916 (39 Stat 862) declared that the mineral interest was paramount on such homesteads (see Leshy 1987, p. 47 n80).

tended to support miners against surface owners.[57] Relying on theories about how easements were regarded under the common law, they developed the concept that, on lands drawn from the public domain, the miner would be the 'dominant' user of the surface.

In Canada, the public-land-policies' exception or severance of mineral rights from agricultural land grants had taken place earlier. It was standard procedure in most provinces throughout the second half of the nineteenth century. Gold and silver had already been reserved to the Crown from the beginning of colonization. From 1859 on, Canadian minerals might be acquired only by following mining-act procedures, not by acquiring settlement grants—resulting in what the Americans were calling a split estate. One of the main reasons, no doubt, was to facilitate the collection of royalties and mineral duties of various kinds. However, between 1908 and 1913 most provinces except Quebec dropped this convention. Past reservations were rescinded and future settlement and other surface grants were held to include mineral rights.[58]

Australia's hard-rock mining rights also allow miners to enter private land to explore for Crown minerals. In fact, the states' hard-rock mining laws go further than the Canadian law in one regard: NSW and certain other states have, since 1888, retroactively allowed miners to explore and mine privately owned minerals on private lands *without* the consent of the owner. The opportunity to do this arises in many parts of eastern Australia, where Crown lands, Crown minerals, private lands and private minerals are mixed together in various combinations. The procedure amounts to treating private lands as if they were Crown lands, thus enabling prospectors to enter them under certain conditions.[59] The intent of the legislation is to speed the development of such minerals. The private mineral owner is entitled to a large share of profit or royalty. As in the US, much litigation arises in such situations in determining 'just compensation'.[60]

One other important aspect of the historical surface-miner conflict needs to be considered. It is hardly surprising that landowners everywhere have hated

[57] More generally, in the US, the widespread passion for general private freehold ownership was reflected in an apparent judicial dislike of 'split' freehold estates and the consequent search and establishment of precedent in favour of the 'dominant' (mining) interest.

[58] For British Columbia, see Cail 1974, p. 72. For Ontario, see Gibson 1933, p. 3. Throughout the nineteenth century minerals had been generally reserved, first on a grant-by-grant basis, later on all grants. However, Barton 1993, p. 68, differs from Gibson on the subject of the effect of an 1869 withdrawal of reservations. From 1880 on Quebec reserved all minerals. In 1883 it acquired more minerals from the seigneurial lands, and in 1982 it expropriated all remaining patented minerals. See also Barton 1933 p. 192.

[59] Some of the legislative history is recounted by Windeyer in *Wade v. New South Wales Rutile Mining Co. Pty Ltd.* (1969), 121 C.L.R. 184–99. I am grateful to Rosemary Hunter for searching and for clarifying this and other cases, debates and legislation. See also Lang and Crommelin 1979, pp. 175–83.

[60] New Zealand had the same law under its 1871 mining act. It was invoked in one high profile case and withdrawn in the current mining law (1991).

the concept of the 'split estate'. Farmers in particular have resented the idea that their holding does not include the minerals beneath, particularly if these deposits turned out to be valuable. Their resentment encouraged them to resistance and to litigation. But these conflicts between the holders of the surface and the holders of the minerals could be regarded as necessary steps on the way to efficient multiple-purpose use of the total resource (land) and to the rights and obligations that govern its use. This subject crops up elsewhere this book, particularly in Chapter 3 on fresh water rights and in Chapter 12 on private forestry rights. Here it suffices to say that if the private sector is to achieve multiple use of a resource, it will often have to rely on localized contracting between the holders of rights to game, trees, soil and sub-soil. To arrange such contracting may be difficult, but the difficulty is greatly reduced when the parties each hold well-defined rights.

Discovery

The first six profile items I have discussed capture the legislative framework, across time and geographic regions, in which a miner holding good title could expect to work. The last two profile items describe the two main conditions, in addition to royalty, rental or local tax payments to maintain the claim,[61] a would-be miner had to satisfy in order to acquire and maintain good title in the first place. The first is the discovery requirement. The second is the work requirement, discussed below. Like the other profile items, the degree of discovery and work required to ensure good title in mining differed across jurisdictions and time.

The discovery requirement was central to the hard-rock claim-staking system. It was a statutory innovation. The previous systems—common law, free mining, camp law—had not made discovery a condition of owning a claim (contrary to some opinions in the literature).[62] What some of these earlier systems, both public and private, had done was to *reward* discovery by granting a claim, either larger in size or more beneficially located, to a discoverer.[63]

[61] In the period of public-land claim-staking mining tenure disposal examined here, these costs were usually fairly negligible. National governments did usually impose a rental and/or royalty on leases, but leasing was rare and confined to particular minerals, mentioned separately below. They did not impose a tax on their grants of mineral rights by patent, but allowed or even encouraged state and municipal governments to do so.

[62] See *O'Reilly v. Campbell*, 116 US 418 (1886); *Erhardt v. Boaro*, 113 US 527 (1885); *Jackson v. Roby*, 109 US 440 (1883); *Jennison v. Kirk*, 98 US 453 (1879). These cases, all subsequent to the 1866–72 laws, have been said to show that the mining districts 'recognized discovery, followed by appropriation, as the foundation of a possessor's title'. Rocky Mountain Mineral Law Foundation 1984, s. 35.02. This is very doubtful.

[63] Rocky Mountain Mineral Law Foundation 1984, s. 35.02, quotes Lindley 1914, p. 335, citing Gamboa (see Chapter 3) as asserting that 'in all ages' discovery has been regarded as conferring rights or claims to reward.

Most lode mining claims were not rewards of this type. They were merely claims staked around a prior discovery.

The American political reasons for requiring *actual* discovery are not hard to guess, as Congressmen were under pressure from both outside and inside the mining industry. Outside the industry, land-settlement interests fought to prevent hard-rock mining law from allowing persons fraudulently to acquire claims for farming or speculation, just as the earlier placer miners had objected to mineral lands going to farmers and speculators posing as farmers during the early homesteading era. Settlers' demand that claims be assigned only where actual mining was feasible led them to give strong political support to the discovery requirement.[64]

Inside the lode mining industry there was a sector-wide feeling that the purpose of mining law should be to promote mining generally, which naturally included explicit rewards to discovery. Although this might seem self-evident, mining law had additional purposes, such as to head off violence and to maintain order among miners and between miners and settlers, all of which might conceivably have been ill served by a strict discovery rule. The creation of the discovery requirement in lode mining suggests, however, that the direct internal interests to promote the growth of the industry held sway. The evidence is paralleled in the courts. Several twentieth-century judicial opinions have confirmed that the spirit of the US government's mining laws had explicitly become the promotion of the growth of mining;[65] and that this promotion entailed a discovery requirement.

How prospectors felt about the discovery requirement depended on their relative optimism about their own chances of making a valuable discovery. Many believed ('pessimistically', as I put it above) they would do best if they could merely acquire and hold land that would turn out to lie next to that of someone luckier than they were. They therefore opposed a requirement that forced them to make a discovery in order to acquire a claim; and they supported the apex rule, hoping that they, or the mining firms who bought them out, could use it against a lucky neighbour. The Congress took the desires of this new class of professional prospectors seriously, for both sentimental reasons and because their continued existence represented the possibility of finding gold and silver on the public lands in addition to the hard-rock minerals such as iron, copper and lead.[66]

[64] On 'fraud', see 54 *American Jurisprudence*, 2nd 'Mines and Minerals' Section 39 (1971). The mining law could be used to acquire a claim in all public lands, not just in lands under a mineral reserve.

[65] *US Borax Co. v. Ickes*, 98 F.2d 271 at 279 (1938). Cf. *Barton v. Morton*, 498 F.2d 288 (1974), affirmed, 419 US 1021 (1974), where the reasoning focuses upon assured compensation for the depletion of the public trust.

[66] Van Wagenen 1918, pp. 286–7, supports this contention when he writes that prospectors were 'the child[ren] and products of the Federal mining law'.

Ironically, sympathy for this group may have led Congressmen to favour the discovery requirement more strongly. Since the new class of hard-rock prospectors did not generally become miners themselves, but rather found and staked claims that firms in the mining industry would buy, sympathetic legislators reasoned that to sell for a good price, and maintain his value to the mining firms, the prospector must have made a real discovery. Allowing likely sites to be staked on spec would result in there being fewer and poorer prospects available for other prospectors. In labour-market language, support for prospectors pointed to a discovery requirement to increase the long-run demand for prospecting.[67]

This support would gather strength from a third group, those developing and financing small mine ventures. They often served as middlemen between the prospectors and the large mining corporations. An enforced discovery requirement offered them an effective reduction in risk: allowing them to shop for a few properties on which were said to lie genuine discoveries rather than for a large number of unproved properties. With a discovery requirement, the claim-staking stage of lode mining would function as an information-producing and sorting process as the staking requirement had in the free mining regimes. Without it, selection and development would both have been assigned to a layer of grub-staking firms whose services were costly to members of the group organizing small mining ventures.

In the debate among these pressure groups, the discovery requirement won out in Congress. It also won out in state legislatures. The precise details of the discovery requirement remained debatable because of the costliness of enforcement. To begin with, the mining world had not agreed on the precise, verifiable meaning of the hard-rock 'discovery'. We will see below (and in Chapter 9 on the oil industry) that the government and the courts first endeavoured to interpret 'discovery' in the most stringent sense, then backed off when they realized that forcing the industry to adhere to such a strict discovery requirement would be so costly as dramatically to limit the ex-ante incentives of even the largest firms to undertake searches. The government's stringent interpretation of a hard-rock mining 'discovery' was formalized in 1894 and confirmed by the Supreme Court in 1905.[68] A claim contained a discovery if the mineral discovered was adequate to justify a 'prudent person' investing in developing it. The concept of prudence was, in the following decades, examined and re-examined in the courts. But the gist remained: a discovery had to be demonstrated to have value before it could satisfy the condition for acquiring (or transferring) a claim or patent.

[67] While various writers discuss the booms in prospecting, few try to link the choice of laws to the fortunes of prospectors. An exception is Van Wagenen 1918, pp. 286–90 and 300–3.

[68] See *Castle v. Womble*, 19 L.D. 455 (1894), a land contest case in which a homestead entryman questioned whether or not a miner had made a 'discovery'. This prudent-man rule was approved by the US Supreme Court in *Chrisman v. Miller*, 197 US 313 (1905). See Leshy 1987, pp. 135–45; Parriott 1956, p. 900, following Lindley 1914.

This interpretation called for a mine-development process at odds with the economic reality of hard-rock mining. The implied process involved two steps:[69] first, elementary prospecting revealed a surface showing that hinted at mineralization. Second, drilling and metallurgical work provided satisfactory evidence of a vein large and rich enough to induce a prudent person to invest in it. But a miner could foresee that the 1894 test—requiring a discovery of defined value at the beginning of the second step—might well deny him a claim before he had time to determine whether or not it was really a find worth developing. He would thus be deterred from taking even the first step. The prospectors and the firms saw this danger set out in *Crisman v. Miller* (1905) and united to demand a change in the law, one that would over-ride the court's interpretation.

In changing the law to provide a discovery requirement that did not deter prospecting the mining lobby saw three possibilities. The first was to invent another instrument—a specialized pre-discovery exploration or discovery instrument, like the wide-area permit in place in Australia, and later in Canada, that would give exclusive occupation of an area containing a suspected deposit to prospectors for a short period. We have already seen why this failed in the US: the prospecting lobby strongly opposed it as a sop to capital. When Congress considered its 1920 Mineral Leasing Act, 30 USC 181, it did introduce rough pre-discovery conditions for acquiring leases of the coal, oil and the other minerals covered by the act, most of which—unlike hard rock minerals—did not require much in the way of exploration. In 1960 Congress seriously considered amending the 1872 Mining Law in order to insert a pre-discovery permit, but was again eventually deterred by the prospecting lobby.[70]

A second possibility was to amend the spirit rather than the letter of the law: that is, to leave the 1872 discovery requirement unchanged but to alter the administrative interpretation of 'discovery'. The Supreme Court did so in 1919 by introducing what became known as the 'foothold' or 'pedis possessio' concept. It allowed the senior party in a dispute over a partial discovery, say an anomaly or surface showing, to retain possession of the claim so long as discovery/exploration was being pursued diligently.[71] The law's implicit requirement became merely that this first step in the discovery and development process must disclose a find promising enough to induce the miner to continue to occupy the area and to diligently work to eventually make a discovery that would pass the prudent-investor test. This is pre-discovery protection of what might be called exploration tenure. It is an unsatisfactory concept that

[69] The discovery and development process, compressed by laws into two steps, is traced in Cairns 1990.

[70] Van Wagenen 1918, p. 312; Leshy 1987, p. 105.

[71] The words 'diligent prosecution of work' are found in *Union Oil Co. v. Smith*, 249 US 337 at 347 (1919).

requires constant intervention of the state courts for interpretation and application. It survives because the mining industry's various pressure groups cannot agree to the Congress's re-opening of the General Mining Law to give the pedis possessio concept a clearer definition.[72]

The third possibility was to persuade Congress to drop or reduce the discovery requirement altogether, as the Australian states had done. But, having fought their way to a law not altogether unfriendly to them, the small prospectors' lobby dreaded re-opening the law because it might allow agricultural interests to gain ground in the subsequent sausage making over laws governing land rights disputes. Advocating different interpretations in court remained the prospectors' preferred approach.[73]

The Canadian provinces' discovery requirements in the late nineteenth century followed the US mining law. They required that before a claim could be registered or recorded it must be shown to contain valuable mineral. In this the provinces favoured some of the larger companies that complained about so-called parasitical nuisance claims next to their developments. Some prospectors agreed, for they wanted to keep the land vacant for repeated exploration until actual discoveries were made. Smaller companies, however, unlike their US counterparts, generally opposed any discovery requirement. They sought to use unproved claims as a source of exclusion and privacy while they explored (trenching and blasting) and assembled low-grade ore sources. Initially the larger mining interests, in tandem with a subset of the prospectors, won out.

The provinces also paid for a real enforcement of the discovery requirement, departing from the laxer US practice. Nelles describes the situation that obtained in 1905. Speculators and insiders had already blanketed the Cobalt (northern Ontario) silver ore body with claims that effectively closed the area to further prospecting. The government responded by invoking the 1897 Ontario legislation that enshrined a discovery requirement.[74] A corps of engineers was dispatched to Cobalt to inspect every claim. Where unsatisfied with the quality of its 'discovery' they proceeded to cancel the claim. Most claims were cancelled, and the area was newly made available for further outside staking.

Nelles writes that thereupon '... half a dozen parties might be seen working on a claim at the same time, and as they realized that they were obliged to

[72] In practice, a discovery is made on one or a few claims, while many other claims are staked to the outer limit of the suspected vein or deposit. The discovery is pursued first by surface methods then by drilling or excavation. This paragraph follows Cameron 1986, p. 210. See also Parriott 1956, p. 900, and, generally, Leshy 1987, chs. 6, 7 and 8.

[73] See Leshy 1987, p. 289 for an account of attempts to reform the Mining Law. The Union Oil case inspired the pedis possessio concept as an alternative to abandoning a discovery requirement altogether.

[74] Barton 1993, p. 134; Nelles 1974, pp. 156–8; LeBourdais 1957, pp. 130, 134.

make a discovery that would pass inspection, every cranny or crack in the rock was searched for cobalt bloom or traces of silver. It is doubtful whether any area of equal size anywhere on the continent has been more minutely or intensely [mined] than the Cobalt silver field.'[75]

The larger firms continued to support the discovery requirement for its protection against externalities and speculation by small firms. But as in the US, the provincial governments gave in to opponents of strict discovery. They gave credence instead to the contemporary small-business or lone-prospector view that over-strict discovery requirements prevented some lode discoveries from being made. Between 1922 and 1958 the provinces had no strict discovery rule. The Canadian courts also followed the US precedent in adopting a requirement that claim-stakers be only in 'substantial' compliance with legislated discovery laws. In fact, the Canadian courts were ahead of the legislatures in backing off the strict requirement. Barton 1993[76] suggests that strict judicial enforcement of discovery had already faded away by 1919.[77]

Australia departed from the US and Canadian experience. Its states never did (and do not now) impose a serious discovery requirement for either a claim or a lease. The governments have long issued a different claim or lease for different minerals, which miners must specify when applying for a lease (also a departure from strict uniformity). Although some states toyed with rules that required claims to be subject to some proof of viability, for instance by being lined up along a vein or 'reef',[78] generally the state governments took a greater interest in whether the holder had observed the rules with respect to size, staking, taxes, rents, royalties and work. This difference persists: modern Australian written claim-granting laws are unusual in that they make few or no references to veins, lodes or even metals. In some jurisdictions the applicants do not need even to convince government officials that their site contains minerals at all. Subject to administrative interpretation and discretion, the multi-purpose rules—stake the boundaries, pay the charges and do the required amount of work—could be used to grow grapes. (Of course, officials do have discretion, so the written laws may conceal an unwritten, *de facto* discovery requirement.)

[75] Nelles 1974, p. 158, quoting Greater Ontario 1908, p. 31.

[76] For dates, see Barton 1993, pp. 75–6, 124, 134 and 139.

[77] For a well-documented account of a more recent event under the no-discovery-needed rule, consider the Joubin-Hirshorn (J/H) opening of the large uranium camp at Elliott Lake Ontario in 1952. Taking advantage of their own investigations and scientific research they in one day flew 75 parties from airports in all corners of the province to stake claims along their predicted line of deposits. Although their spectacular campaign yielded fourteen hundred staked and registered claims, many of them valuable, the area was quickly swamped by the staking of another eight thousand claims adjoining those of J/H. (The Ontario law at the time required staking, but not discovery.) Some of these eight thousand turned out to be the most valuable. In the absence of a discovery requirement and of any sort of pre-discovery protection, J/H was deprived of much of the fruit of its research and risk-taking.

[78] See Van Wagenen 1918, p. 132, on the laying out of hard-rock gold claims in Queensland.

Work and diligence

In contrast to the discovery requirement, the public or Crown lands' hard-rock mining work requirement (also referred to as a 'diligence' requirement or an 'assessment work' obligation) was no innovation. Versions of it had appeared in private common-law mining leases and licences for centuries. It had been adapted in early nineteenth-century public-land leases, and it had been applied by the gold miners in California's camp rules.

The work requirement had always been important to private landowners, who looked to their mining tenants—whether free miners or lessees—to act as their agents in developing their mineral property. Technically speaking, to the extent governments desired to promote discovery and development, they would probably have been better served by enforcing a work requirement than a discovery requirement. (Enforcement can range from collecting an annual payment or fee in lieu of the work not done to declaring the unworked claim abandoned and available for new staking.) It is a low-cost way of learning whether a discovery has been made since, as the opinion in *Cole v. Ralph* (1919) suggests, 'Work presupposes discovery'.[79]

In American hard-rock mining regions of the 1870s, it was the prospectors and speculators rather than the governments who demanded the work requirement as protection against the 'dog in the manger'[80]—the claimholder who refused to abandon his inactive claim. Their demand was easily accepted by congressmen, probably because it brought back memories of the very popular use-it-or-lose-it principle that had been incorporated into homestead law and into early placer-mining law.

Some of the Canadian provinces and the Australian states imposed work requirements similar to those in American mining law. Their rules were usually stated in terms of the number of man-days of work that must be steadily applied per month or per year. In some jurisdictions the amount of work required depended on the mineral discovered or sought. Typically, if the holder had several adjoining claims or lease areas he might concentrate his required work in one of them. The provinces and states frequently changed the details of the work that would satisfy their requirements.

To require that work be done as a condition for obtaining and holding a mining right is intuitive—but did it really increase the rate of mine development? Leshy, writing about the modern American work requirements under the General Mining Law and its offshoots, expresses doubts as to their importance or effectiveness. He points out that the dollar value of the required work

[79] *Cole v. Ralph*, 252 US 286 (1919).

[80] See Leshy 1987, pp. 107–18, and *Chambers v. Harrington*, 111 U.S. 350 at 353 (1884) (cited by Leshy 1987, p. 414 n69).

(or its fee equivalent) was ludicrously low compared to the claim-holder's actual expense of undertaking just a few days work on his property. He argues that the work requirement might have given holders a tendency to open up their claims but that it was generally imposed at far too modest a rate. He suggests that, as late as the early 1970s, there existed in the US thousands, perhaps millions, of inactive claims on public lands, their holders apparently immune to their work-or-abandon alternatives.[81] I have found no authority explicitly asserting that Canadian or Australian work requirements were as feeble as American, but have gained the impression that they were. If this is correct, the work requirement's place alongside the discovery requirement as a condition for acquiring and holding a lode-mining claim must be a minor one.

Characteristics of property rights in the profile of mine disposal law

Having outlined the eight conditions and requirements in the 'profile' of the post-gold rush public mineral land disposal laws, I turn in this part to confront these profile items with the list of characteristics of property rights common to all chapters. The profile items alone and collectively had implications for the characteristics of the resulting mineral right, but the correlation was by no means perfect. In brief, having followed the procedure made up of conditions, requirements and entitlements in the profile, a miner obtained a mining right under the law of the state. This right's value depended on its providing a suitable amount of each of the six characteristics.

Quality of title (security)

One must consider quality of title as providing security both from government actions ('interference' as it is often called) and from the actions of other miners and private parties. Because the new hard-rock laws were formalized by legislation, and were endorsed by exposure in the courts, they brought about a broad improvement in a miner's quality of title. Once the holder had met the initial discovery requirement, and so long as he had maintained the work requirement (and/or paid whatever dues or fees the government demanded) he found himself in a strong position to resist any re-possession of his rights by government, perhaps as strong as the homesteading farmer's position with respect to his land. However, as we have seen, there always remained a risk of government interference or expropriation. This risk was greater in Canada than in the US.

One of the most serious risks a miner faced was that, even after his claim had been granted and was registered, another miner would challenge his holding,

[81] Leshy, 1987, p. 212.

especially (a) when the apex principle was in effect and (b) when his mineral, being a liquid or gas, could not be strictly identified as his property (see Chapters 2 and 9). In addition, the conflicts between the small-prospector lobby and the new capitalistic mining interests meant that neither side was entirely comfortable with the other, both fearing their title might be weakened by government concessions to the other or to outside land interests during a later legislative session. Finally, insecurity in relations with other land holders and users were a risk for miners in all countries, as I discuss further in Chapter 8. Faced with these insecurities, various mining interests have complained that the mining laws have not really given them the quality of title that the land laws have given to users of the surface. However, the tourist who sees giant mines and their mills scattered across the landscape is forced to the conclusion that the owners must have considered their titles good enough to proceed with very large and risky investments.

Exclusivity

The transition to deep alluvial mining and to hard-rock mining, in combination with the more general development of industry during the late nineteenth century, tended to make mines vulnerable to spillovers from the underground, surface or water operations of their close neighbours. As a result, mining operations seemed less exclusive than had those of the primitive riverbed placer miners. On the other hand, developments in public mineral land disposal and mining law—including the granting of exclusive exploration permits and increases in the size of mining claims or rights to hold multiple claims—were designed in part to reverse these effects and protect the mineral right-holders' exclusivity. As we saw in the last chapter, the stage between staking an initial claim and registering it with a granting authority (the camp-cum-government) had traditionally been the most perilous, in the sense of non-exclusive, stage of mining for the placer miner, when he was most at risk of losing his discovery. It was to this stage that some governments, by approximations to two-stage procedures, addressed their attempts to protect the new generation of hard rock miners from interference and trespassing.

In particular, the imposition of the apex principle had notable effects on the distribution of miners' exclusivity. On the one hand, the lucky prospector who happened upon a genuine 'find' (and, if applicable, also the firm who bought him out) gained valuable exclusivity in his rights to much of the lode he had discovered, regardless of whose claim it lay beneath. But the rights of those who had staked around him, and the right of a finder whose 'discovery' claim turned out not to contain the apex, become less exclusive than before the apex rule was introduced. The invasion by the apex holder sometimes imposed on them a complete loss of their rights over the minerals directly beneath their staking.

Transferability and divisibility

The benefits and requirements of the procedures laid down in modern mining laws have greatly strengthened the transferability characteristic of the property rights of miners acquiring claims on public lands. In sharp contrast to the laws that had prevailed in the California-type placer camps, the newer right of individual prospectors (for instance in Australia) to combine their claims into single transferable units made mining holdings just as legally and practically transferable as any other real estate. This was particularly important when mining turned from placer deposits to hard-rock, coal and petroleum sites. There are few complaints in the legal literature about any non-transferability of public-land or Crown-land mineral holdings. The reward to the lucky finder of a lode is not the prospect of profitable mining, but the prospect of sale of the mining right to a syndicate or larger corporation.

Divisibility is another matter. Just as urban zoning laws may prevent real estate from being divided into ever-smaller holdings, so the mineral laws generally have continued to contain provisions banning an extreme subdivision of claims. The general reason is that if claims were regarded as too small, and if there were a limit on the number that could be staked and/or held, prospectors would be less interested in searching for them.

The work requirement had some effect here. As had the use-it-or-lose-it rule in the placer camps, some governments' embrace of a (strict) work requirement to complement or replace the discovery requirement encouraged claim holders to unload some claims so as to avoid the risk and expense of working on them. This conclusion caused them to support laws and court decisions that added to the transferability characteristic even of such informal tenures as claims and exploratory permits.

Duration

Technically speaking, the minerals in a modern claim can be quickly exhausted, so that duration of a right might seem to have a minor importance. But where minerals took longer to extract, duration was of great importance to miners and mining firms. The aspect of mining law that most impacted on the claim's duration was that illustrated earlier: the choice between the freehold patent and the lease arrangement. In the latter arrangement, the mining interest might have to renew its lease periodically, and might find that the legislative or public price regime in which it did so had changed (recall the story of the mining syndicate at Broken Hill). In contrast, a patent was more or less forever, though governments might (as Quebec did in 1982) reclaim the land, thereby decimating the patent's quality of title. Also in the case of a patent, the miner holding it might find his property right to involve *too much* duration (as discussed briefly below), forcing him to endure carrying costs to hold land whose wealth he had already depleted.

On the whole—though not strictly—the hard-rock era's changes in acquisition laws in all three countries brought a definite improvement in the characteristics of the property interest held by the miner. The very fact that many, especially in the US, did not bother to convert their claim to a patent shows how confident they were in their title and its duration and transferability. Even without a patent, their right could arguably be said to possess more of the transferability and durability characteristics than the rights of private landowners under the common law.

The main fly in the ointment was spillovers and external diseconomies. When the industry made the transition to hard-rock mining it entered the field of damage and interference that had for centuries been problems almost exclusively for owners of private coal and metal mines. In some countries, governments granted large acreages to the big mining companies not only for exploration and development but also to provide buffer space between adjoining operations. But more generally, before the age of sustainable development and major environmental concern, governments did not seem to regard such interference and spillovers as their problem. As a result, the standard property rights of hard-rock miners failed to provide all the exclusivity that should have been demanded by the new hard-rock mines and mills.

Concluding remarks on mining rights in public lands

Before the gold rushes, governments' mineral disposal policies were not embodied in specialized land disposal laws. Land alienation was still what it had been under the Westminster model, where the grant of Crown land, at first a prerogative of the sovereign, passed to the government without the involvement of the legislature. In 1783 American public land disposal became a matter for the states and then for Congress, and, eventually, land disposal in Canadian provinces and Australian states became matters for their legislatures. The politicians followed in the royal footsteps, handing out bits of the public domain, including lands containing minerals, at the time and on the terms that pleased them. Ownership of an interest in mineral-rich land was conveyed by a deed that was, to all intents and purposes, like a private deed under the law of property. This was really the sum total of late eighteenth-century 'policy' toward mineral disposal.

In the first half of the nineteenth century there were a few mining acts and private charters, which were noted in Chapter 5. But not until the mid-century gold rushes did pressure begin to mount for rules that went beyond those for common-law conveyancing. Then, all of a sudden (and sometimes in a jurisdictional and legal desert), a class of persons—the prospector/miners—outside the usual land-holding class emerged with a need to be allowed to, basically, *trespass on the public lands* in the interests of fair, orderly and efficient exploration, discovery and production of minerals, particularly precious ones. Given the nature of the 'rush', there was often no time to adequately debate and legislate the needed rules. In Australia, this led to hasty and poorly thought out legislation designed to stem the flow of miners. In California, it led to miners supplying their own law, irrespective of government.

In this chapter I have surveyed how the fundamental features of the placer gold-rush claim-based property right, arrived at in haste and ad-hoc, later became established in the mining laws designed to govern hard-rock mining. Through variations in the eight conditions of the mine-property profile, the laws took on local and national colours. At one stage or another, Ontario ground out different laws for different districts in the province; the United States adopted the apex principle; Australian states encouraged miners to stake claims on private lands; and at an early stage British Columbia appropriated *all* mineral rights for the Crown. In spite of these variations, competition between governments, later to attract the huge, capitalistic mining firms of what was the first major era of globalization, gradually ironed out many of these differences.

There is no doubt that the US mining laws, and particularly Congress' 1872 General Mining Law, became models for the other countries of the period. Yet there were several respects in which US hard-rock law stood increasingly alone. (1) The Congress did not look to mining as a source of revenue. (2) It did not make mining law to promote general economic conditions. (3) It strongly preferred to keep both surface and minerals under claim or under patent (freehold ownership), rejecting leasing and similar 'compromises'. And (4) it aimed to retain certain features of claim acquisition that had been bequeathed to it by the placer-mining camps, especially the individual, small claim and some kind of finder's reward. Essentially, for much of the nineteenth century, the American government acted as though it regarded mining law primarily as an instrument for bringing about an equitable and orderly disposal of the public lands. Mining law was thought of as being an underground version of homesteading law, which was used to make an orderly division of the surface farm land among settlers, and thereby to keep the peace among them. Land and minerals were rewards for discovery and development. Thus, while the Canadian provinces, for example, actively added features to their mining laws in order to promote the growth of the mining communities and refining industries, Washington was—with perhaps the exception of the discovery requirement—satisfied with a law deemed fair by the placer miners and prospectors and more or less accepted, with gradual modifications, by their larger, corporate successors in the industry.

What we have seen since then is the increasing differentiation of the rights provided to miners. In each country, state or province, the differences among the public leasing systems for hard-rock minerals, coal and onshore and offshore oil have progressively widened. Thus, everywhere the procedure by which a mining company acquires rights over a suspected base metal deposit has become increasingly unlike that by which, say, an oil or gas company obtains rights to drill for and produce oil in the Continental Shelf.

The mutations of the procedures for obtaining mining rights from 1860 on in Canada and Australia and to a lesser extent the US also may be seen as appropriate to different stages of a country's, and of the industry's, development. When geological information was scanty and the markets were small or remote, all parties agreed on disposal laws that protected the information rights of each person who undertook to invest in reconnaissance, geological exploration and drilling. This consensus led on to automatic staking and claiming. Then, as the differences in the stock of information and in the methods of obtaining it became obvious, the land-disposal systems for coal, metals, chemicals and oil and gas diverged.

Before ending these concluding remarks, I must introduce a warning concerning the applicability or avoidance of standard public-land disposal laws. With time, the details of disposal systems can become increasingly irrelevant; that is, the amendments to disposal regulations and laws and the decisions of courts may be perfecting a system of public-land acquisition that simply does not affect many active participants in the industry. The general explanation for this is simple. As time passes, more and more of the rights to any likely sources of mineral in the public lands pass into private hands. At the limit, all of a country's 'reserves' could have passed into private holdings carved out by patents and leases. Of course, this limit will not be reached quickly because the increasingly numerous holders of rights will be inclined to let their holdings—with the associated carrying costs and renewal requirements—slip out of private ownership as new public lands are found to be better sources of mineral. Furthermore, some governments, impatient with private speculation, will be led to increase their own carrying costs.

The drift out of public control and regulation is reinforced by the accumulation of geological knowledge. Each year's searches and drilling increase the firms' data, and firms in turn race to out-scoop each other. Many items in this data do not become public in the legal sense but may be held, described and exchanged as firms trade their assets or equity with each other—taking over, merging and optioning. In this way, items of information will drift towards 'junior' companies and specialist firms, confirming their own hunches about where future plays may take place and encouraging them to bear the carrying and renewal costs of holding rights strategically. As metal and energy demand grows and older sources play out, the beliefs and hunches of certain specialist firms are confirmed and their holdings are acquired by senior producing companies. Because these companies acquire their new reserves from specialist junior companies and from individual speculators, they remain more or less indifferent to the government's continually revised procedures and terms for disposal systems. Instead they show an increasing interest in the property characteristics of the claims, leases, freeholds and options granted by *private* owners to private miners and firms and to oil producers.

The evolution of these private rights, from the late medieval period up to the current era, is the subject of the next chapter. Following that, I turn in Chapter 9 to an examination of the development of the coal and oil and gas disposal on public and private lands.

8

Mineral Disposal and Mining Rights on Private Land

Introduction: conflicts and the courts in the development of private mineral rights

In the previous chapters on mining, I examined the historical development of rights to minerals found on 'public' land; that is, on land controlled by the medieval Crown, the colonial powers and their chartered land proprietors, and later the landholding national governments. We saw that, in the earliest days, the supplying behaviour of 'public' landholders was often very similar to that of private land-owners. In this chapter, I return to medieval and early modern England to trace the parallel development in the West of *private* mining rights and contracting, beginning with the English feudal and post-feudal landlords. I turn from the historians' account of the lesser nobility in this period as war-leaders and law-makers to consider them as land-use managers making decisions about their iron and coal resources. They are seen, through economists' eyes, not only setting the terms of their mineral leases but also 'demanding' beneficial decisions in land-use conflicts, mainly from the courts.

In the next section I sketch a largely theoretical account of the lord's deciding whether or not to open up his land to mining, and whether or not to farm out the actual mining operations. From there, I look at the conflicts arising among miners and between miners and their landlords (and the landlords' farming tenants) and discuss the characteristics of the property rights attributed to the various parties to these conflicts. Much attention must be

For this chapter I owe much to Margaret Hall. She participated wholly in research for and drafting of a previous version, and a good deal of her work on development of nuisance and property in mining survives. She must be regarded as the co-author of many parts that follows. In connection with the development of all three mining characteristics, I am grateful for discussions with Michael Crommelin and Peter Pearse as well as Robert Allen, Gary Libecap, David Gerrard, Cole Harris and Robert Cairns.

given to the evolution of the courts, where most of the rights were established and enshrined in precedent, and where, especially in the eighteenth and nineteenth centuries, most demands for changes in the characteristics of mining property rights were presented. As I will show, changes in the characteristics of mining 'property' rights actually emerged primarily as judge-made developments in tort (nuisance) law.[1] Beyond what the courts could supply, we also catch glimpses here and there of the other mining-right suppliers: the government intervening to make or clarify mining laws, and customary mining practices being consulted and upheld.

In the final section of this chapter, I argue that of the six property-right characteristics, the one most sought-after (demanded) by active miners, and the one most often reconsidered by the courts (as suppliers), was restoration of exclusivity: the right to enjoy the full potential reward of a given mineral property free from the intentional or unintentional interference of others. The miners also sought improved quality of title, particularly where title was not directly backed up by government legitimacy as was the case on public lands.

Why did conflicts arise? As already suggested in Chapters 6 and 7, they arose because of changing mineral demand, land-use competition, mining techniques and discoveries of rival and substitute mineral sources. By the dawn of the Industrial Revolution, the natural exclusivity of the shallow medieval excavations had all but vanished. When the intensity of exploration and the depth of mines changed, producers exerted a demand for changes in restrictive laws. Most authors in the natural-resource literature picture mining rights as being at least as exclusive as a farmer's right: each miner keeps to himself as he digs down on his own site. In fact miners could not keep to themselves: their activities gave rise to interferences with their neighbours' workings: flooding their mines, dissipating their oil discoveries and undermining their surface operations.

Private mining, leasing and conflicts

The landholders' choices

Before the nineteenth century English landowners probably saw themselves primarily as private actors making decisions about when and how to undertake mining within a predetermined legal and land-rights system. As feudal duties eroded with time, the 'private' nature of the English land-owner grew more pronounced and more distinct from that of the Crown, which retained and defended its 'public' judicial and law-making powers. Here, I provide a theoretical sketch of the choices faced by a land-owner who found himself possessed

[1] The development of Canadian and Australian private mining rights could be cited here and there, but for the most part their mining laws have dealt with problems and conflicts of the disposal of minerals from public lands. These were discussed in Chapters 6 and 7.

of mineral wealth and wished to exercise his rights to bring it up from the ground.

At the outset the owner—say, a late eighteenth-century holder of a rural estate—would be holding minerals inactively. This is hardly a leap; it is worth remembering that most mineral wealth, throughout history, has been held inactive: by great European land-owning families of the early modern period, by American homesteading farmers and later by the international mining industry. As Leshy wrote about the nineteenth and twentieth-century US mining industry, 'As shown by the vast number of mining claims on which no production has ever occurred, the hard-rock mining industry collectively has a penchant for, even an ingrained habit of, accumulating vast reserves and holding them idle for decades.'[2]

The land-owner faced a two-pronged decision: *when* to cease holding onto the minerals and bring them into production and then, conditional on this decision, *how* to do so. This second decision could involve taking his family into mining directly, making arrangements with a group of free miners (as described in Chapter 6) or working through the real estate market to find a specialized mining firm. In turn, disposal to such a firm could take the form of a lease or of an outright sale of the mineralized property underground, with or without the surface attached. Theory dictates that the agent (the land-owner) would seek to select the pair of actions (when and how) that provided him the greatest stream of returns—the highest discounted present value based on his beliefs and expectations about the extent of mineralization of his lands; present and future prices; present and future availability of investment capital; his own present and future revenue needs; and the transactions costs of each of the alternatives. His calculations and decisions—and those of his peers—would enter into the aggregate or industry demand for strengthening or changing the various kinds of mineral right.

THE LAND-OWNER CHOOSES *WHEN* TO MINE

First, the landlord would need to gain some idea of how long he could expect his mine, once opened, to remain in operation. With this information (say, twenty years), he would estimate his return (the present-discounted sum of the expected net proceeds from each of the twenty years' mining) from commencing mining operations in the current year and in some future year, say five years hence. The difference between these two expected streams of returns was the 'user cost'

[2] Leshy 1987, p. 156. Leshy cites Tussing, Arlon, and Erickson 1969, pp. 40–2. However, I have seen no estimate of the size of the total private mineral reserve in the US (or anywhere else) or of their annual rate of turnover. Clawson and Held 1957, pp. 96 ff. and subsequent editions contain estimates of total public oil land under lease to private owners. They remark that much of the public domain is leased, through brokers, to persons unconnected with the oil and gas industries (who hold them for speculative purposes). These estimates and comments, however, cover only acres under lease, not those under freehold rights or claims.

(foregone profit) of beginning right away—a function mainly of expected future increases in mineral prices or declines in mining costs. The rational land-owner would extend the assumed waiting period until the user cost of starting shrunk to zero, when mineral prices were relatively high and stable and when technological progress in mining did not appear overwhelmingly promising.

The land-owner and his family, whenever they chose not to open up or to sell immediately, were speculating. If, as suggested above, they decided to contract with a mining firm, then that firm too might speculate, for instance by acquiring mineral reserves years before operations were to begin.[3] Speculation often depended on the ebb and flow of information. This was particularly true for speculation in minerals since, unlike many other resources, the mineral landlord's resource was durable and would not deteriorate like a herd of livestock or a stand of timber. For the same reason, mining-related information was also relatively durable; information acquired about operating in the next period had the potential to be valid indefinitely since the physical aspects of the resource would not be changed by postponing operations an extra period. The longer sale or exploitation was delayed, the better the miners' and owner's information about the amount, accessibility or value of each grade of mineral could become.

As well, owners and lessees contended with sharp unexpected changes, as when canals made shipping minerals to remote markets cheaper and faster; or when the cost of mining itself was in the process of change. As a relatively late example, landowners considering when to develop their coal resources around 1800 encountered the possibility that the inventions of Trevithick and Watt might drastically change the expected future profitability of mining on their lands. Taking account of changing technology and markets (and of changing expectations in response to new information about technology and markets) complicates our task of understanding *when* owners found it optimal to offer rights to exploit their holdings in feudal and early modern Europe.

To add to his uncertainty about the user costs of mine openings in different periods, the land-owner also had to begin worrying about externalities: the costs that neighbouring operations could impose on his mine and that his mine could impose on neighbours, the latter opening him up to legal challenges. His mine could also impose externalities on his non-mining tenants and on his and their other land uses. To go into mining was usually to accept the costs of converting a land-owner's green country estate into a black industrial area. If so, the family deciding on when to sell minerals also needed information about surface land values in the future.

[3] The mining literature generally deals with when to mine rather than when to sell. See, however, Gray 1913; Scott 1955, ch. 2; and Scott 1967. The conservation question—when can all operators be predicted to mine?—is the subject of Hotelling 1931 and of a vast 1970s and 1980s energy-resource literature.

THE LANDLORD CHOOSES *HOW* TO DISPOSE OF HIS LAND

Eventually the owner's chosen time for disposal of his minerals would arrive.[4] Ignoring the free-mining option (which, as we saw in Chapter 6 was often determined or limited by tradition), his remaining options were to invest in equipment and take up mining directly, to sell the deposit with or without the land around it or to lease out the mining rights for a period of years.

From the late medieval period on, some great landowners found it relatively easy to adopt any of these alternatives. In sixteenth-century England for example, several great families undertook directly the mining of coal and iron and the metallurgy. To provide the basic manpower for the operations, they advertised for and imported experienced miners and drew on labour available in populated rural districts. In the seventeenth century, a more capital-intensive and less feudally structured age, landowners encumbered with mortgages but less encumbered by feudal obligations to tenants had an incentive to develop and sell mineral leases for revenue. Doing so also helped create a market for a manor's produce. According to Peter Mathias,

> The stewards of landowners such as the Fitzwilliams, Ravenworths, or the Londonderries (or even the Bishop of Durham) became virtually the department managers of great mining concerns. Even if the actual mining operations were usually mined out in concessions, some of the strategy of development as well as much of the capital came from the landlords.[5]

Landlords' own capital was also involved in the management of china-clay development and copper and tin mining in Cornwall. Other great families such as the Lambtons (Lord Durham) and the Howards (Dukes of Devonshire) were heavily involved. 'The most successful cartel in coal-mining was run from the House of Lords by the land magistrates of the north-east coast.'[6]

But by the eighteenth century the land-owning class's various kinds of direct participation in mining were in decline. Most hereditary land-owners had become chary of entering the mining world as principles; and those whose ancestors had done so tended to drop out. Presumably, this was a response to the increasing 'big business' aspects of iron and coal mining in the period culminating in the Industrial Revolution. Mines were larger. Economies of scale found from integrating mining operations with railways and foundries attracted large, risk-seeking investors. A few of the land-owners had the ability and nerve for this kind of entrepreneurial challenge, but most bowed out.

[4] Because the 'private' mineral dealings of European kings and princes are better documented than are those of their subjects, we find many feudal and medieval examples of royal mining partnerships and ventures. As discussed in Chapters 5, the French Crown was the leading example of the state plunging into mining and, in fact, acting like a private revenue-maximizing firm.

[5] Mathias 1989, p. 115.

[6] Mathias 1989, p. 115. See also M. Hughes 1963; and Spring 1951, 1952.

Roy Church's examination of the seven main English coal regions by 1880 found that only 1 per cent of the 'founders' of coal companies were landowners, the rest being businessmen and professionals, some from outside the industry. A half century earlier, in the years between 1800 and 1830, the corresponding figure would have been greater than ten per cent.[7]

EARLY MINING LEASES

The land-owner could avoid direct participation by turning the legal estate over to a miner. Many decided to quit completely: to sell their lands and minerals and move away. Those who stayed faced an additional choice: whether to sell the mineralized land severed from the surface estate or to retain the property itself while selling the mining rights. 'Severing' the underground estate in freehold constituted a sale of the physical subsurface, permanent unless the miner opted to sell the land back to the original land-owner after ceasing his underground operations. The buyer could then mine (or speculate) at his discretion and without being subject to the conditions that would be spelled out in a typical lease. By contrast, 'selling the mining' constituted a leasing arrangement: the landlord allowed someone to come onto his property, engage in mining and take away what was found. This was to be done within a specified period of time after which the land and subsurface reverted to the landlord. This latter arrangement was by far the most common. The lease was variously referred to as a contract or a concession.

Leasing in pre-industrial England

Because leasing eclipsed direct investment as the landowner's preferred method of disposing of his minerals, the historian's interest is naturally drawn to the nature of the lease document, and the rights and responsibilities written into it. It will be shown that, to the extent that the laws applying to private mining and mining rights developed at all during this period, they were mostly supplied by the courts rather than by direct appeals to custom or by legislation from the Crown or the Parliament.

Mining was protected by the general laws of property that applied to rural and urban lands. Until the sixteenth century most mines were little more than small short-lived bell pits and dugouts, widely separated both from each other and from homes and barns.[8] Apart from those in free-mining districts, mines were located in former feudal and church lands. The medieval mining lease usually explicitly confined the miners' rights to the subsurface—the mineral estate—and preserved the rights of surface use for the landlord. The miner,

[7] Church 1986, pp. 450–5.

[8] For a contrast between the mining boom in all kinds of metals in central Europe in the pre-Reformation fifteenth century and the static condition of English mining, see Nef 1964, p. 42 (and his chapter 1 generally).

having neither the financial nor the technical means to remain longer and dig deeper, would work the pit for a year or so before moving on to another location owned by the same landlord. Under these geographically isolated and routine conditions few conflicts arose between mining and other land uses. Rights under the old laws, protecting exclusivity in any kind of property, evidently served pre-Reformation England well enough.

With the Reformation, a widespread surge in mine openings on the lands of the new aristocracy induced many lords to clarify their personal ownership and to acquire more land from the monasteries. They set out to free themselves from the feudal restrictions and entails that stood in the way of their opening their estates to coal, lead and iron miners. In the midst of dealing in increasingly complex property relationships, the inherent exclusivity of the entailed landlord's own rights was being challenged, and the responsibility to the family not to commit 'waste' on the land was becoming more arduous than it had been under the usual family succession arrangements before the mid-seventeenth century. Thereafter, challenges to mismanagement of the estate gained the potential to become formal litigation, and predicting the outcomes of such cases was anyone's guess. It was probably owing to the relatively modest nature of the mines themselves that England did not witness an explosion of lawsuits until the eighteenth century.

Leasing during the Industrial Revolution

By the late eighteenth century lawyers had become quite skilled at helping the land-owning classes circumvent barriers to leasing out their mining: the traditional barriers to leasing inherent in the lord's duties to his farming tenants (sometimes even requiring their consent to miners entering their holdings) plus the newer responsibilities to the widows, children, brothers and sisters catered to by many strict settlements. Having engineered the buying out of customary tenants' and copyholders' various rights to surface and mineral access, the lawyers began drafting bargains with the heir, buying out his claims and those of other family members.

The lords, through their lawyers, went to great lengths to obtain widened leasing powers. The Industrial Revolution was causing a considerable expansion of production and consumption of coal and metals. While the annual output of a coal mine in Tudor England would have amounted only to a few hundred tons, the average figure grew over the next hundred years to ten thousand or twenty thousand tons, especially in the north. There were smaller increases in the sizes of copper and lead mines.[9] These changes were responses to nineteenth-century coal-industry demand: both coal and iron had access to well-paying markets no longer adequately served by central and northern Europe. The improvement of river transport and the digging of canals carried

[9] Nef 1964, p. 129.

this increased demand to ever more remote mining districts and individual mining properties.

Improvements in mining technology also increased the demand for properties. Since the seventeenth century the miner had been able to use water power, or even a primitive steam engine, to hoist coal, lower workers and tools and pump workings dry. In the eighteenth and nineteenth centuries more powerful steam engines were quickly adapted to trams and railroads and applied to dressing, cleaning and concentrating the minerals at the surface. These new production opportunities meant that mines tended to occupy more ground, last longer, go deeper and produce more spoil and waste. Their activities called for new blast furnaces, smelters and factories, all of which had large buildings and service requirements in the form of water, roads, housing and storage.

These various larger-scale operations naturally caused miners to demand such provisions as freedom in the use of the surface for works, more rights of waste disposal and permission to use open-pit techniques. Their demands for duration and flexibility were met through the writing of extremely elaborate leases. These could run to hundreds of pages of covenants, with full and secure provisions for renewal (very occasionally calling for the eventual outright sale of land) and reflecting the more general increase in leasing sophistication accompanied by new waves of commercial buying and settling of farm land, urban development, enclosures of selected commons, continuing subdivision of church estates and changes in the laws of settlement. As I show in detail below, the legal interpretation and adjudication of these leases created the prime right-supplying mechanism within the English mining community—in particular determining which of the detailed *powers* conveyed by holding a right (to manage, to dispose and to take profit) went to the mining tenant as part of the 'mineral estate'.

Evolving conflicts come before the courts

Four main issues and their legal resolutions emerged as question marks about the private mineral property right: underground flooding, removal of surface support, surface damage and appropriation of fluid minerals (the subject of Chapter 9).

The first and fourth of these conflicts mainly arose between adjoining miners. These neighbours were not under contract with each other but shared a common pool or were located within a common water-table. Leaving aside the rights over fluid resources such as petroleum until the next chapter, we can see that flooding disputes were fundamentally different from surface disputes. They were not contractual failures, but rather externality disputes that required resolution through the laws of property and, especially, tort. The second and third types of conflict, by contrast, arose from failed contractual relations between surface owners and their mining lessees. They were resolved by procedures in the law of contract.

All three branches of law—property, tort and contract—were of importance to the development of mining rights. Below, I offer very brief sketches to suggest how far each of them had evolved leading up to the nineteenth century's expansion of mining-related legal activity.

PROPERTY LAW AND THE MINER

Emerging from the medieval Norman preoccupation with the creation of a (vertical) ladder of feudal land rights, property law swung in the middle ages to resolving questions of horizontal (distributional) division. Here I review and expand on the details of the evolution of property law given in Chapter 1, with emphasis on how they applied to mining disputes.

From about 1250 onward the progress of the law of property for handling new kinds of dispute amounted to the development of new forms of action, 'the real property actions'. Initially disputes concerned the rightful owner being physically deprived of seisin; later disputes concerned the question of who exactly *was* the rightful owner—i.e. which party had the better title.

A distinguishing feature of the real property action was that its remedy went beyond an award of damages—it called for a return of the owner's property. However, it had disadvantages as well, stemming mainly from its high cost and its complexity. Furthermore, it was available only to freehold owners. The main alternative to the real property action was to sue for trespass. As its name suggests, this action did provide damages—indeed it provided only damages, not the return of property. The scope of the trespass action was, around 1230, extended by the action of ejectment, which could be brought by a tenant or lessee against someone who interfered with his occupancy.

Later, two improvements made the action of ejectment even more attractive to litigants. For one, the courts began to take the view that damages were not enough. They found that a successful ejectment proceeding could bring also recovery of possession to the tenant. This innovation reflected rivalry between the main courts—that is, 'a fear that if the common-law courts failed to provide a satisfactory remedy for the husbandry [farm] tenant, the Chancellor would [do so in the court of equity]'.[10] The new remedy was fully implemented by 1525. The second improvement in the ejectment procedure was adapting it so that it would be attractive to freeholders as well as to tenants. Clever lawyers found that by using certain 'John Doe' fictions (e.g. pretending that their client was a lessor), they could get their clients' freehold titles tested in an action that nominally was about interference with the right of a lessee. Also, it

[10] Milsom 1976, p. 144.

had the further advantage of offering trial by jury. This strengthening of ejectment swept all other actions out of the courts. By the early 1600s, according to Chief Justice Coke in *William Aldred's Case* (1610): 'All titles of lands are for the greatest part tried in Actions of Ejectments.'[11] As the decades passed litigants and their lawyers also discovered that various trespass actions (from which ejectment was descended) could be used to investigate not only questions of title and the extent and boundaries of properties, but also nuisance, as discussed below.

I come now to property in mines. By the earliest feudal tenure, the lord had rights to everything in, on and over the land or soil. With the transition to the doctrine of estates, these rights manifested as the power to grant (by will or otherwise) either the freehold or the leasehold of any part of his holding, including the mineral part. The quality of the miner's title to his leasehold (his freedom from interference, trespass or disseisin) therefore typically depended on the quality of the title held by the lord who granted it. This could be disputed and was subject to litigation. For example, the miner finding silver was subject to the Crown's claim to noble metals, as established in the Elizabethan *Case of Mines* (1568).[12] Or his landlord might turn out to be liable for waste and so be unable to grant a lease that would deplete the family's lands. Even when the landlord was not impeachable for waste, the title to the minerals might be subject to the customary rights of manorial tenants to access to the surface, or even to the minerals themselves. Apparently these limitations rarely presented actual barriers to mining. Faced with them, a miner or his lord would probably settle with the Crown, the by-passed family members or the injured manorial tenants.

By 1750 actions in the law of property were still the chief methods of dealing with disputed ownership or possession of land—perhaps the main business of the post-medieval courts. However, most property-law cases dealt with what we would today call a distributional question: to whom do the powers of ownership over a piece of land belong? Once the nature of the right was given and accepted, cases were mostly concerned with questions of ownership, title, possession, seisin, estates, conveyances and settlements, as well as family questions that showed up as disputes about succession, trusts and waste. Because such law-of-property concerns were unlike the new rights-based questions of mine flooding, surface support and mine drainage, much of received property law was unsuited for settling mining's unique problems. That property law retained any importance for mining rested on the fact that, with the eighteenth-century boom in mining, there was a lot of pure rent to be captured, shared and assigned. But for our purposes the most significant changes in the characteristics of miners' rights, their duties and

[11] *William Aldred's Case* (1610), 9 Co. Rep. 576, [1558–1774] All E.R. 622, 77 E.R. 816.
[12] *Case of Mines* (1568), 1 Plowd. 310, 75 E.R. 472.

powers, developed in the domains of nuisance or tort law[13] and of contract law, to which I turn next.

NUISANCE LAW

The central contradiction of nuisance law is how to square the privileges of one party's exclusive estate with the limitations necessary for another party's enjoyment of his exclusive estate: if A's exclusive property rights permit him to degrade the quality of B's property, then B's exclusivity is compromised. But for A to refrain from externality-producing activities represents a limitation on his own exclusivity. Perhaps because of this, nuisance law 'has meant all things to all men, and has been applied indiscriminately to everything from an alarming advertisement to a cockroach baked in a pie'.[14] We can, however, offer a general modern definition of (private) nuisance: a substantial and unreasonable interference with the use and enjoyment of another's land.

The historical development of nuisance actions was discussed in Chapter 1. Briefly, they emerged in the eleventh century with the Assize of Novel Disseisin, later the Assize of Nuisance, to which parties whose property had been harmed had recourse for a narrow range of circumstances. Both the plaintiff (the alleged victim) and the alleged perpetrator had to be freeholders. Furthermore, the plaintiff's harm must have been the direct result of some alleged action of the perpetrator (not of something coming from his land).

The seventeenth-century 'action on the case' (or just 'case') evolved beyond the Assize of Nuisance to cover injury to a leaseholder's land, and also injury that was an indirect, or consequential, result of the defendant's actions. The chief disadvantage of choosing to bring an action on the case was its remedy: it was limited to damages (unlike the equity action, with its offer of injunction or abatement). This shortcoming aside, however, the action on the case was widely popular with litigants, for it offered the Assize of Nuisance's 'absolute' protection to any land user, whether he or she was an owner or not: any interference with, or invasion of, the 'natural rights of seisin' would constitute a nuisance akin to modern strict liability.

The task of clarifying these 'natural rights' fell to Sir Edward Coke in *Aldred* (1610).[15] That case concerned a hog sty erected near the plaintiff's house. The defendant had offered an unprecedented utilitarian appeal: 'that the building of the house for hogs was necessary for the sustenance of man: and one ought not to have so delicate a nose, that he cannot bear the smell of hogs'. Coke rejected this, saying:

[13] There was also a small possibility that, in a disputed-ownership case, success might lead through seisin to defining a mine spillover as a trespass, and so remove it from nuisance law to property law.

[14] Prosser 1941, para. 87.

[15] *William Aldred's Case* (1610), 77 E.R. 816. See Coquilette 1979, p. 772; Fifoot 1949, p. 95. See discussion above.

The building of a lime kiln is good and profitable; but if it be built so near a house, that when it burns the smoke thereof enters into the house, so that none can dwell there, an action lies for it . . . This stands with the rule of law and reason . . . *sic utere tuo ut alienum non laedas.*[16]

Coke's statement of a strict liability rule was to be cited for centuries, but it introduced another uncertainty, about the defendant's word 'necessary'. Was the plaintiff's injury a matter of damage to his 'necessity' or merely to a source of his 'delight'? According to Coke: 'For prospect, which is a matter only of delight, and not of necessity, no action lies for stopping thereof, and yet it is a great commendation of a house if it has a long and large prospect . . . But the law does not give an action for such things as delight.'[17] The rule and its discretionary interpretations by the courts remained almost unquestioned law in England and the United States for centuries after *Aldred*.

Did Coke's 1610 decision strengthen the exclusivity characteristic of private miners' rights? Yes, although it may have needed a century to do so fully. So far as we know, no early (pre-Blackstone[18]) nuisance case involved mining—perhaps because of the weak damage remedy in common law and the high cost of an injunction in equity. In any case such obvious nuisances as miners' digging and dumping on a neighbour's land are not found in the court records before 1750. If the reason was not high litigation costs, it might have been that miners' rights in those days already had sufficient exclusivity given the general dispersion and isolation of their mines.

CONTRACT LAW (AND LEASING)

It is surprising that little contracting-based economic analysis has been applied to private mining rights, for miners' contracts to create leases, easements, profits and licences were actually the most important historical source of their powers and obligations. Each contract or lease bound only its two signatory parties, but at any point in post-Norman history there were thousands of them binding. The sanctity of the contract had a long history in England, formal enforcement of contracts having been part of the culture both of Anglo Saxon communities from before the Norman invasion and of the Roman Catholic Church. After 1066 the royal courts of the Norman kings proceeded to develop three forms of action and writs of their own. The first two, the writ of Covenant and the writ of Debt, are of limited interest to this discussion. The third and most important was Assumpsit, which probably arose from general dissatisfaction with the first two.[19] Under this procedure the plaintiff alleged that

[16] Coquilette 1979, from 9 Coke at 58a–59a, 77 E.R. at 821 (citing the *Prior of Southwark's Case* (1498), Y.B. Trin. 13, Henry 7, f. 26, pl. 4, and reprinted in Fifoot 1949, p. 87. The motto *sic utere* was derived from the Roman jurist Ulpian via Justinian in the twelfth century.

[17] Coquilette 1979, p. 821, citing *Bland v. Moseley* (1587) (K.B.).

[18] Coke was cited as the law in *Blackstone's Commentaries* (1765–9).

[19] Plucknett 1956, 633–4.

the defendant had undertaken (assumpsit) to do something but had done it badly (misfeasance) or (after 1505) had evaded or avoided his obligation, perhaps by fraud (nonfeasance). A written contract was not required; the plaintiff had only to show that he had paid in advance or that he had performed his part.

Assumpsit did not go far enough to help a complainant whose agreement did not call for him or her to pay until *after* the defendant had handed over the land. Some judges, in sympathy with the complainants, began to loosen this requirement; others held the line. Inter-court competition for such cases threatened. Finally, in connection with *Slade's Case* (1602),[20] a London meeting of representatives of the competing common-law courts agreed to enforce a contract if the parties had exchanged, or had said they would exchange, valuable consideration. They would, in other words, enforce an alleged contract (even if it was not in writing and even if the plaintiff had not yet performed his part) if it had elements of a barter transaction or quid pro quo. With Assumpsit, contract lost its direct relationship to trespass or tort. Evidence of consideration showed that it was 'reasonable' for the defendant to have made a promise, therefore a contract did exist and therefore the court could enforce it.

I turn to disputes over mining leases and contracts. As discussed above, improvements in the law of property and nuisance had gradually improved the legal position of lessees, including mining lessees, and their complaints did make it to the courts. However, the majority of mining disputes were not about rights to occupy, but instead concerned the meaning of the lease's covenants. Mines were being enlarged and deepened during the terms of a single lease, and miners wanted increasing amounts of space and easier access. Their landlords wanted undertakings to protect the surface and to undertake drainage. Both wanted their lease to contain detailed clauses about such matters—about inspection, rents, royalties, abandonment and lease renewal. Even when leases were specific about these subjects, there was a flow of lawsuits regarding precise meaning and enforcement.

Many covenants had been written in because of uncertainty about where the 'surface' ended and the 'mine' began. This was the general situation of miners' contracts by the middle of the eighteenth century, and it was to lead to the development of surface-rights law in the nineteenth century. As we see below, where the covenants were not clear enough the parties were increasingly subjected to *standardized* miners' 'rights' and 'duties', described or invented by the court as (incidental) rights of property.

Beyond the direct application, the law of contract had a significant impact on the development of mining law in the more subtle sense of its relevance for judicial interpretations of *customary* law—that is, of a right or duty found by

[20] 4 Co. Rep. 92, 76 E.R. 1074.

the court to have been agreed upon in unrecorded, 'reasonable' contracting between an early or original lord and his manorial tenants[21] and to have then persisted through history and across manorial contracts until it became self-evident and generally applicable. With respect to mining rights, the historical accuracy of the theory or fiction of original manorial contracts between tenants and their lords is not as important as is the fact of its employment by parties in seventeenth and eighteenth-century cases. By that time most of the cultivators' rights would have been transferred to and held by modern copyholders (including rival lords, miners or speculators), while their lords would long ago have leased out their rights to mining companies.[22]

Flooding cases and rights

The first of the four main challenges to mineral ownership was underground flooding. Until the sixteenth century the isolation of the miner's small pit protected him from certain kinds of flooding, but did nothing to protect him from 'natural' water problems caused by the penetration of the water table by the first deep mine to arrive in the neighbourhood. Since the water table was geographically large, breaking it was a problem even when, as in the early days, mines were far apart. This was only one of the reasons why in some regions even the earliest miners encountered problems with flooding—in the valleys and in hills of Britain and as well in the lowlands of Flanders, in the Alps and Andes, and even in the American and Mexican deserts.

Flooding could force the abandonment of the reserves at a mine's lower levels. Operational managers faced with this problem often tried to reverse the usual development plan, beginning, as it were, at the bottom and retreating upward as the water level rose beneath them. The losses of ore and coal were lowest in the hills, highest in soggy lowland plains. Most mines did not go deep. In seventeenth-century England and Europe 'the normal procedure in

[21] The word 'manor' covers the several kinds of feudal unit, which include villeins (copyholders, after about 1400), free tenants and landowners, all having a variety of tenurial obligations—military, work and social—to the lord or landlord.

[22] See Macfarlane 1978, pp. 186–7. The seventeenth and eighteenth-century courts adopted a version of the then contemporary idea that private (or social) contract was the key to understanding society, law and the economy. This view was still widely held among legal scholars ('systematizers') in the late nineteenth century, not the least of whom were Maitland, Vinogradoff and Holdsworth. Of course the new wave of political economists, beginning with Smith and Hume, rejected the contractarian idea. Yet even Smith's chapters on the duties of the sovereign (market failure, the role of the public sector) are contractarian in structure. Any claim about the prevalence of local contracts comes up against the actual twelfth-century differences between the manors and villages in the southern (Saxon) regions and those in the northern and eastern (Danish) regions. The idea of local contracts also runs into historical complications when one village had two manors. Thanks to Professor Ian Ross for help on Adam Smith and contractarianism.

attacking silver-bearing ores was to puncture a sloping field with dozens of very shallow pits. As soon as water interfered, a pit was usually abandoned. In this way, hundreds of pits were sometimes sunk in a small area in the space of a few years. Some were so close together that a man could leap the whole distance between them.'[23] Only when silver was pursued by digging shafts did deeper mines—and their associated water problems—become at all common.[24]

To tackle these problems, miners could choose among three general approaches: prevention, gravity draining and lifting (pumping). All three methods were initially very expensive. Draining in particular encouraged high grading and quick extraction in order to reduce draining cost per ton of mineral. The costs encouraged individual operators to look to lifting, adapting the latest pumping engines such as those of Savery (1700), Newcomen (1712) and Watt (1769). The initial expense of installing and operating a steam pump was increased by the royalty on the coal it consumed. But as this cost fell and the reliability of the engines increased, vertical lifting began seriously to compete with horizontal drainage by soughs and adits.

Prevention of damage

COLLECTIVE ACTION BY CONTRACTING: 'COMMAND' VENTURES

Managing a rising water table provides perhaps the classic example of a nonrivalrous public-good (or bad) action. The remedy—pumping or soughing out the water—was subject to the classic problem of free riding among the independently owned mines in a neighbourhood. The solution required collective action. My sources cannot tell me the frequency of such group action undertakings, referred to in many districts as 'command' drainage ventures. The law books and the mining histories tell more stories of districts being flooded together than of pumping together.[25] The following discussion is therefore quite anecdotal.

The first English record I have found concerning collective action is a three-way drainage equal-shares agreement dating from 1407, involving two church landowners and the Blakeston family, in the coal lands of Hett, Durham, to undertake a watergate drainage project.[26] We also find impressive examples of such sharing from Warwickshire and Scotland: 'A sough in Warwickshire running west of Blackwell and Teversal commenced in 1703 was gradually extended until in 1774 it ran for a total length of five miles and had its roof supported by a single line of pit props. Because its cost was shared between several owners it clearly drained a number of pits.'[27] Fordell coal mine in Fife,

[23] Nef 1952 and 1987, pp. 723–4, relying on an article by Schmuller for this information.
[24] See references to Agricola in Chapters 6 and 7 above.
[25] Gough 1967. [26] Galloway 1904, p. 69. [27] Flinn 1984, p. 111.

Scotland was drained by an adit of three and one-half miles, which, with two miles of extensions, drained six pits in all.[28]

It was possible for one relatively small-scale miner to construct a sough such as one bored in a coalfield near Wigan. Such initiatives proved 'a fertile field for disputes'[29] about shared benefits and costs. Bankes, author of a study of this Lancashire coal district, provides information on two hundred years of disputes. It appears that a drainage system was organized and conducted on communal lines from 1573 to 1792, enabling a doubling of output between 1600 and 1700.[30]

Powerful mining interests in a district urged their neighbours to join in centralized drainage operations. The Lowther family, who started coal mining on the coast in Cumberland in the sixteenth century, were command drainage boosters. Writing of the Whitehaven region in the 1630s, John Lowther noted regretfully that, up to that time, development had been hindered by mine fragmentation among small freeholds. Consequently, the needed but costly soughs did not get built. They would have had to be driven through the lands of several people and this would have led to free riding by enabling 'such as have none of the charge to under sell and ruin those who did, so that the working of them under these circumstances was injusticiable and they were lost as well to the owners as to the country'.[31]

While it is not known to what extent changing social pressure encouraged miners to abandon free riding and commit to social projects, we do know that such failures as Lowther mentioned in the seventeenth century were still the rule in the nineteenth century.[32] The Percy Main colliery is a good example. The large and old colliery near Newcastle was working away at the pillars of coal left from previous years. In 1838 water flooded in and 'overpowered' the pumps. The management prepared to dam the feeders (or points) of inflow. But, fearing that this damming would not work, they also sent around a circular inviting nearby mines to meet and to inspect the dams. It seems the neighbouring mines were no longer sealed from one another, so that if one became flooded, they all would: 'The obvious intention of the circular,

[28] Flinn 1984, p. 111. [29] Bankes 1939, p. 33. [30] Id., p. 61.

[31] Hatcher 1993, pp. 115 and 215, citing an 1878 collection of Cumberland documents. Perhaps to avoid this problem, in 1662 the Lowther family began to drive their own 1800-yard level (sough) nearby to drain several of their own coal properties. They held a very long lease from a charity school on much of the district. One of their soughs remained in use for 200 years.

[32] In the late 1500s the Willoughby coalfields in Nottinghamshire were challenged by Nicholas Strelley an owner whose coal lands adjoined Willoughby's: 'Squabbles inevitably ensued, not least because the Wollaton sough was essential for the drainage of all pits in the area, and litigation remorselessly proceeded to Star Chamber, with claims and counter-claims of trespass and sabotage. An agreement was finally entered into which entitled Willoughby to the lion's share of the output of Strelley's collieries in return for allowing the use of his sough.' Hatcher 1993 p. 167. This appears to have been the rare case in which the provider of the drainage could threaten to cut off the neighbour's use.

therefore, was to induce these respective owners to agree to raise a joint fund for the building of a monster [steam-pumping] engine upon Percy Main colliery.'[33] The meeting did take place, but the neighbours used the occasion to criticize the working away of the old pillars below river level. Consequently, the Percy Main owners were forced to add their own large engines to the two already at work, these remaining until the mine finally closed in 1852.

Neighbours could always find some such reason for not working together. The Percy Main's neighbours seem to have perceived the owners' scheme as a threat rather than as an opportunity. But the costs of not cooperating could be substantial. A poignant example comes from the Mexican silver-mining district of Zacatecas. In 1640 Don Bartolomé Bravo de Acuña acquired a group of four mines, long flooded and abandoned. By somehow linking and draining the four he made a fortune,[34] demonstrating to the regional mining community what circumventing free-riding problems could achieve. Yet despite Bravo's example, most other miners did not take collective action. Entrepreneurs 'had the greatest difficulty' in persuading groups to cooperate in pumping water. In one case, pumps were placed 'but the other miners failed to supply the slaves they had promised to work them. Suspicion that the other party to any agreement would gain more from it than he would seems to have prevented the Zacatacan miner from joining with his neighbours in drainage and tunnelling projects for most of the seventeenth century.'[35]

The most famous tale of a failed 'command drainage venture' in the nineteenth century also comes from the New World: the attempt at multi-mine drainage cooperation envisioned in the Sutro Tunnel planned for the Comstock lode near Virginia City (in what is now Nevada), then the source of half the gold and silver produced in the United States.[36] After a business career elsewhere, Adolph Sutro had invented a milling and concentrating process for Comstock tailings and new ore. He became convinced that at least 10 per cent of Virginia City mines needed drainage to free them from the outpourings of 'subterranean springs'. The mines were then relying on steam pumps. To drain them by gravity, Sutro proposed an unusual project: a tunnel to be started in a valley seven miles away and to run to a level two thousand feet below the Comstock surface. The tunnel would incidentally provide an underground route for outward or inward transportation of ore, waste and workers.

Sutro faced financial problems caused by his anticipated free rider problem. While each mine operation, already holding claims under mining-camp law (subsequently validated by the General Mining Law 1866) was enthusiastic about being drained, none was legally bound either to pay for this service or to provide capital. In 1864–5 the owners did approve Sutro's project, but

[33] Dunn 1852, p. 265. [34] Id., p. 135. [35] Id., p. 136.

[36] The tunnel project, and Adolph Sutro himself, are referred to in many places. See especially Stewart and Stewart 1962; and Libecap 1978.

non-commitally. To make his position firmer, in 1865 Sutro persuaded the Nevada legislature to grant him an exclusive right of way for a tunnel and also to require the Virginia City mines to pay him a royalty of two dollars per ton of ore extracted. The following year he persuaded Congress to re-grant his exclusive tunnelling right and to require that the mines not free ride. Even these guarantees were not sufficient to induce investors to finance Sutro's expected five to eight years of excavation until eventually investment funds arrived from England and from the new Virginia City Miners Union (which was pleased that the tunnel promised improved underground conditions for workers).[37]

In addition to his free-riding problem, Sutro faced competition from owners and their affiliates seeking an alternative drainage system to his tunnel. The exclusivity of his tunnel charters did not prevent the mines he hoped to drain from developing their own pumping systems. And the underground transportation he hoped to offer the mines was forestalled by a surface railroad. These substitutes eroded his eventual market. Every month without a tunnel created a decline in the ore he planned to share. When after eight years of excavation the tunnel reached them, some mines' operations had gone below the tunnel level and some were depleted and even abandoned. The remaining mines resented Sutro's project and tried to escape paying a full royalty.

IMPROVING LANDLORDS AND SOLE OWNERS

Of course, a promoter of collective multi-mine drainage could avoid free riding and competition if he had the powers of a landlord. According to Nef, the European noble landlords, whose own large land holdings included numerous mines each under the control of its own lessee, 'found it desirable not to leave such matters to the numerous groups of concessionaires, to be dealt with piecemeal by each group [i.e., partnership]. It was recognized that the drainage of a mining field was actually a single task, which could be met most effectively by a single drainage system'.[38] The pay-off of a comprehensive improvement was well-known, and the European landowners who initiated one were able to attract the contributions of the 'great merchant-financiers of the Renaissance'. These investors accepted shares in the ventures whose pits they helped to drain.[39]

In England owners who invested in the profitability of their lessees' mines were known as improving landlords. Examples proliferate of their large-scale drains for coal, iron, tin, lead and copper. Raistrick provides some details of the de-watering of the lead district of Wharfedale, West Yorkshire.[40] In the

[37] The two-dollar royalty should be seen in light of the fact that the mines were then estimated to be paying ten dollars per ton for pumping. On financing by the royalty and by the miner's union, see Libecap 1978, p. 239.

[38] Nef 1952 and 1987, p. 744.

[39] Ibid. [40] Raistrick 1953, p. 14, and Raistrick 1973.

second half of the eighteenth century the dukes of Devonshire took over the region from the Earls of Burlington and became active developing lead mills and building other facilities. Among these was a three-mile sough, draining perhaps two hundred forty feet below the duke's tenants' lowest drifts, relieving his mines of pumping expense and freeing water power for the mills. New shafts were connected to each other and to the sough, all leased out to new operating partnerships and companies. It seems from Raistrick's account that waiting for individual mines to voluntarily join in coordinated or collective drainage would have been costly.

By the nineteenth century large projects were often shared by the great landowner and his single large-scale mining lessee. 'An important example [of mine owners and landowners combining] . . . was the arrangement of Newton Chambers and Co. and the Earl Fitzwilliam, who together financed a 2,770-metre sough driven for the purpose of draining the Park Gate and Silkstone Seams of coal in South Yorkshire. The cost amounted to £10,000 and the project took six years, beginning in 1838.'[41] Large scale projects also became the domain of corporations. By the seventeenth century, if not earlier (as with the Elizabethan Mines Royal Joint-Stock Company and the Mineral and Battery Joint-Stock Company),[42] private corporations were undertaking multi-mine operations that were large enough to justify deep-mine drainage for all. In 1720 the London Lead Company used its provision of drainage to acquire for itself a position as the de facto manager or owner of an entire lead-mining field in Derbyshire.[43] It took over flooded workings, drained them, explored for deeper veins and ran in soughs.

Though they represented a way around free riding, sole owners' great projects required a great deal of capital. They took on more risk than would have been shouldered by individual parties to a joint project. Their success was threatened by technological or logistic miscalculations and by changes in the industry over the time taken to construct the sough; 'often when [a sough] finally reached the ore veins it proved too high to drain the deeper workings'.[44] Still, sole ownership of regional mining operations in general seems to have made the undertaking of drainage ventures more efficient and lends some weight to arguments in favour of 'natural monopoly'.

[41] Church 1986, p. 320.

[42] Two near-monopolies, established chiefly to mine copper and zinc ores and convert them into brass sheets and rods.

[43] The company relied on a 1629 precedent in the Peak District of Derbyshire, in the Crown-owned mining district. In that case, Sir Cornelius Vermuyden had tackled the flooded Dovegang lead mine. In 1665 the miner's court had given him working rights (as against the free miners to whom the mine belonged), which led in time to the local acceptance of a rule that anyone putting forward a practical scheme for sough drainage could acquire possession. This rule attracted the large London Lead Company, already active in Wales, to the district.

[44] Millward and Robinson 1975, pp. 200–1. Much of this paragraph has been derived from these authors.

MANDATORY COOPERATION AND CONTRACTING

It is rather surprising that the Victorian parliament, which had not hesitated to give powers of compulsory purchase (expropriation) to canals, railways and water suppliers, did not also provide analogous legislation to protect mining promoters' drainage works from free riding. Doing so might have created mine-drainage enterprises with procedures to acquire the land and powers to drain whole districts free of rivals and free riders. In the United States several state governments showed what could be done to encourage drainage. Arizona and Colorado statutes provided for elaborate systems of joint drainage by adjacent owners; Iowa prescribed a royalty to be paid to those ridding a mine of water; a Missouri statute compelled the mine owner either to drain for the benefit of his licensees or to lose his remedy for rent collection.[45]

That such legislation never appeared in England apparently reflected a deficiency of demand. No powerful lobby in England pressed the government to supply rights or institutions that would have given their users *exclusivity* to solve the free-riding and capital-risk problems.[46] The examples of successful English railway charters and American drainage laws show that the lobbying, contracting and organization costs were unlikely to have been prohibitive. Perhaps the majority of mining firms wanted nothing to do with government-supported monopoly. Or perhaps, by the railway age, the firms in the most vulnerable coal districts had already completed cooperative drainage arrangements, had seen them imposed by their sole landowners, or simply foresaw that in the future pumping technologies would be private rather than collective.

The general lesson of this subsection is clear. Where there were divided property rights to a widespread water table, collective tunnelling action rarely emerged or, if it did emerge, met with trouble. Some property holders opted to become free riders on someone else's drainage operations. Others no doubt were deterred from contracting by a lack of information about the amount and division of the total net benefit among the various holders, relative to their costs and benefits without the project. A few examples do exist of field-wide

[45] See examples in Barringer and Adams 1897.

[46] There was Victorian legislation, but it was not to encourage or replace private agreement on drainage, and the statutory regimes created seem to have been both very limited in scope and specific in application. MacSwinney 1907, pp. 537–8, and MacSwinney 1912, p. 72n, refers to legislation to distribute land within the Forest of Dean mines and within certain coal fields (see 1 and 2 Vict. c. 43.) It was expected to lead to arbitration-like awards. In fact, the awards went beyond land distribution to set out surprising arrangements backing the granting of water easements to conduct flood waters. The awards also made rules imposing duties on higher mines not to flood adjacent lower mines. Together these provisions amounted to legislative support for private drainage cooperation. However, they applied only to certain Crown estates in the Forest of Dean and elsewhere. Like the Railways Clauses Act 1845 the Waterworks Clauses Act 1847 and the Railways and Canals Traffic Act 1888 they did not set out to impose responsibilities that would protect the holders of private lands from flooding.

success in voluntary collaboration. Most often, however, success depended on there being some kind of a sole owner. He may have been the landlord of the various independent mines in the field, or he may have been a multi-mine operator. Regardless, the greater exclusivity he enjoyed provided him a practical ability to undertake projects that individual owner-miners on individual holdings could not.

Litigation: property and nuisance

The new technologies and the related economic and physical changes that transformed mining in the eighteenth and nineteenth centuries cut away the miner's natural isolation and increased his exposure to inter-mine flooding—potentially a legal rather than a managerial problem. The increased mining activity, carried on by increasingly intrusive mining procedures, touched off an increasing number of legal disputes.

One might perhaps have expected that the inherent externality problem of flooding—that a new mine adjoining an older mine with a flooded system of tunnels and shafts often found itself overwhelmed by easily identifiable floodwaters from next door—would induce copious legal recourse and eventually regulatory legislation. But there is no record of such a new working suing the owners of an older, abandoned working. It seems the potential flooding of new mines, especially lower mines, was discounted in advance in their leasing arrangements.

In fact, questions of property (seisin and possession) would not have been key issues of liability in flooding disputes. It was becoming clear that property law was best reserved for questions of *title* whereas mine-flooding disputes—regardless of how the mineral estate was defined in the lease—were questions of *nuisance*. But not until 1849, in *Smith v. Kenrick*,[47] would the new general law of nuisance gain application to mine-flooding disputes. Before that time the relevant parts of nuisance law had been developing to deal with pollution, not flooding. As well, Coke's threshold test was being interpreted within the changing context of industrialization. The legal interpretations of 'necessity' and 'unreasonable' changed with the nineteenth-century transition from a rural to an urban society,[48] even as the wording of the rule itself remained constant. The uncertainty created by the shifting definitions possibly discouraged potential litigants.

Eventually, however, nuisance cases did begin making their way to the courts. They obliged the courts to alter their rules for deciding liability, either explicitly or through a building up of precedent interpreting Coke's initial *sic utere* rule. As we will see, the courts chose mainly the latter and their rulings were inconsistent. In a series of cases involving brick-burning nuisance cases

[47] *Smith v. Kenrick* (1849), 7 C.B. 515, 137 E.R. 205.

[48] Brenner 1974, p. 409.

in the mid-nineteenth century, the courts moved toward a 'balance of utilities' doctrine[49] in which the marginal value of brick-burning industry was considered against the rights and losses of the victim of the externality produced by the brickyard. *Hole v. Barlow* (1858)[50] yielded wide latitude to the rights of industry, while *Bamford v. Turnley* (1862)[51] reversed some of these gains to favour the victim. (The reader will note the similarity of this balancing approach to the contemporaneous 'reasonable' approach in water-rights cases in Chapter 3.)

The basic precedent enshrined in these cases also brings back the search for *custom*. The custom concerned was that the modern industrial defendant should be required not to emit a spillover more harmful than what was typical or customary among people in his trade or activity, or more arduous than what could be roughly justified by his contribution to industry and society.

Though for a time the common-law courts showed sympathy to polluting industries, they soon swung back to favour the defendant (or at least to favour the defendant whose property owning was of significant value) by the introduction and implicit enshrining of the 'utilitarian balance' concept in *St Helen's Smelting Co. v. William Tipping* (1865).[52] The company emitted fumes; the complainant lived nearby in a fine estate. The House of Lords (as a court) implicitly endorsed a 'greatest good' principle by weighing the potential loss of jobs and output at the smelter against Tipping's diminished comfort and enjoyment of his estate. It found the latter to be the more serious. It also introduced a distributive-justice idea; that is, that some people in some places had more to lose than similar people in other places and that wealth could confer a stake sufficient to outweigh the 'good' attendant on the smelter's staying open.

This case was very influential. Wealthy landlords saw in it a pronounced improvement in their legal position relative to that of the industrialists. In succeeding cases, the relative *exclusivity* characteristic of industry's land-using rights rose and fell as nuisance decisions favoured and disfavoured industrial defendants.

Contemporarily in the United States, Coke's doctrine also formed the basis of the law of nuisance. As in England, the rule was given an increasingly permissive interpretation throughout the nineteenth century as the courts took into account the same considerations as had the English courts in the brick-burning cases and in *St Helen's Smelting*. As in England, it would be wrong to try to pick a precise date when American courts overthrew *sic utere* in favour of a more defendant-oriented utilitarian rule. Mortimer Horwitz notes how the

[49] Brenner 1974, p. 403.
[50] *Hole v. Barlow* (1858), 4 C.B. (N.S.) 334, 140 E.R. 1113 (C.P.).
[51] *Bamford v. Turnley* (1862), 3 B. & S. 62, 122 E.R. 25.
[52] *St Helen's Smelting Co. v. Tipping* (1865), 11 H.L.C. 642, 11 E.R. 1483.

Kentucky Court of Appeal balanced utilities in the railway case *Lexington & Ohio Rail Road v. Applegate* as early as 1839, but he admits the case stands alone in the pre-Civil War United States.[53] In general, he argues, the strict liability *sic utere* rule dominated during the 'first stage' up to the 1860s. During a 'second stage', he claims that judges began to regard the by-products of economically productive public works as reasonable *by definition*.[54] Throughout the century judges continued to regard conflicts between private parties as subject to the *sic utere* rule, with an ever-stronger seasoning of economic reasonableness, utilitarian balance or both.

American law did strike out to produce a new rule in the twentieth century, an explicit balancing of utilities, as summarized in the American Law Institute's influential *Restatement of Torts* (1939).[55] The *Restatement* defined nuisance as a 'non-trespassory invasion of another's interest in the use and enjoyment of land'. The 'invasion' could be 'intentional' or 'unintentional'. Where a person committed an unintentional invasion, tort rules determining negligent or reckless conduct or abnormally dangerous conditions or activities would apply. Where a person committed an intentional invasion, liability would accrue where the invasion was *unreasonable*—that is, where the utility of the actor's conduct did not outweigh the gravity of the harm he imposed.

[53] See Horwitz 1977, p. 75. 'The law is made for the times, and will be made or modified by them. The expanded and still expanding genius of the common law should adapt it here, as elsewhere, to the improved and improving conditions of our country and our countrymen. And therefore, railroads and locomotive steam-cars—the offsprings, as they will be also the parents, of progressive improvement—should not, in themselves, be considered as nuisances, although, in ages that are gone, they might have been so held, because they would have been comparatively useless, and therefore more mischievous.' *Lexington and Ohio Rail Road v. Applegate*, 8 Dana 289 at 309 (Ky. 1839).

[54] Horwitz 1977, p. 102. Horwitz's perception (of a fairly sharp transition from a stage of English common law that protects traditional and agricultural rural land or stream uses to one in which the judges protected developmental uses) is examined and denied by some later writers. A sharp transition is scarcely visible in nuisance cases in the heavily industrialized mining regions of England, nor is it in American nuisance law applied to mining, although mining law has not been extensively researched. Instead, the modern controversy has focused on Horwitz's interpretation of the stage-like evolution of both property and nuisance law as illustrated by water diversions (see Chapter 3 for more discussion). Among the important critics of Horwitz's thesis is Alan Watson 1990, who asserts that Horwitz misunderstands the English nuisance rules with which he is comparing the changing American law. John Martin 1991 argues that Horwitz is wrong to imply that the changes in water law in New England were matched by changes in other US industrializing states.

[55] The 1939 Restatement balance of utilities test was endorsed by William Prosser in his influential *Handbook on the Law of Torts* (1941) and has been adopted by many American states. A majority of eastern coal-producing states have expressly adopted this doctrine, although it appears that a comprehensive evaluation of its influence has not been conducted (and is certainly beyond the scope of my project here). See Lewin 1990.

Nuisance and inter-mine flooding

SMITH V. KENRICK (1849)

From the preceding survey of the emergence of the exclusivity characteristic in general nuisance law, I turn to its parallels in the specific area of mine flooding. Consider first *Smith v. Kenrick* (1849), which established the liability rule in nuisance for inter-mine flooding in England, and soon after in the United States.[56] As with so many leading cases, the facts in *Smith v. Kenrick* were strange—almost bizarre—and bear close examination. Possibly it was the strangeness that brought the conflict to court. There was certainly no general agreement about the direction that the ruling would take.

The plaintiff Smith's mine (A) was adjacent to and on a lower level than the defendant Kenrick's mine (B). Before Kenrick 'became possessed' of B (one presumes that Kenrick was a lessee), someone called Jones had owned the rights to it. During his possession Jones had made three large holes, called thyrlings, in and through a vertical seam of coal within the border of mine A. This seam otherwise formed a barrier between the chambers of mine A and mine B. When Kenrick took over mine B, there was a large quantity of water in an upper part of his mine, which was fed by springs in the vicinity, perhaps on the surface. This water was separated from the lower, working chamber of mine B by a thick horizontal bar of coal (within and part of mine B). The defendant Kenrick knew that the thyrlings were open and that the effect of removing the horizontal bar within his own mine would be a flow of water down through his chambers, through the thyrlings and into mine A. Nevertheless the defendant did puncture the horizontal bar in order to take the coal, thus 'working his mine in the manner most advantageous to himself'. Consequently, mine A was inundated and its owner sued Kendrick.

In court, the main issue[57] was whether a 'general liability ought to be imposed on the defendant to be responsible for injury done to an adjoining [mine by] water casually introduced into his own, in the course of working it'.[58] There was no indication that the defendant miner was negligent, merely that he had worked his mine in the manner most advantageous to himself.

Rejecting precedents invoked by the plaintiffs,[59] the *Smith* court treated the legal question at stake as essentially novel. However, Cranworth, J. (encountered in *St Helen's Smelting*) held that the principle from *Acton v. Blundell* (1843)[60] was

[56] See Bainbridge 1900, p. 630.

[57] Another minor question was whether the earlier trespass of Jones had imposed some kind of duty on Kenrick. The court found that it did not.

[58] *Smith v. Kenrick* at 223.

[59] These included *Tenant v. Goldwin* (1705), in which the defendant had been found liable for filth from his privy flowing into the plaintiff's cellar, and two previous mine-flooding cases *Haward v. Bankes* (1760) (which involved the same defendant as in the present case, but for which no citation is given) and *Firmstone v. Wheeler*.

[60] *Acton v. Blundell* (1843), 12 M. & W. 324.

applicable. In that case, the improper sinking of a coal pit had the effect of draining water from a neighbour's well:

> We think the same principle is applicable to the present case. The water is a sort of common enemy... against which each man must defend himself. And this is in accordance with the civil [Roman] law, by which it was considered that land on a lower level, owed a natural servitude to that on a higher, in respect of receiving, without claim to compensate, the water naturally flowing down to it.[61]

Leaving aside considerations of support (see next subsection), the owner of an upper mine was entitled to work and remove the entirety of his coal; he would not be liable for any subsequent damage to a lower mine caused by the subsequent natural flow or percolation of water. Cranworth J. said that to find otherwise would be to find that the plaintiff, by working all of his coal (and so removing the vertical barrier) could abridge the defendant's right to work his mine. The 'reasonable thing' for the plaintiff and similarly situated miners to do was to leave a barrier of his own coal to protect his workings: 'It is the custom for the miners on the rise to work for their boundary, and for the miners on the dip to leave a barrier of from six to ten yards to protect them against the water from the mine on the rise.'[62] And this, of course, is what the plaintiff had done; unfortunately, his barrier had been made ineffective by the wrongdoer Jones—for whose act, the court found, the defendant was not responsible.

In a sense, this decision was of a piece with the *St Helen's Smelting* decision discussed above. As in general law, the mining defendant might now plead that a spillover arose from the ordinary practice of his industry in his area. A dictum in *St Helen's Smelting* noted that a plaintiff in an industrial city ought to expect industrial fumes. Similarly, the decision in *Smith v. Kenrick* implied that a plaintiff in an area where mines filled up with water should expect to have to protect himself from flooding. In particular, he should not depend on an exclusivity characteristic in his rights to protect him.

The judgment also strengthened a trend toward utilitarianism,[63] as was also being observed in other, more prevalent, types of nuisance disputes between

[61] *Smith v. Kenrick* at 565. [62] *Clegg v. Dearden* (1848), 12 Q.B. 576 at 995.

[63] The trend of mining law has an interesting parallel with the trend of cattle-fencing rules. Coke's decision had reinforced the older 'fence-in' rule: an owner was liable for the damage done by his cattle if he did not fence them in. In the eighteenth century this rule was carried to the United States and, in the eastern states, strengthened by legislation. However, later, in the western states, courts and legislatures reversed the earlier rule: grain farmers now had to accept a fencing-out responsibility. The usual explanation, from politicians and analysts alike, turned on the nature of cattle ranching in the west. In the west it cost more to fence the sprawling range lands than it did in the east, the value of grain was relatively lower, and the cost of identifying the owner of straying cattle was higher. Following Ellickson (1991), we can say that a fencing rule will differ from place to place, or over time, as though the courts and legislatures were trying to keep down the total of the costs of fencing and transactions. See also Centner and Griffin 1998 and Centner 1997 for a survey of statutory fencing laws.

industrialists and landowners. Each mine might originally have been responsible for preventing its water from ever pouring, in any direction, into any other mine. But the cost justification for this rule gradually disappeared as the density and depth of new, old and abandoned mines increased. Eventually, it would be cheaper for a new mine to be kept dry during the years it was in operation than for the abandoned levels of old neighbouring mines to be kept dry indefinitely. Putting the cost burden on the new mines would also reduce one kind of transaction and information cost: identifying which of several surrounding old mines should be sued when water flowed into a new mine.

Custom may also have developed to keep disputes out of the courts. In the judgment in *Smith v. Kenrick* we hear about the custom permitting the upper mine to work to the boundary. This may have been only one of what Ellickson calls the 'norms' that had evolved in the mining 'culture'. Other norms might have dealt with splitting costs, access, townsite or labour policy. The relative shortness of a mine's life would have affected mining customs and culture in two opposing ways. It would have encouraged a separate culture, as the frequent shifts of operations to new sites would give the operators more lasting professional relationships with each other than with their temporary rural neighbours. Yet it would have worked against the building of a continuing relationship between neighbouring mines, as their relationship was often too short for them to build up trust in the eventual balancing of reciprocal favours and debts. At present, one can only note that the absence of lawsuits and the judicial mention of 'customs' are both consistent with the existence of a mining culture within which respect for flooding norms took some of the place of court enforcement.[64]

RYLANDS V. FLETCHER

Around 1770, in the time of Blackstone, mine-flooding law was in general harmony with Coke's strict liability rule: a defendant must not by his actions on his own property harm a 'necessity' of the plaintiff's property (the 'necessity' being freedom from being flooded). Still, mining law did not actually lead to this precise result. *Smith v. Kenrick* and the decisions that followed it sidestepped the Coke rule by defining the defendant mine as a passive bystander that was not causing, but merely suffering, a flow of water for which it was not responsible and over which (legally) it had no control. This definition gave the flooded miner lesser rights than comparable victims of, say, smoke, fumes or smells.

[64] For a comment on cultural norms as solutions to fencing situations, see Karsten 1998. He examines whether the parties came from the same culture (as do miners in flooded ground and adjoining ranchers). But ranchers and farmers, or miners and farmers, do not. In these circumstances we expect to find few customs and much litigation. See below; and Centner 1997.

In *Rylands v. Fletcher* (1868),[65] the court made an effort to remedy this gap and swing the law somewhat back in favour of the 'victim' (the miner suffering the flooding externality). If a person brought a thing onto his land that would not naturally be there, one that was 'ultra hazardous'—dangerous or liable to cause mischief if not kept under proper control—then he would be liable for damages if it escaped, regardless of whether or not he was wilful or negligent.

The plaintiff Rylands was a flooded miner. But, crucially, the flooding had not come from another mine. Rylands' leased mines had been worked to a point where certain old disused passages were filled with marl and earth. Fletcher, whose mill adjoined Rylands' mining leasehold, had constructed a reservoir on his own land. Shortly after he introduced water into the reservoir, the water broke through and flooded some of the passages in Rylands' mine. Rylands sued Fletcher.

Although the court took some trouble to distinguish the facts in Rylands from those in previous mining cases, it went on to apply the mining rule: the defendant was at fault if the damage that occurred was not 'natural' or if the things that he did were not 'ordinary'. Indeed Lord Cairns, discussing the 'extremely simple' principles he was relying upon, drew on two mine-flooding cases, *Kenrick* and *Baird v. Williamson* (1863). The modern general rule in *Rylands* thus extended the nineteenth-century common-law rules about mine flooding:

> The Defendants... might lawfully have used that close for any purpose for which it might in the ordinary course of the enjoyment of land be used; and if, in what I may term the natural use of the land, there had been any accumulation of water, either on the surface or underground, and if, by the operation of the laws of nature, that accumulation of water had passed off into the close occupied by the Plaintiff, the Plaintiff could not have complained... If he desired to guard himself against it, it would have lain upon him to have done so, by leaving, or by interposing, some barrier between... to have prevented that operation of the laws of nature.
>
> On the other hand if the Defendants... had desired to use it [their close] for any... non-natural use... for the purpose of introducing water either above or below ground in quantities and in a manner not the result of any work or operation on or under the land,—and if in consequence of their doing so... the water came to escape and pass off into the close of the Plaintiff, then it appears to me that that which the Defendants were doing they were doing at their own peril; and, if in the course of doing it, the evil arose... of the escape of the water and its passing away to the close of the Plaintiff and injuring the Plaintiff, then for the consequences of that, in my opinion, the Defendants would be liable. As the case of *Smith v. Kenrick* is an illustration of the first principle... so also the second principle... is well illustrated by another case in the same Court, the case of *Baird v. Williamson* (1863) [15 C.B.N.S. 376, 143 E.R. 83].
>
> [In the latter case] the Defendant, the owner of the upper mine, did not merely suffer the water to flow through his mine without leaving a barrier between it and the mine below,

[65] *Rylands v. Fletcher* (1868), L.R. 3, H.L. 3330.

but in order to work his own mine beneficially he pumped up quantities of water which had passed into the Plaintiff's mine in addition to that which would have naturally reached it, and so occasioned him damage. Though this was done without negligence, and in the due working of his own mine, yet he was held to be responsible for the damage so occasioned.[66]

Rylands v. Fletcher was a mining-law case but its judgment for the plaintiff reached far beyond mining. The new rule was quite quickly applied to a wide range of other hazardous activities, stemming from water, sewage, fires, gas, electricity, fumes, explosives, trees and any activity 'not a matter of common usage'.[67] Today, discussants seem to have forgotten that this rule originated in mining and in nuisance, preferring to write about it as coming from 'bursting reservoir' or wild-animal precedents[68] and as being concerned with accidents and negligence. This neglect may be justified on the grounds that, owing to the defendant coming from outside the mining industry, it actually offered no remedy to the real problem faced by most aggrieved plaintiff miners—flooding from adjacent mines—and condemned them to continue building their own barriers to fence out waters pouring down 'naturally'.

CONTRACT LAW AND MANDATORY COOPERATION

What did contract law offer to disputes about mine flooding? Even if neighbouring operators did not specifically write contracts together, one might imagine that flooding would be amenable to resolution by a kind of enforced 'reasonable' compromise or cooperation between mines, such as a duty to take reasonable care not to cause flooding. But such a duty, which would have decidedly reduced the exclusivity of each mining party's rights, never developed in the courts. The individual mineral estate remained, for the purposes of flooding disputes, highly exclusive, with the applicable legal rules tightly focused on the rights of the individual miner (usually the flooding party), just as they were for the broader class of externality-inducing industrialists.

In the absence of any mandatory rule requiring cooperation, private cooperation schemes, whether casual or formal, could have offered workable solutions to the problem of mine flooding. The agreements would have set out the rights and liabilities of particular neighbouring parties. Perhaps such arrangements did exist; unless they broke down, they would not have shown up in the law reports.[69] If this were indeed the case, we might reason that the hard

[66] *Rylands v. Fletcher*, [1871–73] All E.R. 1 at 12–14.

[67] The phraseology of the *Second Restatement of Torts*.

[68] Ibid.; Halsbury 4th edn. 1973, vol. 34, para. 341.

[69] Merely calling for compulsory participation would not solve these questions. While governments have typically paid for agricultural irrigation and drainage schemes and similar projects with revenue from a property tax based on a measure of farm benefits (i.e., farm size or farm value), they would find no such easy bases in a mine-drainage tax. The distribution of revenues among mines does not necessarily reflect the distribution of damage or of drainage costs by alternative methods.

nuisance custom being applied to inter-mine flooding (as in *Smith v. Kenrick*) actually worked to prevent flooding. Neighbouring miners who wanted to avoid the consequences of the all-or-nothing regime envisioned by the ruling might be driven to contract with one another.[70]

An example of judicial encouragement of contracting and cooperation (though not in a mine-externality case) is found in the twentieth-century case *Leakey v. National Trust* (1980), on the extent of an owner's duty to prevent a neighbour being injured by a natural accident.[71] Discussing the burdens of such a duty, Megaw L. J. offered the hypothetical example of small proprietors on a river charged with the duty to prevent flood-waters harming their neighbours. If the flooding can be easily prevented by minor expenditures the landowner would be '... in breech of duty if he does nothing or does too little. But if the only remedy is substantial and expensive works, then it might well be that the land-owner would have discharged his duty by saying to his neighbours, who also know of the risk and who have asked him to do something about it, "You have my permission to come onto my land and to do agreed works at your expense", or it may be, "on the basis of a fair sharing of expense".' The court is arguing that placing all the duty to take action on one party, up to what is reasonable for that party, need not be burdensome and might provide incentives for the parties to cooperate. By such language, it is suggesting joint action organized by a contract.

In providing incentives, 'might' is the operative word: it was shown earlier that miners who might have contracted with one another to produce a joint drainage operation frequently failed to do so. In general, neither the courts nor the legislators were prepared to compel the other mines to participate in such projects. Moreover, although they might, as in *Leakey*, use their choice of remedy to influence whether parties worked together, they generally edged away from making cooperation a condition of their award scheme. Such problems probably also help explain the common law's failure to develop anything like a 'correlative rights' doctrine for coordinating and harmonizing owners' interests in drainage. More positive state statutory intervention, for instance that in the Sutro tunnel case described earlier, would have required the government to function as had the great English landlords ('sole owners'), compelling their individual miner lessee tenants to coordinate or finance their individual contributions to a total drainage scheme. One can think of many combinations of compulsory levies and government management.

The courts' relative unwillingness to encourage cooperation not only for joint drainage works, but also in order to achieve economies of scale in daily mine operations and to prevent the need for costly self-protection, is

[70] In my sample of mine leases (see Chapter 5, fn. 1), the lessee typically undertakes not to do anything that would tend to drown the mine. See also MacSwinney 1912, p. 249.

[71] *Leakey v. National Trust* (1980), Q.B. 485, [1980] 1 All E.R. 17. Also see Chapter 12.

difficult to explain. There is not yet enough evidence to decisively conclude that the lower courts failed to support efficient industry practices. In light of the infrequency of mining nuisance cases, consider some other possible explanations:

Litigation costs. Conceivably, litigation may have been so costly relative to the costs of prevention—either pumping already accumulated water or simply leaving a barrier of untouched coal to separate the mines—that the courts were rarely presented with the opportunity to forge a law encouraging cooperation in mining.

Penalties and remedies. We know little of the remedies imposed in the lightly reported cases. It may be that courts did skilfully impose them so as to bring about a low-cost joint handling of flooding dangers.

Custom. Litigation may have been avoided because in many mining districts 'customs of the trade' existed by which miners guided their actions. Mine operators were professionals who often worked together; they may have developed an ethic about flood prevention. (On the other hand, their employers were probably strangers to each other and without exposure to custom.) On balance, one finds it hard to believe that neighbouring mines never worked together, regardless of what got said in court or written into law.

Transactions costs to cooperation. Part of the observed enthusiastic welcome for the steam pump may have been caused by the realization that it permitted mines to keep dry without the transaction-costs of coordination with other mines. No matter how the courts cajoled, inter-mine drainage coordination would have been especially difficult when neighbouring mines commenced or ceased operations in different periods.

Surface rights

Of this chapter's four mineral ownership issues, that of 'surface rights' has the longest history, though it is also the most quintessentially modern problem. The surface owner's rights are exclusive up to a point. Beyond that point the miner has rights. Finding where that point is, and enforcing it, is probably the prototype of all miners' property problems. Certainly locating it had been, for hundreds of years, the source of miners' common-law conflicts with customary holders of overlapping surface rights. The legal battles between these groups represented competing demands for exclusivity.

There is a revealing contrast between the surface-rights laws that apply to private land and those that apply to Crown and public land. On public lands, the changing regimes of disposal reflected changing government priorities and the relative strengths of various interested lobbies at a point in time. On private lands, the contrasting evolution saw miners, farmers and courts tackle the *legal* ramifications of the 'split estate'. The parties' options were limited:

conflicts between the mining estate and the surface estate cannot ordinarily be appealed to property law or to nuisance law because the details and characteristics of the miner's right flow from the individual lease or contract and not from the law itself. However, within the domain of contract law, severing landowners' mines from their surface holdings by (typically) a lease of mineral rights created a separate tenement with its own incidental rights of surface ownership. Both in England and in some American states, each 'estate' now existed in abstract isolation, and an interest in any one estate could be conceptualized as mutually exclusive from any other, regardless of their physical proximity to each other.

The contractual act of severance spells out the conditions that apply to the physical continuity between the ore, the rock around it and the surface above. This continuity or oneness of the physical components of the mining area was acknowledged in the following formulation of the miner's necessary infringement on the owner's incidental rights: 'to do all that was necessary for the convenient working of them [the minerals] reasonable care being taken to avoid injury to the property and the rights of others'.[72] Miners recognized that their efforts would ordinarily disturb the surface and essentially pledged to reasonably limit their intrusion on the surface estate.

Customary rights and contracts

I start with customary rights because, when later, in the eighteenth century, the law was called on to deal with surface-rights disputes, *custom* was often more important than ordinary property law or nuisance. The history from which the courts extracted it—the feudal and medieval land-use customs of the manor—could be more revealing than the narrow history of miners. In the early sixteenth century common lawyers had had little use for such custom. They treated it as a troublesome anomaly, strict tests confining it to harmless applications.[73] But only one century later Coke wrote: 'When it [custom] is found true by a jury, and that it hath such antiquity as exceeds the memory of man, then this obtains such privilege as the prerogative of a prince, and is part of the law, and stands with it, and this is reasonable custom... [the reason] stands with the rules and reasons of common law.'[74]

In the seventeenth century, as both minerals and surface areas (the latter for timber)[75] became more valuable, lawsuits multiplied. There was a revival of

[72] *Sheppard's Touchstone*, a statement of the law relied on by the English courts and later by American courts. *Sheppard's Touchstone* 89; 2 Roll Abr. N. 1, 2, 3; 1 Saund. 322; first published in 1641; 7th edn., 1820; 8th edn., 1826.

[73] Based on Plucknett 1956, p. 312.

[74] *Rowles v. Mason* (1612), 2 Browl. 192, 123 E.R. 892 at 893 per Coke C.J.

[75] See *Rowles v. Mason* (1612), 2 Browl. 192, 123 E.R. 892 at 896 per Coke, C.J.: 'it is against common reason, incongruent and against common law, that a copyholder for life may cut and sell the trees, and custom ought to have reason and congruence'.

recourse to manorial custom, involving as it did personal entitlements to strips or plots in the open fields, rights to graze beasts and to take timber, firewood, peat, coal and other minerals in the waste land. 'Good', or enforceable, custom satisfied four criteria: 'immemorial' origin, continuance without interruption since origin, certainty and reasonableness. With such customs, villagers could stand in the way of general presumptions of the lord's ownership rights and access to 'his' land and resources.

By the late eighteenth and nineteenth centuries disputes over mineral-taking were arriving commonly in the common-law courts. In particular, even after the later Enclosure Acts, peasants' copyhold tenure and other remnants of manorial land organization survived. Contrariwise, there were some customary rights that could reinforce and supplement the lords' typical legal rights. For example, in some places a lord might actually enjoy by custom a right to enter the copyholder's own land to dig for minerals.[76] Of these customary rights and the conflicts to which they led, Nef wrote: 'For the settlement of a suit dealing with coal mining one subject was examined by nearly every witness, was cited by plaintiff and defendant alike—the customs of the manor.'[77]

As these customary rights differed from place to place, they were not the 'standard rights' described in Chapter 1. They were also not the standard leasehold conditions and stipulations described earlier under contract.[78] They were legally enforceable (as opposed to 'legal') entitlements. Although variable in particulars, they were widely subjected to consistent tests in the courts. A body of general rules developed by which a manorial custom would be found good or not. The courts also found similarities between a search for reasonableness in a custom and for reasonable intent in a contract. Mainly after the seventeenth century[79] they drew an analogy between the two by assuming that good customs were founded in ancient, unwritten agreements.[80] Their approach is consistent with that of Blackstone who, writing

[76] Typically, the copyhold estate was an estate in the soil, excepting trees and minerals. Ownership of these remained with the lord, but in the absence of a custom entitling him to do so, the lord could not enter onto the copyholders estate to gain access to his property. See Jessel M.R. in *Eardley v. Earl Granville* (1874), 3 Ch. D. at 826.

[77] Nef 1932 and 1966, vol. 1, p. 299.

[78] Id., p. 298, says traditions, including the ancient practices of the metal free miners, were often invoked in coal settlements and disputes but that they had little influence on actual coal outcomes.

[79] See *Rowles v. Mason* (1612), 2 Browl. 192, 123 E.R. 892; the *Tanistry Case* (1608), Dav. Ir. 28; *Simpson v. Bithwood* (1692), 3 Lev. 307.

[80] As one reads the eighteenth and nineteenth-century judgments in mining cases, one is struck by the courts' propensity to appeal to contract or agreement for a rule about underground minerals and water. For example, in *Acton v. Blundell* (1843), 12 M. & W. 324, the court rejects the idea that rules about surface water can apply to percolating waters by remarking that, because the positions, amounts and underground flows are very uncertain, 'there can be no ground for implying any mutual consent or agreements—which is one of the foundations on which the law as to running steams is supposed to be built'.

in the eighteenth century, tells us that Henry II had compiled the common law by collecting the best and most universally applicable of pre-existing English customs and regional laws into a general, uniform body of English law.[81]

While judges might find it convenient to see customs as contract-*like*, they found some contractual characteristics to be missing. Parties subject to a contract could modify it in its next version or renewal to meet a court's objections; but a party claiming under an 'immemorial' custom could not remake it, especially if a court had ruled on it. Hence mining rights shaped by custom lacked the flexibility of those shaped by common law.

The development of a body of property law dealing with the severed mineral estate was guided by a classic appeal to what was assumed to be ancient custom. In *Broadbent v. Wilks* (1744), the court considered the reasonableness of a custom allegedly permitting the lord to throw debris from his mine onto tenants' lands. The key question involved the interpretation of a sort of Social Contract: would the original tenants have entered into an agreement that would permit the dumping of debris on their own lands? The court thought this unlikely, and so found that the alleged custom was unreasonable on the grounds that it could deprive the tenants of the whole profit of their land:

> [The custom is] very unreasonable because it laid such a great burden upon the tenant's land without any consideration or advantage to him, as tended to destroy his estate, and defeat him of the whole profits of his land, and savours much of arbitrary power... and what was said at the Bar touching the public utility of coal pits to the realm cannot be considered, for the pits may be worked without this custom, for aught that appears to the contrary... The objection that this custom is only beneficial to the lord, and greatly prejudicial to the tenants, is, we think, of no weight; for it might have a reasonable commencement notwithstanding, for the lord might take less for the land on account of this disadvantage to the tenants. But the true objections to this custom are, that it is uncertain and likewise unreasonable, as it may deprive the tenant of the whole benefit of the land, and it cannot be presumed at first the tenant would come to such an agreement.[82]

Here we see the court weighing both private (free contract) and public (policy) kinds of reasonableness in order to mediate conflicting rights so as, ultimately, to justify the validity of custom by reference to its reasonableness between the parties (i.e., the reasonableness of the custom as an agreement). Despite the legal rhetoric presenting the court's task as determining whether the custom really existed, the court in *Broadbent* seems also to have been concerned with the public-policy question of whether it *should* exist.[83]

[81] Blackstone (1765), *Commentaries*, Book 1, T. 64. [82] Per Lee C.J.

[83] Modern commentators, especially economists, may be tempted to interpret the judges' 'reasonableness' criterion in deciding the authenticity of custom as a utilitarian impulse—as the best way of bringing out the most socially efficient use of land and resources. This sort of interpretation is consonant with the modern law-and-economics worldview, but it is, I suggest, both anachronistic and incorrect. The flaw lies, I think, in information costs. As late nineteenth-century cases of reasonable use show (see Chapter 3 on water law) it takes time,

More than a century later, *Salisbury (Marquis of) v. Gladstone* (1861),[84] defined a custom as reasonable and, therefore, valid using explicitly contractual reasoning. It concerned a custom whereby a copyholder could dig and remove the clay on his land, which would be made into bricks and sold elsewhere. Accepting that such a custom would tend to destroy the land, the court nevertheless found it reasonable on the basis that the custom applied only to the lord and the copyholder of that particular land. Interpreting reasonableness as evidence of an original agreement, it found that a single lord and his tenant might come to any agreement, even one so absurdly disadvantageous to one party (usually the tenants) that it could not have become far-reaching contractual 'custom':

> This is not, it must be observed, a custom by which any person is affected besides the lord and the particular tenant insisting on it. It is not like the custom ... in *Broadbent v. Wilkes*, a custom to lay coals to an indefinite extent, and for an indefinite period of time, on the lands of other copyholders, whereby their lands might be made practically useless, although they would still be liable to pay their rents and perform their stipulated services to the lord. Nor is it a custom like that set up by the copyholders in *Wilson v. Willes* (1806) (7 East. 121), namely, a custom to take turf in an unlimited quantity from the common for the improvement of their copyhold tenements under which the rights of the other copyholders in the common might be totally destroyed. Nor is it a custom like that insisted upon by the lord in *Hilton v. Granville* (1844) (5 Q.B. Rep. 701), which would have enabled the lord to undermine the houses of the copyholders and, without any notice to them, to cause their houses to fall and crush those residing in them, and that without making them any compensation. The custom here insisted on is one which affects no one except the lord and the tenant insisting on the custom, and I can see no ground for holding that it was impossible or even improbable that it might have been the result of arrangements between the lord and his tenants before the time of legal memory.[85]

Surface-rights litigation: the common law

RULES OF PROPERTY

In the nineteenth century lawyers acting for miners who wanted resolution of exclusivity-related disputes began to rely less on attacking alleged customary rights. Instead, they directed the courts' attention to the rights of miners and of their landlords that were incidental to (attached to) their main property right. The courts' task became to define the incidental rights of the respective estates.

information and confidence to reach a utilitarian land-use solution under which a resource will be used to the maximum benefit of two or more parties. Most judges seem to have lacked this confidence. Even when invited to use their discretion, they looked instead for information, for rules and for precedent. In the absence of these, they took shelter by looking to custom, and the idea that an ancient contract would show what had once seemed satisfactory to two 'reasonable' parties.

[84] *Salisbury (Marquis of) v. Gladstone* (1861), 9 H.L.C. 700.

[85] Per Lord Cranworth (1861), 9 H.L.C. 700.

The usual situation was that the land and its surface had been owned and controlled in freehold by the heirs of the original holder. As we know, the heirs' range of choices included undertaking mining themselves; keeping the surface but leasing out or severing and selling the mining rights; or keeping the mining rights while severing and selling or leasing out the surface. Discovering what these abstract alternatives actually meant on the ground took a good deal of court time. For example, it was not necessarily easy to determine which party owned a severed mineral right once its holder had exhausted the entire mineral deposit.

Incidental rights: reasonable and necessary use

English common law has accepted since the *Case of Mines* that a property right to dig and carry away minerals carried with it such incidental rights 'as are necessary to be used in the getting of the ore'. This remained the law governing surface rights for almost three centuries. Then, with the nineteenth century's increase in mining activity; with the frequent openings and extensions of coal mines that undermined and damaged roads and houses; and with the general changing realities of technology, urbanization and population growth, the courts suddenly had opportunities to expand or pare down the accepted incidental rights of the mineral estate. As late as *Dand v. Kingscote* (1840)[86] the court found the wide range of incidental rights to a coal holding retained when the surface was leased or sold to include 'those matters reasonably sufficient to enable the coal owner to get all the seams of coal to a reasonable profit'. The miner's right was not limited to a description of the route in use at the time of his lease but included, as incident to his liberty to work the mines, a right to build and run a steam engine and railroad to work them:

> ... as all the seams are excepted [from the disposal of the surface], and a right to dig pits for getting those coals reserved, all things that are 'depending on that right, and necessary for the obtaining it' are reserved also, according to the rule in Sheppard.[87] Consequently, the coal owner had, as incident to the liberty to dig pits, the right to fix such machinery as would be necessary to drain the mines, and draw the coal from the pits ... the steam engine which was erected was necessary for winning and working the lower seams, which are the principal seams in that coal field and ... the defendant had a right to erect it.[88]

But, alongside these 'modern' implicit rights, the nineteenth-century courts now attached to the miner's ownership certain implicit (and costly) obligations

[86] *Dand v. Kingscote* (1840), 6 M. & W. 174, 9 L.J. Ex. 279, 151 E.R. 370.

[87] *Sheppard's Touchstone* 100.

[88] A pond and engine house that had been erected were found necessary accessories to the engine, and so lawfully made. Parke B. added: 'It may not be improper to observe that a compensation seems to us to be due for the injury to the soil by making these adjuncts to the pit, the steam engine and its accessories as well as for digging the pits themselves, under the provision in the deed of 1630; whether there is any due for the railroad is doubtful' (151 E.R. 300 at 379). *Sheppard's Touchstone* was a statement of incidental rights relied on by both English and American courts, first published in 1641 and kept up to date into the nineteenth century.

to the surface owner: he might not actually destroy or permanently injure the surface;[89] he might not cause damage through negligence; and he must not remove surface support, even if that necessitated leaving some of his mineral in the ground. Gone was the miner's right to appeal to the customs of the industry. His powers to impose damage had now to arise by clear and unambiguous language in the lease, contract or conveyance.[90]

Turn now to surface rights in the United States. The English common-law doctrine of incidental rights to do what was reasonable and necessary (as refined) was accepted into American law, especially in the nineteenth century judicial tendency to interpret a leasehold or contractual interest in minerals as a standard estate.[91] Surface-right cases were relatively rare in the United States until after the American Civil War, after which the higher market values of mining and of other land uses made conflicts more frequent. The American courts, considering these conflicts, hammered out the doctrine of the dominant estate (more on which below). Their rules can be summarized in the answers to four major questions:[92]

How much of the surface might the miner use or damage? As much as is reasonably necessary for exploration and development of the minerals granted;

Is there liability for surface damage? Not unless the amount of the surface used is excessive or violates an express lease provision;

Is there liability for nuisance? Perhaps, depending on state nuisance laws;

Has the mineral holder an obligation to the surface owner? Yes, to allow such surface uses as do not interfere with legitimate and proper surface uses by the miner.

This American judicial shaping of the dominant-estate doctrine continued into the first half of the twentieth century. The doctrine was reinforced by

89 *Bell v. Wilson* (1866), 1 Ch. App. 303; *Hext v. Gill* (1872), 7 Ch. App. 699 at 714; *Midland Rly. Co. v. Miles* (1886), 33 Ch. D. 632 at 647.

90 *Hext v. Gill* (1872), 7 Ch. App. 699; *A.G. v. Welsh Granite Co.* (1877), 35 W.R. 617 (C.A.).

91 *Cowan v. Hardeman*, 26 Tex. 217 at 222 (1862), noted the 'well established doctrine from the earliest days of the common law' that the right to minerals included a right of entry and 'all other such incidents . . . as are necessary to be used for getting and enjoying them', citing the *Case of Mines* (1568), 1 Plowd. 310, 75 E.R. 472, and *Earl of Cardigan v. Armitage* (1823), 107 E.R. 356. See also *Marvin v. Brewster Iron Mining Co.*, 55 N.Y. 538 (1874). Plaintiff surface owner sought an injunction against a miner whose extensive works (including an open cut near the entrance to plaintiff's house; the persistent deposit of ore and rubbish on the plaintiff's lands; and the erection and maintenance of a blacksmith shop, powder house, stable, steam engine, tram railway and windlass by a deep shaft located a few hundred feet from the plaintiff's house) that had, in some places, caused the plaintiff's surface to fall in. The reasons given in *Marvin* considered the implicit rights of miner and surface owner; the explicit rights created by the original instrument of severance; the nature of the surface owner's right to support; and the English case law on all three issues (although judgment was not given, and the case returned for further facts), citing *Sheppard's Touchstone*: 'It is an old rule that, when anything is granted, all the means of attaining it, and all the fruits and effects of it are also granted.'

92 Welborn 1994, pp. 22–4.

legislation, both state and federal. As with water law, so with mining law: courts and governments increasingly drew into their ideas of rights a utilitarian theory of what was needed in the economy, at the frontier. An extreme judicial statement of policy priorities impressing themselves on the law is found in a frequently cited passage in *Chartiers Block Coal Co. v. Mellon* (1893):

> [If the mineral owner could not reach and work his minerals] the public might be debarred [from] the use of the hidden treasures which the great laboratory of nature has provided for man's use in the bowels of the earth... To place them beyond the reach of the public would be a great public wrong... [T]he question we are considering becomes of a quasi public character. It is not to be treated as a mere contest between A and B over a little corner of the earth.[93]

The right to support

The English judicial discovery of the surface's natural right of support by the mine below is an example of a judge-created property right. From decades of liberally approving the mineral properties' incidental rights to do whatever was 'necessary', in 1839 the English courts began a swing toward the view that parties agreeing to a severance could never have intended that the surface be let down or destroyed, even parties who had inserted in their deed an explicit waiver of a right to support.

In *Harris v. Ryding* (1839),[94] the owner (referred to as 'grantor') had granted the land with an exception of the mines and minerals including a reservation enabling the mineral owner to come onto the surface of the land to 'dig, delve, work for, search, get up, dress and make merchantable' the mines and minerals, along with a clause for 'fair compensation' for harm to the surface. When the miner's workings caused the surface to collapse, the new surface owner sued for the mine's wrongful and negligent working. The miner argued, relying on the fair compensation clause, that his use of the land included a right to collapse the surface. The court found for the new surface owner, interpreting the terms of access as requiring reasonable operation by the miner—one aspect of this reasonableness being that the surface would not be undercut.

The miner also argued that the exception of all mines and 'every part thereof under the land in question' was a reservation of the right to the whole of the mines—a right that could not be exercised if the defendant had to leave props of coal to support the surface. The surface owner countered that, in the case of an exception out of a grant, there is an implied covenant to use the things excepted (in this case, the mines and minerals) so as not to prejudice the surface grantee in the enjoyment of the subject matter of the grant. Hence an agreement to get the minerals while rendering the surface useless could never have been intended by the parties to the conveyance. The court

[93] (1893), 152 Pa. 268, 25 Atl. 597, 599.
[94] *Harris v. Ryding* (1839), 5 M. & W. Rep. 59, 151 E.R. 27.

accepted this latter interpretation. Specifically it reasoned that without the clause giving the original grantor the liberty to come onto the surface in the first place, he would not have been entitled to get every particle of the minerals. So no new right to every last speck of coal was created by the liberty to come onto the surface:

All that the law gives the [original] grantor by virtue of the exception, would be a reasonable mode of getting the mines and minerals... By reasonable intendment... the grantor can be entitled under the reservation only to so much of the mines below as is consistent with the enjoyment of the surface according to the true intent of the parties to the deed, that is, he only reserves to himself so much of the mines and minerals as could be got, leaving a reasonable support to the surface.[95]

Although the miner could not get at it, the remaining coal was, nevertheless the property of the miner:

The case stands thus: here are two persons, one who has the land above—one who has the mines below, with the power of getting those minerals; they are each to enjoy their right of property, and each is to act in respect of those rights of property, upon the maxim that he is to use his own property so as not to injure his neighbour. Then the question is, whether the grantor is not to get the minerals which belong to him, and which he has reserved the right of getting, in that reasonable and ordinary mode in which he would be authorized to get them, provided he leaves a proper support? It appears to me that this is the reasonable construction of the exception, and the reasonable adjustment of the rights of the parties derived out of that exception.

Finally, having dealt with these two arguments, the *Harris* court used an analogy that was to be picked up and explained in the subsequent case of *Humphries v. Brogden* (1850)[96] to describe the miner's rights of access conferred by the grant (including the compensation clause). It was a 'right of the mine owners against the owner of the land which is above it... analogous to that of a person having a room in a house over another man's room, or an acre of land adjoining another man's acre of land; though the latter has the exercise of ownership over the whole [under the terms of the reservation] yet his rights over his exclusive property are not unlimited, but are limited by the duty of so using it as not to do any damage to the property of another person'.

In *Humphries v. Brogden*, the court went further. It declared the right of support to be absolute. The occupier of the surface brought an action against the miner for negligently and improperly working the subjacent minerals,

[95] Per Parke B., see *Harris v. Ryding* (1839), 5 M. & W. Rep. 59, 151 E.R. 27 at 30–1. The opinion also states: 'If... the exception were general without permission to enter upon the land for that purpose... that exception would not give the grantor the privilege of taking the whole of the coal away, so neither will this exception, which gives him the liberty of coming upon the land, give him a right to take away the coal in a careless, negligent or improper way; it only gives him a right to enter upon the land, to take the coal in a reasonable manner.' Per Lord Abinger, C.B., *Harris v. Ryding* (1839), 5 M. & W. Rep. 59, 151 E.R. 27 at 30.

[96] *Humphries v. Brogden* (1850), 12 Q.B. 739, 116 E.R. 1048.

without leaving sufficient pillars and supports, and contrary to the custom of mining in the country. Consequently the surface (which had not been built on) collapsed. It was not proved how the occupation of the different strata came into different hands. The jury found that the defendant had worked the mines carefully, and according to custom, but that the plaintiff should have judgment as he had a right to support from the subjacent strata, and the defendant had a duty (if he removed the minerals) to leave sufficient support for the surface in its natural state. Again, the judges likened the land strata to the floors of a house.[97]

For more than forty years the courts heard arguments about support, back and forth. In *Hilton v. Granville (Lord)* (1844)[98] it was suggested that the right to support was unalterable, even by contract. The case concerned a dwelling house that was injured by mines dug near its foundations. The defendant alleged a custom to work mines, making reasonable compensation to the tenants for use of or damage to the surface by working. The custom (or prescription, if pleaded as such) was found to be unreasonable and so void. Lord Denman C.J., in a non-binding dictum on the case, issued a famous assertion that encapsulated the emerging legal view: 'Even if the grant could be produced in specie, reserving a right in the lord to deprive his grantee of the enjoyment of the thing granted, such a clause must be rejected as repugnant and absurd.'[99]

This absolutist view was not to last. The implication of Denman's opinion, that the right of support was so absolute that its holder might not waive or part with it, opened the portal to a minor flood of cases, which in turn induced later courts to reverse the Denman rule. In *Rowbotham v. Wilson* (1849)[100] and in *Williams v. Bagnall* (1866)[101] judges found firmly for defendants who relied on contractual agreements that the surface might be 'injured' or have its support removed. The final question was whether one might infer from an arrangement to compensate the surface user that subsidence had been contemplated. This was answered in the affirmative in *Aspden v. Seddon* (1876)[102] and again in *Bell v. Love* (1883).[103] Affirming this affirmative view in an 1884 appeal on *Bell v. Love*, Mellish J. drew an explicit analogy between the modern reservation in

[97] *Humphries v. Brogden* (1850), 116 E.R. 1048 at 1054.
[98] *Hilton v. Granville (Lord)* (1844), 5 Q.B. 701.
[99] 6 El & Bl 600.
[100] *Rowbotham v. Wilson* (1849), 6 El & Bl 600 per Campbell L.J.C.
[101] *Williams v. Bagnall* (1866), 12 J.O.R.N.S. 987, 5 W.R. 272.
[102] *Aspden v. Seddon* (1876), 1 Ex.D. 496, 46 L.J.Q.B. 353, 36 L.T. 45, 41 J.P. 804, 25 W.R. 277 (C.A).
[103] In *Bell v. Love* (1883) Lord Watson considered a reservation of minerals in an Enclosure Act. The onus was on the appellant lessees to show that by the terms of the reservation to the lord, they could displace the surface owner's prima facie right to support from the subjacent strata. They did not succeed; the court distinguished *Duke of Buccleuch v. Wakefield* (1870), 4 L.R. 377 (H.L.), in which the mineral owner was found to have a right to work the mines so as to let down the surface on the basis of the act, which included a right to compensation, on the grounds that the reservation clause in *Bell* was less complete and that, most significantly, the

this case and the ancient customary rights for the owner to let down the surface while paying compensation to his tenant:

The right here is simply a right on the part of the owner of the minerals to get all the minerals so as to let down the surface... Then the next thing is, can you annex this condition to that grant, and give a right to let down the surface subject to this condition? I think they may say, 'You shall let down the surface, but [only when] whoever does let down the surface by getting minerals shall pay compensation'. I presume that ever since the ownership of the surface and the minerals has been separated, it has been the common practice to make it part of the conditions, that if the surface is let down compensation shall be paid. I think very numerous cases may be found where it has been proved as a custom from time immemorial for the lord of the manor to be at liberty to get the coal in copyhold tenements, paying compensation for the damage which he may cause by getting it. Sometimes the custom is that the copyholder gets it, or if there is no custom at all, neither party can get it; but I apprehend there may be a well-known and perfectly legal custom that the lord of the manor may get all minerals under the copyhold lands, paying compensation to a copyhold tenant for any damage he may do in respect of the surface in getting them. Enclosure Acts consistently give the same right. That being a perfectly well known right, and existing and binding, in the absence of direct authority to the contrary, we should do very wrong if we held that the right claimed in this case did not exist. It does not impose any unusual burthen.[104]

Through the evolution of these cases, one can see the changing legal views of the special, quasi-contractually derived nature of mineral and surface rights—the power of the lease vs. the power of some assumed 'reasonable' contract enshrined through custom as an inalterable right. Introduced in *Harris v. Ryding* as an obligation of reasonableness, and elevated to the status of an absolute right in *Humphries v. Brogden*, this right to support was brought down to earth—or to negotiability—in *Rowbotham v. Wilson* and after on the basis of the logic of its contractual derivation.

From this array of possible rules, American judges generally adopted the compromise that the right of the surface to natural support was absolute unless the instrument of severance contained an express provision to the contrary.[105]

compensation clause was not intended to enlarge the powers of the mine owner but to cover damage resulting from powers previously reserved or granted. The court found that the reservation carried all the usual powers and surface privileges for working the mines but that this did not include a right to destroy the freeholder's right to support by letting down the surface. About the decision in *Duke of Buccleuch*, the court in *Hext v. Gill* (1872) concluded: 'no one can read the judgment [*Buccleuch*] without coming to the conclusion that, if the provision as to compensation had not been there, the House of Lords, notwithstanding the strength of the other words, would in all probability have come to another conclusion.' *Hext v. Gill* (1872), 7 Ch. App. 699 at 717.

104 *Love v Bell* (1884) 9 A.C. 286.

105 See Comment, 'The Common Law Rights to Subjacent Support and Surface Preservation' (1975), 38 Mo. L.R. 234; and *Marvin*: 'Whatever is necessary for him to do for the profitable and beneficial enjoyment of his own possession, and which he may do with no ill effect to the adjacent surface in its natural state, that he may do though it harm erections

The courts accepted the eventual English rule that the right to support could be waived and that the waiver was a right or estate on its own. Beyond these points in common with English law, the flood of decisions in the American states diverged widely, depending on different theories underpinning, or founding, the right to support. These ranged from adaptations of nuisance law to adaptations of the law of property applying to easements.

SURFACE RIGHTS AND THE LAW OF CONTRACT

In theory, surface disputes could also be argued under nuisance law, as interfering with the use of land by the surface-owning farmer. Preferring an action on the case, and invoking Coke's strict rule, the farmer might have obtained an injunction, or at least damages, as a remedy. However, in practice this was rarely done since all nuisance suits must be made with reference to a specified contract.

In the twentieth century American courts have shaped the rights at stake in surface-rights disputes by regarding their task as the interpretation of contracts and leases, essentially filling out incomplete agreements. The missing details that the judges deduce from the very general wording of the lease are referred to as 'implied covenants'. The lease, together with its implied covenants, assigns to the miners something like an easement over the surface (indeed, the courts use the easement terminology of dominant and servient properties). The implied specifications will be regarded as a set of liberties by the miner and as a set of restrictions by the surface user. In the course of their judgments, the courts regarded the miners' explicit interest in the removal of minerals as the dominant estate. In the course of ruling on the implied covenants, or on the incidental rights of this estate, the courts have produced the so-called 'American rule' of due regard and the doctrine of accommodation.

FROM REASONABLE USE TO ACCOMMODATION

In the twentieth century the duty to show 'due regard' for the surface owner's rights in American common law[106] does not seem to have been onerous. In fact, there is no evidence that a due regard requirement weakened or moderated the doctrine that the owner of the mineral rights held the dominant estate. For one thing, it applies only if and when the surface is being used for

lately put thereon', citing the 'rule' from *Humphries v. Brogden* (1850), 12 Q.B. 739, 116 E.R. 1048, that an owner cannot, by putting an extra weight on his land, render unlawful any operation that, without that weight, would have caused no damage.

[106] See Ferguson 1974, pp. 411, 415–18. See also the similar Pennsylvania Rule that without a specific release in the deed the lessee is absolutely liable for all damage, whether reasonable or not. See *Silvis v. Peoples Natural Gas Co.*, 126 A.2d 706, 60 G.R. 1346 (Pa. 1956). See also *Smith v. Moore*, 474 P.2d. 794 (Col. 1970), in which the court found a right to damage or destroy the surface to exist only if the severance deed is clear and the right is expressed so as to admit no doubt.

purposes that are consistent with the incidental rights of the dominant mineral estate. Indeed, mineral users have successfully prevented farmers and others from making unreasonable use of the surface, where 'unreasonable' is automatically defined as injurious to mining. In *Sun Oil v. Whitaker* (1972),[107] for example, the court held that a farmer could not use surface water if it was needed by an oil leaseholder for flooding operations. In the Texas case *Kenny v. Texas Gulf Sulphur Co.* (1961),[108] the court used arguments from property, nuisance and contract law in finding that, where no alternative existed, the miner's destruction of support was part of his implied right to make a reasonable use of the surface.[109] Writing in 1959, William B. Cassin concluded that in the few cases in which the miner lessee was found to have overstepped his implied rights, the courts did not apply the dominant-estate and due-regard formula, whose absolutist tone was like the mirror image of the English right-to-natural-support rule, favouring the mining over the surface estate. Instead they based their decisions on equity or fairness, referring to the 'concurrence'[110] or 'equality'[111] of lessor and lessee's interests.

A newer approach (accompanied, of course, by changing respective values) may have the potential to produce more even-handed outcomes. In 1971 *Getty Oil Co. v. Jones*[112] departed significantly from the nineteenth-century pattern. It built on the *Kenny v. Texas Gulf Sulphur Co.* ruling discussed directly above. Although *Kenny* had permitted the miner to use a technology that destroyed the surface because no other technology was available to him, the court had at least considered alternative mining technologies and their destructiveness (thereby invoking arguments from tort, as opposed to contract law).[113] The *Getty* court now went farther. Seeking to preserve the surface, it required that the techniques open to both parties be considered. Conceding the priority owed to the miner, it nevertheless required that where the miner had a reasonable economic alternative and the farmer had none, the miner should

[107] *Sun Oil v. Whitaker*, 483 S.W.2d 808 at 817 (Tex. 1972). And see Brimmer 1970, p. 49; see *Lindsey v. Wilson*, 332 S.W.2d 641 (Ky. 1960); the surface owner may use the surface as may be necessary or convenient so long as he does not interfere with the rights of the mineral owner. See *Cosdon Oil and Gas Co. v. Hickman*, 114 Okla. 86, 243 Pac. 226 (1925).

[108] *Kenny v. Texas Gulf Sulphur Co*, 351 S.W.2d 612 (Tex. 1961).

[109] In that case the subsidence was caused by the (at that time) only commercially known process for working. The court found that: '[*Texas Gulf*] is not liable to her [the surface owner] for the subsidence of her surface estate, since the subsidence is (and is so stipulated by the parties) a necessary, natural, reasonable, normal, inevitable, and proximate result expected from the production of sulphur by the Frasch Process.' At 614.

[110] See *Hamon v. Gardner*, 315 P.2d 669 (Okla. 1959).

[111] See *Gulf Pipe Line Co. v. Pawnee Tulsa Petroleum Co.*, 127 Pac. 252 (Okla. 1912).

[112] *Getty Oil Co. v. Jones*, 470 S.W.2d 618 (Tex. 1971).

[113] But the alternative must be available on the same land! So Sun Oil, in a 1972 case, was permitted to run down the farmer's water supply rather than being required to pipe it from a nearby river. See *Sun Oil v. Whitaker*, 483 S.W.2d 808 (Tex. 1972).

use the least harmful mining or drilling technique or else compensate the farmer.[114] But *Getty* went further than this: it required that the miner also consider whether or not there were options open to the farmer on the surface.

This outcome was a significant victory for Jones, the farmer. The evidence suggested that Jones's irrigation system was the only reasonable method for using his property for farming, whereas there were alternatives to Getty's intrusive pumping system (including burying its units at a cost of $12,000, as had already been done by neighbouring operators). The court found Getty's use unreasonable: 'what we have said is that in determining the issue of whether a particular manner of use of the dominant mineral estate is reasonable or unreasonable, we cannot ignore the condition of the surface itself and the uses then being made by the servient surface owner'.[115]

This new doctrine, based on the two parties' duties to each other, has been labelled *accommodation*. It departs from the previous abstraction in which the court was to balance the discrete estates, the mineral holder having incidental rights but no duty to the other party. From the idea of total dominance of the mineral estate, the courts' goal became an increase in equity, giving a better break to the surface user in surface disputes against the dominant mineral estate.[116] Once the courts had yielded to the farmers on balancing the courses open to both parties, judicial attention wandered to balancing other dimensions of the conflict. For example, it was suggested that there should be a more *economic* balancing (or accommodating) of surface uses against mineral values. In fact, today the interests of both the dominant and servient estates have given way, within the courts, to environmental concerns, attempts to preserve ecosystems and habitats for the 'public good'. This important development is considered below.

Obsolescent and uninformed contracting

In the period from 1800 to the present the transferences of property by lease/contract, grant, reservation or exception at the time of severance were largely successful in keeping up with most of the problems of transferring underground rights to miners, except on the subject of surface rights. The agreed surface rights in contracts seemed not to advance as quickly as did other rights in mining law—certainly not quickly enough to prevent the emergence of new sources of irritation and disagreement. The courts drifted away from interpreting the lease

[114] See also *Acker v. Guinn*, 464 S.W.2d 348 (Tex. 1971): 'Unless the contrary intention is affirmatively and fairly expressed, therefore, a grant or reservation of "minerals" or "mineral rights" should not be construed to include a substance that must be removed by methods that will, in effect, consume or deplete the surface estate.'

[115] Id., at 628.

[116] In 1955, this had been regarded as merely an ethical or moral ideal. See Healey 1955, p. 102.

document and, instead, as we have seen, responded with new 'doctrines': natural rights of support, the dominant estate, due regard, accommodation, correlative rights (see Chapter 9) and more.

Perhaps the major impetus for these novelties was that, in many cases, there had been a considerable interval between the situation that held when a contract or lease with its covenants was agreed to and the one that held when the mine was actually developed. As covenants in durable agreements intended to apply to any situation for at least the life of a mineral deposit, contracts were fundamentally not open to judicial reinterpretation in new situations. Yet the demands for exclusivity of the original parties to the contract might be overtaken by any of at least five fundamental changes:

(1) *Changes in technology and demand*: New mining technologies have tended to necessitate more demanding and destructive surface activities. Furthermore, the new technologies tended to upgrade remote and low-grade mineralization into payable ore and so to necessitate operations on parts of the surface that would not have been touched under the old technologies.

(2) *Price changes*: A similar source of change was the rise in demand for mineral products. Because this tended to make profitable those materials once thought not to be worth searching for and removing, it led to plans to open large-capacity workings that had not been considered when the contract was signed.

(3) *Different parties*: Disputes about surface rights sometimes arose between parties who had but a remote connection with those who had negotiated the original severance. Some old properties changed hands several times, perhaps drifting into the hands of distant heirs. The current holders might be only vaguely aware that they were vulnerable to rights to open or extend a mine below.

(4) *Different costs of information and litigation*: When landowners took their split estate to court, they could do so under property, nuisance (tort) or contract law. The legal costs of testing a lease or contract were relatively high. In many cases it was simpler for the parties and for the court to treat the plaintiff surface-owner's claim as though he were claiming that the miner was a trespasser. But not always: this approach would require the landowner to prove that the surface and soil taken by the miner was excessive.

(5) *The changing philosophy of the courts*: Judges in England, evolving the right of support, became increasingly sympathetic to landowners as against their mining tenants and supportive of the railroads, water systems and other surface users. Many American courts on the other hand were as interested as the politicians in the economic development of the frontier, including mining. The language they chose suggests that some of them even regarded old land-owner litigants as harmful parasites slowing down mining and industrial progress. Their hostility led them to welcome

pleadings in which the uniform, or boilerplate, covenants in the leases at issue could be subordinated to a broad property-law approach to rights. Once it was agreed that the miner held rights to a mineral estate, the court could rule on that estate's now-standard incidental rights (and on their limits).

In sum, although an outsider might believe that the extent of the miners' liberty to use the surface was contractually derived and therefore really a question of contract, there were adaptive forces at work, particularly with respect to miners' incidental rights to the surface. In practice the miners (and the oil drillers of the next chapter) held leases that were usually uniform in their provisions and covenants, and these usually referred to general undertakings concerning surface use and access. Thus the miners and oil companies, playing it safe, clung to the contractual provision of their surface access.

Informal surface-rights arrangements as custom

Undoubtedly, the doctrine of the dominant estate and its judicial interpretation created real deprivations for some American land-owning farmers and homeowners.[117] Ranchers and farmers, their eyes on potential royalties and hands out for signing bonuses, agreed to the severing of mineral properties with sweeping incidental rights. In time they learned that the judicial finding of a mineral estate had weakened their recourse if and when their own use of the surface was blocked by the miner's activities to which they had consented. Recently, case law has watered down the power of the dominant estate approach to contracts and conveyances, but it is still there, limiting the exclusivity of the rights of the holder of the surface estate.

Landowners, however, may find they have some protection in custom and cooperation. To prevent miners from using their contractual rights to damage the surface fully, the land-owner may appeal to the 'business norms' established by members of their industry to balance out the needs of miners and land interests. As Brimmer wrote:

> Heedless of this crystallization of the law of surface damages to a holding that the mineral lessee is entitled to reasonable use of the surface, without liability for surface damage except where there has been excessive use of the surface or the operator has been negligent, many Western stockgrowers and farmers have by a bellicose attitude induced mineral lessees to provide monetary compensation that the courts might have declined. In the hope of avoiding litigation or delay, lessees have often paid location damages or surface damages, or bought water from a farmer's reservoir, or provided other compensation such as a new cattleguard as a practical approach toward solution of conflicting interests.[118]

[117] Brimmer 1970, p. 49, concluded that 'judicial interpretation of the lessor–lessee relationship has seemingly whittled the rancher's rights to toothpick size'.

[118] Brimmer 1970, p. 58.

Mineral lessees may decide that making concessions of the type Brimmer describes are cheaper than a trial. Although it is not perfectly reliable, a foresighted damage-paying behaviour has become widespread. Davis claimed that by 1963 this behaviour had, like fringe benefits to employees, 'unfortunately led to a widespread belief that a lessee must, as a matter of law, pay for any and all damages caused [to] the surface of the land'.[119] Welborn supported Davis twenty years later by concluding that 'any landman who works in Colorado can attest that this belief is probably now more widespread than Davis can imagine'.[120] In this way, voluntary payments for damages have become another manifestation of the role of custom (also referred to as norms or practices) supplying exclusivity to the rights of the farmers. Arguably, it may even be more important in determining the relative exclusivity of farmers and miners than doctrines drawn from property law, nuisance law or judicial interpretation of contracts.

Possibilities such as this bring us to Ellickson's famous study of California cattle ranchers. 'A centrepiece of the theory is the hypothesis that, to govern their workaday interactions, members of a close-knit group tend to develop informal norms, whose content serves to maximize the objective welfare of group members. This hypothesis suggests that people often choose informal custom over law not only because custom tends to be administratively cheaper, but also because the substantive content of customary rules is more likely to be welfare maximizing.'[121] The relations among neighbouring miners concerned by flooding could easily help to support this hypothesis.

Of course, the relations between miners and surface owners do not altogether correspond to Ellickson's observed relations among ranchers. A farmer and a miner may have continuous contact during the term of their lease, but not through a succession of leases, so that there is no opportunity for future, repeated, reciprocal relationships between the two. Another related possibility is that the deference to custom forms part of a collective agreement among miners who fear hostile legislation. In the 1970s, an era of high oil prices, the mining industry cut the superadjacent farmers and other surface owners in on their increased profits in order to improve the day-to-day relations between surface-owning farmers and surface-using miners and therefore to reduce the hostility of the farmer's lobby in agitating for legal remedies to curtail miners' rights.

Legislation and environmental land-use law

Before the Industrial Revolution neither Parliament nor the American state legislatures seemed willing to step in to modify or correct the courts' interpretation

[119] Davis 1963, p. 316.
[120] Welborn 1994 at pp. 22–5.
[121] Ellickson 1991, p. 283.

of private rules and contracts. There were exceptions to be found among the nineteenth-century American states. As early as 1874, legislation in Colorado had allowed the surface owner to demand 'satisfactory security' from the miner. This was presumably a bond, but we do not know whether the law was useful, or even enforceable. We must wait till 1923 when, in *Barker v. Mintz*, a Colorado surface owner complained that the 1874 legislation deprived him of otherwise available common-law remedies.[122]

In fact, not until the coal and uranium nationalization, land-use planning and environmental laws of the twentieth century did mining find itself regulated more by government than by contract or judge-made law. In both England and the American states some planning-related permission became needed for the opening of new mines, for the deposit of wastes and for the extension of open-cast or strip mining.

Some of these interventions were highly visible. But on traditional two-way disputes about surface use, American and British governments were generally content to continue to leave the courts in charge. And the American courts continued to rely on—and to develop—the doctrine that the mineral property was the dominant estate. Stephen Dycus (1980) suggests an explanation: in its earliest years, the doctrine actually supplemented or clarified the contracts rapidly being presented to the farmers for signature. At that time, he says, 'So long as the pick and shovel remained the prevalent means of mining... the parties could usually form expectations based upon personal experience with the need to use the surface to recover the minerals, and with the physical effects of mining upon the land. As recently as the middle of this century both parties probably knew what was involved, for example, in the operation of a deep coal mine or a stone quarry, and were thus prepared to bargain knowledgeably about their respective rights.'[123]

This theory helps to explain why, unlike the prospectors and mining firms on public lands encountered in the previous chapter, nineteenth and early twentieth-century miners going on to private lands gave no sign that they wished for legislation to improve their bargains with the landlords. There is no evidence that the miners were in collusion to get permissive contracts and leases, or that landowners united to mount a sort of anti-trust policy against the collective actions of miners (though these generalities do not fully apply to oil lands, discussed in the next chapter).

The current picture is different. In some states, legal and legislative trends, taken together, do seem to be tipping the balance in favour of the surface

[122] The surface argued that the legislation pre-empted the reforms to the absolute dominance doctrine proceeding in the courts from *Barker v. Mintz*, 73 Colo. 262, 215 P. 534 (1923), to *Getty Oil Co. v. Jones*, 470 S.W.2d 618 at 622 (Tex. 1971), discussed earlier.

[123] Dycus 1980, p. 873.

owner. Welborn describes how, in Colorado in 1994, resistance was creating a de facto dominance of the surface estate:[124]

> The [mining or petroleum] landman is usually on the front armed with legal rights which have less and less practical value primarily because enforcing those legal rights often means unwanted litigation with surface owners and local governments—parties who are prepared to litigate because of the perceived value of the surface and the conviction that mineral activity erodes land values and the tax base. This is the present scenario in... areas... of Colorado where the common-law rule of mineral dominance is being tested at every turn.

As well, legislatives have attempted to improve on contractual arrangements by altering the presumptions built into the pre-printed 'broad form' lease—what I refer to elsewhere as the boilerplate deed. The drafting committee of the Model Surface Use and Mineral Development Accommodation Act 1990 based its model act on the accommodation doctrine developed in Texas in Getty, which it declared to be a spin-off of the rule of reason. While the model act designates the mineral estate as dominant, with all rights of access and use of the surface to the extent reasonably required, this is made subject to an obligation to accommodate surface uses where 'technologically and economically feasible'. The doctrine is now law in Utah.

Mainly, however, the end of more than a century of American deference to mining interests and laissez-faire—based on the courts' generous interpretation of the surface utilization 'necessary' for mining and drilling and sheltered by the legislatures' hands-off positions—came when it ran into the demands of environmentalism, beginning in the 1960s. Both in England and in the United States the miner's rights to the surface have been greatly modified by modern environmental policies. Touched off by public revulsion at the damage caused by strip-mining, new laws in both countries require some kind of licensing before mining can commence. Such licensing and zoning requirements entail planning to keep down the scale of the pit as well as to restore the surface and its drainage and vegetation. The miner, of course, must obey these laws; and in some cases the surface user may lose little or nothing of the land. At the same time, these policies have probably reduced the opportunities for the farmers to gain a share of the mining rent or profit by bargaining to give up their surface rights. The contract has come back as the source of the miner's rights to use the surface, but now the miner's bargaining and contracting are as often with the land-use authority as with the surface user or owner.

[124] See *Flying Diamond Corp. v. Rust*, 551 P.2d 509 (Utah 1976): 'wherever there exists separate ownerships of interests in the same land, each should have the right to the use and enjoyment of his interest in the property to the highest degree possible, not inconsistent with the rights of others.' In other words, the mineral owner is required to do what is 'reasonable and practical' under the circumstances. See also *Smith v. Linmar Energy Corp*, 790 P.2d 1222 (Utah Court of App. 1990).

The need for a legislative input into resource extraction and disposal had some recognition in the nineteenth century when central governments commenced regulating the bacteria and toxic chemicals in drinking water. We encounter it again in Chapters 11 and 12 on timber and forest disposal. Increasingly, in the eyes of twentieth-century legislators and voters, the prevention of abusive mining practices was recognized as a public good. It could hardly be supplied by the courts ruling on nuisance cases, for nuisance dealt with individual harms and injuries. Even less could it be supplied under the laws of contract and property.

In response, national governments and local governments took on some land-use zoning and amenity conservation and restoration. These established activities paved the way for mining and pollution control laws, notably, in the United States, the Surface Mining Control and Reclamation Act (SMCRA) of 1977. In this law the government laid down standards for coal removal in enormous surface operations, and for the disposal of huge amounts of waste and overburden in places where they would not harm watercourses, landscape, farming or ranching. It is continually modified and amended by the cooperating state and national governments.[125] The whole programme has made the legislature one of the main, and relatively independent, sources of development of coal-mining rights, especially in terms of their quality of title. Everywhere, rules about the impact on the environment have become a factor in the provision of changes in the miners' powers to produce as they wish. The changes cannot be dismissed as more of what Libecap would simply call the continuing contracting battle between surface owners and miners.[126]

The characteristics of a property right and the evolution of mining rights on private lands

In this chapter I have looked at the supplying of mining right characteristics from the point of view of the demanders. First, external demanders, such as holders of surface lands in active mineral country, sought protection from the spillovers of mining. Second, the miners themselves sought rights that allowed them to get on, cheaply, with their developmental and daily operations and to avoid or resolve conflicts with each other. The two sets of demanders have shopped among the traditional suppliers or sources of rights: the courts, government and custom, manipulating property law nuisance law and contract.

[125] For a detailed discussion of the SMCRA programme's implementation, impact on miners and division among state and national legislatures and bureaux, see Denise Scheberle, 2nd edn. 2004, *Federalism and Environmental Policy: Trust and the Politics of Implementation*, Washington DC. Georgetown University Press, pp. 124–50.

[126] See Libecap 1989, esp. p. 27.

As we have seen, the courts traditionally played a larger role than the government in the shaping of good title and exclusivity.

A main theme of this chapter is that the evolution of a generic miner's title has centred on the evolution of the contract or lease under the judicial strategy for weighing the validity of alleged (ancient) customary land-use rights subject to the law's modern approaches to considering the meaning of a contract. It has proceeded by assimilating concepts and procedures from nuisance law. Much of this assimilation was part of modern mining interests' struggle to free themselves from the medieval laws and customs that limited quality of title in the miner's right. Later, it became a way of responding to the legal and contractual disputes brought about by the notion of the split estate and the rights and responsibilities of the miner to the surface estate.

From this discussion, we can see how nuisance law contributes to the *exclusivity* characteristic of the miner's right. To the ordinary person, this exclusivity is excessive if it permits him to harm others by fouling water, upsetting the landscape, or emitting smoke, noise, dust and smells. Yet unlike the similar spillovers from smelters (as were found in the precedent-setting 1865 *St Helen's Smelting* case), mills and factories, the mine itself was rarely the subject of a suit for nuisance. The general reason was that, unlike these other sources of nuisance, the mine owner was not regarded as having alternative locations to which he might move his operations. Neither was he regarded as having at his disposal less intrusive technologies. The owner had to work where the mineral dictated—as was 'natural'. Consequently, the chief contribution of nuisance law to the exclusivity of the miner's property right was in connection with spillovers *between* adjoining mines, as in the case of flooding.

Exclusivity would also be increased to the extent that adjoining miners contracted with each other to limit the flooding spillovers and to the extent that they contracted with surface parties over the danger of subsidence and collapse. Like *quality of title*, the exclusivity component of the miner's right depended largely on the development of a contract-law approach to his rights and obligations, and in particular on whether miners could cooperate in a contract-like manner. To have a completely exclusive right, the miner needed a tight enough agreement with adjoining right-holders that his entitlement under it could be considered part of his title. The discussion above shows that not only the courts, but also eventually the governments, did take a hand in the interpretation, and so in the preferred drafting, of contracts between miners and surface users.

Mining also required that the *duration* of a miner's lease or contract with his landlord not be shorter than that with his neighbours. This duration was also addressed within the parties' contracted agreement. One might expect that there would be a mechanism for making duration uniform across mines in an area, and indeed the parties were undoubtedly influenced by what was customary at the time for their kind of mineral operation. However, I have found no evidence of explicit area-wide duration-uniformity agreements.

Apart from the need for uniformity, there is little indication that the lives or lengths of the leases were regarded as a general problem. I have mentioned that, in setting the conditions within a lease, both the owner and his mining tenant were in effect speculating: on future mineral discoveries, on future prices and on the technologies they might encounter. At times, one or both of the parties to a lease may well have wished they could annul or cancel their undertaking. Although the contract was there to prevent them from doing this casually, it could often, at a price, be re-negotiated or amended by the party who found the terms most arduous. This gave a *flexibility* (another characteristic) to some miners' contract-derived rights that was missing from court- or legislature-derived rights.

The courts of common law and equity were dedicated to preventing coercion and to protecting individual real property rights. Nevertheless in flooding, groundwater and oil and gas law—conflicts between adjoining mineral users rather than these mineral users and their private landlords—the courts did not develop rules that would induce parties to join their too-small properties into a unit scaled to the magnitude of the resource they were eroding. The courts might facilitate or enforce existing contractual undertakings but they could do little to encourage the establishing of new ones, even though such contracting had the potential to further improve the exclusivity in a miner's right. For that, governments had to step in. Chapter 9, on the development of twentieth-century American oil rights, provides an overview of this type of intervention and its limitations.

9

Rights over Coal, Oil and Gas

Introduction: the energy minerals

Having completed my review of the development of rights to metal mining, I turn in this chapter to the development of rights over the two energy minerals that fuelled the Industrial Revolution and the transition to modern society: coal in the nineteenth and twentieth centuries, and oil and gas from about 1870 through to the present day. The physical properties of oil in contrast to other minerals, and the challenge these presented to the formation of exclusive property rights over it, were introduced in Chapter 2. I return to these concepts, and how they played out historically on US lands, in greater detail here. The treatment of the coal rights on both public and private lands is briefer, for much of the rights-to-coal exposition overlaps with that of the public and the private mining laws discussed in previous chapters.

Coal and petroleum, and the methods and institutions that recovered them, were unique, different from each other and from the metallic minerals previously examined. One reason was that both coal and oil required extraction in far greater quantities by mass and were far less valuable per unit density than even non-precious metals. In gross terms, however, both became enormously valuable—indispensable in ways that gold never had been. A second reason was that neither the coal nor the oil industry depended much on the services of prospectors. Their absence from the scene affected how, and in whose interests, laws governing rights to the minerals developed, and in particular allowed the procedures for granting rights over coal and oil to be less focused on exploration requirements than had been the procedures for other minerals.

Oil rights, of course, had the additional difference from both coal and metal rights that their object—petroleum—was fugacious; its location changed over time within the underground or underwater formation, and it could change ownership through the very act of being extracted. Given the value of crude oil in the late nineteenth and early twentieth centuries, confusion over ownership inevitably led to conflict. The conflicts drove the demanders of rights over the energy minerals to the courts and to the governments to supply rights and institutions with different characteristics from those of the metals and other minerals.

Coal in the industrial age

Coal on private lands

Early coal mining activity was touched on in Chapter 5. In the continental Europe and England of the Middle Ages, a vigorous demand for coal already existed, mostly for use as a household fuel. The search activities of the miners catering to this early demand incidentally produced much more information about location and quality of coal deposits than existed for other minerals. The relative growth of household demand lasted through the late eighteenth century, at which point the demand for coal for industrial purposes, often as coke, was taking off. Just after 1800, domestic uses still accounted for half of Britain's coal consumption, but a hundred years later domestic uses had fallen to only 12 per cent of Britain's total consumption and output.[1] The potential royalty revenues to coal-resource owners (including land-owning governments in overseas coal districts) became increasingly tempting. Consequently the governments of the colonies and emerging nations of the New World began developing procedures for disposing of rights to their coal resources.

Where the coal was located on private land, its disposal to English miners was in the common-law manner described in the previous chapter. Indeed, as coal was for many centuries Britain's chief mineral, the property characteristics and procedures I have documented for 'private mining' emerged mainly in response to pressures from British land-owners and their coal-mining tenants.

In the eighteenth and early nineteenth centuries, overseas settlement and increasing world demand led North America and Australia to begin coal mining for domestic use and for export. The imperial countries granted most of the coal resources to their colonial governments or to favoured private proprietors. In colonies such as Australia the government, acting as if it were an English private owner, granted extensive farming and grazing lands to newly arrived farmers and, following the common law, included in the freehold grants the land below and the minerals therein, including copper and coal. In the next hundred years the various Australian states (colonies at that time) set about recapturing coal rights from old property holdings, and stripping them from new land grants.

[1] These are rough percentages drawn from Mitchell 1984. Mitchell's estimates are based on several basic sources. See B. R. Mitchell 1984, pp. 12–13.

In a second type of disposal, the proprietorship or concession received vast acreages and the freedom to dispose of them to settlers and small miners, or to establish its own mining monopolies—such as William Penn and Associates in Pennsylvania.[2] Later in the nineteenth century, governments began to encourage industrialization by granting similar large land acreages to railroads, including ownership of coal. The railroads were then free either to invent and offer uniform disposal procedures on their lands as though they were governments, or to make large contracts/concessions to a few firms, sometimes their own subsidiaries. Middle and late nineteenth-century examples range from the coal mines of Fort Rupert and Nanaimo on Vancouver Island to the vast coal properties of the American transcontinental railroads in the new western states.

Coal on public lands

As we have seen, the system of land grants described above was supplanted on the United States' federal lands by the claim system. Following on its California gold rush experience, the government applied the gold miners' claim-staking procedures not only to placer and hard rock metals but also to coal. The appropriateness of applying the claim-staking procedure to western coal was not really tested for some years because there was plenty of coal and coal land still on offer in Pennsylvania, Virginia and elsewhere in the Atlantic states. But the delay was also likely to have been a product of the unsuitability to coal mining of the discovery, claim-staking procedures that dominated early western mining law. Many outcrops of coal were already known, indicating extensive beds and seams. Prospecting was hardly needed.

In the next phase, Congress set out to make development possible. In 1864–5 it took coal off the placer-mining law track and enacted a separate disposal act for coal lands.[3] The sales of land for coal could cover up to a hundred and sixty acres, the price at least $20 per acre in a discretionary system of competitive sales bidding for surveyed lands, known (again) as 'survey and sale'. The new procedure applied only on designated 'coal lands'; the traditional free access disposal system was retained elsewhere for gold and most other minerals.

When, at the end of the century, the rising demand for inland coal put these public 'coal lands' into high demand, survey-and-sale transactions under the simple 1864–5 procedure began to involve larger areas and larger sums than had been contemplated, generating public concern and protests from the new

[2] In Nova Scotia coal rights were severed from the Crown lands and in 1784 were granted to Frederick Duke of York in the form of a sixty-year lease. This princely gift was neglected until 1826 when it was sub-leased to the General Mining Association, a private firm. The GMA developed markets in the US and in Europe but did not actively develop its mining capacity. Finally, the Nova Scotia government bought out the GMA and offered mining rights in the current English form, severed from rights to the soil. Thanks to Marilyn Gerriets for information about the Duke's rights.

[3] Leshy 1987, p. 30.

Conservation Movement. In response, two radical innovations changed coal-disposal policy in the first half of the twentieth century. First, in 1906 President Theodore Roosevelt withdrew—or 'reserved'—66 million acres from eligibility for further sales. These lands remained outside any disposal system until 1920, during which time the demand for coal, once again on the decline, was well served by the continued smooth production from older coal lands and private lands. Nevertheless, politicians from the western and mountain states where there were huge known unexploited coal formations in the reserves pressed Congress for legislation that would move their coal out of the reserve and into the disposal process. Their agitation led to the second innovation, as recommended by Roosevelt: the replacement of disposal by survey-and-sale with disposal through leasing. Congress had already tried this system for lead mines between 1824 and 1846, but dissatisfaction by both industry and the public led to its abandonment and replacement by locally organized sale systems.

Now, in 1920, the plan was to remove the reserve and to re-open the public coal lands under leasing, which, since not a complete sale, would allow governments to retain some control over coal depletion and waste.[4] The reopening was enshrined in the Mineral Lands Leasing Law (briefly, the Mineral Leasing Law) of 1920. (It also applied to some other bedded minerals and to oil, as discussed below.)[5] It divided the coal resources for which a miner might apply into two types, each with its own leasing procedure. If a coal mining firm sought rights in a coal area of 'known mineralization', it applied for a production lease directly, or lobbied the government to put up its desired piece of land for disposal by competitive bonus bidding using public auctions or sealed tenders. If instead an applicant sought rights in an area of 'unknown mineralization' (UG or UGS for 'unknown geological structure'), he was subject to an alternative two-stage procedure. After getting a first-stage prospecting permit over a large area, he had to meet a discovery requirement, which granted him a 'preferential right' to one or more production leases in the 'explored' area.

This was the route to low-cost land acquisition by the coal industry. The UG discovery requirement was not hard to meet. It was interpreted by friendly administrators to mean 'knowledge of a lot of coal', enough to keep some miners busy for a while, though not necessarily shown or ascertained to be of 'commercial quantities' or of profitable quality.[6] In practice this gateway test

[4] Ise 1926, p. 310.

[5] Veatch 1911. Leasehold law is explained, with special reference to coal, in Arthur Veatch's extraordinarily complete 1911 survey of the mining laws of Australia and New Zealand.

[6] The phrase comes from Glicksman and Coggins 1995, p. 155. Under the various land-disposal laws, mineral laws and court proceedings, there had been a century of debate about whether lands to be acquired for one purpose or another were 'mineral in character', 'valuable for minerals' and whether the word mineralization implied that mining would be 'profitable', and/or attractive as a 'prudent undertaking'. The 1920 law called for coal to be in 'commercial quantities', departing from the 'prudent undertaking' requirement for petroleum and from the 1872 hard rock law.

was so lax that miners and speculators in UG lands often converted to production leases without providing information on a payable coal deposit.

Thus the eight features of the 1872 US hard rock mining law reviewed in Chapter 7 did not play a major role in the 1920 coal-disposal laws. Governments and bureaucrats bowed to the wishes of the industry and allowed lands where coal was known to occur to be reclassified as 'unknown mineralization' so as to be leased without the mandatory competitive bidding. Some speculators went farther and avoided the Mineral Leasing Act altogether. They acquired coal reserves simply by obtaining an agricultural or homestead land patent—a strategy also being followed by those placer and hard rock miners who wanted to avoid the tougher discovery requirement of the Mining Law in acquiring hard rock minerals.

In 1976 Congress, believing that speculators and miners had obtained too many acres by the two-stage unknown-mineralization route, passed the Federal Coal Leasing Act Amendments (FLCA). This reform made *all* new coal conveyances subject to competitive bidding regardless of the state of knowledge about their mineralization and regardless of the status of the land on which coal was found. Conservationists and many resource economists argue that the amendments came too late. By the early 1970s billions of tons had already entered the two-stage UG process and were in the course of being converted from permit to lease.

Just as conservationists had helped to get coal lands reserved earlier in the century, so environmentalists assisted in the passing of the modified 1970s coal law. Their opposition to coal mining had (and has) two main targets. The first was the open-pit mine with its adverse impact on the surface lands and contamination of surface waters. The second was the transformation of coal into low-level pollution and greenhouse gases upon consumption. In the past few decades, government coal agencies have come under pressure to deal with these problems. In response, successive American governments have attached special environmental regulations and stipulations to coal leases. The current legal opinion holds that, because under the law written in the Mineral Leasing Act the government maintains ownership of coal lands during the life of the lease, there is no legal or business barrier to imposing stringent environmental regulations and shutdowns. (This is in contrast to the 1872 General Mining Law under which the government transfers certain freehold rights to the miner, thereby narrowing the range of regulatory steps it may take afterwards to reduce hard-rock mining's surface, air and water pollution.)[7] According to various industry experts and natural resource economists, efforts to devise an environmentally friendly disposal policy have already 'stymied' US coal leasing.[8]

[7] See Leshy 1987, pp. 45 and 210.

[8] 'Stymied' is the word appropriately chosen by Glicksman and Coggins 1995, p. 162.

Going further, a 1900-style public-land coal moratorium was threatened more than once in the 1990s, even though the practical effect of such a moratorium might simply be to shift the mining of coal, with its attendant externalities, onto private lands. With the new century the focus throughout the world (not just in the US) has swung from protecting the public lands to reducing the emission of greenhouse gases. This aim again brings under active consideration policies that would attach additional conditions to the standard rights of coal mining firms. Coal miners' rights, public and private, have always been subject to conditions more severely imposed than on miners of other minerals—including support and drainage rules, moratoria, mine inspection and special taxes. It seems likely that the newest set of environmental goals will again lead governments to reduce the exclusivity and the quality of title of coal miners' property rights to a degree greater than burdens placed on the other types of mining rights.

This brief review of the changing system of coal disposal and ownership tenures on US coal fields illustrates the range of possible methods by which coal can be disposed from public lands: competitive bidding at one extreme and discovery plus leasing at the other. For completeness, integrated-enterprise and concession arrangements should also be mentioned. Coal is a low-valued bulky product up against potentially high transportation costs that can best be met if the mined coal need travel only a few hundred yards from pit to electric generator, coal-gas facility or metal industry. There are examples in Germany, the US, Canada and Australia where governments (and holders of railway lands) have granted coal concessions extensive enough to keep integrated mining and processing units and town sites in business for many years. In some places the necessary coal has been made available after intense political negotiations among government, coal firms, consumer firms and transportation firms. Sometimes coal industry nationalization is the answer, especially where, as in Australia and Germany, newly mined soft coal is fed directly into electrical generators. Whatever route has been followed, the parties have usually by-passed the formalities of the small production units offered by the coal-disposal and coal-rights legislation. Firms have proceeded by direct negotiation with the government (or perhaps by depending on coal resources held in old tenures, with private land-owners).

Petroleum: oil and gas disposal

Oil and gas production is an international affair, global in every sense. Western producers of oil have included the North Sea nations, Mexico, Trinidad and Venezuela. The major Eastern producers have been Indonesia, Russia, Romania, Iran, Iraq and the Persian Gulf states, in particular Saudi Arabia. As in the previous chapter, however, I focus on the New World economies of the United States, Canada and Australia. This section opens with a focus on public oil land disposal. It then focuses on property rights in fugacious underground minerals on private lands.

Oil drilling and legislation on public lands

Firms in the American oil industry first entered the markets for illuminating oil (such as kerosene) and lubricants. Their 1862 discoveries were in Pennsylvania, concentrated in private holdings on the logging–farming frontier. Over the next decade crude production spread to Ohio, then to the Appalachian hills. Very little American crude then came from public lands. Drillers leased production rights; learned to adapt percussion salt drilling to oil drilling; and arranged for rail transport for their crude and for storage, refineries and shipping docks close to market or port. In their first decade or so, producers relied on the export market. Overseas, their crude met competition from the Baku fields of Russia, and from Romania, Iran, Mexico, Trinidad and Indonesia, some land-based, some offshore.

Gasoline production began in 1863, to be used in lamps. Although there was a huge demand for heating and illuminating fuels, the epoch-defining demand that would eventually emerge for fuelling internal-combustion engines in cars, trucks and stationery plants was barely guessed at by the early gas producers.

OIL DRILLING LAW ON AMERICAN PUBLIC LANDS

From placer law to the two-stage patent; 1860–1910

The disposal of oil rights on American public lands illustrates two important issues of interest to a serious study of property rights development. First we see how the problems of discovery and of appropriation of a fugacious resource led to a disposal law quite different from that used for the placer and hard-rock minerals. Second we see how oil laws changed in sympathy with changes in the oil market and in the economy generally. Whereas the US metal mining law has remained virtually intact since 1872, disposal laws for oil, even more so than for coal, evolved steadily: from claim-staking, to two-stage disposal, to exclusive government concession managed in line with conservation and environmental goals.

At the start, Congress and the courts faced indecision about whether public-land oil and gas rights should fall under the placer or the hard rock rules of the General Mining Law. Of course, it would have made little sense to stake oil claims 'along the vein' as the lode or hard rock mining law demanded. Accordingly, the 1887 courts and Congress decided that the oil claim must be staked according to the mining law's (placer) version. They learned, however, that the placer claim-staking rules were only marginally more appropriate for the discovery and production activities of the oil industry than they were for the coal industry. Five aspects of the poor fit of the placer and hard rock versions of the Mining Law stand out, paralleling somewhat the coal-rights problems suggested earlier.

First, in the pre-discovery stage, while costly exploratory drilling was going on, an oil driller needed better protection from free riders than was offered by a staked placer claim.[9] Second, as we will see, the placer law's small, limited-transferability claims were inefficient when applied to 'pool' development, that is, in fields where several private owners held pieces of oil land whose reservoirs tapped into the same large underground oil formation. There were two separate difficulties: claim sizes were too small; and the mining law would not allow the companies to group them. Third, an oil driller raising capital for development needed greater duration: to be able to hold both unproved and proved land longer than a placer miner needed to hold a claim. Fourth, perhaps because drilling often took place in settled, lowland regions, an oil company necessarily had obligations to and rights against the surface user/owner that were much more complex than those dealt with by placer mining on public lands. Fifth and finally, placer mining law's numerous provisions governing prospecting and discovery had little application to junior companies actually engaged in looking for oil. As with coal, the areas involved were much larger than the personal-sized claims provided by drafters of the 1866–72 law, and had a geography very different than that on which placer miners had worked during the various gold rushes. As McPherson and Owens (1997) put it: 'Oil and gas . . . occur in extensive, relatively undisturbed, nearly flat-lying continuous sedimentary rock formation. The major dimensions are normally parallel to the surface, and the position relative to the surrounding rocks is predictable over relatively great distances. For these reasons, oil and gas present relatively large targets for surface exploration.'[10]

The deficiencies of the placer law affected equally the small wildcatting firms and the oil-field-development giants. Firms of all sizes demanded similar changes from the placer law. In contrast to the divided hard-rock industry—in which some prospectors' goals differed from those of the large mining firms waiting to buy out their finds—the oil industry showed a united front in its dealings with Congress.

Nevertheless, several important groups stood out as demanders of changes in oil-right procedures. The dominant group, of course, was that of the capitalistic drilling companies themselves. They wanted to avoid the absurdities and delays arising when oil development was forced through the acquisition procedures invented by placer miners for alluvial gold mining. They demanded possession of federal oil land with the secure quality of title provided by patenting or by renewable leases of long duration.

In opposition to these companies was a group of members of Congress from eastern states. They had neither oil-industry nor conservation-movement affiliations. For decades a majority of this major block of congressmen had

[9] Ise 1926, p. 297; Leshy 1987, p. 103.

[10] McPherson and Owens 1977, p. 231.

been supporting bills—often western-inspired bills—to assist pioneering settlers seeking low-cost fee-simple acreages on public lands. But now they saw that the emerging oil industry was not personified by the plucky settler or the romantic lone prospector, but was better characterized as a rent-seeking giant looking for profit opportunities similar to those already exploited on privately owned leaseholds in eastern states. Rather than try to win the ideological favour of these eastern-state Congressmen, however, the new industry and its lobby appeased them by offering opportunities for government revenue from oil-land sales or leasehold rents (and, incidentally, better opportunities to support the conservation movement).

The third group of demanders consisted of articulate spokespeople and lobbyists for the conservation movement itself.[11] Though in general the conservationists were focusing their energies on preventing forest depletion by the timber industry, they also criticized the overly rapid disappearance of energy resources caused, they argued, by two factors: (1) the industry finding and producing petroleum too fast and (2) terrifyingly wasteful production methods. Their opposition took two forms. The first was lobbying sympathetic federal politicians to introduce interventions on federal lands similar to those already introduced by state governments requiring waste-reduction measures such as well spacing, prompt casing and/or plugging of old wells on state and private lands.[12] The second, arising from the difficulties of influencing profit-maximizing behaviour once land had been transferred into private hands, was blocking the federal government from opening and disposing of oil lands in the first place. Of course the conservationists were indifferent to or even welcomed the slowdowns created by forcing oil drillers to conform to placer law. Yet, given that the eventual disposal of public oil land was to some degree inevitable, they too came to share the view that retained public ownership and oversight under leasing was preferable to either sale or claim-staking.

Given the hostility to the placer-claim-staking system among the players in this drama, it is not surprising that it met its end early in the twentieth century. The conservationists lobbied and demonstrated until in 1910 President Taft, imitating Roosevelt's reservation of coal lands, withdrew public oil lands from the claim-staking law (a decision upheld by the Supreme Court in 1914). Having failed to prevail through the legal system, some oil interests lobbied for new disposal procedures by which Taft's withdrawn oil lands could again be made available for claiming and patenting.[13] Their first efforts were terminated by a depression in the oil market: flooded markets combined with volatile and generally low oil prices served to darken the industrial lobby's

[11] On the economic goals of the conservation movement, see Scott 1955, ch. 3.

[12] See Ise 1926, pp. 274–90, for a state-by-state description of laws that provided for waste-reducing regulation of spacing, gas pressure, capping and so on, on all lands in the state.

[13] See Leshy 1987, pp. 91–2; and Ise 1926, pp. 321–2. In *US v. Midwest Oil*, 236 US 459 (1914), the Supreme Court declared oil withdrawals to be legal.

vision of federal oil lands as promising commercial sources. As demand for pro-industry reform weakened, Congress opted to bow to the conservationists rather than to the oil industry and, as a result, moved very slowly to update access to the public oil reserves.

Two-stage disposal under the Mineral Leasing Act, 1920

Eventually, prompted by conservationists, oil company spokesmen and sympathetic politicians, Congress accepted a new leasing bill—the one already encountered under the heading of rights to coal. From a historical angle,[14] the lasting two-pronged contribution of the 1920 Mineral Leasing Act was the introduction of a *two-stage procedure* leading to oil *leases.*

As discussed above, leasing obviously meant land ownership was to remain with the government—a policy favoured by the conservationists who sought to weaken the oil driller's quality of title. The Congressional sponsors also established a disposal scheme with production-right characteristics they hoped would lead to less frantic oil-resource exploitation, mainly through *increasing* drillers' exclusivity by cutting down on small-scale wildcatting between major plays and allowing large firms to obtain exclusive control over a wide area for exploration and, eventually, drilling.[15] The disposal scheme contained two distinctions: between the types of procedure by which the firm obtained rights to land (one-stage or two-stage) and between types of land for which a drilling firm could apply. On land classified as having known geological structures (KGS)—generally in areas where oil production was already underway—the production leases were to be apportioned among interested firms by competitive bidding. In areas with unknown geological structure (UGS)—informally known as wildcat areas and located mainly on the frontier—the production leases were to go to miners who first obtained an exploration permit and then followed an updating of the old Mining Law's exploration and discovery route for claims. That UGS production leases could not be obtained without prior exploration permits was the essence of the new two-stage disposal regime, similar to that in other countries, notably Australia.

In introducing these innovations, the government landed itself with a very subjective and difficult classification problem: determining which lands were KGS and which were UGS. Government agencies concerned with public or Crown lands had undertaken such a land-class designation assignment before, for instance in the attempts to identify 'mineral land' in advance of exploration; and 'forest land' with only the evidence that it had a covering of trees.

[14] The Mineral Leasing Act applied to several non-metallic minerals, and so had a number of short-run purposes. For oil, its contemporary purpose was to clear up permit applications by drillers who had started applications before the Taft reservation shut down the granting of 1870s-type oil rights. They therefore had uncompleted claims or applications outstanding under the old mining law.

[15] See Rostow 1948.

Those doing such classification had, unsurprisingly, been subject to pressure from industry and from land-settlement lobbies. So it was too with oil land. Lobbyists pressed for the declaration of particular areas as UGS, so their clients might acquire rights through the two-stage procedure without bidding. As politicians and bureaucrats acquiesced, the demand for tracts by the KGS route diminished and demand for UGS over-the-counter permits intensified.

Under the language and early interpretations of the law, if permits to a given tract of land were being issued, the first applicant automatically had a 'right' to one.[16] However if there were two or more applications covering the same KGS or UGS land, the Department of the Interior early on began conducting lotteries among eligible applicants. Department regulations also called for the successful application to be checked for 'prospective value of the proposed prospecting operations' based on information from Geological Survey reports. This could not have been a serious hurdle for most companies, for the application was for a wildcat high-risk operation. The permit gave the company a two-year right to drill on a designated four-square-mile area of its choosing. A two year extension was possible, and at various dates Congress enacted added automatic extensions, so that the actual maximum duration of exploration permits on UGS land stretched to fifteen years.[17]

If a drilling company did find provable quantities of oil in UGS land, it then had a preference right to a lease of 25 per cent of its permit area at a modest royalty of 5 per cent. Furthermore, it had a right to acquire a lease of the remaining 75 per cent at a standard industry royalty of 12.5 per cent. By contrast, if a finder in already-producing (KGS) area obtained a lease, he would be subject to a 12.5 per cent royalty over the whole tract. These tracts were small by oil-industry standards and there was a limit on the number that could be held at once. There had been no American precedent for the 1920 law's open competitive bidding on KGS land.

Conservationists approved of a number of features in the Act and its amendments: the UGS acreages that could be leased to operators were a good deal larger than what was then typical on private land. The mandated minimum distance or 'spacing' between wells was also greater. Conservationists argued that as these two federal provisions would discourage duplicative offset drilling by neighbouring lease holders they would be more effective than rules for private leases (based on state rules). In addition to setting up well spacing, leasehold tenure and payment by royalty, the Act also provided for maximum

[16] Cragun 1933–4, pp. 57–9. That the application was regarded by many as a right was illustrated in 1935, when this part of the Mineral Leasing Act was amended. The amendment did not cancel pending permit applications but, rather, honoured them in a generous and elaborate phasing-out exercise. For a modern survey, explaining the Bureau of Land Management's lottery, see Paul D. Holleman 1984–5, *Law of Federal Gas Leases*, Vol. 1, Rocky Mountain Mineral Law Foundation, pp. 2-06, 5-24 and 6-10.

[17] Cragun 1933–4, p. 59n.

rates of production for wells and for fields, which conservationists believed would reduce wasteful drilling and operation.

Perhaps most ambitious, the Act contained provisions to reward *unit operation* of fields on public lands with extended lease durations and larger acreages for its leaseholders. Under unit field operation—known under federal encouragement as 'compulsory unitization' even though the firms were and are not actually compelled by law to unitize—a government lessee would negotiate with other leaseholders in his vicinity to form an exploration and production group or 'unit'. The wells could be drilled to maximize group financial return, with both costs and returns divided among the firms according to their proportional shares in the venture.

The changes of 1935: development or wildcatting?

The 1920 leasing law governed oil production on public lands until 1935, when the O'Mahoney-Greever Act (named after the Wyoming politicians who steered it through Congress) scrapped the exploration permit and two-stage oil-land (and coal-land) disposal. Henceforth the choice of procedure for acquiring a lease was to depend only on whether the applicant chose the UGS or the KGS route. In effect, the 1935 law provided the first steps toward a disposal policy based on universal (single-stage) competitive bidding. The government would go on to introduce competitive bidding for offshore oil in the Outer Continental Shelf Lands Act 1953 (OCSLA), for coal in the Federal Coal Leasing Amendment Act 1976 (FCLAA) and finally for onshore oil in the Federal Onshore Oil and Gas Leasing Reform Act 1987 (FOOGRLA).

The 1935 revisions changed the KGS procedure only modestly from that initiated under the 1920 act. Companies acquired their leases in KGS areas by competitive bidding. The leasehold would have an area of less than one square mile, a term of five years (renewable) and an increased royalty rate, up to 25 per cent for some categories of land.[18] The UGS procedure saw a more radical change. With the exploration-permit stage abolished, firms could now apply directly for a lease of requested area with no previous exploration, without discovery and without entering a bidding competition. (The first applicant received a preferential right to receive a lease, an example of the priority principle.)[19] Companies

[18] Apart from their royalty rates and the rentals, all government oil and gas leases carried the same broad-form terms. In this respect they were like private or commercial oil leases: subject to obligations to develop the property 'reasonably' and to drill to protect the property from drainage. Like private oil leases, government leases would not be renewed if development work was not done. On the other hand, one producing well was enough to hold the acreage, as established by the Supreme Court. See *In re L. E. Jones*, 51 L.D. 116 (1925).

[19] 'The person first making application for the lease of any lands not within any known geologic structure of a producing oil or gas field . . . shall be entitled to a preference right over others to a lease of such lands without competitive bidding at a royalty of 12.5 per cent' with power to set higher rates at higher rates of production. See Act of August 21 1935; Public Law no. 297 1/2 - 74th Congress. This is usually cited as 30 U.S.C 226 (a)–(d) as amended.

could now lease a four-square-mile area for ten years, renewable at the private industry's royalty rate of 12.5 per cent—much lower than the 25 per cent rate applied to some KGS lands, a discrepancy that could be regarded as the risk premium inherent in UGS 'wildcat' drilling.

Unsurprisingly, the government found itself gratifyingly inundated by applications for these non-competitive wildcat UGS leases. To handle the flow of requests it administratively divided UGS lands into two further classifications. First, tracts that were widely sought so that a line had formed were disposed of by lottery. As winners might get a valuable property or a worthless site, the lottery attracted speculative acquisitions from outside the industry.[20] Second, UGS tracts that were less sought and did not attract a queue were simply granted 'over the counter' to the first applicant company.

Business historians seem not to have tried to explain the abandonment of the 1920s two-stage UGS procedure in favour of the 1935 Act's three-pronged single-stage disposal process. The abandonment may have been complementary to the Ickes-Roosevelt New Deal depression era oil price maintenance programme, centred on the Interstate Oil and Gas Compact (IOC) cartel. On private and other non-federal lands, most of the oil states that were to form the IOC had already developed well-spacing regulations; efficient-rate production controls based on field technical and geological data; and market-oriented production control 'allowables'—essentially a pro-rationing scheme—that were set and re-set to respond to fluctuations in crude oil prices in the generally weak 1930s oil market. Private producers had argued that the encouragement of public oil drilling, and particularly the attractive exploratory permits under the 1920 Mineral Leasing Law, had undermined their efforts to control the price of oil and maintain their living. Thus, one explanation of the 1935 Act is that the federal government was retaining and cementing widespread bidding on KGS lands in an attempt to support the states' planned control over production on leases on private land.[21]

[20] Anderson 1986, p. 145.

[21] Looking ahead, it is unlikely that fluid substances with lower values, such as brine or fresh water, will pass through the stages discussed in this part and the next. The high values of coal, oil and gas have made it worthwhile for parties to invest millions in lobbying and litigation in order to get the disposal system adapted to rapid exploration and appropriation. (In countries other than those considered here, the parties have ignored existing fragmentary traditional local laws and, instead, have engaged in direct concession-bargaining with rulers.) Furthermore, governments have been attracted by the royalty and/or bidding revenues available and have been prepared to spend millions on attempting to classify areas, on inspection, and on conducting lotteries and bidding competitions. Had the incentive of the high values of oil and gas been missing, all parties might have been prepared to let the disposition of rights drag along in a regulated common-property system (such as the one that exists for the diversion of stream water under common law). These systems survive because the payoff for classifying the resources and giving rights to the more precise discretionary bidding (market) elements is missing. Low final values create limits to how much users will pay to change an imperfect water right into something like today's precise and marketable petroleum lease.

Another possible explanation is that the permits issued under the old law had encouraged speculation and waste.[22] In particular, the easy availability and exclusivity of the permits had encouraged some firms to keep out other searchers while raising capital to drill or speculating on oil prices. Insofar as it induced such behaviour, the law mainly gave temporary shelter to firms that could not afford, and had no real intentions, to drill. Many of these firms defaulted, and others appealed to Congress for special extensions of their permits.[23] Possibly the higher royalty imposed by the 1935 law too was supported by politicians who intended to reduce the eventual payoff to this kind of speculation.[24]

OIL AND GAS PROCEDURES ON CANADIAN AND AUSTRALIAN PUBLIC LANDS

Jurisdiction over petroleum

Petroleum was discovered in Ontario in the nineteenth century. Production there, beginning at the same time as in Pennsylvania, kept pace with local demand until 1903 but tailed off thereafter. After close to a century of intermittent exploration and low-level production of gas and oil, mostly in Western Canada, the major Leduc discovery in 1947 opened Canada's oil boom. By this time, especially after 1930 when the three Prairie Provinces took over the remaining public lands from the Dominion, most public land had come under provincial control. As well, an 1887 act of the federal Parliament had severed underground resources in Crown lands from settlers' surface holdings. Later, minerals beneath the lands that had been distributed as subsidies to the new railroads' lands, along with minerals beneath the remaining Hudson's Bay Company lands, were also severed from their private owners' holdings and 'returned' to the Crown.[25] As a result, although the Leduc discovery and many of the early western discoveries were made on private land, most subsequent discoveries, west and north of Leduc, have been made on provincial Crown land, subject to provincial law-making and control. In the thirty years

[22] Braeman et al. 1975, pp. 232–3.

[23] Davis 1937, pp. 907–8. Congressional extensions had been made in 1922, 1926, 1928, 1930, 1932 and 1935.

[24] At any rate, the low-royalty issue was referred to by Secretary of the Interior Ickes in his contribution to the Congressional debate on the 1935 amendment. He wrote that the two-stage system had not produced much revenue anyway, for the 'royalty and bonus, rightful property of the United States as owner of the mineral deposits, has been granted by the terms of the experimental legislation of 1920 to those who have done little or nothing toward development'. See US Congress, Senate, Congressional Record, 74th Congress, 1st sess., 1935, pt. 11, p. 12,077. Although Harold Ickes handled the legislation on behalf of the administration, a number of books by or about him say almost nothing about the Act. See, for example, Ickes 1953, Watkins 1874 and 1952, and White and Maze 1985.

[25] See Ballem 1973, pp. 1–10, for a brief summary of the dates at which the original landholders began to reserve mineral rights from grants to settlers. See Gray 1970 for pre-war oil and gas in Alberta, for the 1960s, and Crommelin, Pearse, and Scott 1978, tables 1 and 2, for the division of production and acreage in 1970 between private and public owners.

following the Leduc discovery, production began in earnest in Alberta, British Columbia, Saskatchewan, the North West Territories and offshore on both coasts.

Australia's searches for oil produced only gas, shale and condensates until the late 1960s when oil was found in commercial quantities offshore in Gippsland in the Bass Strait. Since then, offshore fields have been found and are producing off northwest Western Australia and in the waters between the Northern Territory and Timor and New Guinea. In the 1950s and 60s there was considerable doubt about the distribution of powers over offshore oil as between the states and the Commonwealth. The distribution became the subject of a vague 1962 joint-jurisdiction agreement. In 1976 the Commonwealth made a vigorous claim to offshore jurisdiction, which was confirmed by the High Court.

Onshore, although discoveries have been made in all states, most production has been in a belt across Queensland, New South Wales and South Australia, licensed or permitted by the respective states. As in the Canadian provinces, much of the ownership of rights to hard-rock minerals, coal and oil and gas in the Australian states was initially held privately by settlers and the successors of other nineteenth-century common-law grantees. And, as in Canada, the governments set out to remedy this early policy by reserving minerals from further land grants or reversing earlier mineral grants. As a group, the states increased their mineral reserves significantly after the Second World War when they began expropriating the remaining privately held mineral rights, especially rights over oil and gas.[26] Today, almost all Australian onshore oil and gas reserves belong to the Crown.

Two-stage disposal systems in Australia and Canada

In this subsection I focus mainly on the development of disposal regimes in Alberta, which would turn out to be the most important oil producer among Canadian and Australian jurisdictions. However, I also want to emphasize the range of modern oil disposal systems in the two countries, with each system reflecting the particular government's needs to attract or to ration oil interests given their resource endowments and bureaucratic capabilities.

In the Alberta region the federal government jumped off with 1914 regulations under the Dominion Lands Act, calling for a survey-and-sale system for leasing large twenty-one-year locations. This system sufficed until 1921 when it was replaced by a two-stage system plus compulsory relinquishment—a requirement to give up three-quarters of the original permit area—both developments probably copying changes in the US leasing system introduced the year before.[27] When in 1930 the province of Alberta gained control over all public resources, its legislators implemented a complicated mix of oil and gas

[26] See Hunt 1989 and Crommelin 1986, p. 296.

[27] Thanks to Rowland Harrison for information about the early regulations in Alberta and in northern Canada, as contained in his preliminary and informal 1996 conference paper, 'Evolution of the Resource Disposition System in the North', Calgary.

reservations, Crown reserves, permits, drilling reservations, acreage relinquishments and natural gas licences.

Perhaps because oil had been a minor product under the province's version of two-stage mineral disposal, the mix was not formally replaced by a simplified bidding system until 1976. Most original and important of the changes at that time[28] was the introduction of a bidding requirement for acquiring an *exploration* permit. In return, the law did away with compulsory relinquishment. Now the highest-bidding company could apply for a production lease for up to the entire permit area, subject to a work requirement and to finding the venture acceptably profitable. Like the federal government's 1921 adoption of a two-stage system, the Alberta government's 1976 provisions seem to have been a response to trends in the US public disposal procedure, in particular the move toward universal bidding, most recently on federal coal lands.[29]

In this policy, Alberta was the first among the Canadian jurisdictions to call for competitive bidding over onshore oil and gas rights.[30] To an extent, this innovation was tailored to the province's economic–geological situation. Alberta no longer needed to attract oil companies with the promise of low-price tenure; indeed, it was coping with an excessive demand for leases. This was less true in other jurisdictions. For example, the 1986 federal lands legislation introduced a new 'significant discovery licence'—a production lease with low carrying charges and a work requirement conditional on oil prices being high enough to cover production costs—as an incentive to promote greater exploration in the northern territories.[31]

To manage its oil fields, and doubtless to match the examples of some American governments, Alberta appointed a Resources Conservation Board. Becoming increasingly powerful, the Board made and administered rules governing well spacing units (and pooling), licensing, maximum allowables for fields and for wells and pro-rationing, as well as half-a-dozen less important related matters. Alberta's pro-rationing scheme was less extreme than the American depression-era IOC (which, as noted above, set out literally to set a price for crude in the nations' markets), but it worked and works on the same theory. Under a procedure called market-demand pro-rationing, the Board gets monthly 'nominations' from refiners of the amounts they require from Alberta

[28] The various kinds of pre-1976 and post-1976 permits and reservations and the related procedures for acquiring and holding them are examined in Crommelin, Pearse, and Scott 1978.

[29] The northern territorial lands still under federal jurisdiction remained on a two-stage basis under the Canada Oil and Gas Act (COGA), which transferred 25 per cent of a permit or lease area to the Crown, and allowed for the land-sharing by checkerboard that had been ruled out under the 1976 Alberta law. In 1986, the new Canada Petroleum Resources Act (CPRA) followed the 1976 Alberta law by introducing some (discretionary) bidding and by removing the required land-sharing.

[30] It introduced 'bonus' bidding for an exploration permit, linked to the automatic granting of a production lease.

[31] See Thompson 1986, pp. 3–34.

at the going price, then distributes the sum of the nominations among the province's pools and wells on the basis of their measured reserves. One might say that its goal is less to move the market-wide price of petroleum to a desired level than to avoid moving it at all.

Since the First World War, various Australian states, notably New South Wales, have also maintained two-stage procedures for oil disposal, presumably developed from the local mining law for hard-rock minerals. (In NSW's case, no discovery was made under it until after the Second World War.) However, within the two-stage framework, procedures differed from each other with regard to matters such as discovery, work and automaticity. Some Australian states favoured a weak drilling requirement, a fierce discovery requirement and an automatic grant of a production lease. Other states, and Alberta in its 1976 reform of disposal law, opted to maintain a drilling requirement. Satisfaction of Alberta's work requirement led to a more-or-less automatic granting of a production lease. In contrast, in NSW and some other Australian states, the production lease was *not* granted automatically. The minister might, at his own discretion, refuse to go to lease even if the firms met the work and (weak) discovery requirements under the law. In Canada, the federal COGA imposed all three requirements: work (drilling), discovery and a rather uncertain grant of a lease (also requiring a significant percentage of Canadian ownership). A government's choice between an exploration requirement and a discovery requirement probably reflected its own expected administrative costs. Alberta and some Australian jurisdictions realized that it was less costly for them to verify an applicant's drilling activity and expenditure than to verify conclusively that the firm in question had made a 'discovery'.

Opinions also differed among jurisdictions as to the wisdom of insisting on partial land divestiture (as reconnaissance permission was converted to an exploration permit, or as the latter was converted to a lease). The US Mineral Leasing Act made provisions for a company to keep the entire permit area if it wished. Alberta from 1921 had called for compulsory relinquishment of exploration land, but later abandoned the rule. The Australian states from the beginning allowed the exploring company to keep the entire acreage if it wished. This inconsistency in approach stemmed from the governments' different incentive strategies. A government that is trying to encourage drilling and discovery awards a very large initial exploration area, correcting this generosity later with a requirement that a good percentage of the large area be returned when exploration is over. In Australia the percentage was zero, probably because relinquishment would have deterred what little exploration and discovery was going on.[32] The US too was under pressure to encourage drilling

[32] Thanks to Jim Cooney for correspondence on this point. The no-relinquishment policy may also have reflected Australian governments' apparently exogenous historical preference for two-stage mineral disposal.

activity (especially during the Depression, even as politicians and conservationists struggled to control the flow of oil from public lands into the market) and so attached no compulsory relinquishment to its generous exploration area. Alberta, by contrast, initially attached a very high 75 per cent relinquishment requirement to its large exploration areas. Theory predicts that later, after drilling greatly increased and production became copious, the government would reduce the exploration area somewhat while perhaps increasing the relinquishment requirement. Instead, the Alberta authorities simply dropped relinquishment altogether and substituted its current bonus-bidding system. Perhaps it deemed the original 75 per cent relinquishment requirement already too high to further increase without facing political consequences.

OFFSHORE OIL AND GAS

Underwater oil drilling and offshore production began very early in many countries, not only off California and Louisiana but also in Trinidad, the Persian Gulf, the Black Sea and the Indian Ocean. Some inland, fresh-water production also took place, for instance on Lake Erie. Offshore drilling was dominated by the great oil companies. They quickly gained international experience in negotiating full-scale oilfield-wide concessions and in picking their way through western-type bidding and exploration-permit leasing procedures.

Both individualistic leasing and government concessions have become the subjects of an extensive literature in resource management, economic development and economic theory. This is particularly true of bidding systems and bidding behaviour. Each proposed change of practice by one national government involves gains or losses of millions of dollars to particular firms or lessors and, of course, touches off a new crop of studies. Here I devote most of my space to a sketch of the much-studied American Outer Continental Shelf (OCS) disposal system, with only a few references to alternative systems in existence. To cover the various bidding systems and the ambitious economic and statistical literature analysing them would carry us too far from the basic subject of property rights.[33]

Any collection of parties looking to set up an offshore oil disposal system must first establish that the country under consideration and its government have dominion over the adjoining submerged lands. Until the mid twentieth century most countries' claims to land and sea were confined to the internal waters of rivers, bays and inlets, plus the area within the outer boundary of the territorial sea. As discussed in Chapter 4, countries had made little progress in agreeing on the width of the territorial sea belt until about 1800, when many of them accepted a distance of three miles from the national shoreline. By 1945 the expanded ability of the oil industry to find and pump oil far out to

[33] One of the basic studies is McDonald 1979; also much cited are studies in Crommelin and Thompson 1977, including Mead 1977. See also Mead et al. 1985, Hendricks 1992 and Porter 1995.

sea, not to mention the desire of naval and fishery groups to broaden the area under which they would be subject to national protection, led several countries to make formal claims and proposals for wider 'contiguous zones' instead of, or in belts beyond, the three-mile belt. Their claims were greatly strengthened in 1945 when US President Truman proclaimed a unilateral appropriation of all the resources of the adjoining 'continental shelf' for the United States. This emboldened a number of countries to make similar claims. Most, following the United States, were interested in gaining and keeping control over 'their' offshore minerals, including oil. A smaller number, such as Iceland, were interested primarily in gaining control over adjacent fishing areas.

Starting in 1956 the new UN intervened and staged a series of international conferences on the Law of the Sea. Each of these led to global conventions. The most recent enshrined the principle that each member nation should control the contiguous sea-bed resources in a vastly increased two hundred mile extended economic zone (EEZ) from its own shores. This proved a boon for Norway and Great Britain whose North Sea oil opportunities were discovered in the 1970s. A recent estimate suggests that more than 60 per cent of the world's oil is currently produced in offshore fields, '. . . in waters of more than half the coastal nations on earth'.[34] Though offshore production seems to have peaked and is probably now declining, some discoveries have yet to be made.

As the oil industry expanded in the US, Canada and Australia (all federations), both the state/provincial governments and the national governments claimed jurisdiction over the minerals in undersea lands near their respective shorelines. The federal-jurisdiction issue arose in the inshore area of the Gulf of Mexico, where Louisiana had selected acreages for leasing and assigned them by competitive bidding as early as 1936. Texas and California followed suit. The federal government was excluded from the transactions until 1947, when Supreme Court judgments began to assign jurisdiction to the national government. In 1953 Congress stepped in with the Outer Continental Shelf Lands Act to assign the inner three miles to the states and to place the rest of the continental shelf under national laws and regulations, essentially adding them to the reserves of public lands. With a number of minor changes, this remains the American federal disposal law. The federal government receives nominations of specific areas from companies that hope to drill in them, and then chooses from among the nominations the offshore areas to be opened up and auctioned.[35] It values them and announces when a sale will take place. Companies have at least three months to consider their strategies—how many

[34] Estimate by Ministry of Energy, Mines and Petroleum Resources, Government of British Columbia, 'Offshore Oil and Gas' February 2006.

[35] For a state-by-state survey of modern laws for the leasing of state submerged lands, see Rocky Mountain Mineral Law Foundation 1991, ss. 60 and 63, esp. pp. 63.37 to 63.39. The 1953 federal legislation borrowed many of its features, including bidding for rights, from the Louisiana law, rather than continue features of the federal UGS disposal rules.

properties to bid on, whether to bid singly or jointly—taking into account their own knowledge of the geology of adjoining tracts and the expected bidding strategies of other companies. The leases have terms of five to ten years. Since the 1950s a number of payment methods have been tried, and more have been suggested, involving various combinations of a floor royalty, a basic rent, an initial cash bid (or bonus bid) and an initial royalty bid.[36] The bonus bid has been the usual method for offshore oil, as for the UGS and KGS systems described earlier.

In Australia and Canada the conflict between the different states and provinces and the national governments over coastal oil resources became intense after 1945. Each country's debate was based on its own history of land appropriation and conquest, so that generalizations can be misleading. In Australia both the state and the central governments have some constitutional and property-law powers over offshore, or 'submerged', oil and gas lands. In particular, a political settlement of the issue in 1979–80 led to arrangements under which the states gained almost complete powers to make laws and grant property within their three-mile territorial seas. Beyond that belt there is a complicated sharing of authority and revenue between the Commonwealth and the adjoining state,[37] but the process is said to be effectively controlled by the former.[38]

In Canada, the land and resources beyond the coastal waters of Nova Scotia, Newfoundland and British Columbia come under the jurisdiction of the Canadian federal government. However, this division has been blurred, and the governments at the federal and provincial levels have subscribed to 'Accords' that propose to share revenue and administration between themselves.

Both countries follow the US in making some use of bidding in selecting the companies to drill and to produce, and both also retain remnants of the two-stage system of rights disposal. Australia's offshore disposal regime is also like the American one in that it is based on formal, standardized individual leasing rather than on bilateral royalty, bonus, concession or agreement bargaining. Nevertheless, in all three federations the formalities of these legislated procedures have rarely been followed in practice, only in part because of the small number of separate offshore projects that either country has attracted. More often, leases to undertake drilling have been negotiated through concession-type bargaining of the sort discussed directly below, in which a contract covering all aspects of the proposed development is hammered out between the government and the company in question. The result, as we will see, is more like a charter or a franchise than the standard right apparently envisaged

[36] See Mead et al. 1985, pp. 5–25. The sophisticated bidding system is described in many other places. Still very useful is McDonald 1979. For a contrast with the highly discretionary British and Norwegian systems in the North Sea, see Dam 1974 and 1976.

[37] See Crommelin 1986, pp. 306–7; and Thompson 1986, pp. 1–28.

[38] Thanks to Michael Crommelin for 1996 correspondence on this.

by the offshore disposal legislation and agreements between the different levels of government. So prevalent was concession bargaining that the itemized 1967 Australian rules for competitive bidding subject to a cash payment or work commitment remained unused in the decades following their passage.

CONCESSION AND AGREEMENT RIGHTS TO PUBLIC LANDS AND OFFSHORE MINERALS

Allocating oil rights by concession has been and is almost entirely at the discretion of the government that holds jurisdiction over the land or sea in question. Counted correctly, the actual number of such concessions around the world, in both single- and multi-country oilfields,[39] is surprisingly large. This is because many projects that have apparently been approved under the general mining or petroleum laws have actually been handled by a contract, sometimes in the form of a special law, with special provisions tailored to the convenience of the government, the firm and the technical requirements of the project.

Modern concessions between governments and private firms update a procedure dating back to the late medieval period. When monarchs owned mineral rights personally and granted them as a part of the royal privilege, the successive charters and concessions were not uniform: each one was negotiated anew. Their fluidity recognized changes in the needs of the monarchy as well as differences between the various mining and drilling costs and mineral values. Later English and colonial administrations inherited the ruler's implied power to sell or rent the minerals of the Crown lands as the governing party wished. Parliament played not even a minor role. Today's petroleum concessions (and also mining agreements) resemble these old disposals in that the legislature may be asked to endorse an agreement or concession, but the administration will have negotiated it almost as a private contract between equals. The move toward concession bargaining was particularly important for petroleum: for many decades the petroleum companies holding concessions have dominated the global supply of crude oil.[40]

Some of the motives that might lead a host government to agree on a blanket concession arrangement with a large oil company rather than encouraging it to compete for an exploration permit under the national leasing law reflect the impoverished circumstance of developing countries. Poorer countries may be anxious to come to a quick revenue-generating agreement, and may also use concession bargaining to drive side-bargains whereby the company provides in-kind services such as roads, schools and hospitals. Others

[39] For instance, the postwar design of the British and Norwegian regimes for the disposal of North Sea oil and gas reflect a similar abandonment of the general law system by which an individual acquires a mineral right by following fixed procedures. Instead, governments offer negotiated contracts or concessions similar to those hammered out between private parties.

[40] The outstanding source is Adelman 1972. See also Bradley 1967.

reflect the circumstances of Norway or Western Australia: developed countries with governments holding sovereign rights over large unexplored and undeveloped areas, going slowly and thoughtfully to avoid waste and premature production and in some cases being out-smarted by the companies.

Concessions and characteristics

Here, briefly, is a review of the effect of concession bargaining on the characteristics of the rights acquired by the company.[41]

- *Security and quality of title*: To many developers, an agreement with the ruling family or political party for permission to drill and conduct auxiliary activities to drilling looks more secure than titles and licences obtained by applying under general laws. The ruling party may share this view. A concession can provide for agreed types of arbitration to replace recourse to local courts unfamiliar with mineral development issues. A government can technically pass new laws that unilaterally amend the terms of a concession, but not without suffering a blow to its reputation in future international dealings. A concession allows both sides to 'lock in'.
- *Duration and exclusivity*: A developer's agreement with a government can tailor the size of the holding to what is essential for a large-scale and long-term project, and establish or strengthen the right of the developer to exclude prospectors, other developers and tourists. According to Crommelin, the areas of most offshore Australian mineral agreements consistently exceed the maximums available under the general onshore mining laws.[42]
- *Transferability and foreign ownership*: To a developer, the concession may provide a way to bypass general rules that otherwise exclude foreign ownership in resource development. To a government, the agreement may also be a way of specifying precisely the acceptable degree of transferability of the company's concession rights to parties unknown to the government; and otherwise of agreeing on and so restricting the activities of a foreign firm in the host country. These are kinds of 'single window' advantage, arising when mining or oil production would otherwise be forced to gain approval under a number of untested laws and bureaux. There may be economies for all the parties, including all their separate bureaux and branches, in getting everyone to design a single agreement. On the other hand, this informality and pragmatism may lead to politically unacceptable inconsistencies between foreign and domestic enterprises.

[41] I have placed this discussion of concession bargaining squarely in the context of oil and gas disposal. But there is also a growing list of concessions or 'state agreements' that bring very similar benefits or advantages to hard-rock mining.

[42] Crommelin 1996, p. 19.

Also worth mentioning is the chief benefit of concession agreements to the state: revenue, and in particular *flexibility* in revenue. The company can be the source of a stream of royalties, in cash or in the form of infrastructure or even social services. Furthermore, the state and the company can cooperate in the maintenance of price, which can be tailored to the public needs of the government or, correspondingly, to the private needs of the ruler or governing family.

The sequence of stages in an oil concession agreement

A typical concession's life may be a half-century or more. As both company and government acquire additional mineral information on the resource and on economic conditions over the course of exploration and development, they may find that the initial features of their concession are no longer optimal, leading to some stages overlapping or being repeated. As a thumbnail, however, the development of a petroleum concession goes through the following stages:

- *Reconnaissance and exploration*: Physical reconnaissance often takes place in virgin country. On the basis of the information the company gathers, it proceeds to a more thorough exploration, including drilling, over a selected area. The government, for whom this exploration may be the most valuable part of the concession, routinely requires that the firm pass on the exploratory information. The company, knowing that the information it gives up will later be used in bargaining between the government and either itself or another company, usually demurs.
- *Conversion*: Usually the company is bound to select only a small part of what it has explored. Thus the famous 1960s concessions in Iran and Saudi Arabia, publicized as company 'monopolies', later had to make room for other companies[43] or for a state-owned oil company.
- *Production*: At this stage the parties re-open their negotiations, using the information gained and shared from the first two stages, concerning the company's plans to develop, produce, sell and ship, and to import staff, equipment and supplies. Depending on how long production is expected to last, the company might also seek arrangements designed to insure contractual security should the life of the oil resource prove to be longer than the life of the government granting the concession. Again, the arrangements may include side-obligations regarding continued production, employment, payments, profits, schools, housing, training schemes or other social policy in populated areas from which the company draws its labour.

[43] For discovery in the Middle East between 1900 and 1938 see W. E. Pratt 1960, 'The Value of Business History in the Search for Oil'. See also the map of Middle East countries in Jacoby 1974, p. 137, which shows where, in the wake of the seven largest companies, 'smaller' oil companies were exploring or developing in 1973.

The government may also demand continuing information disclosure: as production continues, the company naturally acquires further mineral information but may not be willing to disclose it.

- *Conservation of oil and gas*: A petroleum agreement may also include provisions to prevent the waste of oil or gas. In any case, a concession normally covers a large area, usually placing an entire petroleum structure under sole-owner management. Under these circumstances both company and government want to see wells placed in rent-maximizing positions. The better a company's quality and security of title and exclusivity over the entire formation, the lower is its incentive to race other companies into drilling and producing and the more amenable it may be to stipulations on spacing, flaring and rates of production. No doubt realizing this, North Sea governments and certain Arabian governments have for particular fields negotiated secure long-term agreements with a single company or consortium.[44]

Oil and gas on private lands

GOVERNMENT DISPOSAL REGULATIONS VERSUS CONTRACTING

Before and during the Civil War, American national crude output hovered between two and three million barrels. By 1873 it had reached ten million barrels, thereafter growing at more than 10 per cent a year before levelling out in 1891 at almost sixty million barrels and remaining at that level until the end of the century. Substantially all of this production was on leased private land in the east and mid-west of the country, and more crude was expected to be found beneath homesteaded lands.[45]

As discussed above, the physical waste of resources that accompanied the oil boom caused alarm among engineers and technocrats and, by the turn of the century, among the new conservationists. It also produced variants of the conflicts between neighbouring drillers and between drillers and their landlords encountered in Chapter 8.

Although the federal government had eventually responded to problems of waste in oil-drilling activity on federal public lands with its Mineral Leasing Act's provisions to prevent flush production, it fell to the states to handle such waste on private and state lands. Some externalities, conflicts and market imperfections inherent in private leases and contracts led to conflicts and so became subject to the decisions of state courts. Oil-field conflicts were also referred to state politicians, most of whom could not find it in their hearts to intervene to stem the gushers that brought good economic news to the people of their states.

[44] On the theoretical and actual drilling programs of concessionaires, see Bradley 1967, p. 50; Adelman 1972.

[45] Williamson and Daum 1959, p. 730.

Indeed, over the second half of the nineteenth century and the early years of the twentieth, ever-growing armies of invading drilling firms leased, produced and abandoned rights in oil fields, usually on private and homesteaded farmland situated on top of part or (less commonly) all of an underground oil formation. The drillers' contractual obligations to their farmer landlords forced them to drill duplicate wells and to speed up extraction, causing higher expenditure on drilling, pipelines and tanks than would have been undertaken under sole ownership of the formations. Furthermore, the accelerated dissipation of gas caused by competitive drilling called for greater and earlier pumping and secondary recovery expense and reduced the amount of crude oil ever recovered.

Their competitive drilling also caused pricing problems downstream. Through the 1910s and 20s, uncontrolled drilling resulted in a near-total loss of market-oriented producer control over the rate of flow of crude toward the consumer. In the language of characteristics, the problem was a relatively straightforward lack of direct title to oil on private lands under the conventions of the common law, which in turn made oil extraction activity non-exclusive. While a farmer could 'store' the fertility of his land by leaving it fallow, neither he nor his oil-company lessee could store the fugacious crude in its underground formation without running the risk that it might be (legally) drawn from the same underground formation by the matching or offset wells in a neighbouring producer's land. The problem was exacerbated by the limited geological knowledge at that time; producers and farmers often had little idea about the area from which their wells were drawing oil. Oil companies reacted by producing as quickly as possible, pouring the contents of each newly discovered reservoir onto the market and causing price to fall—disastrously, if only a few active fields served a particular market. When their reservoir was exhausted, local prices would rise until a new discovery and race to market pushed them down again. When prices were at their lowest, some desperate producers stored oil from 'flowing' or gushing wells near the wellhead in ditches, behind dams and, later, in wooden or iron tanks.[46]

We saw in Chapter 8 that demanders of characteristics of rights to hard-rock mining turned mainly to the courts to supply acceptable distinctions, characteristics and obligations of the property rights created by mining and property law. In oil, by contrast, the parties' respective 'rights' sprang from their own contractual stipulations as written into their agreements and leases. As a result the courts' role was more narrowly defined. Government regulation made up for the courts' powerlessness—eventually filling the property-right-defining void left by the judges to a greater extent than it had ever been required to do for private hard rock mining rights.

[46] Surface storage was a far more expensive and risky practice than simple storage underground would have been. See Williamson and Daum 1959, pp. 189–94.

THE PRIVATE OIL CONTRACT DURING THE EARLY UNITED STATES OIL BOOMS

To illustrate how the discovery of oil affected landholders, consider the case of an archetypal newly discovered oil field in an American state in the nineteenth century. A drilling company acquired a leasehold right to search for, then to take, oil from land held by a farmer in freehold. The contract granted the farmer a lump-sum premium for signing (also called a bonus or, in England, a fine) whether or not the lessee found and produced oil. It also promised the farmer a stream of royalties based on the value of the stream of oil produced and sold. For both lessee and lessor, the optimal contract involved an exclusivity characteristic in the drilling right, limiting underground interference in or around the property and, conditional on oil being found in profitable quantities, requiring that the driller take care to get it out of the ground before it was captured by wells on neighbouring lands. A farmer also wanted 'strategic' drilling. As neither farmers nor drillers generally knew the shape of the underground oil formation to be drilled, the farmer wanted his lessee to drill to 'offset' successful neighbouring wells. On this matter, the two parties' incentives differed. To both, an extra well meant a protected shared flow on the property, but to the driller it also meant an increase in drilling expense not shared with the landlord.[47]

Given the high stakes involved, bargaining between land-owners and lessees could be a tense affair with lopsided results favouring the smarter or more informed negotiator. Land-owners who had not yet found out about their mineral holdings or who were fearful of losing hypothetical fortunes to their tenants or neighbours often rushed into leases prematurely. The oil company agents (called landsmen) had an incentive to offer the owners bonuses for signing pre-printed lease forms containing standard clauses calling for long durations, minimum lease acreages, a fixed number of wells per acre and modest penalties for failure to drill or produce in the event that little oil was found. Relatively ignorant land-owners might be swayed by the offered bonus. More informed land-owners tried to hold out for clauses strictly compelling their lessees to explore early, to drill early, to offset competing wells and to make the leasehold forfeit if the lessee suspended operations.

As national production surged and oil boom activity swept from state to state, the tendencies of negotiated leases changed, sometimes to the benefit of drillers and other times to the benefit of land-owners. Among the latter, the overall result was one of jubilant winners existing alongside aggrieved losers. The lucky ones captured as much of the resource rent as could be snatched up in a short time. Their good fortune must have helped to persuade governments to shy away from introducing statutory changes in individual rights of capture that would have spread the underground wealth more evenly across land-owners and prevented the luckiest from keeping the lion's share of their sweepstake-like winnings. Yet governments

[47] See Libecap and Wiggins 1984, pp. 87–98.

could not hide forever. For one thing, it became obvious that common-law property rights in land were inadequate to resolve ownership conflicts among land-owners, tenants and neighbours over oil or to protect some land-owners from being exploited by the landsmen. For another, lack of regulation of duplicated drilling and racing distressed conservationists and sometimes the general public as well, failing to stem the industry's alarming waste and over-investment.

LEGAL DISPUTES: PROPERTY, NUISANCE AND CONTRACT

Two kinds of dispute, neatly paralleling those we saw over mineral mining rights in England in Chapter 8, arose in the American oil states: (1) disputes between land-owners and their driller lessees and (2) conflicts between neighbouring rights holders, usually situated on different properties over a common oil formation. In economic terms, the former type of dispute, previewed above in terms of the writing of the contract, was largely a principle and agent problem. The owner, indifferent to the tenant's drilling costs, would try to induce the tenant to drill extra wells and to step up his rate of pumping, thus capturing crude before it was lost to other drillers' wells. The tenant would be willing to incur the cost of drilling more wells only if he thought that doing so would justify his expenses.[48]

I take up the details of the principle-and-agent conflicts between landholders and oil drillers below. Here, my main focus is on the second type of dispute and its resolution in the courts and, especially, in the legislatures: that arising between two or more neighbouring drillers (and, by extension, between their land-owning lessors). As had been the case for disputes over the mining of hard-rock minerals on private land, legal disputes over oil fell into one of three branches of the law, which I discuss separately: (1) property law narrowly defined; (2) nuisance law; and (3) contract law, defined to include a fairly significant body of law devoted to the interpretation of boilerplate leases.

LITIGATION AND DEVELOPMENTS IN PROPERTY LAW

Disputes between neighbouring oil interests emerged over rights to liquid resources flowing by unknown channels between legally separate parcels of land. The disputes involved the lack or breakdown of *exclusivity* over the resource—oil—from which the disputant land-owners hoped to profit. Specialist law firms acting for various industrial interests and landholders emerged and vigorously sought to expand or reinterpret property rules in order to deal with the special problems posed by the exploitation of fugacious minerals. The question was then whether the courts would respond to this agitation by adapting the standard property interests developed for agriculture—licence, freehold, leasehold, profit—to reflect the geological, physical and economic aspects of oil land.

[48] Other owner–tenant disputes concerned use or abuse of the surface (for example, the farmer's ability to tend and harvest his crops while drilling was taking place). Rather than rehash that particular legal history here, I refer readers to the discussion in Chapter 8.

Central to many of these early ownership disputes was the freehold owner's right over the underground formation. Was it exclusive enough to prevent the drainage of 'his' very valuable oil into the wells of his neighbours? Existing common-law rules did not work to efficiently resolve ownership disputes over oil but, as we will see, tended to exacerbate the inefficiencies from missing exclusivity. Essentially, this was because common-pool oil disputes were closer to the Pigovian or Samuelsonian public goods problem than a Coasian problem of simply assigning property rights to enable bargaining. The courts found it more difficult to define and enforce 'reasonable' or equitable behaviour between neighbouring oil owners (i.e. behaviour that ensured each an equitable share of the oil under his land) than they had for water-right contracting disputes. Instead, judges tried to mandate clear requirements that the parties invest in fair but costly adversarial drilling practices, rules of capture, first-come-first-served and winner-take-all kinds of rules—even if, as we will see, the outcomes were not particularly 'reasonable'. Perhaps not surprisingly, the eventual solution was the replacement of litigation by sweeping general government regulation that, while recognizing individual property rights, greatly narrowed the field of choice open to operators and, in a few fields, even forced them to work to maximize a common profit.

Property law and capture: court-made individual rights in oil fields

Oil ownership had been unknown in England, the cradle of common law. Thus, following a pattern we saw when colonial governments tried to create rules of gold placer mining, the US courts in the 1860s and 70s had no direct received doctrine for dealing with the new oil-based cases. They decided that the main problem to unravel was that of origin and ownership of the fugacious resource. The drilling rights lease itself was not novel: in fact, it generally contained the same 'grant' provisions as the mining lease of Chapter 8 (leaving aside the added conditions for immediate drilling and placing offset wells, to be examined below under the searchlight of contract law). However, the leaseholder's property right over a subjacent reservoir of fugacious oil was not similar to the hard-rock miner's right to a mineral deposit. It was closer, in the eyes of the court, to a right over groundwater, and the precedents of English common-law rules that had their origins in still older rules regarding the capture of wild animals. These had given each owner an 'absolute' right to take any amount of water (or game) from his land and use it as he pleased, without regard for others.[49] This right had neither exclusivity nor transferability to another location. When water, like a wild animal, flowed across or beneath a property boundary, it changed ownership as it moved.[50] This was the rule of capture, as it was seized on in mid-nineteenth-century American cases:

[49] *Chasemore v. Richards* (1859), 7 H.L.C. 349; *Acton v. Blundell* (1843), 12 M. & W. 324.

[50] Like the riparian right from Chapter 3, this right was incidental to land ownership; but, unlike riparian rights, there was no duty to give the right holder a 'natural flow' of water. Indeed, the very concept of a stream flowing in a natural course almost never applied to water underground, probably because of the difficulty of proving that either a stock or a flow of any size existed. See *Acton v. Blundell* (1843).

Water and oil, and still more strongly gas, may be classed by themselves, if the analogy is not too fanciful, as minerals *ferae naturae*. In common with animals, and unlike other minerals, they have the power and tendency to escape without the volition of the owner. Their 'fugitive and wandering existence within the limits of a particular tract is uncertain' as said by Chief Justice Agnew in *Brown v. Vandergrift* (1875), 80 Pa. 142 at 147. They belong to the owner of the land, and are part of it, so long as they are on or in it, and are subject to his control; but when they escape, and go into another land, or come under another's control, the title of the former owner is gone. Possession of the land, therefore, is not necessarily possession of the gas. If an adjoining, or even a distant owner, drills his own land, and taps your gas, so that it comes into his well and under his control, it is no longer yours, but his.[51]

As had the introduction of severed mineral estates in England, the rule of capture ran counter to the English/American property law doctrine which held that ownership of a resource on the land stretched *ad coelum et ad inferos*. Surprisingly, there were two ways of interpreting capture. The first way, 'non-ownership', said that even under the old doctrine, the holder of oil or gas rights had never had more than a profit-à-prendre, a right—granted by the landowner, presuming he was not the same as the driller—to go on the designated land, explore and take some of the oil. The new rule of capture was consistent with such a right and did not change it: the holder acquires title as soon as but not before he reduces oil or gas to possession. (This is the version of the law of capture that is referred to in Chapter 4 with regard to the fishery.) The second way, 'ownership in place', also claimed continuity with older mining law, including the *ad inferos* rule. Ownership of the oil and gas in place below is part of the owner's land holding. The only effect of the rule of capture is that the ownership in place is subject to the right of others to drain or remove the oil and gas from the holding.

Of course, neither interpretation much affected the practical effect of the rule of capture doctrine on oilmen's behaviour: overinvestment and overuse of machinery and equipment, waste of gas underground, and flaring.[52] By removing any basis for suing operators whose wells were draining their lands, the rule induced adjacent owners to rapidly deploy the drilling of their own offset wells.[53] The courts' exacerbation of the inefficient incentives inherent in the rapid-fire contracting between farmers and oil companies was made especially explicit in the Pennsylvania Supreme Court's majority opinion in *Barnard v. Monongahela Natural Gas Co* (1907):

What then has been held to be the law?—it is this, as we understand it, every land-owner or his lessee may locate his wells wherever he pleases regardless of the interests of others.

[51] *Westmoreland & Cambria Nat. Gas Co. v. DeWitt*, 18 A. 724 at 732–3 (Pa. 1889). 18A at 732–3; see *Dark v. Johnston*, 55 Pa. 164, 94 Am. Dec. 732 (1867).

[52] Good references on these wastes are Colby 1942, pp. 266–71, and, more generally, Rostow 1948 and Lovejoy and Homan 1967.

[53] This is explained in many places. See Andrews 1940, pp. 175–92; Hardwicke 1935, pp. 351–3; and Kuntz 1962, vol. 1, chapters 1–3.

He may distribute them over the whole farm or locate them on only part of it. He may crowd the adjoining farms so as to enable him to draw the oil and gas from them. What then can his neighbour do? He must protect his own oil and gas. He knows it is wild and will run away if it finds an opening and it is his business to keep it at home. This may not be the best rule, but neither the legislature nor our highest court has given us any better. No doubt many thousands of dollars have been expended in protecting lines in oil and gas territory that would not have been expended if some rule had existed by which it could have been avoided.[54]

Katz, *groundwater and correlative rights*

The rule of capture was—and is—a good defence against a charge that one land-owner has drained reserves from another owner's land.[55] It can be looked at either as a property right or as a simple freedom from liability. However, at least in the United States the common law has changed, limiting this older right by introducing the somewhat undefined doctrine of 'correlative rights'. When an owner and his neighbours in a common pool have 'correlative rights' vis-à-vis one another, they are legally required to work out some way of sharing the pool.[56]

The idea of correlative property rights to an underground reservoir between private parties emerged not in an oil dispute but in the California groundwater case *Katz v. Walkinshaw* (1903).[57] An aggrieved land-owner complained to the court that his neighbour's powerful and elaborate irrigation system had drained the water from underneath his own land. The court self-consciously rejected the 'English' rule of absolute ownership and capture described above. It pronounced this rule to be inappropriate (that is, against the common law's original purpose) in the climate and economy of California, in which water was scarcer than in England and growing ever more valuable. Despite the administrative difficulties inherent in the idea of assigning correlative rights over a 'secret' resource such as groundwater, justice required that the old rule be replaced with a new doctrine of reasonable use, 'limit[ing] the right of others to such amount of water as may be necessary for some useful purpose in connection with the land from which it is taken',[58] and of 'correlative

[54] *Barnard v. Monongahela Natural Gas Co.*, 216 Pa. St 362–5, 65 Atl. 801 (1907). The issue in the case was whether the lessee company had expended enough to protect the land-owning lessor. See Merrill 1940, pp. 299–301.

[55] The literature on groundwater problems and policies is vast. For an economic analysis of quota rights and integration of surface and underground rights, see Gisser and Johnson 1983. For a discussion of Texas's failure to introduce such underground rights, see Griffin and Boadu 1992.

[56] Junger 1958, p. 33. Lucas and Hunt used the word correlative in noting that Alberta's 1980 Oil and Gas Conservation Act s. 4 states that its purpose is to afford each owner the opportunity of obtaining his share of the production of oil or gas from any pool. See Lucas and Hunt 1990, p. 7.

[57] *Katz v. Walkinshaw*, 141 Cal. 116, 70 P. 663 (S.C. 1902), reversed 141 Cal. 116, 74 P. 766 (1903).

[58] Note that a 'reasonable-use' doctrine for stream water had been introduced seventy-five years earlier, in 1827. See Chapter 3 on surface water rights. Note also that a water-rights departure from the common law was not a new idea for California litigants. California was

rights', governing the distribution of an insufficient supply of water 'by giving to each [overlying landowner] a fair and just proportion'.[59]

The *Katz* judgment is complex because at the time California water law recognized both the common law and the appropriative water-right doctrines. Its importance rests on the simple idea that, because other users of percolating (as opposed to flowing) waters beneath their properties were recognized as having correlative rights, no single user had the right to deprive his neighbour of the reasonable use of groundwater. Of course, identifying the actual amounts that were permissible to take was another matter. Cases following the *Katz* judgment have attempted to determine what is reasonable. Clearly, they have been influenced by the reasonable-use judgments for surface water, some of which are discussed in Chapter 3. Trelease finds that state courts have combined correlative rights and reasonableness so as to require the defendant to 'share': that is, to give up a 'reasonable share'; to limit himself to a 'domestic' or 'ordinary' amount of water; or to share equally.[60]

Although *Katz* was a groundwater case, it had, for obvious reasons, large implications for oil well disputes. The *Katz* court was aware of these implications; in fact it had heard them raised by the defence as an argument against adoption of the correlative-rights doctrine, as dealt with, albeit weakly, in the following passage:

> It does not necessarily follow that a rule for the government of rights in percolating water must also be followed as to underground seepages or percolations of mineral oil. Oil is not extracted for use in agriculture, or upon the land from which it is taken, but solely for sale as an article of merchandise, and for use in commerce and manufactures. The conditions under which oil is found and taken from the earth in this state are in no important particulars different from those present in other countries where it is produced... Whether, in a contest between two oil producers concerning the drawing out by one of the oil from under the land of the other, we should follow the rule adopted by the courts of other oil-producing states, or apply a rule better calculated to protect oil not actually developed, is a question not before us, and which need not be considered.[61]

In other words, the court's chief justification for departing from the ordinary common-law rule—the fact that groundwater had a different value in California than elsewhere—would not in itself justify the extension of the doctrine of correlative rights from California's water to its oil. Water produced a benefit to the land, but oil was a trade commodity. As it happened, the Indiana courts had recently found a special characteristic in oil that would justify its own application of a version of correlative rights, once that doctrine was established as precedent by *Katz*.

then still debating its departure from the common law and the succeeding prior-use surface water rules for its substitute appropriative water law.

59 *Katz v. Walkinshaw*, 141 Cal. 116 at 141 (1902).
60 Trelease 1979, pp. 450–4.
61 *Katz v. Walkinshaw*, 141 Cal. 116 at 772 (S.C. 1902).

In 1900, in *Ohio Oil Co. v. Indiana,* the United States Supreme Court had considered the idea of correlative rights to oil in the context of the State of Indiana's constitutional ability to legislate.[62] The case concerned the constitutionality of an 1893 Indiana law forbidding the wasteful flaring of wellhead gas. The court founded the state's ability to legislate on a 'pre-existing' theory of individual correlative rights, an idea that it developed much less fully than had the *Katz* groundwater court.

The background to the case is as follows: In the 1890s 'unlucky' land-owners, those whose leases had been sidelined by drillers who found the oil beneath their lands not worth the cost of drilling or who preferred to get at the oil from a neighbouring property, had supported a campaign to equalize the shares of oil rent from a given reservoir among its land-owners. Judges had been unsympathetic. Turning to legislation, the owners joined forces with some conservation and industry lobbyists who had a different, but in some ways complementary, purpose: to prevent 'waste' such as loss of gas pressure. This coalition aroused some opposition to its campaign from 'lucky' and potentially lucky owners and operators. Those who had become aware of large oil reservoirs beneath their land and looked forward to signing lucrative private leases calculated that mandatory increased sharing of their own bonanzas with the owners and lessees of sidelined properties would harm them more than did the waste of petroleum outlawed by the new legislation.

The constitutional protection of property created tension between the individual property rights of producers and the collective rights of everyone else. The Supreme Court's reasoning in *Ohio Oil* resolved the impasse by recognizing a surface owner's correlative rights to oil and gas from an underlying reservoir: 'a convenient term for indicating that each owner of land in a common source of supply of oil and gas has legal privileges as against other owners of land therein to take oil and gas therefrom by lawful operations conducted on his own land, limited, however, by duties to other owners not to injure the source of supply and by duties not to take an undue proportion of the oil and gas'.[63] The majority opinion held that the state might make laws to protect the pre-existing correlative rights of overlying land-owners:

> As to gas and oil, the surface proprietors within the gas field all have the right to reduce to possession the gas and oil beneath. They could not be absolutely deprived of this right which belongs to them without a taking of private property. But there is a co-equal right in them all to take from a common source of supply the two substances which . . . are united, though separate. It follows from the essence of their right and from the situation of the things as to which it can be exerted, that the use by one of his power to seek to convert a part of the common fund to actual possession may result in an undue proportion being attributed to one of the possessors of the right, to the detriment of the others, or by waste

[62] *Ohio Oil Co. v. Indiana,* 177 US 190 (S.C., 1900).
[63] *Kingwood Oil Co. v. Corporation Commission,* 396 P.2d 1008 at 1010 (Okla. 1964).

> by one or more, to the annihilation of the rights of the reminder. Hence it is that the legislative power... can be manifested for the purpose of protecting all the collective owners, by securing a just distribution, to arise from the enjoyment, by them, of their privilege to reduce to possession, and to reach the like end by preventing waste.[64]

The legislation was therefore valid because it protected (notionally) pre-existing rights. Nevertheless, apart from prohibiting waste of the common supply, the case asserted that the rule of capture continued as the law: 'It is also clear from the Indiana cases that, in the absence of regulation by law, every owner of the surface within a gas field may prosecute his efforts and may reduce to possession all or every part, if possible, of the deposits, without violating the rights of the other surface owners.'[65] Thus *Ohio*, while extending constitutionality to the new legislation, limited but did not abolish the rule of capture of oil. Thereafter, a state could supplant the law of capture with a doctrine of correlative rights as outlined by *Katz*. But if it did not do so, an oil-lease holder had a solid right in law to drain oil from below his neighbour's land.

Since *Ohio*, some American state courts have explored the application of the correlative rights doctrine to disputes between individuals. In general, a neighbour's correlative rights may not so much limit the *amount* an operator may lift from a common pool as the *methods* he may follow in doing so. Probably for this reason, the law of capture has continued to dominate legislative and judge-made rules on entitlements to oil. The appeal to correlative rights is limited to isolated disputes. The influential oil and gas scholar Eugene Kuntz provides a modern definition of what such rights entail, including:

- a right against waste of extracted substances, including negligence in drilling or pumping out of a common formation,
- a right against spoilage of the common source of supply,
- a right against malicious depletion of the common source of supply,
- the right to a fair opportunity to extract oil or gas, and
- the right to conduct secondary recovery operations.[66]

State governments, more than individual mineral claimants, have made use of a doctrine of correlative rights because it gives a constitutional basis for their legislation directly controlling the amounts, rates and methods of private oil production. In Wilson's words: 'In hindsight, it is clear that even though the concept of correlative rights as announced by the United States Supreme Court specifically included rights and obligations concerning waste within an individual reservoir which might have been pled by individual owners seeking injunctive relief, the totality of the circumstances and nearly mob-like actions of owners in multiple fields which prompted the governors of Oklahoma and

[64] *Ohio Oil* at 209–10; and see Wilson 1989a, ch. 18, p. 5.
[65] *Ohio Oil* at 208.
[66] See Kuntz 1962; Wilson 1989a, ch. 18, p. 1.

Texas to act required remedies that the courts could not provide.'[67] Nevertheless, the doctrine merely *allows* states to regulate private production in order to add exclusivity to the rights of demanders. It certainly does find that these demanders already have the exclusivity characteristic in their rights. Nor does it compel the states to legislatively add the missing exclusivity.

NUISANCE

It seems always to have been accepted that the rules of tort could not be brought to bear on the rights of rival oil and gas property holders over common pools. In this respect oil-field drainage was very unlike mine flooding. When a static mine was flooded, property boundaries were clear and questions about 'reasonable' or 'necessary' interference and causation could come into play. But when an oil formation was drained, the meaning of a property 'boundary' had little significance, and this uncertainty was the problem. In the absence of a workable rule setting forth what and how much was included in each oil and gas estate, protections that we might have expected to develop in nuisance were diverted, appearing instead in the doctrine of correlative property rights.

CONTRACT LAW

Contracting and leasing between land-owners and drillers

While limiting the frequency of inter-owner lawsuits, the 'go and do likewise' imperative of the law of capture, especially before being tempered by successive legal modifications to the doctrine of correlative rights, was in fact the direct inspiration for the second type of dispute discussed in the introduction: that arising between land-owners and drillers and usually falling under the domain of contract law. Upon signing a lease or contract with a driller, a land-owner forfeited the right to enter onto his own lands and drill offset wells to keep his product from escaping into a neighbour's active drilling operation. He became dependent on his lessee's doing so in his interest—the principal and agent problem. In the event that a lease did not clearly lay out the driller's responsibility as agent (for instance, as we saw, in cases where the land-owner had limited knowledge of his own lands and/or traded in protective provisions in exchange for a signing bonus), the principals, the owners, quickly appealed to the courts for protection.[68]

I focus here on the traditional two-party contract of the nineteenth and early twentieth centuries, before the advent of wide-scale government regulation. No doubt the earliest drilling contracts contained only a lease's grant provisions: location, for how long and for what payment. But soon, with the

[67] Wilson 1989a, ch. 18, p. 8.

[68] See Merrill 1940, ch. 5, ss. 94 and 95.

understanding that oil was fugacious and that the law of capture applied, land-owners began to demand early and sustained drilling and production efforts from their lessees. In several very early Pennsylvania leases, the owners called for drilling to begin within a stated period and for the lessees to show 'diligence'. It was in the interest of typical producers to spread their risks—to deploy their drilling activities cautiously among their various leaseholds. Such a lessee was too cautious, decided the local courts, when in 1875 a lessor sued for lessee inactivity and won.[69] In this and following cases, the courts, finding that the lessees had not shown the 'due diligence' they had expressly promised, declared their contracts forfeit.

In the 1880s such courts began to detect 'implied' covenants in the leases, to the detriment of the operator/lessees. Even when companies had lived up to the wording of their contractual undertakings to drill and produce (or to pay a delay fee for postponing drilling)[70] they found their land-owners were going to court to press for offset wells or for more drilling. Some sympathetic courts were asked to look for evidence of 'fraud', where a defendant company had, for example, obtained leases on adjoining properties and chosen to pump oil (and pay royalties) on only one of them.[71] Gradually litigation moved the courts toward interpreting the contracts to contain *unwritten covenants* that protected landlords at the expense of their lessees—somewhat as the English courts had done by appealing to 'customary' land-use arrangements as being the probable product of some ancient 'first contract' between a lord and his tenants. Between 1896 (*Kleppner v. Lemon*) and about 1910 the courts of Pennsylvania, Indiana and most of the other oil states rapidly developed a reliance on implicit covenants for their rulings that most holders of certain types of oil lease were bound to drill exploratory and additional wells, to produce diligently, and to prevent drainage.[72] For example, the judges in a 1908 Wyoming case held that '... it was the duty of the lessee, under the implied covenant contained in the lease, to proceed with reasonable diligence to prospect and develop the premises, having due regard to his own interests and those of the lessor'.[73]

In invoking implied contract covenants, the courts sometimes merely filled in what the judges assumed that reasonable parties probably intended, as they

[69] *Brown v. Vandergrift*, 80 Pa. 142 (1875).

[70] *Consumers' Gas Trust Co. v. Littler*, 162 Ind. 320, 70 N.E. 363 (1904). In this and other cases in Indiana, Kentucky and Michigan, it was eventually held that if the lessor rejected the payment of the delay fee, it constituted a breach of an implied covenant to develop.

[71] *Kleppner v. Lemon*, 176 Pa. 502, 35 A. (1896). Lemon, the defendant operator, won the case because it had drilled on two adjoining farms.

[72] For case-by-case accounts see Williamson and Daum 1959 Appendix and especially Merrill 1940, ch. 1 and passim. The modern literature due to H. A. Simons and O. Williamson on implicit contracting has not been much applied to the turn-of-the-century cases on alleged implicit contracting in the oil fields.

[73] *Phillips v. Hamilton*, 17 Wyo. 41, 95 P. 846 (1908).

had done since the seventeenth century under mercantile contract law.[74] Lawyers call this implication of the rulings 'in fact'. Sometimes, however, the courts—and statutes as well—inserted corrections to a bargain they considered to have been fundamentally unrepresentative of the parties' interests or otherwise unfair. This is called implication 'in law'. Many implied covenants found in nineteenth-century American oil and gas leases were of the second type. The courts 'found' them in order to come to the rescue of land-owners who had signed leases that did not say what they 'ought' to have said in order to insure the land-owner an adequate share of the resource rent.

A contested topic in the oil and gas legal literature[75] is whether these 'in law' interventions, and their rationalizations, were justified. In general, the answer given is yes: a solid law was needed because of asymmetric information between potential lessees (landsmen and other industry professionals) and lessors (usually farmers who knew little about oil formations or about oil fields and drainage). Also as we saw, some lessors did not act 'reasonably' as they were attracted by a bonus and confused by the haste to sign—a haste their potential lessees could use to mislead or defraud them. When there was a discovery nearby, the lease procedure for proving that the lessee was not faithfully or reasonably carrying out the lease's express provisions to drill or develop was too slow to protect the land-owner from the loss of his resource. A reasonable operator and a reasonable land-owner rarely shared the same interest in decisions about drilling, developing and land fragmentation. The overall result of the implied-covenant doctrine however was that the operators' powers, originally derived from contract-like leases, became matters of judge-made law, and—as with miners dealing with the doctrine of support in England—were thereby weakened by judges showing sympathy to landed interests.

As a result we may say that the individual parties did not 'bargain for property rights' in the Libecap sense.[76] They had tried: the earliest oil and gas agreements were not true leases under the law of property with indispensable features and incidents attached to them, but undertakings under contract law arrived at through bargaining between the parties. Intervention, first by the courts and later (as seen below) by legislatures searching for 'equitable' solutions, transformed contracting from interpersonal kitchen-table bargaining to litigation over details contained in standard, uniform agreements. In this litigation, under the fiction of 'implicit covenants', the source of many of the operator's powers became, explicitly, a matter for public policy.

[74] In the early seventeenth century, in cases involving bills of exchange in trade between England and the Continent, '... Matters were greatly simplified by merely stating the facts of acceptance, endorsement and so on and then resting the case upon the custom of merchants. In this way there was no need to express in terms known to the common law the rights and liabilities of all parties to a bill.' Plucknett 1956, p. 668.

[75] Such as Lowe 1983, Merrill 1940 or Kuntz 1962. For an analysis of the effect of implicit covenants on subsequent firm behaviour, such as unit operation, see Weaver 1986.

[76] Libecap 1989, pp. 10–28.

Contracting over a common pool

Contracts and contract law did not only regulate relationships between land-owners and drillers. They could also function as a source of rights-delineation and distribution among the neighbouring drillers whose problems we have already encountered in the framework of property law. To what extent, then, did physically adjacent owner-driller pairs contract with each other to prevent such ills as waste, racing and flaring? And what prevented the widespread replacement of their rule-of-capture combat in property law with some form of mutually beneficial (contracted) pool management? In what follows, I first describe the degrees to which field unitization could take place. I then briefly describe some early recorded instances of unified operations in order to show their technical feasibility and historical relevance to the industry and to the development of oil rights. Then I briefly summarize the work of Libecap and Wiggins to help explain why, in spite of the available benefits, widespread voluntary contracting did not in fact emerge in the US oilfields.

There are three well-known options for such collective pooling to take place. The first was simply to replace members' individual go-it-alone production decisions with those of a collective sole-owner under unitized management, technically assuming the whole geological reservoir as the unit of control and production. The second was for members to keep and run their individual operations, but to entrust one or more stages of these operations—such as exploration, pooled drilling or unit secondary recovery (using steam or gas to enhance the natural pressure to drive crude to the wells)—to a co-operative effort. The third was to set up an arrangement under which the parties retained all well discovery and operation but agreed contractually on a collectively efficient system of well spacing and production sharing.

The three procedures are really three degrees of field unitization. The first was referred to as 'voluntary' unitization because it postulated a near-complete unitization brought about by market methods, in the absence of direct government regulation or pressure. We will see that such extensive unitization was rare in practice. The potential gains from co-operative activities—to reduce the waste of oil and gas underground and to achieve economies of scale in operation and investment—were not however always obvious to the pioneering nineteenth-century producers and their lessors. Many considered conservation and waste-prevention to be nothing more than requiring that producers learn to keep gas from flaring and to cap flowing wells, activities that required little collective action to enforce as they imposed little net cost on the producers and land-owners. More important, when a party did grasp the rent-increasing benefits of collective action, he also grasped that he might not individually capture an adequate share of these benefits. Consequently, each pool always had some producers and lessors who resisted unitization under all three alternatives.

I begin with the leases drawn up by land-owners in the 1860s.[77] Self-interest and risk-aversion encouraged farmers to fragment their land and to offer the companies the smallest areas each would accept.[78] This practice of estate fragmentation into multiple leases resulted, in some places, in wells being lined up in rows. Alarmed by the expense, waste and short lives of these small holdings, the operators began to search for land-owners who would sign leases that specified larger drilling areas in return for restricting withdrawals of tubing and plugging abandoned wells. Not all owners would accept these terms and fragmented over-drilling continued.

The sole-ownership ventures of the late 1860s were one kind of response. An example was the Columbia Oil Company's five hundred acre Story Farm. The company leased portions of Story Farm acreage to operators, realizing large profits in 1863–4. As output subsided Columbia re-acquired these properties and drilled new wells, with wide three hundred foot spacing. Half the wells were cased and the water shut off. In 1868 the company had twenty-three pumping wells, all profitable, with low costs. This happy story, unfortunately, does not illustrate either the first or second type of voluntary agreement among producing properties. Columbia was already the sole owner and was acting like a concession holder in a foreign oil field.

Operations on the Tarr Farm field near Titusville, Pennsylvania (1865) were a closer fit to an ideal voluntary unitization of numerous owners' rights. Promiscuous and sometimes vindictive withdrawal of tubing had flooded all producing wells within the oilfield's boundaries, and production was forced to a halt. After several months of negotiation, an agreement was reached between some of the parties, calling for isolation of flooded areas; pumping, sandbagging and casing of all productive wells; and synchronized well operation going forward. When the programme quickly restored production from zero to one thousand barrels a day, it gained support from owners who had been initially reluctant to agree. These owners were nearby and could observe the benefits of cooperation. But in other fields, where the land owners were absent and/or the operators uninformed about the payoff from joint action, opposition was unanimous.

According to Libecap and Wiggins (1985), the simultaneous opening of new fields and the resulting drastic price declines as oil from the newly opened fields flooded the local markets led to more widespread co-operative contracting efforts. Only a few of them succeeded through the First World War. The reasons for the failure were manifold. First, where there were many small firms, private agreements were difficult to reach and to enforce. Possibly a few large

[77] The material about Columbia's Story Farm and Tarr Farm closely follows Williamson and Daum 1959, pp. 161–3.

[78] On the matter of the landowner's theoretical preference for fragmentation of his surface acreage into small oil leaseholds, I am grateful to Lasheng Yuan for discussion and for the analysis in his 1999 University of British Columbia Ph.D. thesis on 'strategic divisionalization'.

firms, coming together from month to month at new showings and fields, might have learned to bargain and work together. By the late 1920s, however, firms were small: the largest oil-field operators among the twelve hundred in Texas and the two hundred seventy in Oklahoma each had less than 10 per cent of their respective state's output. Firms were aggressive and competitive, not cooperative.

Second, information difficulties made firms cautious about entering into unitization contracts. Rationality called for each owner to compare the value of his property *with* and *without* unitization. Formulating an estimate of the *with* value required guessing all the other properties' outputs, then aggregating them with adjustments for economies of scale and obligations under the cooperative contract, into a value under collective management. If an owner estimated the value of his property under non-cooperation to be less than what he could get out of a cooperative regime then he would be willing to enter into bargaining to set up or join the 'collective'. Bargaining brought new difficulties. To get unanimous agreement the parties had to agree on a formula for sharing the total *with* value. One simple procedure was for the total *with* value to be divided in proportion to the *without* values of each field, which would, theoretically, allow all owners to get the same percentage mark-up or rate of return on their opportunity costs for entering into agreement. Achieving this, however, required all bargaining parties to agree on each other's *without* property values, something that individual owners had neither the incentive nor often the ability to do. The implications of the scanty geological information differed from property to property and were evaluated by heterogeneous owners, advisers and professionals. As well, each party had far more information about the flows and geology in the vicinity of his own property than in other vicinities. In addition to (and exacerbated by) these information asymmetries, it was in each party's strategic incentive to exaggerate his *without* value.

A third complication was that most of the many small parties had less to lose from a delay in the introduction of unit management than did the large owners. The combined effect of all these problems was that some parties might, out of ignorance, cussedness or the hope of extorting a larger share by threatening to free ride on the group, hold out against accepting the share offered by the organizers. In fact, the forces working against unitization appear to have prevailed. J. S. Bain found that of three thousand pools throughout the United States in 1947, only twelve were completely unitized. Another forty years after that Wiggins and Libecap (1989) found that only 38 per cent of Oklahoma's and 20 per cent of Texas's production in 1985 came from completely unitized fields.[79]

[79] Bain data for 1947 and Libecap and Wiggins data for 1985 cited in Libecap 1989, p. 96.

One prediction that arises from the previous discussion is that unitization would become more likely in the late stages of the life of an oilfield, once individual values become known with greater certainty to all players, the opportunity costs of holding out fell and information asymmetries weakened. Libecap and Wiggins provide some empirical support for this prediction. Libecap mentions the Empire Abo field where unitization was proposed, and failed, in 1967. He continues: 'A unit contract for Empire Abo was not signed until four years later... when primary production had so declined that the value of all leases was approaching zero and new production could occur only with unitization and related secondary recovery techniques.'[80]

THE ADVENT OF GOVERNMENT REGULATION OF COMMON POOLS

The difficulties surrounding the contractual operation of oil fields, the failure of any kind of private sole ownership to appear and the inability or failure of the courts to fully contain or mitigate these difficulties, suggest why government regulation emerged and became the rule. Initial forays into legislating in the public interest reach back to the origins of the oil boom. Demanders in Indiana and Pennsylvania began pressing for legislative action to mandate the plugging and casing of abandoned wells in the 1860s. This resulted in the first (state) plugging law in 1878.

Little more in the way of such conservation legislation appeared over the next half century. The interruption can be attributed to the more pressing demands of the downstream petroleum industry, some of whose supply was imported and not, therefore, particularly dependent on private US oilfields. In the 1870s the great monopolies and trusts of the world petroleum industry were in their formative years—their market position based to a large extent on their control of transportation on sea and on land. Not surprisingly, state governments directed their political and legislative energies mainly at matters concerning the buying of crude, its distribution by railways and pipelines, its sale to and by refineries and, especially, the exercise of monopoly power. Relatively little legislative attention was paid to practices or disputes in the oil fields themselves. Threats to the exclusivity of owners' contractual rights were left to the courts.

By the 1920s, however, the issue was coming back. Oil production was underway in fifteen states. In some of these states the federal government's public land compulsory unitization rule was dominant. At one extreme, a few states allowed unregulated exploration and production on private lands within the state and a very few introduced leasing laws to benefit marginal landholders. At the other extreme, two or three states introduced rules to reduce waste, chiefly through well-spacing rules. Later in the decade the major oil-producing states introduced legislation to permit or encourage voluntary field unitization (Texas being the

[80] Libecap 1989, p. 107. Empire Abo is one of seven 'Texaco and New Mexico' fields studied by Libecap and Wiggins.

chief holdout). In the 1930s, in conjunction with federal New Deal policies, these states effectively gave up their efforts to bring about unitization and instead cooperated in federally coordinated pro-rationing under the IOC, whereby states divided their private-land allowable production quota among fields and wells according to each one's 'potential'.[81] After the Second World War some states returned to policies of encouraging unitization, called 'compulsory unitization' policies below, even though private oilfield owners were not, for political reasons, actually *forced* to unitize under most conditions. By that time there was more activity on federal oil lands and off-shore oil fields, with the result that firms in the industry had more experience with unit operation and were somewhat more able and willing to apply these methods to lands they held under private lease. Also, fewer new fields were being discovered, which meant that fewer small firms were acquiring mineral rights and that oil-drilling activity was becoming more concentrated. Coordinated arrangements among neighbours therefore depended on the agreement of fewer parties.

The twentieth century also witnessed the emergence and solidification of federal and state regulation, including the very rules that would have been in the armoury of a sole-owner or contractual unit manager, such as spacing rules. The differences, of course, were twofold: (1) most of the governments' quantitative regulations were boilerplate, applied uniformly throughout the whole state rather than tailored to the individual pools as would have been the case under voluntary in-house arrangements; and (2) most of them continued to make it possible for small landholders to grant small-acreage leases.

Though uniformity was the rule within a state, the rules varied *across* states in line with the differing goals of state governments. Some governments sought to please their leading oil firms or regions while others tried to maintain total employment. Still others were mainly interested in maximizing treasury receipts. Often they wound up trying to offer all things to all voters: reducing waste, cutting expenses, maintaining price and giving a break to the owners of small acreages and dry wells. To the extent that unitization can be envisioned as a way of paying small owners *not* to produce, governments took over the role of chief buyer of idleness (much as a government does when it provides an agricultural price-maintenance scheme).

Spacing and pro-rationing legislation

Because they reduce the number of offset wells that lessees are bound to drill, spacing laws have been popular with lessees and unpopular with lessors. This, combined with the US government's traditional sympathies with land interests, probably explains why spacing rules were usually weakened by

[81] Pro-rationing was emulated in Canada on Crown/public lands. Readers should keep in mind that American pro-rationing policies applied on private lands. For a historical survey of the Canadian adaptation (in Alberta) see Crommelin, Pearse, and Scott 1978.

exempting small-acreage properties that the rules would otherwise have prevented from even having a well.

Pro-rationing on private lands was everywhere regarded as more drastic than a spacing law.[82] We encountered pro-rationing in the discussions of American IOC and of Alberta's public land oil disposal procedures above. Indeed, the Interstate Oil Compact, established in 1935, was for nearly half a century until 1972 the dominant example of a legislative control scheme governing output from private oil fields, despite the lack of official federal control (for constitutional reasons) or regulatory intervention. The IOC was born out of individual state pro-rationing actions, and the concern from smaller oil-producing states to limit the ability of Texas, the major producer after 1930, to continue to flood the national market. Oklahoma first introduced pro-rationing in 1928, with variants on its law turning up subsequently in other states, and culminating in the Oil State Advisory Committee—precursor to the IOC—which established state quotas, translated at the state level into field quotas. With the exception of a few crisis periods induced by hold-out states, pro-rationing under the IOC was successful at maintaining a constant price in the national oil market for several decades.[83]

In brief, by reducing their private autonomy, Depression-era spacing and pro-rationing laws made up for oil-land owners' and users' failure to merge or to contract for field management. Government regulation replaced owners' collective decisions on total annual drilling in a unitized field (derived from the legal rights of property) with non-transferable permits (under a spacing law) and quotas (under a pro-rationing law).

Compulsory unitization

There were two precedents for state-legislated compulsory unitization. The first was the voluntary unitization seen in Pennsylvania in the nineteenth century. The second, already discussed, followed from the 1920 Mineral Leasing Act. At that time, the federal government undertook to grant much larger oil and gas leases from its previously reserved public land to those who agreed to create (private) reservoir operating units under government regulatory supervision.

But for the states, private land holding was still the norm. State governments could not follow the federal public lands lead in imposing a unitization scheme or cajole owners into accepting one. They limited themselves to passing laws to

[82] A variant of pro-rationing is the MER or 'maximum efficiency rate'. In contrast to the IOC's (and Alberta's) market-demand pro-rationing, maximum efficiency rate is primarily a physical concept, setting a weekly quota for each well (or each lease or for each operator that allows the field to produce at peak physical efficiency). For a given reservoir, the MER is the combination of annual production rate and number of wells that gives the greatest lifetime total recovery while maintaining an adequate economic rate of return. A change in rate or number of wells that moves the field toward the MER while maintaining the rate of return is not necessarily the same change that would maximize the present value of total operation.

[83] This paragraph is based on information from Libecap and Smith 2004.

make it easier for a group of firms to take the initiative to organize their neighbours into an agreement to manage their shared private common pool. From an institutional point of view, the creation of a mandatory oil-field unit came to resemble the financing of local public works, whereby if a sufficient majority of residents vote for a school or an irrigation system, then the minority must join in and pay the tax costs or contribute land by compulsory acquisition.

The political issue was the required majority. Some states, like Texas, required unanimity—100 per cent support—so that Texas law was for practical purposes non-binding. Wyoming required more than 90 per cent support. Oklahoma, the pioneer state in mandatory unitization on a vote by leaseholders on private land, required only about two-thirds support—low enough, as we have seen, to produce a few unitized fields.

It seems clear that state schemes for unitization on private land have failed because information is held unequally. On federal lands the law called for unitization to begin before the (possibly discrepant) production potentials of the various leases become apparent. The firms involved all have the same information and find themselves on the same *ex-ante* playing field, eliminating their incentive to hold out against equal per-acre sharing. By contrast, on private lands under state law, unitization proceeds only after private leaseholders have drilled and discovered their production capacity, leaving some of them understandably keen to prevent unitization and profit-sharing.

As a closing note, an extensive literature exists on the economics of oil fields, some of which is referenced in the preceding subsections. Much of it provides an analysis of multi-owner, multi-lessee fields and the rough-and-tumble difficulties of getting to a contract in such fields. Only a minor part of this literature deals with the internal dynamics of unitized fields, managed on behalf of the lessees and lessors by their own cooperative or incorporated institution. It is a pity that this latter subject has not attracted more attention, for there is much to be learned by rigorously comparing, say, a fishery managed by its participants, or an aquifer used for irrigation, with an oil field or gas field. It appears, for example, that some governments' oilfield regulations, providing fixed percentage allowables, spacing and maximum rates of production for a field are close analogues of the government-provided parameters that allow fishermen to take over their own resource (see Chapter 4) with rights that are secure, exclusive, transferable and enduring.

The United States oil and gas right profile and characteristics

THE PRIVATE AND PUBLIC OIL RIGHT 'PROFILE' IN THE UNITED STATES

As with coal and metals, the oil right acquired under the government's oil disposal law carried conditions and benefits that can be classified under the eight headings in the mineral right 'profile' introduced in Chapter 7. Because regulation came to impact directly on oil drilling on private land (in ways it did not for other minerals) I also look for how stipulations and benefits differed when oil companies acquired their rights to drill (a) from private land interests and (b) under regulatory supervision.

Free access

In practice the original 1920 Mineral Leasing Law did not give oil miners the same free access that the Mining Law had given to metal miners. Oil prospectors were free to roam around the country and to apply for permits, but the drilling requirement naturally excluded everyone except those with capital and, later, the elite training required to geographically locate oil underground. Prospectors, the class who were most adamant in protecting the right of free access for metals, played no role in the oil industry. After 1935, the two-stage procedure was abolished, reducing the cost of the leasing process to some extent and therefore partially freeing access. For offshore leases, Mead and others have claimed that, in spite of the tremendous cost of bidding, access is not unduly exclusive. For example, in the first twenty years of the offshore disposal procedure, one hundred and thirty two different firms made bids to lease oil patches from the US governments, either singly or in combination with each other.[84]

As for private oil lands, 'free access' as commonly understood naturally played no role. In the absence of contracts giving explicit, exclusive permission to enter and drill, private lands were off limits except by trespass.

Priority principle

Under the 1920 and 1935 disposal laws, the priority principle was retained for UGS lands but rejected for KGS lands for which all applicants, regardless of the seniority of their application, were subject to competitive bidding. This situation lasted until 1987 when the lottery approach was disposed of altogether and nearly all leases were made subject to competitive bidding.[85] Between the passing of the 1935 and 1987 laws, companies had an obvious preference for seeing as much land as possible classified as non-competitive (UGS). Throughout the second half of the twentieth century allegations appeared that lands that should have been put up for bidding were fraudulently classified as UGS and, hence, disposed of by priority (first-come, first-served).[86] A similar situation prevailed for offshore leasing, in which priority never counted but for

[84] Mead 1977; see also Mead et al. 1985.

[85] Tracts not attracting a minimum bid, such as two dollars per acre, continue to be leased free to the first taker, often in large parcels of more than ten square miles. However, by 1987 the proportion of public lands that had not yet been thoroughly searched for oil was very small: the level of industry knowledge was high enough for bidding to be a general disposal method.

[86] *Arkla Exploration Co. v. Texas Oil and Gas Corp.*, 734 F.2d 347 (1984).

which several authors have suggested that some insider advantage in bidding for offshore oil rights may exist for certain types of leases.[87]

Uniformity

The US public oil right features some uniformity of disposal procedure.[88] After the 1920 Mineral Leasing Act undid Taft's oil-lands reservation policy, the public lands became uniformly 'open' (excepting land destined for national-park use). But uniformity was not complete until the abandonment of the UGS/KGS distinction in 1987, since under the 1920 and 1935 laws disposal procedures and royalties differed by subjective land classification. Uniformity has been more solid offshore, where uniformity of procedure and of tract size (5,760 acres) has been federal law since 1953. But there too, much has remained discretionary, not only because of the variants introduced by concession bargaining, but also because the government has treated tracts of land differently in order to conform to various geographically specific conservation rules and endangered species strategies.

As a general rule one would not expect private, often bilateral, negotiations over oil leases to lead to anything like uniformity in disposal or payment procedures. In practice, however, competition among firms seeking drilling acreage pushed the type of lease on offer and the type of property characteristics demanded toward convergence across state lines. For the same competitive reasons, state regulators often adopted similar regulations on wells to those found in neighbouring states. Furthermore, national environmental regulations and standards have forced well drillers to follow many of the same land-use practices everywhere.[89]

Extra-lateral rights

The basic oil ownership problem is that the crude oil flowing in the reservoir obeys no natural boundaries and can legally end up in the hands of drillers situated anywhere on the reservoir. Therefore, no driller, once oil was discovered and the shape of the underground formation realized, could be thought of as holding the dominating position similar to the 'apex' claim on a metal vein.

Patenting

US policy focused on transferring western public lands, including mineral lands, into private hands. The federal oil laws of 1870–2, 1920, 1935, 1953

[87] Porter, Hendricks and others, following Mead, have studied the offshore bids in search of evidence of collusion and/or bias. Porter summarizes with a mixed verdict. Wildcat bidding is highly competitive, bidding for drainage leases less so. One theory is that the special knowledge of owners of adjacent leases gives them the inside track. See Porter 1995, p. 24.

[88] An exception is Alaska, which adopted its own set of rules to promote oil development on state lands.

[89] As noted earlier, most private leases have a term compelling the lessee to drill an offset well if it seemed that adjoining wells would drain the common pool. See McDonald 1971 (a book devoted to policies for preventing waste). See also McDonald 1979, pp. 121–53.

and 1987 all followed dominant oil industry practice on private lands and provided mostly leasehold tenure. Industry demand for freehold tenure through patenting of public tracts of land was weak. Most of the oilfield action took place on private land that had already been severed from the public domain under settlement and homestead laws. By the time oil from federal land (mostly offshore) became important enough to induce muscular lobbying, conservationist demands to keep federal lands under public ownership tended to counteract an industrial push for patenting.

There may be other reasons that patenting did not emerge on public land. One advantage of the patent over the lease is that it stretches out the possible duration of the investment. This consideration becomes less pressing if short-term leases of public land can be easily renewed without running the risk of encountering new regulations or higher royalties on condition of renewal. In the shorter, simpler history of offshore oil rights disposal, the lease has apparently been deemed by industry and policy-makers alike as sufficiently secure.

On private land, we have seen how the disposal of rights took place almost exclusively through leasehold. This is likely the way everybody preferred it since there is in fact nothing in law that would prevent oil companies from buying out private farmers and other land-owners, surface rights and all.

Surface rights

The final feature of the mineral right 'profile' is the inclusion or reservation of surface rights. The general rule for the public oil lessee, like the coal miner, was to hold both mineral and surface rights, just as farmers under the Homestead Act received ownership not just of their fields and pastures but also of the minerals beneath them.

In private land leasing, the lessor could sever his minerals with provisions for the lessee's right of access and with some implied rights for him to continue using his own land without interference from well operations.[90] In fact, the plethora of private leases that emerged in the late nineteenth and twentieth centuries was indirectly caused by the early public-land granting of potential oil lands to western settlers, before the oil worth of the land was known either to the settlers, the drilling companies or the government.

Discovery requirement

In the absence of the priority principle before 1935, the two-stage disposal procedure required a permit holder to establish to the government's satisfaction that 'valuable deposits of oil have been discovered'[91] before proceeding from permit to lease. Politicians learned, however, that claims to have made a 'discovery' meant little unless drilling had actually hit oil. After 1935 the

[90] Corpus Juris Secundum, Mines and Minerals, vol. 58, s. 12, p. 32.
[91] 1920 Act, s. 14.

government abandoned the discovery requirement and it remains unimportant to onshore and offshore oil drilling today. Although governments retain the right to turn down a successful bid or a request from a firm to open up a potential oil patch to bidding on the grounds that the development has not been proved promising, in general the government defers to firms' judgments on where to find and develop oil, even absent a provable discovery. (Of course, in doing so, the government is also influenced by the separate but potentially offsetting concerns of environmentalists and other outside interested bodies.)

In contracting on private land there can be conditions under which a lease is void if the lessee does not make a discovery. If there is no such set of conditions, then the lease will have a fixed term or duration that serves much the same purpose.

Work requirement

Before 1935 a stiff work requirement existed for leases on US public lands. Once the permit was converted to a lease, however, the requirement disappeared with respect to both KGS and UGS lands. After 1935, with the advent of the lottery, the only vestige of the work requirement was found in the requirements for the renewal of a lease. As one inquiry noted, 'The great majority of leases that result in any activity have the first significant ground-disturbing action . . . in the last year of the lease term: the fifth year for competitive leases and the tenth year for non-competitive leases.'[92] A similar rule holds for offshore leases, which allow idleness but lapse after five years if no production has yet taken place. The absence of an additional, continuous work requirement for offshore oil worries observers. They regard companies stacking up inactive leases as a form of non-competitive behaviour, and advocate alternative systems under which companies tender work commitments in the bidding process rather than royalty commitments or cash bonuses to the government.[93]

On private land, by contrast, the lease usually required that the land over which rights were granted would be drilled or at least explored. As we have seen, lessors found it in their best interest to demand diligence in rapid development of their fields. Private leases therefore contained their own 'work requirements', and the courts later universalized the provisions by accepting the necessity of showing 'diligence' as an implied covenant of any private oil lease.

THE OIL RIGHT AND THE CHARACTERISTICS OF A PROPERTY RIGHT

Drilling for oil is even more capital-intensive than metal mining. The companies who undertook to explore and drill over the period I have examined

[92] US National Research Council on Onshore Oil, 1989. Due to speculation, only about 10 per cent of leases acquired on public land were ever explored, and only 10 per cent of these were ever developed. The rest, presumably returned to the public domain when the lease's no-work grace period ran out.

[93] See Erickson 1977, pp. 61–77; Peterson 1977, pp. 27–45.

here faced risks regarding the geology and technology of their operations; about the behaviour of other companies on the same pool; and about the actions and demands of their landlord. Put simply, the more of each of the characteristics of a property right they had, the safer they felt in investing and operating. To conclude this chapter, I survey briefly what was at stake with the five major characteristics:

Quality of title and security

Historically, once preliminary exploration and discovery was carried out on public land, the companies' titles, acquired from the government, were good enough to justify their enormous expenditure on drilling and on transportation.

The same was true on private lands, as the explosion of private land drilling in the late nineteenth and early twentieth century proves. The courts certainly were cluttered with disputes between landlords and lessees, and these sometimes led to companies losing their rights, particularly given the pro-land-owner leanings of many local judges in the US. But most of these disputes were fundamentally about differences of opinion over whether the company had satisfied the terms of the lease and did not reflect a basic tendency of landlord or government to challenge the property rights of a company that obeyed oilfield rules and carried out the contractual requirements to which it had agreed.

Exclusivity

In the American oil states the demand for exclusive access to an underground oil formation, as offered by the law of property, was defeated by the emphasis on the rule of capture.

Though I have not discussed it here, the exclusivity situation in the Canadian and Australian jurisdictions was legally similar. We have seen several examples suggesting how externalities and dependencies among users of a common pool undermined the individual enjoyment of an oil right, and specifically the powers to manage, transfer and (especially) profit from it as desired. As well, the recognition by local courts of implicit covenants in leases, calling for multiple wells, offset wells and pumping, all aggravated the collective dissipation of crude oil in reservoirs. Only the belated application of a correlative rights doctrine made it possible to reduce the destructiveness of this feature of the law of property.

Consequently, to the extent they are built on common-law models, it is fair to say that individual oil rights have very little exclusivity. To compensate, governments have supplied spacing regulations of various kinds, and prorationing to make sure owners all receive a share of the rent they would receive from an exclusive oil right. The provision of rules leading to a unitized oilfield regime is analogous to the provision of a public good. Compulsion is necessary to arrange for the distribution of costs and to prevent free riding on the group;

and the (aggregate) benefits are, by definition, non-exclusive. In the United States, such regulations have been imposed fairly widely on the public lands, but due to state constitutional limitations have been merely encouraged on state and private lands.

These generalizations do not extend offshore. The various international offshore regimes have offered some companies such large acreages, wide spacing rules and long lease terms that the holding companies can be said to be exclusive owners of their pools. This is also true of many concession fields, offshore and onshore, mainly in developing countries. In these arrangements, the host nation agrees that the oilfield must have no wells except those of the concessionaire, producing a very exclusive arrangement.

Duration

Given the rate of interest, an economist can calculate the ideal (present-value maximizing) production path curve for a centrally managed oil pool. If the duration characteristic imposes a finite horizon on the owner's/operator's possession of the well, the maximizing production path will be more temporally rapid; will fail to recover some of the oil in the pool; and will have a lower present value relative to the infinite-production-horizon case.

Prospecting or exploration permits on public lands are issued for short periods, presumably to reinforce diligence and other rules to prevent companies from sitting on their sites like the proverbial dogs in the manger. Typically, if the company shows signs of getting on with exploratory drilling, its term is extended to allow the project to be completed. Once a production well is drilled, a production lease applies a comfortable term of fifteen or twenty years, in most cases renewable. The rules about unitization on public lands usually give individual wells terms that are long enough for the pool to be managed as if they were time-unconstrained, as is optimal under the broad theory laid out in the paragraph above.

On private lands, by contrast, the lessor has every incentive to make the effective term as short as possible in order to bring pressure on the driller lessees to move quickly in order not to lose their legal rights before finishing the drilling project and to capture as much oil as possible from the underlying formation before competing wells dip in. Perhaps counterintuitively, then, it appears that historically most private drilling operations actually finished production well before their legal durations ran out.

Transferability and divisibility

Since an oil lease on public lands is a first cousin to a common-law property interest, it should follow that its holder may transfer it to another lessee at his discretion. In the oil industry, however, the various government regimes attempting to prevent flush production and wasteful offsetting wells sometimes have made transfers subject to Board or ministerial approval.

On private lands, prior to exploration and discovery, the farmer or other landholder was of course free to transfer or divide his interest in land or mineral rights, and parties to a lease could and can transfer their interests to others, subject to the obligation to honour the provisions of the lease as originally signed. Once land was transferred as an oil lease, however, it became subject to state government regulation of the whole district or whole pool. In some cases transferability was allowed but division of holdings forbidden in the interest of not exacerbating the public-good problem associated with efficient joint management. Regulators sought to avoid the political difficulties associated with shutting small land-owners out of drilling by simply refusing permission to divide oil properties into units too small to allow drilling under the government's preferred spacing laws.

[illegible]

Part IV

Rights over Woods-Based Resources

10

Concepts in Forest Property Rights

Introduction

In this fourth and final part,[1] I apply the general approach used for mining rights as presented in Chapters 5 to 9 to the development of forestry tenures in England and the British colonies—first on the public or Crown lands (Chapter 11) and then on private lands (Chapter 12). From the beginning, forest tenures on public and on private lands have been very different. The early Crown made rules for its own lands in an elaborate 'forest law' that was contemporary with the Magna Carta and formed much of the basis for modern public forest rights as they developed in the heavily forested New World. These rules were unlike the feudal arrangements that evolved in private common lands, wastes, domains and parks. These latter customary arrangements became sources for common-law precedent and for later legislation and doctrine governing private forest-land holding, both in England and overseas.

The development of rights over private forests has not yet attracted a full literature of its own. For the discussion in these final chapters my best sources have been from the small literature on the history of forests and forest policy. Authors associated with the conservation movement support state policies of giving property right holders long and secure tenure to foster careful harvesting and long-term silviculture. These authors tell us a good deal about rights and tenures. Authors who mention forests in general or economic history contexts, by contrast, confine themselves mostly to the development and changing welfare of lords and their commoners who were dependent on forest

[1] For the discussion in the following chapter, I have to thank many friends for information and comments. These include the following, but there are others to whom I am also indebted: Douglas Allen (Simon Fraser University), Jamie Benidickson (University of Ottawa), Robert Deacon (University of California), Marion Clawson (RFF), DeLloyd Guth (Faculty of Law, University of Manitoba), David Feeny (McMaster University), Gary Libecap (University of Arizona), H. V. Nelles (O.C.-U.A.), Dianne Newell (University of British Columbia), Peter Pearse (University of British Columbia), Irving Fox (University of British Columbia), David Stewart (Vancouver), Daowei Zhang (University of British Columbia and Auburn), Irene Spry (University of Ottawa). Cliona Kimber helped mightily with the original legal research, and, subsequently, I had help from Ross McKitrick, Catherine Dauvergne, Rachel Mayer, Margaret Hall, Lilliana Biukovic, Leyla Mahdaviani and Ann-Marie Metten.

enterprises (matters of the changing distribution of rights and resources), and to forest harvesting as an element in regional and/or national economic growth. As in the previous sections, my interest is in tracing the evolving privileges held by those who had a right to work in the woods, with a special eye to learning what property right characteristics these holders demanded and achieved, and what obstacles stood in their way.[2]

Among the characteristics needed and wanted by forest users and those concerned about forest productivity and sustainability, *duration* of the holders' rights, the *quality* of their *title*, and the *exclusivity* of their tenures (not only from spreading forest fires but also from government interference) are long-standing and recurring themes. The *divisibility* characteristic, particularly the vertical and multiple use forms of divisibility, also played a large, though perhaps less noticed, role.

In terms of obstacles to economic use of the forest, I focus on two. First, in Chapter 11 for public forests, we will observe the costs and difficulties faced by governments trying to extract optimal rent—for themselves and for society—from the forests. In the nineteenth century, the problem was one of the costs and technical limitations of land classification that made it difficult for New World and frontier governments to create separate tenures for forestry and settlement (and therefore to achieve productive specialization on the public land). This technical barrier, unsurprisingly, did work itself out. But it has been replaced in the late twentieth century by somewhat related government concerns over how, and which, forests should be run in order to serve the public interest, as well as the interests of their private, self-interested users.

In Chapter 12, I turn to the second set of barriers to the creation of fully productive *private* property rights over forests: those arising from the common law itself and its view of trees. The main problem was that, in defining the estates of property holders and their heirs and successors, it made sense to regard trees (timber) not only as part of the holders' lands, but as if they actually *were* land (as opposed, for instance, to chattels). But from the point of view of forest management, it made, and makes, more sense for rights to trees to have their own characteristics, separate from the land or estate on which they grow. The problem shows up again in modern forestry in the absence of a separate, legal 'tree growing tenure'. I argue that this missing tenure can contribute to inefficient or incomplete multiple-use management of forests.

Timber rights and their characteristics

Common law has developed only a few standard interests in private land. Of these, only four apply to forests: freehold (fee simple), leasehold, profit-à-prendre

[2] Thanks to Douglas Allen for discussions on this subject. See Allen 1991.

and licence. As the courts have frequently been called on to define these interests in private land, there is substantial agreement about the features they must have and the features that can be added to them. However, there is no such agreement when it comes to public land.[3] As with mineral rights, governments drafting forest legislation freely created permit, licence, lease, limit, timber sale, concession, contract, and berth interests without much concern for whether or not they correspond to common-law interests of the same names. This also holds true for their proceeds: charge, rent, rental, quitrent, rent charge, royalty, fee, stumpage, due and so forth. Often government agencies have changed the name of an interest simply to advertise their new policies.

Consequently, I am less concerned with the formal titles given to forest tenures and more with the characteristics these tenures conveyed. It is worth reviewing here the six characteristics of rights over the forest:

Duration

In the matter of a temporal hold over a forest right or tenure, what determines the holder's behaviour is expected duration, as lengthened by the probability of low-cost tenure renewal, as shortened by the probability of loss of possession by some date, and as offset by compensation for investments and improvements. The forest-policy literature emphasizes that forest regeneration is very sensitive to two different time periods: the time available for harvesting old stands and the time available for the growth of new stands. We will see that legal titles are sometimes defined to accord with one of these periods—often (and controversially in the era of interest in sustainable development) the second.

Flexibility[4]

A right-holder's power under a given tenure may vary from time to time and from place to place. Over time, the parties to a limited-duration property (estate) may change their initial privileges and duties as the characteristics and maturity of the forest change. Over space, statutes may leave the applicability of certain rules regarding Crown forest management and land use to the discretion of local officials and tribunals. In either case flexibility is a measure of the extent to which the discretionary decisions conveyed with the right remain appropriate to a specific interest in timber: how frequently rights and duties may be changed (over time); or how geographically minute is the decision-unit (over space). An important application of the flexibility characteristic in relation to forestry has, again, to do with the multiple-use forest, discussed theoretically at the end of Chapter 12: how easily forest land can be converted between its many uses and how easily multiple uses can be maintained and accommodated.

[3] In what follows, 'lumberman', 'harvester' and 'logger' are synonymous, as are 'timber' and 'trees'.

[4] See Benidickson 1998 (draft), pp. 44–6; Pearse 1990, pp. 177–90; Bowes and Krutilla 1989; Scott, Robinson, and Cohen 1995, pp. 188–90.

Exclusivity

If a right-holder's right to her patch of forest were perfectly exclusive, then she could exercise her powers without interference from others. Any interference would be liable for trespass or nuisance. As with all the natural resources I have examined so far, this ideal state was rare in practice. We will see, however, that, apart from the risk of spreading fire, the loss of exclusivity from these *physical* spillovers has generally been less important than the loss of exclusivity due to interference from government regulation and taxation, including forced multiple-use. This latter type of impingement on exclusivity dates back to the medieval English forest (where forced sharing of the woods with the lord and with each other under manorial rules led commoners to neglect the trees). It has been on the increase in the North American forests over the second half of the twentieth century.

Quality of title

The forest policy literature emphasizes the value of exclusivity for long-term silviculture and, in this respect, makes little distinction between duration and quality of title—as suggested for the more general case in Chapter 1. As against other private persons, a holder's entitlement is enforced and protected by the laws of property, contract, nuisance and tort. As against the government, a holder's title is protected by regulations about expropriation, compensation and due process. These in turn are enforced and reinforced by political means, by lobbying and mobilizing public opinion. Related to the discussion of exclusivity above, we will see in Chapter 12 that, while forest titles typically convey security against outright expropriation, strong public opinion about conservation and protection of a nation's forest cover has often led to weakened quality of title. Increasingly, governments retain the right to force both holders of rights over private land and users of public forests to engage in sustainable forest practices justified by ecological or conservation goals.[5]

Transferability

Transferability in forest tenures is increased not only by relaxing restrictions on the holder's powers to dispose of the title, but—as was the case for the placer miners in the California camps who were required to sell only to newcomers—also by expanding the set of persons who may acquire and hold a title. The rules regarding the transferability of ownership of forested land are simply the rules regarding the transferability of interests in land in general. But the transferability of rights to use either private or public forests for a single purpose such as logging was, historically, narrowly restricted by feudal-tenure and inheritance laws—a subject I return to directly below in the discussion of vertical divisibility.

[5] See Luckert 1990, and Luckert 1991, and Luckert and Haley 1989 and 1990.

Divisibility

In Chapter 1 it was seen that divisibility or divided ownership can be achieved in three ways, all of which we will encounter in the following chapters: (1) 'horizontally' (or laterally) dividing one parcel of land into several; (2) 'vertically' dividing the ownership rights over the land from those of the things on it (i.e. creating separate temporal estates); or (3) keeping a parcel of land intact while dividing its ownership according to uses, or 'purposes', such as grazing, mining, cropping, logging or fishing—called 'multiple-use' divisibility.

The common law seems to have had little trouble with the idea of severing parts of a parcel of land in these ways. It has regarded property in the trees and buildings and their various uses as incidental to, or at the disposal of, property in the land to which they are attached. The holder of a freehold right in land may dispose of all the property, or he might reserve cutting rights by excepting that part of his holding from the larger bundle of rights over his wooded property (much as we saw some of the great English families do in disposing of their mines and minerals in Chapter 8).

Another historically important arrangement by which timber was made subject to different rights than the rest of the land was in connection with inheritance and succession. Sometimes when inherited land was subject to an entail or came under a strict settlement, the holder of the land might be free to use the farm land as he desired, but constrained to keep the timber in the forest intact, on pain of being sued by his trustees or by his family for 'waste'. In some jurisdictions, these and other forms of life tenancy still differentiate the owner's powers over the uses of the forests from his powers over farmland. The historical importance of entail and inheritance to British forestry, and its later reappearance in US law as a justification for modern forest regulation, is discussed in Chapter 12.

In the legal literature the subject of separating rights to the tree from rights to the land has mostly to do with which party holds a right to cut the trees and for how long the right is valid. Often the right is contractual, not a subject for property law. In Chapter 12 the subject is broadened by considering rights to the *growing* of trees. Under the heading of 'tree tenure' consideration is given to the evolution or creation of property rights to plant, protect, cut and replant trees on land owned by another party. The rights would be a little like the personal right of a commercial nurseryman over his potted flowers and shrubs that grow in the courtyard of a public building.

Multiple-use ownerships and the private–public relationship in forestry

Before moving on to Chapter 11, I want to make a few more introductory remarks about the *versatility* of forest enterprises. It is the sustainable, multiple-use nature of the forest, particularly of the modern forest, that most distinguishes woods-based resources from other land-based non-fugacious resources, and specifically from the underground mineral resources discussed in the last section. The demand for multiple-use forest management comes from strong public interest in forest conservation, and the many services and benefits forests supply to a nation besides timber and wood supplies. From the beginning, owners of forestland made arrangements to accommodate more than one land use—sometimes independently and sometimes at the behest of government. These uses could be as independent as lead mining and sheep grazing, complementary like timber and animal habitat or conflicting, like recreation and tree cutting. After historical periods of woodland specialization and subdivided forest management for single uses, in the early twenty-first century the allocation of forests for multiple purposes is again becoming an urgent goal for some jurisdictions' public policies.

The modern versatility of the forest has led to special types of contract and relationship between the public and private forest sectors. In Chapter 12, we will encounter the modern long-term licence and the Canadian joint-managed forest as examples. Modern governments have additional options for their public and Crown lands. First, they can specify the rights and obligations of uses or users through administrative techniques rather than through property and contract law. For instance, a government can declare a forest to be open to free visitor access but subject to a variety of rules that are enforced by penalties drawn from criminal law. Second, they can tailor user rights to respond to user objections and changing public sector goals. The tenures and charges a government offers need not be standard property rights or standard contracts but simply take-it-or-leave-it instruments, invented or abolished as often as suits political convenience.

When working on the details of new 'tenures' to accommodate multiple use, the managers of public lands combine the power to regulate and the power to innovate. Pollution is prevented by regulation; forest fires are prevented by criminal penalties; visitor access to wilderness or to bodies of water is guaranteed by statutes and regulations. All these may be found with, or even take precedence over, rights nominally conveyed by a timber licence. Because of the government's powers of compulsion, the transactions costs of flexible tenures may be lower than those used by private landlords or tenants. Like the six characteristics of the right, the issues of multiple uses of forest land and competing private and public (government) demands for how forests are to be run and maintained are recurring themes in the final two chapters.

11

Forestry on Public Lands from the Medieval to the Modern Era

The first section of this chapter deals with the English royal forests from the time of the Norman Conquest until the Enlightenment and the start of North American colonization.[1] The rest of the chapter traces the development of rights and tenures over the North American (and briefly the Australian and New Zealand) forests, as adapted from medieval English Forest Law, from the sixteenth century up to the second half of the twentieth century.

Tenure decisions on public lands: the royal forests

Contrary to intuition, assisting wood production was not the chief reason for 'afforesting' original feudal holdings (setting them aside as a royal forest) or for putting the royal Forest Court above the local manorial courts. According to G. M. Trevelyan[2] the court was:

more odious to Norman and Saxon alike than any private jurisdiction. For it represented the King only in his personal and selfish capacity. The forest law and the forest courts of Normandy were transplanted to England, with lamentable results in human suffering and servitude. In the following century as many as sixty-nine forests belonged to the Crown, computed at almost a third of the whole acreage of the kingdom. Inside that vast but thinly inhabited area the King's peace indeed reigned, but in a form hateful to God and man. The special courts of the forest deprived all who dwelt within their jurisdiction of many of the ordinary rights of the subject. Poaching deer was punished under the Conqueror by mutilation, under his successors by death.

The alienation of so huge an acreage of land from national uses and national liberties remained for hundreds of years a source of constant bickering between the King and his subjects. The gradual deforestation of district after district marked the economic and moral progress of the country. When in Stuart times the King's power passed to the

[1] For a short history of French forests, see Reed 1954 and Pincetl 1993.
[2] 1973, p. 149.

squirearchy, the modern 'game laws' grew up, like 'a bastard slip', as old Blackstone called them, of the dying forest laws of the King, less ferocious indeed but equally opposed to the freer spirit of the English law of the day.

It was William the Conqueror who brought this plague into Britain. Trevelyan continues:

He made large forests for deer (wrote the Anglo-Saxon Chronicler), and enacted laws therewith, so that whoever killed a hart to a hind should be blinded. As he forbade killing the deer, so also the boars. And he loved the tall stags as if he were their father. He also appointed concerning the hares that they should go free. The rich complained and the poor murmured, but he was so sturdy that he reckoned nought of them.

Trevelyan, correctly, never mentions trees or woods. Land was afforested almost entirely to create hunting preserves. The woodland was incidental, although its importance in the management of the forest was to increase steadily for centuries. Trevelyan, also correctly, never suggests that the afforested lands were marginal.[3] It is best to assume that they were of average quality for game, cattle, sheep, crops and timber.

From the beginning, then, there was pressure to establish multiple uses. Under William, persons living within each forest became directly subject to the Crown. The resulting 'system was created and maintained by the arbitrary will of the king in face of the hostility of his subjects, who considered that its interference with their liberties was contrary to natural law'.[4] When, much later, North America was colonized, the monarch extended this same prerogative so that he could personally hold the new 'Crown' or public lands and make direct land grants to proprietors.

Seeing to the wood supply was the least of the forester's duties. Woods provided habitat for game: a source of recreational pleasure, but also of venison and other food, skins and furs.[5] Nonetheless, most of a typical royal forest was unwooded, covered by fields, pasture and villages. Each forest was a separate administrative area, headed by a forester and having its own strict forest rules, courts, guardians and wardens. Much of the Norman woodland remained wild and lawless, the haunt of poachers and brigands. The open areas gradually increased, in spite of the forest laws and local rules, as farmers and others arranged legal deforestations and illegal encroachments.[6]

There were opportunities for the royal forests to become a source of revenue through the disposal of rights to timber. Private owners within a royal forest were prohibited from cutting timber on their own acres without permission. Before determining the amounts that could be cut, the forest administration carefully

[3] For a sustained history, see Young 1979.

[4] Grant 1991, p. 7.

[5] See Schlich 1911, p. 645. Schlich was the leading international forestry authority in the late nineteenth century.

[6] See Birrell 1980.

considered the welfare of the animals of the forest. Satisfied on this point, it issued licences to manors and establishments within the forest to cut or sell their own timber—usually for payment, though some were presented to royal favourites. Their provisions were often quite detailed and included some rules about conservation and reforestation. A recurring requirement was for the planting of hedges or the building of fences to protect new growth from cattle. An important variant was a royal order permitting an entrepreneur to buy woods from the owners up to a certain amount and to specify cut and sales. Owners could avoid the delays in obtaining these orders by cutting first and paying fines later.

What of the timber on the Crown's own woodlands? Various monarchs, when desperate for money, occasionally mined these woods for timber, where the severity with which the kings had 'preserved their game reserves had incidentally saved the trees'.[7] A 'commissioner', presumably a sort of agent, would be appointed to sell trees, wood and underwood up to a certain value, with the proceeds remitted to the king. Though we know few of the details of the right conveyed, anecdotes from the period suggest that the buyer's right to the standing trees was of short duration, and suitable trees could not always be found.[8] Although sales were numerous in the thirteenth and fourteenth centuries, they should be seen against the fact that the forests may have covered one third of England. It was later, during the Tudor period, when the forested area had shrunk, that timber sales became a commonplace.

The king gained much new timber when clerical estates were added to the royal forests upon the dissolution of the monasteries. Most of them contained great oaks. Now England saw a wholesale felling of trees to be sold for money. Both the nobles to whom the lands were passed and the monarch him/herself engaged in these sales. According to Albion (1926) and Richardson (1952), Elizabeth I started the selling of 'commercial' licences to cut in the royal woods; and James I, Charles I and Cromwell went further by appointing commissioners to sell the larger forests outright. The extent of this activity may be contrasted with the inactivity of the Crown in mining matters. Elizabeth's Case of Mines had won the monarchy royal prerogative over gold and silver deposits, and various monarchs had created or tolerated free-mining districts where lead and other metals brought in some royalties. But the scope of these mining activities was trivial compared to the Tudor and Stuart real estate operations in forestland. Consequently, the scope of Crown demands had much more impact on changes in forest policy and tree-cutting rights than on the small amount of mining policy and on mining rights.

The massive alienation and destruction of timber in the royal forests and the former clerical estates has been overshadowed in the historical literature by

[7] Albion 1926, p. 107.

[8] One commissioner, Richard de Abyndon, was assigned to sell trees worth £150. See Young 1979, p. 125.

the attention paid to the royal forests as sources of naval timber.[9] The Stuart process of satisfying the Navy's demands for timber involved four sources: private estates, the colonies, the Baltic and the royal forests. Under Cromwell's policy of selling off large areas of the royal forests (Cromwell was such an enthusiastic disposer of forests that he opposed the existence of royal estates), naval purveyors—buying officers from within the Navy—received the right to mark with a broad arrow the timber (especially oak) needed for naval purposes before the areas were sold: this was a revival of the idea of reserving the timber.

Although Cromwell's land-selling policy soon ended, the general policy of naval priority continued. By 1700, in William III's time, the treasury ran the royal forests. Naval purveyors were attached to each forest and, with permission from the treasury, they selected and marked suitable trees. A bureaucratic system of negotiations from the Admiralty and shipyards to the treasury and, thence, to the surveyor-general (head of the royal forests) was saved from total chaos by the existence of much larger, though still limited, competing commercial supplies from civilian woods and estates—a topic to which I return in the next chapter. Indeed, the royal forests rarely provided more than about ten per cent of the oak required by the Navy.[10]

In fact, even within the royal forests, it is doubtful that the naval buyers were bigger players than were civilian licensees. Incidental evidence is provided by the fact that, although there were almost seventy forests, only three were of import as sources of naval timber, all located close to the royal dockyards. Forests further north provided much revenue during the early 1600s from trade timber and coppice sources, but not as naval sources.[11] Yet, while naval documents and various diaries and correspondence (Pepys' for instance) tell a good deal of the system of procuring the Navy's needs from the royal forests, we know relatively little of the characteristics of Elizabeth's civilian licences.

In addition to the concept of naval reservation, two additional aspects of the management and disposal of the English royal forests influenced the later management of timber on the public lands of the New World. First, the administration of the royal forests provided a foretaste of the later drive toward forest privatization. Modern foresters notwithstanding, the Crown did not see itself as a life tenant or trustee. The early monarchy had carved out much forestland to satisfy non-timber, non-revenue purposes, which had become much less important to later governments. In particular, game habitat became less valuable as hunting seems to have lost its fascination for the monarchs. Even more important, meat had become more available in the wintertime from farm sources. Pre-fifteenth-century monarchs could be described as running a sort of land storehouse,

[9] Indeed, the literature often gives the impression that all timber came from the royal forests until Tudor or Stuart times. An outstanding example is James 1981, p. 161, who says almost nothing about private or church woodlands, wastes, chases or parks until about 1482.

[10] Albion 1926, pp. 106, 138.

[11] Albion 1926, p. 107.

granting, regaining and re-granting lands with their woods attached in order to reward (and punish) their subjects, while Tudor and (especially) Stuart monarchs were deterred from selling off virtually all the forest land only by a lack of buyers, the force of hostile public opinion and concern over naval supplies.

Second, it is within this indeterminate holding of Crown lands that the operational meaning of 'licence' developed and with it notions of the characteristics embodied in the right to be conveyed to the lessee of the Crown/public land in order that he could make profitable and safe use of the forest. Over the course of the Middle Ages, duration gradually lengthened; exclusivity increased from the near-non-existence of the early hunting permits to a commonplace under Elizabeth; and divisibility developed as the Crown pondered the compatibility of the chase and wildlife with rights to 'assart' (i.e., clear) land, to grow coppice, to exclude grazing animals, to protect and grow oak for civilian and naval purposes and to sell land while reserving certain uses. Each policy had financial and political consequences for the monarchy (and later for the government as a whole) just as they would for later governments in Canada and the US.

Naval licences and their survival in the New World

Naval licences for timber deserve special attention because the system emerging from naval demand was transplanted to the North American colonies, and also for a time to New South Wales.[12] We can only guess what colonial licences really permitted in the early days of the Thirteen Colonies. Their importance petered out in the new United States, where the timber trade increasingly operated on private lands. However, events conspired to perpetuate the licensing practice elsewhere in British North America where, to this day in the Canadian provinces, much of the timber trade still operates on Crown lands. I conclude by regarding the colonial licence as a property right provided in response to demand for particular characteristics. My hypothesis is that this demand came from the Navy, not from the timber trade or the logger.

The North American naval reserves

When Britain moved some of its forest-management apparatus to North America, some of the purveying system was retained. The monarch's rights

[12] Among Britain's Pacific possessions, Norfolk Island (north of New Zealand) also became an important source of masts for naval (and other) vessels in the early nineteenth century. Norfolk pine became a plantation tree in several parts of the world. Most of the earliest cutting and logging, both on Norfolk Island and later of the Huon pine in western Tasmania, was done in woods near the sea, some of it by the crew of the ship that was to transport it. There does not seem to have been any formal forest property institution (such as the North American licence regime) for most of this trade: gangs of workers and ships' crews simply took what they could carry. Thanks to Neil Byron for information on this subject.

of property over the colonial lands were even more absolute than were his rights over the royal forests in England. In most colonies, however, the Crown's land rights were granted to one great 'proprietor' who then disposed of the lands for his own profit.

To the extent that there was an overarching forest policy in the colonies, it took the form of broad-arrow policies of Naval reservation.[13] The grants of forested land to the proprietors and their assigns were made subject to a reserve. For example, the 1691 charter granted to the Massachusetts colony placed a naval reserve on large white pines, which the Navy wanted for masts. By 1711 this reserve had been extended to all colonies. All Crown grants of land and forests to private holders excepted pines two feet in diameter at breast height. In some places these trees were marked with the famous broad arrow.

From then until the American Revolution the colonists and the naval agents who managed the mast procurement and enforced the naval reserve were in intermittent conflict over its general and particular applicability. The naval reserve was most notorious when the broad arrow interfered with the activities of private landholders on their own lands. This became one of the grievances of 1776. It was probably most economically important, however, when it interfered with commercial logging in the backwoods, on Crown or proprietors' land. There, shippers were busy cutting trees of various species, including pines, for various markets. They resented the threat that their logs could be seized and produced in the Vice-Admiralty Court, which sat without a jury. Officers (called surveyors) and their deputies brought information against those who claimed the logs.[14] However, as information and enforcement costs were extremely high, many builders and lumbermen flouted the regulations.

The Navy did not cut its own masts from its reserves. Instead it granted licences to selected contractors in England who had made successful bids to provide timber. The contractors in turn made their reserves available and/or marked trees for the local lumbermen hired by their American agents. Relatively little about the licences is known with clarity, other than that they conveyed few characteristics relating to a property interest in timber. Their duration was usually one year, giving holders little discretion regarding allocating work or timber over time. They were not very exclusive; more than one contractor could have a permit to find and extract masts in the same area. And they were said to be neither transferable nor divisible.

Well before the American Revolution, licensing and the broad arrow policy was imported into Nova Scotia and New Brunswick. After 1763 it reached Quebec and even Ontario. Ports in Nova Scotia, which were already shipping

[13] The mast policy was part of the timber policy, and it was part of an even broader 'naval stores' policy for procuring tar, pitch and turpentine as well as timber, the former items mainly from the southern colonies. See Albion 1926, p. 250.

[14] The proceedings in three early cases before a Vice-Admiralty judge are presented in Andrews 1938, vol. 4, pp. 247–8.

timber to various markets, had by 1785 begun to ship masts to Britain. In central Canada the Navy improved its administration of the mast policy. The naval reserve continued until well after the Navy's Napoleonic-wars emergency needs had vanished.[15]

Thanks to Wynn, we know something of New Brunswick's experience of the lumber trade. Wentworth, the surveyor-general of naval timber, reserved pine timber fit for naval purposes in all titles to land in both Nova Scotia and New Brunswick. And he endeavoured until 1810 to control mast and timber supplies to England. During this process Crown reserves of whole areas (not just naval timber) were set up and later surveyed.[16] Apparently, the naval cutter's roles and rights did not differ significantly from those that had been developed in New England. For those who were licensed, the forest was like an open access resource with a premium on getting there first. The licensee was assigned a fixed number of pieces but not a fixed location. Accordingly, mastmakers ranged widely through the forest. Enforcement efforts were part of a revenue system that necessarily concentrated on checking logs as they were brought down the river for shipment.

Even in the late nineteenth century the practice of reserving trees and licensing loggers to cut them survived in New Brunswick, at least until settlers who might lay claim to them fulfilled all the requirements for acquiring full title. Not surprisingly, this was a cause of friction between settlers and lumber companies.[17] However, the mast reserves were generally adapted to fit into the colonies' land policy, which was concerned with settlement. As the Ottawa Valley and New Brunswick became the sources for huge export-oriented timber industries, naval priorities were downgraded. This was signalled in 1826 by the incongruous joint appointment of the Upper Canada commissioner of Crown lands and settlement to be also the surveyor-general of mast reserves.

The demand for licence tenure[18]

The short chronology above tells us that licences were used in all the North American colonies to control and market the supply of naval timber. The Crown continued licence tenure in Canada long after the independent United States

[15] On the other hand, Vancouver Island was an important source of masts even though there was no naval reserve of masts or timber there. Gough 1988, pp. 23–4.

[16] Wynn 1981, pp. 138–9.

[17] See Léger 1992, p. 28.

[18] A note on terminology: When land is granted subject to a certain set of terms and conditions, and for certain periods, the set is described as a 'tenure'. Thus the original lumbermen in Canada held rights under a timber-cutting licence tenure. When land was sold outright, there were no conditions imposed by the grantor (the Crown), so the word tenure did not usefully apply. When, in the nineteenth century, the number of leasing and licensing arrangements increased, the word 'tenures' was increasingly used as a sort of collective noun to comprehend all possible arrangements. It is widely used in this sense today within the general field of forest policy/economics.

had begun permanently alienating forested lands. The widespread and consistent nature of licensing in nineteenth-century North America marked something new. The earliest lumber trade had been local and sporadic. Probably many shiploads of logs were cut from Crown land without the cutters possessing a right in the land. Eventually, demanders of a more proper or rigorous tenure—principally the Navy, with the English timber trade and colonial administrators who derived no particular benefit from Crown ownership or public reserves playing only supporting roles—began to press for change.

According to Albion and other naval historians, the Navy board was concerned about a mast shortage. It was therefore impressed by the great pines of the Thirteen Colonies. The Navy was concerned that many of the best stems were being sawed up as lumber or destroyed in transport. In its view, this was wasteful, as sympathetic witnesses (mainly naval contractors) were willing to testify.

To an economist, the charges of wastefulness and poor quality suggest that the price the Navy offered the commercial trade was not high enough to justify catering to it—a topic discussed further in the next chapter with respect to the weak incentives for timber-growing on private forestland in England.[19] In its dealings with the colonies, the Navy's strategy, conceived in eighteenth-century mercantilism, entailed taking trees out of the commercial market and putting them in the naval reserve, a huge bureaucratic undertaking for the time. The Navy licensed dealers and loggers to cut and ship these trees. Thus the licensing system in the colonies was born.

As the Navy both demanded and supplied licence tenure, it met opposition from the settlers and lumbermen in the colonies. History emphasizes that ordinary landowners were outraged by the naval reserve that affected (retroactively) trees on their own land. Besides the 'coercive trespass' onto their private farms and woods, the settlers resented being denied a premium for their superior trees and, indeed, being denied the right to sell them at the price they would fetch on the market. So strong was the settlers' resentment that in practice the Navy discreetly avoided cutting on private land, presumably allowing each settler to eventually dispose of his mast trees at the commercial price. There is nothing in this well-known story to suggest that the settlers, either as landowners or as potential workers, would have favoured licence tenure.

By contrast, the lumbermen probably remained basically voiceless and passive as to the nature of early colonial timber rights. There are misleadingly good official records of their transactions with the Navy and with surveyors of the reserves but very few of their commercial activities. This is a bias in the records, for busy lumbermen tended to steer away from tax or duty collectors and from the Navy mast supply. Most of them 'rampaged' around the forests, combining

[19] Evidence of the Navy's ineptness and failure to constrain corruption is to be found in various naval histories. For an excellent summary of the actual shipments, see Williams 1989, pp. 90–2.

farming, land clearing and commercial lumbering. They sought mast-cutting work when it paid and stole mast trees from the reserve when it did not.[20]

The survival of licence tenure after the Navy

Since it was the Navy and only the Navy that wanted naval reserves and licence tenure, the removal of the former should have precipitated the demise of the latter. Sure enough, the licensing of loggers to cut on public lands vanished in the new United States after independence but survived with the Navy itself in the British-Canadian colonies.

After independence, the individual states claimed the former Crown lands, along with their timber. The idea of a public reserve for masts, timber and stores did not vanish right away. The original naval reserves survived in Massachusetts through 1783 and the concept was revived again when the new republic purchased naval reserve forests in Georgia and later in Florida. Although these were phased out in the 1830s, others were created later in the century. Apparently the new US Navy rarely depended on them, obtaining most of its masts and stores through the same channels as did the commercial shipbuilding industry. At any rate, these relatively minor reserves had no discernible influence on the main currents of tenure or disposition of the public land.[21] The frontier states pursued a policy of complete alienation in the sale of public lands; forests were simply thrown in with land granted to settlers. As could be predicted from my earlier analysis, loggers and settlers did not demand a licence tenure on public lands.

As could also be predicted, the Royal Navy, which stayed on in British North America, maintained its naval reserves policy and the licensing of lumbermen. As the British Crown had made no land grants to them, the new assemblies of the colonial governments lacked the ownership powers and law-making jurisdiction to deal with the public domains. The forestlands were therefore under the jurisdiction of the appointed governors, under orders from the Royal Navy and the secretaries of state in London, who were advised by their local councils.

At first, governors in Upper and Lower Canada presided over a modified seigniorial system, under which new arrivals were granted land (including freehold interests) according to their loyalist or military status, subject to naval reservation. From 1763 to 1827 the governors' appointed surveyors made reserves of oak and pine.[22] In Navy theory, apparently, the logging of

[20] As well, there was considerable local autonomy in forest use, apart from royal and proprietorial authority. See Kawashima and Tone 1983, p. 168.

[21] For information on the earliest US naval reserves, see Hough 1882; Kinney 1916, pp. 372–3; Kinney 1917, pp. 237–9. See also Albion 1926, p. 358. For information on later reserves, see Gates 1968b, pp. 532–4.

[22] In the 1780s and 1790s Wentworth, the naval surveyor general, was active in creating reserves in Nova Scotia. It is not clear whether this activity was pursued by others thereafter or

these reserves—rather than serving the rapidly growing commercial market for squared timbers, logs, stathes and other cut lumber—was to be the mainstay of the Canadian lumber industry.[23] Lumbermen either bought cutting rights from settlers or trespassed on Crown lands. A very few obtained land grants, which included timber, from the local government. In short, although the colonies matured and acquired elected and increasingly responsible assemblies, the formal governance of (and policies for) the forests did not develop at the same pace.

Not until the end of the Napoleonic Wars did London, attempting to assist the Canadian colonial authorities, begin to loosen the Navy's hold on reserves. Colonial officers began to handle timber as a local rather than as an imperial resource.[24] But, as we will see in the next Part, the new regime did not stray far from the naval model. The governments adapted the old licensing procedure both for revenue and for bringing the existing commercial lumberland under control. The adaptations differed from colony to colony. Governor Robinson in Upper Canada at first merely ran a sort of toll gate on the Ottawa River for log rafts being run down to Quebec. In all cases, the legislature's participation was not needed since control over Crown land remained a prerogative of the Crown's representative.

The United States and Canada decide against separate forestland sales

Post-independence, Canada and the United States both decided not to dispose of forestlands by a specific, separate sale. Yet they arrived at this decision from entirely opposite directions. In the United States, farmland was already being sold into freehold ownership. Canada was disposing of cutting rights by licence separately from land. The end result was that many US forest lands wound up under freehold ownership in spite of the lack of a forestland sale law, while in Canada forest lands wound up in licence tenure on Crown lands. Generally, the final difference has been noted in the literature but not the similar no-timber-sale policies that led to it.

It is probably safe to accept the general hypothesis that, all else being equal, the Canadian and the American governments would have preferred to sell specialized rights over forested lands. A specialized sale for forest-related purposes

whether Wentworth had created enough reserves for the following decades. See Fingard 1966–90. For his deputies appointed to Upper Canada, see Lambert and Pross 1967, pp. 30–5. Lambert and Pross believe that these deputies did very little to create new naval reserves either in southern Ontario or in the Ottawa Valley.

[23] On the Nova Scotia growth in squared-timber and wood product trade, see Lower 1933; McCalla 1993, pp. 28–9 and ch. 4, and sources cited by Lambert and Pross 1967, p. 30 n2.

[24] Nelles 1974, p. 11; Lambert and Pross 1967, p. 31. Nelles stands out for noticing the continuity between the naval system and the later licensing system.

would have facilitated orderly, efficient use of land as between farming, mining and forest interests while in theory allowing governments to extract more rent from the land. As well, it seems best to attribute to voters and governments in both nations the same basic preferences for land alienation, especially as they shared preferences with respect to settlement policy, the protective tariff and, later, railways. In what follows, I try to offer a convincing explanation of what prevented them from adopting the forestland sale. I start with a brief chronology of post-independence American and Canadian forest disposal policies. Then I offer a longer exposition of the American problem of classifying forestland. Canada also had this problem to a less serious extent. Finally, I offer an explanation of Canada's licensing policy, which was based on the belief that it would produce more revenue than would a forestland sale policy.

The evolution of land and forest rights in the United States

When the original states began to cede their claims in 'western' territories to the new union government, a federal public domain was created, over which Congress assumed the responsibility for disposing of the lands directly to individuals. As we know, the procedure it adopted assumed that the new owner would be a farmer. There were surveys preceding cash sales by auction, using the grid pattern, the six-mile unit and other details adopted from systems pioneered in New England and allowing buyers to acquire clear title. Indeed, in spite of the size and diversity of the forests being passed into private hands, both the government and settlers were satisfied with the characteristics of the old private common-law freehold interest. The rights to hold and cut timber were to pass with the land.

There was contention about disposal details: the size of the units and their price. There were also ideological differences. The old-line New England conservative Federalist Party argued for charging land prices high enough to select a yeomanry with large holdings and cash to invest. On the opposite side, Jefferson and the anti-Federalists believed in selling the public lands for credit and in small quarter-section holdings. But the practical differences were small. The initial Federalist legislation in 1785 and 1804 embodied Congress's sustained aim: quick, direct disposal. Later Congresses enacted many alterations to the price, land size and conditions of disposal, culminating in the prototypal homestead law of 1862, which was copied in Canada and abroad. Congress also accelerated the alienation of land by adapting methods of indirect land disposal—in particular huge land grants to the individual states and to the railroad companies. As Nelles (1974) aptly remarks of the period: 'The public lands were only public insofar as they were waiting to become private.' This remained the case for timberland until the 1880s when, as we will see below, the new conservation interest urged government to hold back forestland, set up forest reserves and create a forest licence tenure.

A chronology of nineteenth-century Canadian timber law: the lumber industry and users' tenures

The nineteenth-century Canadian governments changed land and trade policies frequently; but the actual individual property rights, or tenures, reacted slowly. Various authors have identified the development of public-land forest policy through four dated 'stages': (1) unregulated open-access forest exploitation (to about 1870); (2) profit- and revenue-oriented disposal (to about 1905); (3) regulation of forest exploitation for fire protection and to lure investors (to about 1946); and (4) forest management for conservation, regeneration and sustainable development (up to now).[25]

The rights and obligations of loggers and lumbermen, modelled on rules applied by the administrators of the naval reserves, slowly changed, eventuating in the implementation of revenue-seeking policies (stage 2); regulations (stage 3); and, finally, contract-like forest management arrangements (stage 4). During each stage outstanding licences held over from the previous stage combined with new tenures, still called 'licences' and still bearing traces of their remote common-law ancestry. But rather than providing a simple right to go onto someone's land and cut trees, at each successive policy stage the licence became the vehicle for an ever-heavier load of terms and conditions, until its origins were all but lost to sight.

Prior to the Napoleonic Wars, the young Canadian colonies had not been significant timber exporters. When the American market opened, timber cut in New Brunswick sold in New England. Mostly, however, the receding New Brunswick forest frontier was oriented toward Britain, as was the timber industry of Lower Canada, weakly competing with the established Baltic timber trade. The forests of the lower St Lawrence valley were rapidly being swept clear. Upstream in Upper Canada, most forested land was cleared by Loyalists and other settlers, who sometimes shipped logs or milled lumber across the lakes to the new American states.

This picture changed when the Napoleonic blockade closed the Baltic to British timber markets. In 1808 Britain radically raised its general duties on European and American timber, thereby creating a valuable preference for colonial (i.e., Canadian) timber.[26] Very quickly, shipping and financial interests began to organize the large-scale export trade of red and white pine logs from New Brunswick and the upper Ottawa Valley via Quebec City. After the Napoleonic Wars, lumbering continued to develop as a major source of paid employment on both sides of the upper Ottawa Valley. Reciprocally, its employees were providing a market for farm produce.[27] The sale of lumber rights, along with the import tariff, was also

[25] For discussion, dating and comparison among authors, see Ross 1995, pp. 63–9.

[26] British tariff protection is discussed in Tucker 1936, ch. 4; and Lower 1933, especially diagram 3.

[27] Recognition of the dependence is captured in some of the official correspondence of the time, for instance, in an 1853 letter from Elgin to Newcastle (quoted by Tucker 1936,

becoming a chief source of government revenue. Consequently, Canadian politicians could not follow American politicians in their settlement-conscious frontier regions and simply ignore the lumber industry's claim to a special procedure for legitimately acquiring timber rights. Following Nova Scotia's entrance into the timber trade, the export economy in the Canadian provinces demanded the development of timber tenure. The development of this tenure meant that, when in 1841 Lower and Upper Canada were united, the great timber boom took place on much the same 'tenures' in Canada East and Canada West.

Initially, as the interest in naval reserves waned after 1815, the forest rules on Crown land became quite lax. In New Brunswick, access to all the Canadian forests was 'defended by regulations on paper only, in reality open to everyone'.[28] But when the expanding industry moved the frontier of forestry well beyond settlement, it became necessary to apply British forest policy in order to maintain control and to obtain revenue. Recall that, according to eighteenth-century British procedure, selected English contractors, suppliers to the royal dockyards, obtained commissions to cut the timber on naval reserves. This theory was still being applied in the early nineteenth century:

> The contractors in turn transferred their rights to Canadian lumbermen or commissioned Quebec merchants to buy timber brought to the Lower Canadian port. The system would probably have worked well enough had not the middlemen who shipped timber for the Navy found that, because of the general scarcity and high price of wood in Britain, there was a growing civilian demand for the product. They began to ship more and more timber from Quebec and diverted an increasing proportion to meet civilian needs. Local lumbermen found the regulations restrictive. They had either to cut on forest reserves under licence from the British contractor or else had to... obtain a grant of land from the colonial government. When these means of acquiring forestlands failed, the lumberman was forced to acquire cutting rights from a settler or trespass on Crown lands.[29]

In the 1820s London, through its colonial governors, created a new method of disposal, first proclaimed in New Brunswick in 1817.[30] Although the Navy's reserves and licences were not abolished, a new system of licensing was created. Locally administered, licences were to create revenue in the form of 'dues' for the colonies. The responsible official was to survey the forests, create reserves (perhaps for the Navy, presumably to prevent settlers from destroying the resource), recommend the locations or districts in which licences were to be issued, set up auctions for the larger tracts and police or enforce the whole system.[31]

p. 72). Lord Goderich, colonial secretary between 1833 and 1834, worried that a high price of land would create a pool of labour, a 'landless' labouring class. See Guillet 1933, p. 239.

[28] Wynn 1981, pp. 138–9.

[29] Lambert and Pross 1967, p. 31.

[30] See Wynn 1981, ch. 6; Lower 1938; and Harris and Warkentin 1974.

[31] See the description of the arrangement for Upper Canada in Reid 1990; and Lambert and Pross 1967, pp. 31–44. Some reserves had been created, but for the most part settlers' rights were to be issued with the timber rights being reserved or severed.

The official granted a licence to a berth for a prescribed amount, subject to a known charge (about one shilling per unit). The transactions costs were very high and confusion prevailed as to what kind of right, and to what, the licence actually conveyed.[32] Moreover, the bureaucratic hurdles entailed in the new system were more than the colonial governments could really handle. The basic requirement for a home-grown policy was to create a workable inventory of licensable berths. Officials simply did not have the staff to do this. Most of the time, governments had to make do with measuring the volume of timber as it was rafted down the river or as it arrived at the port of shipment. Originally, the Crown dues were to be paid at the time of acquiring the licence. Increasingly, as timber values fluctuated widely, the charges were set by competitive auctions or bidding. However, as timber was being scaled and checked as it floated to market, its price could also be charged en route.

The new system worked best in the Ottawa Valley and parts of New Brunswick where inspection of the berth was also instituted. In other places licensing (and charging) was not even attempted. As late as 1839, an Upper Canada surveyor testified that in southern and western Ontario it was impracticable 'to collect any important amount of duties on timber cut upon Government lands . . . and the expenses attending the attempts to do so have borne much too large a proportion of the sum collected'.[33]

Not until the mid-1850s did information collection progress enough to make tolerable the transactions costs of the location-specific and volume-specific licence system institutionalized in the first Crown Timber Acts of United Canada, 1847–9.[34] The legislature had by now acquired (from the Colonial Office and the governor) some control over its revenue and even over the extent of the assault on its forest (as measured either by the number of licensees or by the volume harvested). Under the Acts lumbermen got an exclusive right to cut in specified areas. Although this right's duration was set at one year, the term was renewable on condition that the holder report the amounts cut.[35] This system—private

[32] Consulting the text and documents in Reid 1990, it appears that in Upper Canada much of the Ottawa Valley was thrown open. The buyers or bidders appear to have acquired rights to a number of logs. The proclamation of 1826, and the licences and contract reproduced for 1835 (p. 103), 1836 (p. 129), 1837 (p. 131), and 1842 (p. 137), are all specific as to amount, fairly specific as to place of delivery, and non-specific as to location of camp or lumbering operations. Those acquiring licences must have had some idea where they planned to place their camp, but this 'planning' was not disclosed in their licences.

[33] Lambert and Pross 1967, p. 45, quoting Commissioner of Crown Lands Sullivan reporting to the Assembly in 1839. In 1841 Upper and Lower Canada were united and followed a single forest-rights policy until 1867.

[34] For a short chronology of this period, see the Kennedy Report (Ontario 1947, ch. 1). Kennedy says that Lord Durham's (1839) report focused attention on the profligate disposal of timberland to friends of the colonial administration. Probably this is a reference to Charles Buller's *Report on Public Lands and Emigration* an annex to the Durham Report (Lucas 1912). See also Hansard 81, 15 August 1843, pp. 769–74.

[35] For a yearly table of licences in the Acadian Peninsula, NB, 1875–92, see Léger 1992, pp. 27–40. The average area of a licence was about five square miles. The length of tenure in

timber rights administered on public land—became known internationally as the 'Canadian policy'. The 'policy', of course, was neither conscious nor complete because land settlement by outright grant still had priority on all public land and would continue for another eighty years following the passage of the Crown Timber Acts.

Another problem was that, as in the United States, Crown land had not usually been surveyed in advance nor classified as either lumbering or farming land. Therefore the lands offices could draw little legal distinction between sales to farmers and sales to lumbermen. As well, more and more Crown land was surveyed into towns or counties in advance of immigration. These factors induced lumber operators to don settlers' masks, especially when the price of timber licences rose. An additional New Brunswick complication was that American lumbermen, already familiar with fraudulent patenting of homestead land, found it easy to obtain timber along New Brunswick's boundary rivers by buying out 'settlers' in Canada. Speculators, farmers and loggers joined in obtaining settlement grants for the wood alone, and the earlier, mostly innocuous, trespass of Crown timber was succeeded by much irregular and corrupt purchase or granting of Crown farmland for timber purposes.[36]

In remote British Columbia, a sequence of licence tenures similar to that in eastern Canada did not emerge for another forty years. Instead, as most of its coastal forests were not required for settlement, after 1860 the Colony of British Columbia put its forests on offer as freehold (referred to as Crown-grant) at a low price. Later, the government not only increased the price but also imposed a retroactive royalty. Finally, two decades later, it introduced Ontario's kind of licences (and also long-term leases, discussed below).[37] The expenses and benefits of its licences changed frequently in response to rising and falling market demand between the 1880s and 1907.[38]

New Brunswick steadily increased from one year (prior to 1874) to twenty-five years (by 1893). Côté 1992, p. 44.

[36] The Wakefield approach, which required that a price be placed on grants, was mandated by the Colonial Office in 1827. This had no direct implication for timberland, but it modified the lumberman's choice between directly obtaining a timber berth and indirectly getting timber on a freehold farm. See Wynn 1981, p. 79. On the colonial office's land policy, see Riddell 1937.

[37] The colony, which had copied American water and mining rights, could not 'follow' American timber policy until the US national forests were introduced circa 1900. A few years later the Dominion Department of the Interior administered legislation for Manitoba and the Northwest Territories. Timber was alienated as 'berths'. My thanks to Irene Spry for this information.

[38] For details see Whitford and Craig 1918; and Cail 1974. Scholefield and Howay 1914; Ormsby 1958; and Robin 1972 contain details of the timber booms and the corruption that went with them. Much information is to be found in the important British Columbia Royal Commission Reports of 1911, 1945 and 1976, often referred to as the Fulton, Sloan and Pearse Reports. Carrothers 1938 contains good statistical material on the 1920s and 1930s but is devoid of historical or even economic analysis.

Free-land policies against revenue needs

On both American and Canadian public lands the freedom of governments to add more property-like characteristics to whatever interests they granted to lumbermen was constrained by a high political priority for settlement as well as by a (somewhat lower) urgency of revenue needs.

American land-granting policies centred on settlement: the imperative was to achieve a 'property-owning democracy'. The settler was king, and the various states, territories and (later) railroads competed in offering public lands to attract him. Also, as Douglas Allen has emphasized, there was another aspect of settlement: the occupation of empty lands would forestall and weaken other land claimants, such as those that might come from Mexico, Britain, Russia and (especially) Indian nations and tribes.[39]

Canada competed with the United States for immigrants and settlers, so the rapid-settlement constraint also dominated. The desire for rapid settlement had led the United States to replenish the public lands; to grant settlers full freehold tenure; to pay for prior surveys; and to offer easy procedures, requirements, credit terms and prices. Attempting to follow suit, the Canadian colonies at first rejected the settlement implications of the Canada Act, 1791, with its reserves for clergy, and of the Durham/Buller/Wakefield policy of inducing compact settlement through high land prices. Later, the Dominion, the provinces and the Church began to direct settlement to particular regions, and land policy was used to guide this process.[40] Because of this settlement priority practical politicians in both countries avoided any appearance of depriving settlers of land. Much land acceptable to both settlers and lumbermen was implicitly classified as farmland and reserved. Any allocation of timber to the lumber industry had to be indirect and circuitous (e.g., the countenancing of fraudulent homesteading by lumbering firms).

Canada and the United States did not depend on land-disposal revenue to the same extent. In the United States, Alexander Hamilton's original plans for settlement contained a revenue aspect: land was to be priced, and sales promoted, so as to maximize public revenue. Indeed, there were periods between 1776 and 1837 when land disposal was a significant source of Washington's federal revenue, prompting cash and even land redistributions to the states. Thereafter, however, the government's ability to substitute other sources of federal revenue and its priority for settlement led to cheaper land policies. By the mid-nineteenth century, revenue hardly figured in American land-disposal or timber-disposal policies. Congressional debates on land prices changed as the prices were seen increasingly as devices for selecting among would-be settlers' income-classes, or for selecting areas where settlement was to be encouraged. The grants of federal

[39] Allen 1991.

[40] For a comparison of Canada and New Zealand, both of whom were influenced by Wakefield's settlement theories, see Roche 1984.

land for colleges, railroads and other purposes also testify to Congress's recognition of land's potential value as more than a federal revenue source.

In eastern Canada obtaining forest revenue was a more urgent matter. The 1830s and 1840s were periods of fairly rapid settlement. The colonies, having few sources of revenue, were glad to take over the naval-reserve regime's right to sell timber licences, especially in regions where settlement was not taking place. Since public lands revenues were under royal prerogative, licences were especially attractive to the governing party. Land was sold or licensed by the appointed upper house in the early Canadian legislatures, and revenues flowed back for disposal by the same upper house. Thus, forest revenue transactions avoided the lower elected house's control over taxation and tax revenues. After 1850, when the elected legislatures got jurisdiction over domain revenues, they could decide on the proportion of the colonies' total revenues that were to come from each source. The emphasis on forest revenues was consequently decreased.

American land classification

During the nineteenth century many American loggers and lumber companies employed or contracted with agents—called 'entrymen'—to stake agricultural claims under homestead laws. The social losses from this practice of fraudulently gaining timberland were distributional and allocational. The distributional, or revenue, losses were suffered by the public, who were deprived of the rent of their standing timber.[41] The allocational losses arose from both the poor utilization practices and the rent-seeking expenditures of those acquiring timber illegally. These included the costs of premature cutting, wasteful logging methods (many of which were employed specifically to avoid detection) and distorted use patterns—altogether estimated by Libecap and Johnston (1979) at $17 million, perhaps 60 per cent of total land sale price.[42]

Politicians knew of the public's indignation, yet they did not change the policy significantly until the 1890s. Initial legislative forays into addressing the situation—the Timber Culture Act, 1873, which encouraged Great Plains farmers to grow trees and to settle forested land and the Timber Cutting and Timber and Stone Acts of 1878, which made timber or timberland more available to settlers in certain states—were unimportant or relied on farmers and entrymen to procure timber cheaply for the companies.[43] In particular,

[41] The rent was captured by the companies, by corrupt officials, by entrymen, and also by the genuine settlers who granted their timber to the companies. Many authors have drawn attention to the corruption associated with timber policy at this time. An important attempt at measurement of losses is found in Libecap and Johnson 1979; and Libecap 1989, p. 52. For a detailed account of one region, see Curry-Roper 1989. For one of many accounts of politics, see Lillard 1947, pp. 156–94.

[42] Libecap and Johnson 1979, p. 138, cited by Libecap 1989, p. 59.

[43] Under the Timber and Stone Act, applicants in a few forested states with little farmland could buy land that they swore was valuable chiefly for timber or stone. For the most part this

none of these Acts created a new tenure analogous to the mineral claim Congress had by then adopted on public lands. Such a tenure might have involved a sale of either specially designated forestland or of specially created timber-cutting rights.

Below, I offer and discuss two explanations for the federal government's long inaction. The first is that neither a designated sale nor a timber-cutting right would have reduced taxpayer losses. The necessary policy would have meant incurring costs to classify land, and these costs would have been so high as to cancel the taxpayers' gains, while failing to remove incentives for dishonesty and fraud among loggers. The second explanation is simply that, at least until the organized conservation movement came along, politicians heard less from general forest-preserving interests (including uninformed taxpayers) than they did from the special-interest, rent-seeking factions opposed to a direct timber-sale policy—those who hoped to gain from illegal timber acquisition, and those builders, developers and railroad executives who gained from cheap illegal timber. I discuss these explanations in turn.

CLASSIFICATION COSTS

The American land disposal programme depended chiefly on an active surveying programme conducted in advance of occupation. The programme was carried out by private surveyors under government contract, whose work was a precondition for the disposal of homesteaded land. When surveying moved slowly, squatters were found to have moved miles—and years—ahead of survey parties. Sometimes this led to an intensification of the survey programme; sometimes it led to squatters being allowed to validate their occupation under a pre-emption programme.

Surveying could be sped up by narrowing its objectives, as occurred in areas that the government was anxious to get homesteaded quickly.[44] In a quick survey, surveying parties located rectangular boundary lines (instead of irregular metes and bounds) that were often overlapping. The surveyors' minimal training, the pressure on them to work quickly and the considerable danger and hardship of their work all suggest that they would not have been able to undertake the soil and timber-stand evaluations required for quality land classification.

In the first place, officials and surveyors would have had to predict for which forested acres the lumber industry would be willing to pay enough to make classification and sale, and the denial of settlement claims, worthwhile. They based their decisions on assumptions about available farming methods, tree-cutting difficulties, transportation and markets. While such assumptions might have been trivial in areas like the treeless Great Plains territory, or the

policy channelled the acres from small holders to large companies. For a study of the law's administration and use in Minnesota, see Curry-Roper 1989. For an account of its enforcement, see Lillard 1947, pp. 173–7.

[44] For this and much that follows I am indebted to Allen 1991.

pastureless Lake States, they would have been difficult and controversial in forested lands that were also suitable for farming. As a general rule, wherever the landscape was mixed, transition or mountainous, classifications became matters of judgment—necessarily personal and subjective. We see an example of the practical results of this problem in the US Geological Survey's early attempts to classify land. Generally, the surveyors merely reported those lands that had no access to water for irrigation, but offered no attempt to classify by grass cover, or by more complicated aspects of their suitability for, say, ranching.[45]

Politically, surveying was also subject to a natural contradiction: a system robust enough to satisfy the settlement-favouring public and the land users who had to assent to the classification would have been so expensive that politicians would have sought ways to reduce the cost, which would in turn have made the system less rigorous and therefore more open to challenge by homesteaders denied a piece of 'forestland'. In order to reduce the resulting political risks, the classification policy would have erred in the direction of classifying mixed or marginal land as farm land—presenting only a small change to the single-classification status quo. Already heavily criticized for the slowness, inefficiency and corruption of their one-category pre-emption and homesteading procedures, politicians and bureaucrats were loathe to accept the job of defending the thousands of debatable arbitrary judgments that would result from procedures for dividing the public lands into two categories.

Of course these problems were temporary. In the 1890s Congress, in tightening up the Homestead Act, signalled that the urgency of the free settlement drive had abated. At the same time, it empowered the president to set aside forest reserves, which later became the new national forests. By this time, the need for robustly defensible classifications was less pressing, while classification performance potential was improving. On the one hand, settlement was no longer Congress's single dominating goal. On the other hand, the government was in the position to supply a technically better system of land classification. By the end of the nineteenth century, private surveyors had become more professional, government geological surveyors were in the field, Indians no longer interfered, transportation had improved and many of the remaining unopened regions were transparently identifiable as mountain or desert. An acceptable classification programme was no longer out of reach.

DEMANDERS AND THEIR AVERSION TO LAND CLASSIFICATION

The second explanation I offered for the failure of land classification to emerge until the tail end of the nineteenth century is that there was no effective demand for such a programme. Settlers, lumbermen, politicians and bureaucrats would not have favoured classification, let alone demanded its introduction.

[45] See Gates 1968b, pp. 509–19.

Farmers and settlers. I begin with the lack of demand for classification on the part of farming and homesteading interests. Consider the opportunities and costs facing a settler who acquires land with tree cover. The trees may have been a costly nuisance, but for many settlers they had value too, if for no other use than for odd projects around the farm. Under the single-type land-disposal laws the settler made his own choices about timber use and could seek the most rent from his temporary status as a forest owner. Some users collected it in kind; others captured it in cash when they sold logs, re-sold their cutting rights or sold the land itself. Successful government land classification, which would have prevented farmers from getting acreages with especially valuable timber stands, was not an overly appealing farmer-voter concept.

Lumbermen. The lumber industry would have been more divided in its attitude toward classification than farmers. Many firms should have welcomed schemes that enabled them to get forestland directly, without enduring the costs of fraud or of paying settlers to sell out. Indeed, in 1879 the industry numbered among the proponents of classification.

But there was a drawback. With a classification policy based on a 'settler as king' mentality, early classification efforts would still have given priority to settlement. As a result, the firms would still have found themselves engaging in rent-seeking, bribery, fraud and evasion. Rent-seeking costs—both to buy out good timberland from settlers, as under no classification, and to try to change classification policy in their favour—could be expected to persist in a classification regime, particularly as some timberlands remained unsold in the public-land inventory until after the First World War. The firms' incentive to avoid these costs ex-post would have been greater the more classification policy favoured settlement, which may explain why the lumber industry waited until settlement had lost much of its popular allure in the late nineteenth century before really throwing its weight behind classification.

Administrators and politicians. Seen as demanders, the politicians in government were no more likely than were farmers and loggers to push for land classification. Congress was certainly under some public pressure to stop allowing forests to find their way from homesteaders to the logging industry. But this pressure was far from sufficient to bring about a change in policy by the middle of the nineteenth century: special interests were more influential.

Furthermore, individual politicians had their own personal interests to consider. Many of the officials involved with land disposal held jobs based on rationing land under the homestead law, and feared that their livelihood could be threatened by a workable external classification system. Politicians who patronized these officials took their concerns into account. The politicians' own welfare depended mostly on their ability to read the minds of demanders and opponents of forestland sales. It also depended on how they handled the phenomenon of the land speculation caused by lumpiness in the stream of land coming on the market and by surging and ebbing waves of immigrant-settlers (often carried out through the exchange of land for discounted state war-bonds).[46] Speculators pressed politicians either to approve or to prevent land releases that would affect land prices. Indeed, many politicians were speculators themselves. One might expect these politicians to have preferred the continuance of the homestead system, with its known potential for speculative gains, to a forest-land auction sale system. On the other hand, the probable arbitrariness of forestland classification, and the opportunities for legislative influence on large forestland releases and disposals, would have presented an even wider domain for manipulating speculation.

Though the theory is ambiguous, it is obvious that in practice politicians were slow to embrace classification. An 1880 proposal by a non-partisan public lands commission called not only for classification of timberlands, but also for their sale (as opposed to being free and to being acquired by fraud). The proposal was debated and rejected. Congress, slowly warming to the idea of conservation, was getting into a mood to go beyond classification, but (perhaps like the lumber industry) was not yet ready to abandon earlier qualms. A decade later it finally repudiated earlier doubts by agreeing to reserve forestlands from homesteading or any other form of sale.[47]

Canada: the colonies decide to raise revenue

The section of this chapter on the demand for licence tenure showed how the governor of Upper Canada and his senior advisory council sought revenues that (1) the legislative assembly could not touch; (2) would not interfere with settlement; and (3) were easy to collect. Only the licence to cut timber in the remote Ottawa Valley met these three conditions: it came under the royal prerogative; it did not conflict with settlement; and it called for one convenient payment, which was to be made as the logs passed the 'toll gate' at Bytown. Despite less favourable initial conditions in other provinces, this licensing arrangement gradually became the forest policy of Canada: charge for the right to cut timber rather than alienate the land on which the timber stands.[48]

With time, the system became a better fit universally. As the 1825 schism between the appointed council and the elected assembly disappeared, the latter gained the power to collect revenues both from former prerogative

[46] Economists, aware that speculation is one aspect of efficient market arbitrage over time, often fail to recognize how concerned the nineteenth century was about speculation. In the second half of the century, public land was sold for lumbering in the lake states but not through the Homestead Act. Johnson and Libecap 1980 have shown that a longer-term kind of speculation did take place in that land was bought and kept for ten years before being logged. The authors' technical hypothesis, that forest prices would rise at the rate of interest, was substantiated.

[47] The first suggestion for reservation was made in 1874 by Samuel S. Burdett, Commissioner of the Public General Land Office, 1874–6. On the role of J. W. Powell in proposing classification, see Dana and Fairfax 1980, pp. 39–40.

[48] Reid 1990; Nelles 1974, p. 11; and Lower 1938, pp. 38–46.

domain sources and from taxation. As well, lumbering everywhere moved away from farm districts so that interference with settlement could be reduced. Finally, as colonial revenue sources had now been increased to three—a royalty, an annual rent and an initial bonus fee—collection expenses evened out throughout Upper Canada, Lower Canada and New Brunswick with licensing becoming widespread.

Implicit in the choice of a licence regime was that the Canadian colonies, with the exception of B.C. which came on board later, all decided not to raise revenue by further selling land for settlement or for its timber. This was to some extent a product of the historical and political circumstances. In the mid-nineteenth century Canadians still shared with Americans an enthusiasm for population moving out to the frontier, acquiring land, clearing and developing it.[49] But Canada did not experience the passion for public ownership[50] expressed by the leaders of the new American conservation movement. In this connection I argue that two main points favoured maintaining the licensing regime: (1) where sales for revenue would have called for land classification, the process, while less difficult than in the US, would have faced many of the same drawbacks and (2) where classification was possible, granting licences actually offered more revenue in practice than did land sales.

INADEQUATE LAND CLASSIFICATION SYSTEMS IN CANADA

In some crucial respects, land surveying for classification was more feasible in Canada than in the US. Surveyors were in no danger from Indians and were often, perhaps usually, full-time government employees. Nevertheless, as in the US, the Canadian government would have had to satisfy its political supporters that selling a tract as timberland did not undermine the settlement process. Ontario did in fact designate some land for timber licensing and some for settlement. Its classification was the outcome of a three-party negotiation between the settlement agency, which was often backed by municipalities and developers; the forest agency, which was heavily influenced by lumbering interests; and the provincial treasury, which was concerned with licence revenue.

These three interests were well balanced, and their land-use decisions relied on information that became available when surveys were first conducted at the township-line level (thirty-six square miles), well in advance of settlement

[49] For the advent of the 'forestry' movement in Canada, see Lambert and Pross 1967, p. 182. See also Hodgins and Benidickson 1989, p. 70; and Gillis and Roach 1986.

[50] Thus even when Canadians did eventually match the programme of forest reserves in the United States, their purpose was not to exclude private logging or forest use. See Nelles 1974, p. 200. Writing about British Columbia, Cail 1974 says almost nothing about the impact of the idea of forest conservation. My treatment suffers from a neglect of economies of scale and indivisibilities in forest utilization. Obtaining these might call for public ownership intervention. Fire prevention, for example, can be made less costly by separating forests and settlements; and even in an area of small private woods, fire prevention and control may have public-good aspects. Thanks to Robert Deacon for this discussion.

or logging. Surveying on a finer grid resulted in roads being cut and some lots being taken up by farmers and speculators. This subdivision was what lumbermen wanted to prevent, for it would force them to acquire forested land by buying freehold settlement lots or even by buying cutting rights from small landholders or speculators.[51] These were costly alternatives, so lumbermen opposed any township's desire to conduct fine-grid surveying.[52]

Lumbermen even opposed the original crude township-level surveying, for Ontario's land surveyors usually took an optimistic view of a township's settlement possibilities. Indeed, they had far too little information to do anything else. According to Lambert and Pross, a surveyor sometimes acted in the capacity of 'promoter and Crown Land agent... He had to report on... above all the quantity and quality of land available for agriculture'.[53]

> The surveyors sometimes judged the suitability of land for agriculture by assessing the crops that were already grown in the area; if there were no settlements, they relied on observing the character of the soil and its vegetation... From their reports it is clear that, try as they would to be accurate and unbiased, they tended, on the whole, to give land a better rating for farm purposes than it really merited.[54]

Their optimistic report on township soils would lead the decision makers to survey them on a fine grid. In effect, this decision amounted to the township's being classified against timber licensing, regardless of land variations.

This brief account suggests the weakness of the survey system by which Ontario distinguished land to be given to settlers from land to be marketed to lumbermen. It invited fraud. It could not be trusted to produce a price or value. Like other provinces, Ontario relied on forest users rather than government surveyors to decide which forest lands were the most valuable.

British Columbia was the only colony that actually experimented with forest land sales. Its experience illustrates how selling parcels of land instead of licensing tree cutting did not in itself enable the government to capture the differential rent. The B.C. government could not muster the staff and information to classify different grades of farmland and forestland or to run a

[51] 'It was not unusual for a speculator to hold rights for ten or fifteen thousand acres, and when a new township was surveyed and opened for settlement, to claim a block of it.' Lumbermen could buy settlement land from such a speculator. Later, scrip disappeared and speculators obtained settlement blocks by other means. See Harris and Warkentin 1974, p. 122.

[52] For a review of Ontario land-disposal surveying, see Lambert and Pross 1967, ch. 5. For New Brunswick, see Wynn 1981. For British Columbia, see Cail 1974, ch. 4; Pearse et al. 1974; and Drushka 1985. There is a little material on Quebec in Lower 1936 and in Armstrong 1984, pp. 174–5. It appears that around Georgian Bay, square miles in berths were auctioned for a bonus of about $200 in 1877 but were sold privately for as much as $7,000 in the 1890s. Township-sized berths, therefore, became worth as much as $250,000 in the 1890s, with the annual ground rent of only $36 per township becoming a trivial consideration; the same rent was collected in Quebec. See Angus 1990, pp. 156 and 234–5. For a discussion of the difficulties of classification in New Brunswick in 1917, see Caverhill 1917, p. 2.

[53] Lambert and Pross 1967, p. 62.

[54] Lambert and Pross 1967, p. 66.

bidding disposal process. Despite the presence of military engineers to carry out some of the earliest surveying, there was a shortage of qualified surveyors and no land tax assessors, timber cruisers, scalers, inspectors or map-makers. The colony also had a limited capacity to classify and reserve lands because mineral and township lands were not included in the general land sale arrangement of 1859. Consequently, the government was forced to act as though all forestlands were equally valuable. Timberland and farmland were sold at one price (ten shillings) per acre throughout the Coast and Fraser Valley. This was such a good deal[55] that, when leasing and licensing did become available after 1885, few applications appeared. Land sales continued at a price that was low enough to be within the reach of settlers.

By the 1890s British Columbia's land-office facilities had expanded enough to allow the handling of a huge volume of new timber licences, though forest-quality classification was still not sufficiently advanced to vary the price of the licences by grade, species or location, as necessary to capture most of the forestry rent. (Failure to capture this rent may, however, have had as much to do with the political influence of industry, whose representatives lobbied for, and sometimes had an official role in, land disposal.) Not until 1912 did a more discriminating stumpage timber sale emerge as an alternative to the land sale.

UNREMUNERATIVE CHARGES ON TIMBERLAND GRANTS

Theoretically, outright sales of timberland should have been attractive to the provinces from a revenue point of view. Sales would have allowed the provincial governments to gain the higher price that many and larger buyers would pay for ownership rather than tenancy; the power to levy property taxes on the assessed value; and a release from the responsibility of looking after Crown land. It also seems plausible that, if governments believed that timberland sales would lead to significantly larger revenues than would licensing, then they might well have invested more in surveys and classification. However, there were good reasons for them doubting that higher revenues from sales would materialize.

It is important to understand that, because the government was both landowner and tax collector, the revenue streams from both land sales (freehold) and licences could be divided among the same three components mentioned above: an initial payment (as a uniform statutory price or a negotiated bid price); an annual payment (as a quit rent,[56] tenure renewal fee, property tax or

[55] See Cail 1974, pp. 10 and 92; and Whitford and Craig 1918. Most of those who bought this Crown-granted land have had to pay property taxes since the 1900s. However, they obtained the Coast's best forest land, bearing repeated crops. By 1973, only 6 per cent of the provincial forest land was private, but it produced about 15 per cent of the provincial cut. This large private harvest was liable for only 1 per cent of provincial royalty revenue; indeed, only 40 per cent of this harvest was even liable for royalty. See Pearse et al. 1974, p. 14 table 2.

[56] This is the annual payment known as a *rentcharge* and reserved by the grantor of freehold land. Originally, a quit rent was a rent paid by a grantee to his lord in lieu of feudal or military duties. Both led to payment responsibilities long after the grant or duties had been forgotten.

rental payment); and a royalty. As a point of historical fact, of course, these taxes were not always all feasible. In the early days, as we have seen, the government had mainly to content itself with imposing excise- or royalty-type payments based on log count, or scale, at a central shipping point. Later, without definite shipping points and without knowledge of forest stands, the government was forced to accept what non-competitive lumbermen would bid for cutting rights. Later still, when the government had acquired some independent knowledge of the stands, it could impose an annual rental.[57]

Revenue from a royalty

In Ontario, a royalty ('Crown dues') was paid on timber cut under a licence. In British Columbia after 1888 the same royalty was paid on both freehold and licence timber. Presumably, if all timberland had been sold rather than licensed, there would have been no change in royalty revenue.[58] Hence, if the total revenue stream from licensing had been expected to differ from the revenue stream from selling, the difference must have been found in expectations about the other two components.

Revenue from an annual payment or property tax

Upper and Lower Canada introduced rentals on licences in 1850. In Upper Canada the purpose of the rental, known as a ground berth, was to dissuade licensees from holding timber uncut, and thereby to shorten the practical duration of the timber licences, which had in some cases become very long. Each year the berth was not occupied, the rental rate doubled. In British Columbia, 'leasing' was introduced in 1870, along with an annual rental and renewal fee. The colonies soon had rentals from several vintages of timber

Some American colony proprietors charged their landholders quit rents. Such payments have been abolished in most jurisdictions (though not nationally), but were still strongly in effect in the eighteenth and nineteenth centuries. See Megarry and Wade 1966, pp. 820 and 828.

[57] See, for example, Lambert and Pross 1967; Lower 1973.

[58] The meanings of the words royalty, stumpage and price have varied among periods and among governments, and are typically explained in statutes. The word royalty is nearly always used when the payer holds a long-term lease or licence and pays at the time of cutting or marketing a log at a rate set at the outset: so much per unit (such as cubic foot) for example. But there are instances of leases or licences on which the government might, and did, 'adjust' the rate. Governments had several reasons, economic and political, for making adjustments. One was that when a government kept changing the tenure it was currently offering loggers, it found it necessary to change the rate it was collecting on old but continuing tenures (such as old leases) to an understood proportion of its charge for timber on new types of tenure. Thus the royalty rates on some parcels of land, though contractual, were not usually fixed. Stumpage is/was the name for the current price for timber sold on very short-term timber sales. Some governments set their stumpage rates or prices by a known appraisal formula, taking into account operating costs in the woods, transportation costs, milling costs and market prices for milled products (using known reports or sources of data for these variables). Some writers have criticized the practice of varying royalty rates, and some have defended it. See the Kennedy Report (Ontario 1947, pp. 24–6); Lambert and Pross 1967, p. 144; Robin 1972, p. 90.

leases and licences outstanding, with durations running from one to twenty-one years, nearly all of them renewable. In the second half of the nineteenth century, when speculators acquired timber licences well in advance of the expected cutting date, total licence rental payments were often the largest of the three types of revenue.

On freehold land the equivalent annual-payment to a rental would have been the property tax.[59] While this tax was collected in some Ontario and British Columbia municipal centres, I argue that in the nineteenth century it would not generally have been a rewarding source of revenue.

Much taxable timber lay within surveyed lands in municipal territory, which was organized into townships. Municipal governments had hardly existed in the Canadas until the 1840s, when Lord Sydenham encouraged their introduction in Upper and Lower Canada. (The Maritimes lagged well behind.) As municipal governments proliferated, all colonies followed the United States—each jurisdiction made its own assessments (at first on all property, later on real property only) and set its own rates. As the assessors were subjected to severe political pressure from local property owners, it seems that they protected themselves by applying a uniform per-acre value to all woodlots and to wild (cutover) land.

Where forest stood outside organized-municipality areas (and where owners of large properties won exemption from municipal taxation simply by getting municipal boundaries situated so as to exclude them), the provincial government acted as assessor and tax collector. That is, to the extent it acted at all. By 1913 revenues from such taxes were still trivial in Quebec, Ontario and New Brunswick, partly because freehold timberlands were scattered and poorly registered. British Columbia, which did register all freehold lands, had begun to obtain substantial property tax revenues from its Crown-granted (freehold/patented) forests, but in an amount equal to about one quarter of its licence fee revenue.[60]

Failures of revenue collection thus accrued at both the municipal and provincial level. Admittedly, a government that consistently decided to sell forest-land instead of licensing it could have attempted to set up a fair revenue-producing province-wide assessment procedure. However, given the government's actual failure even to keep forest surveying and mapping ahead of loggers and lumbermen, it seems unlikely that it could have introduced and operated a remunerative property tax.

[59] There are few references on the early property tax in Canada, aside from Perry 1955 who is very brief. In the twentieth century, the property tax has been applied in Canada to both private and licensed timber, collected by municipalities and provincial government. See Wilkes 1954, p. 31; Pearse et al. 1974, p. 30; and Pearse 1976, vol. 2, Appendix C. These authors treat the tax as a burden. Few writers treat it as a source of revenue. In the text, I pass over the difficulty that a property tax on owned timberland would have been different from a rental on licensed land in that the revenue would not have accrued to the provincial government, or not to the provincial agency that collected all three revenue components on licences.

[60] Rowell-Sirois Report, vol. 3, table 18; Perry 1955, vol. 1.

Revenue from initial payment

To make up for the revenue they could not collect from an annual tax or a rental, governments selling timberland outright would have had to charge a healthy initial price for freehold forestland.

In reality, however, this was impossible so long as the government continued to ask a reduced price for settlement land. The government would have been attempting to run a two-price system on marginal land: one for settlers and another for lumbermen. The greater the price differential, the greater would be the incentive for both parties to circumvent the rules by persuading officials to reclassify the forestland or to look the other way when settlers quickly sold out.[61] Furthermore, as the settlement price was then close to zero (and was zero in the western interior), timberland would also have had to be sold at a very low initial price and so would not have produced the desired revenue.

The industry concurred, and therefore supported the sale of timberland. According to an 1854 inquiry into Ontario's experience, when licences were hard to obtain, people acquired land for settlement, stripped it and abandoned it. 'Such settlers did not pay for the timber at the rate the lumberman did. They took possession of the land as squatters, or on credit from the Crown, with no down-payment if in Lower Canada, or with only one down payment if in Upper Canada. The settlers were accused of cheating the government out of revenue it would have had from [licence] timber dues.'[62] In their testimony before a legislative committee, industry representatives took nearby Michigan to exemplify a forest region that also hosted farming. There revenue had been raised from federal lands sold outright to farmers or lumbermen. However, the inquiry did not accept the industry's position and concluded instead that in Canada West more revenue could be raised from licensing and combining annual ground rent with Crown timber dues collected at the time of cutting.

FURTHER DIFFICULTIES WITH TIMBERLAND SALE REVENUES

Four additional difficulties, besides revenue considerations, presented obstacles to a government looking to sell timberland into freehold ownership:

Private political motives

Politicians were not single-minded in their search for revenue. They would also have found occasion to present lumbermen with deeds to forestland in order to buy votes, build mills, finance railways,[63] forestall log exports and

[61] Gates 1968a suggests that this was easy, and Lower 1933, ch. 3, writing about the opportunities on New Brunswick's marginal lands, evidently agrees.

[62] Gates 1968a, p. 297.

[63] In 1907–8, the Canadian Northern Ontario Railway named one of its stations 'Sellwood'. See Hodgins and Benidickson 1989, p. 96.

oblige friends.[64] All of this would have kept prices low and limited the ability of the treasury to recoup timber rents from the lumber industry.

Fraud

Cheating on the part of brokers and administrators was widely observable throughout land sales departments in all countries.[65] However, like must be compared with like. The disposal of timber licences was also subject to cheating on the part of lumbermen, their employees and official scalers. For example, Raymond Léger indicates that as much as three-quarters of the wood exported from the port of Caraquet, New Brunswick in 1878 was not reported for scaling and royalty.[66] The proposition is that land sales and licence systems were both subject to dishonesty whenever the initial price was set high enough to make fraud and evasion worthwhile. It is not obvious that turning to sales would have induced an improvement.

Speculation

When timber prices were low, speculators bought forestland, then captured the rent when the price rose. Fears that rent would end up in a middleman's hands rather than in those of lumberman or government pointed to disposal by low-price licensing. What the government lost at the time of the initial sale or grant would be made up in subsequent rental payments. In general, of course, speculators might not have been as good at predicting prices as the governments feared.

Illiquid, risk-averse buyers

A forestland sale forced buyers to pay before cutting. Furthermore, judging by the duration of nineteenth-century timber licences, the interval between purchase and cutting would have been a long one. Thus, for a given level of risk, the maximum initial price that the government could have obtained from a lumberman for a block of timber would have been lower than a licence's initial price plus its discounted rental stream. Indeed, Nelles suggests, desire to avoid upfront payments, and thereby to postpone the main financial outlays for standing timber until the end of the logging schedule, may also explain the industry's support for a licence system.[67]

Associated with risk-aversion was the problem of asymmetrical information already encountered in Chapter 9 regarding negotiations among private

[64] The 'sprees' of licence granting are reported by Robin 1972, pp. 87–107; and Lambert and Pross 1967, p. 98.

[65] See Libecap and Johnson 1979; and Libecap 1989, pp. 53–7.

[66] Léger 1992, p. 31.

[67] Nelles 1974, p. 15, based on the report of the 1854 select committee to the legislature. See Gates 1968a, p. 297. Nelles gives less weight than do I to the probability that the government actually maximized its revenue by not selling forestland.

owners of land above an oil reservoir. Though the government and lumber firms might have worked out a way to share some risks (for instance of forest fire), they would keep information about the forest and its value to themselves while bargaining. The badly informed party would be exposed to the greater risk: for firms, of bidding too much; for governments, of accepting too low a bid. As between large and small firms, the latter could probably acquire forest information cheaply, but on a small scale, while the former could better spread the risks. As between the government and firms, very large firms might bear risk better than a provincial government; smaller firms would do less well. This suggests a publicly optimal policy of selling timberland to large firms and licensing the use of it to small firms.[68] Looking below at the allocation of large-scale 'agreement' and 'concession' tenures (which can be thought of as approximating a sale more closely than a very long-duration licence), we will see some evidence that this is, in fact, what took place.

In summary, the colonies opted against the large-scale disposal of timberland in fee simple for a variety of reasons, including the transactions costs for land classification and assessment, survey, grading timber stands, inspection and enforcement, the expense and difficulty of which together made the revenues from the large-scale sale of timberland less attractive. Entry into the logging industry was easy, requiring neither a skilled labour force nor a lot of capital. And the governments were in a hurry. They may well have decided it was better to collect small, continuous payments from licensing scores of small firms than the theoretically large payouts from selling land and timber to a few larger firms.

Private tenures on public lands: pulp leases, concessions and agreements

Eventually Canadian governments decided to augment their short-term, small-scale licences with long-term, large-scale pulp leases, timber concessions and agreements, thus adding new duration characteristics to users' rights to public forestland. These new tenures provided the holders with a private interest in a single use of the public forests and lands. In the late nineteenth century they were used to encourage investment in new manufacturing facilities in the wilderness. By the mid-twentieth century they were being granted only to those who made commitments to sustained yield from the granted area. Today the idea of large-scale private forest management remains ascendant in Canadian public policy, and new variants are being proposed that will relieve government departments of still more of the burdens of forest-use planning, protection and silviculture. This 'Canadian-made' agreement tenure

[68] Thanks to R. T. Deacon for discussions about the relevance of risk and risk aversion.

differs fundamentally from the modern American policy that, we will see, focuses on either making forests strictly private (farm woodlots and industry forests) or on keeping them strictly public (national forests). It is somewhat ironic, then, that the basic model for the modern Canadian agreement tenure in fact came from the US in the form of the cooperative sustained yield unit (CSYU), which is discussed below.

Using licences to attract mills to Ontario and B.C.

In early nineteenth-century Canada, the wood cut under licence tenure could be assigned to any market or use. At first, much wood went abroad in the form of logs, round or squared. Some went as pulpwood or cordwood. A little went to local mills, to be shipped in the form of staves and cut lumber or in the form of ships' holds.

MODIFYING LICENCES AND CONCESSIONS IN ONTARIO

Late in the nineteenth century provincial governments began promoting three policies to encourage the milling of Crown wood within Canada. First was negotiation with the United States to reduce or remove its protective tariffs on Canadian lumber. Second came taxing or directly forbidding the shipping of raw material from Canadian forestry units to American mills. The third policy was the subsidizing of sawmilling in Canada—the focus of this subpart. Through their promotional efforts, the provincial governments introduced incentives that guaranteed the permanent survival of licence tenure, while greatly modifying its characteristics from those we have previously encountered in the early Canadian forest industry. The new sawmill and pulp mill licences, combining elements of a lease and a profit-à-prendre to cut trees, gave the licensee exclusive use of very large acreages of forest.

Each licence was individually negotiated and packed with location-specific features. At first, the incentive to sawmilling consisted only of a provision of the licence that the licensee not export the logs. Then, with the advent of the pulp industry, governments began to use their power as landlords to enter into specific agreements with potential pulp and paper manufacturers. Ontario did so between 1892 and 1905.[69] Investors received access to suitable pulp species in areas where lumber species (such as pine) had already been licensed to lumbermen. Again, the agreements were backed up by a complete prohibition of exports from Crown lands.

As a magnet for Ontario investors willing to invade American pulp and paper markets, the new tenure was not a success. Trade recessions and American tariffs discouraged prospective investors, though not speculators. Three of

[69] References for Ontario include Lambert and Pross 1967, ch. 13, pp. 250 ff; Nelles 1974, pp. 83 ff; Hodgins and Benidickson 1989; Lower 1936; and Armstrong 1984.

the first four companies actually to get under way collapsed. The speculative buyers found no takers, and an embarrassed government could do nothing more than grant extensions of the agreements. By 1905, 'three mills were in ruins and the five promised seemed unlikely to materialize'.[70]

Not until after the Great War was Ontario's pulp and newsprint 'boom' renewed. Between 1919 and 1926 three giant concessions were made and the earlier ones extended, each negotiated in confidence in order to bypass the formalities of the original legislation. Although American investors did raise the possibility of outright purchase of the timber, a wary Ontario government stood firm on retaining land ownership.[71]

B.C. LICENCES AND LEASES

After the 1860s gold rush, the B.C. government faced different opportunities and constraints from those facing their contemporaries in Ontario and Quebec. Like Ontario, the province was eager for population growth. But on most of the steep, rocky forested land, conflict between settlement and logging was not an issue, so that the government had a free hand to devise land-disposal systems and tenures for logging only. The resulting experimentation produced the bewildering succession and proliferation of forest tenures referred to earlier.

After 1870 forest was handed out through small-area licences and large-scale leases conditional on sawmill construction. In order to attract mill investors to British Columbia, the terms of the leases were made steadily more inviting. Their duration, starting at thirty years, was soon lengthened and was easily renewable at carrying charges that were found to bring in considerable revenue. Investors with the largest sawmills paid cutting royalties at the lowest rates and their leases granted them the largest forest acreages. When pulp and paper mills became investment opportunities, a special pulp lease was devised. And, as in Ontario, when the new American tariff became an impediment to investment in the province, the government reinforced the mill leases with a log-export ban, forcing cut logs to go through the provincial mills.

The attractiveness of British Columbia's mill leases tempted politicians and governments to grant them to speculators with a very free hand. Robin (1972) describes the leasing programme in the 1880s as one of 'reckless alienation, [a] Potlatch'.[72] The handout era rose to a crescendo in 1907, when public alarm caused Richard McBride's government to suddenly withdraw further land from leasing or licensing. By then over 150 billion board feet of timber had been alienated in licences and leases, far more than would be used by B.C. industry over the next twenty-one years.[73]

[70] Nelles 1974, p. 116.
[71] Nelles 1974, p. 384.
[72] Robin 1972, pp. 60–1.
[73] Whitford and Craig 1918, p. 88.

DEMAND FOR DURATION IN TIMBER TENURES

In neither Ontario nor British Columbia were the pulp mill agreements originally linked to sustained-yield forest management. Although the companies promised to protect the timber against fire, they were not deemed responsible for preparing the forest for another harvest: new pulp mills were treated as though they were new mines. Not until the 1920s in Ontario did the government begin to talk about 'perpetual' industries. In British Columbia, where quicker tree growth should have made more plausible the linking of acreage, stand, mill capacity and duration, similar talk was not heard until the 1940s. In short, the provinces' mill and pulp leases were intended to promote fire protection and industrial growth, not sustained-yield forestry.

Perception of their strictly extractive purpose goes a long way to explaining why large property-conscious American investing firms were prepared to accept the characteristics of licence, lease or contract for their planned mills. The leases had a very long duration—from twenty to a hundred years—long enough to amortize the required expenditure on mill and townsite. They were easily renewable for a charge, though neither transferable nor divisible. The large-scale new interests also promised more exclusivity, at least from neighbours' fire risk.

They also seemed to offer more security (quality of title) from further regulatory involvement until the time when the spent land could be relinquished back to the government. Of course, in the heat of politics, the government might change the contract by raising the rents or the investment or the required forest management. The Ontario and British Columbian provincial governments did try several times in the decades that followed to withdraw land or disown covenants in their bargains with forest tenure holders.[74] Nevertheless, the leases were thought to have, on average, greater quality of title than had the older timber licences.

Apparently, the balance of these advantages and disadvantages was not overwhelming. After 1907, some years passed before Ontario or British Columbia found many investors willing to take on their new tenures, though whether industry was gloomy about tenure or more generally about the future of pulp and paper is unclear. The politicians, of course, had their own demands: they wanted to hold on to Crown forestlands and let them under agreement licence. Licensing, leasing, contracting: all these temporary tenures gave governments, wary of the possibility they could be outsmarted by the specialists who sought their concessions, more than one chance to impose their preferences, and, if necessary, to recapture their lands if the industry's side of the lease was not being met. The ability eventually to re-grant the cleared land made the tenures generally more acceptable to the electorate in its early twentieth-century pro-settlement mood.

[74] See, for example, the Kennedy Report (Ontario 1947, p. 106).

The new mill tenures also coincided with intense public support for forest maintenance. In the United States this demand was emerging in the form of the conservation movement, and it was paralleled, even anticipated, in eastern Canada by a concern over the perceived excessive destruction of provincial forestlands.[75] There emerged a public demand for conservation (forest management), protection (from fire), and reservation (from settlement and from speculative alienation)—though not yet sustained-yield management.[76] Demands for conservation focused on existing trees rather than future generations of trees. Still, the government saw that to respond to this demand to conserve, protect and reserve its timber it would have to retain the ownership.

Finally, as was the case for the simple licensing tenure already discussed, governments may have perceived long-term leasing as a better source of revenue than sales.[77] Under the best of circumstances, it would have been difficult to capture the public's share of the future rent in a single concession negotiation; the up-front finance requirements would have strained the timber industry investors' capacity to raise the funds and handle the risk. In general, a government that wished to raise its charges or to introduce a new kind of charge or appraisal formula facilitated the change by giving the changed tenure a new name, at the same time changing details of its property-like characteristics and of the lessee's privileges and forest-protection duties.

In fact, government revenue expectations were bound to be disappointed anyway. After the first boom of 1905–7, the new leases, and particularly the generous pulp leases, produced almost no revenue until well after the First World War.

Modern industrial agreement tenures

After the Second World War (or just before it, in New Brunswick's case),[78] the provinces' policies swung toward long-term forest management on a plantation-like model. The offers of long-term mill leases were refashioned into long-term 'agreements' with large enterprises, while smaller licence holdings became subject to planned cutting schedules.

Leading the way was the report of British Columbia's Sloan Commission, which in 1945 recommended the use of large-scale 'forest management

[75] See Scott 1973, pp. 244–54, 254–62; Lambert and Pross 1967, pp. 150–99; Gillis and Roach 1986; Ross 1997, pp. 5–6.

[76] There is an extensive American literature on the origin of 'reserves'. See Ise 1920; Hays 1959; and, for a more recent survey, Hage 1989. For Canada see Benidickson 1983; and Lambert and Pross 1967, p. 173. Historically, the term was rarely intended to mean that logging would be prohibited or that the wilderness would be preserved (as in a natural park). However, after a block of land had been 'reserved' for some years, various interest groups would invent purposes for which it had been created.

[77] The very brief discussion here reflects a re-reading of the chapters in Nelles 1974 on Ontario timber disposal, and to helpful conversations with Mike Percy and Ron Shearer. On British direct investment in timber, see Paterson 1976.

[78] See Michael Howlett, in Ross et al. 1995, pp. 64–5.

licences' (FMLs). These were inspired by the US Forest Service's Cooperative Sustained Yield Unit (discussed directly below), which pooled public acreage with private parcels to be held and managed jointly by the Forest Service and the private owner. This concept was soon almost completely rejected in the United States. But in Canada, first British Columbia then the other major timber-producing provinces designed and negotiated similar forest management agreements with major pulp, paper and sawmilling companies.[79]

UNITED STATES EXPERIENCE: THE CSYU

The American federal government's brief experimentation with the Cooperative Sustained Yield Unit (CSYU) represented a substantial change from the short-term timber-sale tenure then offered to loggers in the US national forests.[80] By the 1920s and 1930s the new US national forests were managed by the US Forest Service. The Forest Service was zealous in awarding blocks of national forest timber to the winner in competitive bidding; it did not pay much attention to the location or size of these blocks, nor did it pay much attention to the political connections of the bidders. This impersonal procedure was opposed by those who wished each national forest to be designated as the timber source for a specific neighbouring community. The Forest Service had also seen its efforts to advance the practice of sustained yield forestry in the national forests, as well as in large and small private forests, blocked by Congressmen sympathetic to or aligned with private industry.

In 1944 leaders of the Forest Service and their congressional friends introduced a compromise that was accepted by the forest industry. A new law authorized setting up two types of sustained-yield units, both of which would reduce the Forest Service's open competition for national forest timber by dedicating large parts of any forest to ensuring employment stability in the local community, and gave the Forest Service a sought-after voice in the management of private forest holdings. Only the second type, the CSYU, is important here. In a CSYU, the silviculture of acres and stands in a private forest might be combined with that being conducted in an adjoining national forest. The owner(s) would join the Forest Service in working out a long-period cutting and regeneration plan for the combined unit. The chosen private firm—conceived as an integrated logger-miller-shipper—would get sole access to high-quality national forest timber stands at an agreed stumpage price. In return, it would open and log its own marginal over-age, remote, high-altitude stands, which otherwise would not be commercially attractive.

[79] The provinces' alacrity was not surprising, for, as we have seen, Ontario and Quebec had inter-war experience in awarding large-scale pulp licences and leases. For some, the introduction of the new management agreement approach was part of an existing programme to tidy up the older pulp agreements. See Lambert and Pross 1967, ch. 19, pp. 390–423.

[80] In this section I have been much assisted by conversations with Dr Marion Clawson. I also acknowledge assistance from Dr John Walker, Simpson Lumber Co.

The new tenure did not please all members of the Forest Service elite, for by negotiating with private owners, the Forest Service lost complete authority over its own lands and their eventual competitive disposal. On the other hand, the Forest Service gained opportunities to persuade major integrated firms to take and process large amounts of neglected old-growth forest as well as to manage their own lands according to Forest Service standards.

Between 1944 and 1946 the Forest Service had the experience of negotiating a CSYU with Simpson, a large Seattle firm, and of seeing their trial joint management plans ripen into a cooperative unit as envisaged in the legislation.[81] The unit covered a large tract of national forest on the Olympic Peninsula of Washington State. Lyle Watts, the chief forester, pushed for agreement against the public and political furore that surrounded the effort as well as against the bitter and disappointed opposition from small communities, companies, and unions whose people were to be excluded when Simpson attained its monopoly. Several more cooperative units were negotiated, but in the end only the Simpson unit survived. It is still in operation. There are other large forestry units in the United States, but their management is not integrated into that of neighbouring public forestlands.

CANADIAN POST-WAR TENURES

For the rest of the story we must cross the boundary from Washington into British Columbia. There, C. D. Orchard, soon to become chief forester of British Columbia, and the Sloan Commission were proposing a similar joint tenure to the B.C. cabinet.[82] Under the resulting tenure the province's forest management licences (later renamed tree farm licences, concessions or agreements) combined Crown lands with a firm's licensed lands and its own provincial freehold lands. The public-service forest administration and the company each retained the ownership of its lands and timber, but joined with the other in an agreed management plan for the whole. (Later, in practice, some tree-farm units were set up entirely on Crown land.) Once the initial plans were approved, the firm became the manager and the public service bowed out.

The chief novelty of the new policies was their emphasis on long-term forest management[83] rather than on orderly long-term liquidation. Such long-run management was perceived to require economies of scale, each mill's wood supplies obtained from following a 'working circle' within the forest. The necessary large scale was achieved by adding new public timber acreage to

[81] Clary 1986, pp. 126–46. Many thanks to Walker and Clawson for guidance here.

[82] For a one-sided history of the forest management licence proposal in the Sloan Report, see Mahood and Drushka 1990.

[83] Formally, forest inventory and stand management were introduced to Ontario pulp licences in the 1930s, but they were not taken seriously. See Lambert and Pross 1967, p. 407.

the 'private' timber already held by the firm.[84] In the American prototype, the cutting of the separate national forest and company acreages had been 'co-ordinated', but in the various Canadian provincial versions, public and private holdings were pooled so as to lose their original identities.

By 1990 similar agreements existed in nine provinces (the exception being PEI with its 2,500 square miles of mostly private forest). They typically cover large territories: in 1990, one proposed in Alberta exceeded 73,000 square kilometres, more than double the size of Belgium. Terms range up to twenty years or more and are automatically renewable, at expiry or before. Though the firms' duties and obligations vary by province, they typically require the holding company to prepare management and working plans that, when approved, become part of the agreement. The holder assumes forest management obligations, including keeping forest inventories, planning, road building and maintenance, forest protection and reforestation. As well, the holder undertakes to pay annual rentals and royalties and/or stumpage and perhaps local property and school taxes.[85]

THE AGREEMENT'S PROPERTY-RIGHT CHARACTERISTICS

Invented and negotiated by the government, the agreement tenure can be interpreted legally as an interest in land; as a concession of the type found today in some developing countries; or as a lease-type contract.[86] Seen through the eyes of an economist, the agreement can be sized up by considering its characteristics. Its duration, when automatic renewal on meeting certain standards is taken into account, is longer than that of the preceding pulp licences and certainly longer than that of the individual licence. It typically has great exclusivity, at least in the sense that other firms are shut out from the same timber.

However, compared to the all-embracing estate of the textbook freehold owner in sole possession from the sky to the centre of the earth, the owner of the agreement tenure is constrained in his private choices and his powers to manage, dispose and take income from his property. He must adjust his management to state requirements regarding roads, the environment, watersheds, wildlife and fishing as well as to the holders of licences to make different uses of the same land. He may be subject to an Allowable Annual Cut (AAC) of varying flexibility. His quality of title is probably considered to be about the same as for most other government franchises, permits and licences—that is, less than the security of a freehold interest. And, unlike

[84] For the public debate on redistributing existing licences and new acreage in British Columbia, see Mahood and Drushka 1990. For Ontario, see Lambert and Pross 1967, p. 402.

[85] This brief sketch of the terms and conditions of management agreements follows Pearse 1990. It ignores exceptions and special arrangements. For a more detailed account, see Luckert and Haley 1989.

[86] For a discussion of the cases concerning whether an agreement is an interest in land in the sense of the common law or whether it is a mere contract, see Ross et al. 1995, pp. 136–87.

freehold, the typical agreement explicitly limits the holder's transferability and divisibility through provisions that forbid the rights over the land to be re-assigned or sub-divided, by legal conveyance or by reorganization of the firm, without government permission.

PROVINCIAL POLITICAL PREFERENCES FOR AGREEMENT TENURE

The previous discussion suggests that industrial investors would prefer freehold ownership to the agreement tenure. Why, then, have the provinces persisted in offering agreement tenures while retaining final ownership of the forestland? There are two general explanations, both related to the government's attempts to retain control over forest utilization. The first, the government's desire to protect and regulate non-timber forestland users, is discussed below. The second is the goal, carried over from the older licences, to see investment in the forests. From the point of view of hard-pressed politicians, attaching an investment condition to forest disposal ensured construction and development and gave governments something other than roads and post offices to offer frontier voters. The relatively long-term employment opportunities the timber processing firms brought with them (with the attached stream of visible political decisions to be made during the course of the lease) made agreements so politically valuable that some provinces kept them on offer for years, waiting for industry takers.

There were alternative ways for governments to insure that they saw investment in the public's woods. Public enterprise remained an option. During the period when Ontario was setting up Ontario Hydro,[87] Crown investment and operation of the pulp mills powered by the new utility could have created many patronage opportunities for politicians. However, there were good reasons to avoid public enterprise in pulp: the difficulty in raising the capital and maintaining large-scale public operations in the backwoods.[88] There was also a constitutional difficulty in channelling forest revenues into financing forest regeneration. Although forest inquiries repeatedly asserted that more revenue must be ploughed back to keep the forest capital intact, provincial treasuries generally resisted giving forest management preference in the allocation of the general revenue fund.

Agreement licences proved a way out of this dilemma. Politicians who could not get the provincial treasurer to spend directly on sustained yield in effect forced him to do so indirectly when firms deducted the same expenses before handing over agreement revenues. A similar problem had emerged in the US when Congress equivalently refused to plough back revenues to the US Forest

[87] See Nelles 1974, p. 384, and passim.

[88] There was an attempt at public mill ownership in British Columbia after the Second World War. In Ontario in the 1930s the collapse of Abitibi had given the provincial government a chance to take over the firm. Later, the Kennedy Report (Ontario 1947) did in fact propose a joint industry-government operating company in each watershed. See Lambert and Pross 1967, p. 402.

Service, in part because the Forest Service plans included the costly harvesting and rehabilitation of the most marginal forests. (This reform provoked temporary interest in the CYSU initiative.) Clearly, politicians had incentive to reject the public-enterprise alternative.

In principle, politicians and governments could have indulged the firms' desire for ownership by selling forested blocks outright, subject to specific (anti-speculative, pro-investment) conditions contained in a side contract. Either a conditional sale or a licence arrangement would bring the same three basic benefits: construction in the wilderness, future manufacturing employment and a stream of rental and royalty revenue. In practice the conditional sale would have been enormously complicated and difficult to enforce without the explicit threat on the government's part of foreclosing or nullifying the agreement. An agreement licence also permitted the government certain important additional information and verification privileges such as the right to visit or inspect periodically; to get internal reports on plant and forest; and even to veto company decisions. Finally there is the matter of transactions costs. Under both an agreement and a forest sale, the politician incurs the 'static' transactions costs of enforcing the conditions of mill building and operation as well as the 'dynamic' transactions costs of guiding the firm's land and forest practices under changing and unknown conditions. It is arguable that both these classes of transactions costs will be lower if the government keeps the ownership than if it sells it.

Altogether, then, it is not surprising that the provincial governments more or less unanimously decided in favour of licence tenures rather than sale of forest land into private ownership.

The environment, multiple use and agreement tenures

Beyond timber, citizens want from the forests such things as genetic diversity, grazing range, fish and wildlife habitat, watershed and flood protection and space for recreation and study. Some of these demands are for commodity-like services relating to individual participation and enjoyment. Others, however, include not only services that are tangible but cannot be appropriated by individuals (ranging from scenery to watershed protection), but also some that are intangible and abstract, such as tribal and national symbolism, ecosystem integrity and 'sustainability'.

Governments and monarchies always had two ways of meeting these various public demands: their land-disposal powers and their law-making powers. The former were sometimes very convenient. Nineteenth-century governments withdrew Crown Lands into 'reserves' that were then available to meet public demands for providing various aspects of nature. Alternatively, where land could serve two or more purposes, or could serve private and public purposes together, governments could use their law-making power to impose the multiple use of forested land on individuals. For example, under medieval and some customary Forest Law, some contractors' rights to cut certain timbers were superimposed on a matrix of existing rights (held by others) to harvest other trees, to hunt and fish, to graze animals and to offer access to villages, churches or mining operations.

The philosophers of the US and Canadian conservation movements did not concern themselves with multiple use—that is, with the eighteenth century European idea of conserving all aspects of whole landscapes—until the 1920s. Of course, there had always been common-sense recognition of complementarity (e.g. in trapping and forestry; inland fisheries and forestry; and rangeland and forestry); however, most attention, from Arbor Day onward, was given to protecting the forests as future sources of timber.

In the United States and (especially) in Canada, the conservation movement, after rather broad beginnings, narrowed its forest policy goals to reservation. The United States established its forest reservations in 1891. Ontario and Quebec followed suit between 1897 and 1904 on the model of the upstate New York State forests. Across North America there seemed to be enough space for each new demand, as it emerged, to be served by specific new reserve, park or monument. The turn-of-the century debates on the creation of Yellowstone and other Rocky Mountain national parks showed an inclination to assign some forested areas for recreation, others for water-shed protection, others for the military, and the rest for the lumber industry.[89]

It was not until the First World War[90] that conservationists and governments realized that there was just not enough forested land to separately satisfy each demand for dedicated single-purpose tracts of land. As well, some of the various purposes could actually be served best by joint production on the same parcel of land. Since some of the uses were to satisfy public good demands, governments found themselves needing either to create multiple-use forests on public land (tended by public-service foresters, gamekeepers or park wardens) or to use their legislative and police powers to force citizens to manage their own private forested lands for multiple purposes. They mainly opted for the former. Using their landlord powers, governments began to insert a few multiple-purpose conditions into their timber licences. Legislative

[89] See Hodgins and Bendickson 1989, ch. 4; Benidickson 1998 (draft). On Algonquin Park see Lambert and Pross 1967, ch. 14. On Banff and other national parks, see the essays by Robert Craig Brown et al. in Nelson 1970. On the conservation movement in Canada, Nelles 1974, pp. 182–214; and Lambert and Pross 1967, pp. 150–73 provide splendid chapters. Although these refer to central Canada, something of the movements in the other regions can be gleaned from the volumes and reports of the Canadian federal Commission of Conservation after 1909.

[90] A historical study of land policy by L. C. Gray, who had been active during the war decade, excluded from its list of 'shortcomings' during a century of US federal land alienation any mention of failure to implement multiple-use (cited in Johnson and Barlowe 1954, pp. 57–60; N.B.: Johnson and Barlowe had been Gray's colleagues).

and police powers were limited to occasional experiments in rural zoning or town and county planning.

After the Second World War the demands on forested-land for multiple use changed sharply. Industry still wanted access to standing timber; some firms still campaigned for fire prevention and forest regeneration; and farmers and ranchers still sought rangeland. The new demand was for the simultaneous protection of wildlife habitat, recreation and scenery (especially in old-growth stands), watershed and general ecosystem health and sustainability. While most of these could, in the long run, be regarded as joint products with timber (for instance, through the clearing of old-growth stands to quicken regeneration), in the short run they could not. Generally, the provision of more mature trees to satisfy non-timber demands either reduced the output of the timber industry or raised its costs.

Now the government had to arm itself with both its landlord powers and its police-legislative powers. The deeds it negotiated with its tenants, the holders of its licences and agreement tenures on public lands, were loaded with conditions, rules and codes aimed both at protecting the forest ecosystem and at making other users' access to and enjoyment of the forest easier. Governments have made some forays into wielding legislative and police powers to bring about similar results on private land. Nevertheless, the demand for sustainable forestry and multiple use has probably further entrenched politicians' preference for licence tenure over expanded private ownership.

Conclusion: changing demands and the future of agreement tenures

I set out to write this chapter with the preconception that the major demanders of pulpwood agreement tenure over the past two centuries in Canada were the politicians and bureaucrats, not the investors. After all, the agreement policy was largely promotional and was aimed at a type of potential (large) investor not yet on the scene to resist politically. The small firms present when governments were putting the licensing regimes in place were less interested in undertaking pulp mill enterprises than in conducting their logging operations at their own pace under individual licences. And whatever their ex-ante objections might have been, it turned out that the larger-scale segments of the logging industry were attracted to the prospect of locking up large reserves for their own future harvest without the risks and credit difficulties pertaining to the high initial price of buying land.

Eventually, pulp mill tenure was so successful from the politician's point of view that it was adapted for a new purpose when, in the 1940s, sustained yield became the goal. Whether industry remained cheerful about the role cast for it under agreement tenure—acting like an owner with a future in the land but without holding a real ownership interest—is less obvious. But the point is moot since the provinces have increasingly refused to act as land sellers. At the same time, Canadian provinces have, in recent decades, assigned a much larger role to the forest user than at any time in the history of the public forests. As of the late 1990s firms were being asked to take over the government's role as landlord of the small logging and lumbering businesses that operate still holding older small licence and timber-sale tenures—a subject to be further discussed below.

As well, provinces show signs of wishing to delegate some role in dealing with multiple-purpose forest allocation. So far neither the provincial landlords nor the industrial tenants have produced robust theories about how to accommodate changing wildlife, hunting, recreation and environmental goals to their older tree-growth and tree-harvesting targets. Political problems and principal-and-agent problems abound.[91] Whether governments can design variants of the large-scale agreement tenure that will be able to deal with these problems at reasonable costs remains to be seen. If not, then we may see future forests divided between those the public sector runs for multiple purposes and those private firms run for single, private purposes.

The timber sale: the final tenure on public lands

The remaining tenure to be explained is the modern timber sale, which emerged in the first decades of the twentieth century in the US as an alternative to the Canadian licence system, but has made some inroads into Canadian forest policy. I begin with the US, which followed two paths: one led to the agreement licence discussed in the previous part, the other led to the short-term timber sale discussed here.

The United States National Forest

In his appraisal of pre-Great War US public-land disposal policies, Lewis C. Gray wrote, 'Perhaps the most fateful and potentially tragic development was the consistent adoption of alodial [absolute] tenure in fee simple...the almost unrestricted right of use and abuse of land has resulted in devastation of a major portion of our forests,...and the social dislocations that flow from these.'[92] After the Civil War Congress had continued with its policy of freehold land disposals, now mainly west of the Mississippi. Homesteading and land sales both flourished, and sometimes land was disposed of practically free. Not until the final decades of the nineteenth century did widespread political dissatisfaction with the vanishing of public lands, with fraud and with the devastation of great forests lead to the decline of disposal in fee-simple. Congressmen were sandwiched between interests that wanted to keep the lumber boom going by

[91] See Haley and Luckert in Scott et al. 1995, pp. 54–80.

[92] Gray in Johnson and Barlowe 1954, p. 57. On Gray's stand on land use and land classification, see Gates 1968b, p. 598.

making public timber available through the homestead system and those that wanted to slow down in order to preserve what remained of the forests. Gradually the latter agenda prevailed. With the approval of Congress, successive early twentieth-century administrations set aside 200 million acres of forestland.

By that time, altogether about 1,500 million acres (forested or bare) had been, at one time or another, within the federal public domain. Of these about two-thirds, 1,000 million, had been disposed of. After 1850, this included about 300 million that were passed on via the states or the railroads to encourage land development expenditures; and after 1862 it included about 600 million that were sold, auctioned, pre-empted or homesteaded directly. Of these immense areas only 14 million were ever earmarked as timberland (after 1878); all other forested tracts had been granted indiscriminately and/or fraudulently as agricultural land. Indeed, as we have seen, with the exception of the limited provisions of the Timber and Stone Act (1878) and a few attempts by the states and railways to classify land under their domain, no real broad-ranging method of identifying or classifying forestland was ever developed.

About one-third of the original 1,500 million acres had not been disposed of by 1891 when large-scale reservation began. Some of these acres simply remained unwanted, but most were reserved as Indian reservations, public grazing lands, national forests, wildlife habitats and state public lands.[93] The government now had to find some method by which to dispose of these reserved acres. The method it eventually settled on was the timber sale.

I believe Fernow and Pinchot, two of the chief national forest-policy architects, shaped the US timber sale by adapting the systems they had seen on the Continent.[94] Much of their research was embodied in legislation in 1897. Their goal was the protection and restoration of the American forest. Of course, their freedom to design a new institution was constrained by local politics and revenue needs. They had to win over the support of nearby wood-using communities, and they also had to raise revenue to pay for forest-protection activities. In the end they created a professional Forest Service—an arm of the Department of Agriculture that was also of service to private forest owners—and used it for an internalized silviculture in which only the cutting activities were contracted out.[95]

[93] The numbers are taken from research by L. C. Gray, now in Johnson and Barlowe 1954, chs. 2 and 3. See also tables in Gates 1968b.

[94] See Fernow 1911, p. 123, on forest administration in Germany. Fernow's books are too rarely cited. Pinchot was much at home in France. On the importance of various European models to Pinchot and Fernow, see Miller 1991.

[95] A subsidiary activity was to distribute the public lands among uses: settlement, grazing and recreation. For decades many outside experts believed that the highest and best use of any land was agriculture: 'It is neither desirable nor necessary to use land needed for cultivation or pasture for forest purposes.' 'During the next 25 years [1950–75] about 25 to 30 million acres of the more fertile of these lands may have to be diverted from forest to crops and improved pasture.' See Johnson and Barlowe 1954, pp. 223–4. Like the Forest Service, these land economists forecast timber 'needs'. They assumed there would be exports but no imports. Experts inside the Forest Service, however, tended to assume that all the land in its forests was to be allocated to silviculture.

For all their insistence on the historical importance of the exclusivity of private forests, it was the public domain as a whole that Fernow and Pinchot wished to manage. (They were convinced that there were economies of scale in fire protection and silviculture, and they had a horror of patterns broken up by patches of settlement.) Under their large-scale public ownership, there would be long-range growing and cutting plans to remove the over-mature trees, take forest revenue and allow the new Forest Service to get on with building a stock capable of being cropped perpetually.

Consequently they saw the timber buyer as someone who contracted to remove selected, marked and designated timber. His cutting and removing were to be supervised. Instead of being hired for money, he would be paid in kind with the trees he cut minus the stumpage[96] he paid to the Forest Service, proportioned to the amount cut and/or based on the net value or rent after subtracting cutting costs. The whole operation was to be specified in advance by the Forest Service. In principle the logger had no voice in choosing the stand to be cut.

The timber sale, like the logger's interest in forested land, lacked almost any measure of four of the main characteristics of property rights. Its duration was very short, and it had neither transferability nor divisibility. Exclusivity in decision-making was non-existent since any decisions were subject to ubiquitous scrutiny and veto by the Forest Service.[97] On the other hand, because the payment by stumpage was set by bidding or calculated on the basis of local circumstances, the timber sale as a disposal institution had greater flexibility than had tenures calling for royalties or rentals at uniform rates across all forests. It also gave some quality of title, which perhaps could be regarded as comparable to the mining claims being issued by the federal government.

Twentieth-century modifications

Over time, the US national forests came to offer an interest that gave a region's largest operator, mill owner or pulp producer property characteristics more like those of the Canadian volume licence or leasehold of the 1900s. A major reconsideration occurred after the Great War when the forest service's logs were not selling rapidly: less than 1 per cent of the national cut of 'sawtimber' came from the public forests. In the 1950s the figure had risen to about 20 per

[96] The origin of this word, and concept, in the United States is handily traced in the *Shorter Oxford Dictionary* to a price paid for standing timber (1848) or for the tax payable for the privilege of cutting timber on state/public lands. A few years later (1854), it appears to have meant simply the value of standing timber without the land. These three concepts are not the same, but together they provide a private property antecedent for the word used in national forest procedures. Of course, Fernow and Pinchot would also have been familiar with German and French words with identical meanings. See Dana and Fairfax 1980, pp. 62–3.

[97] See Megarry and Wade 1984, p. 633.

cent and in the 1970s to about 35 per cent.[98] Two timber sale characteristics were modified during this 'learning' period: duration and exclusivity. When operations reached into tougher country and required more logger up-front investment, loggers demanded freedom: more exclusivity in the sense of control over the pace of logging, and more time to get the job done—eventually five years. Although Forest Service timber sales were competitive, they were predictable; a large buyer could, and can, rely on getting his accustomed share of the periodic cut.

There were other modifications, especially for small operators. For instance, some national forests now allow for disposal of cut logs, rather than of standing timber. The government manages the timber stands, oversees the harvesting, and keeps possession of the cut log until it reaches a yard at the forest gate similar to those run by owners of very large private forests. In these, the individual logger-contractor-hauler is paid by the hour and is as much an employee as a client.[99]

The United States timber sale decision and the Canadian licence

In early debates over how to use and allocate the national forests, some champions of setting up reserves praised the 'Canadian scheme'. To people in the United States this meant any system under which private enterprise got access to the trees but the public retained the land itself.[100] We may ask, then, why Fernow and Pinchot chose European-style timber sales rather than the Canadian-type area licences.

To begin, it is worth thinking about the differences between a Canadian licence and a US timber sale. In the early 1900s a Canadian licence entitled the holder to enter a given plot and cut trees. The volume to be cut was not stated in advance. The licence's duration was often more than one year and easily renewed. On a US timber sale, by contrast, the holder entered the land to cut a volume of timber stated in advance and subject to a shorter duration (so the lumberman was essentially 'in and out'). In Canada most of the payments were deferred, becoming due during the period before, or at the time of, cutting. In the United States most of the payment was due in advance. In both countries, the logger's interest might be issued or sold by competitive auction, subject to a calculated upset or minimum price. In Canada, the auction price was a bonus on top of rental and royalty-like payments. In the United States, the auction price, or stumpage, was commonly the government's whole method of billing.

There are several possible explanations for Fernow and Pinchot's rejection of the Canadian licensing model. One is revenue maximization: they may have

98 See Clary 1986, pp. 29–30; and Clawson 1979, p. 182.
99 Mead and McKillop 1976, pp. 95–100.
100 Ise 1920, p. 110; Gates 1968b.

reasoned that a competitive timber sale would bring in more revenue than would the kind of licence disposal they saw in Canada. In the short run at least, this was incorrect. In fact, not until the 1930s did US timber sales actually deliver a higher price than the reserve (upset) price.

A better explanation might be the Forest Service's intention of closely monitoring harvesting. This had certainly not been the intention of earlier licensing systems. The US national forests were set up in a 'custodial' atmosphere of intense dedication to the ideal of scientific forestry.[101] The planners doubted that their principal-and-agent problem could be answered by delegating any stage of the silvicultural process to the discretion of contractors. The conservation movement had a low opinion of the nation's small lumbermen, who were just then ending a twenty-year orgy of land-sale fraud, speculation and cut-and-get-out logging. It was only natural that the service should prefer to suppress the logging industry's freedom, transforming the firms into little more than one-year casual contractors possessing a minimal property interest.

Having settled on the more restrictive timber sales, however, the government still retained discretion for setting the conditions of the sale to the mutual benefit of itself and the industry. The principal-and-agent question was whether the sale mechanism should 'lease' the forest to an operator for a medium term or should 'employ' the operator in a one-season timber sale. Judging from the historical record, a safe assumption seems to be that the Forest Service sought to achieve maximum revenue subject to a selected forest practice standard, rather than maximum net revenue (rent or profit), an emphasis criticized by a long series of commentators, especially Marion Clawson. Loggers got economies of scale from being able to spread their operations over more than one year, and also may have indulged the idea that they could benefit from rising timber prices by bidding early and selling later.[102] For a given volume, then, loggers would bid more for an *n*-year contract than for n one-year contracts, thus increasing Forest Service revenues.

Aside from price, the service had to be concerned with its monitoring costs. In general, longer contracts required less frequent but more thorough inspections, generating economies of scale in monitoring up to a point. Plotted on a diagram, as the period of contracts is lengthened from one to *n* years, frequency costs fall and thoroughness costs rise, probably generating a U-shaped total cost curve with respect to duration: very high for almost instantaneous removal of the given volume, lower for durations long enough to give some possibility of correcting and/or effectively penalizing bad practices, and perhaps rising for very long durations.

These economies can explain why the Forest Service eventually lengthened the duration of its timber sale contracts from one to five years or more.

[101] Clawson and Held 1957, p. 29, use the word 'custodial' for this early period.
[102] Clawson and Held 1957.

The original insistence on almost-instantaneous contracts shows how much the Forestry Service's planners had doubted that loggers could be induced to adopt and not short-change desired logging practices. They also had underestimated the costs they would face of frequent renewals, inspections and supervision of the industry.

Canada: from area licences to timber sales and agreements

From the early days of licences, the Canadian provinces' disposal systems featured confusing sequences of forest tenures.[103] Many old area licences, granted in the nineteenth century with long durations, were held and renewed without cutting. Timber sales not unlike the US Forest Service timber sales were introduced early in the twentieth century. They were mostly issued on an area basis. When, in the 1940s and 1950s, the provinces adopted 'sustained yield' goals (and associated regulations) for their forest tenure policies, they began to calculate an allowable annual cut for each administrative district. This volume was divided among individual volume timber sales with short lives and volume licences with longer terms. In British Columbia the licences were issued with terms between ten and twenty-five years with payment by stumpage or Crown dues, a more flexible system than the former fixed-royalty payment. In most provinces the stumpage rate can be set by competition. But actual competition is rare and the rate is set administratively, using an appraisal formula that takes into account site-specific production and transportation costs as well as market prices.

The provinces' sustained-yield policies require that someone undertake to start and protect a new crop. In New Brunswick, the government farms out management tasks in some provincial forests. In Saskatchewan and Ontario the provincial forest services take direct responsibility for reforestation. In most provinces, especially British Columbia, a great many management obligations rest with the holder of the previous licence including road building, harvesting, reforestation and fire protection.

The trend has been to assign an ever greater responsibility to the licence holder. The small holder has not been expected, or given an incentive, to manage the crop or see it through from one cutting to the next. Indeed the provinces have tailored the Canadian volume licence to the needs of larger firms, those combining logging and processing. Pulp and paper companies, which usually are the holders of major management agreements, and tree farm operators have also become important holders of volume licences, mainly through the acquisition of smaller firms. The 1991 Peel Commission found 60 per cent of B.C.'s total expected cut on Crown lands to be in the hands of large firms.

[103] Thanks to Peter Pearse, David Haley and Martin Luckert for discussions of the features of various categories of licences in Canada.

The Australian experience

In this chapter the focus has been on the extensive Canadian public and shared public–private forest, with some comparative discussion of the emergence of the US national forests. In keeping with the geographical range of other chapters, however, I present here some brief comments on the development of forest tenures in the former British colonies of Oceania.

To start with, the native trees were quite different from those mentioned so far, and varied across the continent: rain forests in Queensland, eucalyptus in the wet areas of New South Wales and Victoria and widespread but thin stands of conifers in the dry interior. Starting around 1800, Australia's experience with forest harvests is notable for the rapid disappearance and regrowth of forests in periods as short as fifty years, and for the introduction and plantations of other species from Europe and North America.

As in North America, in the 1880s and 1890s, governments began to take interest in preserving and maintaining the remaining forests, extensive parts of which had been cleared. In the 1880s New South Wales set up forest reserves, and in the 1890s South Australia established a Department of Woods and Forests both to conserve existing stocks and to establish new ones. The Monterey pine (from California) was to become a mainstay of the Australian (mainly domestic) timber industry, both from private and public lands. By 1917 all states had established government forests and reserves with timber supply as their goal.

Following the North American pattern, it was only from the 1970s that forest policy on these reserves came to reflect the preferences of naturalists, conservationists and environmentalists. The tenures adopted by state governments also reflect the North American experience. In Tasmania, the state set up vast public–private shared logging concessions. These are very similar to the Canadian tree farm and agreement tenures discussed above. In all other states, for both natural and plantation forests, the state forestry agencies now issued licences to sawmillers and other users—they were in effect wood-supply contracts. Apart from the short duration—ten years, renewable—the licences were much like those established under the Canadian provinces' licencing systems. But over the course of fifty years the state systems evolved in the direction of the American national forests. Their licences became quotas, quantitatively fixed, almost as rights. They became tradeable, mostly among sawmills and other users, and developed a market value. Some states, trying to reduce the total cut, have set out to buy back the quotas at their market values—much like the fishery buy-back schemes discussed in Chapter 4.

Concluding remarks: demands and alternatives

Focusing attention on Canada, in the last two parts we have seen two ways in which early and mid-nineteenth-century Canadian licence tenure evolved. In some circumstances, the provincial governments, as landlords, saw the licence as too small and therefore inadequate to performing the functions desired by the government. These same governments enlarged the tenure, in scope and in physical area, first to the pulp-mill tenures of the Great War period, then to the agreement tenure of the 1940s created in response to the new, modern demand for sustained-yield forestry.

A major theme of this chapter has been how and why the provinces went out of their way to avoid outright forested-land sales. They were not able to prevent lumbermen—mostly small operators—from acquiring directly or by re-sale the freehold of timberland that lay within municipal boundaries or in nearby surveyed townships. But they forced larger firms, seeking to establish large-scale operations in unsurveyed forest, to acquire timber by obtaining a volume timber licence. In theory, this licence could not be acquired through favouritism, and had to be sold at public auction. Following the US practice of retaining public control over allowable harvest volume, its acquisition allowed its holder to enter the land and remove a specific amount of timber over a specific period of time (measured by a cutting plan). The holder deferred to rules for forest protection and land and water conservation as well as to other users.

The natural downside of this system was that it returned the duties of multi-purpose forest management and enforcement, which had previously been assigned to the holders of large-scale agreement tenures on public lands, back to provincial bureaux. These duties dragged the various provincial forest services into detailed surveying, planning, inspection and revision, implying an actual reduction in the exclusivity enjoyed by holders of timber sales and an increase in the combined administration and organization costs of government and industry.

Given that the holders of timber sales were not necessarily integrated with any mill, and given that they had their own independence and enterprise, the question naturally arises as to whether there exists an alternative that allows public control of the land to continue while allowing and ensuring that private operators take over tree growing as well as tree harvesting. The very low discounted value of merchantable trees to be harvested in, say, seventy-five years makes it difficult to imagine such a tenure becoming popular. I conclude this chapter with a few possibilities for how such an arrangement might be achieved.

The traditional farm woodlot, based on international experience, is not usually well managed but is at least protected.[104] The so-called taxation tree farm is a system under which landowners who practise silviculture on a small private landholding are rewarded with a reduction in land taxes. Tree tenure is a traditional arrangement found in some developing countries by which one party can own rights to plant and harvest an orchard, a small plantation, or a

[104] On American private (non-industrial) forests, see various writings of Marion Clawson. On Swedish non-industrial forests, see Hansing and Wibe 1992, pp. 157–70.

stand of trees on land over which another person has surface ownership.[105] I discuss it further in the next chapter with respect to private forest tenure. The community forest is encountered in India and China, though a few examples are also found on provincial public lands in Canada. Under this arrangement a village, having an exclusive right over an adjoining forest area, takes responsibility for its management and regeneration and also for distributing rights of use among the villagers.[106] The question with regard to all such models is whether the social and opportunity-cost obstacles are large enough to prevent examples of them from appearing on public lands in the West.

[105] For a survey, see Bruce and Fortmann 1992, pp. 477–9.

[106] See Thomson, Feeny, and Oakerson 1986, on patterns of common and community property in Asian forests (followed by three other papers on similar subjects); Agrawal et al. in Ostrom et al. 1994, on rule-making and rule-breaking in Indian community forests; and Hyde 1992, in Nemetz 1992, pp. 431–52, for a survey of social forestry.

12

Forestry on Private Lands from the Medieval to the Modern Era

In this chapter[1] I survey the development of the interests held by users of private forests, starting again with the medieval English forest.[2] It is tempting to think of the royal forest as a private (feudal) forest that happened to be owned by the king. But, in fact, the differences between the royal forests and private forests were great: rights in the former stemmed from 'forest law' under the royal prerogative, not from manorial customs or from the common law. This key difference obliges us to turn our back on rights to use the royal or public forests and to examine the emerging rights in the private woods.

Private woods and the common law

The private woods in England

Apart from stands in the royal forests, most of England's trees were located in manorial woods. Typically, these consisted of the private woods, over which the lord, in conjunction with the other right-holders in his family, held title, and a broader wood shared by the lord and his manorial tenants. In the former, some species of trees that had grown to maturity, especially oak, ash and elm, were honoured by the designation 'timber'. Some old stands or groves were coppiced or pollarded to produce smaller dimensions: charcoal or firewood. These were enclosed and carefully preserved. A few whole woods were divided into compartments, cut cyclically and fenced against animals for at least their first years of growth.

[1] Parts of this chapter are based on explorations by Cliona Kimber. Thanks to DeLloyd Guth, David Stewart, Margaret Hall and Lilliana Biukovic.

[2] See especially Trevelyan 1973.

The common woods and wasteland[3] were governed by custom. The lord was restricted in the same ways as when he attempted to dispose of coal and other minerals. Although he 'owned' the whole manor, including the land and all attached to it, law and custom required him to recognize commoners' rights to make certain uses of the resources, and to maintain rights over routes of access to the resources. If he granted rights to an outsider to enter and take from the woods and forests without the consent of the commoners, he was obliged to pass on to them something of what he was paid. (Usually he passed on very little, so that a rise in price was of no interest to commoners. Indeed it was bad news because more of their wood would be stolen.)[4]

The lord's possible encroachments aside, villagers (commoners) who had appropriate rights pastured animals on the commons and 'gleaned' coal, peat, nuts, soil, stone and acorns, among other things. As it was with private mining rights, so it was for timber and wood rights: the custom of each manor provided the various classes of village freeholders and commoners with defined entitlements to use the space and resources as they needed, subject to their rank. The amounts and timing of entitlements varied widely within and among villages. Rights with respect to the trees were given the general name of 'estovers'. These included housebote (wood for house and building repairs), ploughbote (for farm implements), haybote (fences) and firebote (fuel). In some manors a person's share would be not only defined but quantitative, the whole amount being 'stinted', or rationed, among various classes of persons.[5] On others, the lord had a right to all the timber (classified as above) wherever it had grown, in the common waste or forest and in the villagers' own holdings.

Historians say that in the long run the lands over which the commoners had rights to take trees or timber were bare. As the total amounts that might annually be taken from the common woods were not exactly proportioned to the sustainable capacity of the manorial wastes, commoners and their livestock gradually reduced the growing stocks on most commons as well as on their individual holdings to sparsely treed grassland. The failure to regrow

[3] See Peterken 1981, ch. 2. There were other private woods within the village. These were assigned to the priest or owned by the few free landholders. Maps have understated private woods (and common woods) relative to fields and meadows. There is a suspicion that they were measured in different (larger) units than were fields and meadows, perhaps twice as large, to avoid taxes. See Maitland 1907, pp. 406 and 437.

[4] Thomas 1983, ch. 5.

[5] Eventually, the assortment of villagers' customary entitlements in different regions was classified by the common lawyers. Some were regarded as easements, but most were regarded as commons or profits of estovers. But the classification of a title did not make uniform its sources or its amount as between villages. For useful summaries of types and sources (e.g., whether commons appendant or appurtenant) see Megarry and Wade 1984, ch. 15, especially pp. 851–912. On medieval forest stinting in England and Switzerland, see Stevenson 1991, pp. 122 and 155.

trees was recognized as a problem in two royal statutes, the Statute of Merton (1235) and the Statute of Westminster (1290), ambitious attempts to restrict grazing from spreading farther. We do not know whether they were effective. The encroachment of grazing varied among manors, depending largely on the respective lords, the extent of creation of individual holdings, and on their village courts.

The extent of the commoners' neglect is somewhat surprising. We do not hear of their woods ever being actively managed or coppiced. Evidently, neither the lord nor the village courts could assign and enforce sufficiently exclusive rights to encourage an individual to take the kind of responsibility for specific trees or copses that he had for strips of ploughland. There are also almost no recorded incidences of commoners selling timber from common land, suggesting that economic and socio-economic conditions did not provide sufficient encouragement for or protection of joint management of common woods (again in contrast to jointly managed ploughland). It will be suggested below that timber and lumber prices may simply have been too low to make wood or timber production for the market worthwhile. It is a complicated question.

The poor shared quality of title experienced by lords and their commoners goes a long way toward explaining the decline of English forests as timber producers in the late middle ages. Perhaps more surprising is the fact that the decline of English commercial forestry did not stop with changes in property holding institutions, and the rise of freehold. The process of manorial enclosure, especially after 1600, steadily reduced the number of villages where people retained estover rights in common woods and wastes and increased the number of private parks, woodlots and copses. Indeed by the mid seventeenth century a new flow of timber and wood products from planted and managed woods began to reach the market, though by this time the English forests were no longer the chief source from which English users obtained timber and other wood products.

However, the lord's rights over his own forest estate were shrinking throughout the period for other reasons: specifically, the restrictions of the system of bequest and succession. From the early eighteenth through the nineteenth centuries, family lawyers perfected the 'strict settlement' system of inheritance, designed to meet owners' passions for keeping the estate in the family, and keeping its buildings and landed features intact.

The details of the strict settlement were examined in Chapter 1. Briefly, family heads had for centuries been bequeathing estates by entailing them. But the legal profession—with the help of sympathetic judges—had learned how those in the next generations might 'bar the entail' so that an entailed property might actually be broken up and its assets sold. The strict settlement, which adopted and essentially turned on its head the procedure of barring entails, was the answer.[6] Under the simplest version of the system, each head of family became, under the arrangements made by his father, a tenant for life and his son the heir in entail. When the son reached his majority his father would offer him a sizeable income until he succeeded to the estate. In return, the son would agree to bar the existing entail and bequeath the estate to his own son, in a new entail. He, like his father, become a tenant for life and in turn passed the property to his son (the grandson in the trio) entailed, at which point the process repeated. Thus the goal of the originator of the procedure would be achieved: every man in the succession would become a tenant for life, the lord and master of the estate, but without property rights sufficient to enable him to dispose of any part of it.[7]

The upshot was that the life tenant for the time being was responsible for keeping the estate intact. He might not cut the timber, open and work a mine, remove buildings or even redistribute the uses to which the fields were put—even if he could show that such changes would improve the estate to be acquired by his heir and later family life tenants. To take such action could make him, or the estate trustee whose job was to oversee succession and carry out provisions to keep the estate intact, 'impeachable for waste'. Lords who were impeachable for waste—in the late nineteenth century perhaps the majority of owners of estates with large areas of forest—might be prevented from participating in the market for wood products in the United Kingdom.

Some writers, such as Gordon (1955), believe that the poor quality of title to private forest properties—first due to manorial obligations, later due to the strict settlement—were widely detrimental to the practice of forestry: 'the adverse influence of the land laws prevailing in the eighteenth and nineteenth centuries has been much underrated in the standard forestry textbooks'.[8] Gordon says that such stultifying circumstances prevented forest culture from being learned, let alone practised. Other historians, such as Albion, have made a partly complementary argument that English forest husbandry was hurt by the tendency of private land-owners to strip their woods in order to pay old debts and support the average lord's growing number of dependants

[6] The will and the settlement went well beyond providing for the succession: they contained numerous provisions for the widow, daughters and younger sons and their marriages, and spread out to bequests or gifts to remote family members. The father–son settlement could contain undertakings by the son to look after these dependants. The burdens could be large, so that the son when he became the lord would suffer by his inability under the settlement to sell the timber, minerals or land. If the strict settlement was worded to allow him to 'waste' the woods, he would do so, thus incurring blame for 'stripping' the forest (see below). Of course, there were other owners who stripped their forest simply to find cash for themselves.

[7] Given the situation of rights and incomes into which he was born, the strict settlement between the father and his son made the son better off. For a discussion see Megarry and Wade's description in various editions of *The Law of Property*, chapter 8.

[8] Gordon 1955, p. 7.

beyond the circle provided for by past or current strict family settlements.[9] Of course, as suggested in the paragraphs above, many owners would have been prevented by their inheritance obligations from 'stripping' their woods, at least rapidly. Only a minority, perhaps some of those holding their forests in freehold tenure, could legally have cleared and sold all the woods and timber. Nevertheless, the potential restrictions down the family line on the ability to optimally raise and harvest timber trees on an estate would have encouraged lords to strip their lands when they could rather than engage in sustainable forest husbandry.

Historians have gone so far as to argue that these tendencies, in conjunction with the Crown's destruction of its own forests through the issuing of commercial licences and outright alienation (see Chapter 11), resulted in a seventeenth and eighteenth-century 'timber famine' in England, a topic I return to directly below. Nevertheless, the effect of strict settlements has almost certainly been exaggerated. To begin, the restrictions on timber-felling were not absolute. Although most strict settlements apparently provided that the estate's life tenant should keep the timber trees intact, this provision was not a legal necessity. From the seventeenth century the heirs to life estates could be exempted by their fathers from impeachability for some or for all kinds of waste.[10]

As well, it can be seen from an examination of the cases that by mid-eighteenth century, judges, far from upholding the medieval rules forbidding waste, were now prepared to limit their application. Judges almost always found entails and strict settlements to be enforceable, variously noting that they worked a hardship on some members of some families and also led to inefficient use of the woods but that the courts could do nothing about it. However, the judges were more activist about many-generation entails and strict settlements because they disliked the idea of the family founder's 'dead hand' reaching from the past to dictate who should enjoy and control the family's estate and so what use should be made of the nation's forest resources. In *Packington's Case* (1744), the Lord Chancellor went so far as to say that, while it might be in the interest of large families to have powers to impeach for waste, 'the common law thought it for the interest on the public to limit these rights, as timber might thereby circulate for shipping and other uses'.[11] The

[9] In fact, Albion offered what could be thought of as the complement to Gordon's argument. Gordon says that impeachability for waste worked only too well, and so deprived British forests of management. Albion says impeachability for waste was not *sufficiently* rigorous to prevent damage and overcutting in the British forests, thereby depriving England of a maturing growing stock of trees. See Albion 1926.

[10] Megarry and Wade 3rd edn. 1984, p. 97.

[11] (1744), 3 Atk. 215, 26 E.R. 925. On the other hand, in *Marker v. Marker* (1851), 68 E.R. 389, the court said that 'the excessive use of the legal power incident to an estate unimpeachable of waste [was] inequitable and unjust, and this court therefore controls it'. See (V1851), 9 Hare 1, 68 E.R. 389.

liberalizing attitude persisted in the courts; for instance a softening of the rule against waste of timber was achieved in 1891 with *Dashwood v. Magniac.*[12]

Government intervention was also an option. In mid-nineteenth century Parliament passed a series of Settled Land Acts that modified the testator's powers to create and perpetuate a strict settlement and its associated impeachability for waste. The legislature could also act without government, by passing a private Act of Parliament, a 'cheap, expeditious, and very effective' procedure.[13] In a sense, in turning to the courts and the Parliament, the lords demanded and sometimes received changes in the characteristics of their property rights: an improved quality of title and more of both transferability and flexibility. These improved rights should have made good long-term forestry practices more appealing and preserved the resource, though by this time England had long since ceased to be a serious source of timber on either home or foreign markets.

The alleged English timber shortage revisited

In my view, the historians' consensus of a sustained timber 'shortage' or 'famine' due to supply-side considerations, such as poor property rights, does not stand up well to the kind of scrutiny that relies on economists' concepts.[14] I argue instead that, to the extent that the market for British timber during the period was weak, the problem was also due to demand side conditions, under which, for many years, becoming a timber grower and seller simply did not pay. As discussed in the previous chapter, the literature on the alleged timber crisis is dominated by evidence about the Royal Navy's difficulties in securing adequate supplies of timber toward the end of the eighteenth century.[15] The failure of the royal forests to provide as much timber as wanted led the Navy to search the colonies and other nations for suitable timber—pine for masts and oak of over twenty-one years for ships' knees and crossbeams. As we saw in Chapter 11, the Navy was stubbornly unreceptive to substitutes, and its refusal to pay market prices when they jumped to wartime levels, and its bad credit, were instrumental in diverting high-quality masts and timber from the dockyards to other users. Essentially, its refusal to deal at a market price at home and abroad created much of the apparent 'shortage' experienced by naval shipbuilders.[16]

[12] [1891] 2 Ch. 306. The Court of Appeal's majority decision was merely confirming this development.

[13] *Packington's Case* (1744), 3 Atk. 215, 26 E.R. 925.

[14] For general sources on the history of forestry in England, see James 1981; Rackham 1980 (and other works); Nisbet 1909; Thomas 1983; and Scott 1983. All contain extensive bibliographies.

[15] See Albion 1926, p. 45. Fernow 1911 was among the first writers on the history of the forests and forestry. A professional himself, he did not always accept the modern idea that the role of a forest is to produce wood or timber rather than to store trees.

[16] See Albion 1926, pp. 41–4.

Competing with the Navy were many domestic and industrial wood users, especially the charcoal-using mineral-refining industries and the urban construction industry. As for the amounts needed by the iron industry, the economic historian T. S. Ashton maintained that tree felling for charcoal, carried out by the iron and glass industries from 1550 to 1700, was a chief cause of the destruction of British woodlands, the shortage of fuel supplies, and what he regarded as the approach of the total exhaustion of private wood resources.[17] Charcoal production certainly must have drawn some timber from the naval shipbuilder, though other writers than Ashton say the Navy was not in direct competition for the underwood relied on by the mineral-industry fuel users.[18]

As for the third element in the demand for timber, the construction (building) industry did not prove to be a direct rival of the Navy and the iron industry. It sought mainly Baltic softwood lumber, popular for its price, quality and availability. Not only was the Baltic trade apparently better organized and more reliable than the domestic trade, but its provision of milled, rather than hand-sawn, products was much desired for low-cost building. So complete was the dependence of British builders on foreign timber that historians have used the volume of imports to measure the extent of eighteenth-century house building.[19]

Taken together, these conditions could not have looked overly attractive to the land-owners and dealers on the supply side of the timber market, irrespective of their own imperfect property rights over the trees. Whether these suppliers took timber out of the woods, and whether they supplied it to the Navy, depended in part on the opportunity costs of leaving their trees standing—the price the Navy was willing to pay and the willingness demonstrated by the charcoal-using (iron) and building industries to compete for this timber, perhaps bidding the price up. Adam Smith ascribes the tepid pace of private timber production in England both to a low price (commanded, perhaps by the Navy and presumably relative to the opportunity cost of keeping herds of cattle in the woods), and the difficulties of forest management on unfenced common lands. However, he suggests that market mechanisms did eventually encourage plantations on certain lands. This is how it looked from Scotland:

> As agriculture advances, the woods are partly cleared by the progress of tillage, and partly go to decay in consequence of the increased number of cattle... Numerous herd of cattle, when allowed to wander through the woods, though they do not destroy the old trees, hinder any young ones from coming up, so that in the course of a century or two the whole forest goes to ruin. The scarcity of wood then raises its price.[20]

[17] Ashton 1951; Slater 1968. There is good evidence that the price of fuel did rise and that the growth in demand from iron producers did create a new sustained demand for coppice and managed woodlands. But this is not the oak 'timber' and shapes that the Navy sought.

[18] See Flinn 1958; Hammersley 1973.

[19] For aspects of the Baltic trade, see Albion 1926, p. 10; Flinn 1958, p. 151; and Rackham 1980, ch. 9.

[20] Smith 1793, vol. I, p. 260.

Earlier, when in the 1660s John Evelyn had written his famous Sylva (for the Royal Society), he could describe wood-management practices already in use by those landlords who had entered into timber-growing: enclosures, fence-building, growing and sale of wood and timber.[21] These are only two suggestive contributions to a very undecided literature. Writing about the period, Rackham (1980) details leasing of underwood and arrangements with wood and fellmongers to cut wood and timber. Albion (1926), saying very little about waste and other property limitations, maintains that selling timber was the easiest way for a land-owner to raise money. Chalkin (1974) cites some builders' supply shop advertisements from the time, offering both domestic and imported timber for sale, and says that such signs were commonplace at that time.

Granted, the failure of price to rise to profitable levels, caused perhaps by the steadily growing importation of wood and timber and the Navy's monopsonist-like behaviour, prevented a full recovery of output from the neglect of earlier centuries before enclosure, leaving the Navy and the British charcoal-dependent industry relatively vulnerable to wartime shocks to imports from the Baltic. The point, however, is that the 'shortages' that emerged during Baltic shipping crises do not, in my view, support the theory that defects in the property rights and markets of the timber trade alone can be blamed for a state of British 'timber famine' complained of by the Navy and the iron and steel industry. This remains an open question.

Common law and forest property

The three modern tenures under which private timberland is held—freehold, leasehold and (in England) copyhold—were hammered out in the nineteenth-century courts on both sides of the Atlantic. The freeholders included the manorial landlords and their 'free' tenants (those in the manor whose forbears had held land with few or no responsibilities to the lord and whose title increasingly approximated fee simple). With the enclosures and the industrial revolution this class of landholders included an increasing number of individuals who had simply purchased rural or forested land outside of manorial relationships. Their title, unregistered then as now, had to be achieved by the tedious process of proving that it had been obtained from someone who had a good title, dating back to Norman land gifts and grants.

Those in the copyholder class were for the most part holders of the land rights of their commoner ancestors in manorial tenures, or of commoners from who such land rights had been purchased. They would have received a piece of land on the estate at the time of enclosure, roughly similar in the

[21] See Thomas 1983, pp. 199–200, for a discussion of Evelyn and for an account of whether forestry paid. A century later, Young 1771, p. 336 writes of a plantation owner in East Anglia who, by planting appropriate species, can 'cut down the trees he planted himself'.

characteristics of property to a freehold (at least after the sixteenth century) but chiefly governed by the customary law of the manor from which the land was severed.[22] By the nineteenth century it was easy to confirm their titles, as they would have been recorded in the manorial court rolls. Some new landholders acquired their woods by buying land from freeholders, some from copyholders.

The leaseholder class, by contrast, had whatever rights and duties they had agreed to in drawing up their contract with the landholder. The security of their titles was protected mainly, though not exclusively, by the common law of contract—though leases did over time gradually gain something closer to the legal standing of other modern tenures. Usually leases specified minutely what rights or duties a lessee had over the old and the growing trees found on the lands he had leased. We will see below that in the nineteenth century one issue was whether those who had as entrepreneurs contracted to cut the forest for the owner had in effect become leaseholders.

THE LEASEHOLD AND WASTE

Just as most owners had duties under the family settlement to maintain their lands and woods in the interest of their families and heirs, so most lessees had duties to their lessor/owner concerning their use of the woods. These duties were explicit or implicit conditions in the lease, making the lessee liable under common law if he did not return the land to its lessor in good condition. If the written lease said nothing on the subjects of what care must be taken and what could be removed from the land, then the law made the lessee automatically 'impeachable for waste' and so constrained not to harvest treed areas for timber or even wood (or to be compensated for improvements he made to the land).[23] Mostly, however, the parties bargained in advance over how timber and coppice were to be managed and wrote down their responsibilities and expectations over the condition of the land in their agreement.

The costs of initial bargaining were naturally higher than they would have been had the parties adopted a standard or boilerplate agreement. But apart from these costs, there is little evidence that placing a woodland under a lease lessened the user's rights. If the owner's powers vis-à-vis the rights of others in his family allowed him to cut a stand of trees, then they also allowed him to lease out the stand so that his tenant might do the cutting in his stead. The silvicultural and economic management of the stand were the same either way.

FREEHOLD AND SETTLEMENT

A major question under settlement law became how impermissible 'waste' was to be distinguished from permissible forest utilization by the current generation

[22] Simpson 1986, p. 164.

[23] For an extreme example (a tenant who had planted 10,000 trees), see Hughes 1965, p. 132.

holding the estate. Out of the disputes over the meanings of settlements and leases a body of interpretation gradually emerged. It was established that 'wood' (or underwood) was legally a fruit produced on an annual/cyclical basis by various methods of coppicing and pollarding and was therefore a source of the life tenant's present income. On the other hand, large dimensions called 'timber'—defined as trees of over twenty feet and of species fit for construction (especially ashes, oaks and elms)—had to be allowed to grow to maturity over a long period and must therefore be considered part of the land and inheritance itself, very often bound by strict settlement to be passed intact to the heir. Arriving at this basic distinction seems to have been helped by the law of tithes, notably by the case *Sowby v. Mullins* (1575).[24] Based on the doctrine that tithes should be paid on the income or yield of each parishioner's land, not on the land itself or its components, the *Sowby* decision had held that no tithes should be paid on the inheritance, the stand or stock—thus confirming that a stand of timber trees was legally part of the land. Hence, if the land were part of a family estate, to cut the trees would be to deprive future generations of that part of the land, i.e. to commit waste.

Wood, on the other hand, could be bought and sold and was subject to the annual tithes levied on all of the parishioner's income. As early as 1571 the cutting of underwood (and, incidentally, some timber trees) was recognized as not necessarily constituting waste.[25] Apart from tithes, we see evidence of the same distinction between wood and timber being made in the terms of leases for wooded land and in contracts for timber from woods where growing trees were also to be found.[26]

COMMONERS AND COPYHOLDERS

Timber from the common woods was never easily marketable. There is no period in which the commoners could be said to have 'produced' wood in the sense that they produced and sold wool, meat or crops. As we saw above, commoners in the pre-enclosure era had little incentive to practise forest husbandry or make positive investments in the woods, instead lopping and topping trees and hedgerows in pastures for various estovers, while animals took the grass. As for coppice, each acre seemed to be allocated on an all-or-nothing basis: managed coppice for market sale by the lord or common woods for the commoners' own uses. It appears that the commoners' own courts,

[24] *Sowby v. Mullins* (1575), 17 Eliz.

[25] Bewes 1894, p. 76. According to Bewes, the leading case in this area is one reported in the Year Book 11 Hen. 6, Mich. No. 3. See Bewes 1984, p. 75.

[26] Rubin and Sugarman 1984. The legal nature of these cutting rights was arranged with members of the wood trade, including timber merchants, woodmongers and building suppliers. It was much in evidence from the thirteenth century. The law made it clear that the family's strict settlement and protection from waste did not apply to those other lands that the father happened to own but were not part of the estate of inheritance.

which were active in managing the open fields, played mostly a negative role in the woods, enforcing the limitation of the right of estovers to certain privileged commoners and rationing or stinting the amount (bote) each could take. This enforcement did perhaps help preserve some stands of trees in the common and waste.[27]

This, then, would seem to have been a serious source of 'property failure'—one evidenced by the deterioration both of common land and of the remaining standing trees, scrub and coppice. Mitigations did appear as manorial tenants' status became the status of copyholders. Some lords found it possible to ignore the rights of their rural copyholders—though this was difficult when the copyholders became non-villagers of some standing and wealth who could take legal action, or even pool their rights. In general, however, timber was not valuable enough to justify investment either in management or in demanding private rights to grow and to manage.

Five characteristics of the timber right in England

Here I present some important trends in the evolution of the characteristics of each of the kinds of forest-tenure right just sketched.[28] My emphasis here is on changes by the common-law process rather than by legislation. While we have seen that direct legislative decisions brought about major changes in public forest tenures, we will now see that legislated regulation of private forest property was often arbitrary and non-enforced. The cases and the court decisions were what mattered.

The evolution of quality of title over woodland rights has been little different from that of the holders over the rest of their estates. The security in ownership of English freeholders, leaseholders and even commoners developed from early tenures for services to the Crown toward more individual rights. These were partly defined by a few important statutes scattered over the centuries, but mostly by the courts' routine enforcement of freehold ownership and customary possessory rights, and contract law.

Transferability and divisibility were valuable to owners for various personal reasons. One was arranging the succession. Another would have been the facilitating of the sizing of tracts of land into larger holdings, or of subdividing them into smaller holdings, in order to match them to the scale

[27] An excellent account of management of one manor's common over several centuries is provided in Hill-Manetas 1983. This manor vigorously protected coppice for bote—an unusual practice. However, this manor was within a royal forest, and Hill-Manetas implies that the commoners were being regulated from above. Thompson 1993, pp. 103–4 and 143 n1, describes the conflict between a commoner and the lady of the manor over liberties in Epping Forest; the lady won, pollarding the hornbeams, thus denying the residents' right of lopping trees up to a certain height.

[28] The discussion of *flexibility*, the sixth characteristic is postponed until the section on multiple-use forestry.

and desired mix of the lord's forest purposes: lumbering, hunting, grazing and so on. The question was the extent to which the right holder could 'stratify', or 'partition', his property interest to create separate transferable rights for sub-holders with particular forest purposes—for instance, 'severing' the right over hunting and selling it or else disposing of all the land but 'excepting' and retaining the right to cut oak lumber.

The transferability and divisibility characteristics of a forest holder's right changed over time in much the same way as those over arable or grazing land. In an early medieval period, the various use and access rights of his manorial customary tenants meant that the lord could not sell or lease the woods separately without the permission of his overlord or his tenants. After about 1650 he might take the matter to Parliament for a private bill. Otherwise, to transfer and or divide his rights over his own forest lands and timber stands he had to resort to short-term and to long-term leasing. Gradually enclosure, implemented in England first by voluntary and later by statutory division and fencing of common lands and of whole manors, meant that the general law allowed an increasing number of landholders to divide and sell or lease their estates (subject to the potentially arduous constraints of inheritance laws) while excepting or reserving their woods.[29]

The final two characteristics to be discussed, the duration and exclusivity of a forest right, are sufficiently important and complex to deserve their own subparts.

Duration as a property litmus test

To the professional forester, the duration of title has an importance relating to the period needed for trees to grow to their ideal rotation age. He needs a duration long enough to ensure that he will not lose out on his investment through the need to harvest prematurely or face seeing his rights over the land on which the trees are growing revert to a previous or future owner. But to the historian of forest law, the important questions in cases and disputes have centred on the length of much shorter periods: sometimes the time required for an immature stand to finish growing, but usually the time required or contracted for harvesting a stand of timber—often on the order of two to five years.

I have already noted that, in hammering out a theory of the estate, the courts debated the question of whether a private forest was like a production facility for growing the owner's timber or like a storage area within which the owner kept his inventory of mature timber. If the former, the soil with its trees

[29] In the chapters on mineral rights, I record the disputes between miners and surface owners. The courts developed the concept of 'the dominant estate' to describe whether a surface occupant or a miner should have the right to get in the way of the other. Though the original land holding may have been severed in the same way as for mining, there is little to suggest that similar clashes arose.

would be comparable to a building, a fixed asset, included and described in many documents simply as 'land'. If the latter, the space would contain items comparable to movable assets on a farm: seed, livestock, implements and stocks of harvested crops, all referred to, usually, as 'inventory' or 'personal property'. In this case, the owner's or lessee's right would require only a year or so for storing and cutting, and maybe additional time to accommodate speculation in timber prices. If an outsider paid a forest owner for the right to cut and remove the trees, and if there were a dispute about non-performance, the question might arise about the ownership of the trees: if they were not yet cut, who owned them? And who owned the land beneath them? The answer typically boiled down to a matter of the duration of the contracted cutting operation. As well, the law of real property has no 'inventory' (or stock in trade) classification: a timber stand must either be attached to and so part of the owner's land, or it must be his personal property. The two issues, regarding duration and regarding inventory, are actually one. The courts were slow to agree on how long the stand must be held for it to be recognized as affixed to the soil. Below I look at how the issues resolved themselves in England, the United States and Canada.

RESOLVING THE ISSUE IN ENGLAND

The issue of the legal classification of a stand of trees seems to have arisen, perhaps in the Tudor period, when cutting timber for domestic and local building gave way to cutting it for a market. The new class of dealers who bought and sold timber from abroad and from English woods ran into legal conflict over their contracts with the owners of English woods and brought their disputes as cases before the English courts. The contract in question might have been the result of one of four possible kinds of transaction: (1) a signed conveyance of freehold interest in all or part of a parcel of forested land; (2) a signed conveyance of a lease of the same land; (3) a licence to enter land to cut and remove trees (generally revocable and non-transferable); or (4) a transferable commercial contract selling the trees, with detailed provisions about entry, delivery and timing and with cutting to be done by either the owner or the buyer.

From the cases, it appears that all four types of transaction were familiar in England. They all had uncertain results, leading to disputes and to litigation concerning one question: what was the nature of the interest in land acquired by the lessee/licensee/buyer/contractor in the actual case? For all four types, the question at issue became whether the intention, the signing and the duration combined to implement the transferee's acquiring an interest in a stand of trees (seen as goods, chattels, personalty) or an interest in the trees (seen as an incident of land, realty). Since the technology and risks of timber-cutting were not very different from those of building construction, and since the stand of timber itself was not very different from the stock-in-trade of various kinds of dealer and merchant, one could reason that, when an English dealer bought timber from a landowner, he had bargained for a chattel interest. After about 1600, about half of the courts agreed with this reasoning in their opinions. The rest of the courts favoured the view that the contractor was acquiring an interest in land, comparable to a lease of mines and minerals. The landlord, like those observed in Chapter 8, had stratified his integrated interest in land. For the next three centuries decisions on this point were unpredictable, but the facts of the cases are informative.

The first reported English case taking the interest-in-land view was *Andrews v. Glover* (1562).[30] An interest had been granted by the lady of the manor in return for a fixed yearly payment. The grant conveyed both timber and underwood/coppice: 'all those her woods, underwoods and hedgerows . . . upon and within the manor'. The duration was for her life, though in two later cases the periods during which the trees might be removed were of only five years[31] and twenty years,[32] respectively. Despite the clarity of these time limits, the courts held that they could not bar the grantee-buyer from cutting the trees at a later date. Possibly, the grantor could sue for damages if cutting took place after the court-imposed time limit. But the trees were no longer hers. In the court's understanding the grant of a common-law timber-cutting right had actually conveyed a durable real interest in trees, though its duration was only for the crop of trees existing at the time of the contract.

This interest-in-land right conveyed complete transferability, at least after 1615 when, in *Stukeley v. Butler* (1615), timber trees were in the space of five years sold by the Earl of Sussex to a buyer and then by this buyer to four subsequent buyers. Although much litigation about who had acquired what arose from these sales, the right's transferability was not in dispute. *Andrews* was confirmed. *Stukeley* also established that the buyer was licensed to enter on the Earl's land and cut trees, though perhaps only for the limited time stated in the grant.[33]

This interest-in-land view of the outcome of a contractual transaction prevailed through the nineteenth century.[34] It was fortified in *Scorell v. Boxall* (1827),[35] which established that even a contract to allow growing underwood could be seen as an interest in the land. In *Lavery v. Pursell* (1888), the judge went so far as to say: 'I am bound of course by the English law to say that a tree is not a chattel'; he then went on to establish the similarity in point of law

[30] 74 E.R. 505.
[31] *Stukeley v. Butler* (1615), 80 E.R. 316.
[32] *Anon.* (1584), 74 E.R. 250.
[33] *Wood v. Manley* (1839), 113 E.R. 325, 11 A. & E. 34 at 37, 38. In *James Jones and Sons Ltd. v. Earl of Tankerville* (1909), 2 Ch. 440 at 442, it was found that the implied licence, which was akin to a quasi-easement, was irrevocable.
[34] From *Teal v. Auty* (1820), 2 B. & B. 99, 129 E.R. 895, to *Lavery v. Pursell* (1888), 39 Ch.D. 508.
[35] *Scorell v. Boxall* (1827), 1 Y. & J. 396, 148 E.R. 724.

between a stand of trees and a mine (at 516–17). A final victory for this view was registered in *Morgan v. Russell & Sons* (1909), in which the court found that the buyer of a pile of mine and mill cinders had acquired an interest in land.[36]

The alternative view was the interest-in-trees, chattel or personalty view. After early setbacks, it was revived in *Mayfield v. Wadsley* (1824)[37] and in *Smith v. Surman* (1829),[38] in which a sale of coppice was classified as a mixed contract for goods and chattels. The owner did not intend to dispose of the trees until he had cut them himself and they were movable. Mr. Justice Littledale added that, even if the contract had allowed the buyer to do the cutting, it would still not have given him an interest in land.

This point of view was frequently referred to in the tax cases that stretch forward with increasing frequency until the 1960s in the British High Court. The tax collector typically sought to treat the proceeds from timber sales as taxable income. The leading procedure for deciding this matter became the double test suggested in *Marshall v. Green* (1875):[39] when in doubt about whether a contract is for an interest in chattels, consider the duration: the length of time within which the trees are to be removed. If removal is to be 'immediate', then the contract is for a chattel; if it is to be prolonged so that the trees may continue growing in size or value, then the contract is for an interest in land.

The centrality of contract duration was established in the New Zealand case *Kauri Lumber Co. v. Commissioner of Taxes* (1913).[40] The verdict held that a sale for severance within or over a long period is an interest in land and a capital asset for tax purposes, while a sale for immediate cutting is an interest in trees and a stock-in-trade for inventory or tax purposes. Later cases showed this to be a workable rule, but no definite rationale emerged until 1957 in *Hoods Barrs v. Inland Revenue Commission*: 'wherever at the time of the contract it is contemplated that the purchaser should derive a benefit from the expected further growth of the thing sold, from further vegetation and from the nutriment afforded by the land, the contract is to be for an interest in land; but where the process of vegetation is over, or the parties agree that the thing should be immediately withdrawn from the land, the land is to be considered as a mere warehouse of the things sold, and the contract is for goods.'[41] The criterion is not defined as a fixed, absolute duration, but as a period long enough for the trees to grow in value or to otherwise change their quality and quantity from what they were at the time of contracting.

[36] *Morgan v. Russell & Sons* (1909), 1 K.B. 357.
[37] (1824), 3 B. & C. 356, 107 E.R. 766.
[38] (1829), 9 B. & C. 561, 109 E.R. 209.
[39] [1875] 1 C.D.P. 35, [1874–80] All E.R. 2198. In cases where *Marshall v. Green* was not yet available, the courts sometimes referred to *Smith v. Surman* 1829.
[40] [1913] A.C. 771.
[41] [1957] 1 All E.R. 832.

DURATION AS A TEST OF PROPERTY IN THE UNITED STATES

The evolution of the duration and transferability characteristics of timber rights in the United States took a different path from that in England, but wound up with much the same relationship. Earlier it was seen that after the American Revolution most of the lands of the new United States were at the disposal of the state and federal governments. In the populated areas those to whom these lands were granted vigorously cleared them in the course of setting up farms and communities. The wood was sometimes little more than a bonus for domestic use. More generally, much of the organized timber trade depended on stands of old growth and second growth that had been left behind on relatively small holdings and on farm woodlots. Not until the mid-1800s did the bulk of the lumber or timber industry move into the backwoods of the Atlantic states, whence it jumped to the northern Midwest, the south and out to the mountain and Pacific states (which were already exporting by ship).[42]

Toward the end of the nineteenth century, as the largest and oldest trees were cut, market demand appeared for smaller dimensions and then for pulpwood. By the time of the Great War American industry was increasingly drawing timber and wood from hundreds of thousands of farm woodlots and other small holdings, augmented by a few thousand holdings of very large tracts in the backwoods and hills. On the latter, the tree-cutting operations were integrated with sawmills and pulp and paper mills under the same ownership.[43] Almost all the exploited forest, old-growth or cutover, was private. The large recently established national forests were still unimportant sources.

Not surprisingly, those involved in these waves of clearing and settlement initiated many transactions in lands all or partly covered in trees. They ranged from outright sales of whole farms to friendly permissions to cut a few trees. Some led to disputes and of these a relatively small number proceeded to litigation. The disputes seem to have arisen mainly when an owner selling his land reserved or excepted the timber for his own alternative disposal or when he made an agreement to get his trees cut and sold while retaining ownership of his land. In both cases, just as in England, the basic legal question was over what kind of right the contractor/buyer had acquired: an interest (however temporary) in land, or a chattel interest?

The American courts scanned the English common-law cases and mainly adopted the interest-in-land view. But there were exceptions to the rule. In *Owen v. Lewis* (1874)[44] the Indiana court found that although the contract was for measured timber to be removed, the buyer had acquired an interest in land

[42] For a handy bibliography of the earliest of these migrations of the timber industry, see the references in Blackmer 1995, pp. 263–9.

[43] These integrated private forests were models for the Canadian 'agreement' forests described in the previous chapter.

[44] *Owen v. Lewis*, 46 Ind. 488 (1874). *Marshall v. Green* (1875) was not then available and the *Owen* court relied on *Smith v. Surman* (1829), 109 E.R. 209.

because the trees were attached to the land at the time of contract. However in the similar case of *Fish v. Capwell* (1894)[45] the Rhode Island Supreme Court found that the Indiana court had erred in *Owen v. Lewis*. Following the test in *Marshall v. Green* (referenced above) it argued that the buyer in *Owen* had plainly been after wood, not land. Soon after this, as in England, duration became the test characteristic. In *Hurley v. Hurley* (1909),[46] a court found that standing timber to be removed immediately or within a reasonable time[47] passed as a chattel. American cases continued in this vein into the 1980s, with the duration-based rule, from *Marshall v. Green,* becoming ever-firmer. The different state courts did not give much weight to whether the deal was in writing,[48] or to whether the owner or the contractor was to do the cutting. If the intention was for the trees to remain growing on the land until the right-holder chose to cut them down, then an interest in land had been transferred to him, with the rule applicable to both leases and licences.

DURATION AS A TEST IN CANADA

In turning to cases in Canada we must remember that most of the Canadian forest is on public land. Private forests constituted only 5 per cent in the country as a whole in 1945. There is, however, provincial variation. In Nova Scotia, the fraction of private land is about 75 per cent and in New Brunswick it is about 55 per cent (of which half is in large holdings and half in areas of less than a hundred acres).[49] In spite of the provincial differences, private case law was of limited importance to the forestry industry. Where private conflicts did arise, they were mainly over contracts offered to cut a landowner's standing trees, as in the English cases. Although the courts followed English precedents, in any decade the outcomes were most like those then coming from courts in the American states.

In brief, a line of Canadian cases from 1880 to the 1990s produced the default rule that title to a stand of trees was an interest in land.[50] Two landmark cases were *McPherson v. US Fidelity and Guaranty Co.* (1915), which contained a notable survey of English cases to that date,[51] and *Beatty v. Mathewson* (1908).[52] In the latter case, Mathewson sold Beatty all timber standing on his

[45] *Fish v. Capwell et al.* (1894), 29 A.C. 840.

[46] 110 Va. 31, 65 S.E. 472 (1909).

[47] Note that the word 'reasonable' is not found in English forest cases; its use suggests a test drawn from contract law. It allowed courts to find that, say, ten years might not be so long as to undermine a claim that the parties had intended a quick removal.

[48] Kinney 1917, p. 141, for example, maintains that, with an unsigned or parol agreement, an interest in the land might pass even though severance of the trees was to be made by the vendee.

[49] See Huber 1985. Part of what is summarized here is based on Bankes 1983 and on my discussions with him. Ljiljana Bukovic has helped me to review the material.

[50] An important early citation refers to *Summers v. Cook* (1880), 28 Gr. 179.

[51] 24 D.L.R. 77.

[52] *Beatty v. Mathewson* (1908), 40 S.C.R. 557.

property, together with the right to enter onto the land for cutting and removing it, but did not spell out the time in which the cutting had to be done. The majority in *Beatty* held that the transaction was a sale of a chattel interest together with a right to remove within a reasonable time. In dissent, Mr. Justice Duff held that the deed granted an estate in fee simple in the contracted timber.

Duff's opinion has been followed in later cases. In most modern cases the Canadian courts have likened contracted timber rights to those over a building, a mine or a barn. Likewise, they have reasoned about the right over trees by analogy with those over crops in fields,[53] natural gas, mines and buildings. In other words, a timber contract is taken to convey an interest in land regardless of the duration of the contract.

DURATION AND 'TREE TENURE': PERSONAL PROPERTY OR REAL PROPERTY?

From the discussion above we see that what roughly emerged from the cases in England, the US and Canada was a workable rule for assigning the cutter's rights: personal property if the cut was to take place in the near future and real property if the cutting was to take place at a later date. The litigation was about the result of agreements concerning extraction, as though the forest were a mineral resource.

The courts have not, however, been asked to rule on lease-like rights that give the holder long-duration powers to grow and harvest cycles of trees but give him no powers over the land to be used for other purposes; interests that would allow and encourage tenants to specialize in a repeated cycle: plant, grow, thin, harvest. They have not had the opportunity to create or refine what might be called a 'tree' interest in land, an interest in trees with duration sufficient to plant and 'farm' on the soil of another party. In part this was because the forest lessee users, as demanders, did not complain that their tenures were too short. But some experts still are inclined to blame short tenures for the short time horizons of many owners and for generally poor forest management. In 1979 Marion Clawson famously pointed out that sales of timber from a small US property, typically farm property, took place at intervals of eleven to thirty three years. Yet the average length of farm 'tenure'—the period of possession by one farmer—was then only seven years. He reasoned that until tenure durations increased, other problems for tree growing could be neglected as insignificant by comparison.

The missing tree interest in land is not completely unknown, though versions of it, known as 'tree tenures', tend either to be regionally constrained

[53] Courts have sometimes been tempted to make their point by saying that even a crop in a field could be an interest in land. In *Kirk v. Ford* (1920), 53 D.L.R. 644, an owner sold the right to cut hay on his land, with no time limit. The sale was found to be an interest in land.

(there are examples in the southern US and Sweden) or else found mainly in the Third World, especially in Borneo and India. Some tree tenures are temporary, while others are like a stable distribution of land-based activities among different holders.[54] There is also a vast and diverse category of community-owned and/or community-managed forests, some located in Europe (e.g., Switzerland) but most located in the Third World. I do not discuss these here.

In the southern American states and Sweden, tree-tenure type arrangements are ones in which, as usual, a pulp mill or sawmill obtains wood from owners' forests or woodlots. The difference from the usual situation is that, if the tree-tenure arrangement has been fully worked out, it is the mills that manage the woods and grow the trees; the owners provide the land. In regions where the tree tenure idea has not been universally applied the mills grow and manage only some of the forests from which they obtain their wood supply; they obtain the rest by purchase from other owners.

Across the roughly 190 million acres in the southern US states, the forest industry owns 38 million, leases 3 million, and obtains roadside supplies at something close to 135.[55] It is on this 135 million acres that we can find approximations to and variations on the tree tenure idea. Industry has some 'contracted' relationships with large non-industry investor landholders and some looser 'rights of first refusal' with smaller landholders and small farmers.

These kinds of procurement, taken together, have much in common with what Anderson (1948) described as buyer direct intervention in forest management. The lands are held and used by farmers and specialized land-holding investors for a number of purposes. Only one of these need be growing the mills' wood supplies. The obligations and rights of the mill and of the owners are spelled out in their contracts; there is as yet no law-of-property tree-growing tenure. The southern-state example suggests that the details of such a tenure will be worked out by usage, as the land-owners learn to combine tree-growing for the mills with other uses for their acreages. If the contractual relationships between mills and farmers have high coordination costs and/or are ambiguous about roles and obligations, then the parties may become demanders of legislation to define and enforce their respective rights.

I offer this glimpse of a future tree-tenure property right in order to contrast it with present doctrines about holding rights over trees and timber. First, under tree tenure, ownership of a stand of growing trees would not be a part of or incident to ownership of the land. The whole point of the arrangement would be

[54] For an excellent survey with a useful bibliography, see Bruce and Forstmann 1992 (on tree tenures, see, in particular, pp. 492–3). On the Norwegian separation of ownership from rights to make particular uses of certain forests, see Berge and Sevatdal 1994. See also Jessup and Paluso 1986. The whole subject of community forest is extensively discussed in the 'common-property' and natural-resource governance literature associated with the Ostroms' workshop at Indiana University. See, especially, Feeny 1982 on the common forests of Thailand.

[55] The data here are from various sources, especially Professor Daowei Zhang (personal communication). See also Stoddard 1961.

that the trees are not legally attached to the land. Second, although the duration of the tree-growing operation under tree tenure may stretch over many years and many rotations, the mills' rights would otherwise be similar to those held for shorter periods by parties whose aim was not to grow, but to harvest an existing stand (described in litigation in the previous subsections). It might indeed be similar to what was once regarded as a chattel interest but became, following the Duff dissent in Canada, an estate in fee simple in the (future, at the time of contracting) timber. Third, consideration of the possibilities and legal problems of tree tenure shows the relevance of the duration characteristic in the mills' tree-growing rights. The mills will not be interested in the tree-growing opportunity unless, by long tenure or guaranteed inexpensive tenure renewal, they can keep control of their forest management. Fourth, under tree tenure the land-owner may find himself providing acreage for several land and forest enterprises, of which tree-growing is only one. If so, his piece of land may wind up under several tenures, a mixed portfolio of profits, easements and leases each with its own duration. Some interest or estate may be in effect for a very short (perhaps annual) duration, while others may be all but permanent.

Exclusivity of rights over forested land

From the duration characteristic and its evolution, I turn to the exclusivity characteristic in the private forest user's right. Exclusivity in private forest rights has two almost-independent meanings. First, the amount of exclusivity in his property right is an indicator of the right holder's freedom from physical externalities and spillovers flowing in from adjoining forest properties. Forest fires are an example, discussed below. Such exclusivity has been changed from time to time through modifications in property-right and/or nuisance law. Second, strong exclusivity implies independence from government interference with forest operations, including financial implications such as tax levies. Environmental regulations governing tree-spraying and wild-animal habitat are two of a widening class of examples. In what follows, it appears that the forest holder's right's exclusivity of the first, physical, kind may have been slowly on the increase in the past 150 years; but exclusivity regarded as independence from government regulation and taxation has been declining.

It is important to note that when external changes such as increased public concern with fire prevention on private lands or changes in private-forest taxation rules have threatened their woodland operations, right-holders' search for relief has not taken the traditional form of a demand for more exclusive rights. Instead, foresters have directed their collective lobbying powers toward obtaining positive correctives and exemptions: public help with fire protection; with the costly requirements of environmentally friendly forest management; and even with taxation.

EARLY-MODERN EXCLUSIVITY AND LACK OF INDEPENDENCE

Turning to 'original' conditions, we observe first the exclusivity inherent in four kinds of right to hold or use forested land: freehold, leasehold, custom and contract (licence). Legally, the lords and lesser freeholders had exclusive use of their domains, including their freehold woodlands, subject to their duties to their overlords and to the customary privileges of commoners. Small freeholders and lessees in England and in North America had to put up with many partial rights over their woodland holdings, varying from those customarily reserved by their lord for timber, game or assarting to those later granted by the Crown and legislature to outsiders for road rights of way, urbanization, canal easements and public footpaths. Commoners had customary rights in the woods but little exclusivity against each other or against outsiders. Finally, land holders acquired exclusive rights under contract to cut designated trees or stands but could acquire almost no exclusivity in their access to their operations in forested land.

From these original, non-exclusive, conditions the amount of physical exclusivity in pre-twentieth-century private forest rights cycled. In the earliest medieval period, a forest owner lording it over those with customary rights to make various marginal uses of his forest had little cause to worry that he would be harmed by these uses on the lands and woods of his neighbours. But if we pick up forest rights around 1600, in Coke's time, we find a significant increase in the owner's damage caused by others, and reciprocally, his liability to others for harm originating in his woods. Two centuries after that we find a significant decrease in an owner's liability, unless he was shown to have been negligent or unreasonable. That brings us to the twentieth century, when a forest owner's liability for harmful spillovers has again increased, approaching what it was in Coke's time. In short, so far as the influence of liability for spillovers is concerned, the physical-exclusivity characteristic of forest owners' rights did not evolve steadily, but cycled in response to the uneven pace of change in external events.

These cycling eras of tort-law liability are complicated by the steady shift over the same period of forest ownership, from that of a relatively few nobles and manorial land-owners to that of ordinary freeholders and copyholders. The greater density of independent forest holdings would have implied more spillovers and less exclusivity in their operations. In what follows I offer brief discussions of three more 'modern' challenges to the exclusivity of their rights. It would have been rewarding to have integrated them into a declining-feudalism framework, but that would have been a life's work. The three are: spillovers between adjoining properties; demands for publicly conscious forest policy; and pressures from tax policy.

SPILLOVERS AND NUISANCE BETWEEN ADJOINING FOREST PROPERTIES

In Chapter 8 we saw that the booms in mining, and their 'neighbourhood effects', inspired considerable litigation and so serious demands for more exclusivity of rights provided to miners and owners by changes in property and tort law.

Although there were many more people with forest-property rights of one kind or another, they did not give rise to a similar demand for changed exclusivity in their rights. The forestry version of nuisance doctrine holds that the owner should not use his wooded land in such a way as to create or contribute to the injury to others, perhaps making allowances for his behaviour being 'reasonable' and for a balancing of equities on both sides. One can imagine a forest owner transgressing nuisance law by causing or allowing fire, falling trees or pesticides to damage the ability of adjoining forest property to provide income, amenity or wildlife habitat.[56] It can be observed, however, that with regard to fire and falling trees the established law of nuisance was of a lesser importance in providing physical protection than was the fast-emerging law pertaining to negligence.

Loss of owner independence and falling trees

The hazard of falling trees has only a tangential relationship to forestry rights per se, for trees in a timber stand rarely fall outside their owner's estate. But this hazard does provide material for a single-issue case study of nuisance law's emergence as a limitation on the exclusivity of the land occupant's rights.

The changing physical exclusivity of a forest-owner's rights was provided by the changing decisions about the liability of his neighbour, usually the defendant in damage cases. Here I follow the law-historians' record of changes in liability. The falling trees did not harm the forest-owner, but his potential liability for falling trees did cramp his style and so reduce his powers to make independent decisions in his forest property. By the time of *Rylands v. Fletcher* (1868) (see Chapter 8), the law as applied to mining had reached the position that the defendant was not liable for a flow of harmful floodwaters if the flow was deemed 'natural'.[57] The effect of a spillover's naturalness culminated in Britain in *Giles v. Walker* (1890),[58] where weed seeds blew from one property on to a neighbouring property, causing harm. Following the Rylands precedent, the judges found for the defendant because the seeds and the wind were 'natural'.[59]

We next see the emergence of a general duty in the United States in the working of the doctrine of 'due regard' for neighbouring property and persons, widely applied around 1900 both in the US and Canada.[60] It was followed by the emergence, in the new field of product liability, of a duty to prevent harm in the absence of a contractual relationship. In 1916 in New York State, Judge Benjamin Cardozo in the notable *MacPherson v. Buick Motor Co.*,[61] held that an automobile manufacturer was liable to a 'remote' (unconnected by any busi-

[56] See Brubaker 1995, pp. 29–53.
[57] 7 C.B. 515, [1847–60] All E.R. 273, 137 E.R. 205.
[58] 24 Q.B.D. 656, 59 L.J.Q.B. 416.
[59] L.R. 3, H.L. 3330.
[60] *Reed v. Smith* (1914), 17 D.L.R. 92 (B.C.C.A.); *Patterson v. Board of School Trustees* [1929] 3 D.L.R. 33 (B.C.C.A.).
[61] 217 N.Y. 832 (1916).

ness relationship) purchaser for a 'foreseeable' injury caused by a negligently made product, a position reaffirmed in the 1928 *Palsgraf v. Long Island R.R. Co.*[62] using the same language. The Cardozo cases were favourably cited by Lord Macmillan and Lord Atkin in the equally famous British product-liability case *Donoghue v. Stevenson* (1932).[63] Their decision was somewhat broader than Cardozo's in that it established a duty of care. It not only dwelt on foreseeability, but it also referred to a positive duty to foresee.

These ideas about a general duty of care found their way into disputes about care over falling trees in England via *Leakey et al. v. National Trust for Places of Historic Interest or Natural Beauty* (1980).[64] Rocks and debris from the trust's hillside property crashed down and damaged the house on the Leakey property below. When Leakey sued, the trust pleaded, as had been usual, that the damage had been caused by natural material moved by natural processes. In the new spirit of *Donoghue*, the Court of Appeal rejected the argument, asserting that in English law there was now a general duty of occupiers to prevent hazards on their land, whether the hazards were natural or man-made.

In jurisdictions across the Atlantic, there is some confusion in the tort law over how to deal with an owner's responsibility to inform himself about his own potential liability in nuisance. A recent British Columbia falling-tree case illustrates. For six months, the defendant in *Hayes v. Davis* (1991)[65] had been aware of the possibility that his trees might be broken or uprooted in a wind storm, but did nothing to minimize the harm that his neighbour eventually suffered from their collapse. Citing *Leakey* (1980), the court found liability in nuisance. Such a finding leaves open opportunities for arguments by the defence concerning not only how much preventive action would be 'reasonable' for this defendant, but also, and particularly, about how much effort he ought to have made to acquire knowledge of any hazard.[66]

Hayes (1991) has almost completed the destruction of the defence that consists of arguing that, when the source of a hazard is 'natural' and unknown, it is not the defendant's business. Admittedly almost all falling trees cases are applicable in populated suburban areas (trees falling in the forest are rarely a nuisance for an adjoining landowner). However, in principle the defendant forest owner's right to choose how to use and manage his own land is diminished by this direction of the law, for he must go out of his way to take into account not only the known but also the possible effects on others of natural accidents occurring on his own forested holdings.

[62] 248 N.Y. 339, 162 N.E. 99 (1928). See also Bohlen 1929.
[63] [1932] A.C. 645, [1932] All E.R. 1 at 101.
[64] [1980] 1 All E.R. 17 (C.A.).
[65] 25 A.C.W.S. 3d 1348.
[66] These matters feature in follow-up cases like *Doucette v. Parent* (1996), file no. 1842/193 (Ontario Court, General Division).

Loss of physical exclusivity and forest fires

The spillover damage caused by falling trees is trivial compared to that from forest fires.[67] Yet, as was the case for the development of law governing falling trees, there were few forest-fire cases. As a result, the common-law courts never produced polished forest-fire law precedents, relying instead on town fire cases.

English woodland fires were rare and small. They often occurred in open moorland rather than in stands of trees. As Rackham wrote before the era of global warming, after his examination of thousands of years of woodland history:

> Our woodlands are more difficult to burn than almost any of the world's forests. As stubble-burning farmers demonstrate every year, native woods are almost fireproof even in exceptional droughts... Pine is the only tree that can easily be burnt standing. Even if the wild wood contained enough small logs to add to the fire hazard in a long dry spell, we can hardly suppose that it would be burnt in the present climate.[68]

By the fifteenth century an action on the case was available for 'trespass' by (urban) occupiers who 'negligently used fire' and, contrary to custom,[69] allowed it to escape. In this early invocation of negligence we see two elements affecting the ever-changing fire law: fire, properly contained, is useful, and its proper use is governed by 'custom' or ordinary practice. Nevertheless, appeal to these ideas did not succeed as a source of defence against liability in late medieval and early modern Britain. Instead, defendants tried to prove that the fire under dispute was set by a stranger or was an act of God. Liability for a fire they were judged to have started was almost absolute.[70]

This rule was much too narrow, creating a 'period of dry precedent which is so often to be found midway between a creative epoch and a period of solvent philosophical reaction'.[71] The dry precedent was that whoever had started the fire must have been negligent and therefore was liable. At the end of the

[67] For a theoretical analysis of the effect of the risk of fire on a planned series of forest rotations, see Reed 1984. This kind of fire problem seems not to have attracted as much attention from forest economists and lawyers as it once attracted from foresters and from the industry. In the indices and contents of some forestry-economics textbooks and handbooks, the word 'fire' never appears. The same is true of other disciplines. Environmentalists seem unconcerned about forest fires except as a source of pollution emissions. Convenors of recent conferences surveying modern issues in forest policy omit fire from their programmes altogether. Reed 1984, p. 184 concludes that the effects of the probability of fire on the plans of an owner are the same as is adding the risk of fire per period to the rate of discount per period.

[68] Rackham 1980, pp. 103–4, is describing the propensity to burn since about 500 BC. For a quick summary of the modern forest fire situation in Great Britain see Mayhead 1990, whose expert survey, strikingly, makes absolutely no reference to the responsibilities or rights of individual forest owners.

[69] *Beaulieu v. Finglam* (1401), Y.B. 159, cited by Fleming 1987, p. 232; *Tuberville v. Stampe* (1697), 1 Salk. 13 at 91.

[70] Fleming 1987, p. 232.

[71] O.W. Holmes, *The Common Law* 1881, p. 89, cited in Plucknett 1956.

seventeenth century a demand had emerged for a widened set of recourses to defendants in fire cases, allowing an accused party to claim either that he had not set the fire or that, in doing so, he had not been negligent.[72]

Instead of introducing such a new doctrine, Parliament went off in another direction, providing a new law, the Statute of Anne, 1707,[73] amended in 1775. Rather than excuse the defendant if he had not been negligent, it excused him if the fire were accidental. This new defence led to much confusion, especially as, taken at face value, it would seem to excuse a negligent occupier who failed to deal with an accidental fire or who negligently started a fire that then spread accidentally. Some courts held that the statute simply did not apply to some fires. In other cases, it simply reinforced a judicial tendency to presume that, until proven otherwise,[74] fire was the intended work of the defendant. Yet it provided no rules for looking into why he would have set a fire.

Indeed, the statute raises questions about why Parliament had intervened to pre-empt the development of judge-made law to refine the occupier's duties to deal with natural fires; his rights to set useful fires; and the possible responsibility of neighbours to adjust to, or fence out, escaping fires. Parliament could have been responding to some lobby group, such as city developers and landlords, though it is not immediately obvious whether such a lobby would have been in favour of or against expanded liability for fire.[75] One cohesive group whose short-run fortunes did obviously depend on whether accidental fires were excused from liability was the insurance industry. The new class of insurers would have been better placed than anyone to know about the frequency of accidental and other fires, and would have had much to lose from the spread of fires from properties they were covering (though, again, not if they were more likely to cover properties that became victims of fires). The arrival of the insurance industry seems just the kind of change that would explain Parliament unexpectedly negating strict liability without a word on what was to take its place when a non-accidental fire was both useful and reasonable.

Given the difficulty of the Statute of Anne as a guiding policy, British and American courts adopted a policy of trying to determine reasonable behaviour. Indeed, according to Wiener (1963), the early American courts often cited the Law of Anne and its successors in fire cases but actually tended not to give accidental causes the status of an exception to the more general development of tort law when looking for evidence of care and lack of negligence. At about the time of the 1770 amendment to the English accidental-fire statute, the

[72] *Tuberville v. Stampe* (1697), 1 Ld. Raym. 264, 91 E.R. 1072.

[73] 6 Anne, c. 31, s. 67 (1707) going on to 14 Geo. III, c. 78, s. 76 (1774–5), the latter is commonly known as the Fires Prevention (Metropolis) Act.

[74] *Becquet v. MacCarthy* (1831), 2 B. & Ad. 951, 109 E.R. 1396, cited in Fleming 1987, p. 322.

[75] A smaller group—for instance landlords whose properties had kitchens—would have been easier to organize if it could find a policy upon which its members agreed. See Olson 1965.

American skies were often black with the smoke of land-clearing and field-cleaning.[76] Courts became accustomed to looking for carelessness beyond habitual burning. For example, in 1811 in New York State, a defendant whose fallow-burning had spread was found not liable unless he was also negligent.[77] In a stream of subsequent cases the defendants strove to show 'reasonable care', 'due diligence', 'ordinary caution', or 'honest motives' in setting and minding a fire. By 1882 in New Jersey, in one of a series of railroad cases the court had turned completely away from strict liability: 'in the absence of negligence in kindling or guarding a fire, one is not liable at common law for a conflagration caused thereby'.[78] These US courts paid little attention to whether a fire started in woods, a railway or a building: negligence was the common element. For example, in 1911 a fire begun in a derrick set a meadowland ablaze. The derrick's owner was liable, because negligent, in that 'the season was dry, the fire was in August, and the meadow... was dry and easily ignited. The soil itself burned easily.'[79] There is no reference to either strict liability or accident.

This tendency has persisted since then in Canadian and American law.[80] With regard to the shaping of owners' property rights, the ruling doctrine is that a forest owner who shows reasonableness about his use of fire retains much of the exclusivity of his ownership right. But what behaviour pertaining to fire will be found reasonable? Legally, a land-owner gambling with using fire or holding forest land that could ignite under the right circumstances faces numerous uncertainties: when a fire will strike, how far it is likely to spread, how much damage it will do and how much preventative action he must undertake to avoid being found legally negligent.

So far these uncertainties seem uninsurable. In particular, the insurance industry has not provided inspection or set standards because, as in 1700 so in the twentieth century, fire damage to stands of trees is not a risk normally covered by European or American private insurers. At most insurance is used to cover an owner's sawmill, equipment and likely fire-fighting expenses. According to Herbert (1922), no US insurance for woodlands even existed until 1915,

[76] The later 1825 Miramichi fire in Maine and New Brunswick, arising from land-clearing and slash-burning, ranged over 1.2 million hectares of uncut forest and spruce-budworm-killed stands. One hundred and sixty people were killed. In 1871 a Wisconsin and Michigan fire killed 1,500 people (B.C. forest service data). See Holbrook 1943 for a survey of American forest fires. See Carroll and Raiter 1985 for an account of a lawsuit, with a modern bibliography.

[77] *Clark v. Foot* (1811), 8 Johns. 421.

[78] *Read v. Pennsylvania R. Co.*, 44 N.J. Law 280 (1882). A series of cases also made the defendant liable if he had not actively worked to prevent a fire escaping or spreading to a neighbour's land.

[79] *Jordan v. Welch*, 61 Wash. 569, 112 Pac. 656 (1911).

[80] Modern Canadian examples: *Canadian Pacific Forest Products v. Munn Lumber* (1998), 49 B.C.L.R. (3d) 57 (C.A.), showed that a fire was due to the defendant's carelessness. The defendant's actions fell short of executing a duty under the felling contract. *Canadian Forest Products v. Hudson Lumber Co.* (1959), 20 D.L.R. (2d) 712 (B.C.S.C.), showed that nuisance and strict liability (*Rylands v. Fletcher* (1868), H.L. 3330) might both apply if the defendant were carrying on a business in an unreasonable manner and/or was negligent.

and a New Hampshire company that did successfully offer policies in 1917 went out of business. To explain these failures, Herbert suggests inadequate statistics on loss experience.[81]

If the insurance industry stays clear of forest fires, what about government? Forest owners have encouraged state and provincial governments to institute forest fire services and to create standards. Once an outside-the-industry standard is created, the courts may be willing to use it in determining when the defendant's behaviour has been reasonable and when it has been negligent. An illustration is provided by the 1911 Oregon Forest Protection Act.[82] It banned some forest-use practices and, more usefully, listed actions that should be taken to prevent or handle a spreading fire. In *Department of Forestry v. Jepson and Sons Logging Co.* (1983), an Oregon appeal court found that the private defendant's actions regarding a slash fire fell within what the statute calls making 'every reasonable effort' to extinguish the fire. Had they not, the firm would have been found negligent and so strictly liable.[83]

Further confusing matters, standards set by governments do not replace the common law, but merely supplement it. Conflict between statute and precedent emerged most strikingly in a B.C. case, *Tahsis Co. v. Canadian Forest Products* (1968).[84] As in an earlier, similar case, *Coates v. Mayo Singh Lumber Company* (1925),[85] the defendant was conforming to statutory requirements to burn slash. Nevertheless, because the judges decided that the defendant did not take 'all reasonable precautions',[86] the company was found liable according to common law.

This information on the increasing fire liability of defendant owners reveals a declining exclusivity in their rights (and a rising exclusivity in the victim's rights). There is no doubt that the toughening of the forest-fire laws and of the associated liability rules reduced the exclusivity of forest ownership. Where once he could choose whether to manage or neglect his forest as he wished, the

[81] Other sources include Fernow 1902, pp. 263 and 467 who discusses the fire policies offered by an exceptional private firm, though admitting it had not many takers. Phoenix, a UK fire insurer had offered forest fire policies but dropped them. A good discussion of the failure of private insurance of forest fire is in Duerr 1960, pp. 479–87, suggesting that lending institutions may themselves organize coverage for the stands on which they have made a loan. Modern forestry texts scarcely ever mention fire insurance as a cost.

[82] See Or. Rev. Stat. 1983.

[83] *Department of Forestry v. Jepson and Sons Logging Co.*, 64 Ore. App. 390, 668 P.2nd 461 (1983). I omit the complication of *contributory* negligence in this case, as it is not as important in forest fire cases as in others. Negligence law per se tends to prevent the defendants from pleading that the victim was also negligent.

[84] (1968), 70 D.L.R. (2d) 476 (B.C.S.C). See also Wiener 1968, pp. 235–44.

[85] *Coates v. Mayo Singh Lumber Co.* [1925] 4 D.L.R. 345. See also *Silver Falls Lumber Co. v. Eastern and Western Lumber Co.*, 149 Ore. 126 at 150–2 (1935).

[86] *Rylands v. Fletcher* (1868), L.R. 3, H.L. 3330. A 1945 Ontario statute granted permits for summer operations (when the woods were otherwise closed) on condition that holders must furnish 'proof of innocence' if a fire broke out. See Lambert and Pross 1967, p. 221.

changing fire laws forced him to take precautions. Nevertheless forest fire has not been conspicuous in nuisance or tort litigation, in spite of the damage it has caused. Determining culpability for fire is not governed by a serious, specific body of case law. I offer seven explanations to explain this incongruity:

- There were few cases. Forest fires were not common in England. Tort and nuisance law regarding fire developed in the cities rather than in the countryside. Even in North America, where forest fires were a serious problem, the development of property law and negligence law was in response to 'demanders' who were concerned with city fires, not forest fires.
- As discussed above, insurance companies, never having really accepted forest fire risks, have not participated in the shaping of liability rules and concepts.
- In the forest fire cases, human action was rarely found to blame. Many fires had a natural origin and/or had been properly tended. Often the owner suffered greater loss than the neighbour who suffered the legal nuisance.
- Rural owners of woodlots had little wealth or property to attract lawsuits. The exception was the railway (which, I suggest, attracted a number of lawsuits far out of proportion to damage flowing from locomotives and rights-of-way, particularly with regard to fire).
- The criminal law was very difficult to apply. It was difficult to establish that a fire has been set if the actor had taken care to conceal his activity. The absence of insurance company investigators is important.
- Burning of slash and cleared wood was branded as 'incendiary behaviour' by some victims and by foresters, but was often regarded by rural communities and courts as reasonable burning and made little headway in the courts.
- Industrial owners of forests concentrated their demands on getting legislatures to finance forest fire fighting services and the reduction of natural hazards.

These factors have created a striking difference between the breadth of miner's rights and those of woodland-owners. As seen in Chapter 8, wealthy owners of mineral properties faced a constant stream of litigation for damages caused by their mines, both from adjoining (often older) mines and from nearby surface owners. When legislatures have stepped in, it has been to modify the drift of court decisions in contract and tort. Forest law disputes were much rarer, so there was little recourse to judges or to legislatures. When intervention has occurred, the initiative for change in forest law and liability often came from the legislatures, acting as both demander and supplier, or from outsiders such as environmentalists. Consequently, any loss of exclusivity and independence by forest owners due to adverse decisions, fines and regulations has not been as extensive as the loss of exclusivity in the mining industry.

LOSS OF EXCLUSIVITY DUE TO GOVERNMENT REGULATION OF PRIVATE FOREST MANAGEMENT

There exists an extensive professional and popular literature devoted to describing government actions both to 'save our forests' from over-cutting, fire, insects and other perils, and to reserve private woodland for purposes other than those their owners had intended. In some places, these policies are weak: educational and propagandistic. Elsewhere, however, they are strong, regulating private actions and providing for enforcement. These policy, or regulatory, intrusions and the uncertainty they create reduce the exclusivity characteristic in the forest owner's rights.

Forest regulatory policy has a long history. Before the days of environmentalism, in 1948 R. L. Anderson produced a useful three-way classification of the many ways European governments then actually imposed 'controls' on private woodlands: (1) command and control, (2) assistance and (3) direct management. Command and control ranged from prohibiting certain practices to compelling the adoption of whole systems of management. Assistance (for small holders) took the forms not only of education and advice, but also of credit, subsidies, awards and tax abatements. Direct management could range from cooperation in, to full-out takeovers of, activities to stabilize soil and control pests. Today, the 'need' for these methods of influencing private owners' silviculture is somewhat reduced, for owners have learned that some mandatory practices are to their own profit. At the same time, public demand for conservation and the precedence of environmentalism, ecology and multiple-use over profitable timber production has made intervention more attractive to politicians and bureaucrats.

In what follows, I break the focus on forest history in England and its former colonies to notice developments in government regulatory intervention in pre-twentieth-century Europe. Developments in Europe, and particularly France, would have a major impact on the development of New World forest policy.[87] Almost certainly there was no officially imposed regulation of private forest management in Europe until around 1500. Where private woods were tended at all, it was to preserve animals for the hunt and to exclude outsiders from hunting. Of course, land-owners did make rules about their own holdings. Some early silvicultural writings offering guidance to the lords' servants still exist. But private forests were rarely or never subjected to regulation or policies from the government.

In the 1600s and 1700s not only Britain but also Denmark, France, Sweden and Norway, having various reasons for fearing timber shortages, introduced controls on private cutting and clearing. In Britain the law applied narrowly, governing only private holdings within the royal forests. As seen in Chapter 11, there was no lack of English and Scottish law-making for the royal forests. Parts of them were under private management, as estates, parks and chases and

[87] For surveys of early policies see Fernow 1911, James 1981, and Anderson 1950. See also Scott 1983.

were technically subject to the savage forest laws and charters. However, owners and holders could pay for permits and licences to use their trees and land according to their own goals, so it is difficult to guess how far the Forest Charters and Forest Laws actually regulated management of the increasing number of 'private' wooded lands.[88]

One regulation that did apply to (non-royal) private forests set out how large trees were to be replaced.[89] In France sixteenth-century edicts placed all forest land under royal jurisdiction, but not until Colbert's drastic law in the next century were regulations actually issued. Although these were uniform for all forests in all provinces, they were not enforced everywhere and were weakened by exemptions and amendments issued over the next fifty years.[90] Denmark in the fifteenth century began to ban the felling and sale of trees on private land until they had been marked by State officials. This intensive policy was vigorously enforced and copied elsewhere.

Everywhere, the best-enforced laws (comparable to England's Statute of Merton) were designed to prevent the erosion of private woods under the onslaught of nearby holders who, under the pretence of custom, treated the lands as open for grazing and wood supply. This exclusivity was reinforced during the individualistic phase early in the French revolution. Soon after that, French policy was reversed as privileges ranging from access to pasture (with rights to burn to encourage grass) to rights to take trees for household fuel, commercial charcoal and timber were revived and strengthened. Then late in the nineteenth century the French government again reversed the policy. It re-introduced exclusive rights, withdrawing grazing privileges. Other western European countries also acted to restore exclusivity, over the protests of local villagers.

It was these latter-day exclusive European forest policies and regimes that so appealed to Pinchot, Fernow and other evangelists of the North American forestry and conservation movements. The European examples helped persuade the leaders in North American jurisdictions similarly to regulate the comparatively vast forests of the New World, both private and public. Their policies emphasized the danger from forest fires rather than from public grazing or over-cutting. Fires, Pinchot said, were the most effective barrier to the introduction of forestry (management) on private lands: 'Laws, generally good, to prevent damage from forest fires, have been enacted by practically all the states, but their enforcement has unfortunately been lax.'[91] For other aspects of fire and policy, see Scott 1983. For a contemporary view, see Pinchot's 'Forests and Forestry' in the *Encyclopedia*

[88] See Anderson 1967; Thomas 1983, ch. V; Albion 1926.

[89] 35 Henry VIII, c. 139. See James 1981, pp. 125–8 and 305–12.

[90] See Freeman 1994 for an account of how French regulatory policies were implemented. Note that although France and the Swiss cantons are well-known for the very early and sustained policies to prevent damage from avalanches and erosion, Freeman's work casts some doubt on whether, in France, these policies were maintained.

[91] Pinchot (1911). For other aspects of fire and policy from a more modern perspective, see Scott 1983.

Britannica, 11th edn. (1911), vol. 10, p. 656. The fire danger was perhaps best understood in California, where in 1885 a Board of Forestry began to work at controlling the alarming wildfires. In the next decade most other states started to participate in education, assistance and fire-protection controls and facilities.

Apart from vigorous fire regulations and some protective rural zoning laws in the lake states, however, command and control regulation of private woodland did not really begin in North America until after the Second World War. The availability of timber reserves in the US national forests; the distractions of the Depression and the War; and, particularly, concern over whether controls were constitutional[92] had caused American state governments to leave privately owned woods alone.

Then in 1945 *Dexter v. Washington*[93] paved the way for a new era of widespread regulation. Washington State's drastic (by the standards of the time) legislation had called for owners to replace cut trees with new seedlings (thus preventing cut-and-run harvesting in private forest land). *Dexter* tested the constitutionality of the law. In light of my previous discussion of rules against waste, the pro-government verdict in *Dexter* rested on an unusual argument. Modern forestry literature had painted an English landholder's impeachability for waste as an evil, weakening his powers of management and disposal. In the *Dexter* decision, however, the judge held impeachability for waste as beneficial, preventing an improvident life tenant, say, from depriving future family generations of timber. He saw the Washington law against cutting small-dimension timber as similar to a prohibition of waste in that it protected the state's public interest against the narrow, short-run intentions of the owner. The analogy was shaky, but it served to support the main argument that, being in the public interest, the law was within the state's constitutional jurisdiction.

Within a few years a number of states had followed Washington and implemented similar laws. The emphasis on these laws is important because, in North America generally, private woodlands had been the least regulated kind of realty. (In fact, with a few provincial exceptions, this remains the case in Canada with its paucity of private woods.)[94] In many jurisdictions

[92] See Hays 1959; Ayer 1973; Worrell 1970. Regulatory laws were a state responsibility. They could be challenged for being a 'taking' of private property rather than an implementation of the government's police powers. The opponent of a proposed regulation attempts to show that, as it confiscates a parcel of private land or the profit from it, it must be accompanied by compensation (possibly by a fair expropriation procedure). The supporters of the regulation attempt to show that it is not a confiscation but a reasonable restriction on private action in the interest of promoting the public good.

[93] *Dexter v. Washington*, 338 US 863, 94 L.Ed. 529, 70 S. Ct. 147 (1949).

[94] The main exceptions are fire laws and the 'agreement tenures' discussed in Chapter 11, under which private forest areas contributed to a mixed ownership enterprise become subject to contractual or government regulations. For a discussion of some failures of private forest regulation in Canada, see Huber 1985, pp. 79–101; Wear and Hyde 1992. See citations in Sedjo 1983, pp. 124–200. For more on Canadian application of agreement tenure, see Zhang (1994). In 1999, British Columbia broke the low-regulation tradition by introducing regulations to conserve soil, to protect water quality and to preserve fish and wild habitat on certain tax-reduced, managed private lands.

forest-practice regulation had been non-existent or badly enforced. We may ask whether the government regulatory policies that did emerge decreased the exclusivity of owners' rights. To the extent that firms owning small properties were compelled to do things on their land that they would otherwise not have done—leave trees they would have cut, plant land they would have neglected, and thin stands and burn slash they would have ignored—the answer is yes. However, most of the post-*Dexter* regimes were comparatively modest by today's standards, focused on the relatively narrow goals of land and timber-stand management. Exclusivity has been further eroded by more recent types of regulation forcing the adoption of sustainable, environmental or pro-ecological policies. Most owners are now affected by 'multiple use' controls within and between forest properties (access for recreation, hunting, hiking, fishing); water supply and quality; flood prevention; air quality; amenity and land-use zoning; fish and wildlife species protection and habitat; and ecosystem stability. For instance, Section 9 of the US Endangered Species Act 1973 and 1994, which is used to empower the federal government and its agencies to regulate the development and modification of woodland habitat, has been a much more sweeping and better-enforced restriction on private land use than were pre-war state or federal forest-practice acts.[95] The incidental effect is that as the scope of regulation has broadened, the exclusivity of forest property ownership has contracted.

FOREST TAXATION AND EXCLUSIVITY

No investigation of owners' property rights in forests would be complete without taking note of the threat that heavy taxation may pose for forest management, and whether changes in that threat can be interpreted as gains or losses of exclusivity and independence in the owners' property rights.

First I must note that forest taxes and tax bases are highly variable. Internally, forests are not homogeneous, so that any given tax will probably be seen by the owner/manager as bearing most heavily on particular stands: the trees in one area, of one species or of one age-class. As well, any given tax may bear more heavily on one owner's woodland property or enterprise than on another's, even within a small geographical area. In these ways, taxes can affect forest owners' behaviour. A higher forest-land tax rate, for example, may suggest to owners that they should discontinue growing one species of tree, or should shorten the rotation age of a planted stand of trees or should reconsider the size of their holding or the number of purposes for which they are using the land.

These are Ricardian or high-grading effects, to be seen when any tax is applied to any heterogeneous thing or activity. A tax-rate increase motivates owners to abandon products and enterprises having relatively low returns

[95] For surveys see Thompson 1997.

and to specialize in a reduced programme of forest activities. However, forest taxpayers have alternatives to adjusting their behaviour to tax designs and rates: they can incur top-level transactions costs (including lobbying or litigation costs) to get the tax or the tax rates reduced or the tax base changed. Success may restore their independence and exclusivity in choosing their regime of forest management.

An annual tax

The base for an annual tax, such as land tax, local rates or property tax, may include the whole value of the forest stand in that year. Modern theoretical treatment of this tax, parallel to common observation, concludes that it has a 'carrying-charge effect'. Strictly levied, it can induce taxpayers to avoid it by harvesting the stand earlier than if there were no tax. This is known as 'cutting out from under the tax'.[96]

A brief examination of the history of the annual land tax, however, suggests that forest owners have understood this effect and persuaded ('demanded' of) those who set tax rates and those who collected them to remove or reduce their tax burden on the growing forest. Their demands were often successful: the historic European tax collector did not in fact re-value the stand every year as it grew; indeed he did not levy the tax against the value of the stand at all, but against the land's value as soil.

In England Henry VIII's administration was brought to an increasing dependence on taxes voted by Parliament. One after the other, the 'tenths and fifteenths', 'subsidies' and land tax were introduced, each to be levied on all property, personal and real, county by county. After a few years, difficulties of assessment, taxpayer resistance and corruption led to the simplification of each of these, confining them to real estate, chiefly buildings. Collection was also simplified by assigning an annual quota, either of assessed valuation or of revenue, to each county. Accordingly, the tax collector assessed each major piece of property at the same nominal value year after year, vastly understated in the case of the estates of the nobility and great landlords. Roughly speaking, forests were valued by the acre along with cleared and farmed land and pasture. If the trees grew up, or were cleared, the estate's taxable valuation did not change.

This was also true for Elizabethan local rates and for the national land tax of the seventeenth and eighteenth centuries. The lack of complaints recorded in the historical literature on taxation suggests that the land-owners chiefly concerned, active in Parliament and in county affairs, were able to see to it that their estates, including their forests, were under-assessed. In the nineteenth century

[96] There are many theoretical articles and conference papers in the literature of forest taxation. For surveys, mostly with bibliographies, see Scott 1983, ch.12; Scott 1959 (in Ballaine 1959); Duerr 1960, pp. 430–70; Heaps and Helliwell 1985; Johannsson and Lofgren 1985, pp. 130–3 and 149–50; Pearse 1990, ch. 10.

the tax burdens of British land-owners gradually changed from liability for national land taxes to liability for national income tax. As for local land taxes, or rates,[97] the great families persuaded Parliament that forest land should everywhere be assessed at its value for agriculture, regardless of the amount of timber standing on it. Again this prevented a 'carrying charge' effect of too-early cutting to avoid the tax.[98]

In late nineteenth-century North America the carrying-charge effect of the general local property tax on forest growth was frequently referred to. Couching their complaints in the language of the emerging conservation movement, forest owners around 1900 complained that the property tax reduced the likelihood that they would plant and preserve trees. In the 1930s the US federal government set a committee under Professor F. R. Fairchild to study this idea. Its report confirmed that the tax was actually having the effect that carrying-charge theory predicted.[99]

In most jurisdictions today the property tax has much the form objected to since the 1900s. But there are important exceptions. Some property taxes have been replaced by local severance taxes and by yield taxes. Some have been modified by assessing forested acres at their bare-land value or their farmland values, as in Europe. As well, the burden of local taxation is relatively lighter than in the 1930s. In any case rural forest owners are not as sensitive to the weight of total taxation as they were during the depression. The reviled property tax is no longer commonly regarded as an absolute deterrent to good forest practice. In general, private forest right holders appear to have been successful at preventing the land tax from determining how and when to grow their trees. In terms of characteristics, the land tax is now imposed in a fashion or at a rate that does not take away the right-holder's managerial exclusivity and independence.

Tax on wealth and subsidies

As with land taxes, so with death duties, inheritance and succession taxes, estate duties or capital taxes—all these lump-sum taxes on asset values can deprive the forest-owner of the power to make independent decisions and drive him to try to escape from their burden by changing the way he grows and harvests trees.

In Britain death duties were not generally burdensome for private estate planning until the 1890s. At that time light succession duties gave way to a

[97] See Seligman 1925, pp. 38–42 and 452–9; Braddick 1994, chs. 2 and 3; Sabine 1990.

[98] I omit a discussion of the history of land tax in Scandinavia and on the Continent. For a survey, see Grainger 1950.

[99] See Fairchild 1935. This report was based on actual data. In this respect it stood above such later reports and discussions as the 1947 Kennedy Report on Ontario forest policy, reports that lacked the empirical evidence needed to confirm the simple theories on which their criticisms were based.

heavily progressive estate tax on practically all inheritable wealth. It could be said that to be an owner of woodland was to invite heavy taxes (although the woodland was also a source of liquid cash with which he could pay the new duties and other taxes on the rest of his estate). In the long run the late-Victorian taxes on wealth and the uncertainty about them assuredly discouraged the accumulating of forest capital by planting and silviculture. It suggested liquidation.

Top-level complaints from the affected land-owners and also from a public interested in maintaining and restoring the woodlands of Britain eventually elicited a sympathetic response in the government. Until the late 1800s owners of major estates showed almost no interest in treating their woods as timber plantations. Hunting and shooting were the chief uses. Government was indifferent, at least until the First World War, when a demand for wood products produced new policies, including what was in the 1920s to become the Forestry Commission with responsibilities for Crown forests along with revision of the assessment of estates subject to death duties. During the Second World War concern about timber supply produced further policy changes. By 1950 a forest 'dedication' scheme had been installed bringing further advantages to good forest practices, this time by subsidy—including loans, planting grants and maintenance grants—rather than tax concession. Dedication is said to have brought about an almost-miraculous boom in tree-planting and woodland maintenance over the next thirty years, primarily to create a source from which wealthy land owners might be able to pay their other death duties and receive income from their land.[100]

Consequently we may say that although the dedication scheme, and similar arrangements in other countries, have reduced the incentive to give up forest management, their rules and stipulations have not widened the taxpayer's freedom of decision about how to use his land. In a way, an independence-removing regime of wealth taxation has been replaced by an independence-removing dedication scheme and its successors. The owners have done with their forests what either the tax regime, or the tax-freedom regime, has dictated.

Personal and corporate income taxes

The third type of tax that might influence forest management and change the exclusivity of owners' rights was the income or profits tax.[101] These take, annually, a percentage of the rent earned in the forest. Mostly, they are levied at rates that rise with the base (the rent or profit) to be taxed (i.e. are progressive),

[100] See James 1981, Grainger 1950. The literature gives more attention to the condition of the woods than to linking changes in taxation and property laws to planting and cutting data. See Scott 1983. On Scotland, see Anderson 1967. For a survey, including US estate and inheritance duties, see Gregory 1987, pp. 159–86.

[101] The Canadian 'logging tax' is a minor variant. See Moore 1958.

though some are proportional. Progressivity in this kind of tax tends to induce the taxpayer to cut his trees at a younger age than he would under a proportional rate because the expected marginal harvest income from allowing a given tree to mature is reduced by the higher marginal tax to be paid on the gain.

In response to the groans and complaints of owners, who object to both income taxes in general and to their progressivity, governments have offered correctives. The US federal taxation of forest income is an example. In an effort to avoid the impact of income taxes on loggers who were clear-cutting mature stands, Congress introduced the depletion allowance, already available to the US mining industry against corporate and personal taxable income, and the capital-gains exemption, applied to forest operations under the 'Bailey amendment' to tax legislation from 1943 until 1986. Like the British exemption of forest operations from death duties, the Bailey amendment was an over-correction, one that touched off a boom in woodland planting and maintenance, especially by pulp and paper firms.[102] The Bailey amendment actually spurred not only further lobbying for tax exemption and lower tax rates but also gave rise to a direct demand by property holders for changed forest laws and tenures. Companies that until the 1940s had either processed timber from their own lands or had bought pulpwood and logs locally now searched for financing and property rights that would make them eligible for capital-gains treatment in wood supply. Among these were the southern pulpwood tree-growing agreement for the use of farmers' and private lands that we encountered earlier in the chapter.

These accounts of reactions to general taxes suggest that, although it seems plausible that the introduction or expansion of a distortionary tax would have touched off a political campaign for an adjustment of forest tenure or new demands for changed characteristics of the property right, historically it rarely did so. Instead, it seems, new taxes fuelled campaigns aimed directly at winning further tax reductions and exemptions. These campaigns were so successful that now, whenever there is lobbying of politicians by rights-holders in England, the US or Canada, they draw attention to their hardships from imports, adverse tariffs, transport costs, and environmental burdens, not from taxes. Indeed the general historical literature on forests, timber trade or woodlots rarely mentions taxes. A striking early example of the non-issue is the magnificent British Imperial and Local Taxes report of 1899. In response to a memorandum by Sir William Hamilton, thirteen economists and taxation experts, including Sidgwick, Marshall, Edgeworth, Bastable, Gonner and

[102] Before the Bailey amendment came into force, a sort of capital-gains treatment had been available for the company or owner that held trees then sold them to be processed elsewhere, but not for the company that planted and held them for their own processing. See Boyd and Daniels 1985. The amendment was backed by an industry association, introduced by influential senators, passed healthily in both houses, vetoed by the president but passed again into law by the Congress. For an account see Steen 1978.

Cannan, wrote long comments about, among other issues, the incidence of taxes on land, and the effect of a change in taxes. Not one of the thirteen mentioned forests or forest taxation. Either the British forest owners had already used their considerable political power to reduce much of the burden of taxation on tree-growing (as they would continue to do so over the next thirty years), or the issue had simply never become sufficiently pressing, given the low priority placed on timber-growing in nineteenth-century England, to warrant the economists' theoretical attention.[103]

The same basic pattern is true of modern commentators on the health of North American forest management. I have consulted Canadian royal commission reports, and Canadian and American conference volumes with titles like 'Emerging Issues', 'Agendas for Future Research' and 'Outlook' for the forest industries, as seen in the 1950s, the 1970s and the 1980s: few of them mention forest taxation. This disregard is also found among environmentalists and environmental economists. They are concerned about the powers of forest-right holders, but they have not asserted that forest taxation is an important determinant of ownership behaviour. I conclude that this is mainly because owners' political lobbying has prevented it from becoming important. However, it may also stem in part from the fact that forest owners and users often react passively to the tax in a way that furthers a general conception of the public interest: the loss of exclusivity in his ownership right induces every owner simply to do what all the other owners are doing by way of adjustment to the tax.

Multi-user, multi-purpose forests

Introduction and definitions

The purpose of this section is to take account of the role of property rights when, in a single forest area, a number of specialized right-holding firms each produces one forest product (or makes one use or pursues one purpose). The forest is not naturally divided spatially into product sub-areas, and we can safely assume that each firm draws, or could draw, its product from the whole area. (There may be more than one firm specializing in each product.) Consequently, as each right-holding firm exercises its powers it interferes with and/or complements all the others. After a brief historical overview, the exposition here is largely abstract.[104]

[103] Of course, many economists have developed theoretical models showing how different types of taxes could and can distort management. See Heaps and Helliwell 1985. However, it is worth noting that most forest-economics textbooks do not give much emphasis to taxation issues. Incidentally, they also give less attention to importance of *exclusivity* of tenure and property and more to the importance of short lease *duration*.

[104] Although I make use several times of the concepts used in the formal analysis of the management of a single-purpose stand of a single species of tree, my exposition is basically

The word 'multiple' and its synonyms need a little refining here. In modern usage, a forest is a large wooded area composed of different species of trees, some the source of valuable products and some not. Marketable products can be taken from various parts of the trees, and at different ages: from nuts to coppice to Christmas trees to pulpwood and saw timber. The variety of purposes implied by this variety of tree products could justly be called multiple-purpose. But this variety is matched by the variety of other kinds of harvest: berries, grasses, mosses, wildflowers, herbs and fungi for example, and of both private uses and public indivisible uses: hunting and fishing, hiking, camping, 'recreation', water-shed protection, species preservation and climate modification. Finally, because the forest usually occupies a large area, parts of it are in demand merely for rights-of-way running through it.

Historical notes on multiple use

When the Normans took over English lands from their Saxon rulers, the forests began to lose their open wild-land character and came under 'ownership'. Most of them began to serve their users in more ways than one. The royal forests were unenclosed, containing whole individually held villages and farmlands. Hunting was the dominant purpose for which the kings and their lords held their forests. Their strict game-protective forest laws confined farming and banned most forest activities. However, the absolute nature of these laws encouraged the introduction of formal and informal ways around them: the offer of approximations to permits and even to leases. In search of revenue, the king and his forest administrators at first sold bribe-like exemptions from certain forest-law provisions. Later they used their forest-law courts to levy 'fines' for regular forest-law 'transgressions' by farmers and gatherers.

Later, too, land-owning aristocrats leased out or licensed rights to undertake non-hunting activities on their estates, parks and wastes (reinforcing their value by enforcing the laws against trespassing and poaching). Indeed, they might even have rented out the hunting itself. Apart from granting these tenures, the owners might, like the king, gain revenue in fines and penalties for tolerating other uses, such as taking wood for fuel. Within the villagers' lands, of course, multiple-purpose use of woodlands and wastes was not the exception but the rule. As between the lord and his tenants, these informal arrangements tended to become honoured as the customary woodland rights and traditional levies discussed earlier. Eventually the lords' woodlands diminished as narrow fringes were grubbed up or assarted and, later, as large areas were cleared and sold outright.

In England, as in the rest of Europe, increasing population pressure was causing agriculture to succeed hunting as Europe's dominant land use. Common

non-technical. The economic theory of forest management is important but can be repellantly mathematical and is a subject fit, mostly, for forestry professionals.

law allowed landlords and yeomen owners to make firm time-limited contracts with outsiders for timber and for non-timber purposes. We have already seen that a seventeenth-century owner might transfer rights to entitle others not only to the hunting but also to water diversion, mining, timbering, gathering fuel, fishing and grazing. The contracts were bilateral, in danger of non-renewal, lacking much of the quality of title conveyed by a landlord's lease of a whole farm or forest. But they allowed for a diverse, easily arranged multiple use of the land.

In spite of this flexibility, by the nineteenth century the total area of multiple-use wooded land was diminishing. In England the main reason had been the enclosure of pasture and its sub-division into small fields and into suburban lots. The holdings that supported domestic-animal grazing and game-animal habitat alongside timber production were being progressively squeezed or fenced out. As the new private owners had single purposes, no concurrent blossoming occurred of ownerships of rights to woodland attributes, with each right tailored to a special purpose. In both England and the New World (where, by the turn of the twentieth century, the private sources of much of the world's consumption of wood products were located) enclosure and specialization in land use diverted the increasing public demands for certain non-timber services to specialized public lands and parks. Even these were not truly multiple-use, for they were dedicated primarily to recreation.

The process of sub-dividing private forests into small single-purpose holdings was reversed in the twentieth century. As consumers' demands developed beyond food, clothing and shelter, some small private holdings and specialized uses were reconverted back to multiple-purpose holdings. They offered rights-of-way, private camping and recreation, fishing, hunting, foraging and, collectively, protection of wildlife habitat and of watershed. These uses were within and among the stands of trees; they led their owners to protect some stands and to clear others. In England few attracted their owners to go in for tree-planting and growing. Consequently, the holding of much private forest and woodlot, which since Norman times had alternated irregularly between multiple- and single-purpose uses, was and is again being sought for its multiple purposes.

Deciding on the multiple uses of a single forest

A central idea here is that the observed combination of ages and purposes in almost every multiple-purpose forest is the result of earlier decisions and actions, and not predetermined in some way by 'nature'.

A sophisticated way to think of the multiple uses of woodland is as their having been intentionally combined into sought-after mixes of uses. This begins with accommodating a single use. Consider the simple benefit–cost problem of deciding how much to expand the extent to which the areas of a forest are used for a particular purpose or output relative to all the others. In classic economic theory, the optimum for any one use is where its marginal net gain as its area is expanded equals the marginal net loss of the use(s) that must make way for it (assuming land is adaptable). For example, the use of the forest for flood-damage avoidance should be expanded until the value of the additional flood damage it will avert is just equal to the value of the reduced proceeds from timber harvesting that it necessitates. Proceeding further, the optimum mix of all possible uses is attained when the marginal gains from flood-damage avoidance are equal to the marginal value of every other forest land use that must be sacrificed, and when a similar equality exists between the marginal products and losses of all pairs of these other forest land uses. In the jargon, the mix is juggled until there has been a maximization of the 'forest rent'.

I narrow the analysis down to deciding on the amount of timber to be cut as a crop. It is not enough to adapt the procedure above merely to select the number or the area of trees. The output and value of a tree, and of a stand of trees, depend on their ages and sizes. A tree cut when it is still growing (part of a young stand such as coppice) will produce rather different wood products (poles, pulp chips) than when it is mature (beams and plywood among other things). The mix of those trees to be cut young and those to be held until maturity is chosen by maximizing the present values of the stands' rents. In the choice involved, the trees are allowed to age, comparing the increase in the present value of holding them for saw timber with the loss from not cutting the trees earlier for pulpwood and other purposes. If he knows the dollar values of trees of different dimensions, a forester can calculate the best age for using one tree or for using trees grouped in a stand.

Even this is not the end of the calculation. In one small area, the timber-growing stretches over years, while nearly all alternative uses of the area would be enjoyed continuously. Therefore, the tradeoff between timber uses and other uses of the forest area (such as recreation and flood-prevention) depends on the age and size of the forest and the amount of time a harvester can enjoy or must defer other activities while a given stand comes to maturity. The planner may also need to look beyond the forest. Steps taken to maximize a forest's rent can affect the rest of the local community and its economy, for instance through a stream of employment.[105] Strangers to static economic theory should be warned that the theory described above, being static, describes the owner's sought-after mix of uses, but it does not describe how, when or in what time horizon to get there. The actual process for developing and changing the mix of uses is referred to in the next subsection.

[105] Conditions for the community's welfare can be calculated abstractly. For example, only if perfectly competitive market prices exist for such inputs as labour and capital, and for the final outputs of each of the forest uses, can a forest planner assume his private forest interest will coincide with the larger social optimum through an ideal allocation of the forest across its uses, and of all resources across all sectors.

In reality, the mix of most existing multiple-use woodlands was never deliberately planned and executed. Instead, a succession of owners/farmers/managers gradually introduces, or permits, various uses, not necessarily taking account of the tradeoffs between them. The forest one observes may have developed in response to unexpected changes in the market values and in the technologies of the various uses that could change the optimal mix or the appeal of a certain use. For example, during the life of most mature stands of trees today, values for pulpwood and for recreation have increased relative to the planned or expected values of the timber for lumber for which the stand may have been started. These stands may therefore have values and uses that differ from those their owners expected at the time of their planting or clearing the previous stands.

After these brief notes on the idea that existing multiple-purpose forests do not just occur, but have been shaped by previous decisions and changing conditions, I return to the subject of the evolution of property rights, and how the rights held by the various users are affected by, or may expedite, the establishment of a forest mix.

Two extremes of economic organization

SOLE OWNER VS. ATOMISTIC FOREST USERS

The determination of the mix of forest uses actually chosen and/or achieved by a forest user depends on the type of economic organization in which he finds himself. The question is somewhat similar to the economic theorist's problem for the entire economy: what degree of concentration of ownership and control enables firms producing different goods to compete or cooperate most efficiently? In what follows, I focus on the two extremes of industrial organization: sole ownership of the forest (for all its uses) and atomistic individual ownership of areas within the forest, each for a single use. In the first case the rights of the individual owner include powers to do all that is necessary to manage and exploit the forest for its many purposes. In the second case the rights of each of the many owners include powers that enable him to make a particular use of his component of the forest.

Apart from the exchange of spillovers with neighbouring owners, the theoretical forest sole owner acts with complete autonomy. It may be assumed that his firm alone produces all the various goods and services; plants and harvests trees of various species and dimensions; builds fences, roads, bridges and picnic tables; and engages in fire-prevention. An obvious example of such a sole owner is the farm owner who has a large woodlot.

As a variant, a sole owner may centralize some but farm out other production tasks of some of his forest's goods and services. In particular, the harvesting of trees could be turned over to the crews of a wood merchant or of a pulp mill or sawmill. The right conveyed might be purely contractual, recognized only by the two parties, or it might be a standard property right such as an easement, a profit or a lease. The decision about the proportions in the mix of forest uses and purposes would, however, be the sole owner's. His agreements with all his partner firms could specify how each was to adjust to the needs and rights of all the others. In such a way, the sole-owner could make use of his forest, holding basic rights over all but decentralizing some of the activities to divisions of his own 'firm' or to firms that hold, with limited duration, of him. As the basic owner, he would have stronger powers of coordination and lower transactions costs than if he and his tenants and contractors merely had market relationships.

Compare this situation to that of a forest shared by relatively many use-based 'firms', with the rights of no firm or use being dominant. In the extreme (atomistic) case, the activities of each kind of firm stretch over the entire forest area. Each firm's property rights are described in terms that may include units of forest-land use and/or yield for a specified purpose. The various independent users must bargain and agree with each other as to the extent and style of their uses of the trees and of the land. In a less extreme case, each firm holds and is confined to one of the small tracts into which the forest has been divided. In this case it can bargain with its neighbours to gain access to their soil, roads or forest stands suited to its enterprise and products. Compared with the extreme atomistic case described above, the initial conditions for this less-extreme case do not seem fanciful. Once can easily find examples of forests carved up into smaller holdings. However, compared with the sole-owners case, this case faces one serious constraint: under common-law property law, an owner cannot grant one or more standard property rights to a tree or trees alone (except, as we have seen, near the time of cutting). The trees and the land are legally one. The owner might sever from his forest land a building or the grazing or the mining. But he cannot sever and hand over a stand of growing trees,[106] unless unity of tree and land are changed by statute. He can contract with the tree-owning neighbouring landowner, like the southern US pulp mills contracting with the owners of farm woodlots seen earlier, but he cannot buy space on which to plant and harvest rotations of his own trees without acquiring the land outright.

[106] A possible historical exception was the ability of the owner in fee simple to lease or sell the *exception*. Many of the sixteenth and seventeenth-century cases on this subject turned on the fact that the 'owner' was actually a tenant for life. If so, it was not so clear that he would be entitled to sell the excepted forest away from the soil. In most cases on excepted and reserved forest rights what the parties, and the courts, had in mind was a right to harvest standing trees rather than a (novel) right to create a timber-growing estate which would engage the right-holder in the full cycle of planting, growing, harvesting and replanting. Cases are discussed in Coke's Institutes of the Laws of England, Part 2, p. 642. See *Liford's Case* (1615), 11 Co. Rep. 46b, 77 E.R. 1206; and, as the last word, *Dashwood v. Magniac* (1891), 2 Ch. 306 at 327 per Chitty J. I have long been greatly indebted to Nigel Bankes for his 1985 research report on these cases.

TRANSACTIONS COSTS AND SOCIAL OUTCOMES UNDER THE TWO OWNERSHIP REGIMES

Formally, in a sole-ownership forest operated by one firm, the mix of uses and purposes is decided centrally and is made operational by issuing instructions to division managers. In the real world, the central decision-makers would get much of their information from these managers, would consult them, would encounter their cooperation and strategic behaviour and would impose monitoring and enforcement on them. Going through all these stages, the sole-owning firm can run into extensive 'organization' costs.

In the atomistic forest, on the other hand, the combination emerges formally from interaction and competition among the specialist firms rather than from forest-wide planning. Each firm, seeking to establish a rate of output, will run into physical conflict or complementarity with the outputs of other firms. Each firm holds property rights. The extent of their activities is determined in their bargaining with each other about the areas they are to use, the amounts of their outputs and the information they may share; and by the stratagems they follow (including the withholding of information). Property and tort law play a role in constraining their bargaining and its enforcement.

To compare them, we assume that both types of forest organization face the same final demand markets and the same original input costs of labour and capital goods. Both must engage in some strategic behaviour to gather information about optimal use (the sole-owner with his branches and his contractors, and the atomistic firm with the neighbouring independent co-users) of the forested land. Ronald Coase (1937 and 1960) famously suggested that the atomistic small firms (if they are numerous and if they have appropriate property rights) will together converge on the same mix of inputs, forest uses and outputs as the sole-ownership firm. This is an important conclusion. From the point of view of the allocation of resources, elementary theory says it may not matter whether the rights in the multiple-use forest are held by one firm or by many.

However, we must now follow Coase to take account of the variable institutional costs faced by the two types of organization. A sole owner, in choosing his optimal use-mix, will be dependent on the inflexible information, communication and enforcement costs typical of that within large conglomerates. For multiple firms to contract their way to the same mix also would involve information and bargaining costs, with the number of stipulations and conditions that need to be contained in each lease or contract increasing in the total number of forest users and uses. Once the details of such costs are considered, it no longer seems so likely that the total costs and chosen total matrix of products of the sole owner and the set of independent owners will be the same.

We ought also to consider the anti-Coase argument of market failure: most simply in the possibility that the sole-owner and/or atomistic forest structures are confronted by non-competitive final markets. As well, if the relations between divisions of a sole ownership are defined by various degrees of strategic behaviour and obstructiveness, while bargaining between firms in the atomistic structure is defined by varying degrees of monopoly and market power, then it is quite unlikely that the equilibrium mix of uses and outputs will be the same between the two.

Whether or not the Coasian result leads to similar (constrained)-optimal use of the forest under the two extremes of management, in either case we can expect one other general result to hold: the under-provision of public and non-market goods. The extent of under-provision may still differ across organization types. What looks like a public good to a small firm in an atomistic organization (such as ecological stability, water quality or fire prevention) may look like a necessary, private cost-item to a sole owner. Such considerations suggest that, in a comparison between the extremes of organization, the sole ownership would face fewer disincentives in providing non-market goods since it internalizes more of their benefits. By contrast, in theory, there would be no voluntary provision of such goods in an extreme atomistic forest organization, in which the individual firms received only a vanishing share of the benefits of the public goods, unless the firms are required to do so by government subsidies, regulations, or taxes. In both types of organization, however, we would expect at least some degree of under-provision relative to the social optimum.

RE-ORGANIZATION

We are unlikely to encounter a forest whose multiple-use management occurs at either of the extremes discussed above: a single large private property owner or a complex of special-purpose firms. The reason is that, in the process of reorganizing toward the two extremes, changes in tastes and technology change the optimal mix of uses and thus the long-run equilibrium structure. In the long history of forest use, the non-market purposes of kings, aristocrats, village courts and local and national governments have imposed idiosyncratic ownership structures that are resistant to market pressures to improve the mix of outputs. Also, if adaptations in the mix of uses are 'sticky' or hard to change quickly, forest organizations that were once well-adapted to a particular mix of forest outputs may be hit by an external change in market demands or alternative land uses that render them suddenly inefficient. In response, large owners may contract out or sell off their rights to use some of their forest's features and attributes. Similarly, to reduce their information and bargaining costs and improve coordination, small single-purpose firms operating in a forest may merge, set up joint operations or sell their rights and go out of business, thus moving away from the atomistic extreme.

ASSOCIATED AND APPROPRIATE PROPERTY RIGHTS

Under either regime, the ease with which the forest organization can be changed depends on the characteristics of the property rights available to be held by users. For example, a sole owner with full freehold land and tree ownership could easily dispose of some of his powers over some forest uses. In contrast, the same user holding only a licence-based right with low transferability of his rights to make certain uses of the forest would ordinarily be unable to spin off his powers to other firms.

Regardless of the initial, historical, form of forest organization, the achievement of an efficient rent-earning mix of forest uses depends on obtaining and installing use rights with appropriate characteristics—particularly transferability and divisibility. We can think of firms shifting the mix of forest uses, as between many and few, large and small, so that there are actually four extremes: atomistic, with either many or few forest activities; and sole-ownership, again with many or few forest uses. Because of limited capacity and rising institutional costs, actual forest organizations will ideally find a comfortable intermediate form such as those we observe around us, where a few 'firms' or actors are responsible for one or more forest uses on the same piece of land. With sufficient transferability and divisibility of rights, the form need not be fixed. The actors can adjust as their abilities, their desires for non-market goods, market prices and the availability of finance dictate.

Finally, in addition to the ability to shift between types of property ownership (or concentration levels), I return briefly to 'tree growing tenure'—without which, in fact, a multi-owner forest organization would be a poor shadow of the theoretical 'atomistic' forest organization sketched above. The worldwide rarity of 'tree tenure' means that even where many individual pairs or groups of neighbouring forest users have good title that can serve as the basis of their trade and negotiations, they run up against the timber firm that, under current property-law concepts, owns both its land and its appurtenant growing trees. This dominant firm will, like a monopolist, limit the range of forest-use mixes. As a general proposition, I suggest that unless such a property right is introduced, all private multiple owner forests must neglect some of the forest-use purposes and products that could be easily undertaken by a sole owner.

A cooperative organization to reconcile multiple and competing uses of the forest: the condominium

In the previous subparts I argued that both the sole-owner and atomistic structures of forest management have associated shortcomings. The trouble with the sole-ownership extreme is its insulation from factor and input market influences. The trouble with the atomistic extreme is that the many firms' coordination agreements are subject to extensive transactions costs of information, bargaining, monitoring and enforcement. We might argue that forest users would prefer to be organized as a sole owner, while the public interest, as represented by a benevolent government, is better served by an atomistic arrangement, except in cases where the ideal mix of uses produces a natural monopoly. Here, I explore a cooperative alternative, emulating the condominium or strata-title organization of apartment houses introduced in Chapter 1, and somewhat similar to the idea of unitized oil fields in Chapter 9 and sea fisher organizations in Chapter 4. In all these cases, there is collective ownership of the main resource and responsibility for its maintenance against damage from internal or external sources. The members have individual (private) property rights to their share or part of the resource, for instance a catch quota or stand of trees. The members' shares in the main resource are roughly proportional to the amounts of their individual property rights.

Consider 'condo-like' forest ownership more directly. For share rights in common to the building and its services, substitute share rights in common to the land and the forest. For rights to the individual apartments, substitute rights to make different, separate, uses of the forest. If the initial condition before the condo was set up was an atomistic ownership of rights to various forest uses, the various owners join to take over the land and to own and manage the tree stand, including its regeneration. There is no need to suffer from the absence of the 'tree-growing' property right mentioned above. Of course, the multiple-purpose forest is not exactly analogous to a condo building. In particular, a condo building is able to separate its owners' physical spaces by floors and walls. A condo forest (or fishery) on the other hand will have the private activities of its members perhaps interfering with one another, and, even if they do not impose externalities, will share the same physical space. Nevertheless, I suggest that placing a whole forest under a condo-type organization would offer a remedy to some of the problems associated with atomistic holding and with its opposite, ownership concentration.

For one, externalities, conflicts and disappearances between and among neighbours would amount to less than in a forest with atomistic ownership. Since information about the forest would be freely accessible to all members, the scope for strategic behaviour in negotiations between, say, the owners of camping rights and the owners of hunting rights would be greatly reduced. As a second merit, some of the negotiation would be political rather than formally commercial, more like working on a general peace treaty than reconciling a set of bilateral bargains. Where arriving at a final general mix of forest uses might be blocked by a dispute between a few of the owners who could not agree on a contract in the atomistic forest, under a condo-like majority voting arrangement the organization as a whole could dilute the power of 'trouble-makers'.

A condo-like organization would also provide the flexibility needed to adapt the mix of forest uses over time. It would, in effect, combine the best characteristics of sole ownership with those of atomistic ownership. Coordination of uses, and the provision of infrastructure and public goods would be mostly determined within one large corporation, thus greatly reducing transactions and information costs, while the mutual shareholding in the whole forest would decrease the disincentives of free-riding. Management of the trees and of tree-growing, could, where desired, be permanently separated from that of the land. The members could decide whether to treat timber-growing as a dominant use to which all other uses would have to adjust, or to treat it as just one of the uses of a given area of land. As in an atomistic forest, the members would escape from a contractual, dependent, relationship to the sole owner, but would avoid the temptation to combine in order to acquire market power. Each would have a right defined as property, be it only to make the use of the forested land for a distinct purpose, and each would have a stake in others' making optimal use of their own rights. Their individual rights would have long duration, security, transferability and divisibility. Also, because of the coordination provided by their condo organization, their individual rights would have more exclusivity than under the atomistic organization.

Conclusions: the private forest right and its characteristics

This chapter has traced the development of the rights of private forestland holders in England and in North America from the Middle Ages to the late twentieth century. The separation of private woods from the Crown forest domain began with the Normans. In their division they created the King's own forests (later the public or Crown forests), and the various kinds of wood within the feudal manor. These eventually took on the properties we now associate with private woodlands, as freehold interests gradually supplanted feudal and colonial tenures, leaving owners with powers to manage, dispose and take income from their own timber or woods. As with mining rights, the development of rights over private woodlands depended on decisions by the courts and the amassing of case law and legal theory in property, nuisance and tort. Governments, concerned with promoting industry, conserving existing trees, increasing the uses being made within a forest, protecting the public from fire and other forest dangers, taking a share of the forest rent and encouraging forest rejuvenation, made a typically belated effective appearance.

To conclude the discussion in this chapter, I return once more to the characteristics of the property right in forest to summarize how the duration and exclusivity of the typical forest right changed over time, with particular attention to the roles played by top-level transaction costs and by disposal practices on public forestland. The effect of the courts on the forest property right and its characteristics ran through two channels. In one, forest users demanded changes in the characteristics of their property rights so as better to adapt to nuisance and other torts. In the other, the rules of nuisance law became in themselves elements in the characteristics of the forest-user's right.

Duration

Whereas 'duration' with regard to rights to use the public forest had been part of a policy to induce investment in mills and in protecting and managing the woods (see Chapter 11), its significance in the private forest has been different. As seen earlier, clarity about duration of a private right was wanted not to give the holder time to rear a timber stand, but to give a contracting party time in which to complete the cutting of a mature stand. The courts' long association with questions about this contract produced the concept that contractors can have real-property rights in timber that are severed from the real-property rights of the owner of the soil. This was a breakthrough, but it has not yet been extended to apply to very long tree-growing durations. Leased private rights in land of a duration long enough to encompass planting, harvesting and planting again do exist today, but they have not yet been tested or identified in the common-law courts.

Exclusivity

In exclusivity of the forest owner's right, the contrast with the developmental pace of rights to mines and mining is startling. Whereas mining rights closely followed and sometimes led the development of nuisance law through the nineteenth and twentieth centuries, forest rights generally lagged well behind both general product-liability (negligence) and nuisance law over the period. Neither individual accidents nor sweeping forest fires provoked litigation significant enough to challenge the exclusivity and independence of the forest holder's rights (although we can discern the courts alternating between periods of strict liability and periods when nuisance was excused by 'accident' or by deficiency of information).

In the twentieth century the exclusivity of private forest rights was explicitly shaped by a variety of statutory forest-practice, disease control and forest-fire regulations, by taxation and by subsidies. Many of the underlying policies are actually more concerned with rural social and economic betterment than with tree-growing. The regulations and associated tax abatements and subsidies are valued by politicians for the spending and stability they bring to backward areas. Forest improvement is sometimes the chief local target for 'social' spending.

An alternative theory holds that government forest-practice and forest-protection regulation activity is a response to the rent-seeking lobbying of larger milling companies whose goal is to ease the burden of protecting their timber by increasing the public role in forestry management (for instance, having the government spray against insects or protect against fires). The evidence does not clearly show that this kind of government activity has actually increased the long-run supply of timber and other raw material, as would be expected if the private costs of supplying timber fell. Consequently, theories holding that large-firm wood users have effectively demanded the intrusive regulations and policy-programmes that impinge on their exclusivity await empirical support.

Top-level transactions costs

Finally, an examination of how the characteristics of the forest property right changed over time should not ignore the role played by top-level transactions costs: effectively, the price demanders paid for an increase in their rights' duration and/or exclusivity. These costs may well explain the forest industry's poor performance relative to mining in achieving a well-defined, well-adapted and efficient set of private property interests. At several points I have mentioned that timber and wood were not valuable enough to justify costly litigation or lobbying to change the right. In England, wood products could be imported. Later, in urban North America, they could be replaced by supplies from frontier timber regions, by old-growth, by farmers' woodlots and by substitutes.

Late in the nineteenth century most English woodland estate owners finally got rid of their owners' impeachability for waste, of the strict settlement and of most copyhold and commoners' rights. Freehold powers became pretty well absolute in England and the United States. Since then, private owners have shown little desire to obtain new characteristics in their rights; their reforming zeal and lobbying investments have been directed at taxes, tariffs and building codes, not at deficiencies in property rights. They agree with rights-holders in the mining industry that the rights they have today (not greatly different from those of two centuries ago) should, in the interest of continued investment, employment and production be kept clear of government interferences.

Has governmental regulation been the mother of forest property rights?

Finally, we may ask whether government regulation has, in effect, substituted for the private property rights as spelled out in common law. In Chapter 4 on rights in the sea fisheries, we observed a period over which government regulation was introduced, perhaps to stand in for the individual property rights precluded by high transactions costs. When landing quotas and other property-like interests are introduced, the characteristics of the new private interest can be traced back to the characteristics of the previous regulatory licences. Here, public regulation was the mother of the new private right.

Nelson (1986) has offered a related point about US public forests. Government did not 'regulate' the logging industries of the various regions in the nineteenth century but it did keep them small and active by making licences and leases obtainable by anyone who met the timber-disposal conditions. This openness of public auctions and other selection procedures worked against the interests of the larger companies that sought a secure flow of wood for their processing plants. Somewhat like the fishery story, the companies that had endured the quick sale of land rights and the absence of long-duration property rights helped to alter the land-disposal system. Gradually, they acquired something like automatic renewal of their atomistic leases. In effect, Nelson argues, they had acquired long-run property rights over an area or a flow of wood; the governments' land disposal procedures designed to favour small-scale participants actually worked to increase the duration and quality of title of the rights held by the increasingly large mill firms.

By contrast I would argue that the rules and procedures of the public forests have not been the mother of private timber rights. On the one hand, rights in the public forests are still usually farmed out as short-term cutting rights, expiring when the timber has been removed. Short-term leases, licences and contractual arrangements like those on public lands do exist in the private forestry sector, but their form owes nothing to that of disposal and issuing of rights in the public forest. In particular, the comprehensive freehold rights of modern forest owners are little different from those granted in fee simple centuries ago. This property interest was refined in the common law, and adopted in the assignment of title (or 'patent') to individuals by both public and private holders. Thus, the characteristics of licences and the other disposal rights we encountered in Chapter 11 for the public forests were not smoothly transmuted into the characteristics of today's rights of private forest ownership, thereby justifying the different treatment of the public-land derived property rights of Chapter 11 and those private rights dealt with in Chapter 12.

Bibliography

Acheson, J. M. 1975. 'The Lobster Fiefs: Economic and Ecological Effects of Territoriality in the Maine Lobster Industry', *Human Ecology* 3: 183–207.

Adelman, M. A. 1972.*The World Petroleum Market 1947–69*. Baltimore: Johns Hopkins.

Agnello, R. P., and L. P. Donnelly. 1977. 'Some Aspects of Optimal Timing of Intraseason Catch'. In L. G. Anderson, ed. *Economic Impacts of Extended Fisheries Jurisdiction*. Ann Arbor, MI: Ann Arbor Science Publishers Inc., pp. 209–21.

Agrawal, A. 1994. 'Rules, Rule Making and Rule Breaking: Examining the Fit Between Rule Systems and Resource Use'. In E. Ostrom et al. *Rules, Games and Community Pool Resources*. Ann Arbor, MI: University of Michigan Press.

Agricola, G. 1556. *De Re Metallica*. Translated and edited by H. and M. Hoover, London 1912 and New York: Dover 1950.

Albion, R. G. 1926. *Forests and Sea Power: The Timber Problem of the Royal Navy 1652–1862*. Cambridge: Harvard University Press (1965, Hamden, CT: Archois Books).

Alchian, A. A. 1965. 'Some Economics of Property Rights'. *Il Politico* 30: 816–29. Reprinted as chap. 5 of A. A. Alchian, *Economic Forces at Work*. Indianapolis: Liberty Press, 1977.

——. 1977. *Economic Forces at Work*. Indianapolis: Liberty Press.

Allais, M. 1957. 'Methods of Appraising Economic Prospects of Mining Exploration over Large Territories', *Management Science* 3, no. 4: 285–347.

Allen, C. K. 1958. *Aspects of Justice*. London: Stevens.

Allen, D. 1991. 'What Are Transactions Costs?', *Research in Law and Economics* 14: 1–18.

Allen, G. 1981. *The Japanese Economy*. London: Weidenfeld and Nicholson.

Allen, R. C. 1992. *Enclosure and the Yeoman: The Agricultural Development of the South Midlands, 1450–1850*. New York: Oxford University Press.

Anderson, L. G. 1999. 'ITQs in Share System Fisheries: Implications for Efficiency, Distribution and Tax Policy'. In R. Arnason and H. H. Gissurarson, eds. *Individual Transferable Quotas in Theory and Practice*. Reykjavik: University of Iceland Press, pp. 169–84.

Anderson, Owen L. 1986. 'Federal Oil and Gas Management in the United States'. In J. O. Saunders, ed. *Managing Natural Resources in a Federal State*. Toronto: Carswell, pp. 139–57.

Anderson, M. L. 1950. *State Control of Forestry under European Democracies*. Oxford: Oxford University Press.

——. 1967. *A History of Scottish Forestry*, 2 vols. London: Nelson.

Anderson, T. L., and P. J. Hill. 1975. 'The Evolution of Property Rights: A Study of the American West', *Journal of Law and Economics* 18: 163–79.

Andrews, C. M. 1938. *The Colonial Period of American History*. New Haven: Yale University Press.

Andrews, L. M. 1940. 'The Correlative Rights Doctrine in the Law of Oil and Gas', *Southern California Law Review* 13, no. 2: 175.

Andrews, M. 1933. *The Founding of Maryland*. New York: Appleton-Century.

Angell, J. K. 1877. *A Treatise on the Law of Watercourses: With an Appendix, Containing Statutes of Flowing, and Forms of Declarations*, 7th edn. Boston: Little, Brown, and Company; reprinted Holmes Beach, FL: Gaunt, 2000.

Angus, J. T. 1990. *A Deo Victoria: The Story of the Georgian Bay Lumber Company, 1871–1942*. Thunder Bay, ON: Severns Publications.

Appelbaum, S. 1972. 'Roman Britain'. In H. P. R. Finberg, ed. *The Agrarian History of England and Wales*, vol. I, Part II. Cambridge: Cambridge University Press, pp. 3–268.

Arbuckle, M., and K. Drummond. 1999. 'Evolution of Self-Governing within a Harvesting System Governed by Individual Transferable Quota'. In R. Shotton, ed. *Use of Property Rights in Fisheries Management*. FAO Fisheries Technical Paper 404/2, pp. 370–82.

Armstrong, R. 1978. *The Asbestos Industry in Quebec 1878–1929*. Ph.D. thesis. Quebec: Laval University. Mimeo.

——. 1984. *Structure and Change: An Economic History of Quebec*. Toronto: Gage.

Arnason, R. 1990. 'Minimum Information Management in Fisheries', *Canadian Journal of Economics* 23: 630–53.

——. 1995. *The Icelandic Fisheries: Evolution and Management of a Fishing Industry*. Oxford: Fishing News Books.

Arnason, R., and H. H. Gissurarson, ed. 1999. *Individual Transferable Quotas in Theory and Practice*. Reykjavik: University of Iceland Press.

Arrow, K. J., and R. C. Lind. 1970. 'Uncertainty and the Evaluation of Public Investment Decisions', *American Economic Review* 60: 364–78.

Ashton, T. S. 1951. *Iron and Steel in the Industrial Revolution*, 3rd edn. Manchester: University Press, 1963.

Ault, D. E., and G. L. Rutman. 1979. 'The Development of Individual Rights to Property in Tribal Africa', *Journal of Law and Economics* 22, no. 1: 163–82.

Ausness, R. 1983. 'Water Rights Legislation in the East: A Program for Reform', *William and Mary Law Review* 24, no. 4: 547.

Ayer, J. D. 1973. 'Public Regulation of Private Forestry: A Survey and a Proposal', *Harvard Journal on Legislation*, 10: 407–29.

Baildon, W. P., ed. 1890. *Select Civil Pleas, AD 1200–1203*. London: Selden Society.

Bainbridge, W. 1841 to 1900. *The Law of Mines and the Ownership of Minerals*. London: Butterworth.

——. 1841 to 1900. *The Law of Mines and the Ownership of Minerals*. London: Butterworths.

Baker, J. H. 1986. *The Legal Profession and the Common Law*. London: Humbledon.

Ballem, J. B. 1973. *The Oil and Gas Lease in Canada*. 2nd edn. Toronto: University of Toronto Press, 1985.

Bankes, J. M. 1939. 'Records of Mining in Winstanley and Orrell, near Wigan', *Transactions of the Lancashire and Cheshire Antiquarian Society*, 84.

Bankes, N. D. 1983 'Non-Crown Timber Rights in Ontario', *Canadian Institute of Resources Law*. Typewritten memorandum. Calgary.

Barringer, D. M., and J. S. Adams. 1897. *The Law of Mines and Mining in the United States*. Boston, MA: Little, Brown, and Company.

Barton, B. 1986. 'Cooperative Management of Interprovincial Water Resources'. In J. O. Saunders, ed. *Managing Natural Resources in a Federal State*. Toronto: Carswell, pp. 235–50.

——. 1993. *Canadian Law of Mining*. Calgary: Canadian Institute of Resources Law, University of Calgary.

Barzel, Y. 1989. *Economic Analysis of Property Rights*. Cambridge: Cambridge University Press.

Beaglehole, E. 1968. 'Property', *International Encyclopedia of the Social Sciences*. New York: Macmillan.

Bean, M. J. 1983. *The Evolution of National Wildlife Law*. New York: Praeger.

Becker, L. C. 1977. *Property Rights: Philosophic Foundations*. London: Routledge.

Beddington, J. R., and R. B. Rettig. 1984. *Approaches to the Regulation of Fishing Effort*. FAO Fisheries Technical Paper FIRM/T243. Rome: FAO.

Belshaw, C. S. 1957. *The Great Village*. London: Routledge and Kegan Paul.

Benidickson, J. 1983. 'Private Rights and Public Purposes in the Lakes, Rivers and Streams of Ontario 1870–1930'. In David H. Flaherty, ed. *Essays in the History of Canadian Law II*. Toronto: University of Toronto Press, pp. 365–417.

——. 1998. 'Forest Management and Environmental Values: Ontario's Old Growth Forests' (draft June 1998). Ottawa: Faculty of Law, University of Ottawa.

—— 2000a. 'Forest Management and Environmental Values: Ontario's Old Growth Pinelands'. *Journal of Environmental Law and Practice* 9: pp. 93–117.

——. 2000b. 'Sustaining Old Growth Pinelands in Ontario: Pathways to Reform'. *Journal of Environmental Law and Practice* 9: 199–226.

Berge, E., and H. Sevatdal. 1994. 'Some Notes on the Substance and Terminology of the Norwegian Law of Common Property', *Common Property Resource Digest* 30: 8–11.

Berkes, F. 1986. 'Marine Inshore Fishery Management in Turkey'. In US National Research Council, *Sharing the Fish: Toward a National Policy on Individual Fishing Quotas*. Washington: National Academy Press, pp. 63–83.

Berman, H. J. 1983. *Law and Revolution: The Formation of the Western Legal Tradition*. Cambridge: Harvard University Press.

Berton, P. 1958. *Klondike: The Life and Death of the Last Great Gold Rush*, also titled *The Klondike Fever*. Toronto: McClelland and Stewart and New York: Knopf (1959). Revised edition, 1972.

Bess, R. and Harte, M. J (2000) 'The Role of Property Rights in the Development of New Zealand's Seafood Industry', *Marine Policy*, 24, pp. 331–9.

Bewes, W. A. 1894. *Law of waste. A treatise on the rights and liabilities which arise from the relationship of limited owners and the owners of the inheritance with reference to the tenements*. London: Sweet and Maxwell.

Birch, A. L., and R. B. MacLock. 1992. 'Water Conservation and Transferable Water Rights: Australia and Alberta', *Canadian Water Resources Journal* 17, no. 3: 214–22.

Birrell, J. 1980. 'The Medieval English Forest', *Journal of Forest History* 24: 78–85.

Blackmer, S. D. 1995. 'Of Wilderness and Commerce: A Historical Overview of the Northern Forest', *Vermont Law Review* 19: 265–81.

Blackstone, Sir William. 1765. *Commentaries on the Laws of England*, 1st edn. Reprinted 1966: New York: Oceana; and London: Wildy, originally published, Oxford: Clarendon.

——. 1809. *Commentaries on the Laws of England*, 15th edn., with the last corrections of the author, and with notes and additions by Edward Christian. London: T. Cadell and W. Davies.

Blainey, G. 1962. 'The Gold Rushes: The Year of Decision', *Historical Studies, Australia and New Zealand* (May).

Blainey, G. 1978. *The Rush That Never Ended: A History of Australian Mining*, 3rd edn. Melbourne: Melbourne University Press.

Blomquist, W. A. 1992. *Dividing the Waters: Governing Groundwater in Southern California*. San Francisco: ICS Press.

Bohlen, F. 1929. 'Liability of Manufacturers to Persons Other Than Their Immediate Vendees', *Law Quarterly Review* 45: 343.

Boldrewood, R. 1880. *The Miner's Right*. Printed serially in Australia 1880; London: Macmillan 1890. Sydney: University Press 1973.

Bonfield, L. 1983. *Marriage Settlements, 1601–1740. The Adoption of the Strict Settlement*. Cambridge: Cambridge University Press.

Bowen, H. R. 1943. 'The Interpretation of Voting in the Allocation of Economic Resources', *Quarterly Journal of Economics* 58: 27–48.

Bowes, M. D., and J. V. Krutilla. 1989. *Multiple-Use Management: The Economics of Public Forest Lands*. Washington, DC: Resources for the Future.

Boyd, R., and B. Daniels. 1985. 'Capital Gains Treatment of Timber Income', *Land Economics* 61, 4.

Bracton, H. de. 1230. *De Legibus et Consuetudinibus Angliæ (Bracton on the Laws and Customs of England)*. 4 vols. S. E. Thorne, trans. Cambridge, MA: Published in association with the Selden Society, The Belknap Press of Harvard University Press, 1968–77.

Braddick, M. J. 1994. *Parliamentary Taxation in Seventeenth-Century England*. London: Boydell.

Bradley, P. G. 1967. *The Economics of Crude Petroleum Production*. Amsterdam: North-Holland.

—— 1970. 'Some Seasonal Models of the Fishing Industry'. In A. D. Scott, ed. *Economics of Fisheries Management: A Symposium*. H. R. MacMillan Lectures in Fisheries. Vancouver: University of British Columbia, Institute of Animal Resource Ecology, pp. 33–44.

——. 1986. *Report of the Mineral Revenues Inquiry (in regard to The Study into Mineral (Including Petroleum) Revenues in Western Australia)*. Perth: Mineral Revenues Inquiry. Typescript.

Braeman, J., R. H. Bremner, and D. Broady. 1975. *The New Deal*. Vol. II: *The State and Local Levels*. Columbus, OH: Ohio State University Press.

Brajer V., A. Church, R. Cummings and P. Farah. 1989. 'The Strengths and Weaknesses of Water Markets as They Affect Water Scarcity and Sovereignty Interests in the West', *Natural Resources Journal* 29, no. 2: 489–511.

Braudel, F. 1985. *Civilization and Capitalism 15th–18th Century*. Vol. 1, *The Structures of Everyday Life*, revised edn. London: Collins Fontana.

Brenner, J. F. 1973. 'Nuisance Law and the Industrial Revolution', *Journal of Legal Studies* 3: 403.

Brenner, R. 1974. 'Nuisance Law and the Industrial Revolution', *Journal of Legal Studies* 3: 407.

Breton, A. 1991. 'The Organization of Competition in Congressional and Parliamentary Governments'. In A. Breton, et al. eds. *The Competitive State*. Dordrecht: Kluwer, pp. 13–38.

——. 1996. *Competitive Governments: An Economic Theory of Politics and Public Finance*. Cambridge: Cambridge University Press.

Breton, A., and A. D. Scott. 1978. *The Economic Constitution of Federal States*. Toronto: University of Toronto Press.

Brierly, J. L. 1963. *The Law of Nations*, 6th edn. Oxford: Clarendon Press.

Brimmer, C. A. 1970. 'The Rancher's Subservient Surface Estate', *Land and Water Law Review* 5, no. 1: 44–64.

Bromley, D. W. 1989. *Economic Interests and Institutions: The Conceptual Foundation of Public Policy*. New York: Blackwell.

Brose, E. D. 1993. The Politics of Technological Change in Prussia: Out of the Shadow of Antiquity. Princeton: Princeton University Press.

Brown, J. N. Elliot. 1907. 'The Evolution of Law and Government in the Yukon Territory', *University of Toronto Studies in History and Economics* 2, no. 4: 1–18.

Brubaker, E. 1995. *Property Rights in the Defence of Nature*. Toronto: Environment Probe London.

Bruce, J. W., and L. Fortmann. 1992. 'Property and Forestry'. In P. N. Nemetz, ed. *Emerging Issues in Forest Policy*. Vancouver: University of British Columbia Press, pp. 471–96.

Buchanan, J. M., and G. Tullock. 1962. *The Calculus of Consent*, Ann Arbor, MI: University of Michigan Press.

Burgess, D. F. 1989. 'The Social Opportunity Cost of Capital in the Prese Labour Market Distortions'. *Canadian Journal of Economics* 22, no. 2 (May): 245–62.

Burke, D. L., and G. L. Brander. 1999. 'Canadian Experience with Individual Transferable Quotas'. In R. Shotton, ed. *Use of Property Rights in Fisheries Management*. FAO Fisheries Technical Paper 404/1, pp. 151–60.

Cail, R. E. 1974. *Land, Man and the Law. The Disposal of Crown Lands in British Columbia 1871–1913*. Vancouver: University of British Columbia Press.

Cairns, R. 1990. 'The Economics of Exploration for Non-Renewable Resources', *Journal of Economic Surveys* 4, no. 4: 361–95.

Calabresi, G., and A. G. Melamed. 1972. 'Property Rules, Liability Rules, and Inalienability: One View of the Cathedral', *Harvard Law Review* 85: 1089–128.

Cameron, E. N. 1986. *At the Crossroads: The Mineral Problems of the United States*. New York: Wiley.

Campbell, B. A. 1974. 'Licence Control Programs in Other Countries ...' Licence Limitation in BC Report Number IV, Canada Department of the Environment. Vancouver. Mimeo.

Campbell, H. F. 1989. 'Fishery Buy-Back Programs and Economic Welfare', *Australian Journal of Agricultural Economics* 33, no. 1: 20–31.

Campbell, H., K. Menz, and G. Waugh, 1989. *Economics of Fishery Management in the Pacific Island Region*. Canberra: ACIAR.

Campbell, H. F., and A. D. Owen, eds. 1994. *The Economics of Papua New Guineas' Tuna Fisheries*. Canberra: Australian Centre for International Agricultural Research (ACIAR).

Carlos, A. M., and F. D. Lewis. 1999. 'Property Rights, Competition, and Depletion in the Eighteenth-Century Canadian Fur Trade: The Role of the Canadian Market', *Canadian Journal of Economics* 32: 705–28.

Carroll, F. M., and F. R. Raiter. 1985. 'The People versus the Government: The 1918 Cloquet Fire and the Struggle for Compensation', *Journal of Forest History* 29: 4–21.

Carrothers, W. A. 1938. 'Forest Industries of British Columbia'. In A. R. M. Lower, ed. *The North American Assault on the Canadian Forest*. Toronto: Ryerson, pp. 227–345.

Caverhill, P. Z. 1917. *Classification of the Crown lands of New Brunswick*. Montreal: The Federated Press Ltd.

Centner, T. J. 1997. 'Reforming Outdated Fence Laws: Good Fences Make Good Neighbors Only If They Are Fair', *Journal of Environmental Law and Litigation* 12: 267–304.

Centner, T. J., and R. C. Griffin. 1998. 'Externalities from Roaming Livestock: Explaining the Demise of the Open Range', *Journal of Agricultural and Resource Economics* 23: 71–84.

Chalkin, C. W. 1974. *The Provincial Towns of Georgian England.* London: Arnold.

Cheung, S. N. S. 1969. 'Transaction Costs, Risk Aversion, and the Choice of Contractual Arrangements', *Journal of Law and Economics* 12, no. 1: 23–42.

Chitty, J. 1812. *A Treatise on the Game Laws, and on Fisheries*, 2 vols. London: W. Clarke and Sons; reprinted New York and London: Garland Publishing, 1979.

Christy, F. T., Jr. 1964. 'The Exploitation of a Common Property Natural Resource: The Maryland Oyster Industry'. Unpublished Ph.D. Dissertation, University of Michigan.

——. 1973. *Fisherman Quotas: A Tentative Suggestion for Domestic Management.* Occasional Paper No. 19, Rhode Island Law of the Sea Institute.

Christy, F. T., Jr., and A. D. Scott. 1965. *The Common Wealth in Ocean Fisheries.* Baltimore: Johns Hopkins Press.

Church, R. 1986. *1830–1913: Victorian: Pre-Eminence.* Vol. 3 of *The History of the British Coal Industry.* Peter Mathias, ed. Oxford: Clarendon.

Clark, C. W., and G. R. Munro. 1980. 'Fisheries and the Processing Sector: Some Implications for Management Policy', *The Bell Journal of Economics* 11, no. 2: 603–16.

Clark, Colin W. 1976. *Mathematical Bioeconomics: The Optimal Management of Renewable Resources.* New York: John Wiley and Sons.

Clark, I. N., and A. J. Duncan. 1986. 'New Zealand's Fisheries Management Policies'. In N. Mollet, ed. *Fishery Access Control Programs Worldwide.* Proceedings of the Workshop on Management Options for the North Pacific Longliners held on Orcas Island, April 1986. Fairbanks: Alaska Sea Grant Report.

Clark, I. N., P. Major, and N. Mollett. 1989. 'The Development and Implementation of New Zealand's ITQ Management System'. In P. Neher et al. *Rights Based Fishing.* Dordrecht: Kluwer, pp. 117–45.

Clark, M. 1979. *A Short History of Australia.* New York: New American Library.

Clark, S. D. 1942. 'Mining Society in British Columbia and the Yukon'. Reprinted in *British Columbia: Historical Readings*, W. P. Ward and R. A. J. McDonald, eds. Vancouver: Douglas and McIntyre, 1981.

Clark, S. D., and I. A. Renard. 1970. 'The Riparian Doctrine and Australian Legislation', *Melbourne University Law Review* 7: 475–506.

Clary, D. A. 1986. *Timber and the Forest Service.* Lawrence, Kans: University of Kansas.

Clawson, M. 1979. *The Economics of US Nonindustrial Private Forests.* Baltimore: Resources for the Future.

Clawson, M., and J. Knetsch. 1966. *Economics of Outdoor Recreation.* Baltimore: Johns Hopkins.

Clawson, M., and B. Held. 1957. *The Federal Lands: Their Use and Management.* Lincoln: University of Nebraska Press.

Cleary, D. 1990. *Anatomy of the Amazon Gold Rush.* Houndsmill, Basingstoke, Hampshire: Macmillan in association with St. Antony's College, Oxford.

Coase, R. H. 1960. 'The Problem of Social Cost', *Journal of Law and Economics* III: 1–44.

Cohen, D. A. 1982. 'The Relationship of Contractual Remedies to Political and Social Status: A Preliminary Inquiry', *University of Toronto Law Quarterly* 32: 31–108.

Colby, W. E. 1942. 'The Law of Oil and Gas', *California Law Review* 30, no. 3: 245–71.

Connor, R. 1999. 'Trends in Fishing Capacity and Aggregation of Fishing Rights in New Zealand under Individual Transferable Quotas'. In R. Shotton, ed. *Use of Property Rights in Fisheries Management.* FAO Fisheries Technical Paper 404/2, pp. 267–78.

——. 1999. 'Are ITQs Property Rights?' In R. Shotton, ed. *Use of Property Rights in Fisheries Management.* FAO Fisheries Technical Paper 404/2, pp. 29–38.

Cooley, R. A. 1963. *Politics and Conservation: The Decline of the Alaska Salmon.* New York: Harper and Row.

Cooper, L., and L. Joll. 1999. 'The Scalefish Fisheries of Northern Western Australia: The Use of Transferable Effort Allocations'. In R. Shotton, ed. *Use of Property Rights in Fisheries Management.* FAO Fisheries Technical Paper 404/2, pp. 445–53.

Cooter, R., and T. Ulen. 1988. *Law and Economics.* Glenview, IL: Scott, Foresman.

Copes, P. 2000. 'ITQs and Fisheries Management: With Comments on the Conservation Experience in Canada and other Countries'. Invited address to the Unión del Comercio, la Industria y la Producción of Mar del Plata City, Argentina, 29 June 2000. Discussion Paper 00-1. Vancouver: Simon Fraser University Institute of Fisheries Analysis.

Coquillette, D. R. 1979. 'Mosses from an Old Manse: Another Look at Some Historic Property Cases about the Environment', *Cornell Law Review* 64: 761–9.

Cordell, J. C., and M. McKean 1986. 'Sea Tenure in Bahia Brazil'. *Proceedings on the Conference on Common Property Management.* National Resource Council, Washington DC: National Academy Press: 85–114.

Corpus Juris Secundum. 1998. Mines and Minerals, vol. 58. M. J. Canavan, ed. St. Paul, MN: West.

Côté, S. 1992. 'Naissance de l'industrie papetière et mainmise dur la forêt: le cas de Bathurst'. In L. Anders Sandberg, ed. *Trouble in the Woods: Forest Policy and Social Conflict in Nova Scotia and New Brunswick.* Fredericton, NB: Acadiensis Press.

Coull, J. R. 1993. *World Fisheries Resource.* London: Routledge.

Crabbé, P. J. 1979. *Analyse économique de la réglementation de l'exploration dans la loi des mines du Québec.* Communication a présenter au Congres de l'ACFAS Montreal. Ottawa: University of Ottawa. Mimeo.

——. 1983a. *Economic Analysis of Quebec's Mining Legislation.* Paper delivered to meeting of CEA Vancouver. Ottawa: University of Ottawa Economics Department. Mimeo.

——. 1983b. 'The Contribution of L. C. Gray to the Economic Theory of Exhaustible Natural Resources and Its Roots in the History of Economic Thought', *Journal of Environmental Economics and Management* 10: 195–220.

——. 1985. 'Turgot's "Brief on Mines and Quaries": An Early Economic Analysis of Mineral Land Tenure', *Natural Resources Journal* 25, no. 2: 267–73.

Cragun, J. W. 1933–4. 'Title to Oil and Gas Lands Under the Federal Leasing Act', *George Washington Law Review II*: pp. 55–64.

Craine, Lyle E. 1969. *Water Management Innovations in England.* Baltimore: The Johns Hopkins Press.

Crommelin, M. 1982. *A New Era of Concessions? The Government Agreement in Australia* typescript. Melbourne: University of Melbourne Law School.

——. 1986. 'The US Rule of capture: Its Place in Australia', *AMPLA Yearbook Extract.* Melbourne: Australian Mining and Petroleum Law Association Ltd.

——. 1996. 'Development Alternatives: The Feasibility of a Single Window' (unpublished conference paper). Melbourne: Faculty of Law.

Crommelin, M., and A. R. Thompson, eds. 1977. *Mineral Leasing as an Instrument of Public Policy*. Vancouver: UBC Press.

Crommelin, M., P. H. Pearse, and A. D. Scott. 1978. 'Management of Oil and Gas Resources in Alberta: An Economic Assessment of Public Policy', *Natural Resources Journal* 18, no. 2: 337–90.

Crowe, A. F. 1930. *Mines and Mining Laws of British Columbia*. Calgary: Burroughs.

Crutchfield, J. 1955. 'Fishermen's Unions and the Anti-Trust Statutes: The Economic Issues', *Journal of Industrial and Labour Relations* 8, no. 4: 531–6.

——. 1956. 'Common Property Resources and Factor Allocation', *Canadian Journal of Economics and Political Science* 22: 292–300.

——. 1965. 'Economic Objectives of Fishery Management'. In J. Crutchfield, ed. *Public Policy Issues in Natural Resources: The Fisheries*. Seattle: University of Washington Press.

——. 1979. 'The Economics of US Ocean Policy', *American Economic Review* 69, no. 2: 266–72.

Crutchfield, J., and G. Pontecorvo. 1969. *The Pacific Salmon Fisheries: A Study in Irrational Conservation*. Baltimore: Johns Hopkins Press.

Crutchfield, J., and A. Zellner. 1962. *Economic Aspects of the Pacific Halibut Fishery*. Fishery Industrial Research Report. Washington: US Department of the Interior.

Cruz, W. D. 1986. 'Overfishing and Conflict In a Traditional Fishery: San Miguel Bay, Philippines'. In US National Research Council, *Sharing the Fish: Toward a National Policy on Individual Fishing Quotas*. Washington: National Academy Press, pp. 115–35.

Curry-Roper, J. M. 1989. 'The Impact of the Timber and Stone Act on Public Land Ownership in Northern Minnesota', *Journal of Forest History* 33, no. 2: 70–9.

Cushing, D. H. 1988. *The Provident Sea*. Cambridge: Cambridge University Press.

——. 1993 *Population, Production and Regulation in the Sea*. Cambridge: Cambridge University Press.

Cushing, J. D., ed. 1978. *The Earliest Printed Law in Pennsylvania*. Wilmington, DE: Michael Glazer.

Cutting, C. L. 1955. *Fish Saving: A History of Fish Processing From Ancient to Modern Times*. London: L. Hill / New York: Philosophical Library, 1956.

Dam, K. W. 1974. 'The Evolution of North Sea Licensing Policy in Britain and Norway', *Journal of Law and Economics* 17, no. 2: 213–63.

——. 1976. *Oil Resources: Who Gets What How?* Chicago and London: University of Chicago Press.

Dana, S., and S. Fairfax. 1980. *Forest and Range Policy*, New York: McGraw-Hill.

Darby, H. C. 1977. *Domesday England*. Seventh volume of series on the geography of England as revealed by Domesday. Cambridge: Cambridge University Press.

Davidse, W. P. 1999. 'The Development Towards Co-Management in the Dutch Demersal North Sea Fisheries'. In R. Shotton, ed. *Use of Property Rights in Fisheries Management*. FAO Fisheries Technical Paper 404/1, pp. 198–202.

——. 2000. 'The Effect of Transferable Property Rights on the Fleet Capacity and Ownership of Harvesting Rights in the Dutch Demersal North Sea Fisheries'. In R. Shotton, ed. *Use of Property Rights in Fisheries Management*. FAO Fisheries Technical Paper 404/2, pp. 258–66.

Davies, K. 1975. *Law of Compulsory Purchase and Competition*, 2nd edn. London: Butterworths.

Davis, L., and C. Davis. 1963. 'Selected Problems Regarding Lessee's Rights and Obligations to the Surface Owner', *Rocky Mountain Mineral Law Inst.* 8: 315.

Davis, B. G. 1937. 'Fifty Years of Mining Law', *Harvard Law Review* 50: 897–908.

Demsetz, H. 1967. 'Toward a Theory of Property Rights', *American Economic Review* 57, no. 2: 347–59.

Dennen, R. T. 1976. 'Cattlemen's Associations and Property Rights in Land in the American West', *Explorations in Economic History* 13: 423–36.

Derham. P. J. 1987. 'The Implementation and Enforcement of Fisheries Legislation'. In G. Ulfstein et al., eds. *The Regulation of Fisheries: Legal, Economic and Social Aspects*. Strasbourg: Council of Europe, pp. 71–81.

Devlin, Rose Anne, and R. Quentin Grafton. 1998. *Economic Rights and Environmental Wrongs—Property Rights for the Common Good*. Cheltenham: Edward Elgar.

Dewar, M. E. 1983. *Industry in Trouble: The Federal Government and the New England Fisheries*. Philadelphia: Temple University Press.

DeWolf, G. A. 1974. *The Lobster Fishery of the Maritime Provinces: Economic Effects of Regulations*. Bulletin 187. Ottawa: Canadian Department of the Environment, Fisheries and Marine Service.

Downs, A. 1957. *An Economic Theory of Democracy*. New York: Harper.

Drushka, K. 1985. *Stumped: The Forest Industry in Transition*. Madeira Park, BC: Harbour Publishing.

Duerr, W. A. 1960. *Fundamentals of Forestry Economics*. New York: McGraw-Hill.

Dunbar, R. G. 1983. *Forging New Rights in Western Waters*. Lincoln, NE: University of Nebraska Press.

Dunfield, R. W. 1985. *The Atlantic Salmon in the History of North America*. Ottawa: Department of Fisheries and Oceans.

Dunn, M. 1852. 'A Treatise on the Winning and Working of Collieries'. Newcastle. No publisher.

Dycus, J. S. 1980. 'Legislative Clarification of the Correlative Rights of Surface and Mineral Owners', *Vanderbilt Law Review* 38: 871–95.

Easterbrook, W. T., and H. G. J. Aitken. 1956. *Canadian Economic History*. Toronto: Macmillan.

Eckert, R. D. 1979. *The Enclosure of Ocean Resources*. Stanford: Hoover Institution.

Eggertsson, T. 1990. *Economic Behavior and Institutions* Cambridge: Cambridge University Press.

Elder, J. R. 1912. *The Royal Fishery Companies of the Seventeenth Century*. Glasgow: James Maclehose and Sons.

Ellickson, R. C. 1973. 'Alternatives to Zoning: Covenants, Nuisance Rules, and Fines as Land Use Controls', *University of Chicago Law Review* 40: 681–781.

——. 1991. *Order Without Law: How Neighbors Settle Disputes*. Cambridge, MA: Harvard University Press.

Ely, N. 1964. 'Mineral Titles and Concessions'. In *Economics of the Mineral Industries*, 2nd edn. American Institute of Mining and Metallurgy and Petroleum Eng. York, PA: Maple Press.

English, B., and J. Saville. 1983. *Strict Settlement: A Guide for Historians*. Occasional Paper No. 10. Hull, PQ: University of Hull.

Erickson, G. K. 1977. 'Work Commitment Bidding'. In M. Crommelin and A. R. Thompson, eds. Mineral Leasing as an Instrument of Public Policy. Vancouver: University of British Columbia Press.

Eswaran, M., and A. Kotwal. 1985. 'A Theory of Contractual Structure in Agriculture', *American Economic Review* 75: 352–67.

Fabretti, G. 1995. 'La Cittadella d'argento', *Ulisse* 2000, pp. 44–57, based on G. Fabretti. 1995. *L'Arte della Cultivazione del rama e de l'argento,* Massa Maritima. Florence: Cantini.
Fairchild, F. R. 1935. *Forest Taxation in the United States.* USDA Miscellaneous Publication 218. Washington: United States Department of Agriculture.
FAO. 1995. *The State of World Fisheries and Aquaculture.* FAO: Rome.
——.1999. *Use of Property Rights in Fisheries Management.* Proceedings of the FishRights99 Conference held at Fremantle, Western Australia, 11–19 November 1999. FAO Fisheries Technical Papers 404/1 and 404/2.
Faraday, M. 1991. *Ludlow 1085–1660: A Social, Economic and Political History.* Chichester, Sussex: Phillimore.
Farrow, R. C. 1949. 'Water Rights in British Columbia', *Transactions of the Second Resources Conference,* Victoria, BC: Department of Lands and Forests, pp. 42–8.
Feeny, D. 1982. *The Political Economy of Productivity: Thai Agricultural Development.* Vancouver: University of British Columbia Press.
——. 1988. 'The Demand and Supply of Instititutional Arrangements'. In V. Ostrom et al., eds. *Rethinking Institutional Analysis and Development.* San Fransisco: ICS Press.
Fenn, P. T. 1926. *The Origin of the Right of Fishery in Territorial Waters.* Cambridge, MA: Harvard University Press.
Ferguson, F. E. 1974. 'Severed Surface and Mineral Estates—Right to Use, Damage or Destroy the Surface to remove Minerals', *Rocky Mountain Mineral Law Institute* 29, no. 14: 411.
Fernow, B. E. 1902. *Economics of Forestry.* New York: Crowell.
——. 1911. *A Brief History of Forestry.* Toronto: University of Toronto Press.
Field, B. C. 1985. 'The Optimal Commons', *American Journal of Agricultural Economics* 67, no. 2: 364–67.
——. 1986. 'Induced Changes in Property Institutions'. Amherst: University of Massachusetts. Mimeo.
——. 1989. 'The Evolution of Property Rights', *Kyklos* 42: 319–45.
Fifoot, C. H. S. 1949. *History and Sources of the Common Law: Tort and Contract.* London: Stevens and Sons Limited.
Finberg, H. P. R. 1969. *Tavistock Abbey: A Study in the Social and Economic History of Devon,* 2nd edn. New York: Augustus M. Kelly.
Fingard, J. 1966–1990. 'Wentworth'. In George W. Brown, ed. *The Dictionary of Canadian Biography,* vol. 5. University of Toronto Press, pp. 848–51.
Fisher, S. G. 1895. 'The Administration of Equity through Common Law Forms in Pennsylvania', *Law Quarterly Review* 1: 455–65. Reprinted in J. H. Wigmore et al., eds. 1908. *Selected Essays in Anglo-American Legal History.* Boston: Little Brown, pp. 810–23.
Fisher, W. W., M. J. Horwitz, and T. Reed. 1993. *American Legal Realism.* New York: Oxford University Press.
Fitzpatrick, D. 2000. 'Property Rights in Relation to Fishery Licences in Australia from a Legal Perspective'. In R. A. Shotton, ed. *Use of Property Rights in Fisheries Management: Proceedings of the Fish Rights 99 Conference.* Freemantle: Western Australia, 11–19 Nov. 1999. FAO Fisheries Technical Paper # 404/2.
Fleming, J. G. 1987. *The Law of Torts,* 7th edn. Sydney: Law Book Company.
Flinn, M. W. 1958. 'Growth of the English Iron Industry 1760–1960', *Economic History Review* II: 144–53.

——. 1984. *The History of the British Coal Industry,* vol. 2. *1700–1830 The Industrial Revolution.* Oxford: Clarendon Press.

Foster, H., and J. Mclaren, eds. 1995. *Essays in the History of Canadian Law,* vol. VI: *British Columbia and the Yukon.* Toronto: University of Toronto Press.

Foster, H. D., and W. R. D. Sewell. 1981. *Water: The Emerging Crisis in Canada.* Toronto: J. Lorimer.

Frankel, M. M. 1969. *Law of Seashore, Waters and Watercourses, Maine and Massachusetts.* Forge Valley, Massachusetts: Murray Printing [cited in Johnson, 1981].

Freyfogle, E. T. 1989. 'Context and Accommodation in Modern Property Law'. *Standard Law Review* 41: 1529–56.

Gaffney, M. 1968. 'Water Law and Economic Transfers of Water: A Reply', *Journal of Farm Economics* 44: 427–34.

——. 1969. 'Economic Aspects of Water Resource Policy', *American Journal of Economics and Sociology* 28: 131–44.

——. 1992. 'The Taxable Surplus in Water Resources', *Contemporary Policy Issues* 10 (October): 74–82.

Gallob, J. 1991. 'Birth of the North American Environmental Transboundary Plaintiff', *Harvard Environmental Law Review* 1, no. 15: 85–148.

Galloway, R. 1904. *Annals of Coal Mining and the Coal Trade,* 2 vols. Newton Abbot; reprinted David and Charles, 1971.

Gamboa, F. X. de. 1761. *Commentaries on the Mining Ordinances of Spain.* Translated by Richard Heathfield. 1830.

Gates, L. F. 1968a. *Land Policies of Upper Canada.* Toronto: University of Toronto Press.

Gates, P. W. 1968b. *The History of Public Land Law Development.* Washington: Public Land Law Review Commission. Reprinted Washington: Zenger Publishing, 1978.

Gates, W. 1951 and 1969. *Michigan Copper and Boston Dollars: An Economic History of the Michigan Mining Industry.* Cambridge, MA: Harvard; New York: Russell and Russell, 1969.

George, P. 1987. 'Ontario's Mining Industry 1870–1940'. In *Progress without Planning: The Economic History of Ontario from Confederation to the Second World War,* I. M. Drummond, ed. Toronto: University of Toronto Press.

Gerriets, M. 1991. 'The Impact of the General Mining Association (Company on the Nova Scotia Coal Industry, 1826–1850', *Acadiensis* 31, no. 1: 54–84.

Gertenbach, L. P. D. 1962. 'Regulation of the South African West Coast Shoal Fisheries'. In *Economic Effects of Fishery Regulation.* Fisheries Report No. 5. Rome: FAO.

——. 1973. 'License Limitation Regulations: The South African System', *Journal of the Fisheries Research Board of Canada* 30, no. 12: 2077–84.

Gibson, D. 1968–69. 'The Constitutional Context of Canadian Water Planning', *Alberta Law Review* 7: 71–92.

Gibson, T. W. 1933. *The Mining Laws of Ontario and the Department of Mines.* Toronto: Kings Printer.

Gillis, M., and R. Beals et al. 1980. *Tax and Investment Policies for hard Minerals: Public and Multinational Enterprises in Indonesia.* Cambridge, MA: Ballinger.

Gillis, R. P., and T. R. Roach. 1986. 'The American Influence on Conservation in Canada: 1899–1911', *Journal of Forest History* 30, no. 4: 160–74.

Gislason, G. S. 1999. 'From Social Thought to Economic Reality: The First 25 Years of the Lake Winnipeg IQ Management Program'. In R. Shotton, ed. *Use of Property Rights in Fisheries Management.* FAO Fisheries Technical Paper 404/2, pp. 118–26.

Gisser, M., and R. N. Johnson. 1983. 'Institutional Restrictions on the Transfer of a Water Right and the Survival of an Agency'. In T. L. Anderson, ed. *Water Rights: Scarce Resource Allocation, Bureaucracy and the Environment.* Cambridge, MA: Ballinger, for Pacific Institute for Policy Research, pp. 137–66.

Glanville, Ranulf de. 1130–1190. *The Treatise on the Laws and Customs of the Realm of England commonly called Glanvill.* G. D. G. Hall, ed. and trans. Oxford University Press, 1993.

——. 1187. *The Treatise on the Laws and Customs of the Realm of England commonly called Glanvill*, 16th edn. G. D. G. Hall, ed. and trans. Oxford University Press, 1965.

Glick, T. 1972. *The Old World Background to the Irrigation System of San Antonio Texas.* El Paso, TX: Western University Press.

Glicksman, R. L., and G. C. Coggins. 1995. *Modern Public Land Law.* St Paul: West.

Godwin, R. K., and W. B. Shepherd. 1984. 'Forcing Squares, Triangles and Ellipses into a Circular Paradigm: The Use of the Commons Dilemma in Examining the Allocation of Common Resources', *Western Political Quarterly* 32: 265–77.

Goodlad, J. 1999. 'Industry Perspective on Rights-based Fishing: The Shetland Experience'. In R. Shotton, ed. *Use of Property Rights in Fisheries Management.* FAO Fisheries Technical Paper 404/1, pp. 229–34.

Goody, J., T. Thirsk, and E. P. Thompson. 1976. *Family and Inheritance: Rural Society in Western Europe.* New York: Cambridge University Press.

Gordon, H. S. 1951. 'The Trawler Question in the United Kingdom and Canada', *Dalhousie Review* 31: 117–27.

——. 1989. 'Darwin and Political Economy: The Connection Reconsidered', *Journal of the History of Biology* 22, no. 3: 437–59.

Gordon, W. A. 1955. *The Law of Forestry.* London: HMSO.

Gough, B. M. 1988. 'Forests and Sea Power: A Vancouver Island Economy, 1778–1875', *Journal of Forest History* 32, no. 3: 117–24.

Gough, J. W. 1967. *The Mines of Mendip.* New York: Kelley.

Gould, G. A. 1989. 'Transfer of Water Rights', *Natural Resources Journal* 29, no. 2: 457–78.

Grafton, R. Q. 1996. 'Performance of and Prospects for Rights-based Fisheries Management in Atlantic Canada'. In B. L. Crowley, *Taking Ownership: Property Rights and Fishery Management on the Atlantic Coast.* Halifax: Atlantic Institute for Market Studies, pp. 145–81.

Graham, M. 1943. *The Fish Gate.* London: Faber and Faber.

Grainger, M. B. 1950. *Forest Taxation in Europe and New Zealand,* Information Series No. 11. Wellington: New Zealand Forest Service.

Grant, R. 1991. *The Royal Forests of England.* Slough: Allan Sutton.

Gras, N. S. B. 1930. *The Economic and Social History of an English Village.* Cambridge, MA: Harvard University Press.

Gray, E. 1970. *The Great Canadian Oil Patch.* Toronto: Maclean-Hunter.

Gray, L. C. 1913. 'The Economic Possibilities of Conservation', *Quarterly Journal of Economics* 27: 497–519.

Gregory, C. E. 1980. *A Concise History of Mining.* New York: Pergamon.

Gregory, G. R. 1987. *Resource Economics for Foresters.* New York: Wiley.

Gregory, H. E., and K. Barnes. 1939. *North Pacific Fisheries*. New York: Institute of Pacific Relations.

Griffin, R. C., and F. O. Boadu. 1992. 'Water Marketing in Texas: Opportunities for Reform', *Natural Resources Journal* 32, no. 2: 265–88.

Griffith, J. A. G. 1977. *The Politics of the Judiciary*. Manchester: Manchester University Press.

Grunsky, H. W. 1913. *Water Legislation and Administration in British Columbia*. Report of the Minister of Lands. Victoria, BC: British Columbia Ministry of Lands, pp. D117–D125.

Guillet, E. C. 1933. *Early Life in Upper Canada*. Toronto: Ontario Publishing Co.

Gulland, J. A. 1977. *Goals and Objectives of Fishery Management*. Rome: Department of Fisheries, Food and Agricultural Organization of the United Nations.

Habakkuk, H. J. 1950. 'Marriage Settlements in the 18th Century', *Transactions of the Royal Historical Society* 4, no. 32: 15–30.

Hage, W. 1989. *Storm over Rangelands: Private Rights in Federal Lands*. Bellevue, WA: Free Enterprise Press.

Halsbury's Laws of England, 4th edn. 1977. London: Butterworth.

Hammersley, G. 1973. 'The Charcoal Iron Industry and Its Fuel 1540–1750', *Economic History Review* 26: 593.

Hannesson, R., and S. I. Steinshamn. 1991. 'How to Set Catch Quotas: Constant Effort or Constant Catch?', *Journal of Environmental Economics and Management* 20: 71–91.

Hansing, J., and S. Wibe. 1992. 'Rationing the Supply of Timber: The Swedish Experience'. In P. N. Nemetz, ed., *Emerging Issues in Forest Policy*. Vancouver: University of British Columbia Press, pp. 157–70.

Hardin, G.'The Tragedy of the Commons', *Science*, 162: 1243–1248.

Hardwicke, R. E. 1935. 'The Rule of Capture and its Implications as Applied to Oil and Gas', *Texas Law Review* 13: 391.

Harper-Fender, A. 1981. 'Managing the Use of a Common Resource: the Crees of Saskatchewan', *Journal of Economic History* 41: 163–70.

Harris, J. R. 1964. *The Copper King: A Biography of Thomas Williams of Llanidan*. Liverpool: Liverpool University Press.

——. 1988. *The British Iron Industry 1700–1850*. London: Macmillan.

Harris, M. 1953. *Origin of the Land Tenure System in the United States*. Ames: Iowa State College Press.

Harris, R. C. 1968. *The Seigneurial System in Early Canada: A Geographical Study*. Madison: University of Wisconsin Press/Québec: Les presses de l'université Laval.

Harris, R. C., and J. Warkentin. 1974. *Canada Before Confederation*. New York, Toronto and New York: Oxford.

Hart, J. F. 1998. 'Property Rights, Costs and Welfare: Delaware Water Mill Bill Legislation 1719–1859', *Journal of Legal Studies* 27, no. I: 455–71.

Hartwick, J., and N. Olewiler. 1986. *The Economics of Natural Resource Use*. New York: Harper and Row.

Harvey, P. D. A. 1965. A Medieval Oxford Village: Cuxham, 1240 to 1400. London: Oxford University Press.

Hatcher, J. 1973. *English Tin Production and Trade before 1550*. Oxford: Clarendon Press.

——. 1993. Before 1700: Towards the Age of Coal. Vol. 1 of The History of the British Coal Industry. Oxford: Clarendon Press.

Hayek, F. A. 1960. *The Constitution of Liberty*. Chicago: University of Chicago Press.

Hays, S. 1959. *Conservation and the Gospel of Efficiency, 1890–1920*. Cambridge: Harvard University Press.

Healey, H. H. 1955. 'Rights of Mineral Owners in Surface', *Rocky Mountain Mineral Law Institute* 1: 85.

Healy, J. F. 1978. Mining and Metallurgy in the Greek and Roman World. London: Thames and Hudson.

Heaps, T., and J. H. Helliwell. 1985. 'The Taxation of Natural Resources'. In A. J. Auerbach and M. Feldstein, eds. *Handbook of Public Economics*, vol. 1. Amsterdam: North-Holland.

Heaton, H. 1936. *Economic History of Europe*. New York: Harper.

Heizer, S. 1999. 'The Commercial Geoduck Fishery in British Columbia'. In R. Shotton, ed. *Use of Property Rights in Fisheries Management*. FAO Fisheries Technical Paper 404/2, p. 228.

Hendricks, K. 1992. 'Joint Bidding in Federal O. C. S. Auctions', *American Economic Review Papers and Proceedings* 82: 506–11.

Herbert, P. A. 1922. 'Standing Timber Insurance', *The Timberman p. 122* (Cornell U. Forestry Thesis).

Herfindahl, O. C. 1959. *Copper Costs and Prices: 1870–1957*. Baltimore, MD: Johns Hopkins Press for Resources for the Future.

Herskovits, M. J. 1952. *Economic Anthropology: A Study in Comparative Economics*. New York: Norton. Originally published in 1940 as *The Economic Life of Primitive Peoples*.

Hey, D. 1986. *Yorkshire from A.D. 1000*. London, New York: Longman.

Higgs, R. 1982. 'Legally Induced Technical Regress in the Washington Salmon Fishery', *Research in Economic History* 7: 55–86.

Hill, A. V. 1967. *Tides of Change: A Story of Fishermen's Cooperatives in British Columbia*. Prince Rupert, BC: Prince Rupert Fishermen's Co-operative Association.

Hill, C. 1975. *Pelican Economic History of Britain*. Vol. 2, *1530–1780: Reformation to Industrial Revolution*. London: Penguin Books.

Hill-Manetas, L. 1983. 'The Destruction of Sustained-Yield Woodsmanship on Loughton Manor'. In H. K. Steen, ed., *History of Sustained-Yield Forestry*. Portland, OR: Forest History Society, 392–400.

Hilton, R. 1966. *Medieval Society: The West Midlands at the End of the Thirteenth Century*. London: Weidenfeld and Nicolson.

Hirshleifer, J., J. DeHaven, and J. Milliman. 1960. *Water Supply: Economics, Technology and Policy*. Chicago: University of Chicago Press.

Hodgins, B. W., and J. Benidickson. 1989. *The Temagami Experience—Recreation, Resources and Aboriginal Rights in the Northern Ontario Wilderness*. Toronto: University of Toronto Press.

Holbrook, S. H. 1943. *Burning an Empire, the Story of American Forest Fires*. New York: the Macmillan Co.

Holleman, P. D. 1984–85. *Law of Federal Gas Leases*, Vol. 1. Rocky Mountain Mineral Law Foundation.

Holt, J. C. 1992. *Magna Carta*, 2nd edn. Cambridge: Cambridge University Press.

Holt, R. A. 1988. *The Mills of Medieval England*. Oxford: Blackwell [Raftis].

Honoré, A. 1987. *Making Law Bind*. Oxford: Oxford University Press.

Horwitz, M. J. 1977. *The Transformation of American Law 1780–1860*. Cambridge, MA: Harvard University Press.

Hough, F. 1882. *Elements of Forestry*. Cincinnati: R. Clarke and Co.

Howarth, W. 1990. *The Law of Aquaculture: The Law Relating to the Farming of Fish and Shellfish in Great Britain*. Oxford and London: Fishing News Books.

——. 1987. *Freshwater Fishery Law*. London: Financial Training Publications.

Howay, F. W., and E. O. S. Scholefield. 1914. *British Columbia*, Vol. 2 by F. W. Howay. Vancouver: S. J. Clarke.

Howe, C. W., C. Boggs, and P. Butler. 1990. 'Transaction Costs as Determinants of Water Transfers', *Colorado Law Review* 61: 393–405.

Huber, P. B. 1985. *Promoting Timber Cropping: Policies Toward Non-Industrial Forest Owners in New Brunswick*. Montreal: Institute for Research in Public Policy.

Huffaker, R. G., N. K. Whittlesey, and J. Hamilton. 2000. 'The Role of Prior Appropriation in Allocating Water Resources into the 21st Century', *International Journal of Water Resources Development* June 2000: 265–73.

Hughes, E. 1965. *North Country Life in the Eighteenth Century*, 2 vols. London: Oxford University Press.

Hughes, M. 1963. 'Lead, Land and Coal as Sources of Landlord Income in Northumberland Between 1700 and 1850'. Ph.D. thesis, University of Durham.

Hughes, R. 1987. *The Fatal Shore*. New York: Knopf.

Hunt, C. D. 1989. *The Offshore Petroleum Regimes of Canada and Australia*. Calgary: Canadian Institute of Resources Law, University of Calgary.

Huppert, Daniel D. 1982. 'Living Marine Resources'. In Gardner M. Brown Jr. and James A. Crutchfield, eds. *Economics of Ocean Resources: A Research Agenda*. Seattle: University of Washington Press, pp. 44–6.

Hutchins, W. A. 1928. 'The Community Acequia: Its Origins and Development', *Southwest Historical Quarterly* 31: 261.

——. 1957. 'The Common Law Riparian Doctrine in Oregon Legislative and Judicial Modification', *Oregon Law Review* 36: 193–220.

——. 1971. *Water Rights Laws in the Nineteen Western States*. Vol. 1. Washington, DC: United States Department of Agriculture.

Hyde, William F. 1992. 'Social Forestry: A Working Definition and 21 Testable Hypotheses'. In P. N. Nemetz, ed. *Emerging Issues in Forest Policy*. Vancouver: University of British Columbia Press, pp. 431–52.

Ickes, H. L. 1953. *The Secret Diary of Harold L. Ickes*. New York: Simon and Schuster.

Innis, H. A. 1936. 'Settlement and the Mining Frontier'. In *Canadian Frontiers of Settlement*, vol. 9, part II. Toronto: Macmillan, pp. 171–413.

——. 1954. *The Cod Fisheries: The History of an International Economy*, revised edn. Toronto: University of Toronto Press.

——. 1955. *Empire and Communications*. Toronto: University of Toronto Press.

Isay, R. 1933. 'Mining Law', *Encyclopaedia of the Social Sciences*, Vol. IX–X: 513–18. New York: Macmillan.

Ise, J. 1920. *The United States Forest Policy*. New Haven: Yale University Press.

——. 1926. *The United States Oil Policy*. New Haven: Yale University Press.

Jackson, R. V. 1977. *Australian Economic Development in the Nineteenth Century*. Canberra: Australian National University Press.

Jacoby, N. 1974. *Multinational Oil: A Study in Industrial Dynamics*. New York: Macmillan.

James, N. D. G. 1981. *A History of English Forestry*. Oxford: Basil Blackwell.

Jamieson, S. M., and P. Gladstone. 1950. 'Unionism in the Fishing Industry of British Columbia', *Canadian Journal of Economics and Political Science* 16, no. 1: 4–11.

Jenkins, J. G. 1974. *Nets and Coracles*. Newton Abbot: David and Charles.

Jessup, T. C., and N. L. Peluso. 1986. 'Minor Forest Products as Common-Property Resources in East Kalimantan, Indonesia'. In US National Research Council, Common-Property Resource Management. Washington.

Johannes, R. E. 1978. 'Traditional Marine Conservation Methods in Oceania and Their Demise', *Annual Review of Ecological Systems* 9: 349–64.

Johannsson, P. O., and K. G. Lofgren, 1985. *The Economics of Forestry and Natural Resources*. New York and Oxford: Basil Blackwell.

Johnsen, D. B. 1986. 'The Formation and Protection of Property Rights Among Southern Kwakiutl Indians', *Journal of Legal Studies* 15, no. 1: 41–68.

Johnson, N. K., and C. T. DuMars. 1989. 'A Survey of the Evolution of Western Water Law in Response to Changing Economic and Public Interest Demands', *Natural Resources Journal* 29: 347–89.

Johnson, R. N. 1999. 'Rents and Taxes in an ITQ Fishery'. In R. Arnason and H. H. Gissurarson, eds. *Individual Transferable Quotas in Theory and Practice*. Reykjavik: University of Iceland Press, pp. 205–16.

Johnson, R. N., and G. D. Libecap. 1982. 'Contracting Problems and Regulation: The Case of the Fishery', *American Economic Review* 72, no. 5: 1005–22.

Johnson, R. N., M. Gisser, and M. Werner. 1981. 'The Definition of a Surface Water Right and Transferability', *Journal of Law and Economics* 24, no. 2: 273–88.

Johnson, V. W., and R. Barlowe. 1954. *Land Problems and Policies*. New York: McGraw Hill.

Joncas, L.-Z. 1883. *The Fisheries of Canada*. Ottawa: Canada Department of Agriculture; London: W. Clowes.

Jones, R. A., P. Pearse, and A. D. Scott. 1980. 'Conditions for Cooperation on Joint Projects by Independent Jurisdictions', *Canadian Journal of Economics* 12, no. 2: 231–49.

Junger, P. D. 1958. 'The Wyoming Oil and Gas Conservation Act: Private Rights and Public Policy', *Wyoming Law Journal* 13, no. 1: 3.

Karsten, P. 1998. 'Cows in the Corn, Pigs in the Garden, and the "Problem of Social Costs:" "High" and "Low" Legal Cultures in the British Diaspora Lands in the 17th, 18th and 19th Centuries', *Law and Society Review* 32: 1.

Kawashima, Y., and R. Tone. 1983. 'Environmental Policy in Early America: A Survey of Colonial Statutes', *Journal of Forest History* 27, no. 4: 168–89.

Kent, J. 1828–1896. *Commentaries on American Law*, 4 vols., various editions; reprinted New York: O. Halsted, 1997–2002.

Kerridge, E. 1969. *Agrarian Problems in the Sixteenth Century and After*. London; New York: Allen and Unwin.

Kidd, Scott. 2006. 'Keeping Public Resources in Public Hands: Advancing the Public Trust Doctrine in Canada', *Journal of Environmental Law and Practice* 16, 2, pp. 187–207.

Kinney, J. P. 1916. 'Forest Legislation in America Prior to March 4, 1789', Bulletin 370 of the Agricultural Experiment Station, Cornell University, in *Use and Abuse of America's Natural Resources*, Stuart Burchey, ed. New York: Arno Press, 1972.

——. 1917. *The Essentials of American Timber Law*. New York: Wiley.

Knack, S. 1996. 'Institutions and the Convergence Hypothesis: The Cross-National Evidence', *Public Choice* 87: 207–28.

Kuntz, E. 1962. *Treatise on Law of Oil and Gas*, 2 vols. Cincinnati: Anderson.

La Croix, S. J. 1992. 'Property Rights and Institutional Change During Australia's Gold Rush', *Explorations in Economic History* 29: 204–27.

Lacasse, J.-P. 1976. *Le claim en droit québécois*. Ottawa: University of Ottawa Press.

——. 1985. *Le Droit Minier* series 'Titres Immobiliers' Document 6c. Quebec: Chamber of Notaries.

Lake, J. A. 1962. *Law and Mineral Wealth: The Legal Profile of the Wisconsin Mining Industry*. Madison: University of Wisconsin Press.

Lambert, R. S., and P. Pross. 1967. *Renewing Nature's Wealth: A Centennial History of Public Management of Lands, Forests and Wildlife in Ontario, 1763–1967*. Toronto: Government of Ontario.

Lambert, S. 1971. *Bills and Acts: Legislative Procedure in Eighteenth-Century England*. Cambridge: Cambridge University Press.

Landes, W. M., and R. Posner. 1987. *The Economic Structure of Tort Law*. Cambridge: Harvard University Press.

Lang, A. G., and M. Crommelin. 1979. *Australian Mining and Petroleum Laws*. Melbourne: Butterworths.

Langdon, J. 1991. 'Watermills and Windmills in the West Midlands, 1086–1500', *The Economic History Review* 44, no. 3: 424–44.

Langford, P. 1989. A Polite and Commercial People: England 1727–1783. Oxford: Clarendon Press.

Lauer, T. E. 1958. 'The Riparian Law as Property'. In D. B. King, T. E. Lauer, and W. L. Zieglar, *Water Resources and the Law*. Ann Arbor, MI: University of Michigan, pp. 533–614.

——. 1963. 'The Common Law Background of the Riparian System', *Missouri Law Review* 28, no. 60: 60–107.

——. 1970. 'Reflections on Riparianism', *Missouri Law Review* 35: 1–25.

Lawson, F. H., and B. Rudden. 1982. *The Law of Property*, 2nd edn. Oxford: Oxford University Press.

Le Bourdais, D. M. 1957. *Metals and Men*. Toronto: McClelland and Stewart.

Leal, D. 1996. 'Community-run Fisheries: Preventing the Tragedy of the Commons'. In B. L. Crowley, ed. *Taking Ownership: Property Rights and Fishery Management on the Atlantic Coast*. Halifax: Atlantic Institute for Market Studies, pp. 183–220.

Léger, R. 1992. 'L'impact de l'industrie du bois sur le territoire et la main-d'oeuvre de la Péninsule acadienne, Nouveau-Brunswick, 1875–1900'. In L. Anders Sandberg, ed. *Trouble in the Woods: Forest Policy and Social Conflict in Nova Scotia and New Brunswick*. Fredericton, NB: Acadiensis Press, p. 28.

Leshy, J. D. 1987. *The Mining Law: A Study in Perpetual Motion*. Washington, DC: Resources for the Future.

Lewin, J. L. 1990. 'The Silent Revolution in West Virginia's Law of Nuisance', *West Virginia Law Review* 92: 235–353.

Lewin, T. 1931. 'The History of Government Property in Minerals in the United States', *St. Louis Law Review* 16: 245–52.

Lewis, G. R. 1907. *The Stannaries: A Study of the English Tin Miner*. Cambridge, MA: Harvard University Press.

Libecap, G. D. 1978. *The Evolution of Private Mineral Rights: Nevada's Comstock Lode*. New York: Arno Press.

——. 1979. 'Government Support of Private Claims to Public Minerals: The Case of Western Mineral Rights', *Business History Review* 53: 364–85.

——. 1989. *Contracting for Property Rights* Cambridge: Cambridge University Press.

Libecap, G. D., and R. N. Johnson. 1979. 'Property Rights, Nineteenth-Century Federal Timber Policy and the Conservation Movement', *Journal of Economic History* 39: 129–42.

Libecap, G. D., and J. L. Smith. 2004. 'Political Constraints on Government Cartelization: The Case of Oil Production Regulation in Texas and Saudi Arabia'. In *How Cartels Endure and How they Fail: Studies of Industrial Collusion,* 2004, pp. 196–223, Cheltenham, UK and Northampton, MA.: Elgar.

Libecap, G. D., and S. N. Wiggins. 1984. 'Contractual Responses to the Common Pool: Prorationing of Crude Oil Production', *American Economic Review* 74, no. 1: 97–108.

Liew, D. S. K. 1999. 'Measurement of Concentration in Canada's Soctia-Fundy Inshore Groundfish Industry'. In R. Shotton, ed. *Use of Property Rights in Fisheries Management.* FAO Fisheries Technical Paper 404/2, pp. 279–87.

Lilburn, B. 1986. 'Management of Australian Fisheries: Broad Developments and Alternative Strategies'. Canberra: Australian Fisheries Service, Department of Primary Industry. Mimeo.

Lillard, R. G. 1947. *The Great Forest.* New York: Knopf.

Lindley, C. H. 1914. *A Treatise on the American Law Relating to Mines and Mineral Lands,* 3rd edn. San Francisco: Bancroft-Whitney.

Lindner, R. K., H. F. Campbell, and G. F. Bevin. 1990. 'Rent Generation during the Transition to a Managed Fishery: The Case of the New Zealand ITQ System'. Typescript. Wellington: New Zealand Fishing Industry Board.

Lounsbury, R. G. 1934. *The British Fishery At Newfoundland: 1634–1763.* New Haven: Yale University Press.

Lovejoy, W. F., and P. T. Homan. 1967. *Economic Aspects of Oil Conservation Regulation.* Baltimore, MD: Johns Hopkins.

Lowe, J. S. 1983. Oil and Gas Law in a Nutshell. St. Paul, MN: West Publishing Co.

Lower, A. R. M. 1933. 'The Trade in Square Timber', *Contributions to Canadian Economics* 6.

——. 1936. 'Settlement and the Forest Frontier in Eastern Canada'. In W. A. Mackintosh and W. L. G. Joerg, eds. *Canadian Frontiers of Settlements,* vol. IX. Toronto: Macmillan. Reprinted Millwood, NY: Kraus Reprint Co., 1974.

——. 1938. *The North American Assault on the Canadian Forest.* Toronto: Ryerson.

——. 1973. *Great Britain's Woodyard: British America and the Timber Trade.* Montreal: McGill-Queen's University Press.

Lucas, A. R. 1990. *Security of Title in Canadian Water Rights.* Calgary: Canadian Institute of Resources Law.

Lucas, A. R. and C. D. Hunt. 1990. Oil and Gas Law in Canada. Toronto: Carswell.

Lucas, C. P., ed. 1912. *Lord Durham's Report on the Affairs of British North America.* Oxford: Clarendon Press.

Luckert, M. K. 1990. 'The Perceived Security of Institutional Investment Environments of Some British Columbia Forest Tenures', *Canadian Journal of Forest Research* 37, no. 5: 1441–62.

——. 1991. *Tenures for Mixed Wood Management: A Framework for Policy Analysis.* Working Paper No. 164. Vancouver: University of British Columbia Forest Economics and Policy Analysis Research Unit.

Luckert, M. K., and D. Haley. 1989. *Funding Mechanisms for Silviculture on Crown Land; Status, Problems and Recommendations for British Columbia.* Working Paper no. 131-A. Vancouver: Forest Economics and Policy Analysis Research Unit, University of British Columbia.

——. 1990. 'The Implications of Various Silvicultural Funding Arrangements for Privately Managed Public Forest Land in Canada', *New Forests* 4: 1–12.

Lueck, D. 1989. 'The Economic Nature of Wildlife Law', *Journal of Legal Studies* 18, no. 2: 291–324.

——. 1994. 'Common Property as an Egalitarian Share Contract', *Journal of Economic Behavior and Organisation* 25, no. 1: 93–108.

Lund, T. A. 1980. *American Wildlife Law.* Berkeley: University of California Press.

Lyons, C. 1969. *Salmon: Our Heritage.* Vancouver: British Columbia Packers Ltd.

Maass, A., and H. B. Zobel. 1960. 'Anglo-American Water Law: Who Appropriated the Riparian Doctrine?', *Public Policy* 10: 109–56.

Maass, A., and R. L. Anderson. 1978. *... And the Desert Shall Rejoice.* Cambridge, MA: MIT Press.

Macaulay, T. B. 1885. *History of England.* New York: W. L. Allison.

Macfarlane, A. 1978. *The Origins of English Individualism: The Family, Property and Social Transition.* Oxford: Basil Blackwell.

Macgillivray, P. 1997. 'Individual Vessel Quotas in the Halibut Fishery of British Columbia'. In Laura Jones and Michael Walker, eds. *Fish or Cut Bait!* Vancouver: The Fraser Institute.

MacGrady, G. J. 1975. 'The Navigability Concept in the Civil and Common Law: Historical Development, Current Importance, and Some Doctrines that Don't Hold Water', *Florida State University Law Review* 3, no. 4: 511–615.

Macpherson, C. B. 1962. *The Political Theory of Possessive Individualism: Hobbes to Locke.* Oxford: Clarendon Press.

MacSwinney, R. F. 1907. *The Law of Mines, Quarries, and Minerals*, 3rd edn. London: Sweet and Maxwell.

——. 1912. *The Law of Mines, Quarries, and Minerals*, 4th edn. London: Sweet and Maxwell.

Mahood, I., and K. Drushka. 1990. *Three Men and a Forester.* Vancouver, BC: Harbour Publishing.

Main, O. W. 1955. *The Canadian Nickel Industry.* Toronto: University of Toronto Press.

Maitland, F. W. 1886. 'The Mystery of Seisin', *Law Quarterly Review* 2: 481–96.

——. 1907 and 1975. *Domesday Book and Beyond* (reprint). London: Collins Fontana.

——. 1909. *The Forms of Action at Common Law: A Course of Lectures.* Cambridge University Press.

——. 1911. *The Constitutional History of England.* Cambridge: Cambridge University Press.

Major, P. 1999. 'The Evolution of ITQs in New Zealand'. In R. Arnason and H. H. Gissurarson, eds. *Individual Transferable Quotas in Theory and Practice.* Reykjavik: University of Iceland Press, pp. 81–102.

Mann, F. A. 1959. 'Outlines of a History of Expropriation', *Law Quarterly Review* 75: 188–219.

Mann, John F., and Melvin Blevins. 1986. 'Groundwater Management in the San Fernando Valley Basin'. Paper presented at the Annual Meeting of the Cordilleran Section of the Geological Society of America. Los Angeles, California.

Marceau, N., and G. Myers. 2005. 'On the Early Holocene: Foraging to Early Agriculture', WP 05-02 Montreal, CIRPE'E, University of Quebec at Montreal.

Marglin, S. A. 1963. 'The Social Rate of Discount and the Optimal Rate of Investment', *Quarterly Journal of Economics* 71: 95–112.

Marshall, A. 1920. *Principles of Economics*, 8th edn. London: Macmillan; reprinted 1949.

Martin, J. 1991. 'Water Law and Economic Power', *Virginia Law Review* 77: 397–426.

Mathias, P., and J. A. Davis, eds. 1989 and 1990. *The First Industrial Revolutions*. Oxford, 1989 and Cambridge, MA: Basil Blackwell, 1990.

Matthiasson, T. 1999. 'The Icelandic Debate on Fisheries Management and Resource Rent Distribution'. In R. Arnason and H. H. Gissurarson, eds. *Individual Transferable Quotas in Theory and Practice*. Reykjavik: University of Iceland Press, pp. 185–204.

Mattei, U., and F. Pulitini. 1991. 'A Competitive Model of Legal Rules'. In A. Breton et al., eds. *The Competitive State*. Dordrecht: Kluwer.

Matthews, R. C. O. 1986. 'The Economics of Institutions and the Sources of Growth', *Economic Journal* 96: 903–18.

Mayer, C. J., and G. A. Riley. 1985. *Public Domain, Private Dominion: A History of Public Mineral Policy in America*. San Francisco: Sierra Club Books.

Mayhead, G. J. 1990. 'Fire Protection in Great Britain', *Commonwealth Forestry Review* 69: 21–7.

McCalla, D. 1993. *Planting the Province: The Economic History of Upper Canada 1784–1870*. Toronto: University of Toronto Press.

McClurg, T. 1997. 'Bureaucratic Management versus Private Property: ITQs in New Zealand after 10 Years'. In L. Jones and M. Walker, eds. 1997. *Fish or Cut Bait*. Vancouver: Fraser Institute.

McDonald, S. L. 1971. *Petroleum Conservation in the United States: An Economic Analysis*. Baltimore, MD: Johns Hopkins.

——. 1979. *Leasing of Federal Lands for Fossil Fuel Production*. Baltimore, MD: Johns Hopkins.

McDonnell, J. 1981. *Inland Fisheries in Medieval Yorkshire 1066–1300*. York: University of York, Borthwick Institute of Historical Research.

McDougal, M. S., and W. T. Burke. 1962. *The Public Order of the Oceans*. New Haven: Yale University Press.

McEvoy, A. F. 1986. *The Fisherman's Problem: Ecology and Law in the California Fisheries, 1850–1980*. Cambridge: Cambridge University Press.

McIlgorm, A., and M. Tsamenyi. 1999. 'Rights based Fisheries Development in Australia: Has It Stalled?' In R. Shotton, ed. *Use of Property Rights in Fisheries Management*. FAO Fisheries Technical Paper 404/2, pp. 148–54.

McKechnie, W. S. 1913. *Magna Carta: A Commentary on the Great Charter of King John*, 2nd edn. New York: Burt Franklin; reprinted 1958.

McLaren, J. P. S. 1983. 'Nuisance Law and the Industrial Revolution: Some Lessons from Social History'. In F. M. Steel and S. Rodgers-Hasnet, eds. *Issues in Tort Law*. Toronto: Carswell.

McManus, J. C. 1975. 'The Costs of Alternative Economic Organization', *Canadian Journal of Economics* 8, no. 3: 334–50.

McMurran, J. 1999. 'Property Rights and Recreational Fishing: Never the Twain Shall Meet?' In R. Shotton, ed. *Use of Property Rights in Fisheries Management*. FAO Fisheries Technical Paper 404/2, pp. 184–7.

McPherson, J. L., and O. E. Owens. 1977. 'Mineral Leasing in a Private Enterprise System'. In M. Crommelin and A. R. Thompson, eds. *Mineral Leasing as an Instrument of Public Policy*. Vancouver: University of British Columbia Press.

Mead, W. J. 1977. 'Cash Bonus Bidding for Mineral Resources'. In Crommelin and Thompson, eds. pp. 46–60.

Mead, W. J. et al. 1985. *Offshore Lands: Oil and Gas Leasing and Conservation on the Outer Continetal Shelf.* San Francisco: Pacific Institute for Public Policy Research.

Mead, W. R. 1958. *An Economic Geography of the Scandinavian States and Finland.* London: University of London Press.

Mead, Walter J., and W. McKillop, eds. 1976. *Timber Policy Issues in British Columbia.* Vancouver: University of British Columbia Press.

Meany, T. F. 1979. 'Limited Entry in the Western Australian Rock Lobster and Prawn Fisheries: An Economic Evaluation'. In P. H. Pearse, ed. Symposium on Policies for Economic Rationalization of Commercial Fisheries. *Journal of Fisheries Research Board of Canada*, pp. 789–98.

Megarry, R. W., and H. W. R. Wade. 1966. *The Law of Real Property*, 3rd edn. London: Stevens.

——. 1984. *The Law of Real Property*, 5th edn. London: Stevens and Sons.

Merrill, M. 1940. *Covenants Implied in Oil and Gas Leases*, 2nd edn. St. Louis: Thomas.

Meyer, M. C. 1984. *Water in the Hispanic Southwest: A Social and Legal History 1550–1850.* Tucson, AZ: University of Arizona Press.

Meyers, C. J., and A. D. Tarlock. 1980. *Water Resource Management*, 2nd edn. Mineola, NY: Foundation Press.

Mikesell, R. F. 1979. *The World Copper Industry. Structure and Economic Analysis.* Baltimore, MD: Johns Hopkins.

Miles, E., and L. Geselbracht. 1987. 'Fisheries and Conflicting Uses of the Sea'. In G. Ulfstein et al., eds. *The Regulation of Fisheries: Legal, Economic and Social Aspects.* Strasbourg: Council of Europe, pp. 149–78.

Milgrom, P., and J. Roberts. 1992. *Economics, Organisation and Management.* Englewood Cliffs: Prentice Hall.

Miller, C. 1991. 'The Russians are Coming!' *Journal of Forestry* 89, no. 3: 23–7, 42.

Millward, R., and A. Robinson. 1975. *The Peak District.* London: Eyre Methuen.

Milsom, S. F. C. 1976. *Legal Framework of English Feudalism.* London: Cambridge University Press.

Mitchell, D. L. 1991. *Using Water Better: A Market Based Approach to California's Water Crisis.* San Francisco: Bay Area Economic Forum.

——. 1993. Water Marketing in California: Resolving Third-Party Impact Issues. San Francisco: Bay Area Economic Forum.

Mitchell, B. R. 1984. *Economic Development of the British Coal Industry 1800–1914.* Cambridge: Cambridge University Press.

Mollat du Jourdin, Michel. 1993. *Europe and the Sea*, trans. Teresa Lavendar Fagan. Oxford: Blackwell.

Moloney, D. G., and P. H. Pearse. 1979. 'Quantitative Rights as an Instrument for Regulating Commercial Fisheries', *Journal of the Fisheries Research Board of Canada* 36: 859–66.

Moore, A. M. 1958. *Forestry Timber and Taxes in Canada.* Tax Paper No. 11. Toronto: Canadian Tax Foundation.

Moore, S. A., and H. S. Moore. 1903. *The History and Law of Fisheries.* London: Stevens and Haynes.

Morrell, W. P. 1941 and 1968. *The Gold Rushes*, 2nd edn. 1968. London: Adam and Charles Black.

Moss, K. N. 1924. '"Mining Leases" in Mining Association of Great Britain', *Historical Review of Coal Mining*. London: Fleetway.

Munro, G., with A. D. Scott. 1985. 'The Economics of Fishery Management'. In A. V. Kneese and J. L. Sweeney, eds. *Handbook of Natural Resource and Energy Economics*. Amsterdam: North-Holland, pp. 623–75.

Munro, G. R., and P. A. Neher. 1995. 'Institutional Changes and the Management of British Columbia Fisheries'. In A. D. Scott et al., *Managing Natural Resources in British Columbia*. Vancouver: University of British Columbia Press, pp. 80–94.

Murphy, E. F. 1961. 'A Short Course on Water Law for the Eastern United States', *Washington University Law Quarterly* 2: 109–14.

Needler, A. W. H. 1979. 'Evolution of Canadian Fisheries Management'. In P. H. Pearse, ed. Symposium on Policies for Economic Rationalization of Commercial Fisheries. *Journal of Fisheries Research Board of Canada*, pp. 716–24.

Nef, J. 1932 and 1966. *The Rise of the British Coal Industry*, 2 vols. London: Routledge. Reprinted London: Frank Cass; and Hamden, CT: Archon, 1966.

——. 1952 and 1987. 'Mining and Metallurgy in Medieval Civilisation'. Vol. II, Ch. X of the *Cambridge Economic History of Europe*, M. M. Postan and Edward Miller, eds. Cambridge University Press, 2nd edn. 1987.

——. 1964. *The Conquest of the Material World*. Chicago, IL: University of Chicago Press.

Neher, P., R. Arnason, and N. Mollett, eds. 1989. *Rights Based Fishing*. Dordrecht: Kluwer.

Nelles, H. V. 1974. *The Politics of Development—Forests, Mines and Hydro-Electric Power in Ontario 1849–1941*. Toronto: Macmillan.

Nelson, J. G., and R. C. Scace, eds. 1970. *Canadian National Parks: Today and Tomorrow*. Montreal: Harvest House.

Nelson, R. H. 1986. 'Private Rights to Government Actions: How Modern Property Rights Evolve', *University of Illinois Law Review* 2: 361–86.

Nemetz, P. N., ed. 1992. *Emerging Issues in Forest Policy*. Vancouver: University of British Columbia Press.

Netting, R. 1976. 'What Alpine Peasants Have in Common: Observation of Communal Tenure in a Swiss Village', *Human Ecology* 4: 135–46.

New Zealand. 1992. *Sustainable Fisheries: Tiakiana Nga Taonga a Tangaroa*. Report of the Fisheries Task Force. Wellington: Department of Agriculture and Fisheries.

Newell, D. 1986. *Technology on the Frontier: Mining in Old Ontario*. Vancouver: UBC Press.

Nisbet, J. 1909. *Our Forests and Woodlands*. London: J. M. Dent.

North, D. C. 1990. *Institutions, Institutional Change, and Economic Performance*. Cambridge: Cambridge University Press.

North, D. C., and R. Thomas. 1977. 'The First Economic Revolution', *Economic History Review* 30, no. 2: 229–41.

Nunn, S. C. 1985. 'The Political Economy of Institutional Change: A Distribution Criterion for Acceptance of Groundwater Rules', *Natural Resources Journal* 25: 867–91.

Offer, A. 1981. *Property and Politics, 1870–1914: Landownership, Law, Ideology and Urban Development in England*. Cambridge: Cambridge University Press.

Olson, M. Jr. 1965. *Logic of Collective Action; Public Goods and the Theory of Groups*. Cambridge: Harvard University Press.

Ontario Committee on Taxation. 1967. *Report*, Vol. 3, Chapter 32: 'Revenue from Mines', pp. 303–48.

Ontario. 1947. *Report of the Royal Commission on Forestry* (Kennedy Report). Toronto: Kings' Printer.

Oosterhoff, A. H., and W. B. Rayner et. al. 1985. *Anger and Honsberger Law of Real Property*, 2nd edn. Aurora, ON: Canada Law Books.

Ormsby, M. A. 1958. *British Colombia: A History*. Toronto: Macmillan.

Ostrom, E. 1988. 'Institutional Arrangements and the Commons Dilemma'. In Vincent Ostrom, David Feeny, and Hartmut Picht, eds. *Rethinking Institutional Analysis and Development: Issues, Alternatives and Choices*. San Francisco: International Center for Economic Growth.

Ostrom, E. 1990. *Governing the Commons: The Evolution of Institutions for Collective Action*, rev. edn. New York: Cambridge University Press.

Ostrom, V., D. Feeny, and H. Picht, eds. 1988. *Rethinking Institutional Analysis and Development: Issues, Alternatives, and Choices*. San Francisco: International Center for Economic Growth.

Ouellet, F. 1980. *Economic and Social History of Quebec, 1760–1850: Structures and Conjonctures*. Ottawa: Carleton University Press.

Page, Francis M. 1934. *The Estates of Crowland Abbey: A Study in Manorial Organisation*. Cambridge: Cambridge University Press.

Parriot, J. D. 1956. 'Mining Rights in Public Lands', *Texas Law Review* 34, no. 4: 892–908.

Paterson, D. G. 1976. *British Direct Investment in Canada, 1890–1914*. Toronto: University of Toronto Press.

——. 1977. 'The North Pacific Seal Hunt, 1886–1910: Rights and Regulations', *Explorations in Economic History* 14, no. 2: 97–119.

Paterson, D. G., and J. E. Wilen. 1977. 'Depletion and Diplomacy: The North Pacific Seal Hunt, 1880–1910'. In Usleding, Paul, ed. 1977. *Research in Economic History*. Greenwich, Conn.: J.A.I. Press.

Paterson, J. 1863. *Fishery Laws of the United Kingdom*. London and Cambridge.

Payne, R. L. 1994. 'A Glance Into the Future of the World Canned Tuna Trade', *Marine Policy* 18, no. 5: 407–21.

Pearse, P. H. 1976. *Timber rights and Forest Policy in British Columbia*. Report of the Royal Commission on Forest Resources, 2 vols. Victoria, BC: Queen's Printer.

——. 1979. 'Property Rights and the Regulation of Commercial Fisheries'. Vancouver: University of British Columbia Economics Department Resources Paper No. 42.

——. 1982. *Turning the Tide: A New Policy for Canada's Pacific Fisheries*. Final Report of the Commission on Pacific Fisheries Policy. Vancouver: Canada Department of Fisheries and Oceans.

——. 1990. *Introduction to Forestry Economics*. Vancouver: University of British Columbia Press.

——. 1991. *Building on Progress: Fisheries Policy Development in New Zealand*. Wellington: Ministry of Agriculture and Fisheries.

Pearse, P. H., A. V. Backman, and E. L. Young. 1974. *Crown Charges for Early Timber Rights—First Report of the British Columbia Task Force on Crown Timber Disposal*. Victoria: B.C. Forest Service.

Pearse, P. H., and J. E. Wilen. 1979. 'Impact of Canada's Pacific Salmon Fleet Control Program', *Journal of Fisheries Research Board of Canada* 36, no. 7: 765–9.

Pennington, R. R. 1973. *Stannary Law: A History of the Mining Law of Cornwall and Devon*. Newton Abbot: David and Charles.

Percy, D. R. 1988. *The Framework of Water Rights Legislation in Canada*. Canadian Institute of Resources Law, University of Calgary Faculty of Law, Calgary.

Perry, J. H. 1955. *Taxes, Tariffs and Subsidies: A History of Canadian Fiscal Development*, 2 vols. Toronto: University of Toronto Press.

——. 1989. *A Fiscal History of Canada: The Post War Years*. Toronto: Canadian Tax Foundation.

Peterken, G. F. 1981. *Woodland Conservation and Management*. London: Chapman and Hall.

Peterson, F. M. 1977. 'Economic Theory of Mineral Leasing'. In Crommelin and Thompson, eds. pp. 27–45.

Pincetl, S. 1993. 'Some Origins of French Environmentalism: An Exploration', *Forest and Conservation History* 37: 80–89.

Pisani, D. J. 1986. 'Federalism, Water Law and the American West, 1886–1928'. In H. N. Scheiber, ed. *Perspectives on Federalism*. Berkeley Institute of Government Studies, pp. 117–48.

——. 1992. *To Reclaim a Divided West: Water, Law and Public Policy 1848–1902*. Albuquerque, NM: University of New Mexico Press.

Plucknett, T. F. T. 1956. *A Concise History of the Common Law*, 5th edn. London: Butterworth.

Porter, R. H. 1995. 'The Role of Information in US Offshore Oil and Gas Lease Auctions', *Econometrica* 63, no. 1: 1–27.

Posner, R. 1977, 1986. *Economic Analysis of Law*. Boston: Little Brown.

——. 1980. 'A Theory of Primitive Society, with Special Reference to Law', *Journal of Law and Economics* 23, no. 1: 42–52. Reprinted in R. A. Posner, *The Economics of Justice*. New York: Little, Brown, 1983, pp. 192–203.

Postan, M. M. 1972. *The Penguin Economic History of Europe*. London: Penguin.

Powell, J. M. 1976. *Environmental Management in Australia, 1788–1914: Guardians, Improvers and Profit: An Introductory Survey*. Melbourne: Oxford University Press.

Powell, R. R., and P. J. Rohan. 1968. *Powell on Real Property*. New York: M. Bender.

Pratt, W. E. 1960 'The Value of Business History in the Search for Oil'. Ed: none given, *Oil's First Century*. Cambridge, MA: Harvard Graduate School of Business.

Prosser, W. 1941. *Handbook on the Law of Torts*. St. Paul, MN: West Pub. Co.

Rackham, O. 1980. *Ancient Woodland, Its History, Vegetation and Uses in England*. London: E. Arnold.

Raistrick, A. 1953. 'The Lead Mines of Upper Wharfedale', *Yorkshire Bulletin of Economic and Social Research* 6: 1–16.

——. 1973. *Lead Mines in the Mid-Pennines: The Mines of Nidderdale, Wharfedale, Airedale, Ribblesdale and Bowland*. Truro: Barton.

Raistrick, A., and B. Jennings. 1965. *A History of Lead Mining in the Pennines*. London: Longmans.

Ramsay, G. D. 1965. *Wiltshire Woollen Industry in the Sixteenth and Seventeenth Centuries*, 2nd edn. London: Cass, Frank Publishers.

Rankin, M. T. 1991. 'Despoiling a River: Can the Law Help to Sustain the Fraser River?' In A. H. J. Dorcey, ed. *Perspectives on Sustainable Development in Water Management:*

Towards Agreement on the Fraser River. Vancouver: Westwater Research Centre, The University of British Columbia, pp. 391–416.

Reed, J. L. 1954. *Forests of France.* London: Faber.

Reed, W. J. 1984. 'The Effects of the Risk of Fire on the Optimal Rotation of a Forest', *Journal of Environmental Economics and Management* 11, 2, pp. 180–90.

Reid, R. M., ed. 1990. *The Upper Ottawa Valley to 1855.* Ottawa: Carleton University Press.

Renzetti, S., and D. Dupont. 1999. 'An Assessment of Impact of Charging for Provincial Water Use Permits', *Canadian Public Policy* 25: 361–78.

Repetto, R. 2001. 'The Atlantic Sea Scallop Fishery in the United States and Canada: A Natural Experiment in Fisheries Management Regimes'. Discussion paper. New Haven: Yale School of Forestry and Environmental Studies.

Rettig, R. B. 1984. 'License Limitation in the United States and Canada: An Assessment', *North American Journal of Fisheries Management* 4: 231–48.

Rettig, R. B, F. Berkes, and E. Pinkerton. 1989. 'The Future of Fisheries Co-Management: A Multi-Disciplinary Assessment' in Pinkerton, Evelyn, ed. *Co-Operative Management of Local Fisheries.* Vancouver: UBC Press, pp. 273–9.

Richardson, W. C. 1952. *Tudor Chamber Administration 1485–1547.* Baton Rouge: Louisiana State University Press.

Rickard, T. A. 1932a. *Man and Metals: A History of Mining in Relation to the Development of Civilization,* 2 vols. New York: McGraw-Hill.

——. 1932b. *A History of American Mining.* New York and London: McGraw-Hill. Reprinted Johnson and Co., 1966.

Riddell, R. G. 1937. 'The Land Policy of the Colonial Office', *Canadian Historical Review* 18: 385–405.

Robin, M. 1972. *The Company Province: The Rush for Spoils.* Toronto: McClelland and Stewart.

Robinson, W. L. 1985. 'Individual Transferrable Quotas in the Australian Southern Bluefin Fishery'. Juneau: National Marine Fisheries Service, US Department of Commerce. Mimeo.

Roche, M. M. 1984. 'Reactions to Scarcity: The Management of Forest Resources in Nineteenth-Century Canterbury, New Zealand', *Journal of Forest History* 28, no. 2: 82–91.

Rocky Mountain Mineral Law Foundation. 1960, 1983, 1984, 1985, 1991. *American Law of Mining,* 2nd edn. Cheryl Outerbridge, ed. Denver, CO: Matthew Bender.

Rogers, G. W. 1979. 'Alaska's Limited Entry Program: Another View'. In P. H. Pearse, ed. Symposium on Policies for Economic Rationalization of Commercial Fisheries. *Journal of Fisheries Research Board of Canada,* pp. 783–88.

Rose, Carol. 2003. 'Joseph Sax and the Idea of the Public Trust', articles of Issues in Legal Scholarship: Joseph Sax and the Public Trust, The Berkeley Electronic Press, 2003.

——. 1990. 'Energy and Efficiency in the Realignment of Common-Law Water Rights', *Journal of Legal Studies,* 19: 261–95.

Rose-Ackerman, S. 1985. 'Inalienability and the Theory of Property Rights', *Columbia Law Review* 85, no. 5: 931–70.

Rosen, M. 1990. 'The Political Economy of Water Markets', Association of Environmental and Resource Economists, *AERE Newsletter,* pp. 10–14.

Ross, M. M. 1995. *Forest Management in Canada.* Calgary: Canadian Institute of Resource Law.

——. 1997. *A History of Forest Legislation in Canada*. Calgary: Canadian Institute of Resource Law.
Rostow, E. V. 1948. *A National Policy for the Oil Industry*. New Haven, CT: Yale.
Royce, W. F. 1988. 'The Historic Development of Fisheries Science and Management', *Marine Fisheries Review* 50, no. 4: 30–9.
Rubin, G. R., and D. Sugarman, eds. 1984. *Law, Economy and Society, 1750–1914: Essays in the History of English Law*. Abingdon: Professional Books.
Ruddle, K. 1989. 'The Organisation of Traditional Inshore Fishery Management Systems in the Pacific'. In P. Neher et al. *Rights Based Fishing*. Dordrecht: Kluwer, pp. 73–85.
Ruddle, K., and R. E. Johannes. 1985. *The Traditional Knowledge and Management of Coastal Systems in Asia and the Pacific*. Jakarta: UNESCO.
Ruskin, J. 1871–84. *The Works of John Ruskin*. Vols. 27–9, *Fors Clavigera*. E. T. Cook and A. Wedderburn, eds. London: George Allen, 1907.
Russell, A. 1864. *The Salmon*. Edinburgh: Edmonston and Douglas.
Rutherford, J. B., D. G. Wilder, and H. C. Frick. 1967. *An Economic Appraisal of the Canadian Lobster Industry*. Ottawa: Fisheries Research Board of Canada.
Rydz, D. L. 1979. *The Parliamentary Agents: A History*. London: Royal Historical Society.
Sanders, T. C., ed. 1876. 'De Legge Aquilia'. In *The Institutes of Justinian*, 5th edn. London: Longmans, Green and Co., 1952, p. 492.
Saunders, J. O., ed. 1986. *Managing Natural Resources in a Federal State*. Toronto: Carswell.
Sax, J. L. 1990. 'The Constitution, Property Rights and the Future of Water Law', *University of Colorado Law Review* 61: 257–82.
Sax, J. L., and R. H. Abrams. 1986. *Legal Control of Water Resources*. Minneapolis: West Publishing Co.
Schaab, W. C. 1983. 'Prior Appropriation, Impairment, Replacements, Models and Markets', *Natural Resources Journal* 23: 25–42.
Scheberle, D. 2004. *Federalism and Environmental Policy: Trust and the Politics of Implementation* 2nd edn. Washington, DC: Georgetown University Press.
Scheiber, H. N. 1973. 'Property Law, Expropriation and Resource Allocation by Government: 1789–1910', *Journal of Economic History* 33, no. 1: 232. Reprinted in L. M. Friedman and H. N. Sheiber, eds. 1988. *American Law and the Constitutional Order: Historical Perspectives*. Cambridge, MA, and London: Harvard University Press, pp. 132–41.
Schlager, E. 1990. *Model Specification and Policy Analysis: The Governance of Coastal Fisheries*, Ph.D. Dissertation, Indiana University Bloomington: Workshop in Political Theory and Policy Analysis.
Schlager, E. C., W. Blomquist, and S. Y. Tang. 1994. 'Mobile Flows, Storage and Self-Organized Institutions for Governing Common Pool Resources', *Land Economics* 70, no. 3: 294–317.
Schlich, W. 1911. 'Forests and Forestry', *Encyclopedia Britannica*, 11th edn., vol. 10.
Scholefield, E. O. S., and F. W. Howay. 1914. *British Columbia from the Earliest Times to the Present*, 4 vols. Vancouver: S. J. Clarke.
Schubert, H. 1957. *The History of the British Iron and Steel Industry from c. 450 B.C. to A.D. 1775*. London: Routledge and Kegan Paul.
Schumpeter, J. A. 1942. *Capitalism, Socialism and Democracy*. New York: Harper and Row.
Schwartz, G. 1981. 'Tort Law and the Economy of Nineteenth-Century America: A Reinterpretation', *Yale Law Journal* 90: 1717.

Schworm, W. E. 1983. 'Monopsonistic Control of a Common Property Renewable Resource', *Canadian Journal of Economics* 16, no. 2: 275–87.

Scott, A., J. Robinson, and D. Cohen eds. 1995. *Managing National Resources in British Columbia: Markets, Regulations and Sustainable Development.* Vancouver: University of British Columbia Press.

Scott, A. D. 1955. 'The Fishery: The Objectives of Sole Ownership', *Journal of Political Economy* 63, no. 2: 116–24.

——. 1957. 'Optimal Utilization and Control of Fisheries'. In Ralph Turvey and Jack Wiseman, eds. *The Economics of Fisheries.* Rome: FAO; reprinted in V. L. Smith, ed. *Economics of Natural and Environmental Resources.* New York: Gordon and Breach, 1977, pp. 155–69.

——. 1964. 'Food and the World Fisheries Situation'. In Marion Clawson, ed. *Natural Resources and International Development.* Baltimore: Johns Hopkins Press, pp. 127–344.

——. 1965. 'The Valuation of Game Resources: Some Theoretical Aspects', *Canadian Fisheries Reports* 4. Ottawa: Dept. of Fisheries, pp. 27–49.

——. 1967. 'The Theory of the Mine Under Conditions of Certainty'. In Mason Gaffney, ed. *Extractive Resources and Taxation.* Madison: University of Wisconsin Press.

——. 1973, 1983. *Natural Resources: The Economics of Conservation,* 2nd edn. Ottawa: Carleton University Press.

——. 1982. 'Regulation and the Location of Jurisdictional Powers: The Fishery', *Osgoode Hall Law Journal* 20, no. 4: 780–805.

——. 1983. *Natural Resources: The Economics of Conservation,* 3rd edn. Ottawa: Carleton University Press.

——. 1984. 'Property Rights and Property Wrongs', *Canadian Journal of Economics* 16, no. 4: 555–73.

——. 1985. 'The State and Property: Water Rights in Western Canada'. In D. Cameron, ed. *Explorations in Canadian Economic History: Essays in Honour of Irene M. Spry.* Ottawa: University of Ottawa Press, pp. 157–89.

——. 1991a. 'British Columbia's Water Rights: Their Impact on the Sustainable Development of the Fraser Basin'. In A. H. J. Dorcey, ed. *Perspectives on Sustainable Development in Water Management Towards Agreement in the Fraser River Basin.* Vancouver: Westwater Research Centre, The University of British Columbia, pp. 341–90.

——. 1991b. 'The Market for Characteristics of Property Rights'. In A. Breton et al., eds. *The Competitive State.* Dordrecht: Kluwer, pp. 221–55.

——. 1993. 'Individual Water Rights in an International Water Market'. In J. Windsor, ed., *Water Export: Should Canada's Water Be Sold?* Cambridge, ON: The Canadian Water Resources Association, pp. 141–81.

Scott, A. D., and Johnson, J. 1985. 'Property Rights: Developing the Characteristics of Interests in Natural Resources'. In A. D. Scott, ed. *Progress in Natural Resource Economics.* Oxford: Clarendon Press, 376–403.

Scott, A. D., and P. Neher. 1981. *The Public Regulation of Commercial Fisheries in Canada.* Ottawa: Economic Council of Canada and Department of Supply and Services.

Scott, A. D., and M. Tugwell. 1981. 'The Maritime Lobster Industry'. Case Study No. 1, Technical Report No. 16, The Public Regulation of Fisheries in Canada. Ottawa: Economic Council of Canada.

Seale, S. J. E., and A. R. Thompson. 1979. *Institutional Arrangements for Managing the Oyster Resources*, vol. IV of A. H. J. Dorcey, ed. *The B.C. Oyster Industry: Policy Analysis for Coastal Resource Management*. Vancouver: Westwater Research Centre.

Sedjo, R. A. 1983. *Government Interventions and Social Needs and the Management of the US Forests*. Washington: Resources for the Future.

Seligman, E. R. A. 1925. *Essays in Taxation,* 10th edn. New York: Macmillan.

Sen, A. K. 1967. 'The Social Time Preference Rate in Relation to the Market Rate of Interest', *Quarterly Journal of Economics* 81: 112–24.

Sewell, W. R. D., and L. R. Barr. 1977. 'Evolution in the British Institutional Framework for Water Management', *Natural Resources Journal* 17, no. 3: 395.

Shackleton, M. 1986. *The Politics of Fishing in Britain and France*. Aldershot: Gower.

Shaw, A. G. L. 1970. *Great Britain and the Colonies, 1815–1865*. London: Methuen.

Sheppard, W. 1641. *Sheppard's Touchstone of Common Assurances*, 8th edn. 1826.

Shinn, C. H. 1884 and 1965 *Mining Camps: A Study in American Frontier Government*. New York: Scribners. Reprinted as a Torchbook Edition with R. W. Paul, ed. New York: Harper and Row, 1965.

Shotton, R. ed. *Use of Property Rights in Fisheries Management*, FAO Technical Papers 404/1 and 404/2, Rome 2000.

Shupe, S. J., G. D. Weatherford, and E. D. Checchio. 1989. 'Western Water Rights: The Era of Reallocation', *Natural Resources Journal* 29, no. 2: 414–34.

Simpson, A. W. B. 1986. *A History of the Land Law*, 2nd edn. Oxford: Clarendon Press.

Sinclair, S. 1960. *License Limitation and British Columbia: A Method of Economic Fisheries Management*. Ottawa: Department of Fisheries Canada.

Slater, G. 1968. *The English Peasantry and the Enclosure of the Commons*. New York: Kelley.

Smith, A. 1793. *The Wealth of Nations* 7th edn. London: Strahan and Cadell, Vol. I, p. 260.

Smith, D. N., and L. T. Wells. 1975. *Negotiating Third World Mineral Agreements: Promises as Prologue*. Cambridge, MA: Ballinger.

Smith, P. 1986. *Harvest From the Rock: A History of Mining in Ontario*. Toronto: Macmillan.

Spatt, C. S. 1983. 'Comment on the Cooter Paper', *Public Choice* 41, no. 1: 139–44.

Spence, C. C. 1970. *Mining Engineers and the American West*. New Haven and London: Yale University Press.

Spring, D. 1951. 'The English Landed Estate in the Age of Coal and Iron: 1830–1880', *Journal of Economic History* 2, no. 1: 3–24.

Spring, E. 1964. 'The Settlement of Land in Nineteenth Century England', *American Journal of Legal History* 8: 209–23.

——. 1977. 'Land-owners, Lawyers, and Land Law Reform in Nineteenth Century England', *American Journal of Legal History* 21: 40–59.

Steen, H. K., ed. 1978. 'Capital Gains for Forest Lands: Origins of the 1944 Tax Legislation', *Forest History* 22: 147–53.

Stevenson, G. G. 1991. *Common Property Economics: A General Theory and Land-Use Applications*. Cambridge: Cambridge University Press.

Stewart, R. E., Jr, and M. F. Stewart. 1962. *Adolph Sutro: A Biography*. Berkeley, CA: Howell-North.

Stigler, G. 1971. 'The Theory of Economic Regulation', *Bell Journal of Economics and Management Science* 2: 3–21.

Stoddard, C. H. 1961. *The Small Private Forest in the US*. Washington: Resources for the Future.

Stokes, A. H. 1883. *Lead and Lead Mining in Derbyshire*. Reprinted in *Transactions of the Chesterfield and Derbyshire Institute of Mining, Civil and Mechanical Engineering*, vols. 8–10, 1880–1883. Sheffield, England: Peak District Mines Historical Society, 1964.

Sugden, R. 1985. 'Spontaneous Order', *Journal of Economic Perspectives* 3, no. 4: 85–98.

Swenson, R. W. 1968. 'Legal Aspects of Mineral Resources Exploitation'. In *History of Public Land Law Development*, Mason Gaffney, ed. Washington, DC: Public Land Law Commission/Zenger.

Symes, D. 1999. 'Rights-based Management: A European Union Perspective'. In R. Shotton, ed. *Use of Property Rights in Fisheries Management*. FAO Fisheries Technical Paper 404/1, pp. 276–83.

Tarlock, A. D. 1985. 'The Law of Equitable Apportionment Revised, Updated and Restated', *University of Colorado Law Review* 56: 381.

Taylor, G. W. 1978. *Mining: The History of Mining in British Columbia*. Victoria and Seattle: Hancock House.

Thomas, G. 1920. *The Development of Institutions under Irrigation, with Special Reference to Early Utah Conditions*. New York: Macmillan.

Thomas, K. 1983. *Man and the Natural World*. New York: Pantheon.

Thompson, A. 1986. 'An Overview of Oil, Gas and Mineral Disposition Systems in Canada'. In *Proceedings of 32nd Annual Rocky Mountain Mineral Law Institute*. New York: Bender, Chapter 3, pp. 3-1 to 3-78.

Thompson, B. H. Jr. 1997. 'The Endangered Species Act: A Case Study in Takings and Incentives', *Stanford Law Review* 49: 305–79.

Thompson, E. P. 1991 and 1993. 'Custom, Law and Common Right'. In E. P. Thompson, *Customs in Common*. London: Penguin, pp. 97–184.

——. 1993. *Customs in Common*. London: Penguin Books.

Thompson, F. F. 1961. *The French Shore Problem in Newfoundland: An Imperial Study*. Toronto: University of Toronto Press.

Thomson, D. B. 1983. 'Fishermen and Fisheries Management'. In FAO 1984.

Thomson, J. T., D. H. Feeny, and R. J. Oakerson. 1986. 'Institutional Dynamics: The Evolution and Dissolution of Common Property Resource Management'. In US National Research Council, *Common-Property Resource Management*. Washington, pp. 391–424.

Thorpe, F. N. 1909. *The Federal and State Constitutions, Colonial Charters and Other Organic Laws of the States, Territories and Colonies Now or Heretofore Forming the United States of America*. Washington: Government Printing House.

Tober, J. A. 1973. 'The Allocation of Wildlife Resources in the US 1850–1900'. Yale Ph.D. thesis; reprinted Ann Arbor: University Microfilms International, 1977.

Trebilcock, M. J. 1984. 'Communal Property Rights: the Papua New Guinean Experience', *University of Toronto Law Review* 34: 377–420.

Trelease, F. J. 1974. 'Trelease, the Market Water Code, The Wise Administrator and the Goddam Bureaucrat', *Natural Resources Journal* 14: 207.

——. 1979. *Cases and Materials on Water Law*, 3d edn. St. Paul, MN: West Publishing Co.

Trevelyan, G. M. 1973. *History of England*. London: Longman.

Tucker, G. N. 1936. *The Canadian Commercial Revolution, 1845–1851*. New Haven, Yale University Press; London: H. Milford, Oxford University Press.

Turner, M. 1980. *English Parliamentary Enclosure*, Folkestone: Archon Books.

Turris, B. R. 1999. 'A Comparison of British Columbia's ITQ fisheries for Groundfish Trawl and Sablefish: Similar Results from Program with Differing Objectives, Designs and Processes'. In R. Shotton, ed. *Use of Property Rights in Fisheries Management*. FAO Fisheries Technical Paper 404/1, pp. 254–61.

Turvey, R. 1964. 'Optimization and Suboptimization in Fishery Regulation', *American Economic Review* 54: 64–76.

Tussing, Arlon R., and G. K. Erickson. 1969. *Mining and Public Policy in Alaska*. College, Alaska: Institute of Social, Economic and Government Research, University of Alaska, pp. 40–2.

Umbeck, J. R. 1977. 'The California Gold Rush: A Study of Emerging Property Rights', *Explorations in Economic History* 14: 197–226.

——. 1981. *A Theory of Property Rights: With Application to the California Gold Rush*. Ames, IA: The Iowa State University Press.

Unger, R. W. 1980. 'Dutch Herring, Technology and International Trade in the Seventeenth Century', *Journal of Economic History* 40: 253–79.

United States, National Research Council, Committee on Onshore Oil and Gas Leasing. 1989. *Land Use Planning and Oil and Gas Leasing on Onshore Federal Lands*. Washington, DC: National Academy Press.

Van Wagenen, T. F. 1918. *International Mining Law*. New York: McGraw-Hill.

Vanberg, V. 1986. 'Spontaneous Market Order and Social Rules: A Critical Examination of F. A. Hayek's Theory of Cultural Evolution', *Economics and Philosophy* 2: 75–100.

Veatch, A. C. 1911. *Mining Laws of Australia and New Zealand*. US Geological Survey Bulletin 505. Washington, DC: Government Printing Office.

Von Tunzelmann, G. N. 1978. *Steam Power and British Industrialization to 1860*. Oxford: Clarendon.

Waite, P. B. 1971. *Canada 1874–96: Arduous Destiny*. Toronto: McClelland and Stewart.

——. 1985. *The Man from Halifax: Sir John Thompson, Prime Minister*. Toronto: University of Toronto Press.

Walford, L. 1958. *Living Resources of the Sea: Opportunities for Research and Expansion*. New York: Ronald.

Walters, C., and P. H. Pearse. 1996. 'Stock Information Requirements for Quota-management Systems in Commercial Fisheries', *Reviews in Fish Biology and Fisheries* 6: 21–42.

Warriner, K. 1987. 'Regionalism, Dependence, and the BC Fisheries: Historical Development and Recent Trends'. In P. Marchak, N. Guppy, and J. McMullan, eds. *Uncommon Property*. Toronto: Methuen, pp. 326–49.

Watkins, T. A. 1874 and 1952. *Righteous Pilgrim: The Life and Times of Harold L. Ickes*. New York: Holt.

Watson, A. 1990. 'The Transformation of American Property Law: A Comparative Approach', *Georgia Law Review* 24, no. 2: 163–221.

Wear, D. N., and W. F. Hyde. 1992. 'Distribution Issues in Forest Policy'. In P. Nemetz, ed. *Emerging Issues in Forest Policy*. Vancouver: University of British Columbia Press, pp. 297–314.

Weaver, J. L. 1986. *Unitization of Oil and Gas Fields in Texas*. Washington, DC: Resources for the Future.

Weber, M. 1923 and 1961. *General Economic History* translated Frank H. Knight. New York: Collier.

Welborn, J. F. 1994. 'New Rights of Surface Owners: Changes in the Dominant/Servient Relationship Between The Mineral and Surface Estates', *Rocky Mountain Mineral Law Institute* 40: 22–1.

Wesney, D. 1989. 'Applied Fisheries Management Plans: Individual Transferable Quotas and Input Controls'. In P. A. Neher, R. Arnason, and N. Mollett, eds. *Rights Based Fishing*. Dordrecht: Kluwer.

White, G., and J. Maze. 1985. *Harold Ickes of the New Deal*. Cambridge, MA: Harvard University Press.

White, D. J. 1954. *The New England Fishing Industry*. Cambridge, MA.: Harvard University Press.

Whitford, H. N., and R. F. Craig. 1918. *Forests of British Columbia*. Ottawa: Commission of Conservation, Canada.

Wiel, S. C. 1911. *Water Rights in the Western States*, 3rd edn. 2 volumes. San Francisco: Bancroft-Whitney.

——. 1918. 'Origin and Comparative Development of the Law of Watercourses in the Common Law and in the Civil Law', *California Law Review* 6: 245, 247–8.

——. 1919. 'Waters: American Law and French Authority', *Harvard Law Review* 33, no. 2: 133–67.

——. 1936. 'Fifty Years of Water Law', *Harvard Law Review* 50: 252.

Wiener, N. 1968. 'Timber Catastrophes—The Lawyer's Job', *Willanette Law Journal* 2: 235–44.

Wildsmith, B. H., K. J. Spears, and W. G. Wharton. 1985. *Individual Entitlements in the Tidal Fisheries: Some Legal Problems*. A report prepared for the Department of Fisheries and Oceans. Halifax: Dalhousie University Faculty of Law.

Wilen, J. E. 1989. 'Rent Generation in Limited Entry Fisheries'. In P. Neher et al. *Rights Based Fishing*. Dordrecht: Kluwer, pp. 247–63.

Wilkes, G. C. 1954. *Taxation of the Forest Industries in Ontario*. Toronto: University of Toronto Press.

Williams, D. R. 1977. *'The Man For A New Country': Sir Matthew Baillie Begbie*. Sidney, BC: Gray's.

Williams, M. 1989. *Americans and their Forests: A Historical Geography*. Cambridge: Cambridge University Press.

Williamson, H. F., and A. R. Daum. 1959. *The American Petroleum Industry: The Age of Illumination 1859–1899*. Evanston: Northwestern University Press.

Willison, G. F. 1952. *Here They Dug the Gold*. London: Eyre and Spottiwoode.

Wilson, K. 1989a. 'Conservation Acts and Correlative Rights: Has the Pendulum Swung Too Far?' *Rocky Mountain Mineral Oil Institute*, 35, ch. 18.

Wilson, K. W. 1989b. *Irrigating the Okanagan: 1860–1920*. Unpublished M.A. thesis, University of British Columbia Department of Geography.

Wirth, F. P. 1927. 'The Operation of the Land Laws in the Minnesota Iron District', *Mississippi Valley Historical Review* 13, no. 4: 438–98.

Worrell, A. C. 1970. *Principles of Forest Policy*. New York, NY: McGraw-Hill Book Company.

Wright, J. 1966. *The Galena Experiment*. Madison: University of Wisconsin Press.

Wynn, G. 1981. *Timber Colony: A Historical Geography of Early Nineteenth Century New Brunswick*. Toronto: University of Toronto Press.

Yamamoto, T. 1995. 'Development of a Community-Based Fisheries Management System in Japan', *Marine Resource Economics* 10, no. 1: 21–34.

Yamamoto, T., and K. Short, eds. 1992. *International Perspectives on Fisheries Management with Special Emphasis on Community Based Management Systems Developed in Japan.* Proceedings of the JIFRS/IIFET/ZENGYOREN Symposium on Fisheries Management, Tokyo, 26 August–3 September 1991. Tokyo: National Federation of Fisheries Cooperative Associations (ZENGYOREN).

Young, A. 1771. *The Farmer's Tour Through the East of England,* 4 vols. London: W. Strahan.

Young, C. 1979. *The Royal Forests of Medieval England.* University of Pennsylvania Press.

Yuan, L. 1999. 'Essays on Strategic Divisionalization and Decentralization'. Ph.D. dissertation, University of British Columbia.

Zaslow, M. 1971. *The Opening of the Canadian North 1870–1914.* Toronto: McClelland and Stewart.

Zerbe, R. O. Jr. 1987. 'The Joint Production of Fairness and Efficiency', (typescript draft) University of Washington.

Zhang, Professor Daowei. 1994. 'Implications of Tenure for Forest Land Value and Management in British Columbia'. Ph.D. dissertation, University of British Columbia.

Zimmerman, M. 1969. 'Inter-Provincial Water Use Law in Canada: Suggestions and Comparisons'. In D. Gibson, ed. *Constitutional Aspects of Water Management.* Vol. 2. Research report, Agassiz Centre for Water Studies.

Table of Cases

Chasemore v. Richards (1859), 7 H.L.C. 349, 11 E.R. 140
Chrisman v. Miller, 197 US 313 (1905)
Clark v. Foot, 8 Johns. 421 (N.Y. 1811)
Clegg v. Dearden (1848), 12 Q.B. 576 at 995
Coates v. Mayo Singh Lumber Co. [1925] 4 D.L.R. 345
Cole v. Ralph, 252 US 286 (1919)
Colorado v. New Mexico, 459 US 176 (1982)
Connecticut v Massachusetts (Commonweath of), 282 US 660, 51 S.Ct. 286, 75 L.Ed. 602 (1931)
Consumers' Gas Trust Co. v. Littler, 162 Ind. 320, 70 N.E. 363 (1904)
Cook v. Vancouver (City) [1914] A.C. 1077 (P.C.)
Cosdon Oil and Gas Co. v. Hickman, 114 Okla. 86, 243 Pac. 226 (1925)
Cowan v. Hardeman, 26 Tex. 217 at 222 (1862)
Cox v. Matthews (1673), 1 Ventis 237, 239, 86 E.R. 159, 160 (K.B.), referred to in *Wheeldon v. Burrows* (1879), 12 Ch. D. 52
Dand v. Kingscote (1840), 6 M. & W. 174, 9 L.J. Ex. 279, 151 E.R. 370
Dark v. Johnston, 55 Pa. 164, 94 Am. Dec. 732 (1867)
Dashwood v. Magniac [1891] 2 Ch. 306, [1891–4] All E.R. 1906
Department of Forestry v. Jepson and Sons Logging Co., 64 Ore. App. 390, 668 P.2nd 461 (1983)
Dexter v. Washington, 338 US 863, 94 L.Ed. 529, 70 S.Ct. 147 (1949)
Donoghue v. Stevenson [1932] A.C. 645, [1932] All E.R. 1
Doucette v. Parent (1996), file no. 1842/93 (Ont. Ct., Gen. Div.)
Dougleston Manor v. Bahrakis, 89 N.Y. 2d 472 (1997)
Duke of Buccleuch v. Wakefield, (1870), 4 L.R. 377 (H.L.)
Duke of Norfolk's Case (1681), 3 Ch. Cas. 1, 2 Ch. Rep. 229, 2 Swans. 454, 460
Duke of Somerset v. Fogwell [1826] 5 B. & C. 875
Eardley v. Earl Granville (1874), 3 Ch. D. at 826
Earl of Cardigan v. Armitage (1823), 107 E.R. 356
Eastern Oregon Land Co. v. Willow River Land and Irrigation Co., 187 F 466 (D. Ore. 1910), reversed, 201 F. 203, 119 C.C.A. 437 (US 1912), affirmed, 204 F. 516, 122 C.C.A. 636 (US 1913)
Embrey v. Owen (1851), 6 Ex. 353, 155 E.R. 579 (Exch.)
Erhardt v. Boaro, 113 US 527 (1885)
Firmstone v. Wheeler, 2 D. & L. 203
Fish v. Capwell et. al. (1894), 29 A.C. 840
Flying Diamond Corp. v. Rust, 551 P.2d 509 (Utah 1976)
Foster v. Warblington [1906] 1 K.B. 648 (C.A.)
Geer v. Connecticut, 161 US 519 (1895)
Getty Oil Co. v. Jones, 470 S.W. 2d 618 at 622 (Tex. 1971)
Giles v. Walker (1890), 24 Q.B.D. 656, 59 L.J.Q.B. 416
Greyes Case (1594), Owen 20
Gulf Pipe Line Co. v. Pawnee Tulsa Petroleum Co., 127 Pac. 252 (Okla. 1912)
Hale v. Oldroyd (1845), 14 M.&.W. 789, 153 E.R. 694 (Exch.)
Hamon v. Gardner, 315 P.2d 669 (Okla. 1959)
Harris v. Ryding (1839), 5 M. & W. Rep. 59, 151 E.R. 27

Haward v. Bankes [1760] 2 Burr. 1113, 97 E.R. 740 (K.B.)
Hayes v. Davis (1991), 25 A.C.W.S. 3d 1348
Hext v. Gill (1872), 7 Ch. App. 699 at 714
Hilton v. Granville (Lord) (1844), 5 Q.B. 701
Holker v. Porritt (1875), 10 Exch. 59 (Eng.)
Hole v. Barlow (1858), 4 C.B. (N.S.) 334, 140 E.R. 1113 (C.P.)
Hoods Barrs v. Inland Revenue Commission [1957] 1 All E.R. 832
Hough v. Porter, 51 Or. 318, 95 P.732 (1908) and 98 P.1083 (1909)
Humphries v. Brogden (1850), 12 Q.B. 739, 116 E.R. 1048
Hurley v. Hurley, 110 Va. 31, 65 S.E. 472 (1909)
In re Hood River, 114 Or. 112, 227 P. 1065 (1924)
In re L.E. Jones, 51 L.D. 116 (1925)
In re Willow Creek, 74 Or.592, 144 P.505 (1914), modified on rehearing, 74 Or.592, 146 P.475 (1914)
Jackson v. Roby, 109 US 440 (1883)
James Jones & Sons Ltd. v. Earl of Tankerville (1909), 2 Ch. 440
Jennison v. Kirk, 98 US 453 (1879)
Jordan v. Welch, 61 Wash. 569, 112 Pac. 656 (1911)
Katz v. Walkinshaw, 141 Cal. 116, 70 P. 663 (S.C. 1902), reversed 141 Cal. 116, 74 P. 766 (1903)
Kauri Lumber Co. v. Commissioner of Taxes [1913] A.C. 771
Kenny v. Texas Gulf Sulphur Co., 351 S.W. 2d 612 (Tex. 1961)
Kensit v. Great Eastern Railway Co. (1884), 27 Ch. D. 122 (Eng.)
Kingwood Oil Co. v. Corporation Commission, 396 P.2d 1008 at 1010 (Okla. 1964)
Kirk v. Ford (1920), 53 D.L.R. 644, [1920] 3 W.W.R. 91
Kleppner v. Lemon, 176 Pa. 502, 35 A. (1896)
Laing v. Whaley (1858), 3 H.&.N. 675, 157 E.R. 639 (Exch.)
Lavery v. Pursell (1888), 39 Ch.D. 508
Leakey et al. v. National Trust for Places of Historic Interest or Natural Beauty [1980] Q.B. 485, [1980] 1 All E.R. 17 (C.A.)
Lexington and Ohio Rail Road v. Applegate, 8 Dana 289 at 309 (Ky. 1839)
Lifford's Case (1615), 11 Co. Rep. 46b, 77 E.R. 1206
Liggins v. Inge (1831), 7 Bing. 682, 131 E.R. 263 (C.P.)
Lindsey v. Wilson, 332 S.W.2d 641 (Ky. 1960)
Lord Norbury v. Kitchin (1862), 3 F.&F. 292, 176 E.R. 132 (Cr. Cir.)
Love v. Bell (1884), 9 A.C. 286
Lutrel's Case (1625), 4 Co. Rep. 86a, 76 E.R. 1065 (K.B.)
Lux v. Haggin, 69 Cal.255, 10 P.674 (1886)
Marker v. Marker (1851), 9 Hare. 1, 68 E.R. 389
Marshall v. Green [1875] 1 C.D.P. 35, [1874–80] All E.R. 2198
Marvin v. Brewster Iron Mining Co., 55 N.Y. 538 (1874)
Mason v. Hill (1833), 5 B.&Ad. 1, 110 E.R. 692 (K.B.)
McCartney v. Londonderry & Lough Swilly Railway Co. [1904] A.C. 301
McPherson v. US Fidelity and Guaranty Co. (1915), 24 D.L.R. 77
Merritt v. Brinkerhoff, 17 Johns. R. 306 (N.Y. 1820)
Midland Rly. Co. v. Miles (1886), 33 Ch. D. 632

Miner v. Gilmour (1858), 12 Moo. 131, 14 E.R. 861 (P.C.)
Morgan v. Russell & Sons (1909), 1 K.B. 357
National Audubon Society v. Superior Court of Alpine County, 189 Cal. Reptr. 346 (1983)
New Jersey v. New York (State of), 283 US 336, 51 S.Ct. 478, 75 L.Ed. 1104 (1931)
Nuttall v. Bracewell (1866), 2 Exch. 1
Ohio Oil Co. v. Indiana, 177 US 190 (S.C. 1900)
O'Reilly v. Campbell, 116 US 418 (1886)
Ormerod v. Todmorden Mill Co. (1883), 11 Q.B.D. 155 (Eng.)
Owen v. Lewis, 46 Ind. 488 (1874)
Packington's Case (1744), 3 Atk. 215, 26 E.R. 925
Palmer v. Mulligan, 3 Caines 307 (N.Y. 1805)
Palsgraf v. Long Island R.R. Co., 248 N.Y. 339, 162 N.E. 99 (1928)
Pasco v. Canadian National Railway Co. (1985), 69 B.C.L.R. 76 (S.C.)
Patterson v. North Vancouver Board of School Trustees [1929] 3 D.L.R. 33 (B.C.C.A.)
Pells v. Brown (1620), Cro. Jac. 590, 2 Rolle 216
Pennington v. Brinsop Hall Coal Co. (1877), 5 Ch. D. 769 (Eng.)
Phillips v. Hamilton, 17 Wyo. 41, 95 P. 846 (1908)
Platt v. Johnson, 15 Johns. R. 213 (N.Y. 1818)
Prather v. Hoberg, 24 Cal.2d 549, 150 P.2d 405 (1944)
Prior of Southwark's Case (1498), Y.B. Trin. 13, Henry 7, f. 26, pl. 4
R. v. Steer (1704), 6 Mod. Rep. 183, 87 E.R. 939
Read v. Pennsylvania R. Co., 44 N.Y. Law 280 (1882)
Red River Roller Mills v. Wright, 30 Minn. 249, 15 N.W. 167 (1883)
Reed v. Smith (1914), 17 D.L.R. 92 (B.C.C.A.)
Regina v. DeLéry et al. (22 December 1883), *Legal News* 6, no. 51: 402–08
Rowles v. Mason (1612), 2 Browl. 192, 123 E.R. 892 at 893 per Coke C.J.
Rowbotham v. Wilson (1849), 6 E1 & B1 600 per Campbell L.J.C.
Rylands v. Fletcher (1868), L.R. 3, H.L. 3330
Rylands v. Fletcher [1871–73] All E.R. 1
Salisbury (Marquis of) v. Gladstone (1861), 9 H.L.C. 700
Sampson v. Hoddinott (1857), 1 C.B.(N.S.) 590, 140 E.R. 242 (C.P.)
Sands v. Trefuses (1638), Cro. Car. 575, 79 E.R. 1094 (C.P.)
Saunders v. Newman (1818), 1 B.&Ald. 258, 106 E.R. 95 (K.B.)
Scorell v. Boxall (1827), 1 Y. & J. 396, 148 E.R. 724
Seymour v. Courtney (1771), 5 Burr. 2814
Shury v. Piggot (1625), 3 Bulstrode 339, 81 E.R. 280 (K.B.)
Silver Falls Timber Co. v. Eastern & Western Lumber Co., 149 Or. 126 (1935)
Silvis v. Peoples Natural Gas Co., 126 A.2d 706, 60 G.R. 1346 (Pa. 1956)
Simpson v. Bithwood (1692), 3 Lev. 307
Smith v. Kenrick (1849), 7 C.B. 515, [1847–60] All E.R. Rep. 273, 137 E.R. 205
Smith v. Linmar Energy Corp, 790 P.2d 1222 (Utah Court of App. 1990)
Smith v. Moore, 474 P.2d. 794 (Col. 1970)
Smith v. Surman (1829), 9 B.&C. 561, 109 E.R. 209
Sowby v. Mullins (1575), 17 Eliz
St Helen's Smelting Co. v. Tipping (1865), 11 H.L.C. 642, 11 E.R. 1483
Stockport Waterworks Co. v. Potter (1864), 3 H.&.C. 300, 159 E.R. 545 (Exch.)

Stukeley v. Butler (1615), 80 E.R. 316
Summers v. Cook (1880), 28 Gr. 179
Sun Oil v. Whitaker, 483 S.W.2d 808 (Tex. 1972)
Tahsis Co. v. Canadian Forest Products Ltd. (1968), 70 D.L.R. (2d) 376, 65 W.W.R. 641 (B.C.S.C.)
Tanistry Case (1608), Dav. Ir. 28
Teal v. Auty (1820), 2 B.&B. 99, 129 E.R. 895
Tenant v. Goldwin (1705), 2 Ld. Raym. 1089 at 1092, 92 E.R. 222 at 224 (K.B.)
Tuberville v. Stampe (1697), 1 Salk. 13, 1697 Ind. Raym. 264, 91 E.R. 1072
Tyler v. Wilkinson, Fed. Cas. No. 14312, 4 Mason 397, 24 F. Cas. 472 (C.C.D.R.I. 1827)
Tyson v. Smith (1838), 9 A.D. & E. 420
US Borax Co. v. Ickes, 98 F.2d 271 (1938)
Union Oil Co. v. Smith, 249 US 337 (1919)
Wade v. New South Wales Rutile Mining Co. Pty Ltd. (1969), 121 C.L.R. 184–99
Walsingham's Case (1579), 2 Plowden 547, 555, E.R. 805, 816–17
Ward v. Creswell (1741), Willes 265
Westmoreland & Cambria Nat. Gas Co. v. DeWitt, 18 A. 724 at 732–3 (Pa. 1889)
Wheeldon v. Burros v. Matthews (1673), 86 E.R. 159 (K.B.)
William Aldred's Case (1610), 77 E.R. 816
Williams v. Bagnall (1866), 12 J.O.R.N.S. 987, 5 W.R. 272
Williams v. Morland (1824), 2 B.&.C. 910, 107 E.R. 620 (K.B.)
Wilts and Berks Canal Navigation Co. v. Swindon Waterworks Co. (1872), 20 W.R. 353 (Ch.)
Wolstanton and A.G. of Lanc. v. Newcastle Under Lyme Corp. [1940] 3 All E.R. 101
Wood v. Manley (1839), 113 E.R. 325, 11 A.&E. 34
Wood v. Waud (1849), 3 Ex. 748, 154 E.R. 1047 (Exch.)
Wright v. Howard (1823), 1 Sim.&St 190, 57 E.R. 76 (V.C.)
Year Book (1473), 18 Edw. 3
Year Book (1477), 17 Edw. 4
Year Book (1528), 19 Hen. 8

Index

Index